THE TIME OF LIBERTY

A book in the series

LATIN AMERICA OTHERWISE
Languages, Empires, Nations

SERIES EDITORS
Walter D. Mignolo, Duke University
Irene Silverblatt, Duke University
Sonia Saldívar-Hull, University of Texas, San Antonio

Mexico underwent extraordinary changes as it fought Spain to become an independent nation, yet we know relatively little about how subaltern peoples experienced and responded to independence. Writing with a double focus on the urban, mestizo population of the city of Oaxaca and on the largely native and rural population of Villa Alta, Peter Guardino explores how urban mestizos and indigenous peasants responded to and engaged in the emerging political world of nineteenth-century nationalism. Mining a rich array of sources, Guardino provides a fine-grained picture of these momentous years.

Bringing together social sectors — urban and rural, indigenous and mestizo — Guardino is able to challenge long-standing assumptions about subaltern politics and the broader contests shaping the early years of Mexico's independence. We learn about peasant activism, when previous histories told us it didn't exist; and we learn about complex adaptations and maneuvers by subaltern peoples, when previous histories spoke of simple responses. With great theoretical sophistication and sensitivity to the dynamics of ideologies and power, Guardino has presented an "otherwise" narrative of popular political culture and its consequences in these extraordinary times.

ACKNOWLEDGMENTS

Although researching and writing a work of history can sometimes be a lonely business, no person really completes such a work alone. This book, like others of its kind, is the product of a wide variety of institutions and individuals who supported the research, thinking, and writing that it represents.

Institutions provided the financial resources that are crucial for such an endeavor. Much of the research was funded by an Advanced Research Grant from the Social Sciences Research Council and the American Council of Learned Societies. A National Endowment for the Humanities Fellowship allowed me time to complete the bulk of the writing. Indiana University contributed on different occasions two Summer Faculty Fellowships, two Research Leave Supplements, and a Grant-in-Aid of Research.

Two different research assistants, Timothy Schmitz in Bloomington and David Carbajal López in Mexico, lent very timely help that allowed me to profitably use sources I might otherwise have been unable to fully explore.

One of the great pleasures of this project was the opportunity to spend long periods of time working in Oaxaca, with its exceptionally pleasant ambiance and superb archives. Thus I am particularly indebted to my friend and fellow historian of Oaxaca, Jeremy Baskes, who originally suggested that I locate this project there and provided me with my first knowledge of key Oaxacan archives.

During my many stays in Oaxaca a number of the region's historians and ethnohistorians, including Carlos Sánchez Silva, Maria de los Angeles Romero Frizzi, Daniela Traffano, Francisco José Ruiz Cervantes, Luis Castañeda Guzmán, and Ronald Spores, have shared their time and knowledge with me, providing orientation about archives and Oaxacan history. Luis Castañeda Guzmán graciously allowed me to use his personal archive. These historians also welcomed me into their seminars and provided great insight both during their conversations and through their writings. I simply cannot thank them enough. Three other specialists on Oaxaca, John Chance, Silke Hensel, and Yanna Yannakakis, also helped me again not only through their published work but also through various conversations conducted via electronic mail.

I already mentioned the quality of Oaxacan archives, and many of the historians just mentioned have participated in the continuing task of preserving and organizing those archives. They and other Oaxacan colleagues have worked extremely hard for over twenty years, securing funding from private and public sources as well as spending arduous hours sorting through piles of neglected documents. Even though they explain to me that there is much yet to be done, I am simply amazed by what they have already accomplished in one of the most impoverished regions of what is still a relatively poor country. Moreover, the service personnel of both Oaxacan archives and those in Mexico City have often impressed me with the helpful and professional way they handled my countless requests for more documents. These people work very hard for little pay, and they are to be commended for their love of the Mexican cultural patrimony they preserve and protect.

This project benefited from conversations with a variety of colleagues, often following lectures or papers where I presented preliminary results and ideas. The institutional context for these lectures and papers was provided by, in chronological order, the Conference on Latin American History, Indiana University, the Latin American Studies Association, the University of Michigan, the University of Chicago, El Colegio de Michoacán, El Centro de Investigaciones y Estudios Superiores en Antropología Social, La Universidad Autónoma Metropolitana-Itztapalapa, El Seminario de Historia de Oaxaca, the Oaxaca Summer Institute, the University of Florida, Wofford College, El II Congreso Internacional sobre los Procesos de Independencia en América Española, La Universidad Veracruzana, La Universidad Centroamericana, the Boston Area Latin American History Workshop, and the University of California at San Diego. I would particularly like to thank Christon Archer, William Beezley, Karen Caplan, Manuel Chust, John Coatsworth, Brian Connaughton, Antonio Escobar Ohmstede, William French, Nils Jacobsen, Seth Meisel, Juan Ortiz Escamilla,

Jaime Rodríguez, José Antonio Serrano Ortega, Eric Van Young, and Josefina Zoraida Vázquez.

Many years ago I was lucky enough to attend graduate school with a group of outstanding people who happened to share an interest in the popular politics of early-nineteenth-century Latin America at a time when that interest seemed unusual indeed. I still think of Michael Ducey, Aldo Lauria Santiago, Charles Walker, and Richard Warren as my closest peers and friends. From their point of view this may not seem such an honor, as it means that I pick their brains frequently and repeatedly ask them for favors. Clearly, though, this book would not be what it is without their support and insight.

Arlene Díaz, Jeffrey Gould, Daniel James, and my other colleagues at Indiana University deserve a great deal of credit, not only for their encouragement and support on the current project, but for making Indiana University such a nurturing climate for research.

Michael Ducey, James Cypher, Jeffrey Gould, Florencia Mallon, John Tutino, Charles Walker, Richard Warren, and Jane Walter read this manuscript in its entirety. Each had valuable comments and I feel the work has benefited greatly from their intelligence, experience, and patience.

My children Rose and Walter kept me laughing during the long process. They made it impossible to think about the book for several hours each day, helping to preserve their father's mental health and undoubtedly improving the final result.

Jane Walter, my wife and life partner, was with me every step along this long path. Her support was unending, and she was the person who sacrificed the most to keep this project moving forward, especially when she became a temporary single parent during my long absences on research trips. Although Jane no longer considers herself to be a historian, she has also always been a terrific colleague, challenging me both to hone my thinking and to communicate more clearly. Words are not enough to thank her for her contributions to this book.

Although the institutions and individuals above all helped make this book possible, I alone am responsible for any errors.

INTRODUCTION

༄ Spanish American politics underwent a dramatic cultural transformation between the middle of the eighteenth century and the middle of the nineteenth. Around 1750, society and state were envisioned through paradigms of royal sovereignty and colonial corporate and ethnic difference. By the 1850s, society and state were idealized through images of popular sovereignty and republican citizenship. The most obvious manifestation of this shift in political culture was the replacement of an absolutist monarchy with various forms of republican government. The new republican model gave Spanish American economic elites the opportunity to control government and write laws. Yet, the cultural transformation of politics did not affect only elites. Spanish America's impoverished majorities also experienced and participated in the dramatic revolution in political culture.

The transformation of Spanish American politics that began in the eighteenth century was sparked by the Enlightenment and competition among European powers, which together changed the ways in which Spanish American political elites viewed politics and the state. These political elites, at times voluntarily and at other times by default, altered the largely hegemonic set of political ideologies that underpinned the colonial order. The political innovations were fundamental, but the impulse that drove them came largely from the most powerful social groups. To examine this historical situation, then, is to explore what happens when a hegemonic system is transformed not by resistance from subalterns but instead by the actions of political elites.

From Colonial Corporatism to Republican Equality in Spanish America

The drastic shift in the way elites conceptualized and justified Spanish American politics affected the ways in which urban plebeians and rural indigenous peasants spoke and acted politically, and so changed popular political culture. As I understand the phrase, *political culture* encompasses both practices and discourses.[1] Political practices are very diverse, and include both actions that are openly political, such as voting or supporting a political party, and actions whose political nature is not quite so obvious, such as evading taxes and suing adversaries. Notably, actions also have discursive dimensions because they often have symbolic meaning as well as practical effect. The political discourses discussed in this book include obvious forms like speeches and newspaper editorials as well as less evident forms such as the arguments plaintiffs made in the courts. The definition of *politics* here is a very broad one, encompassing a variety of ways in which people sought to shape their worlds by influencing or replacing governments.

Political culture is deeply historical, rooted in past traditions and events, but it is never static. Political culture is perpetually changing because it is constantly contested. Although it is possible to describe the political culture dominant in one or another historical moment, we need to keep in mind that freezing that moment is no more than a convenient artifice. Historical struggles and events continue to shape an era's political culture, and to analyze any political culture we need to study political history. One useful way to think about political culture is that it is comprised of repertoires. This notion, introduced by Charles Tilly, emphasizes the changing and learned nature of political culture.[2] People learn, improvise, and invent new discourses and tactics, and they employ them to pursue goals.

From the beginning of the 1990s, many historians of Spanish America have been attracted to the problem posed by the radical change in political culture that characterized the late eighteenth century and the early nineteenth. These historians are a diverse group based in Europe, North America, and Latin America.[3] Some emphasize the importance of continuities in Spanish American political culture and the ways in which the earlier corporatist political culture was incompatible with the newly fashionable norms of liberal republicanism. Generally these historians posit a fairly sharp dichotomy between modern politics and traditional politics in Spanish America, and they imply that this gap was an important cause of Spanish America's notorious political instability in the nineteenth century.[4] Others in turn believe that Spanish America developed an important liberal political tradition, and some even argue that political instability resulted not because the transition to liberal republicanism was hindered but because it was too far-reaching.[5]

Despite these basic differences, the burgeoning historiography on Spanish America's rapidly changing political culture also seems to be developing some consensus views. Historians emphasize the incompleteness of the transition to liberal republicanism, the way people synthesized or syncretized older and newer political vocabularies, discourses, and arguments. Thus, for instance, Antonio Annino writes of "liberal political syncretisms"; Annick Lempérière discusses the ambiguities caused by the persistence of an older political terminology based on classical sources even as the means and ends of politics changed drastically; Marco Bellingeri sees a "hybrid synthesis of old privileges and new liberties"; and Michael Ducey sees "a complicated duality" of older and newer forms of political identity.[6] The incompleteness of the transition stems directly from the historical nature of political culture. Even elites attempting to drastically change Spanish America's political culture could not simply wipe the slate clean. As we will see again and again, people tended to interpret new ideologies and events on the basis of older notions and proven strategies.

Some historians continue to believe that the urban and rural poor were too ignorant, isolated, or traditional to participate in politics or understand the dramatic political changes of the period.[7] However, a host of studies have shown that at least in some regions subalterns learned, and learned to use, many of the new discourses and arguments that were introduced beginning in the late eighteenth century. These included visions of citizenship and nationality as well as liberal arguments about individual liberty.[8] Subalterns also participated in elections after the establishment of republics. The point is not that the post-Enlightenment liberal state represented a new era of freedom for the downtrodden masses, but instead that subalterns working to survive and improve their lives were sensitive to the new political ideas bandied about by elites.

With this book I hope to advance this thread of research in several ways. First of all, the book offers a systematic treatment over a long period of change. In the middle of the eighteenth century, most critiques of corporatist political culture were confined to marginal intellectual circles, but soon afterwards these critiques began to influence Spanish colonial policy. By 1850 the corporatist vision had not been entirely stamped out, but it had lost the support of political elites. Examining the intervening period should help us understand not only the causes of innovation, but the mechanisms through which change operated. Moreover, studies of state formation and political culture in the period have without exception focused on either urban areas or rural regions. This book will compare the city of Oaxaca with a key part of its rural hinterland, the mountainous and largely indigenous district of Villa Alta. These two places were subject to the same laws throughout the period, but they contained different social and ethnic groups as well as significantly different political traditions. The comparison should help us understand what kinds of events and underlying cultural features shaped how people received, interpreted, and used the new liberal republican political culture.

I chose to study the Oaxaca region for several reasons, but two of the most important are related to other historical contributions. Most of the historians arguing that rural and urban subalterns learned to use the new political repertoires of republicanism have examined periods and regions whose politics were eventful and often violent. For instance, Guerrero, the region I researched for my first book, was the scene of continual rebellions and dissident social movements from the late colonial period through the 1850s.[9] This kind of political trajectory quickened the pace of change there. In choosing Oaxaca and Villa Alta for study, I deliberately tried to select places that did not experience so much upheaval. I believed that examining more sedate areas would allow me to see the quieter political engagement and accommodation that was probably the norm. Close examination revealed that neither the city of Oaxaca nor the district of Villa Alta were quite as calm as the national historiography had led me to believe, but even so their relative stability did permit me to investigate many of the more subtle and routine ways in which new political norms were disseminated, understood, and used. I also wanted to find places with extensive surviving documentation, in particular documentation that would allow me to see how politics changed *within* indigenous villages. Villa Alta's well-preserved and indexed district judicial archive allowed me to do this to a surprising degree, even though the sheer number of villages in the district precluded a systematic search for municipal archives. My partially successful effort to understand the political dynamics inside villages during the late eighteenth century and the early nineteenth makes this study unique within the existing historiography.

MAP 1. Map of Mexico

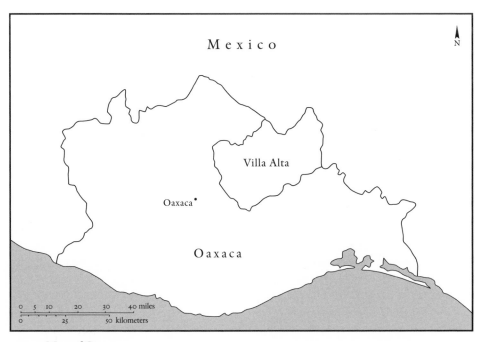

MAP 2. Map of Oaxaca

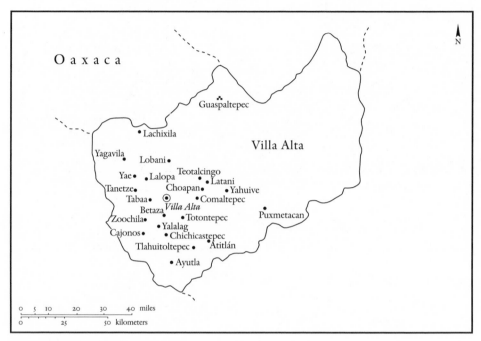

MAP 3. Map of Villa Alta

The dramatic shift in the basis of the state in Spanish America also raises a theoretical problem. Social scientists working on a variety of different eras and regions have examined what is often called *hegemony*, the way in which the state and ruling elites are able to shape political and social conflict by establishing a common discursive framework. Much of the early thinking on this idea was inspired by Antonio Gramsci, and some intellectuals suggested that hegemony prevented class conflict by inflicting a kind of false consciousness on subalterns, preventing them from realizing their true interests. For the last couple of decades this version of hegemony has remained popular only as an object of critique.[10] More commonly, social scientists have argued that hegemony does not prevent conflict so much as it sets the boundaries of debate. William Roseberry suggested in the early 1990s that

> we use the concept *not* to understand consent but to understand struggle, the ways in which the words, images, symbols, forms, organizations, institutions, and movements used by subordinate populations to talk about, understand, confront, accommodate themselves to, or resist their domination are shaped by the process of domination itself. What hegemony constructs, then, is not a shared ideology but a common material and meaningful framework for living through, talking about, and acting upon social orders characterized by domination.[11]

Similar visions of hegemony have become quite common in historical works on Mexico.[12]

Historians and social scientists typically deploy the concept of hegemony to help them understand domination and resistance. In particular the concept stresses how the very manner in which domination is justified shapes the resistance to it. Hegemony channels resistance in directions that make a given social order difficult to overthrow, and it shapes the way subalterns discuss their grievances and possible solutions. Generally, however, historians and social scientists have not yet placed much attention on situations where hegemonic frameworks are fundamentally altered by the powerful. If hegemony regulates the ways in which elites and states interact with subalterns, and the way subalterns address states and elites, what happens when the basic justifications of the ruling order shift? The literature is remarkably silent on this problem.[13] For example, postcolonial theorists are very concerned with hegemony in various guises, and they are often quite provocative and creative. Yet they are concerned less with the aftermath of colonialism on the ground than with colonial domination and the ways it shapes cultural knowledge. When postcolonial theorists do write about the end of colonialism they do not emphasize how the change in the way states are justified affects subalterns. Instead they stress the continuity of domination, arguing that native elites replace colonial elites but replicate colonial systems of power.

Needless to say, not all visions of hegemony are static. Among Latin Americanists, for instance, Florencia Mallon and William Roseberry have emphasized the historical nature of hegemony, showing that hegemony can be viewed as a process rather than an outcome.[14] Although this is a very useful approach for studying domination and resistance, the image of continual struggle and change does not say much about what happens when ruling elites replace earlier discursive frameworks from above. Instead the image of hegemonic process stresses continual struggle and adjustment from both above and below.

Few historians of Latin America have turned to situations where more drastic changes occurred. Mallon has studied the period in Peru and Mexico, 1850–1910, in which she believes "the first serious attempts" were made to "construct nation-states around hegemonic national-democratic discourses."[15] Yet, by 1850 Spanish America had already experienced the Bourbon Reforms, early Spanish liberalism, wars of independence, and decades of efforts to construct republican states. Although at times the Mexican liberals of the 1850s argued that Mexico's political and social structure was essentially unchanged from the days of darkest colonialism, this was far from the case. A 1999 article by Sergio Serulnikov examines the ways in which the new colonial project of the Bourbons "was performed and negotiated at its most concrete level, and how subaltern groups engaged and challenged state power."[16] However, this valuable piece concentrates on the Bourbon era, and does not venture into the explicitly republican projects that dominated after Latin American countries severed their ties with Spain. In recent years many historians have addressed the relationship between subalterns and the state that emerged from Mexico's 1910–1920 revolution.[17] These studies are extremely interesting and many of them are theoretically sophisticated. Yet, although the Mexican state after 1920 liked to argue that the new political order was revolutionary, in many important ways it replicated the authoritarian liberalism that had dominated the country before the Revolution. In other words, the revitalized Mexican state actually showed a great deal of philosophical and discursive continuity with earlier hegemonic projects. This continuity, in fact, was probably the key to its successes.

Thinking about hegemony can help us understand domination and resistance as well as changes in political culture. However, there are some dangers inherent in this effort. First of all, as many authors have pointed out, we need to be careful not to accord hegemonic frameworks a coherence that they lack. Hegemonic frameworks or projects were not concrete structures organized around ironclad logic. Although we can see them as constructed, they were not planned by engineers. They often contained inconsistencies and even contradictions introduced by the messy accretion of values and experiences.[18] Although often intellectuals and politicians worked to bring order to hegemonic projects, their efforts were kept in check by a strong tendency towards entropy, driven by the creative resistance of subalterns and the very messy real world where governing actually took place.

The problem of consciousness also presents a danger in these analyses. As we write about the efforts of elites to form and impose hegemonic projects on the one hand and the ways in which crafty subalterns reinterpret and resist those projects on the other, we enter a linguistic terrain that privileges a conscious instrumentality. This instrumentality is perhaps most visible in the image of repertoires introduced earlier. Thinking about political repertoires forces us to consider innovation, improvisation, and learning. However, it also assumes that there is a social actor or musician choosing the tunes played. Although certainly both elites and subalterns often thought about how they could convey their messages and achieve their aims, we should also keep in mind that people both do and say things because words and actions have cultural meanings and fill emotional needs.[19] I do not mean to imply that the elites and subalterns of the past were somehow less rational than the people who study them today. People in both the past and present constantly slide back and forth between conscious actions and culturally scripted expressions of emotions. None of us are entirely free actors.

ꕔ Methodologies

The most obvious methodological difficulties for this kind of research stem from the effort to research the politics of urban plebeians and indigenous peasants. Although the actions of these subalterns were often recorded and even their words sometimes made their way into the historical record, how do we know what they believed? James Scott has argued that at least sometimes the "public transcript" of what subalterns say to elites in official venues differs greatly from the "private transcript" of what subalterns believe or what they say to each other when they are beyond the hearing of the powerful.[20] Many of the actions discussed in this book were described on paper by literate government officials and thus form part of the public transcript. Furthermore, every quotation from a subaltern was either written for a government audience or recorded as court testimony. In all cases the authors of the quotations aimed either to prompt government officials to action or to avoid negative actions. In other words, these actions and quotations were fully part of the public transcript.

Eric Van Young has expressed doubt that there could be a wide separation between the public arguments of indigenous peasants and their private beliefs on the same issues. Van Young argues that such a separation could only be sustained by a continuous and conscious duplicity unfettered by cultural or psychological constraints.[21] Adding to this, I would argue that even the lies subalterns told in the public transcript reveal important clues about subaltern views of their lives because such tales had to be plausible not only to the audience but to the storyteller. Thus, they can tell us about the actions and causes that subalterns believed to be possible. Moreover, although certainly subalterns framed their arguments with particular audiences in mind, so did elites. Why should we hold our research on subalterns to higher standards than our biographies of Lincoln or Juárez?[22] Certainly indigenous peasants and urban plebeians were in less advantageous positions, but in neither case can we expect the words historical subjects said or wrote to faithfully reflect some pure version of what they were thinking. In the very acts of speaking and writing people shape their thoughts to make them intelligible to the audience they want to reach, and of course to influence that audience. In this way our knowledge of the political beliefs or attitudes of historical and even contemporary subjects is always limited, and we need to remain conscious of those limits.

The problem here is very daunting, but we need to keep in mind not only the limits of what we can know but also the limits of the project in which we are engaged. In this book, I am trying to understand how popular political culture changed in a particular period. Along with this, I also aim to probe what happens when hegemonic frameworks are overhauled by the powerful. Neither purpose requires knowledge of the political *beliefs* of subalterns, because in effect both political culture and hegemonic frameworks are very much part of what Scott calls the public transcript. They concern what people said and did, not what they believed, a distinction that is already part and parcel of the most common views of hegemony. In other words, it is not necessary for me to know whether or not subalterns internalized the arguments of the dominant political culture. Instead I am interested in how subalterns used those arguments, and the evidence for examining this question is very good.

Lest this appear a sophism, let me flesh it out with some extreme examples of statements that are useful to us even if we doubt that their authors believed them. Rumors and lies can tell us a great deal about political culture.[23] Rumors and lies are obviously not the same thing, but they are related by their reliance on plausibility. Rumors depend on their plausibility to survive and propagate, as the ones that do not seem plausible die out, and liars shape their stories in the hope that they will be believed. Obviously neither rumors nor lies are "true" representations of historical reality, but both can help us understand the political cultures and hegemonic frameworks within which they are devised, because they tell us what is believed to be possible.[24] In both cases the value of these statements to us is quite independent of whether or not their authors believed them.

Another methodological pitfall that is specific to historical research on indigenous peasants is what we might call the ethnographic temptation. Beginning in the early twentieth century, ethnographers fanned out among the indigenous villages of Mexico. These often-skilled researchers usually lived with the villagers for months and even years, and they have published a wealth of detail about indigenous life and politics. Certainly ethnographers also stood in a power relationship with their subjects, and arguably anthropological subjects were no more likely to reveal their "true" beliefs to ethnographers than they were to judges. For these reasons alone historians should treat ethnographic publications with due caution. However, there is also another reason we need to be cautious about ethnography. As I discuss in chapter 2, it is very tempting to project the detailed information ethnographers provide about twentieth-century peasants backward onto the latter's ancestors. After all, our own biases about rural people in general, and ethnic "others" in particular, suggest that they lead timeless existences, in which culture does not change. Moreover, indigenous subjects themselves encourage this belief when they often justify cultural practices and even the possession of particular resources as originating in a past too distant to remember. Nevertheless, indigenous societies also have a history, and the documentary evidence argues that change has been as important as continuity. For this reason I have treated ethnographies with particular care. Although I cannot claim that the historical research was not influenced at all by twentieth-century insights into indigenous peasant life and politics, I have tried to make certain that my research was not limited to the paths suggested by those insights.

If we are ever going to understand how the dramatic shift from corporatist monarchy to republican liberalism affected popular political culture, and therefore how one hegemonic discursive framework was replaced by a radically different one, it will be through research on specific sites and practices. Although sometimes dramatic events called forth dramatic statements, more mundane conflicts over resources, rights, and obligations generated most political action and discourse. The points of contact between the general political principles managed by theorists and the lives of ordinary people often existed in interactions that of and by themselves seem quite trivial. The larger contours of political culture and hegemony are exposed to scrutiny only in what often seem like minor quarrels.

For these reasons the rich and sometimes relentless exposition of details is the only manner in which I can answer questions about how popular political culture changed and what that means for understanding how hegemonic frameworks shift. It is also the only way in which I can provide adequate context for the words of politicians, plebeians, and peasants. Moreover, the corporatist political culture of colonial New Spain not only respected local diversity, it almost demanded such diversity by privileging custom as a form of law. Even when later political theories sought to standardize political practices, the new rules were actually put into effect through hundreds of conflicts and negotiations. In examining detailed cases we can see how people actually used symbols and ideas that are otherwise doomed to remain abstractions to us.[25] For this reason this book has a very tight regional focus. It discusses the broad issues through detailed analysis and comparison of two rather small places, the city that is now known as Oaxaca and the district of Villa Alta in the same region. Oaxaca and Villa Alta are probably no more representative of the great changes taking place in Mexican political culture than any other two regions. At best they show us some of the forces at work throughout the country and some of the possibilities that could be realized in other locations.

Historical comparison is difficult for several reasons. In this case, many will find it difficult to believe that the crucial shifts in the underlying justifications of political order could have had any impact on popular political culture. Some of this skepticism is no doubt based on an exaggerated estimate of the cultural gulf between elites and subalterns. However, I am willing to bet that most readers will find it easier to believe that this gulf was bridged in the cities than that it was bridged in the countryside. After all, one of our most inveterate prejudices is the notion that rural and particularly indigenous people live conservative, timeless, "natural" lives, removed from the bustle and perhaps corruption of cities. Yet, as Eric Wolf began trying to tell us in the 1950s, rural people, even impoverished peasants, have always lived their lives within larger political and economic systems.[26] Research published in the last twenty years has portrayed indigenous peasants not as simply passive victims but as often very sophisticated interlocutors who dialogue and bargain with the powerful.

Still, it will surprise many that the major difficulty I have had in comparing the ways in which indigenous peasants and urban plebeians acted and spoke politically stems from the fact that indigenous peasants are much better-documented. The urban poor do not show up in the documents in particularly articulate ways. Although it was possible to discover a great deal about what others said to plebeians, plebeians themselves apparently did not make political statements, or at least statements that show up in the archives, with anything like the frequency with which their rural colleagues did so. There seem to have been three reasons for this difference. Most obviously, urban plebeians lacked collective institutions that could voice and hence document their political arguments. Although some plebeians belonged to guilds and confraternities, these corporate organizations litigated infrequently. In contrast, soon after the conquest indigenous corporate villages flooded the colonial court system with arguments, and this propensity to litigate continued throughout the colonial period and beyond.

However, collective organizations did not provide all the political discourse seen in this book. Individuals also made political statements in courts, during protests, and during arguments. Indigenous individuals seem to have done so with much greater frequency, or at least had their statements recorded with much greater frequency. The reason again seems to be related to the strength of indigenous corporate villages. Villages not only provided an institutional voice for peasants, they also made demands on peasants. As we will see, villagers were bound up in a complicated web of obligations to the village and its patriarchy. These obligations occupied a significant portion of the time families had available to guarantee their own subsistence, and thus villagers were very sensitive to any perceived inequities in their distribution. The conflicts that arose were often ventilated in courts and thus captured in documents.

Finally, indigenous villagers also had rights to resources that in turn led to conflicts on both collective and individual levels. Villages held territorial rights, and they lobbied incessantly to preserve those rights against the pretensions of outsiders. In the case of Villa Alta, villages most often came into conflict with other villages during these struggles over land, since there were few other landowners in the district. Land was also an important generator of conflict within villages, because individual families argued over the rights to particular plots of land within village territories. Although legally families held only usufruct rights to these plots, in practice plots were inherited and therefore were expected to remain within families for generations.[27]

Obviously the different frequency with which urban plebeians and indigenous peasants show up in archives presents problems for any comparison. Moreover, plebeians and peasants tend to show up in very different ways. Often, indigenous peasants are documented as named individuals making specific arguments and carrying out specific acts. In contrast, urban plebeians, both in the colonial period and after independence, appear in the records as faceless masses subject to the scrutiny and concern of more literate and wealthy neighbors. During the transition to independence, concern and scrutiny are supplemented by efforts to mobilize plebeians, but again the plebeians themselves remain quite anonymous and often voiceless. Not surprisingly, the reader will find in these pages that greater space is devoted to the arguments of indigenous peasants, and that generally their portrayal here seems more convincing. This outcome is frankly unavoidable even if it is unfortunate. Yet I believe that there is enough material here to allow some valid comparisons.

ꝼ⃝ Overview

Chapters 1 and 2 lay out the basic social structure and political culture in the city of Oaxaca, then called Antequera, and the rural district of Villa Alta. In both chapters the aim is to present a baseline picture of what political culture looked like before the impact of the Enlightenment and the Bourbon Reforms. Chapter 1 examines Antequera, a commercial, religious, and administrative center that dominated the mostly mountainous province of Oaxaca. Socially, it was highly differentiated and highly stratified. The wealthiest inhabitants of the city tended to use race to distinguish themselves from their social inferiors, but race was not a particularly important part of the way plebeians lived and spoke about themselves. Despite this difference, the people of the city shared a common colonial political culture defined by patriarchy and bolstered by religious belief. Antequera's political culture organized the city into many corporate groups. This social and political structure was periodically demonstrated to the populace through various public displays, but the actual institutions of government were not particularly powerful.

Colonial Villa Alta, the subject of chapter 2, differed in important ways. The overwhelming portion of this rugged district's population consisted of indigenous peasants living in corporate villages. The manufacture of coarse cotton cloth tied these indigenous peasants to the vice regal economy, and a credit and marketing system dominated by regional royal officials organized this production. Indigenous officials selected by elders who had completed years of service in various offices governed the dozens of small villages of Villa Alta, and service to the village was central to political identity. However, conflicts over this system of service and government were common and often severe. Moreover, villages and village government were even more obviously patriarchal than colonial political culture as a whole. Peasants participated in an indigenous Catholicism that reaffirmed village identity even as it tied the villagers to a colonial Catholic church represented by the parish priest. Indigenous peasants engaged in politics through appeals to Spanish courts as well as riots and less serious confrontations. Conflict within villages was common despite nominal political values that abhorred such factionalism.

Chapter 3 examines the impact of the late-eighteenth-century Bourbon Reforms on political culture in both Antequera and Villa Alta. These imperial reforms aimed to increase revenue and reorganize colonial society. They also worked to change colonial political culture, reducing the power of corporate institutions. In Oaxaca, specific reforms made Antequera the official political center of the province even as they reduced the economic control exercised by the city's elite. The efforts to increase revenue collection gave further impetus to the decline in racial identity among its plebeian population. In Villa Alta, the Bourbons attacked the credit and marketing system centered on royal officials, allowing indigenous peasants greater economic freedom. Bourbon officials also worked to curb indigenous religious practices that seemed economically wasteful, and they sought to regularize the way indigenous peasants paid parish priests. Yet all of these dramatic reforms were limited by the fact that Bourbon reformers saw themselves as bureaucrats rather than politicians. They made no effort to mobilize indigenous peasants or urban plebeians to support the implementation of their policies. Bourbon intellectuals simply did not believe that such people could help carry out their project. Moreover, the Bourbon project itself contained key contradictions. In particular, the drive to maximize revenue collections led Bourbon officials to revitalize some corporate institutions and even limit the individual economic freedom they believed would lead ultimately to prosperity. In the end, the impact of Bourbon initiatives on the political culture of the urban poor and indigenous peasants was quite limited.

Chapter 4 traces an even more tumultuous period. Between 1808 and 1821, a series of momentous events shook politics throughout New Spain. First, international politics temporarily stripped the empire of its royal family. Spain's independence itself seemed to be at risk, and soon Spanish liberals constituted a new government that became the center of the empire. Spanish liberals were even more committed to change than Bourbon reformers had been, and they instituted a series of revolutionary measures that promised to make the empire a constitutional monarchy and collapse its racial hierarchy. Yet even before these reforms were implemented in New Spain, social conflicts and the crisis of legitimacy caused by the absence of the royal family sparked a more violent sort of revolution there. The insurgent leaders wanted to make New Spain autonomous under the monarchy, and they also sought to end the domination of Spanish-born elites. The insurgency had a wide social base, and subaltern insurgents often held even more drastic visions of what society should look like after the war. During the decade of war various political forces worked to mobilize urban plebeians and rural peasants to support the monarchy, embrace liberal reforms, or oppose the colonial government. These events and efforts led to important changes in the ways Antequera's plebeians and Villa Alta's indigenous peasants spoke and acted politically. Urban plebeians in particular were attracted to the increasingly popular idea that all men were equal, a notion introduced in efforts to mobilize support for the captive royal family but reinforced by the doctrines of both Spanish liberals and Mexican insurgents. The other major legacy of the 1808–1821 period was an increasing level of political tension and political intolerance that stemmed from apocalyptic visions of possible political futures.

These issues are explored further in chapter 5, which analyzes urban politics after independence. Urban political culture was shaped by the new media and tactics that entered the political repertoire after independence. These included newspapers and elections as well as new kinds of civic ceremonies. Mexico became a republic, and the city of Oaxaca, formerly Antequera, experienced the rise of two virulently opposed political parties whose partisan rivalry dominated the political landscape. Their rivalry largely arose from the introduction of electoral politics, and it was fueled by each party's fear that the other would undermine Oaxaca's core social values. Both parties worked to mobilize Oaxaca's relatively poor urban majorities, and both had significant success. These trends represented a democratization of urban politics. However, this democracy was not coupled with pluralism, and as a result the party with the upper hand usually sought to repress its rival. Therefore, elections became much less important in determining who held power in the state, and, not surprisingly, opposition politicians turned to other tactics. Oaxacan politics largely came to depend on the physical control of the city, and that physical control in turn depended on the identity of military leaders selected by whoever controlled the national government.

Chapter 6 examines the impact of new republican forms of political culture on Villa Alta's indigenous people. Notably, indigenous villagers did not participate in the fiercely partisan politics that dominated urban Oaxaca. Villagers used republican egalitarianism to reform the system of village service that underlay village politics, but the continuation of the principle of service helped them maintain village identity. Local government also changed in important ways as republican norms subverted the power of village elders. This subversion led to severe conflict in many villages, but eventually such conflict subsided as villagers learned to meld the earlier prestige of the elders with the new procedures of republican government. In some villages new types of leaders who based their power on their knowledge of Spanish and legal procedures came to exercise long-lasting influence. Villages continued to remain subject to outside government, but they often resisted state demands. In general, republican government made important alterations in the political culture of indigenous villagers in Villa Alta while allowing the retention of key features of indigenous political culture, particularly village government and the ethic of community service.

The dramatic shifts in the way Mexico's rulers legitimated their actions beginning with the Bourbon Reforms and continuing during the construction of republican government had important consequences for the political actions and arguments of urban plebeians and indigenous peasants. When Benito Juárez and the other great liberal politicians of the 1850s and 1860s launched their sustained effort to build a new liberal national state, they sometimes argued that Mexican culture and politics had reached the middle of the nineteenth century virtually untouched by the Enlightenment and new modern political norms. Nothing could be further from the truth. Mexico's political culture had been transformed in the previous century, and it would have been unrecognizable to anyone from the earlier era.

Popular political culture in the middle of the century did not fulfill the "modern" expectations of liberal politicians, and it certainly did not match the blueprints that various generations of earlier reformers had laid out. Nevertheless, judging from the party politics of urban plebeians and the communal disputes of indigenous peasants, much indeed had changed.

CHAPTER One

Society, Economy, and Politics in
Colonial Antequera

𝔍🐦 For most of the colonial period the city of Oaxaca was known as Antequera. Antequera, home of roughly 18,000 individuals in the middle of the eighteenth century, was situated at the junction of three of southern Mexico's most fertile valleys. By 1750 these valleys were shared, often grudgingly, between landed Indian villages and small estates owned by Spanish or Creole families.[1] The strategic location of Antequera, however, also gave it access to several mountainous zones where hundreds of Indian villages predominated. The city served as an administrative and commercial center for these varied rural areas.

The city was tied to the country in various ways. The bishop who served as spiritual leader for the entire province lived in Antequera. This man wielded important spiritual influence and significant, though often informal, political power. The city also was the seat of a *corregidor*, a Spanish official who governed parts of the surrounding valleys. Rural people often came to town to pursue lawsuits or contract lawyers to make arguments in the corregidor's court. Although the Spanish colonial apparatus did not directly employ many people, it did make the city an attractive site for commercial activities, which, as in many early modern cities, were more important than direct production. The city's elite directed the most prominent commercial network. These Spanish and Creole merchants channeled the labor-intensive goods produced by the province's indigenous majority into wider markets. The cooperation of individual royal officials allowed merchants to control this trade. Yet, as important as these merchants were, they shared commercial activities with other social groups. Peddlers traveled to village markets throughout the province, offering better prices and taking payment in cash. Antequera also hosted the largest of the weekly markets that tied together the different Indian communities of the valleys. Antequera's market, held on Saturdays in the city center, was a meeting place for city and country. Villagers, including some from adjacent mountainous districts, could sell their surplus of crops and handicrafts and buy the items they needed. For villagers, Antequera was the place to buy fireworks or rent costumes for patron saint celebrations. In the city they could also contract specialists who aided in these celebrations, created religious objects, or decorated sacred spaces. The city's population included fireworks makers, musicians, gilders, silversmiths, and painters.[2] Some rural people immigrated to the city, although in the second half of the eighteenth century the rate of immigration was slow.

A few elite families dominated the social landscape of the city much as their imposing mansions dominated the geography of the city's center. These prominent families earned the bulk of their wealth through commerce, but some also maintained landed estates in Oaxaca's valleys. They cultivated ties to colonial officials in the different districts of the province.[3] Officials were able to maintain commercial monopolies in their districts, lending indigenous producers cash, tools, and work animals in exchange for the right to buy products at fixed prices. One lucrative product was cochineal, a dyestuff produced by indigenous males who cultivated special species of cacti, seeded them with insect larvae, and then laboriously collected and dried the mature insects. Cochineal was in great demand both in New Spain and in Europe, where it provided the bright reds of popular fashion. A second lucrative good was coarse cotton cloth, produced by indigenous women in mountain districts, especially Villa Alta. This textile was an important item in regional markets and clothed much of the region's population. It was also popular in the mining districts of central and northern Mexico.

The urban population of Antequera produced tools, furniture, shoes, cloth, and clothing. The latter two categories were particularly prominent in the late colonial period. Urban textile production increased dramatically in the 1740s and soon the city boasted hundreds of working looms and tailor shops. Earlier in the century some wealthy members of society had owned *obrajes*, large textile workshops staffed by bound labor. However, by the middle of the century master artisans who employed apprentices and journeymen produced most textiles, along with many other urban products. Antequera's guild of cotton weavers was incorporated in 1757, and it joined over a dozen other guilds in the city.[4]

The available documentation makes it easier to enter into the cultural and social worlds of Antequera's elite than to enter those of the mass of the population. Clearly the members of the elite took care to preserve their sense of difference from the rest of society. They built imposing mansions near the city center and financed the even more impressive religious buildings for which the city is still known today.[5] The wealthiest of these families preserved the family holdings in *mayorazgos*, preventing partible inheritance from dissipating their patrimony.[6] Elite families also controlled the town council, whose posts were all either inherited or bought from the Crown. These families seemed to perceive themselves as Spaniards surrounded by a sea of darker people. They were often headed by immigrants from Spain who married Creole women but taught their Spanish nephews how to run their businesses. They also took care to preserve their *limpieza de sangre*, or purity of blood, which they needed to demonstrate in order to assume important religious posts or inherit seats on the town council. Limpieza de sangre was generally demonstrated through the testimony of prominent friends of the family. For example, Geronimo de Alemán, royal constable of the city, testified on behalf of Don Ignacio Nicolas de Lazarte in 1737 that Lazarte's mother was a product of the marriage between a Spaniard and a prominent Creole, and his father Don Juan de Lazarte was

> from the city of San Sebastian, Province of Guipusio, *hijodalgo* [hidalgo, noble, son of something] of known home and house lot, due to which his father and other ancestors obtained the honorary posts of that place, and said Don Juan has been Alcalde Ordinario of this city with great acceptance of the whole population, showing through his very upright actions his nobility, cleanliness, and descent from old Christians, free of all bad race, showing the same his wife Doña María Antonia with her virtue and modesty, and her Christian behavior, arranged so publicly. Everything in this statement is known and no one is ignorant of it.[7]

Clearly there is something formulaic in this incantation, but formulas can also tell us much about those who invoke them. The concept of purity of blood had originally developed in Iberia on religious grounds as a means of placing officials above suspicion of covert Jewish or Muslim belief. Yet the emphasis in Lazarte's statement is on the connection to Spain and to prominent families there, and the absence of any blood tainted by origin in Africa or America.

Readers familiar with the growing literature on the concept of honor in Latin America will not be surprised to know that elite families, and those that aspired to elite status, took their honor very seriously.[8] They struggled to prevent their daughters from marrying men considered to be less than honorable, or at least not financially eligible for elite status.[9] They also went to court when they felt others had insulted them. In 1797 Don Rosendo Antonio Monteagudo tried to pay a servant's debts to José García, the baker the servant had previously worked for. García threatened to kill Monteagudo for being a "liar," an insult that led Monteagudo to take him to court.[10] In 1765 Doña Josepha de Aguero, widow of Don Mathias Joseph, became involved in an angry argument with her business partner Don Manuel de Cossio. She accused him of calling her a "filthy pig" that he wished "the devil to take in body and soul." She leveled criminal charges, asking the judge to punish him for "shaming himself with people of the quality and distinction that I have."[11] Such clashes over honor were closely related to the elite's position in a multiethnic, socially stratified society. This relationship can be seen clearly in the complaint of Doña Isabel de Lorenzana, wife of Don Pedro Antonio Gaytuzzo, against Pioquinto Vacas in 1754. She had sought to defend one of her servants against his mistreatment, but Vacas insulted her, telling her to "screw herself." When she answered that "only mulattos and low people used that term," he called her a "mulata bitch, vile and very low person." After he refused to apologize she took him to court, saying, "In this city my nobility and that of my husband Don Pedro are well known, such that no one can allege ignorance because they are public and notorious" and "the injuries, verbal or physical, done to noble persons should be punished severely, especially when the aggressor is a person of low sphere and quality."[12] As Anne Twinam points out, "honor was profoundly important because it rationalized hierarchy, the division of Hispanic society between a privileged few and a deprived majority." In her words, although other social groups in Latin America "might have their own versions of honor . . . only colonial elites reserved it exclusively for themselves."[13]

Exactly who was it that the city's elite defined their honor against? One group of importance was the province's indigenous population, scattered in hundreds of villages. Another, more immediate, group was the plebeian population of the city itself. The elite often viewed the behavior of this group as distasteful, disorderly, and dangerous. In 1762 Spaniard Manuel

Nieto de Silva y Moctezuma, "decent and reputable person," accused of carrying arms illegally, responded that he did so "for his defense as a gentleman, given that there are so many lazy and vagabond people in this city, who assault anyone at any hour of the day or night."[14] Responding to the elite's concerns, in 1776 Viceroy Antonio María de Bucareli commiserated with them about "harmful effects brought by the idle life which your wretched plebeians are given to" and went on to lament the fact that plebeians insulted and obstructed the town officers who sought to control them.[15] However, elite descriptions of the mass of the population are generally vague as well as fearful. Moreover, they can give us no clues about how the members of the "plebe" saw themselves and their social world.

The common people of cities like Antequera are very difficult to research because few documents provide information about them. In fact, despite our prejudices to the contrary, we know much more about the lives of indigenous peasants than we do about plebeians because indigenous peasants were much more likely to bring disputes before the judicial system. Lacking both property and the tight web of obligations that governed indigenous peasant life, plebeians almost never became involved in civil court cases. Most legal petitions brought to the courts by plebeians stem from criminal cases, and the petitioners are often the accused.[16]

Still, the testimony of witnesses in criminal cases, and the identity of those witnesses, provide clues about the lives and concerns of the urban poor. These documents strongly suggest that plebeians did not share the elite's preoccupation with race. In the streets of Antequera individuals of different ethnic identities and economic positions conducted economic and social transactions or bustled past one another on urgent business. The plush fabrics and capes of the relatively wealthy mingled with the simple "shirt and pants" of peasants.[17] Indians who lived in the valley villages or further afield entered the city to work, to sell and buy, and to see authorities. The plebeians who resided in the city were racially heterogeneous, and many plebeians were of mixed or indeterminate race. They included Indians who had immigrated to the city from the mountains and valleys of the province, the descendants of slaves brought from Africa, and many people with mixed Indian, African, or Spanish genetic and cultural heritage. There seems to have been no effective residential segregation in the city. Several neighboring villages were being gradually absorbed into the city in the eighteenth and nineteenth centuries. These villages retained traditional village governments but were usually called suburbs or barrios in the documents. They remained centers of Indian population and were often first ports of call for immigrants from other indigenous villages, but mestizos and mulattos also lived there and some Indians lived in the more central neighborhoods of the city.[18] In court cases it was common for witnesses from several racial categories and occupations to testify about the same events even when they took place in residential neighborhoods. The list of witnesses and participants in a 1769 brawl in the Barrio de los Alzados includes Joseph Lorenzo de Orozco, a mestizo porter; Juan Ramos, a cochineal peddler; Indian Manuel de la Trinidad, a tanner; Indian María Dominga Ruiz; and Juan de Antonio Jesus, a mestizo tanner.[19] The poor of different racial backgrounds and occupations seem to have lived more or less elbow-to-elbow.[20]

Witnesses in criminal cases and even people dictating their wills did not generally identify individuals by race. Often they did not know the last names of their neighbors, but identified them through their parentage, occupation, or nicknames like "Lightning" and "Worst." For instance, when the mestizo Obaldo Antonio Savedra dictated his will in 1765, he was owed many small sums by people such as "Dionicio the Silversmith, Francisco the Candle maker, Bartholo the Candle maker, Antonio the Mason," and so on.[21] Witnesses offered similar forms of identifying people in criminal cases, for instance "Bernarda the Chocolate-maker."[22] For most plebeians, race was an abstract category that was only recorded or even assigned to them when they were called as witnesses or married.[23] As John Chance has shown, there were very high rates of racially mixed marriages in the city.[24] Clearly the social and economic networks of the mass of Antequera's population stretched beyond racial categories. It is striking, for instance, that in 1764 Carpio Antonio de Matos, a mestizo dealer in building supplies, would choose "Vicente de Zarate alias Concepción . . . free pardo resident of this city, master button maker" to execute his will.[25] Retail merchants and master artisans seem to have associated freely with people of various races and occupations. To the extent that racial hierarchy was important to the hegemony of the colonial state, that hegemony was limited in urban Antequera.[26] Elite visions of racial hierarchy simply did not resonate with plebeian Antequerans.

In general, the documents suggest that Antequera was divided between a relatively small elite that stressed its racial identity and many people of more modest means who rarely thought about race at all. Connections between these groups appear to have been tenuous. The mercantile elite seems to have been oriented outward, culturally toward Spain and economically toward the villages of the province, where they worked through Spanish officials and associates.[27] Although R. Douglas Cope has argued that Spaniards and Creoles in colonial Mexico City enjoyed extensive patronage connections with plebeian clients, that does not seem to have been the case in Antequera.[28] Various convents and confraternities owned much of the urban real estate that plebeians rented, and the mercantile elite seems to have avoided investment in urban rental property. Moreover, they did not lend money directly to the city's population, although they did make some loans to shops which in turn allowed purchases on credit. Instead, most people of modest means turned to their peers for loans.[29] Certainly many poor Antequerans worked in the homes and shops of master artisans we might think of as middle-class, but this latter group did not share the wealth and worldview of the elite mercantile families.[30] Both the lack of direct economic connection between elite and plebeians and their dramatically different perspectives about race would have significant consequences when government came to be based on popular elections in the early nineteenth century.[31]

ʃ❧ *Political Culture and Politics in Colonial Antequera*

Antequera's merchant elite and plebeians may have had different visions of the importance of race, but the city's inhabitants seem to have largely shared a vision of political structure and political legitimacy. Moreover, they also shared religious beliefs that were important to politics. Social order and social life were based on linked ideas about justice and salvation. The wealthy and the poor worshiped in the same churches, venerated the same saints, appeared in the same courts, and used similar arguments to sway judges and, ultimately, the king. The colonial state and its attendant political culture enjoyed a significant degree of hegemony, but this hegemony did not prevent conflict and resistance. Instead, hegemony contained conflict and resistance by controlling the ways in which people could express political goals.

Colonial political culture before the Bourbon era was at the same time bizarrely complex and absurdly simple. It was complex because individuals belonged to a myriad of overlapping corporate organizations, each of which had a separate relationship with the king. Corporate organizations ranged from the large and vague "Republic of Spaniards" and "Republic of Indians" to religious orders, guilds, Indian village communities, and professional organizations. Sometimes membership in an organization entitled one to trial in special courts. More often it simply entitled one to trial under different laws and regulations. Moreover, the pre-Bourbon legal order favored customary practice over innovation and typically new laws were enacted without abolishing old laws. As a consequence, contending parties could almost always support their case with some legal precedent.[32] The thicket of legal identities and laws makes court records challenging reading.

At the same time, colonial political culture was built on some very simple but powerful metaphors. The king was seen as ruling his subjects as a father rules his children. As an important consequence, the king was always assumed to be benevolent. In this model, any violations of justice were clearly the result of mistaken policies or evil officials, and the point of political action was to bring these problems to the attention of the benevolent monarch so he could correct the abuses or mistakes. The only metaphor that rivaled the familial one was that of society as a body, with the king as its head. Yet this corporal metaphor again emphasized loyalty, as the arm or leg could not hope to govern the body.[33] These metaphors had important consequences. Subjects had no rights versus the king. They could approach the king, and his courts, only as passive petitioners. Moreover, loyalty was prized above obedience. Officials could refuse to implement royal orders and laws if they believed them to be impractical or mistaken. Conflicts were often resolved through negotiation, and repression was a last resort. In fact, the ability of the colonial state to repress was remarkably weak until the Bourbon reforms, and far from strong even after that.[34]

Urban residents did not come face to face with these tenets of colonial political culture as often as indigenous peasants did. City dwellers were much less likely to be involved in lawsuits or criminal court cases. Their rare appearances in court, and thus in the documentary record, tended to result from disputes between individuals rather than conflicts over collective rights. Yet the colonial system demonstrated its principles to urban residents on a remarkably regular basis. As Dorothy Tanck de Estrada argues, the principal forms of communication in colonial culture were predominantly oral and visual rather than written.[35] Royal laws and decrees were paraded through the cities and read aloud in strategic spots. Colonial authorities also spent large sums presenting civic and religious ceremonies on important occasions. Some were annual, while others marked liminal political moments. Annually, the whole society was represented in Corpus Christi and Holy Week ceremonies and processions as well as the annual feast of Antequera's patroness, the Virgin of the Soledad. On the latter occasion the city's royal standard-bearer carried the royal banner at the head of the city's faithful. Liminal political moments that inspired ceremonies included the arrival of new bishops, the accession of new popes, news of Spain's victories in international wars, and funeral rites for deceased kings as well as oaths of obedience to their successors. On all of these occasions the king had a very potent symbolic presence.[36]

We will never know how the mass of Antequera's population experienced these ceremonies. Although they were designed to inspire emotion, and official observers sometimes reported on the reactions of the crowds, there is no trustworthy evidence about how urban people perceived the ceremonies. What we do know is that the colonial state and church took them very seriously. Sonia Lombardo de Ruiz has discovered a contemporary statement that neatly captures this attitude. Viceroy Revillagigedo argued in the late eighteenth century that "the people do not have any other ideas than those formed by external symbols, and along with them their esteem, subordination and obedience rise and fall. For this reason ceremonies are so recommendable and important, not only in political matters but also in the spiritual."[37] Thus, authorities designed the ceremonies carefully and spent large sums on them. For example, when Antequera's city council learned in December 1746 of the death of King Felipe V, they immediately declared public mourning and ordered stores to sell appropriate cloth at low prices so that the population could dress properly. The official funeral, the oath to his successor Fernando VI, and the thanksgiving mass, however, were postponed until February so that proper arrangements could be made. Even so, the town council members were not satisfied by their efforts, which had been hampered by an epidemic and famine. A year later they planned new ceremonies, to include a week of bullfights, coaches depicting allegorical scenes provided by different guilds, and a night of fireworks.[38] To officials, the ceremonies were important in preserving the general patterns of social order, but they also believed that the ceremonies should exactly demonstrate hierarchies within the colonial political and social order. Thus, throughout Spanish America, royal and local officials debated and even sued each other over protocols and their exact placement in ceremonies.[39]

The king was *assumed* to be benevolent but he was *known* to be distant, at least physically.[40] His principal representative in Antequera was the corregidor, who administered the territory and presided over its principal court. The corregidor also presided over the meetings of the town council. Unlike the king, the corregidor was a visible presence in the city, where he could be seen moving around the center or occupying the most important place in civic and religious ceremonies. He was enormously powerful, and for elite merchant families in particular his favor could be an important source of wealth. Yet his actions and judgments could always be appealed, to the Audiencia (the high court of New Spain), the viceroy, and ultimately the Council of Indies and the king. A titled legal advisor helped those corregidors who had not studied law preside over cases. This provision suggests how important law was as a tool of colonial hegemony. Most people who sued in the corregidor's court used lawyers, but doing so was not required, and more than a few legal petitions found in local archives seem to have been composed through the verbatim transcription of the emotional appeals of relatively poor individuals. In these petitions, as well as those written by lawyers, the corregidor, like the king, was appealed to as a benevolent patriarch.

The *ayuntamiento*, or city council, was one of the most visible corporate bodies of the polity. The officers of the ayuntamiento were members of the local elite. Some of the posts had been bought from the Crown early in the colonial period, and were then passed down within families. The Crown also sold a few posts as they became vacant. Regular elections in which sitting members could vote filled other positions.[41] The colonial ayuntamiento is a bit of a puzzle for those accustomed to more modern political forms. It was at the same time very important and remarkably powerless. The colonial ayuntamiento represented local interests to the king and maintained order on a daily basis, but it met infrequently at best. For example, it is telling that the town council minutes of 1746, 1747, and 1748 are contained in a single volume with 182 folios, while its post-independence city council required more than 600 folios for just its 1824 minutes. Yet the ayuntamiento could be important. In the drought year of 1746 the council invested 12,000 pesos in buying grain to sell at below-market prices.[42] It provided nightly police patrols that were the only effective police presence in the city. Moreover, council members represented the city symbolically in an amazing number of religious ceremonies. These were carefully recorded in the 1806 minutes. There were nineteen major ceremonies and processions that required the presence of the entire council. These included the various Holy Week ceremonies, the Feast of the Ascension, Corpus Christi, the Feast of the Virgin of the Soledad, and other major saint days. A further thirty-nine religious celebrations required the presence of at least one council member. The members divided these minor obligations among themselves. Of course, civic ceremonies, such as funeral rites for kings, required the attendance of all members.[43]

Posts on the ayuntamiento were prized. Those that were filled by the voting of the town council sometimes led to heated disputes. The others were quite expensive. In 1798 four posts were auctioned for between 1,300 and 1,525 pesos each, sums that exceeded an entire decade's income for the vast majority of city residents. The *alcaldes ordinarios* (council members) who policed the city sometimes found their duties laborious and expensive. As Intendant Antonio Moya y Pesas noted in 1791, the posts involved expense because alcaldes paid the officers who aided them in policing the city and could not spend as much time on their own business. They also had to personally patrol the city every night.[44] It is therefore puzzling that council posts were so desirable. Service in the royal administration as corregidors or alcaldes mayors for rural areas could be profitable, because these officials used their political power to manipulate markets, but town council members did not have the power needed to reap direct profits. Rather, the appeal of municipal posts seems to have stemmed from the prestige and honor associated with them. Such posts were the exclusive province of the wealthiest and most prominent families, which is precisely what made them valuable. Seen this way, the apparently onerous requirement that town council members participate in processions and ceremonies becomes in fact the reason that the posts were so prized.

The town council was the maximum local expression of corporatist society and political culture in Antequera, but it was far from the only one. People of relatively modest means also had access to corporate identity. Guilds were among the most visible kinds of corporations. Available records do not allow us to confidently determine how many guilds operated in Antequera. The constitutions of most seem to have been lost, and the only more or less systematic counts of guilds result from Bourbon efforts to collect tribute from them. Still, it is instructive that such a list details thirtyseven guilds in 1810, including one that grouped three trades.[45] These guilds provided a number of urban goods and services, and they were not seen as socially equal. Water carriers, masons, and carpenters, for instance, were not as wealthy as silversmiths, nor were their occupations considered as prestigious.[46] Defying the norm, as of 1757 the guild of pulque-makers included both Indians and Spaniards.[47] The members of a particular guild were not necessarily economic equals. For instance, in 1783 the cotton weavers' guild included masters, journeymen, and apprentices. Masters owned the largest shops, which contained as many as four looms, and employed several journeymen and/or apprentices. Journeymen also owned some shops, but none owned more than a single loom.[48] Some guilds in Antequera never had formal constitutions. All guilds, both formal and informal, sought to regulate their trades. They controlled entry into their trades by requiring apprenticeships and entrance exams, and they vehemently denounced interlopers. However, it is unclear how effective guilds were at preventing competition and setting prices.

Guilds were also important for other reasons. They sometimes represented their members in appeals to political authorities. Such appeals usually stemmed from their efforts to restrict their trades. Each guild also held annual elections, typically choosing a judge, one or more inspectors, and sometimes a steward.[49] Only masters could vote in elections, and these annual meetings alone probably did not provide a strong basis for group identity or political sociability. However, the evidence suggests that most guilds also met at other times of the year, and that guilds could have been important loci of identity. Each guild had a patron saint for which it organized devotion. The guilds also participated in the more general religious ceremonies of Antequera, underwriting and sometimes building floats and statues to carry or drag in procession. For instance, for the funeral procession of Jesus held on Good Friday, each guild provided a sumptuously dressed statue of an angel, along with food and drink.[50] Of course this expression of religious fervor could also be a burden. In 1757, the pulque-makers' guild petitioned to be released from this obligation. The guild officers alleged that they were not really a guild because they were merchants rather than practitioners of a mechanical art. They also argued that the officers of the guild had to carry the statue themselves because most guild members preferred to sell pulque to the crowds assembled for the procession.[51] Some guilds also had their own confraternities, or *cofradías*, which both helped organize the veneration of their patron saints and served as spiritual welfare institutions.

ꝰ Religion and Society

Religion and state, often termed the "Two Majesties," were not neatly separable in colonial Antequera. In the words of Annick Lempérière, in colonial Mexico the function of government was "above all spiritual, but its temporal dimension was no less important: in conditions of misery and discord, men do not achieve salvation."[52] Religious rhetoric permeated all forms of political discourse. In colonial Mexico, as William Taylor points out, religion "provided a focus for authority, a cosmic model for human order in a society where one's dying thoughts still turned to confession and salvation, and an institutional framework for expressing social relationships and mediating inequalities."[53] Yet the relationship between religion and politics also worked in the other direction. Few religious decisions and developments were totally removed from political considerations. In what was probably Antequera's most important protest movement during the colonial period, many city inhabitants backed Bishop Angel Maldonado's effort to avoid reassignment in 1712. They held public demonstrations on his behalf, prevented the bells of most of the city's churches from being rung to celebrate the arrival of his designated successor, and staged sarcastic street plays.[54] Faced with this opposition, the viceroy backed down, and Maldonado remained as bishop. Moreover, there was no sharp line between religious and civic ceremonies. Both stressed the sacred nature of political and social order.[55]

Antequera's massive cathedral shared the central plaza with the government palace and various mercantile establishments. However, on a day-to-day basis, perhaps the most visible symbols of Antequera's religious devotion were the city's convents and monasteries with their associated churches. There were seven monasteries for men and five convents for women. The grandest of all was Santo Domingo, which still dominates the city's urban space. Hundreds of friars, monks, and nuns inhabited the monasteries and convents, and many faithful attended mass at the chapels attached to them. Yet relatively few Antequerans could aspire to join religious orders. Entering a religious order required wealth, and most convents were only open to persons of unquestioned Spanish ancestry. The only exception, the Convent of Our Lady of the Angels, was established for the daughters of indigenous nobles.[56]

Although relatively few Antequerans could join convents, many were able to fulfill religious and social needs through another type of organization. The city was home to thirty-six cofradías, each of which was headquartered at one of the city's churches. Some churches had as many as four confraternities, although one or two was the norm.[57] Cofradía membership offered individuals forms of sociability and some recognition of their piety and good conduct. It was not uncommon for an individual to be buried in the habit of his or her cofradía, as the master hatmaker Pedro Miguel Ramirez was in 1791.[58] Cofradías were in one sense a kind of spiritual insurance. They assured their members that someone would seek out the parish priest to administer last rites, that someone would say masses for their souls, and that someone experienced would negotiate with the parish priest about funeral expenses.[59] For example, the members of the Cofradía de San Anastacio paid weekly dues to finance masses for the souls of live and dead members and sometimes extra dues in Holy Week to pay for the cofradía's role in the celebration. If a member received last rites, his comrades accompanied the priest bringing the sacrament with lamps and music. Moreover, when a member died his family received between fifteen and twenty pesos as well as candles and space in the church for burial.[60] Members of the Cofradía de Nuestra Señora de los Angeles paid one half-real weekly and in return received a funeral and burial with twelve mourners, two masses said for their souls, and a sackcloth burial shroud. If they died outside the city they would receive instead twenty masses said for their souls. A further two masses were said yearly for all living and dead members.[61] Cofradía members could reassure themselves that they would receive a relatively dignified passage from this world to the next, and aid in their efforts to achieve eternal life. Antequerans seem to have seen these rituals as crucial in helping to expiate sin and assure salvation.[62] The sentence of one accessory to homicide included a sum to be paid for twenty-five masses for the soul of the victim.[63] In 1761, as the daughter of Joseph de Lazo, a mestizo, was dying, he went to the house of a priest in search of "a candle for her Soul." The priest did not have one, and in the words of Lazo his daughter Angela died "at the age of twelve years one month and nineteen days in which there was no candle."[64] The heartbroken statement of Lazo suggests the importance of the services cofradías provided for the dying and dead. The Cofradía de Nuestra Señora de Los Angeles also paid the priest's fee when members married.[65] These benefits were not acts of charity. They were spelled out for the members in contracts they received upon joining the confraternity, and failure to pay duties cancelled the obligation.[66] Confraternities kept careful track of dues for this purpose.

Confraternities were not only linked to churches, they were also sometimes tied to particular occupations. For example, the Congregación de San Nicolás, based in the cathedral, grouped secular priests from throughout the diocese. Its members had masses said for their souls and received three reales a day if they became ill.[67] In 1755 almost every member of the Cofradía de la Santísima Trinidad was a tailor.[68] The Cofradía de Santa Verónica was founded at the instigation of blacksmiths in 1773, although its constitution also allowed the admittance of other people.[69] In addition, some cofradías were racially exclusive. When they were founded in the seventeenth century, the Cofradías de las Nieves and la Sangre de Cristo were composed of mulattos, and the Cofradía de Jesus Nazareno was limited by its constitution to Indians of the barrio of Jalatlaco.[70] Yet there is no evidence that this racial segregation survived into the eighteenth century.

Although some cofradías limited membership, in general cofradías were the most nominally egalitarian institutions in colonial society, an institutional artifact of the Christian doctrine that all individuals had the potential to reach eternal life. Juan Javier Pescador suggests that these brotherhoods, as they were called, should be seen as spiritual families. In his detailed study of the records of a Mexico City parish, Pescador found that the growing popularity of cofradías in the eighteenth century democratized death, giving relatively humble people access to a dignified burial in the interior of the church.[71] The most arresting evidence of this apparent egalitarianism is the fact that many cofradías admitted women as full members.[72] This admittance was not just the result of widows retaining their husbands' rights, as sometimes happened in guilds. Women were admitted to cofradías as individuals, and they made up a substantial proportion of the membership. The Cofradía of Santa Barbara, for instance, had 82 females and 32 males on its rolls in 1767.[73] In 1787 the enormous Cofradía de Jesus de los Desamparados had 1,486 members, including 972 women.[74]

The available records do not allow us to know how many Antequerans belonged to cofradías, or what percentage of the adult population was covered. Certainly the total membership of cofradías was over 2,000 and there were probably fewer than 9,000 adults in the city. Cofradías were thus not confined to the elite. Explaining the popularity of cofradías is not simple. Membership brought some prestige or at least recognition of one's piety. Cofradías also had an important role in the community social life manifested in public religious celebrations. In 1787, for instance, the Cofradía de Jesus de los Desamparados spent 571.5 pesos on last rites and death benefits for members, but it spent more, 713.5 pesos, on other religious celebrations. This fiscal datum suggests the relative weight of individual and community ritual for cofradías.[75] Moreover, the support cofradías provided for the major expenses of individual religious life could also be found elsewhere. Families could borrow money for such occasions, and church rules allowed the impoverished some relief from expenses. The cathedral parish also offered a "parochial agreement" under which individuals paid about half the monthly dues cofradías required. In return they received funeral rites and masses for their souls. This particular agreement may have been designed with lower-class women in mind, as unlike many cofradía constitutions it also paid for marriage.[76]

The historiography of cofradías has concentrated heavily on their economic role, tracing the investments cofradías made and conflicts over the control of their wealth.[77] Yet cofradías were important institutions in Antequera's political culture throughout the period examined in this book. They held annual meetings in which members selected officers who administered finances and benefits. The records suggest that women as well as men sometimes voted in these elections.[78] At first, some cofradías limited voting rights to founding members. As founding members died, the survivors gradually extended voting rights to other longtime members.[79] During the colonial period royal officials were required to attend all cofradía meetings, although it is hard to tell whether this order was scrupulously followed. At the very least the Bourbons felt compelled to reissue the order in 1791.[80] The available records are silent about the topics discussed at cofradía meetings. One assumes that voters chose officers on the basis of demonstrated piety and honesty. Perhaps officers needed some degree of literacy in order to keep cofradía records. Juan Javier Pescador found that in Mexico City's Santa Catarina parish even humble cofradías were led by wealthy parishioners who apparently served as a charitable duty. However, the administration of cofradías took place through many minor officers who actually collected the weekly or monthly dues.[81] We do not know if cofradía members also met to plan religious celebrations, as they often do today. In any event, they were one of the most important social institutions of urban Oaxaca.

Religion justified the social and political organization of Antequera, and religious activities in turn required a great deal of political and social organizing. Yet numerous documents remind us that religion was also an important part of the emotional life of individuals. Urban Oaxacans lived in an uncertain world, where death was never far away. For them, Catholicism not only justified the social order, it also held out the promise of eternal life. Probably not every individual took part in all of the religious events that filled the annual calendar, or even attended weekly mass. Yet it is hard to be unmoved by documents like those describing the obligations cofradías had on the illness and death of their members, or wills that began by bequeathing the deceased's soul to God. Even the semiliterate request of the convict Polinar Gonzalez to be released from unjust imprisonment suggests the importance of individual religiosity. Addressing the judge, Gonzalez invoked as intercessors the Señora de Athocha and the Señora de Guadalupe, adding, "To whom I commend the important life of Your Excellency, asking that they give you True Light to rule as you should rule in the duty of your ministry, and that Our Sovereign (God) gives you more and more laurels, and afterwards, eternal life."[82]

Nevertheless, the documents can tell us only so much about individuals' religious feelings. Wills, for instance, might be formulaic, or at least owe as much to the religious beliefs of the person recording the will as to those of the person who nominally authored the document. The careful provision for the religious ceremonies of last rites and funerals through cofradía membership might indicate the need to keep up outward appearances as well as genuine concern about eternal life. Polinar Gonzalez and others who invoked religious intercessors in court and wished long lives for their judges might have been insincere, wanting only to curry favor. However, as Stephanie Wood points out, one kind of evidence of religious fervor is much more difficult to dismiss.[83] Like the indigenous peasants of Central Mexico Wood discusses in her work, Antequerans owned numerous religious objects which were recorded in their wills and probate proceedings or when creditors embargoed their goods to extract payment. Religious items seem to have been important for individuals of varying socioeconomic positions. In 1810 Doña María Josefa Gonzalez Mimiaga, part of the highest strata of Antequera's society, included dozens of religious paintings and statues together worth more than 900 pesos in her dowry of 4,820 pesos. When the master silversmith Diego Ruiz was unable to pay his debts in 1745 his creditors embargoed forty-one small religious paintings and a crucifix among his other goods. The mestizo fish merchant Obaldo Antonio Savedra, son of an indigenous leader of the barrio of Jalatlaco, prepared his will in 1765. His possessions included nineteen small religious paintings, twelve small religious statues, and three larger religious statues. When an unnamed indigenous woman of Jalatlaco dictated a deathbed will in 1810 it included a cross, two statues, and thirty religious paintings.[84] The demand for such religious objects must have been formidable, which makes it easier to understand how Antequera's economy supported thirty-six painters in 1792.[85]

꩜ *Gender, Society, and Politics*

Gender played an important role in colonial political culture. The king and by extension his agents in the New World were held to govern society as a father does his family.[86] As Steve Stern explains, authority within the family was the fundamental metaphor for authority in society, and gender not only differentiated men from women, it also served to order hierarchies among men and among women. Political authority was justified in gendered terms.[87] Not surprisingly, gendered language abounds in the political arguments and appeals preserved in the colonial documents that provide evidence about life in Antequera. This visibility of gender presents a marked contrast with the relative absence of living women in the same documents.

Women sometimes appear as witnesses or victims, but generally the documentation makes them seem rather passive. Because women were supposed to be governed by family patriarchs, they had little direct contact with the state institutions that generated documentation.

In fact, the women who seem most active are those whose patriarchs were missing. In 1743 María Josepha, a free black woman, tried to protect her mulatto son from habitual mistreatment at the hands of his owners. She worked to arrange for his sale to a new owner, but was stymied by the high price set by his current owners. She appealed to the court to set a new price, and her appeal successfully led to the sale of her son.[88] As a free and apparently unmarried black woman, María Josepha seems to have been one of the few women not directly subject to a male. When other women approached the courts it was often because their patriarch was absent due to death or disability. Women in such situations appealed to royal officials, and by extension the king, to act as the fathers or husbands they lacked. In a poignant example, the Indian girl Francisca de Aquino from the Indian barrio of Jalatlaco appealed to authorities for her release from prison. Apparently she and her father had been imprisoned for some crime she claimed to know nothing about, and now her mother was ill and needed her help. Francisca stated, "I have no other shelter but God, and after God Your Excellency, because my Father is imprisoned in this Royal Jail and my Mother is in the Village very ill." She goes on to call herself a "Poor girl" and says that she hopes that "Your Excellency as my Father and Lord" will free her from prison.[89] Doña María Ballados appealed to officials in a similar though less compelling situation. Her husband, though alive, was disabled, and now she asked that the small shop she ran to support the family be exempt from taxation.[90]

Sometimes even a patriarch who was not physically disabled might be unable to solve problems, and women had to appeal beyond him to the government. In 1801 the nuns of the Convent of the Concepción were distressed at the physical state of the convent. They directed their plea for a new building to both their confessor and the head of the provincial government. The confessor is repeatedly referred to as "Our Beloved Father," and in the document this outpouring of familial reverence seems to extend to the colonial official as well.[91]

Women could also appeal to the government to make claims on the wealth of deceased patriarchs. Typically such claims were made against the executors of wills, and they were often based on a family relationship. Not surprisingly, the arguments used were very gendered. When Doña Ana

María Armendariz protested her family's effort to cut her out of her father's will, her lawyer pointed out that the executors had not given her any money to tide her over while they executed the will. He asked, "Should she beg, or should she serve, or should she prostitute herself?" The lawyer pointed out that in the absence of an inheritance Ana María would support herself "with the labors of her sex" but since the family had money she should have her share.[92] In at least one case the claim a woman made on the wealth of a deceased patriarch was based less on a family relationship than on services rendered. María Josefa de Lions argued that she served her relative Don Felipe Singuenza for eight years before his death. She nursed him through his various chronic illnesses, cooked "special and exquisite foods" for him, and served him as "seamstress, laundress and many times tailor, sewing the new and old for him and his son, whom [she] cared for the same as the mother who bore him would have been able to," all without any salary but the room and board that any person would pay the lowliest servant boy. Now she demanded that the executors of Singuenza's will treat her fairly, compensating her for her time and labor.[93]

Nevertheless, lower-class women who appealed to royal courts against even lower-class men entered a realm where the patriarchal sympathy of judges was overmatched by the gendered social hierarchy. In 1766 Joseph Rodriguez, a free mulatto, was accused of wounding María Antonia, an Indian, with a knife. His lawyer attacked María Antonia's credibility as a witness, calling her "a neophyte Indian, and a woman," and sarcastically adding that he admired "the fact that she's been lifted up and sanctified so much."[94] When a mulatto slave, Josepha Juachina de la Encarnación, was brutally raped while washing clothes in a river in 1743, her owner gave her permission to complain to the court against Joseph Manuel Ximenes, alias Peores, a morisco shoemaker. In his defense Ximenes explained that he was only "playing" with the "mulatilla," and did not rape her.[95] The documents on these two cases do not indicate their outcome, a frequent occurrence that suggests that either the plaintiffs lost heart or that some kind of agreement was reached before trial. Other cases indicate the especially difficult task faced by women who came into conflict with their own patriarchs. When Raphael Ximenes, a butcher, accused his wife of infidelity in 1784, his own legal petition freely admitted that he had punched her two or three times, an act of violence that he apparently expected the court to set aside while it pursued the adultery case.[96] An even more telling case came up that same year. María Michaela Yrigoyen accused her husband Juan Manuel Espinosa of committing incest with one daughter and trying to seduce another. Even as María Michaela pursued the case, Juan Manuel took advantage of a general royal pardon, freeing himself of legal responsibility. Moreover, the court pressured María Michaela to reconcile with Juan Manuel, and she did so on the condition that he stay away from the houses of their daughters, who were apparently living on their own. Juan Manuel soon violated this agreement, and María Michaela feared he was again soliciting their daughters. She asked that he be imprisoned again, and tried to renew her incest complaint. The court refused, saying that it had no authority to overturn a general royal pardon. The judge did again warn Juan Manuel to stay away from his daughters, but one suspects that this warning had little effect without the possibility of punishment.[97] At least some women were very aware of the bias of the courts toward their patriarchs. In 1770 Don Juan Berdejo wounded his pregnant wife, Juana de Dios, in her words "without telling her the cause." Juana explained that she had decided to approach the judge "not to complain, but instead to inform your majesty, so that you can determine what you will."[98] Although this woman seems uncertain about whether her husband should be punished, she also seems doubtful about whether the court can offer her anything. These doubts were justified, as the file ends immediately after her petition, implying that the court took no action.

꒒ Conclusion

Modern historians have written many works about colonial political culture in the Hapsburg era, and probably few of the points raised here will surprise specialists.[99] Still, rather than replicate earlier work, the intention here has been to outline the ways in which this political culture manifested itself to the inhabitants of Antequera. What did they know about the political theories of Thomas Aquinas, Francisco Suárez, or Francisco de Vitoria, the great intellectuals who built the ideological framework for colonial politics? How did they know it? What difference did this knowledge make for the way they approached politics? What other things about life in Antequera shaped their political experience?

Although the mass of the city's population, and perhaps even some literate Antequerans, did not read political theory, the basic tenets of the hegemonic political culture seem to have been well known. People were familiar with the importance of corporatist bodies in politics and society, because these groups were demonstrated very visibly in the major civic and religious festivals that marked the passage of time. People also seem to have understood the patriarchal metaphor that bound and justified political actions and appeals. Individuals used patriarchal language in almost every appeal for the redress of problems. However, what is less clear is how images of patriarchy were taught. Perhaps the choreographers of civic and religious festivals used techniques to visually demonstrate patriarchy. Such techniques were not overtly discussed in the surviving documents, but they may have been so naturalized that their discussion was unnecessary. Perhaps the metaphor of the family infused sermons, especially on political occasions such as oaths to the king.[100] The general principles of the political culture were also encoded in the titles of the king that prefaced royal decrees, which were read aloud and posted in ceremonies in the central plaza. Yet ultimately the most important sites for the teaching of the family metaphor of politics were probably the families people lived in on a daily basis.[101]

The colonial political culture of Antequera was by design hierarchical, yet this hierarchy was not by any means neat. Individuals belonged to society through their membership in corporatist bodies, and those bodies were not ranked in relation to each other. The people of mixed race who occupied the lowest tiers in the city's economic structure did not necessarily consider themselves the political subordinates of the wealthy. Even when members of the town council policed the streets at night, their authority derived from their service as ministers of the *king's* justice rather than from their own usually lofty social and economic status. Their position at the top of the political order was based on their relationship to the king. That relationship may have seemed very durable in the middle of the eighteenth century, but it would become more questionable within a few short decades.

CHAPTER TWO

Society, Economy, and Political Culture in Colonial Villa Alta

🔊 The present-day state of Oaxaca has long been known for its indigenous population, which was the majority group for almost the entire history of the region and today still constitutes a prominent minority. The presence of this indigenous population has dominated the region's intellectual, cultural, and economic life for centuries, and it shapes the way governments and intellectuals have presented the region to outsiders. Not surprisingly, the massive indigenous population has also dominated the historiography of the region. Oaxaca has an impressive and growing tradition of ethnohistory in which international, national, and local scholars have all participated.

Although this will be the most ethnohistorical chapter of this book, for several reasons I do not seek to make a contribution to that tradition. First, John Chance has already written an impressive ethnohistory of the district and period that concerns me here.[1] In fact, it was in part the availability of his study that drew me to the district in the first place, and although I disagree with a few of Chance's interpretations, his pioneering book in many ways forms the groundwork for this chapter. Second, my interest in political culture draws me in directions that Chance and other ethnohistorians have not emphasized. Although writing about the political culture of the region requires me to explain many things about the economy and society, I will always do so with an eye to how those things are related to the way the indigenous and nonindigenous people of the region acted and expressed themselves politically.

The focus on political culture necessitates another telling departure from the concerns of ethnohistory. Generally, ethnohistory stresses local variation and focuses on probing the society and culture of a particular ethnic group. However, examining the political culture of such a group, in this case the indigenous peasants of the district of Villa Alta, pulls attention away from the local and toward aspects of culture shared beyond localities. These include characteristics shared among different villages, between different indigenous linguistic groups, and even with Spaniards, Creoles, mestizos, and mulattos in the district, the Oaxaca region, and New Spain as a whole. Although political norms may have varied from village to village, the available records do not document such variations. Moreover, the evidence of significant differences between the political cultures of distinct indigenous linguistic groups is weak. The documents essentially restrict me to discussing the political culture of this mountainous rural region as if all natives shared one political culture that differed from, but at key points was congruent with, the political culture of Spaniards, Creoles, mestizos, and mulattos. This model is certainly imperfect, but for the moment it remains impossible to improve on.

Change over time presents an even more difficult problem. As I argued in the introduction to this book, political culture is constantly changing in response to social pressures and intellectual influences. Yet clearly there are historical periods in which change is much more rapid. In the case of Mexico, one of those periods began with the Bourbon reforms and continued through the Wars of Independence and the introduction of republican government after independence. To get a sense of how that period changed political culture, we need to establish a kind of baseline from which we can observe change. This chapter aims to establish this baseline, constructing an image of society and political culture in rural Oaxaca in the middle of the eighteenth century. I will do this by primarily using documents produced from the early eighteenth century through the moment when the Bourbon reforms began to affect politics in the region. That moment is not easy to determine. Historians have questioned the neat periodization that considers the Bourbon reforms to have started with the introduction of the intendancy system. They have pointed out earlier changes, including fiscal reforms and the secularization of parishes held formerly by regular orders.[2] Still, I would argue that for the purposes of this book the important impact of the Bourbon reforms in Villa Alta came in the middle of the 1790s. Although the region's parishes were secularized earlier, this process did not have nearly the political impact of the Real Ordenanza de Intendentes and its prohibition of colonial officials' credit monopoly.

Thus the baseline picture presented here can be considered valid from roughly 1730 to 1795.

Considering change over time brings up yet another issue. The greatest temptation faced by historians of Mexico's indigenous people is the existence of ethnographies produced through participant-observation in the twentieth century. Although the area covered by the colonial district of Villa Alta has not been one of the primary targets of ethnographic research, researchers working in the region have produced works of exceptional quality. Julio de la Fuente, one of Mexico's most important anthropological pioneers, began research in the region in the 1930s, and de la Fuente was followed by other ethnographers of note, including Laura Nader, Philip Parnell, and Etzuko Kuroda.[3] Yet, however tempting it is to turn to authorities who were able to question the contemporary inhabitants of the region about customs and uses, I do not believe that this is a valid way to research the region's distant past. Too much had changed in the meantime. Although our own cultural common sense unconsciously biases us toward viewing indigenous peoples as unchanging remnants of the past, and indigenous peoples today often stress their adherence to timeless tradition, the historical evidence suggests that change has been at least as important as continuity. For this reason I have treated ethnographies with great caution. In the footnotes for this and subsequent chapters I will sometimes compare the evidence and interpretations I present with those found in ethnographies, and I will reflect on what the historical evidence suggests about contemporary society. However, I will not project contemporary evidence backward to fill in the blanks the historical documents cannot fill. In a few cases I will refer to documents produced in the nineteenth century to explain points I make about the period covered in this chapter, but I will minimize this procedure and point out whenever my evidence is actually drawn from a later period.

ᔥ Society and Economy in Villa Alta

The colonial district of Villa Alta was one of the most heavily indigenous regions of New Spain. According to María de los Angeles Romero Frizzi, in 1742 there were 8,221 indigenous families, and 26 families of Spanish, mestizo, or mulatto origin. There were, in other words, 316 indigenous families for every nonindigenous family.[4] John Chance found that in 1781 there were 179 people who were not Indians living in the region, of a total population of 47,135. Stated another way, more than 99.5 percent of the region's people were of indigenous origin.[5] Few nonindigenous people were born in the region, and even fewer migrated in from other parts of New Spain. In contrast, many indigenous men traveled within and sometimes outside the region, and some migrated to the city of Antequera.[6]

Geographically, the region is extremely rugged even by Mexican standards. A series of jagged mountains and deep valleys rise from Oaxaca's central valleys and then fall to the east toward the plains of Veracruz. Many of the region's rivers run toward Veracruz, eventually draining into the Gulf of Mexico. In the colonial period many villages found it easier to travel and trade with populations in Veracruz than with ethnically similar populations in Oaxaca.[7] Until the 1960s most trade to both the east and west was conducted on the backs of mules that moved on narrow mountain trails where steep climbs and descents often alternated with the crossings of rapid streams. In the colonial period some streams were fordable, but others were traversed by rope bridges.

The rugged terrain creates a number of microclimates with differing elevations and rainfall. The effect is almost like that seen in the Andes, where steep terrain provided indigenous peoples with the possibility of producing crops in a variety of climate zones. Andean peoples in the past usually took advantage of this opportunity by establishing colonies in different climate zones. In Villa Alta, sometimes a single village held land spread over 2,000 vertical feet in a compressed area, allowing people to farm plots at various elevations.[8] In some cases villages also held relatively distant lands, typically on the Veracruz plains. Generally, however, the inhabitants acquired goods from different ecological zones through trade rather than the satellite communities that defined the Andean peasant economy.[9]

There were no haciendas and only a few mines in the district. Indigenous peasants could and did cultivate a wide variety of products, but most were so cheap relative to their bulk and weight that geographic barriers prevented their long-distance trade. Given the plentiful labor supply, the logical solution was for indigenous peasants to concentrate their labor by elaborating two products of relatively high value per pound. Some indigenous peasants produced cochineal, a valuable dyestuff derived from the dried bodies of insects that were raised in cacti patches. Yet by the second half of the eighteenth century cochineal production was losing importance in the district.[10] Most peasant families produced coarse cotton cloth instead. In fact, the district was famed as a source of cotton cloth, and cloth from Villa Alta supplied the wardrobes of the plebeians of Antequera and the workers of mines and haciendas far away in central and northern Mexico.[11] Yet the demand for textiles and the availability of land to grow cotton did not magically build an industry. The industry was instead built with the backs and hands of the region's indigenous men, and, especially, women.

Historical documents do not provide much evidence of how cotton was cultivated. Cotton was grown in the lowland areas of the district and in neighboring areas of Veracruz or Oaxaca.[12] Within the Villa Alta district we can identify villages like Candayoc, Puxmetacan, Latani, Choapan, and Sochiapan as centers of cotton cultivation, and we know that as the textile industry grew land suitable for cotton became more valuable and was more often at issue in land disputes.[13] It seems likely that indigenous men were the actual cultivators of cotton, and they certainly transported it to the villages where it was processed. A variety of sources reveal that indigenous women processed the cotton into cloth. They removed the seeds by flailing the cotton.[14] Women then spun thread from the fibers using a spindle and wove the cloth using back-strap looms. Processing the necessary cotton and weaving a single piece of coarse cotton cloth, or *manta*, took an indigenous woman at least a week and more often much longer, depending on her skill and the burden of her other duties.[15] Men grew cotton and other crops, but the elaboration of textiles was women's work. Each manta that left the region on the back of a mule was the distillation of many hours of an indigenous woman's labor. Women were the most important commodity producers in Villa Alta's colonial economy.

The district exported thousands of yards of coarse cotton cloth to Antequera, Mexico City, and the Bajío every year. Items imported for the use of its indigenous inhabitants included agricultural tools, mules, oxen, and wax, as well as fine cloth from Europe or Asia, used to clothe the statues in village churches. Nevertheless, relatively few Spanish merchants lived or even operated in the region. At any given moment just one or two Spanish merchants lived there, and a few more visited periodically.[16] How can we explain this contradiction? The answer is twofold. Part-time indigenous merchants who carried goods on their own backs or those of their mules to and from the main Saturday market in Antequera handled a significant amount of commerce. Yet this conduit could only account for a small percentage of the trade we know existed. The most important part was conducted by the *alcalde mayor*, the Spanish official who administered the district for the crown. Villa Alta's alcalde mayor dominated the trade of the district, working to collect and export the largest number of mantas he possibly could. He accomplished this in two ways. When it was possible, he required the Indians to pay their tribute in mantas rather than in money, and set the price at which they valued such mantas.[17] The alcalde mayor also engaged in the *repartimiento de mercancías*. He established a legal commercial monopoly in the district, requiring that each village accept certain amounts of raw cotton, tools, mules, oxen, wax, and fine cloth and repay him in coarse cotton mantas. The alcalde mayor set the prices of the goods he delivered to the Indians and the price at which he accepted their mantas. He also used his authority to discourage Spanish and mestizo merchants from operating in the district.

The alcalde mayor who ran the repartimiento had direct ties with wealthy merchants in Antequera and Mexico City.[18] In fact, a posting as alcalde mayor of Villa Alta was prized as a particularly lucrative post because it was possible to use the repartimiento for two different products, mantas and cochineal. These products complemented each other well because cochineal fetched a high price when open sea-lanes to Europe allowed its export, while mantas fetched a high price precisely when wars shut the sea-lanes, especially in the late eighteenth century. In those periods the coarse cotton cloth of Villa Alta did not have to face competition from European textiles in the Mexican market.[19]

As Jeremy Baskes points out, in an important way the repartimiento functioned as a credit system.[20] Indigenous families received loans that they later repaid with the fruit of their labor. The repartimiento was not really the system of forced sales it has often been portrayed to be. Nevertheless, the repartimiento did not function like credit systems in contemporary economies. Each alcalde mayor had a monopoly on the provision of credit in his district, and this allowed him to effectively set both the price of credit and the price of the goods that were bought and sold.[21] Moreover, it is difficult to ignore the often brutal ways in which the alcaldes mayores and their agents collected debts. Indians who refused to pay repartimiento debts were jailed or sometimes whipped.[22] The alcaldes mayores ultimately made the decisions about who owed them what, since as the highest judicial officers in the district they adjudicated most civil suits.[23] This same power was used to discourage other merchants from operating in the district. Although the aggrieved could appeal to higher authorities, doing so was an expensive and uncertain enterprise. The alcaldes mayores sometimes administered the repartimiento through indigenous government officials, and these officials were often held responsible for debts.[24] Generally, the repartimiento facilitated a certain identification between commerce and government power in local political culture. For instance, in 1768 the village government of San Andrés Yaa raised money for a lawsuit by carrying out a miniature repartimiento within the village. In another example a Spanish official opposed to the repartimiento and the officials who ran it referred to one of them derisively as a "store clerk of the said official invested with judicial power, carrying a staff," the symbol of royal power.[25]

Despite all the coercive aspects of the system, it is also necessary to acknowledge the other side of the repartimiento equation. The system allowed indigenous peasants to borrow capital in the form of money and needed goods. Some of these goods, like raw cotton, tools, and mules, were of obvious economic utility. Yet in Villa Alta the alcalde mayor also used the repartimiento to supply Indian villagers with products whose importance was symbolic. As María de los Angeles Romero Frizzi points out, the ritual observances of community Catholicism required goods like wax for candles and fine cloth to clothe the images of the saints. Villagers acquired these goods from the alcalde mayor and paid for them with the product of their labor.[26] The repartimiento, in other words, supported the religious observances that Indians thought essential to community identity and well-being as well as individual salvation.

Alcaldes mayores made considerable efforts to reduce independent commerce in their districts. They wanted to limit competition for desirable goods, and, as Baskes points out, it was particularly important for them to prevent independent merchants from buying products that were already pledged to pay repartimiento debts.[27] In Villa Alta, some alcaldes mayores harassed competing merchants, but they were unable to prevent other Spanish merchants from working in the district. These merchants provided some competition as buyers of mantas and sellers of various products. Still, it was difficult for them to collect debts without the coercive power of the alcalde mayor, and this limited their operations.[28] Indigenous merchants also engaged in trade, and in fact one reason that alcaldes mayores often sold mules through the repartimiento was that many indigenous families supplemented their income through trade. There was a steady trade in which individual indigenous men bought modest amounts of mantas and brought them to Antequera for sale. Indigenous merchants also bought raw cotton in cotton-producing lowland villages for distribution to mountain women. Indigenous men and women participated in an active circuit of village markets or *tianguis*, and villages prized the right to hold such markets. Although most of the buyers and sellers in these markets were indigenous peasants, Chance astutely points out that their greater importance in the eighteenth century arose from the efforts of peasants to meet external demand for mantas and, to a lesser extent, cochineal. As families devoted more time to producing these goods they often had to use some of the money they earned to buy food they no longer had time to grow.[29] Villages cultivated or collected a variety of foodstuffs determined by their specific ecological circumstances, and they traded these foodstuffs at tianguis. Notably, although the Spanish settlement of Villa Alta held a market, it was dwarfed by those of its indigenous neighbors. Villa Alta, unlike the capitals of many of New Spain's districts, never became a market town.[30]

The district of Villa Alta also played a very minor role in colonial New Spain's mining economy. Throughout the colonial era Spanish entrepreneurs periodically worked a series of small and poor mines. Most gave up after a few years. Beginning in the 1770s, Juan Francisco de Echarri operated a much more ambitious enterprise at Santa Gertrudis for a number of years, but it is not clear that his success stemmed from the discovery of a richer vein of silver. It seems more likely that he began operations at the right time, when Bourbon officials were willing to subsidize mining operations by holding down the price of inputs like gunpowder and mercury as well as forcing indigenous peasants from the surrounding villages to take turns working at Santa Gertrudis.[31] Either way, Echarri's operation was still dwarfed by the great mines of Taxco, the Bajío, Zacatecas, and points further north.

ʃ꙰ Politics in Villa Alta

Every indigenous peasant in the district of Villa Alta was subject to a village government, or *república de indios*, and the system of village government was crucial to the political culture of Indian peasants. Even their relationship to the king was filtered through village politics. Although it is likely that forms of local government existed before the arrival of the Spaniards, it was the Spaniards who established the most obvious patterns of indigenous village government. They instituted elections and set up village governments as key intermediaries between individual Indians and the colonial government.[32] Village governments came to be extremely important to indigenous people, and the various general rules put in place by Spanish law were reinterpreted and modified to further indigenous purposes. However, village government in New Spain also aided colonial officials greatly in their efforts to administer and tax the colony's vast indigenous population. One telling bit of evidence of this is the fact that officials sometimes sought to implant the institution in areas where nothing similar had existed previously. Although strong village governments could help indigenous villagers protect resources from powerful outsiders, they also were one of the most important parts of the infrastructure of colonial rule.[33]

Village governments were very active in the lives of peasants, and the highest village officials were continually busy. Throughout their year in office they policed the village, adjudicated minor crimes and disputes, validated wills, supervised the weekly market if there was one, organized communal public works and the labor they required, and managed community funds. Three times a year they collected the royal tribute. They organized and financed annual ceremonial activities, such as those surrounding their own inauguration, Holy Week, Corpus Christi, and the feast of their village patron saint. Village officials also often participated in various legal actions involving the village.[34]

In one aspect, political culture in Villa Alta was quite different from that of most of rural New Spain or for that matter most of the province of Oaxaca. The different population centers of the district all had their own village governments. By the middle of the eighteenth century Villa Alta did not follow the more typical pattern where some villages were head towns, or *cabeceras*, and the majority were subject towns, or *sujetos*, that owed loyalty and often labor service to the head towns.[35] The one exception to this rule may have been the Chinantec portion of the district, an ethnic and geographical area that contained about 10 percent of the settlements and 7 percent of the population as of 1789.[36] For this area a few documents have surfaced that refer to cabeceras and sujetos. However, on close examination the documents do not refer to the head town / subject town relations in civil affairs seen in much of New Spain. Instead they describe goods, money, and labor smaller Chinantec villages provided to support the parish priests who lived in larger towns, and religious services in those towns on ritual occasions. There is a hint of political authority here, as the documents complain about the head town, not the priest, and suggest that the leaders of the head town are making the rules about who owes what, but that is still a far cry from the situation seen in much of New Spain, where subject towns had reduced political power in all matters.[37] Documents from later periods suggest that residents reported to parish seats for the publication of laws and the proclamation of new constitutions, but again this did not necessarily indicate practical political subordination.[38]

Generally, then, the picture of politics in colonial Villa Alta that emerges from the documents is one in which indigenous peasants lived in small villages, and each village had its own relatively autonomous village government. Not surprisingly, this kind of diffusion of power suggests democracy to many modern observers. Unfortunately, appearances can be deceiving. Indian village government, in Villa Alta as in the rest of New Spain, was not democratic. Villages were fraught with hierarchies of gender, of age, and, in Villa Alta, of birth.[39] Wealth could also be an important determinant of political power, although it seems to have been less important in Villa Alta than elsewhere because differences in wealth among villagers were minimal there. Although villagers often stressed the importance of unity, there is little evidence that significant decisions were based on consensus.[40]

Village officials found themselves in some sense at the intersection of two political worlds. They were selected by a relatively small group of electors within their village. However, they understood their authority to emanate not from the village but from the world beyond the village. For instance, in 1750 the governor of the village of San Juan Yae referred to himself as "the governor named by God and the King," and in 1769 the village officials of San Juan Tabaa argued that their power to govern was conferred on them by "the King our Lord."[41] Moreover, Spanish colonial officials tried to ensure that Spanish-speaking peasants with good habits filled the highest village posts.[42] They may have been successful in enforcing their second criterion, but the evidence suggests that only some village officials spoke Spanish well enough to appear before colonial authorities without an interpreter. Spanish colonial officials also preferred village officials who were relatively wealthy, because officials were liable for any tribute they were unable to collect from villagers.

Although the authority of village officials was supposedly conferred on them by the king and God, that authority did not go unchallenged. Villagers were often defiant, and sometimes abused officials verbally. For example, in 1789 Nicolas Mendes and his wife told village governor Felis Mendez to "go to shit" after the governor insisted that Nicolas provide the labor he owed the village.[43] In 1806 Juan Ximenes stood in the village square of Santo Domingo Roayaga, shouting that Alcalde Pedro Mendez was living with an unmarried woman.[44] On some occasions village officials were even physically abused, although more often than not the abuser himself also held a post.[45] One particularly dangerous task seems to have been collecting tribute or other money owed to village government. In 1789 Alcalde Antonio Agustin of Tepuxtepec attempted to collect some religious fees from Miguel Pedro. Pedro beat Agustin, took away his staff of office, and stomped on it, saying there were many pieces of wood like it in the brush.[46] In the same year Regidor Joachim Lucas of Totontepec was collecting tribute when Miguel Gomez and some friends began to threaten him. A physical confrontation ensued when more officials arrived to help. Gomez struck Alcalde Gabriel Feliciano and threatened to defecate on him.[47]

It is therefore not surprising that, although the authority of village officials might emanate from lofty places, it often could be exercised only through the use of force or the threat of force.[48] Officials regularly inflicted corporal punishment on villagers. The documents frequently leave the impression that the authority of village officials was so tenuous that they needed to react severely to any public disrespect. Although sometimes people were flogged for other crimes, most victims of physical punishment in the villages of Villa Alta seem to have been people who publicly defied the authority of village officials. In a telling case from Santiago Lalopa, Antonio Lorenzo clashed with village officials in 1750. According to the officials, Lorenzo refused to attend a mandatory meeting and then refused to pay a fine for missing the meeting. He was jailed before being placed in the public pillory and lectured about his duties as a member of the village. He responded by shouting defiance, and at that point officials ordered that he be flogged, arguing that he had lost "the respect due to Justice."[49] Village officials also sometimes whipped those who complained about them to Spanish authorities.[50] No one was exempt from corporal punishment. Women were punished, as were former officials.[51] When Salvador Hernandez of Santiago Yagallo was jailed for refusing to pay a tax in 1791, his wife confronted officials and called them "robbers" and according to officials made "a thousand foolish remarks." They then gave her "three little lashes like a school girl." Hernandez claimed that officials had whipped his wife twelve times, taking their son from her arms to do so.[52]

The violence village officials meted out, and that directed at them, suggest that officials were not chosen by consensus. In fact, the processes through which men obtained village office were often conflictive. These processes were centered on a cargo system. Males served the village in a series of offices, beginning with lowly ones such as sweeping the village square daily.[53] Each period of service was one year, and ideally a man would take a yearlong break from service after each period in office. In theory, faithful and honest labor in an office qualified one for service further up the cargo "ladder," until one eventually reached the pinnacle, the office of village governor. After that, one became a *principal* or principal man, sometimes called an *anciano* or elder.[54] The principales or ancianos were exempt from further service, and they also chose all officeholders. These elders exercised patriarchal authority over all villagers, male and female. These cargo systems still exist in many Mexican and Central American villages, and anthropologists have often described them.

The basic outline of the system was established during the sixteenth and seventeenth centuries when the Spanish colonial government set up municipal governments modeled after those of Spain. Although Spanish lawyers were clearly cognizant of this origin, by the eighteenth century the system had been shaped by indigenous needs and experiences, particularly through the proliferation of offices.[55] In the twentieth century these systems typically combined religious and civil offices, but in a 1985 article William Taylor and John Chance argued that religious offices were not added to the system until after the middle of the nineteenth century.[56] Recently María de los Angeles Romero Frizzi has contradicted this view, pointing out that it is unlikely that the role of religious offices in the cargo system would be mentioned in documents directed to Spanish authorities who were uninterested in them.[57] In fact, a few references tie religious offices to the cargo system in colonial Villa Alta. In the most telling example, in 1760 the elders and officials of Santa María Yaviche described the village cargo system as including "constables, as much of the Church as of the civil government," equating the low-ranking guardians of the church building with those of the municipal offices.[58] Also, in 1798 several men of Camotlán argued that their children should not serve in a low religious office after having already served in a higher civil office. This document thus suggests that at least for these men, there was an emerging consciousness that religious and civil offices were arranged together on a scale that men climbed through their life cycle.[59]

The documents also suggest that some religious offices that required special expertise acquired at a family's expense exempted their holders from service in the civil cargo system. For instance, schoolteachers, who in the middle of the eighteenth century taught catechism classes and sometimes Spanish, were exempt from other service. The same was true of *cantores*, or members of the church choir. In both cases the families of these men invested precious resources in educating them for these special tasks, and they expected compensation. The same is true of one civil office, that of village scribe, which again was filled by a man educated beginning in his youth. In all of these cases the offices did not expire annually. The scribe was chosen by the village administration, and many times scribes served for a number of years. Religious officers like schoolteachers and cantores served at the pleasure of the parish priest, although in the case of schoolteachers villages often were able to influence who held the office.[60]

In the twentieth-century cargo systems observed by anthropologists, all males entered the system at the same level, making them at least nominally egalitarian. In eighteenth-century Villa Alta, however, this was not the case. In each village a handful of families were considered nobles, and their youths entered the cargo system at higher levels, bypassing the tedious and laborious posts at the bottom of the ladder. Often they also claimed exemption from other forms of service to the village.[61] Surprisingly, noble families do not seem to have had substantially more wealth than commoner families. John Chance suggests that these families did not own substantial lands before the Conquest, and their status tended to decline thereafter. Although they often called themselves "caciques," they were not powerful or wealthy like caciques in some parts of Mesoamerica. By the early eighteenth century, references to lands held by the nobility cease appearing in the records.[62]

If nobles were not wealthier than commoners, what made them nobles? This deceptively simple question aroused controversy in most villages throughout the eighteenth century and the early nineteenth. Essentially, nobles claimed privileges based on their descent from the founding members of their villages. These privileges were passed on through males.[63] Those who claimed noble status heavily emphasized the idea that they were descendants of the founding fathers, and often they referred to commoner families as "*advenedizos*," literally "upstarts" or "parvenus," even though the commoner families do not seem to have been recent migrants.[64] Noble families were making a very powerful claim, because the primordial titles of villages in fact emphasized the role of founding males, who migrated from place to place, establishing relationships with the founders of other villages, and eventually embraced Christianity before settling down and acquiring land titles from the Spanish Crown.[65] The relationship between noble lineage and faithfulness to Christianity may also have been important to some families. When the Yescas of San Juan Yae sought to confirm their noble status in 1766 they asked witnesses two questions. The first question was whether their ancestors had served in high posts in village government without serving in the lowest posts on the cargo ladder. The second was whether their ancestors were "reputed to be good Christians, without having committed the crime of idolatry." The family was claiming primacy over other indigenous villagers by employing an argument that was commonly used in New Spain's political culture to assert the primacy of whites over people of indigenous or African descent.[66] Commoners agreed with the basic notion that nobles descended from village founders, but they also believed that this lineage had to be proven in royal courts, and they placed great emphasis on the resulting documents, which according to commoners at least should confirm specific privileges. Thus in 1816 the commoners of Santiago Lalopa asked those who claimed noble status to show "their patents of nobility, titles, or dispatches, the only way they can confirm their nobility," while in 1796 the commoners of Santa María Yaviche argued that two families could not be true nobles because they lacked any documents that qualified them as such.[67]

Hereditary nobles were not the only group that enjoyed higher status in these communities. In each village a group of principales was set above the mass of the population. Although generally age was held in high esteem in these villages, not all elderly men achieved the status of principal because not all were selected to serve in the higher offices in the cargo system.[68] Just to add to the confusion, as the indigenous nobility grew weaker in the eighteenth century, some villages began to also call them principales, a move that soon led to controversy.[69] In any event, the principales were the most powerful men in the community. They selected the holders of all cargo system offices, up to and including the *gobernador*, the political leader of the community. The principales also deliberated about important community decisions, and key meetings required their presence.[70] For this reason villagers sometimes called the principales *vocales*, those with a voice or those who were allowed to express themselves.[71] Privileges also came with that status. Principales were exempt from further service in the cargo system, and in some villages they were exempt from other forms of community service. Principales were perceived to be the most respectable and honorable men of the village.

Below the principales was the mass of the population. By definition, they were plebeians or *macehuales*, but they were also called *sirbientes, mozos, mosetones,* or *muchachos.*[72] *Sirbiente*, or servant, emphasized the idea that they should provide menial labor for the village. *Mozo* and its derivative *moseton* implied the same but added the further connotation of youth. *Muchacho* denoted youth, but we have to keep in mind that *youth* is a relative term. In these villages, men over thirty were often referred to as muchachos as long as they had not served in enough offices to reach the status of principal. These relatively young men had neither voice nor vote at village meetings.[73] In theory they could improve their status only by serving faithfully in cargo posts, gradually working their way up in the village hierarchy. In practice, the events of the late eighteenth century and the early nineteenth brought them significant challenges and opportunities.

Beginning in the middle of the eighteenth century, the cargo system became very controversial in many of the villages of the district. Conflicts over the cargo system generated most of the litigation involving peasants in the district between 1750 and the end of the colonial period. These disputes were very complicated and changed substantially over time. Understanding their dynamics can help us understand indigenous political culture and its relationship with Hispanic political culture and authority in the district. Each of these disputes centered on the question of what kind and what amount of service different groups owed their villages, although in many cases the conflicts came to include disagreements over political power within communities.

The earliest manifestations of these conflicts were the efforts of noble families to preserve their privileges. By the middle of the eighteenth century, between one and three families in most villages claimed descent from the village founders. Although documents mention the family names involved, it is not at all clear that they were referring to nuclear families. Indigenous forms of kinship are difficult to ascertain from the Spanish language documents, but it seems likely that the number of nobles in any given generation was larger than the number of families named. Around the middle of the century these families began seeking confirmation of their privileges in the district court. It is impossible to ascertain the origins of the controversies from these suits. Each case has two possible origins. Either village elders were infringing on the privileges of cacique families by making their children perform services they considered beneath them, or families whose claim to cacique status was dubious were attempting to gain recognition as nobles. In each case a family or set of families claimed the privileges of nobles, and the village government denied these claims.

Spanish authorities were sometimes frustrated by these cases, because the litigators were tenacious even though so little seemed to be at stake. John Chance argues that individuals and families sought higher status to gain profits from the repartimientos issued while they were in office, but there is no direct evidence of this motive.[74] In contrast, almost all the petitions of those who claimed noble status explicitly state opposition to serving in lower offices in the cargo system or other forms of community service. For example, in San Juan Yae in 1766 the members of the Yesca family argued that they were "all caciques and noble persons and as such exempted by the Laws of the Kingdom from occupying themselves in *tequios* [village work parties] and low offices like those of messenger and others of that nature, which are filled by the macehuales" and that some officials had made them serve in such low offices.[75] These conflicts were important to peasants because time spent holding office or performing other community service was not available for the economic activities needed to survive and accumulate wealth.

Spanish authorities seem to have backed the pretensions of families in about half the cases, and in several others villages tried to cut short litigation with written agreements that explicitly stated the rights of noble families.[76] It seems doubtful that most of these families could truly trace their ancestry to the earliest inhabitants of their villages. On the contrary, many individuals who had earned exemptions from service by climbing the cargo ladder and becoming principales tried to pass their exemptions on to their children. In effect they were taking advantage of the fact that the privileges of "real" caciques had fallen to the point where they were essentially the same as those of principales who had earned their status. In some cases the new pretenders enjoyed the support of more established cacique families, probably because the latter needed allies in villages that were becoming increasingly hostile to their own claims. In a few villages, constant clashes over the principales' efforts to pass on to their children exemptions gained through service led to the establishment of specific privileges for the children of these principales, but these agreements were the exception, not the rule.[77] In contrast, more often the rights of caciques decayed to the point where some lawyers equated them with principales, arguing, as one did for Yaviche in 1760, that there were two kinds of principales, a few that inherited the status and the rest who achieved their status by serving in the cargo system.[78]

Many of the disputes over privileges pitted the claimants against the village government charged with organizing services. For this reason it is not surprising that those claimants came to see influence in village government as crucial to gaining or maintaining exemptions from laborious duties. The converse is also true. Macehuales, sometimes with the aid of principales who had served in the cargo system, sought to prevent nobles or supposed nobles from having privileged access to village government. The result was a series of electoral disputes that broke out in the very villages that were already divided by clashes over status and privileges. Village governments were elected at the end of the year, typically by the principales, although again cacique families claimed ancient privileges. In the resulting disputes, cacique families tried either to claim a right to vote denied by their enemies, or tried to claim the right to actually hold high offices in alternating years. For example, at the end of 1774 the principales of San Juan Yae conducted the election for the following year without asking any caciques for their votes, claiming that the caciques were not elders. Spanish officials threw out the election results, however, when they discovered that several caciques had in fact already served in the high offices that also qualified them as being principales.[79] In 1814 in Lalopa those who claimed to be caciques held the election without the other principales. When the excluded principales complained, the Spanish judge conducted an election himself, taking votes from all principales. The cacique faction lost across the board, but they protested so strongly that the judge was forced to choose the officers himself, naming some from each group.[80]

Many villages in other parts of New Spain, and indeed even in other regions of Oaxaca, experienced electoral clashes between plebeian and noble Indians in the eighteenth century, and generally historians have found a tendency for plebeians to seek more political power during the period.[81] It is tempting to see these disputes in Villa Alta as being part of the same general trend. Nevertheless, there seems to be a significant difference. In Villa Alta these electoral disputes occurred only in villages that had already seen protracted conflicts over the cargo system. In other words, the efforts of some villagers to avoid onerous duties to the village seem to have been driving political conflict in these villages.[82]

Villagers expressed great discomfort about conflicts within villages, as indigenous political culture prized unity greatly. Thus it is not surprising that they often tried to end electoral disputes and other conflicts about the privileges of different groups with their villages by reaching agreements. These agreements were written down and deposited with the alcalde mayor in Villa Alta, which in and of itself is testimony that unanimity was more an ideal than it was a commonplace of village political life. These agreements sometimes regulated the duties of people in different groups. Other times they specified that higher offices should rotate among the different factions.[83]

ꝫ Identity, Service, and Territoriality

The cargo system and other forms of community service were crucial to the social identities of the district's indigenous people. Probably there was some sense of a general difference between indigenous and nonindigenous people, although there were so few Spanish, Creole, or mestizo people in the district that villagers almost always refer to them by name in documents without describing their ethnicity. There also may have been a sense of common identity among those who spoke mutually intelligible dialects, but many cultural characteristics did not follow linguistic boundaries.[84] Yet, although social identities were complicated and interlocking, there is little doubt that in Villa Alta, as in much of New Spain, people identified most strongly with the other residents of their village.[85] One of the best ways this can be seen is in the prevalence of community endogamy, which according to John Chance approached 100 percent in some periods.[86]

Another way in which the importance of village identity can be seen is in the relative rarity of legal or political documents generated by more than one village. Yanna Yannakakis points out that earlier in the colonial period the region's indigenous nobles participated in wide-ranging kinship networks that allowed cooperation among various villages, and one late-seventeenth-century petition was even filed on the behalf of ninety communities.[87] Yet by the 1750s these alliances had become very rare. Of the hundreds of later documents in the district, provincial, and national archives, only five even pretend to speak in the name of more than one village. Moreover, four of the five are a bit less than they seem. In 1808 Joaquin Perez Gavilan presented a complaint against the district administrator. Perez Gavilan claimed to represent "the commons of natives of Santiago Amatepec, Xaltepec, and rest of the Jurisdiction of Villa Alta," but in fact he had established power of attorney for only three villages.[88] In 1815 eleven villages presented a joint complaint against the district administrator, but it was soon revealed that actually their parish priest had written the complaint. Although the fact that the parish priest wrote the complaint does not mean it did not represent the views of the various village governments, it does suggest that the intervention of an outsider like the priest was necessary to form the kind of alliance this joint action implies.[89] When the village of Santo Domingo Tepuxtepec complained in 1799 about an interpreter of Mixe who worked for the district administrator, they claimed that his manipulations and extortions harmed both their village and the others where Mixe was spoken, but they did not seek support from other villages for this claim.[90] In 1796 Raymundo de los Santos petitioned the court, identifying himself as the representative of five villages of the parish of Ayutla, but on further examination the document in question only concerns one of them.[91]

In Villa Alta, as in the rest of Mesoamerica, territoriality was essential to village identity.[92] Each community was identified with a particular stretch of territory, comprised of both agricultural land and the wilder lands around it used for pasture or to gather natural products. The importance of this identification between territory and community was a significant barrier to wider forms of identity. It was very common for neighboring villages to litigate fiercely over their boundaries.[93] This litigation was often time-consuming and expensive even when the lands in dispute were quite modest. Conflicts over territory were not, however, confined to the courts. On many occasions disputes over territory became physical battles. Sometimes a dispute was initially aired in the courts and then continued in the fields and on the mountain paths, and sometimes the opposite was true.[94]

Villagers believed that their rights to specific territory were guaranteed by very old primordial titles. This belief endured even when the document in question was not in the hands of the village, and villages often petitioned the courts to find and return to them documents that had been lost, typically during previous litigation.[95] Strikingly, these primordial titles were not particularly effective as evidence in court, as they did not conform to the accepted conventions of legal documents, and they specified dates and events that Spanish lawyers could disprove easily.[96] Their cultural significance was much greater than their legal significance. In effect, primordial titles in Villa Alta were the founding stories of their communities. These titles probably were committed to paper relatively late in the colonial period, but they recorded oral traditions about how a particular community had come to exist and to occupy a particular piece of territory. Introduced to the written records as weapons in land disputes, they offer a cloudy window on indigenous beliefs about community and identity in the district.

For example, Yaneri submitted a primordial title to the courts as evidence in a land dispute in 1815. The document, composed in the first person plural, was written in Zapotec but translated for the court's use. In the narrative, four founding cacique *abuelos*, or ancestors, travel through the district meeting the founders of other villages. They then travel to Spain in 1514 and meet "King Fernando Cortés." The king returns to New Spain with them along with three priests and the first alcalde mayor of Villa Alta. The four ancestors witness the baptism of the Spanish in Veracruz, and the construction of a church there. Then they travel to Mexico City for the founding of the Audiencia and the construction of the cathedral. They travel to Oaxaca and witness the baptism of the caciques of the valley, and then to Villa Alta where they are present for the construction of the church and the seat of district government. There the ancestors accept Christianity along with the caciques of other villages. They are inaugurated as village officers and given the *varas*, or staffs of office, that symbolize that power.

They also organize the first *tequio*, or labor service that all villagers owed for public works. The caciques found churches in various communities. The ancestors then conduct a careful journey along the boundaries of Yaneri's territory, meeting the caciques of other villages and marking limits with crosses. At the very end of the document the story returns to the issue of Christianity, explaining that they have described what happened "when the word of God came."[97]

This kind of story bolstered the claims of noble families by identifying them with the founders of their villages and the first Christians. In addition, as María de los Angeles Romero Frizzi points out, each of these stories links the origins of the village with the arrival of the Spanish and Christianity. In doing so it places the foundation of the village at the dawn of a new age, a "new sun." The key moment in the origin story was the construction of the first church of the village.[98] The very ownership of the land was closely tied to indigenous versions of Christianity. When a village rented land to indigenous peasants from another village, it specified that the rent should be paid in goods like wax for the candles of the village's patron saint, or in some cases cash that was likewise spent to support the religious rituals honoring the saint.[99] In the words of Dorothy Tanck de Estrada, "in celebrating its saint the village celebrated itself." These religious rituals were very elaborate, and their celebration could be quite costly for villages.[100] Although in the late eighteenth century Spanish officials would come to see them as a waste of precious resources, for indigenous peasants such rituals were crucial symbols of community identity.

Service was central to community identity. Note that in the primordial title of Yaneri one of the first things the ancestors did after the establishment of village government was to organize the tequio. This work might consist of preparing or maintaining the roads that linked a village with its neighbors and their crucial markets. It also might consist of making building materials to be used in public works or sold to finance other village needs.[101] Other routine forms of mandatory community service were the positions in the cargo system and periodic turns serving the local priest. Even more effort was needed for special projects, such as reconstructing churches ruined by earthquakes, fires, or storms. The combined burden of these various mandatory public duties must have been a major portion of the time indigenous peasants had available for work.

Community service weighed heavily on the peasant household economy, but there seems to have been general agreement on its importance. For one thing, community service was a practical necessity for the maintenance of autonomy from neighboring villages. Communities needed to keep order, collect royal taxes, maintain a municipal building and church, pay the priest in goods and services, and support important religious celebrations, especially that of the patron saint. It is impossible to imagine villagers accomplishing these goals without mandatory community service. Yet the practical necessity of labor for the community was matched by its symbolic importance. The obligation to serve had been established by the ancestors who founded the village, and good children of the village were required to respect those customs. Although villagers could and did argue about the specifics of custom, they never denied the importance of custom, at least before the Bourbon reforms emboldened a few dissenters.[102] Community service was required of all who wanted to be members of the community, and those who refused to serve faced severe disapproval. In Santiago Lalopa, for instance, families that were absent from the village for long periods and did not perform community service might return to find that their house had been dismantled and the materials used for public works projects.[103]

꒰꒱ Gender and Political Culture

The obligation to serve the community was an obligation of the nuclear family, not the extended family. It was individual men who climbed the cargo ladder, even though women performed much of the actual labor of community service. The husband-and-wife pair was the most important unit in the economic, social, and cultural systems that governed village life. A man could not hope to survive and prosper without a wife, and vice versa. Almost everyone in these villages married.[104] Widowers were perceived as having about half the economic potential of married men, and widows were seen as being even worse off.[105] The documents sometimes suggest that husbands and wives were viewed as two halves of the same person. A rare but evocative case is found in an 1805 document. The officials of Santo Domingo Yojovi jailed Miguel de Castro for various offenses. He complained in a petition to the court in Villa Alta, explaining the origins of his conflict with the local government. In the middle of his explanation the voice of the petitioner changes from Castro to that of his wife. In other words, a narrative that starts out by identifying the author as Castro suddenly begins to speak of him as "my husband." This oddity drew no comment from the Spanish judge, who treated the case like any other dispute.[106]

The evidence of the importance of female labor to community service is overwhelming. First of all, a wife was considered crucial to the successful completion of posts in the cargo system, probably because the time a man needed to fulfill cargo duties required his wife to expand her role in the everyday family economy. For instance, in Yagallo single men entered the cargo system but could serve only as messengers, the lowest posts in the system.[107] A more telling indicator of the importance of wives is that village officials could resign in the middle of their terms only if they were widowed. In 1786 the principales of Yatoni accused Gobernador Francisco Vicente of neglecting his duties. He responded that he had had great difficulty doing his job because his wife had died and he "had no one to help him." Vicente was allowed to resign.[108] Moreover, although for the most part wives were not directly involved in the duties of cargo holders, such as collecting taxes, jailing delinquents, or carrying messages, their labor was crucial in the other two service institutions of village life. They often participated in public works under tequio. Women also served turns as temporary domestic servants for parish priests, sometimes with their husbands.[109] There they performed the laborious household tasks that made them so crucial to the peasant economy. They gathered fodder for the priests' animals, fetched wood, drew water, and prepared food, particularly through grinding corn and preparing tortillas. Women's roles here again underline the crucial role of the husband-and-wife pair in the village economy. They had to take turns serving the priest precisely because the priest did not have a wife. As officials of the village of San Francisco Cajonos put it in 1798, if the women of the village did not make tortillas for the priest, "the priest himself would have to do it."[110] The possibility was so unthinkable for everyone involved that it was ludicrous.

Women were important in the service systems that allowed the village to fulfill its obligations and maintain its cohesive identity. In the words of Steve Stern, "popular understandings of and arguments about legitimate and illegitimate authority rested on profoundly gendered foundations." Like the larger Spanish colonial empire of which it was a part, each village was structured as a patriarchy, with the elder village leaders as its fathers. Older men governed younger men, and all men governed women.[111] The villagers were, in their oft-repeated words, "children of the village," a phrase that emphasizes patriarchy. Not surprisingly, gendered rhetoric abounded in village political discussions. Most often this gendered rhetoric took the form of familial metaphors in which wise political fathers received respect and obedience from the community.[112] Yet in moments of tension gendered rhetoric could take on more critical tones. In 1806, when Juan Ximines of

Santo Domingo Roayaga clashed with village authorities over his service obligations, Ximines publicly said that "he was not a woman for the Justices to make use of and the village gave the justices pleasure the way women gave pleasure."[113]

Although political rhetoric was often gendered, women themselves had a much-diminished public role in the official politics of the community. Women certainly gained prestige as their husbands climbed the cargo ladder, but they themselves never became principales with formal political rights. Women participated in disputes, but always in support of their families. They might intervene physically to defend a husband or child. More often they defended their family verbally, as when the wife of Salvador Hernandez called the officials of Santiago Yagallo robbers when they tried to collect a tax from her husband, or when the wife of Nicolas Mendes told the justices of Santiago Camotlán that they could go "to shit" when they tried to make him serve in a lowly cargo post.[114] Yet women seem more often to have been the victims in these conflicts. Authorities struck at their husbands or fathers by physically punishing their women. In 1801, when Juan Simon Lopez was embroiled in a dispute with the authorities of San Cristóbal Lachirioag, the governor of the village had his daughter Leocadia publicly whipped and confined to jail.[115] In other cases the wives of officials were injured when they rallied to the defense of their husbands. In 1789 Pedro Miguel attacked Antonio Agustin, alcalde of Tepuxtepec. When Agustin's wife came to his aid, Miguel then attacked and injured her.[116]

Women also stepped to the front precisely at the moments of greatest tension, when some substantial portion of the community physically confronted an abusive official or other threat. In Villa Alta, as in other parts of New Spain, women often took prominent roles in village riots.[117] In a perceptive analysis of riots in late colonial Morelos, Steve Stern argues that the very etiquette of revolt was gendered. Women took the forefront to defend their families, running physical risks to emphasize the importance of the occasion and to convince the men to take decisive action as patriarchs.[118] The prominent role of women in riots in Villa Alta probably had similar roots. The participation of women may have also symbolized unanimity. Although gender was one of the most important ways that villages were divided, women found their interests to be aligned with those of the men when the village confronted corrupt authorities, abusive priests, and the territorial pretensions of rival villages.

Familial relationships were also very patriarchal. Customs surrounding marriage and family emphasized the respect and service that young people owed their elders. Before marriage, young men spent a period serving the parents of their fiancée. After marriage, the young couple lived with the male's parents for several years, and the bride was effectively the domestic servant of her mother-in-law.[119] Not surprisingly, patriarchal norms governed a couple's life even after they set up their own household. Patterns of married life in Villa Alta seem similar to those analyzed by Steve Stern for Morelos. Women expected men to provide economic resources for them and their children. Men expected women to provide domestic labor and other help in economic matters. Both desired fidelity. Stern calls this set of expectations and interests a "contested patriarchal pact," and he shows how ideas about economic rights and sexual rights became interwoven as women sought to make contingent the rights males claimed as absolute.[120]

Village authorities did what they could to ensure marital harmony, working as the patriarchs of the village family. Judging from early-nineteenth-century evidence, village officials were required to attend all weddings, and the highest official lectured the newlyweds on their duties as a married couple.[121] Village officials also intervened after the marriage. They sought to reconcile quarrelling spouses, especially when domestic violence became severe. Although officials might also punish a man who beat his wife excessively, the documents give the sense that restoring marital harmony was a higher priority than physically protecting women. Most cases where criminal proceedings were initiated end without a sentence or even a verdict.[122] Religious officials also severely sanctioned sexual infidelity, flogging repeat offenders.[123] Perhaps the most severe sanction for sexual infidelity fell on the children that resulted. In at least one village, San Juan Yae, male children whose fathers were unknown were obligated to serve on the lowest rung of the cargo system for their entire lives.[124]

ﻌ Religion and Community

Religion was crucial to the political culture of colonial Villa Alta. For two centuries the Spanish had struggled to Christianize the Indians of the area. In the early eighteenth century some well-publicized incidents made it clear that indigenous worshipers were continuing community religious practices modeled on their pre-Hispanic predecessors. However, by around the middle of the century, after renewed Spanish efforts, most community religious practices were based on Christian rituals. Although private religious practices probably retained pre-Hispanic elements, Christian public rituals not only flourished, they became central to community identity.[125] These public rituals served to reinforce the independence of communities, but at the same time they linked each community to a wider Catholic church. The priests crucial to public ritual came from beyond the district, and their duties required that they serve several villages at once. These priests brought with them different expectations of proper religious practice and also attempted to oversee other areas of indigenous life that the priests considered crucial to the salvation of souls. Priests developed allies in communities, but their relations with their parishioners were often less than comfortable.

The public religious rituals that flourished in the eighteenth century were dominated by devotion to patron saints. Each village had its saint, and often groups of villagers called barrios also adopted patrons. Every saint had his or her day, when the community celebrated the saint's protection and in doing so affirmed its own solidarity. We know little about the process through which communities became linked to particular patrons. In Villa Alta early Dominican missionaries had great influence, but it seems likely that groups of villagers sometimes selected patrons for their barrios long after the initial evangelization of the community. In either case patron saints were celebrated by expensive festivals that included masses, processions, dances, and fireworks, as well as special meals for important groups in the community or even the whole village.[126] Expenses in money and labor included payments to the priest, the decoration of the village with foliage, bonfires, fireworks, and clothing for the saint's image, as well as candles for veneration, the fabrication or rental of costumes for dancers, the purchase of special food and drink, and of course its preparation by the women of the village. Although festivals for patron saints seem to have been the most lavish, significant festivals were also held at the more universal feasts of the Catholic calendar, including Holy Week, Corpus Christi, the Purification, Holy Spirit, Rosary, and Nativity.[127]

As public Christian rituals grew in popularity and became more elaborate, villagers began to develop new ways of financing and organizing them. The most important institutions were confraternities, or cofradías, and the very similar brotherhoods or *hermandades*.[128] The cofradías of Villa Alta were very different from the cofradías of Antequera, which we have seen both supported public religious devotions and served as a kind of spiritual insurance, paying for the funerals of their dues-paying members. In rural districts like Villa Alta, cofradías spent almost all their income on public ritual. Although the earliest cofradías in the district, founded in the 1730s, supported periodic masses for the souls of all members, soon the focus shifted altogether to the celebration of patron saints and, in some cases, the decoration of church interiors.[129]

Religion was crucial to community identity for the indigenous villagers of Villa Alta, but paradoxically it also brought powerful outsiders to their communities on at least a periodic basis. The district was divided into twenty parishes, and each had at least one priest.[130] Every priest administered to a flock of one to three thousand indigenous peasants. Priests resided in parish seats but visited the other villages of their parish for rounds of religious devotions. Sometimes the residents of outlying villages were obligated to attend celebrations in the parish seat, typically for the more universal feasts like Holy Week. In New Spain's colonial Catholicism the vast majority of parish priests were creoles or mestizos. Although some were well-educated by the standards of the time, others were not, especially in Villa Alta, where the parishes were both poor and isolated.[131]

Parish priests filled one of the most difficult roles in the colonial system. Although they sometimes brought family members to live with them in their parish seats, generally they were isolated from the urban centers of Spanish culture in New Spain. The priests lived what many perceived to be lonely lives, surrounded by indigenous people whose language they did not necessarily speak.[132] These indigenous people always seemed alien, and during the inevitable moments of conflict they could be positively threatening. In the Spanish colonial system, priests were supposed to have great influence over their parishioners, leading them to salvation by correcting their errors, and, especially in the late colonial period, supervising the acculturation of Indians to more Hispanic ways of life. Yet, isolated as they were, priests were themselves inevitably subject to indigenous influence.[133] Even in the area of religion, where priests felt they were specialists with privileged knowledge, they were under continual pressure to bow to indigenous expectations. The cultural pressure of indigenous society on priests' daily life was even greater. For instance, all their meals were prepared by indigenous peasant women, who were a constant presence in the priests' households as they conducted their domestic duties. It also seems likely that when priests fell ill they turned to these same women to nurse them back to health.

Villagers and bishops agreed that the most important duty of parish priests was to provide indigenous people with access to the sacraments.[134] In Catholic doctrine these sacraments were essential to salvation, and priests were the only humans empowered to preside over them. Moreover, indigenous peoples also saw masses in particular as crucial to the cult of the patron saints that protected villages and fortified community identity. In addition to celebrating masses for the patron saints of the various villages in his parish, each priest celebrated Sunday mass in at least one village each week. Priests also said mass in the parish seat on the most important occasions of the Catholic liturgical year. The obligations of priests did not end with mass, however. They heard the confession of each parishioner at least yearly. They also endeavored to provide last rights to dying parishioners whenever it was possible. They baptized infants, and in many cases presided over the burial of deceased parishioners. Conscientious priests spent many hours traveling through often-difficult terrain to minister to their flocks.[135]

One of the most important duties of parish priests was to teach Catholic doctrine to their parishioners. Most of them taught in cooperation with schoolteachers. In the middle of the eighteenth century, village schools were entirely religious in character. The schoolteacher helped the children of the village memorize the Catholic catechism.[136] In many cases the schoolteacher was himself a native of the village, and he taught the catechism in whatever indigenous language was spoken there.[137] The evidence suggests, however, that schoolteachers also knew how to read and write Spanish, and they probably were also entrusted with the few children whose parents were willing to invest in literacy.[138] Generally parish priests chose the schoolteacher, but often they had to make their selection from among the few candidates who had acquired sufficient knowledge. Village government also sought influence over the naming of teachers in cases where villagers helped pay for the schooling. Schoolteachers were often exempt from serving in the cargo system and tequio, although the specifics of their exemptions and payment varied from village to village.

Much less is known about another kind of religious specialist, the cantores, or singers, who led the singing at mass and assisted the priest. They may also have presided over other religious ceremonies when the priest was not present, although this type of irregular practice is not documented. Cantores, like schoolteachers, were trained as children in the specialized knowledge they needed. As Toribio and Diego Perez of Camotlán put it in 1798, "We spent our own money so that our children would be taught how to sing." For this reason cantores were often exempt from service in the cargo system.[139]

The priests' most important collaborators in the villages were the *fiscales*, who in Villa Alta mostly served as religious and moral policemen. Priests usually chose the fiscales, and they expected the fiscales to serve as their eyes and ears. A fiscal looked out for lewdness, sexual immorality, abortion, failure to attend mass, and unorthodox religious practices.[140] In theory fiscales referred cases to the priest, and inflicted punishment only on the priest's orders. In reality, fiscales often administered punishment without specific orders from the priest. They, like the civil officers of the village, had the right to administer corporal punishment by flogging offenders. Such beatings could be extremely brutal. Often fiscales served for years with the apparent acquiescence of a community, but those who were too zealous in administering punishment could lose community support. Although technically only priests could remove them from office, in practice some found it difficult to continue to serve in the face of widespread opposition. Moreover, at least some priests allowed villages to elect their fiscales.[141]

Priests often clashed with groups of their parishioners over how they were paid for their services. Priests were generally paid according to the work they did, and the large number of ceremonial occasions requiring their presence meant that individuals and communities sometimes paid more to the priest for his services than they did to the king in taxes.[142] In the early eighteenth century most parishes paid priests according to customary arrangements in which they supported the daily life of the priest with food and services and also compensated him in cash for masses and sometimes other sacraments. These arrangements prevented priests from having to pay cash for food or domestic labor. Beginning in the mid-eighteenth century some indigenous peasants began to attack customary agreements, and the pace of those assaults increased as the century wore on. Several factors precipitated these conflicts. The most important was that the burden of supporting the priest in these customary arrangements was unequally distributed among indigenous peasants. Following village customs about service, it was those younger peasant families who did not inherit exemptions from service who had to take turns providing food and labor to parish priests. Like other service obligations, this duty took time away from the things families had to do to ensure a margin of subsistence and a measure of economic well-being. Moreover, in customary arrangements the labor and food required to support the priest was distributed among the various villages of his parish. The inhabitants of outlying villages shouldered an inordinate burden because they had to travel to the parish seat to fulfill their obligations.

The inequalities in the distribution of the services owed to priests generated discontent about the situation, but most likely those grievances would not have resulted in widespread legal action if the laws did not encourage such suits. Unfortunately for parish priests, the letter of the law already did not support these customary relationships, and legal changes in the eighteenth century were even more unfavorable. From the early seventeenth century on, it was illegal for parish priests to demand unpaid service from their flocks.[143] This law conflicted with practice in indigenous parishes throughout New Spain. Yet even though the law was not often enforced, it gave a very good legal argument to every group of peasants who wanted to overturn the customary arrangements under which they served the priest. Their legal chances were improved in the eighteenth century, when the various dioceses of New Spain began publishing *aranceles*, or schedules of clerical fees. Theoretically villages had the option of paying their priest according to these strict schedules, which established how much cash had to be paid for each mass, funeral, baptism, and so on. It is not clear when the Diocese of Oaxaca published its first schedule, although one group of peasants stated that it had been during the administration of Bishop Angel Maldonado, who served from 1702 to 1728. In any event, by the middle of the century legal specialists in the district seat were certainly aware of the existence of an arancel, and villagers seeking relief from services found it easy to get a copy of the document.[144]

The temptation to see these conflicts as clashes between greedy priests and overburdened villagers is very strong. However, this vision does great injustice to a much more complex reality. Disputes between peasants and priests rarely pitted priests against a monolithic village. Maintaining the priest, like the other burdens of communal life, was a constant source of tension among indigenous peasants. Generally customary arrangements burdened macehuales and the young more than they did elders and nobles. Moving to a fee schedule would mean that each villager would pay for his or her own private ceremonial needs, like weddings, baptisms, and funerals. The change would be less drastic for communal ceremonies like masses on Sundays and feast days, because even under customary arrangements priests usually received cash for these services. Thus elders and nobles often favored customary agreements, and in each dispute the priest had significant allies in the village. One example of how conflicts over payments to the priest were embedded in more general tensions over the distribution of the burdens of community life is seen in the village of San Juan Yae in 1774. Different groups of villagers signed what was in effect a peace treaty that specified exactly what kinds of services each group owed in both the cargo system and support of religious observations. The sixteenth point of this detailed document was an agreement not to seek enforcement of the arancel under the current parish priest, and not to seek it under subsequent priests unless they mistreated the villagers.[145]

The relationships between indigenous peasants and the parish priests who served them were sometimes close and effective, but they always had the potential to sour. Disputes over payment were only one possible cause of tension. Indigenous parishioners were sometimes upset by the abusive behavior of priests. They complained to diocesan authorities about priests who did not fulfill their obligations. In 1783 the village of Talea charged that its priest, Manuel Nuñez Iracheta, neglected his duties in order to travel to a nearby market town to gamble. The bishop ordered Nuñez Iracheta to refrain from gambling or frequenting places where gambling occurred.[146] In 1804 the officials of Santa Cruz Yagavila accused their priest Mariano de Arlanzon of not only neglecting his duties but also spreading rumors about the village.[147] Indigenous peasants also became upset when priests administered excessive or arbitrary corporal punishment. The government of Santo Domingo Latani criticized the parish priest in 1799 for imprisoning and whipping his parishioners without cause as well as beating the fiscal with his fists.[148] Often complaints about maltreatment surfaced in villages where some peasants were trying to change the payments made to a priest. Perhaps priests who neglected their spiritual duties or were quick to use violence exhausted the store of good will that made customary arrangements for payments work smoothly. Yet it is also possible that the legal efforts of some parishioners to enforce a strict schedule of fees were so threatening to priests that they began to see themselves as surrounded by adversaries.

In the worst cases the relationship between priests and peasants could deteriorate so much that the latter rioted. Riots against priests were rare, and priests were never injured in riots.[149] However, a riot could be extremely intimidating for a priest stationed in a remote rural parish, far from the nearest person he identified with ethnically, and much farther from any public force capable of confronting a mob of enraged parishioners. These riots, far from spontaneous or atavistic explosions, took place in villages that had witnessed prolonged disputes with their priests. With a riot parishioners sent a very strong signal to authorities that their relationship to a particular parish priest was no longer tolerable.

Given the problems that parish priests faced, it is not surprising that many of them had a very low opinion of their parishioners. Even when they were not threatened, parish priests often worried about the tendency of indigenous peasants to resist innovation. Struggling to increase attendance at his parish school, Juan Jose Siguenza, the pastor of San Juan Tanetze, criticized parents who said they needed their children's labor. Showing little patience for the difficulties of family economics, Siguenza called the parents and the village government "insolent and excessively free."[150] Francisco María Ramirez, pastor of Santiago Zoochila, argued that "Indians, Jews, and men of bad faith" were almost synonymous.[151] Yet some priests were of a very different opinion. Joseph Mariano Davila Bustamante, an experienced priest newly appointed to the parish of Latani, praised his parishioners in 1783 as "Indians who were angelic as much for their blessed obedience as for their great affection for the Divine worship."[152]

Davila Bustamante's praise of the religious devotion of his parishioners raises key questions about the indigenous peasants of Villa Alta. How orthodox was their Christianity, and what was the role of pre-Hispanic beliefs in their religious thought and practice? These questions are difficult to answer. John Chance argues that by the late eighteenth century communal pre-Hispanic rituals had given way to new syncretic rituals centered on saints and festivals, even though individuals turned to shamans for ceremonies oriented toward private goals.[153] The problem of "idolatry," as the Spanish called it, certainly surfaced less frequently in the courts as the century wore on. In some incidents indigenous peasants accused each other of this crime during other disputes. Such accusations were typically vague and authorities apparently did not investigate them.[154] The last detailed accusation I have been able to find took place in Tepuxtepec in 1767. Magdalena de la Candelaria, a mulata who had lived in the village before being expelled in 1763, went to a priest and described an annual community ceremony in which new village officials sacrificed turkeys and a dog to two stone figures on a hill just outside town.[155] The documents are mute about whether church authorities took this accusation seriously enough to initiate an investigation.

Even this kind of detailed report of unorthodox religious practice will never allow us to understand the religious beliefs of indigenous peasants. Religion was simply too subtle and complicated to be captured in the available documents. Even peasants engaged in overtly orthodox rituals might have understood them in ways that were quite alien to written theology. The most obvious examples of this problem are found in the communal cult of saints, but the same could easily be true of such individual ceremonies as baptism, confession, or funerals. As William Taylor puts it, "Indian understandings were not carbon copies of Spanish intentions."[156] Church authorities were aware of this, but they often were not able or willing to exert great effort to make belief, as opposed to practice, more orthodox. After all, the gradual Christianization of Europe itself had been greatly aided by Catholicism's tolerance of local religion.

✦ Spanish Colonial Authority in Villa Alta

The maximum Spanish colonial authority in Villa Alta was the alcalde mayor, who governed the district from the small village of Villa Alta. Generally these men were natives of Spain who took up the post after serving in the military.[157] Although they were most likely loyal to the Crown on matters they considered important, the reason most alcaldes mayores took this isolated post was financial. The region's production of cotton textiles, and to a lesser extent cochineal, made the task of administering it very lucrative. Alcaldes mayores sometimes required that tribute be paid in the form of cotton mantles rather than cash, a practice that allowed them to speculate in the textile market.[158] More importantly, an energetic man could use the repartimiento to amass a considerable fortune during his term as alcalde mayor. It was easy to ally oneself with one or more wholesale merchants to control trade in the district and siphon off indigenous production. In many regions of New Spain alcaldes mayores chose Spanish or Creole business partners as their lieutenants, officials who exercised their power in outlying parts of the district.[159] For some reason the pattern seems to have been less important in Villa Alta than elsewhere, as references to lieutenants in the documents are rare.

In the absence of Spanish or Creole lieutenants resident among the far-flung villages of their domain, alcaldes mayores turned to a very different type of people to help them administer the district. In most cases they relied on the officials of the many indigenous community governments. But what happened when those officials did not appreciate the mandates of the alcalde mayor? In those cases alcaldes mayores employed a number of irregular officials called *sahuiches*. The sahuiches were commissioned for specific tasks as they were needed. They were sent to collect the repartimiento debts or tribute, to arrest criminals, or to enforce judicial edicts in land disputes.

Sahuiches were chosen from the population of Analco, a small village adjacent to the settlement of Villa Alta. Analco was founded in the sixteenth century by Tlaxcalan auxiliaries who accompanied the Spanish conquerors. Its inhabitants performed a series of unpaid services for the Spanish town of Villa Alta, as well as being hired as sahuiches, and they were exempt from tribute. The Tlaxcalan influence was diluted over the following centuries by a stream of migrants from various locations in Oaxaca, but its memory remained powerful, and Nahuatl was still spoken there in the eighteenth century.[160] In the first years after the Conquest the men of Analco helped put down uprisings in various parts of the district, and even late in the colonial period sahuiches sometimes brought arms on their missions.[161] In 1761 the village government of Analco petitioned to defend its royal privileges, obtained "because our ancestors came in company of the Spanish conquerors capturing this entire Kingdom." They added that as descendants of Tlaxcalans they continued to serve as a militia to put down riots or rebellions, and claimed that they were soldiers of a presidio, entitled to autonomy and exemptions from taxes.[162]

Although Spanish officials were skeptical of the notion that the inhabitants of Analco were presidio soldiers ready to put down Indian rebellions, clearly the people of Analco saw themselves as quite different from the peasants of the other villages of the district. For one thing, whatever their native tongue the people of Analco generally also spoke Spanish. However, the best evidence of how distinct the men of Analco felt from the other Indians of the district is their behavior. Sahuiches were famed for abusing indigenous villagers. They demanded that villages provide them with food and shelter for free. Sahuiches also reportedly captured peasants to extort money from them, raped or seduced indigenous women, whipped Indians, and mocked indigenous authorities.[163] Repeated tales of such abuse eventually led Bourbon officials to outlaw the use of sahuiches, but even so the practice continued.[164]

The alcalde mayor also needed help in administering his court in the village of Villa Alta. For example, a bailiff ran the district jail. Although some indigenous peasants spoke enough Spanish to represent themselves or serve as witnesses in court, others needed interpreters. In 1791 the district administrator paid Juan Antonio Basquez one hundred pesos annually to serve as interpreter of Mixe, and Josef Mariano de Medina one hundred and fifty-six pesos each year to interpret Zapotec. Apparently at least Basquez thought his salary was insufficient, for a few years later the village of Tepuxtepec complained that he constantly extorted more money to smooth the process of judicial proceedings and routine administrative business. He also apparently insisted that the various Mixe villages of the district provide him with unpaid personal servants. Basquez made more money on the side preparing legal petitions for those who lacked the necessary literacy.[165]

Although Villa Alta was a small village, the presence of the alcalde mayor made it the center of royal authority in the district. This point was underlined in various ceremonies. From the Conquest through at least the late seventeenth century, indigenous peasants traveled to Villa Alta to participate in two festivals. In January the fiesta of San Ildefonso, the patron of Villa Alta, commemorated the Conquest, and in June the feast of Corpus Christi modeled the place of various groups in the colonial order.[166] Although these festivities do not show up often in late colonial documentation, as late as 1781 at least some villages were required to participate in the feast of San Ildefonso, with their "flags, drums, bugles and other musical and festive instruments that they customarily use."[167] Alcaldes mayores also required newly elected officials and other village leaders to travel to Villa Alta for an inaugural ceremony in early January. As representative of the king the alcalde mayor handed them their varas, or staffs of office. The alcaldes mayores also received cash gifts in this otherwise symbolic transaction, a fact that many indigenous peasants resented deeply.[168] The ceremony underlined how the authority of village officials derived from the king and not from their election by the principales.[169]

꧁ Researching Indigenous Political Culture

Political culture, the set of discourses and practices characterizing politics, is neither monolithic nor static. It is very much a historical creation, and this is as true of the seemingly isolated and traditional indigenous peasants of Villa Alta as it was of the residents of European cities.[170] Generally speaking, the available sources do not allow us to discern people's core beliefs about politics or anything else. However, the sources document people's public statements about politics, and much about their actual political practices. These public statements and practices are in fact what actually define political culture, which is ultimately about what people say and do rather than what they think. In other words, for understanding political culture and how it changed over time, people's private beliefs are strangely irrelevant.

The principal sources for investigating political culture in colonial New Spain are judicial ones. In the case at hand, I consulted documents from a variety of archives, but by far the most fruitful was that of the district court in Villa Alta. The district court archive holds the vast majority of the cases initiated or pursued by the residents of the district. Generally other archives on the regional and national level document only the subset of cases that were appealed to higher authorities. Although the material available in the district archive is superior to that found on the regional or national level, it certainly does not reflect all of the political arguments people made. Pursuing a problem in district court cost both time and money. It is reasonable to assume, therefore, that people took cases to district court only when more local means of resolving a dispute were ineffective.[171] Since these local processes were for the most part verbal and were not recorded, the district court archive is our best source for local indigenous society.[172] Moreover, the records of the district court provide very good evidence about the problems that came before Spanish authority, and thus they record key interactions between the broader colonial political culture and local practices.

Even so, the district court records, as well as the records of cases that were pursued at higher levels in the judicial system, present a series of problems for research. One of the most important is that very often a case file seems incomplete. After some initial arguments by one or both sides in a conflict, the file simply ends, with no resolution. The most likely explanation of this is that the plaintiff dropped the suit or criminal complaint, and the incomplete record was shelved. Perhaps the plaintiff realized that whatever could be gained by a victory did not justify further expense. Sometimes the plaintiff or plaintiffs simply lacked the resources needed to pursue a case further. Yet it seems likely that in many cases the parties involved came to some kind of agreement that was satisfactory enough to both sides to end their engagement with the Spanish legal system. Undoubtedly they faced great pressure to compromise, for as we will see indigenous political culture valued village harmony very highly. One problem this entails for the researcher is that often it is impossible to discern the reactions of Spanish judges to the arguments put before them.

Two different kinds of legal documents capture the political discourses of indigenous peasants. Indigenous peasants testified directly in court. Such testimony was sometimes recorded for civil cases and almost always in criminal cases. Usually the testimony began with information designed to identify the witness, including their name, age, and whether they were married. After that the testimony was recorded in the third person, and sometimes explicit questions were also recorded. In many cases, an interpreter appointed by the court translated this testimony. Courts represented a set of very uneven power relationships where indigenous peasants were at a disadvantage. How do we sift through direct testimony to discern fragments of the subaltern voice? Circumstances sometimes help. Defendants occasionally stood up for their side of the conflict with apparent disregard for the consequences. One rule of thumb is that if defendants said something that made them look bad to the judge then they were almost certainly speaking their own minds. Moreover, witnesses for the plaintiff or complainant also testified, and the person who initiated the case was often among them. They were less afraid of the court because they had approached it themselves. Furthermore, witnesses often included information that was useless to the court. Such information apparently helped them structure their tales and make sense of events for their own purposes. This type of information is particularly valuable and often illuminates aspects of political life not directly related to the case. Frequently such tangents cropped up when the lawyers let a witness spin his or her own tale without interrupting with further questions. Finally, the emotional content of people's testimony is also important, even if we cannot quantify it. The raw emotion of some accounts lends them an air of gritty reality that makes them more believable.

Transcripts of direct testimony are not the most common or most useful documents found in judicial records. In both the Spanish court system and its republican successor, judicial decisions were supposedly based on the careful examination of written documents.[173] All civil and most criminal files begin with legal petitions, which contemporaries often referred to as *escritos*, or writings. These documents were submitted by an aggrieved party. Each begins by identifying the nominal author or authors, including their place of residence and any titles or posts they held. The subsequent narrative explains the abuses or crimes being protested. All of these legal petitions were written in the first person, and they were often written and submitted to the court soon after the events they describe. All were signed by the nominal authors, or signed on their behalf. However, it is often hard to pin down the actual writers of documents.

In the easiest cases, the handwriting of a document closely matches one of the signatures that follows it.[174] Yet these cases are fairly rare, and even in cases where petitioners could sign their names in clear script it is not uncommon for the petition to be composed in someone else's handwriting. In many cases escritos were written by village scribes, peasants who acquired literacy as well as knowledge of the Spanish administrative and judicial systems so they could serve their village.[175] The Spanish grammar and spelling of *escribanos* often suggests that it was not their first language and that their training was not extensive. In fact, the existence of a few Zapotec language documents even late in the colonial period indicates that in at least some villages aspiring escribanos learned to read and write Zapotec before learning Spanish.[176] One legal petition was written in Zapotec in 1815, and that year the village of Yaneri submitted a primordial title written in Zapotec.[177] Generally, however, late colonial documents in Zapotec seem to have been intended for use inside a given community. These include, for instance, the 1807 cofradía accounts of San Mateo Cajonos, accounts of the money Santiago Teotlaxco spent on a court case in 1751, records of a land rental by San Miguel Metepec in 1720, a 1720 will from San Bartolome Zoogocho, an 1808 description of an internal land transfer in San Juan Lachiroag, and another internal land document from the same village in 1815.[178]

Certainly many of the people of the district spoke only indigenous languages. Yet the evidence scattered among the hundreds of documents in the district judicial archive also indicates that a large group of people spoke Spanish and could testify without the aid of interpreters. Spanish seems to have been particularly common among noble families.[179] The prevalence of literacy is much more difficult to gauge. Dorothy Tanck de Estrada estimates that the literacy rate for adult males was 9.5 percent in central Mexico at the end of the colonial period, but it might have been lower in a region like Villa Alta.[180] In Villa Alta, it was not uncommon for many men in a single village to be able to sign their names clearly, but is that strong evidence of functional literacy? Perhaps the cases where indigenous peasants used *pasquines* in political disputes are better evidence. Pasquines were criticisms, often satirical, that were written and then posted in a public place for people to see. Their prominence would arouse discussion, and probably literate people would read them aloud to curious friends and neighbors. Although pasquines were anonymous and usually subversive, the basic idea of posting a written document publicly was derived from the manner in which royal decrees were disseminated.[181] Although the repeated mandates of Spanish civil and religious officials that all children learn to read and write Spanish were only partially successful, some peasants clearly saw literacy as a powerful political and social tool.[182] Families often spent considerable resources educating their sons. Literate men could gain political power, and by serving as village scribes they could avoid more onerous village duties.

Even so, it is clear that much peasant legal action, and many of the documents it generated, involved the activity of intermediaries. These intermediaries can be divided into three groups. The first were the *tinterillos*, or, literally, "ink pot men." They were literate men with some knowledge of the legal system. For instance, Juan Antonio Basquez, an official interpreter of the district court, also served as a kind of lay lawyer, converting the oral complaints of indigenous peasants into the written form acceptable to the court.[183] Unlike real lawyers, tinterillos rarely signed the documents they produced, and often it is difficult to say when a particular document was written by a village scribe and when it was written by a tinterillo.[184] Because Villa Alta did not generate enough legal business to support even one educated and titled lawyer, these shadowy figures were a necessity there. Yet many Spanish colonial authorities and their republican successors viewed tinterillos with disdain. They believed tinterillos egged on spurious and misinformed lawsuits, draining money from already impoverished communities and clogging the legal system.[185]

Indigenous peasants also employed titled lawyers, especially when they appealed to courts in Mexico City or Antequera. Peasants employed lawyers for some cases argued in the district court in Villa Alta, although doing so increased the time and expense involved in a lawsuit. Peasants could use such lawyers precisely because the legal system worked through written documents rather than oral arguments. An individual or group could travel to the city of Antequera and explain their complaint to a lawyer. The lawyer would then prepare an escrito, shaping their tale to emphasize the appropriate legal points. The group then could sign the document and take it to Villa Alta to present to the alcalde mayor. Lawyers signed many of these documents along with their clients, but even when they did not their intervention can often be detected in the clear hand or precise legal references of a document. Little is actually known about the relationship of these Creole or Spanish lawyers to their indigenous clients. Clearly lawyers made money, but they also received other tokens of respect. In a rare example of correspondence between a lawyer of Antequera and his indigenous clients, in 1807 Licenciado Manuel Fernandez Pantaleon asked the leaders of a Cajonos barrio for more information about a case and thanked them for the two hens they had sent him.[186]

Priests, as we have seen, sometimes had very tense relationships with their parishioners. Yet such tensions were not universal, and priests were uniquely positioned to help indigenous peasants be heard in the legal system. They were very literate and often had firsthand knowledge of indigenous peasants and their problems. Some priests were acquainted with lawyers, while others had a decent grasp of royal legislation important to peasants. Thus it is not surprising that they sometimes aided peasants in lawsuits, or produced documents for peasants. In 1812 Joseph María de Paz, the pastor of Santa María Yahuive, said he had often helped his parishioners find lawyers. In 1815 the priest Francisco María Ramirez wrote a legal petition for his parishioner, while in 1789 Pastor Francisco María de la Sierra wrote a lengthy complaint on behalf of his flock.[187]

The role of these intermediaries in the preparation of documents poses a difficult question for historians. How well do these documents reflect the arguments of indigenous peasants? Certainly the legal arguments, terms, and metaphors seen in documents are akin to those found in documents produced by Spanish lawyers, administrators, and bishops, but this commonality is not always evidence of the hand of intermediaries. Even village scribes shaped their petitions with an awareness of the audience they needed to persuade. Generally it seems that even documents definitely written by intermediaries on behalf of indigenous peasants at least partially represent the views of the peasants. Certainly the intermediaries packaged the opinions of peasants for the particular audience they were addressing, or as María de los Angeles Romero Frizzi puts it, they "translated their words into the legal terms of Audiencia lawyers."[188] However, it is unlikely that tinterillos, lawyers, or priests made arguments without dialogue with the peasants who employed them. Moreover, in cases where escritos were followed up by the questioning of their nominal authors, files rarely show contradictions between documents written for peasants and their subsequent testimony.

Arguing that the views of indigenous peasants found their way into legal documents does not imply that the views of all indigenous peasants were voiced there. Even when the authors of a given document claimed to represent an entire community, that document might have been produced by a few people with more individual goals in mind. Taylor calls these individuals "legal entrepreneurs."[189] Spanish authorities were very sensitive to this possibility, and some indigenous peasants aware of this sensitivity levied similar charges against their opponents. Yet we should not let the suspicions of Spanish authorities blind us to the complexities of the ways in which legal action was generated. A search for charges of "legal entrepreneurship" in documents produced by indigenous peasants reveals a few of the nuances. Sometimes Indian peasants accuse a village scribe or other figure of instigating court action for selfish reasons.[190] Yet in other cases the person so accused argued that he was reluctant to organize a lawsuit but was convinced that it was his duty to defend his fellow villagers. In an evocative case, Juan Martinez, a young man from Santiago Lalopa, found himself in the middle of a heated conflict between the highest officials of the village and the village's commoners when he penned an escrito for the latter in 1801. Martinez had begun to study for the priesthood in Antequera, but after dropping out he returned to the village. When questioned about the motive of his involvement, Martinez explained that "his Father told him that he had to make some legal appearances in the name of the commons, and defend it in whatever was necessary, that it was necessary to obey and bow his head for whatever was necessary."[191] In a culture that emphasized obedience to elders and offered young men a chance for economic and social independence only after years of loyalty to their fathers, this was an offer that Martinez could not refuse.

Throughout New Spain, Indian peasants were famed for their litigiousness, a characteristic that both Spanish colonial officials and their republican successors deplored.[192] The explicit motive of authorities who sought to reduce the number of lawsuits pursued by indigenous peasants was the high cost of legal activity, and this expense was an important factor in explaining why some indigenous peasants resisted participation in lawsuits filed in their name. Others took issue because they disagreed with a particular argument or felt it was prejudicial to them. In either case resistance usually took the form of refusing to pay a share of the costs, which included both money and time lost in journeys to and from Villa Alta or Antequera. Village governments pursuing legal action had various ways of financing it. According to one witness, in the early nineteenth century the government of Yahuive paid for lawsuits by carrying out a repartimiento, forcing residents to sell it cotton cloth or raw cotton at low prices, and then selling the goods acquired at the market price.[193] More commonly, villages imposed what were called *derramas*. Derramas were temporary taxes or assessments in which each family paid a determined amount. Officials pursuing lawsuits enforced derramas as they did other taxes. Families that refused to pay faced the confiscation of their goods, jailing, or flogging. Unfortunately these actions often led to another round of legal activity, as the aggrieved parties protested their mistreatment.[194]

As Enrique Florescano argues, the courts were schools where Indians "learned to manage the laws, the procedures and the legal memory of the conqueror."[195] In them indigenous people learned what they needed to forge their own legal arguments. One feature of Spanish colonialism that helped indigenous peasants form effective legal arguments was the fact that the colonial legal system granted indigenous custom the force of law when it did not contradict the goals of the colonial church or state.[196] Yet indigenous people, even those who were illiterate, also often demonstrated knowledge of the written law of the colonial system.[197] Spanish authorities took great pains to make new laws and royal orders known to the general populace and not just Indian leaders. Important orders were read aloud in indigenous languages, typically in the parish seat. Sometimes orders were read at tianguis, the regional markets attended by many indigenous men and women. They were also posted outside the offices of village governments.[198] Indigenous villagers showed a sometimes-surprising memory of important orders and rules. In a striking case, in 1816 the village of San Baltazar Yatzachi told the judge Luis Fernandez del Campo that in the year 1690 they had obtained an order prohibiting Spanish officials from confiscating their mules. After a bit of historical research Fernandez del Campo found the relevant order in the archive.[199] This kind of incident suggests how indigenous villagers constantly built political and legal arguments out of custom, memory, and royal law, mapping their place in the colonial order to the best advantage they possibly could.

Taking problems to court was a strategy that assumed that they could be solved or alleviated within the basic boundaries of the colonial order. Villagers knew that Spanish authorities and the abstract king they represented would not hand down decisions that threatened the colonial system. Surprisingly, riots, the most violent political strategy villagers pursued, were similar in this regard, expressing appeals to colonial authority rather than resistance to the colonial system.[200] In fact riots often took place at critical junctures in ongoing lawsuits, where they served to signal the depth of peasant commitment. Spanish colonial authorities recognized the limited aims of riots, and tempered their response accordingly. They did not try to repress rioters with armed force. Generally Spanish officials waited patiently, only later trying to identify and punish leaders while simultaneously working to calm tempers by addressing the problem that sparked the protest.[201]

Even though officials did not believe riots threatened the colonial order, those closest to indigenous peasant life pointed out that riots were quite common, due to what one priest called "the rebellious character of this kind of people."[202] Riots and near riots were an important part of the political life of these villages. Sometimes in the documents it is difficult to distinguish a threatened riot from an actual riot, as riots began when a group of people gathered and uttered threats.[203] Often the action stopped there, but other times the fury of the crowd exploded into physical violence. Although such occasions seemed quite threatening to the targets of riots, in hindsight very few people received even slight injuries. At times it seems that riots were more like demonstrations than rebellions.

The basic pattern of riots in Villa Alta conforms closely to that reported by William Taylor in his 1979 study of riots in New Spain.[204] In each riot, a community or some part of it gathered to protest some action or series of actions. In many cases the target was an outsider or group of outsiders.

These targets included, for instance, sahuiches, priests, or indigenous peasants from another village. Sometimes the targets of riots were internal. Community officials or even individuals engaged in unpopular actions also drew the ire of peasant crowds. In many cases the riot took place in the center of a village, and began when someone rang the church bells, signaling a severe threat to the village.[205] The exceptions were cases where a community was defending its territory against another village or against the efforts of Spanish authorities to set a boundary it considered unfavorable. In these situations the action often took place at the very edge of a village's territory.

Riots were collective acts. In each riot dozens of people came together to achieve a goal. Although every member of a community did not necessarily participate, each riot certainly involved a substantial proportion of the population. The collective nature of the act is suggested by one term used for riot. Cajonos Zapotec, Nexitzo Zapotec, and Mixe, three of the indigenous languages spoken in the area, all included the words *chinalagui*, *chinalahues*, *chinalahui*, *ichina lahuiy*, or *chinalaque*. Given the fact that these indigenous words were embedded in Spanish-language texts, it seems entirely possible that the differences among them are simply differences in opinion about how to write the same word in the Roman alphabet. This was a common problem even for the names of villages. These words were used to denote riots, village meetings, village work parties or tequios, and the community chest.[206] The use of the same term for these seemingly disparate occasions implies that for indigenous peasants these actions were akin, and were defined by the collective action of the village.

The collective nature of riots can also be seen in the prominent role played by peasant women. Generally the political activity of indigenous peasant women was hidden. They had no official role in village elections, and they did not participate often in lawsuits, even when such suits dealt with their labor service to the community or the cotton textile industry in which women were so heavily engaged. Nevertheless, they were very often at the forefront of groups of rioting peasants.[207] When a Spanish official tried to establish a boundary line between two villages in 1791, the women of San Pedro Cajonos rioted, preventing him from placing a marker.[208] In 1805 the effort of an official to establish a boundary between Talea and Juquila had exactly the same result.[209] The participation of women in riots above all underlined the unanimity of communities faced with dire threats to their resources.

Political culture in colonial Villa Alta was based on a series of core values, some of which were shared with the political culture of the Spanish empire. Probably the most important of these values was the legitimacy of the king. The king was a beloved but abstract figure, the very embodiment of justice. The king was perceived to be above any policies set by the colonial government, and even protests against those policies were directed to the king.[210] In this patriarchal order, the king was the ultimate paternal figure, although lesser authorities were also seen as fathers.[211] The legitimacy of all lesser authorities, including village officers, was seen as originating in that of the king. This ultimately royal legitimacy was very closely intertwined with loyalty to God. The reign of God and that of the king were often referred to as the two majesties, or "both Majesties," and in 1750 the governor of San Juan Yae said he had been named "by God and the King."[212] In a 1701 ceremony recognizing the rental of village lands, Alcalde Jose de los Angeles of San Francisco Cajonos reminded the renters that they should recognize "that first there is God, and after God the King who is the one chosen and named for the superior government so that the children do not damage themselves."[213] References to God's law and God's love appeared often in political arguments, and we have already seen how village nobles based their claims for privileges on the idea that as founders of the village they had brought Christianity to the other families.[214]

Indigenous villagers stressed a close connection to the king. For the most part they seem to have avoided the organic metaphor of the body politic, in which they might be viewed as the arms or legs while the king was the head.[215] However, indigenous peasants argued that they had a right to petition for the king's attention. They were the king's vassals, and the relationship was embodied in what is sometimes called the tributary pact, in which indigenous peasants exchanged tribute for the king's protection. Thus, for instance, the government of Zoogochi stated in a 1709 document, "We are and will be loyal and humble tributaries of his Majesty."[216] This tributary pact was elaborated very specifically in the 1786 Real Ordenanza de Intendentes, a document that recapitulated what royal officials saw as valuable about colonial political culture even as it attempted to reform it. The Real Ordenanza refers to Indian tribute as "the Royal Tribute that they pay my Sovereignty in recognition of the vassalage and supreme protection that is conceded to them."[217]

Both the wider political culture of the Hapsburg world and the more local political mores of indigenous peasants placed great value on custom. Under the Hapsburgs, custom, even indigenous custom, had the force of law when it did not contradict royal edicts.[218] Not surprisingly, indigenous arguments that stressed custom are common in the documents. Very often indigenous peasants referred to practices as existing "desde inmemorial tiempo," or as long as could be remembered.[219] Many indigenous peasants believed, in the words of a Spanish official, that "to be good children of the Village it is necessary to follow the ancient customs."[220] Yet we need to keep in mind that valuing custom was easier than determining whether a particular practice was actually customary. It was not uncommon for different groups of villagers to argue this point.[221] Elders were the guardians of custom, and respect for elders was a key political value of the community. As we have seen, in these intense patriarchies, men were placed over women and older men ruled younger men. Men did not acquire respect and political power until they had served years in the cargo system, gradually climbing to the higher offices. Men also had little economic power until they had faithfully served their fathers for a number of years after marriage. Before these conditions were satisfied, men were considered muchachos or mozos, youths of little consequence.[222] Not surprisingly, the premium put on the opinions of the aged made these communities tend toward conservatism, particularly in their relations with outsiders. The emphasis on tradition and the views of the elders slowed the pace of change, emphasizing cultural survival rather than opportunities for gain. This conservatism would remain an obstacle for the Bourbon reformers, Spanish liberals, and republican ideologues who tried to change indigenous political culture over the next century. Still, as we will see, communities sometimes needed expertise that was not available among the elders, and this would remain an avenue of political advancement for the young and a conduit for change from the outside.

Community harmony and unanimity were also key political ideals, but in this case the ideal often differed from practice. Internal conflict made villagers very uncomfortable, and they sought to contain such conflict in various ways. The stress put on tradition and the opinions of elders undoubtedly served this purpose. When conflict nonetheless arose, villagers worked to compromise, as we have seen in various cases. Although we have no information about internal judicial processes in colonial villages, undoubtedly they were able to contain many potential conflicts, preventing them from reaching the system of Spanish courts that began with the district court in Villa Alta. Notably, Hispanic political culture in the colonial period also abhorred conflict, and saw competing groups within a polity as "factions," an attitude that François-Xavier Guerra explains as a result of the importance of the metaphor of the political body.[223] In her contemporary ethnographic study, Laura Nader attributes what she calls the "harmony ideology" of Villa Alta villages to their Hispanic Christian legacy.[224] Whether or not indigenous peasants' censure of political conflict within communities originated in Hispanic political culture, by the eighteenth century villagers had adapted and assimilated this view into their political culture. Although at times the ideal of harmony led to calls for individuals to defer to the consensus of the majority, in practice deference was more often directed toward the village elders and other leaders.[225]

If the ideal of organic harmony had held true, there would have been no need for meetings of groups smaller than the whole community. One of the manifestations of the ideal was the notion that such meetings were by their very nature illegitimate. Insult was added to injury if a meeting was held in a clandestine fashion. Thus the government of Santa María Asunción Lachixila, complaining about its adversaries in a lawsuit about religious practices, was indignant that "the always rebellious ones, particularly Narsizo Cruz, with those mentioned previously, began to rile up the village holding nocturnal meetings in the house of Narsizo Cruz, to prepare to sue us."[226] Criticism of such meetings continued well into the nineteenth century because their existence indicated that a village was divided.[227] However, this strong criticism did not prevent meetings from happening, precisely because the ideal of organic politics was a practical impossibility. There was so much at stake in the decisions of village government that dissent was inevitable, and successful dissent required organization.

William Taylor points out that the words used for groups within villages, *parcialidad* and *bando*, owe much to "colonial preoccupations with order and wholeness."[228] Although *bando* was sometimes used in Villa Alta, *parcialidad* was the more common term. *Parcialidad* emphasized the idea that a group was only part of a real community. In other parts of New Spain the term was sometimes used for a large residential division within a community, but in Villa Alta parcialidades were kinship groups and political factions. For instance, the priest Joseph Clemente Lopez, on observing a 1789 election, reported that San Juan Tabaa was divided into two parcialidades, and proceeded to list the members of each. In the complicated discussion that followed he continually identified the parcialidades only as the first and the second. Clearly Lopez was describing factions or parties rather than residential divisions.[229]

Villages were divided in various ways, and one of the most obvious barriers to the idealized unified village was gender. Men and women clearly had different positions in society, and this undoubtedly generated different perspectives on a variety of issues. Yet the weak evidence available of women's opinions suggests congruence rather than divergence. As mentioned previously, women tended to be publicly prominent at moments of intense community unity, particularly during riots. Although their testimony about marital disputes, particularly in domestic violence cases, tells us some about their visions of gender roles in the community, women apparently had little need, desire, or opportunity to organize publicly to assert or enforce these visions.

Probably the most common division in communities was between nobles, or those who claimed noble status, and commoners. As we have seen, these divisions could be intense, and they generated many lawsuits. One of the interesting aspects of these disputes is that they also provide most of the evidence on the role of kinship in village politics. In many of the cases fathers sued on behalf of their sons, and in others the plaintiffs mentioned other blood relationships, particularly as brothers. What we cannot know, however, is how indigenous notions of kinship were translated into the Spanish terms used in court. John Chance points out that relatives the documents label as siblings may very well have been cousins.[230]

Some villages were divided into barrios. In many parts of New Spain the term referred to residential units, basically neighborhoods. However, this was rarely the case in Villa Alta, where only a couple of references to barrios as residential units exist, each from a report written by a priest whose understanding of local society may have been weak.[231] Notably, in one of these cases the barrios are named for saints, a fact that correlates neatly with the more common usage of the term in the district. As John Chance points out, contemporary barrios are basically religious organizations, very similar to cofradías. Barrios finance the festivities for their patron saints.[232] Most of the primary sources for the colonial period are consistent with this vision, although they do not rule out the possibility that barrios might also have organized spatially. Much of the documentation about barrios was generated by disputes over the worship of saints and its attendant expenses. This was even true in the very rare case of Santa María Lachixila, which had a "Barrio Zapoteco" and a "Barrio Chinanteco," suggesting that village residents belonged to two different linguistic groups.[233]

Over and over the records prove that the communities of Villa Alta were not the unified, harmonious bodies envisioned in indigenous political ideals. In fact, the most interesting documentation about life in the villages was generated precisely because villages were not unified, and villagers could not resolve their differences without turning to Spanish authorities.

Communities could be very conflictual places, where the authority of village leaders was so tenuous that they often had to turn to corporal punishment to enforce respect for their authority. Yet it would be wrong to assume that all villages were always cauldrons of ferment and discontent. Undoubtedly in many cases consensus was achieved, if grudgingly, and even if everyone did not agree with some decisions and practices, they were willing to go along to get along. The fact that most of the documents useful to us were generated by conflict within villages can bias us toward looking at such conflict as the norm. Yet the ideal of unanimity and harmony persisted into the twentieth century, suggesting that it was achieved often enough to continue to be tenable as a value.[234]

꩜ The Symbols of Political Life in Indigenous Villages

One of the most important political symbols in village life was the village government building, placed in a central location in each village. Here the gobernador judged disputes within the community. The building also served as a meeting place for principales during elections, and was in fact considered the only legitimate place for meetings. When the whole village met for some reason it met in front of the office. The building included a jail that was used to punish offenders, and the stocks used to punish more serious cases were found either in the jail or in front of the building. If officials flogged a community member it was again in front of the village offices. These village offices were almost always called the "*casas reales*," or "royal houses," a term that emphasized the idea that the power of village government came from the king. In one of the few cases where the offices were not called the casas reales they were referred to as the "house of God and the King."[235]

The village church was typically near the government offices, often on the same plaza. Sometimes people met in the churchyard or cemetery. Usually the village children were taught in the cemetery or in some shelter annexed to the church.[236] Nearby was a house for the priest, which would be decently solid if the priest lived in the village but might be in worse condition if he only stayed there occasionally while making his rounds among the villages of his parish. The church and related buildings, like the casas reales, were centers of community activity, mostly because so much of community life revolved around religion and religious festivities. Although some villages also had chapels in outlying areas, together the casas reales and the complex of religious buildings formed the most potent symbolic center of political and social life as well as the physical space where political activity was most likely to take place.[237] Moreover, in villages that held a weekly market the venders always set up in the same area.

The most important political symbols in indigenous villages were the varas, or staffs of office, sometimes called *bastones*. These symbols had both indigenous and Spanish origins. Gonzálo Aguirre Beltrán points to the importance of similar staffs in Nahua and Maya culture, while Carmen Cordero Avendaño argues that Mixtec religion also featured a similar symbol.[238] There is no evidence for the importance of staffs in the Villa Alta district before Spanish contact, but the idea seems quite plausible. Yet these staffs of office were also key insignia in Hispanic political culture. For both Spaniards and Indians, varas represented the authority of municipal officials.[239] Perhaps the tremendous power of these staffs, which remain important in many indigenous communities of the Americas today, derives from their dual origins.[240]

Every year the newly elected officers of each village traveled to the district seat of Villa Alta, where the alcalde mayor handed them their staffs in a ceremony that emphasized their connection to the king. An individual received the vara when he took office, and gave it up when he left office. The vara was the principal symbol of office, and stood in for the office in documents. When in 1750 a group from Lalopa wanted the alcalde mayor to remove the village's alcaldes from office, they asked the priest to write to the alcalde mayor "in order to take the staffs from those Alcaldes for being against the common good."[241] The size of these staffs varied. Typically those of gobernadores were larger and more richly decorated than those of alcaldes and other officials.[242] Varas were closely connected to the king, and their possession showed that the power exercised by village officials was derived from the king.[243] Possession of the vara was also a practical sign that an individual or group was engaged in official village business. Its presence was required at all official village meetings. When an official set out to patrol the village, his authority was not recognized if he was not carrying the vara.[244] Respect for the vara was a symbol of respect for the king and justice. As the village officials of Santiago Yagallo suggested in 1806, they were obligated to "work for the honor and respect of the vara that [they carried] and for the good Government and subordination of those subject to it."[245]

These highly charged symbols often figured in confrontations within communities.[246] Officials brandished varas during arguments, and sometimes also used them to strike people. In 1773, Antonio Gutierrez Teran arrived in San Juan Tabaa to collect repartimiento debts for the alcalde mayor. He called for Alcalde Salvador Lopez to bring fodder for his animals. Lopez ignored the order, and Gutierrez began to beat him. Lopez picked up his vara, apparently to defend himself, and Gutierrez threatened to imprison him. Lopez responded that Gutierrez could not jail him because "the vara he carried was that of the King." He called for help and a crowd formed, forcing Gutierrez to desist.[247] Disrespect for the vara was a potent sign of disrespect for its holder. When Alcalde Antonio Agustín of Tepuxtepec tried to arrest the drunken Miguel Pedro in 1789, Pedro exclaimed that "there are a lot of those staffs in the woods." Treating the staff of office as a mere branch, he took it away from Agustín and proceeded to beat him with it.[248] Yet the vara itself was a symbol of, among other things, the power of village officials to punish their charges. When Francisco Macario complained about punishment he had received from the village officials of San Francisco Cajonos, they replied to the alcalde mayor: "What use are the varas that the king has given us, and Your Majesty in his name, if they do not serve to punish the defects of the subalterns?"[249]

Although relatively few people in indigenous communities were able to decipher written words in Spanish or an indigenous language, documents were also very potent symbols in these communities. As we have seen, primordial titles that described the founding of communities were key icons of community identity. Although they were often presented to courts as proof of territorial boundaries between communities, their form suggests that their most important function was symbolic. They were a depository of community memory, but as Angeles Romero Frizzi points out they were most of all part of "a process of re-elaborating the past, making it adequate to the colonial moment."[250]

However, primordial titles were not the only documents that were potent symbols in indigenous political culture. Indigenous people recurred to Spanish courts over many issues, and because the Hispanic legal system worked almost entirely through documents, documents came to symbolize the king's will on a variety of matters.[251] Indigenous villagers became practiced at reading such legal documents, able to distinguish between the claims presented in courts and judicial decisions.[252] We have seen, for instance, how commoners insisted that those who aspired to noble status prove their claims with documents. In embracing the colonial courts as a legitimate and at least occasionally effective mechanism for adjudicating conflict, indigenous villagers came to see documents as talismans of power. Legal documents took on, in the words of María de los Angeles Romero Frizzi, a "sacred and political role."[253] Given this, it is not surprising that village authorities considered disrespect for such documents a notable crime, worth emphasizing in their complaints to Spanish superiors. The officials of Camotlán complained in 1789 that Nicolas Mendes and his wife had said that they should go "to shit . . . with their papers that they have in the court that are not worth anything."[254]

❧ Conclusion

The preceding pages have presented a relatively static picture of society and politics in Villa Alta in the eighteenth century. Three hundred years after the Conquest, some of the basic values and features that governed life were more or less set. Society and politics were intensely patriarchal, and custom was given great respect. The king was an important presence, and his will was invoked to justify all forms of authority and even community identity. Community identity was also underpinned by the duty of community service and devotion to particular forms of Christianity.

However, life and politics for the indigenous majority continued to change throughout the colonial period. Nothing was written in stone. During the eighteenth century, community rituals shifted away from overtly pre-Hispanic bases toward a reinforced cult of the saints. This new basis of community identity required greater services from Spanish and Creole priests, but the burden of supporting priests was unevenly distributed. This problem was a source of tension and change in communities. The controversial position of community nobilities was an even greater source of dissension. Conflict over how communities would fulfill new ritual burdens and how other community duties would be divided seems to have generated pressure toward a democratization of power and responsibility in the community. Commoner families wanted the weight of community life to be divided among as many families as possible, and their efforts met fierce resistance. In other words, these isolated, overtly conservative indigenous villages generated strong and conflictive forces for change.

In addition to these largely internal dynamics, external factors also changed communities. The physical isolation of the district did not effectively separate it from the colonial system. The growing importance of the cotton economy connected the villages ever more tightly with the outside world. Although we remain largely ignorant of the effect of this trade on life inside the communities and families of the region, it is reasonable to assume that the growth of an economic complex in which women were the most important producers of commercial products affected gender relations in the community. Even this newly strengthened connection to the colonial world was not immune to transformation. The regional economy's reliance on the repartimiento de efectos for credit and marketing was particularly vulnerable in an age of economic and political thought that viewed monopolies with suspicion and believed economic potential would be better realized if producers were allowed greater freedom. Other intellectual tides of the eighteenth century also affected the communities. In particular, the importance of Catholic priests to community rites, identity, and politics was another potential source of innovation and conflict in a moment when some political philosophers were suspicious of their role.

Yet ultimately it was indigenous peasants' relationship to the colonial political system that would provide most of the impetus for changing local political life in the coming decades. The political culture of indigenous peasants relied heavily on communities' relationship with the king as a source of legitimation. It also relied on the colonial courts to resolve many practical conflicts that could not be contained within the different communities. The colonial political system and its political culture were entering a sustained period of conscious innovation, and the reforms enacted with royal authority would present problems and opportunities to different constituencies, including different groups of indigenous peasants in Villa Alta. Soon thereafter political events would destroy the colonial system, altering politics in Villa Alta in even more profound ways.

CHAPTER Three

Bourbon Intentions and Subaltern Responses

ꕥ In the late colonial period Spain's leaders moved to dramatically change the way the colonial state functioned. Above all, they worked to increase the revenue Spain's overseas possessions remitted to the mother country. Yet the measures they took to extract more wealth from Spanish America may not have been the most important features of these so-called Bourbon reforms. Inspired by Enlightenment thought, Bourbon reformers also modified some of the ways that the state justified its actions, changing Hispanic political culture by making new kinds of arguments powerful. Moreover, Bourbon thinkers also examined colonial society with a critical eye. They introduced social reforms that threatened to change the relationships among various kinds of colonial subjects. These social reforms had fiscal ends, but they brought into play new arguments that colonial social actors could use for their own goals. The era of the Bourbon reforms was a period of great ferment throughout Spanish America, but the period's impact on popular political culture in Oaxaca was uneven.

The period of the Bourbon reforms has drawn a remarkably sustained degree of interest from historians. David Brading, one of the most influential twentieth-century historians of colonial Mexico, focused the historical gaze on the period in his 1971 *Miners and Merchants in Bourbon Mexico*. Brading also set out one of the key themes of Bourbon historiography when he titled one chapter "The Revolution in Government." In this chapter Brading argued that the efforts of Bourbon reformers to bring colonial government and society under the control of the metropolis were so far-reaching that they in effect constituted a second conquest of America, this one at the expense of the native-born Creole elite.[1] Much of the historiography of the period has followed this line of inquiry, focusing on the placement of European-born Spaniards in key positions and the correspondingly reduced influence of Creole elites on colonial policy and, especially, its enforcement.

Historians have also probed the impact of the Bourbon reforms on the mass of the population. They have concentrated on two areas of Bourbon policy. Some historians, perhaps most notably Scarlett O'Phelan Godoy, have focused on Bourbon fiscal policy, showing how Bourbon efforts to collect more taxes affected the popular economy and led to unrest.[2] As they strove to collect more excise taxes from the population, Bourbon officials also moved very aggressively to increase the number of people required to pay tribute.[3] Another group of historians has examined Bourbon efforts to reform the cultural habits of the colonial population, especially those of the urban poor, as the state took an "increasing role in the lives of ordinary people."[4] Pamela Voekel, examining Bourbon efforts to change popular mores in Mexico City, argues that Bourbon officials were engaged in nothing short of "radical social engineering to produce a more rational and productive citizen."[5] These historians have placed particular emphasis on Bourbon efforts to reign in popular amusements like the theater, ball games, and bullfights, as well as public drinking habits.[6] However, in Antequera concerns about the popular mores of the urban poor were expressed only sporadically, and there was no concerted Bourbon effort to reign in drinking or other plebeian habits. It seems likely that traditional social controls were stronger in this quiet provincial city than they were in the bustling metropolis of Mexico City or the raucous mining towns of the Bajío.

The most important changes that Bourbon ideals and policies brought to Oaxacan political culture were not directly related to either fiscal measures or new state surveillance of social mores. More fundamentally, the Bourbons worked to consciously change the basic relationship between the governed and the governors. They sought to bring order to a Hapsburg political system that had been based above all on a slow and intricate dance between an enormous variety of colonial actors and royal power. The Bourbon quest for new efficiencies may have been driven by fiscal concerns, but the most dedicated reformers believed they needed to bring colonial society under control with what Felipe Castro Gutiérrez calls a "new authoritarianism."[7] In the words of Sergio Serulnikov, for colonial political culture the Bourbon reforms represented a "new hegemonic project, a profound reformulation of the colonial pact."[8] The Bourbons made a series of efforts to reduce the power of colonial corporate institutions, including the Catholic Church, Indian villages, and guilds. They also introduced novel arguments into political discourse. For example, the Bourbons sought to increase economic efficiency even if that sometimes meant reducing old privileges. They also favored law over custom, a major departure from their predecessors.

Nevertheless, as Josefina Vázquez cautions, we should be wary of exaggerating the coherence and impact of the Bourbon project.[9] The policies we associate with the Bourbons were implemented over a long period of time, and most Bourbon innovations were tempered somewhat by the overt and clandestine opposition of interested parties in New Spain. Government functionaries appointed under the Bourbon kings often worked in a "climate of ideas nurtured by enlightened rule," but they remained individuals whose approaches to specific problems varied greatly.[10] Moreover, in their efforts to strengthen law over custom, Bourbon officials often sought to codify the desirable elements of the Hapsburg system rather than write totally new legislation. Bourbon efforts contained a series of contradictions that limited their impact. For instance, sometimes Bourbon officials' desire to increase economic activity led them to strengthen corporate bodies or even invent new ones. Pursuing economic growth, the Bourbons endorsed forced labor for specific projects even as they worked to create an economy of individuals pursuing their own best interests. Finally, and most importantly, the Bourbons did not seek collaborators in New Spain's society. Arguably, many elements of the new order the Bourbons sought to create had potential constituents in New Spain's population. Yet ultimately Bourbon officials' disdain for all colonial subjects, and colonial subalterns in particular, prevented many of their initiatives from being naturalized into New Spain's political culture.

The establishment of the intendancy system had paradoxical effects for politics in Oaxaca. The intendancies inserted a new layer of provincial colonial officials between the viceroy and district administrators. These new intendants were expected to be able to curb the abuses of district officials by providing more direct supervision than was possible when a viceroy might have to directly oversee hundreds of alcaldes mayores. Before the Bourbon reforms Antequera's political role in the province was limited. The city was the seat of the bishop, so its ecclesiastical courts were important for disputes involving religion or priests. The city was also the center of an indigenous marketing system, especially for nearby valley villages. Many long-distance merchants who financed the repartimiento trade in mountain districts lived in the city. Yet the highest-ranking official in Antequera was a corregidor who had no authority over royal officials in outlying districts. Moreover, no secular court serviced the same districts. Thus indigenous peasants from Villa Alta sometimes contracted lawyers from Antequera, but those lawyers prepared written arguments to present to the court in Villa Alta or the Audiencia in Mexico City. With the Bourbon reforms, an intendant took up residence in Antequera, and the city became for the first time the political capital of the province.[11] The intendant took over the duties of the alcalde mayor of Antequera itself, so people actually living in the city did not face a new political authority. The story was different for indigenous peasants and authorities in regions like Villa Alta. The alcalde mayor there was replaced by a subdelegado, but this official was supervised by the intendant in Antequera, and for the first time indigenous peasants could appeal to a secular court in Antequera. The political geography of Oaxaca thus took a form that is recognizable today, in which the city of Antequera (now called Oaxaca) governs a vast hinterland. Yet other factors mitigated the change. Perhaps the most important was a perceptible decline in the role of Antequera's merchants in commerce in areas like Villa Alta. Alcaldes mayores had maintained close relationships with the merchants of Antequera who financed their repartimientos. These merchants put up the bonds alcaldes mayores were required to post before taking up office, and they became in effect the business partners of the alcaldes mayores. Silke Hensel has found that the new subdelegados had substantially weaker ties to the merchant elite of Antequera.[12]

One of the principal manifestations of the Bourbon appetite for revenue was their effort to increase the collection of the royal tribute. To collect more tribute from indigenous peasants, the Bourbons revised tribute rolls and began demanding tribute from single males over the age of eighteen.[13] Revising tribute rolls had radical implications in the Andes, where indigenous families that had migrated to new villages were forced to pay more, but it had little effect in Oaxaca or other parts of New Spain, where such migration was less common.[14] The effect of collecting tribute from single indigenous men older than eighteen was miniscule, because almost all indigenous men married early. The Bourbons' renewed efforts to collect tribute from mulattos had greater consequences in Oaxaca, although not the consequences that policymakers intended. The Real Ordenanza de Intendentes stipulated that mulattos and blacks should pay three pesos annually, 50 percent more than Indians.[15] Despite the efforts of Bourbon officials to collect this sum, it appears unlikely that much additional revenue was obtained, at least not in Antequera. In 1700, as much as 27 percent of Antequera's population fell into the newly taxed categories. By the 1792 census, only 14 percent of the population was so classified. Over the intervening period many mulatto or black families succeeded in passing as Creoles or mestizos.[16] It is likely that Bourbon efforts to collect tribute more aggressively accelerated this process, although we have no reliable data on the proportion of the population classified as mulatto in later years. According to John Chance, guilds, which were supposed to collect tribute from any members who owed it, "revised the racial designations on their membership lists, with the result that large numbers of workers now denied that they were subject to tribute."[17] In effect, the Bourbon effort to collect tribute only contributed to the demise of an urban system of racial identification that was already melting away.[18]

Informed by the new principles of political economy, some Bourbon policymakers were very critical of the guild system, but the Bourbons, unlike their liberal Spanish descendants, did not abolish guilds or make other direct attacks.[19] Still, guilds were under considerable economic pressure in the late eighteenth century. They found it increasingly difficult to maintain monopolies in their trades even as Bourbon efforts to collect tribute from urban mulattos placed more demands on guild officers. For instance, in 1805 the officers of the hatmakers' guild complained that women and boys had also begun to make hats, and that guild officers spent too much time collecting tribute. They also complained that the officers were liable for any tribute they were unable to collect. In essence, Bourbon policies had made guild office more onerous even as economic competition reduced the benefits of guild organization. As a result some guild officers began petitioning for relief from their duties.[20] The plight of guild officers was sometimes worsened by Bourbon efforts that reduced guild prerogatives. In Spain, the royal government opened guild trades to women in 1779, although the decree was not made effective in Mexico City until 1799 and was not published in Oaxaca until 1816.[21] In 1791 officials abolished the guild of fireworks-makers, claiming that if Mexico City did not have such a guild Antequera should not. For two years, however, the administration continued to rely on the former officers of the guild to collect tribute, a fact that says volumes about the tensions between Bourbon discomfort about the excessive number of corporations in society and the Bourbon drive to maximize government revenue.[22]

The Bourbons also moved to augment the military capacities of the colonial state, mostly by reforming the colonial militia and increasing its size. In Villa Alta these efforts had no effect on local society because the vast majority of the inhabitants were Indians ineligible for militia service. The effect of these initiatives on the urban society of Antequera is more difficult to estimate. An urban militia unit was formed in the 1760s, and from the 1770s it provided a small force to help civil judges enforce order. The principal problems seem to have been public drinking and raucous behavior.[23] Ironically, however, militiamen enjoyed the *fuero militar*, the right to be judged in military courts, and their officers insisted that they were not subject to the discipline imposed by civil judges. This insistence that militiamen had special rights of course filtered down to the troops. On the Day of All Souls in 1799, an alcalde tried to stop a drunken fight between two men on a public street. The combatants united and turned on him, insisting that he leave them alone since they had the fuero militar. A comrade joined them, and after the alcalde arrested all three they proceeded to vulgarly insult the alcalde, their commanding officer, and the two officials' spouses.[24] The vast majority of militiamen were artisans of mixed racial origins, while the city's elite dominated the ayuntamiento. Given this, it is tempting to see militiamen's defense of their privileges as an expression of resentment against people who considered themselves superior.[25] As we will see in the next chapter, there is clear evidence that militia service was associated with this attitude in the 1810s. However, in the Bourbon period the picture is more complicated. First, Creole militia officers also clashed with the civil authority represented by the ayuntamiento and the intendant. The officers claimed that civil officials undermined their efforts to enlist men in the militia, and that civil officials sometimes used the militia not to enforce order but instead to reinforce their egos with honor guards. These officers viewed the members of the ayuntamiento in particular as their social inferiors. There are hints here that in Oaxaca, as in colonial British America, militia rank was used as a marker of elite social status.[26] Second, militia service was never popular, and it became especially onerous in the rare moments when deployments out of the city were planned.[27] Many evaded militia service, and officers' complaints that the ayuntamiento was obstructing enlistment suggest that the city's elite was trying to protect its labor supply from Bourbon military efforts.

ꝥ Subdelegados, Repartimiento, and Cotton

Probably the most important Bourbon initiative for rural Villa Alta was the abolition of the repartimiento. The repartimiento system had been controversial for decades, and an effort was made to abolish it in 1751. Parish priests and Oaxacan bishops were among the system's most vociferous critics. They believed that it impoverished the Indians and that the threat of punishment for those unable to pay repartimiento debts damaged Indian communities. In the 1770s and 1780s, Bishop José Gregorio Alonso Ortigoso repeatedly asked the Crown to abolish the system. The 1786 Real Ordenanza de Intendentes must have seemed a fitting answer to his entreaties. The alcaldes mayores were replaced by subdelegados, and all officials were explicitly forbidden from engaging in the repartimiento.[28]

However, as Brian Hamnett showed in his 1971 book, the repartimiento was difficult to kill. Although Antonio Mora y Peysal, Intendant of Oaxaca from 1787 to 1808, was a fierce opponent of the repartimiento, his efforts to stamp it out faced tremendous opposition. Not surprisingly, Antequera's merchants, who stood to lose the huge profits they had gained with their partnerships with the alcaldes mayores, led that opposition. Their fears were justified, as the ties of local merchants to the new subdelegados were substantially weaker than those they had enjoyed with the alcaldes mayores.[29] Yet, even the new subdelegados were sometimes opposed to this Bourbon reform. This was particularly true of Bernardo Bonavia, who became subdelegado of Villa Alta in 1790 and was soon one of Mora y Peysal's fiercest enemies. The two men tangled over a variety of issues over the years, but the origin of their animosity seems to have been the intendant's efforts to prevent Bonavia from enriching himself with the repartimiento in Villa Alta.[30]

In Villa Alta, the repartimiento trade in cotton and finished textiles was closely intertwined with the operations of royal government. In 1790, even the prisoners in the district jail were hard at work ginning cotton and spinning yarn for mantas.[31] Yet the most important obstacle to ending the repartimiento was the problem of compensating subdelegados for their work upholding royal authority in isolated areas. Their salaries were supposed to be taken from Indian tribute, but even if they could collect the official maximums their income would be thousands of pesos short of what their predecessors had earned through the repartimiento. The gap was too bitter a pill for many subdelegados to swallow. Bernardo Bonavia was a vociferous opponent of the repartimiento in early 1790 when he was interim intendant of central Mexico.[32] After he took office as subdelegado of Villa Alta later that year he proceeded to implement his own repartimiento, installing an ally in a store and forcing indigenous villagers to accept credit. Bonavia also worked to exclude other merchants from the district. The subdelegado, not content with his now-illegal gains, also lobbied the royal government to restore the legal repartimiento, arguing that without it the Indians of the district would produce less.[33]

Bonavia's complaints were seconded by many colonial officials in New Spain, and in 1794 the government decided to allow royal officials to advance credit to Indians as long as the loans were voluntary.[34] This nebulous provision was difficult to enforce. Not surprisingly, Bonavia's successor, Bernardo Ruiz de Consejares, also worked to extract as much profit as possible from the district. As he explained to a potential backer, he would use the repartimiento during his five-year term "by means of the approval of his Majesty and the case concluded that finds that Justices can distribute as they did before as long as they do so justly."[35] Ruiz de Consejares and several business partners or employees lent money or goods to indigenous peasants, accepting debt payments in cotton, mantas, or cash.[36] Complaints soon followed. Even when indigenous creditors stated that they had voluntarily accepted credit, they complained that Ruiz de Consejares used the power of his office to imprison them when they were unable to pay their debts.[37] Moreover, indigenous creditors had now learned that stating that they had been forced to accept repartimiento credit would give them a further powerful argument against the subdelegado. When officials investigated Ruiz de Consejares, they tried to find out "if the Indians have been compelled to receive the goods with the usurious earnings, damages, and ill-treatments that have been described." Savvy complainants realized that the effective answer to this question was yes.[38] In 1801 royal officials prohibited Ruiz de Consejares from continuing his practices, and published this prohibition throughout the district in both Spanish and the various indigenous languages. However, they allowed him to collect the money he was already owed. This sum was enormous. As of 1804, three years after he had stopped lending and left office, Ruiz de Consejares was still owed 24,624 pesos from 110 villages in Villa Alta and three villages in neighboring Teotlitlan del Valle.[39]

Josef de Gordon, who served as interim subdelegado for about a year, succeeded Ruiz de Consejares in office. Gordon had a long history in the region. He was a merchant who had managed a store in Choapan for Pablo de Ortega, the last alcalde mayor. Ortega had also named Gordon his royal lieutenant in Choapan. In a 1789 complaint, the local priest accused Gordon of administering corporal punishment to Indians with whom he had business disagreements. A detailed petition from the village seconded this complaint.[40] There is no direct evidence, however, that as subdelegado Josef de Gordon extended credit to Indians, and it seems unlikely that he would have been able to so soon after the new prohibition inspired by Ruiz de Consejares. In fact, the only evidence that the repartimiento continued after 1801 is from an 1805 case in the village of Yovego. Francisco de la Cruz complained that the village government had forced credit on the villagers and even punished a *regidor* who argued that they could not do so. The village government replied that the accusation was "false, because the debtors of the village have only been compelled to work to pay their creditors, whether they are from Villa Alta or other places."[41] No matter which side we believe, the positions expressed here suggest how the issues of credit and government coercion were intertwined in the district.

The repartimiento was the principal way in which Spanish colonial officials exploited the cotton economy, but it was not the only one. Subdelegados were responsible for collecting the royal tribute. Indigenous people had long been allowed to pay their tribute in either cash or goods as they preferred, but now that access to the cotton trade through the repartimiento was becoming more difficult, the new subdelegados of Villa Alta began pressuring Indians to pay their tribute in mantas. Doing so allowed the subdelegados to acquire mantas at a price they themselves set. The officials could then sell them on the market and pocket the difference in price before covering the tribute owed with cash. This practice was almost instantly controversial. In 1791, after barely a year in office, Subdelegado Bernardo Bonavia was repeatedly accused of requiring Indians to pay their tribute in mantas. The villagers of San Baltazar Yatzachi el Alto, San Baltazar Yatzachi el Bajo, and San Bartolomé Zoogocho argued that the time their women put into making mantas combined with the price of the necessary raw cotton made this practice very expensive. They also complained that the subdelegado rejected mantas he considered too small, increasing the work of their women. The parish priest of Betaza seconded this complaint.[42] Bonavia responded much as he did with the repartimiento. He insisted that this practice be legalized, claiming that if he did not require the Indians to pay their tribute in cloth they would no longer manufacture it. His superior, the intendant Antonio Mora y Peysal, argued against Bonavia, saying that the Indians could and would supply the market with mantas without the intervention of government officials. Bonavia was immediately ordered to allow the Indians to pay the tribute as they liked.[43] Perhaps he followed this order, and perhaps he respected orders not to implement the repartimiento. However, when Bonavia's tribute accounts were audited in 1799, he had on hand hundreds of mantas valued at 6,324 pesos.[44]

Bonavia's successor, Bernardo Ruiz de Consejares, definitely did require villagers to use mantas to pay their tribute. The same 1801 royal order that again prohibited the repartimiento ordered Ruiz de Consejares to stop forcing Indians to pay tribute in the form of mantas.[45] Even then the practice seems to have continued. In 1806 the government of the village of Santo Domingo Roayaga required villagers to pay the tax with mantas.[46] The document does not, however, specify that the subdelegado insisted on the practice. It is quite possible that the village government, responsible for paying the tribute to the subdelegado, was speculating in mantas for personal gain or to cover village expenses.

In theory, the subdelegados appointed under the new Bourbon colonial regime were to be less rapacious then the alcaldes mayores they replaced. With a decent salary derived from the legal collection of tribute, subdelegados would be less tempted to profit from the repartimiento and from the many fees alcaldes mayores had imposed on their indigenous charges. Yet subdelegados were drawn from essentially the same pool of candidates as the alcaldes mayores, and many had similar expectations of what might constitute adequate compensation for years of service in outlying districts. In fact, some subdelegados even used provisions of the Real Ordenanza de Intendentes to justify new fees or new versions of old ones. One issue that fell into this category in Villa Alta was the annual ceremony in which colonial officials inaugurated new village governments. In this *feria de varas*, as it was called, the village officials traveled to the village of Villa Alta and were handed their staffs of office by the alcalde mayor or subdelegado as representative of the king. For many decades alcaldes mayores had forced the new officials to pay a fee on this occasion.[47] The fee was exactly the kind of exaction subdelegados were supposed to abstain from. However, the Real Ordenanza de Intendentes actually gave savvy subdelegados an opportunity to continue the practice. It required that the subdelegado or another Spaniard commissioned by him preside over village elections, and explicitly stated that only elections supervised this way were valid. This provision was supposed to help prevent conflicts in village elections, and it was closely followed by another that explicitly stated that Spanish officials should not charge for approving village officers.[48] Nevertheless, Bonavia, the new subdelegado of Villa Alta, did not travel to the 110 villages of the district to preside over their elections, and he did not name Spanish commissioners to replace him in this duty. Instead he waited for the new officers to travel to Villa Alta, and then he charged them for approving their election. Moreover, the interpreters of the district court also charged villagers for their services on this occasion. Bonavia's successors continued this practice until the end of the colonial period, and several reports to the intendant on this matter went unheeded.[49]

The new subdelegados continued other practices that drew complaints from indigenous peasants.. They continued to rely on sahuiches from the village of Analco to collect tribute or repartimiento debts as well as to arrest prisoners and carry out other judicial orders. These sahuiches remained abusive toward indigenous villagers, demanding personal service and food from the villages they passed through.[50] By 1801, the Audiencia was sick of hearing repeated complaints about the sahuiches, and it specifically prohibited subdelegados from using "the officers called sahuiches." Intendant Antonio Mora y Peysal elaborated on this, prohibiting the sahuiches from going to villages for any reason.[51] Another particularly sore point for indigenous peasants was the subdelegados' use of corporal punishment against those who protested their decisions. A group of villagers reported in 1791 that Bonavia whipped his opponents, and another group complained in 1808 that subdelegado Juan Antonio Llaguno used the whip with unusual cruelty, even lashing village officials to the point of death.[52]

ʃ❧ The Bourbon Reforms and Religious Life

Bourbon policymakers have long been known for their desire to reduce the weight of religion in Mexican social and cultural life. They instituted a series of controversial measures to reign in clerical influence over the population and curb excessive or irregular demonstrations of public piety. However, it would be an error to portray these Bourbon reforms as an all-out assault on religion. If some secular officials saw the measures as a coherent policy, they were probably a minority. Decisions about religious matters, like many other Bourbon measures, instead flowed more or less independently from new assumptions about both state and society. Moreover, many of the people of New Spain had varying attitudes about different parts of the package. Bishops sometimes encouraged the entire gamut of operations, but more often they avidly participated in the reform of religious practices while doing little to encourage Bourbon efforts to reduce the political role of the church.[53] Some parish priests had similar attitudes, while others believed that reducing public religious displays endangered the souls of their parishioners. The lay faithful also had differing attitudes. Some opposed both sets of changes. Others saw the state's new desire to reduce the power of priests as a potential tool in their own disputes with their pastors. Finally, yet another group realized that the Bourbon campaign against some public religious displays gave them leverage in their efforts to distribute service obligations more fairly within their communities.

Many Bourbon administrators believed that the only way to reform the empire and make it competitive with other states was through the full exercise of royal authority. They saw the church as a conservative force, and they viewed parish priests as obstacles to royal power.[54] Although these attitudes surface in many documents, a close look at the actual interplay between Bourbon functionaries and parish priests suggests that at least sometimes their mutual animosity came about in more contingent ways than this generalization suggests. For example, when Villa Alta's new subdelegado, Bernardo Bonavia, first began corresponding with the district's parish priests in 1790, he was on excellent terms with at least some of them. Father Pedro Lucas Parra y Arteaga of Betaza called Bonavia his "friend," and Bonavia in return sent Parra vegetables and greetings from his wife along with his regrets that he would have to enforce the new Bourbon ban on some village fiestas. Their relationship began to cool a bit only after Parra continued to argue that the festivities were important in maintaining the Catholic faith of the Indians and Bonavia criticized the excessive expenditures of Indians on such matters.[55] Soon Parra and the other parish priests realized that Bonavia also planned to continue the repartimiento, and several of them began a rather bitter campaign against both Bonavia and the prohibition of fiestas. In 1793, a priest named Juan Pio Alvarez wrote to the viceroy that Bonavia was "a public and severe enemy of the priests." He then went on to criticize Bonavia for harassing all the priests of the district, prohibiting fiestas, and implementing a usurious repartimiento.[56] Bonavia's position also hardened. He complained that it was the priests who abused the Indians. Moreover, in a key move, he apparently arranged for various villages of the district to sue their priests over clerical fees. Eleven villages initiated such suits in the district court between July 1794 and August 1795. At least one of them did so with the aid of Juan Antonio Basquez, an interpreter Bonavia employed in the court.[57] Bonavia, as we saw above, was not exactly the most avid Bourbon reformer when it came to provisions that reduced the profits and power of royal administrators, such as the abolition of the repartimiento. He eventually became a strong backer of curbs on the power of the clergy, but the documents suggest that this attitude became stronger only as he began to see the district's clergy as a powerful obstacle to his personal interests. Moreover, although the attitudes of Bonavia's immediate successors towards priests are not nearly so evident, there is some evidence that at least one subdelegado favored priests. In 1808, subdelegado Juan Antonio Llaguno was even accused of obstructing the efforts of several villages to force their priests to follow the official schedule of fees, and in an 1806 case he tried to get Santiago Amatepec to compromise with its priest over fees and other problems.[58]

In the last decades of the colonial period, Villa Alta's indigenous peasants often sued parish priests over payment. In case after case, parishioners sought to substitute strict schedules of fees established on a diocesan basis for customary arrangements under which they compensated priests with food and labor.[59] Though these disputes had also surfaced earlier in the century, we can attribute at least part of this final wave of colonial lawsuits to general Bourbon policy, even if we take into account the personal conflict between Bonavia and priests. William Taylor points out that the Bourbons were generally inclined to organize society and politics with fixed principles, and that they often encouraged litigation as a way to encourage the triumph of law over custom.[60] The Real Ordenanza de Intendentes ordered bishops to form fixed schedules of fees and submit them to the Audiencia for approval. It also ordered the viceroy to enforce them.[61]

There was a very strong difference between the attitudes of high church officials actually appointed by the Bourbons and the rank-and-file priests who struggled to make a living in rural parishes. In Oaxaca, Antonio Bergoza y Jordan, the bishop for the last decade of the colonial period, was a staunch royalist who backed official policy to the hilt. Bergoza y Jordan routinely insisted that the pastors of Villa Alta follow the official schedule of fees.[62] His subordinates were less compliant with Bourbon wishes. They sued in the Audiencia to prevent the publication of the schedule of fees, claiming that it would confuse the province's Indians. The Audiencia ordered the publication, and Bergoza happily complied.[63]

Although certainly some Bourbon functionaries promoted the switch from customary arrangements between priests and parishioners to strict schedules of fees, they could succeed only if they could convince indigenous villagers to work for the change. In chapter 2 we saw that in fact villages often split over the issue. Under customary arrangements, generally elders and nobles contributed less to the maintenance of the priest than did young commoners. Also, the outlying villages of a parish often felt that their duties under customary arrangements were particularly onerous because they had to travel to the parish seat to provide labor for the priest. In cases where groups of villagers successfully forced a priest to follow the fee schedule, what we see is less a forceful imposition of fixed rules from above than political movements through which some villagers take advantage of new Bourbon tastes to substantially modify the burden of community life.[64]

This dynamic can be very difficult to see in the documents, precisely because the legal process generally called forth petitions or escritos that claimed to represent the voice of entire communities. Those are the kinds of documents that surfaced when Bonavia swung his weight behind the drive for fee schedules in 1794 and 1795. One file contains petitions from eleven villages. Each is quite short and formal, and none tells us much about the messy internal politics of the villages.[65] Although this does not necessarily mean that the documents were not composed at the behest of at least some people in the relevant communities, the interpretation of such documents requires a degree of caution.

A more believable document was produced by Rafael Perez in 1798. The document was written in the name of Perez, five other individuals, and unnamed "associates" of the village of Santa María Lachixila. They complained that their women were forced to grind maize for the priest, and that they also had to provide food and fuel for his household. The complainants argued that the labor demanded of their women was illegal involuntary service, and that this way of compensating the priest violated the official schedule of clerical fees.[66] These petitioners did not represent the entire village, and here we can see how the reaction of indigenous peasants to the various Bourbon measures that touched on religion was bound up with tensions in the village over who bore the burdens of community life. Given this, it is not surprising that priests often had at least some allies in indigenous villages during these disputes.[67]

Tensions over the burdens of community life also helped shape the impact of the Bourbons' drive to curb religious celebrations they considered excessive. In the late eighteenth century, Bourbon officials, bishops they appointed, and even many parish priests turned against the dances, processions, and feasts that were so important to both indigenous religiosity and community identity. Earlier, Spanish missionaries had encouraged these activities as the best way to implant Christianity in the sometimes-hostile soil of indigenous Mexico. Now the celebrations were seen as unorthodox and the source of excessive expenditures that prevented indigenous peasants from being more productive.[68] Yet once again the attitudes of the officials who were charged with overseeing indigenous life were mixed. José Gregorio Ortigoza, bishop of Oaxaca from 1775 to 1792, and a fierce critic of these celebrations, made strong efforts to curb them during his visits to

Villa Alta in the late 1770s and early 1780s.[69] Yet, as late as 1789, Pablo de Ortega, alcalde mayor of the district, praised Indians who insisted on celebrating the feast day of San Juan Bautista, patron of their village, Tabaa, as "devout."[70]

When Ortega was replaced by the district's first subdelegado, Bernardo Bonavia, the situation changed rapidly. Bonavia proceeded to enforce the prohibitions against dances and feasts that were not authorized by the viceregal government. In his words, "the King does not want the Indians to go into debt for these feasts, which are not limited to the religious service, but include dances, banquets, and other expenses."[71] Bonavia also forbade Indians from outlying settlements to build arbors in the parish seat for the Corpus Christi procession and prohibited residents of the town of Villa Alta from lighting their houses with candles to celebrate the feast of the Virgin de los Remedios.[72] The initial reaction of at least some parish priests was incomprehension. For instance, Pedro Lucas Parra y Arteaga wrote his friend Bonavia to ask him if it was true that Bonavia did not want his parishioners to celebrate the feast of Santa Rosa. Priests like Parra y Arteaga soon mounted a defense of the celebrations, arguing that they were essential to prevent the return of idolatry. As Father Juan Pio Alvarez argued in response to Bonavia's action, if the strong French church had been destroyed by the French Revolution, it was possible that with "such weak fundamentals among the Neophytes of this district, their faith might weaken and fail."[73] This quote from Alvarez is a reminder that most of these religious practices were in fact relatively new. As John Chance points out, they were instituted by priests and adapted by the Indians to their needs after the early-eighteenth-century demise of pre-Hispanic community rituals.[74] The opposition of parish priests to the abolition of these customs could not reverse Bourbon policy. Bishops continued to support it, and the belief that these festivities were indigenous practices of dubious orthodoxy undoubtedly was promoted in the very seminaries that trained the next generation of parish priests. In 1812, Joseph María de Paz y Mendoza, pastor of Yahuive, criticized the indigenous dances performed on feast days as "bad teaching for the innocents" and called them scandalous.[75] By then his attitude was probably fairly common among his peers.

Up to this point, what we have seen is a determined attack on some forms of indigenous religiosity, an assault led by the Bourbon state but soon seconded by the Mexican church. Serge Gruzinski sees this as a second effort to acculturate Mexico's Indians, and he details indigenous resistance to this effort in the Archdiocese of Mexico.[76] Many indigenous peasants in

Villa Alta also resisted these efforts to change cherished religious and communal ceremonies. However, there is another side to the story.

Indigenous communities in Villa Alta did not stand united against these Bourbon reforms. The new Bourbon initiatives to limit certain kinds of religious ceremonies instead added another element to communities that were already grappling with the problem of how parish priests should be compensated, as well as how the burdens of community life could best be distributed among the villages of a parish or among the members of individual communities. Most of the documentation generated by Bourbon limitations on religious ceremonies clearly shows that some villagers sought enforcement of the measures. For example, the village of San Juan Tabaa was fiercely divided over the celebration for its patron saint in 1789. The village government, embroiled in a dispute with the parish priest over fees, decided not to hold the celebration. A group of villagers met and raised money to pay the priest for the mass. This group also held the traditional procession. In retaliation the village government imprisoned them.[77] In Father Juan Pio Alvarez's long 1793 complaint to the viceroy about the subdelegado Bernardo Bonavia, he explained that the villagers of San Juan Yetzecovi, one of the outlying settlements of his parish, refused to construct arbors in the parish seat for Corpus Christi. When he scolded them about this, they argued that the obligation had been removed, and when he insisted, they told him they would explain the case to the subdelegado. Bonavia backed the village.[78] In 1798, more than twenty-seven villagers from Santa María Lachixila petitioned against their village's "bad custom" of demanding excessive money for fiestas. They pointed out that these festivities were illegal, and they also complained about their village's failure to follow the legal schedule of fees for paying the priest, arguing that the labor their women performed in making tortillas for the priest amounted to "involuntary services." In a second escrito they detailed the expenses, which included a feast for the entire village, the rental of costumes for the dances, and clerical fees, and they called the tradition "some corrupt practices . . . with the title of custom."[79] These were hardly situations in which indigenous peasants defended their ceremonies against Bourbon sensibilities. Instead we see groups of villagers using Bourbon decrees to press their cases about clerical fees, the distribution of burdens between parish seats and outlying settlements, and the distribution of community service and expenses within their villages. The villagers who appealed to Bourbon sensibilities this way were no less "Indian" than those who defended traditional religious expressions which were themselves recent colonial creations. Cultural expressions and political relationships had been evolving since before the Conquest, and the challenges and opportunities that the Bourbon reforms presented for different groups became part and parcel of this history.

The Bourbon efforts to reduce the role of priests in daily life, regulate clerical fees, and limit excessive religious celebrations had relatively little impact in the city of Antequera. Parish priests there did not clash with civil authorities over their powers. Urban Bourbon officials did not campaign to reduce religious processions or other celebrations. There was some effort to more closely regulate cofradías, but most urban cofradías had been established legally and were already closely supervised. Generally, the status of the city as the longtime seat of a bishop meant that, even before the Bourbon reforms, its religious activities were more Hispanic and more carefully policed than those of outlying areas. Moreover, the looming presence of the bishop probably curbed any overzealous activity on the part of civil officials. Finally, it is worth mentioning that Antonio Mora y Peysal, the intendant of Oaxaca from 1787 to 1808, often was allied with the church hierarchy on issues like the repartimiento. All of these factors meant that the Bourbon period brought little activity on the religious front in Antequera.

ℑ❧ The Bourbons and Education

The Bourbon effort to increase the number of primary schools and improve the instruction they provided generated activity in Antequera. In 1786, Juan Sanchez Cavehonda pointed out that in Antequera the only primary school was located in the convent of Belemites. Arguing in a typically Bourbon way that "the education of Youth, especially small children, is one of the points most interesting to the State," Sanchez Cavehonda suggested that the city's many convents be required to establish primary schools.[80] The convents resisted, but in the next decades the city council tried to provide at least some support for primary education. The council worked to furnish a space for a school and find a teacher.[81] However, references to the school are sporadic, and it is not clear that a school was operational during every year. Moreover, it is doubtful that this lone school could have provided education for more than a relative handful of Antequera's school-age children.

Arguably, efforts to educate rural indigenous children were more sustained and perhaps even more effective. Bishops and priests had long supported village schools to teach catechism. In the middle of the eighteenth century Bishop Diego Felipe Gómez de Angulo and his successor Buenaventura Blanco y Helguero both worked to insure that such schools also taught Spanish. Notably, their efforts predated the Bourbon state's 1770 decision to implant the Spanish language in Mexico's Indian population.[82] Again, the available records do not indicate how common village schools were in Villa Alta before this Bourbon decree, but there were certainly at least some, most probably in the parish seats. As discussed in the previous chapter, the principal goal of such schools was to teach indigenous children the catechism, and the basic method used was repetition.

In 1784 the Bourbon state placed the responsibility for naming teachers in the hands of its district administrators. Not surprisingly, this transfer of control from church to state was controversial. Priests argued that the subdelegados named their economic dependents as teachers.[83] They also claimed that subdelegados set high salaries that unnecessarily burdened peasants. In 1793, Father Juan Pio Alvarez complained that Bernardo Bonavia had named as schoolteachers "vicious and vagabond men given to drunkenness and some bachelor Indians from the Barrio of Analco who are 16 or 17 years old." He criticized Bonavia for making these schoolteachers functionaries in his illegal repartimientos.[84] These complaints fell on deaf ears, and subdelegados continued to name teachers. However, they soon found this task to be more a burden than an opportunity. It was difficult to provide mestizo or Creole teachers enough compensation to lure them to live in isolated Indian villages. Moreover, those teachers often clashed with the villagers over their pay and the faulty attendance of peasant children. The evidence suggests that within a few years the reluctance of mestizos or Creoles to teach in Villa Alta's villages led the subdelegados to effectively hand the task of hiring teachers over to village governments. These governments then chose men who had acquired Spanish-language skills, and compensated them with small salaries supplemented by relief from village service requirements. For instance, Juan Miguel, the teacher in the village of Jareta in 1805, was named by the village and did not participate in the cargo system. In 1806 the village of Santo Domingo Roayaga fired their teacher, Juan Ximines, and replaced him with another who "better understood and wrote the Castillian language." After Ximines lost his job the village government forced him to participate in the tequio.[85] Even when subdelegados exercised their right to name teachers, there was no guarantee that a teacher could remain in his post without support from the village government. In 1804 the subdelegado named a mestizo blacksmith, Jose Felis Salgado, schoolteacher for the village of San Pablo Ayutla. In 1811 the village government complained that he did not teach the children but instead made them do agricultural work. They argued that Salgado had not taught a single child to read and doubted that he himself actually could read. They suggested that the current subdelegado test him by making him read or write a letter. The government wanted to name a local villager who could teach the children Spanish and also teach them the catechism in Mixe, the local language. Subdelegado Julian Nieto Posadillo removed Salgado and gave the post to the villager Clemente Jose.[86]

The reluctance of indigenous peasants to make their children attend school has often been noted. Spanish officials constantly struggled against the failure of parents to send their children to school.[87] It is very tempting to see the evasion of school as indigenous resistance to cultural change, especially in the late colonial period, when the Bourbons were promoting schools as a means to modernize and acculturate New Spain's Indians.[88] However, the peasants' reluctance has been sometimes exaggerated and often misunderstood. Many parents did see the point of having all children learn the catechism in their own language. Those with a little more means and ambition also wanted their sons to learn to read and write Spanish. However, these desires were balanced by other concerns. First, parents did not want their children to be mistreated, and they suspected nonindigenous teachers of being particularly harsh to their children. For instance, the residents of three Villa Alta villages complained in 1791 that the schoolteachers named by the subdelegado "much mistreat the children because they are not his ethnicity."[89] Second, parents often had to pay for schooling, and indigenous peasants were quite poor. They resisted payment by withholding their children from school.[90] Third, and perhaps most importantly, the time of children was highly valued. Childhood was not a part of the life cycle dedicated to play or education. Even five- or six-year-old children were able to make substantial contributions to a family's economic well-being. What was needed was not their physical strength or stamina, which was of course limited. Instead they could lend a family their energy and attention. For young girls, this meant doing the lighter chores for the mother and often amusing or watching the smallest children while the mother did heavier work like preparing food or producing cloth. Young boys had a special task. One of the biggest threats to indigenous crops was the depredation of animals. Domestic animals were not fenced in, and neither were crops. Young boys kept them out of the fields, either by herding the animals or watching the fields.[91] Young boys also watched the fields to protect them from daytime raids by birds and other pests. Indigenous peasants simply could not afford to give up a substantial proportion of their crops to animals. Spanish observers tended to scoff at this excuse for lack of attendance at school, but of course they did not have to make a living farming in Mexico. For instance, in July of 1783 the parish priest Juan Jose Siguenza scolded the governor of Cacalotepec for not making children attend school. The governor replied that the children were needed to watch over the cornfields. Siguenza complained that this was a poor excuse, since not all children who failed to attend school were in the fields.[92] Yet July was a critical moment in the agricultural schedule, in which the maize was nearing maturity and was thus a terrific target for hungry pests.

As the above cases suggest, the identity of village schoolteachers varied. Villages often preferred to hire village residents.[93] These were men who had probably acquired literacy and knowledge of Spanish from previous schoolteachers. In the early 1790s, Subdelegado Bernardo Bonavia apparently named Hispanicized Indians from the village of Analco as schoolteachers in several villages. In this way, Analco's men filled a variation of their traditional role as intermediaries between Spanish power and culture on the one hand and the area's indigenous population on the other.[94] More often the schoolteachers who were sent to a village from the outside were literate mestizos or whites of relatively low status. In two cases they were blacksmiths who apparently supplemented the income they acquired from making or repairing tools with their salaries as schoolteachers.[95] A schoolteacher who was popular might hold the post for many years. Felipe Morales taught in the village of Tepuxtepec for at least nine years.[96]

What did indigenous peasant children learn in village schools? This question is both extremely important and extremely frustrating. We know that even with the Bourbon emphasis on acculturating Indians most schoolteachers continued to stress the memorization of the basic catechism. Teachers from outside the village taught the catechism in Spanish rather than indigenous languages, but they continued to use the catechism written by the Jesuit priest Gerónimo de Ripalda in the sixteenth century. Although in a few parts of New Spain teachers also used history books, there is no evidence of anything like this in Villa Alta.[97] Benito Juárez pointed out that the curriculum of the urban primary school he attended in Antequera in 1819 consisted of "reading, writing, and memorizing Padre Ripalda's Catechism."[98] In this sense the Bourbon efforts to educate New Spain's youth were hardly a step toward a new Enlightenment republic of letters. Indigenous students also used a small reading book called the "Cartilla" which showed how the letters of the alphabet formed words.[99] Advanced students used the "Catón," another small book. The Catón, like a catechism, was written in dialogue form. The lead character, Cato, instructed his disciple about "not the wisdom of that ancient Cato and the moral philosophers, but instead the wisdom [he] learned from the Gospel, wherein is contained the eminent science of Christ." Explaining proper prayer and conduct for Christians, the book also counseled obedience to both God and the authorities God gave to society. Those authorities were to be obeyed even when they were "evil."[100]

✺ The Bourbons and Political Culture

Together, the Bourbon reforms constituted a new hegemonic project for the colonial state. Bourbon administrators altered government practices in a myriad of ways, and they made significant efforts to change colonial society. The basic justifications for policy also shifted considerably. Yet Bourbon officials did not seek opportunities to educate the majority of the population about the new order. As we have just seen, they did not, for instance, take advantage of their renewed emphasis on schooling to indoctrinate youngsters about the new relationship between the king and his subjects. Although Bourbon plans and justifications are well-documented, our sources on Bourbon projects are policy debates carried on in letters and reports that were not accessible to even the literate among the vast bulk of New Spain's population. The Bourbons, unlike their early republican successors, did not publish manifestos.

However, many people in New Spain came to know a great deal about the new hegemonic project. Even impoverished and often illiterate subjects developed understandings about the new order of things. They had to do so precisely because they were not powerful. Subalterns needed to be sensitive to the new criteria the powerful used to make and justify decisions because they had so much at stake in those decisions.[101] Because the Bourbons made little effort to make the new project known to subalterns, subalterns learned of and responded to the reforms primarily through their activity in the judicial system. Enrique Florescano calls the colonial court system a school where Indians learned how to use laws, and at no point was this more true than during the Bourbon reforms.[102] Although judges did not explain the reasoning behind their decisions, their legal advisors did.[103] These explanations were transmitted to subaltern plaintiffs through lawyers, tinterillos, and village scribes. Even the urban poor took disputes they could not resolve to court, and listened carefully to how authorities justified their decisions.[104]

The colonial court system was extremely active during the Bourbon period. The Bourbons wanted to standardize the rules under which colonial society operated, and for that reason in their decisions they generally favored law over custom.[105] This Bourbon taste tended to encourage litigation, because even if current custom did not favor their case, plaintiffs could find and cite some law that would. The Bourbons were busily issuing new decrees and regulations in their effort to modernize the Spanish empire, so those arguing in court and the officials justifying court decisions often had recourse to relatively new laws. These included, for instance, the new schedules published for clerical fees, but the principal example was the 1786 *Real Ordenanza para el establecimiento e instrucción de intendentes de ejército y provincia en el Reino de la Nueva España,* commonly known simply as the Real Ordenanza de Intendentes.[106] As its full title suggests, this lengthy document not only explained the attributes of the new provincial officials relied on to enforce the Bourbon reforms, it also instructed them about how to fulfill their duties. It contained many provisions about how all kinds of government were supposed to function in the colony. In some ways the Real Ordenanza was as detailed as the written constitutions that would become so common in the nineteenth century.

However, it would be mistaken to see the Bourbons as determined revolutionaries who sought to totally remake colonial government. In the Spanish system, older laws often remained on the books indefinitely. The Bourbon penchant for laws over custom frequently led them to favor old laws over custom. In fact, in the words of William Taylor, "Bourbon administrators invoked Hapsburg law to justify their reforms whenever possible" even though they saw themselves as reformers determined to change government.[107] Some Bourbon reforms were in effect restatements of older provisions that had fallen into disuse, and generally Bourbon reformers wanted to build on those Hapsburg policies that had proven effective.[108] Moreover, the officials the Bourbons relied on to actually govern New Spain were not committed radicals fresh from the salons of France. This was particularly true of bishops and priests, but even such key civil officials as subdelegados were drawn mostly from the same pool of officials who had administered local New Spain before.[109] In fact, the documents generated at the various levels of the regime suggest a fairly strict hierarchy. Intendants and their advisors tended to be quite committed to the new order of things, and conversant with the philosophy, but subdelegados generally were not. Audiencia members, viceroys, and their advisors could be found at various places along this scale.

Bourbon judges and the lawyers who argued before them were well-educated about the rather enormous number of royal laws and decrees generated during the first two centuries of the colonial period, and they were certainly willing to use them. However, the general taste for systemization and standardization that sometimes led them to Hapsburg-era legislation also made them wary of arguments based on custom or current practice. Moreover, they could be particularly vicious when opponents used evidence that did not stand up to the new standards of rationality. During an 1815 dispute over land with the neighboring village of Zoogochi, San Pedro Yaneri presented a primordial title that described the village's foundation by a group of ancestors who had accepted Christianity and accompanied Cortés. Luis Castellanos, one of the most active lawyers in late colonial Antequera, responded for Zoogochi. He blasted the primordial title, comparing the dates and events it described with the dates in common histories of the Conquest. He was especially irritated by the idea that the ancestors of Yaneri met Cortés before the latter set foot in New Spain. Castellanos' critique was signed not only by the lawyer, but also by two indigenous officials from Zoogochi.[110]

The new kinds of argument and language that characterized the Bourbon period could be utilized by indigenous peasants as well as titled lawyers. However, one cannot trace these arguments by simply looking for the terms we associate with the Enlightenment. In fact, the terms used in arguments changed relatively little, because the theorists of the Hapsburg order and those of the Spanish Enlightenment drank from the same well of classical political vocabulary. In other words, older documents also often contained words like *republic*, *despotism*, or *liberty*.[111] Many times, it is hard to trace the intellectual genealogy of a particular argument, even when the author is someone we can otherwise associate with the new ways of thinking. For instance, in 1796 the lawyer Manuel Mimiaga, who later became an important Bourbon functionary in Antequera, complained of the "despotism" of the subdelegado Bernardo Ruiz de Consejares when Ruiz changed a decision about an inheritance in Villa Alta.[112] However, Mimiaga's argument would not have been unusual even if it had been made a hundred years earlier.

Sometimes documents produced in the Bourbon period use the shared vocabulary in novel ways. William Taylor, for instance, has pointed out that colonial law had long shown Indians ways to use *liberty* in political arguments. However, when Joseph Nuñez, a lawyer, deployed the term on behalf of a group from San Juan Tabaa in 1784, he used it in a new way. The village had just elected a new set of officers, and the "committee members and principales" who had voted for them instructed them to continue the village's effort to prevent its members from being forced to labor in a nearby mine. The new officers refused, and the "committee members and principales" promptly held a new election. Their lawyer insisted that they could do this, because in "all our Nations, and almost all other nations" it was considered the duty of officials to "carefully consider the defense of the Patria and the liberty of its inhabitants." Nuñez based his argument on an interpretation of Roman history, suggesting the renewed interest in history inspired by the Enlightenment. Moreover, the effort to have the election overturned was entirely without precedent. The combination is not one that would have been possible earlier in the century. Strikingly, the argument was more successful with the indigenous officeholders than it was with royal authorities. It fit well with aspects of indigenous political culture that stressed respect for elders and the need to uphold the rights of the village against outside threats. The officials who had been elected in the first election agreed to continue the village's lawsuit against the mine, and they were allowed to take office. Even so, the intendant's legal advisor in Antequera stated that he was very reluctant to allow indigenous villagers to overturn elections, and undoubtedly if the dispute had continued the intendant would have ruled against Nuñez and the plaintiffs.[113]

The laws had protected Indians from "involuntary service" or "personal service" for many years, but Bourbon notions about the utility of individual liberty gave those laws greater credence. There was always a contradiction in the villages of Villa Alta: involuntary service for individuals was illegal but involuntary service for communities was considered essential to political, social, and religious life. Both the Bourbon penchant for individual liberty and the effort to force priests to follow fixed schedules for fees increased the number of complaints against involuntary service. In the 1784 San Juan Tabaa case, Joseph Nuñez also argued that labor drafts for a mine were a form of illegal involuntary service. In 1799 the village of Santo Domingo Tepuxtepec complained that Juan Antonio Vazquez, an interpreter for the court in Villa Alta, forced Mixe men and women to work in his house in Villa Alta, exploiting their "personal services against all law, Justice and equity," and imprisoning those who resisted.[114] Most often, though, these charges were made about service for priests, perhaps because Bourbon judges already pushing schedules of clerical fees were particularly open to them. In 1794 the lawyer Mariano Perez de Tagle complained about the "involuntary services" the villagers of Santiago Yaveo were forced to give their priest, and in 1798 a group of Indians from Santa María Lachixila complained about the "involuntary services" that their women had to perform for their pastor.[115] Bourbon judges were inclined to see these kinds of services not only as violations of Hapsburg law and obstacles to their effort to standardize the rules of social life but also as affronts to the personal liberty Indians would need to become productive contributors to the glory of the Spanish empire.

The Bourbon period brought another new wrinkle to the political vocabulary used in Antequera and Villa Alta. Although in retrospect it is clear that both the royalist Bourbon reforms and the French Revolution emerged from similar philosophical roots, in the 1790s Bourbon theorists, policymakers, administrators, and religious officials all saw the French Revolution and indeed the French Enlightenment as examples of political and religious madness.[116] Although this was particularly true during the periods when the Spanish state was at war with France's revolutionary armies, the Bourbons always worked to keep the French contagion at arm's length. Thus it is not surprising that political actors sometimes tried to associate their adversaries with the Enlightenment and the French Revolution. When Bishop Gregorio Omaña y Sotomayor appealed to his parish priests for funds for the war against France in July 1793, he spoke of the atrocious crimes committed by the revolutionaries against their king, his family, sacred images, and indeed the Catholic religion. The war against France was a "Holy War, because the cause of God also has an interest in it." Omaña pointed out that France's royal family was executed only after the church had been severely attacked, and he railed against "modern and worldly French."[117] A month later Juan Pio Alvarez, one of the priests Omaña had appealed to, was complaining about Subdelegado Bernardo Bonavia's enforcement of the royal order against excessive religious celebrations. He argued that such an order would leave New Spain exposed to the destruction of Catholicism already seen in France.[118] These kinds of images also found their way into the arguments made on behalf of indigenous villagers. The lawyer Manuel Mimiaga, arguing for the right of the village government of San Francisco Cajonos to punish villagers who defied its authority, stated that if villagers were not forced to subordinate themselves to superiors, one result might be "the recent unfortunate revolutions of the French Nation."[119] This kind of argument suggests how the spirit of the times infiltrated popular political culture through official propaganda and the arguments made by the literate in court.

𝕾 *The Limitations of the Bourbon Reforms*

The Bourbons formulated and set in motion dramatic changes in the political culture of New Spain. They viewed the older Hapsburg colonial order as inefficient and sometimes unjust. In their view, only drastic reforms would allow the Spanish empire to compete on the world stage. These reforms would change not only the relationship between the governed and their rulers, but also relationships among the king's many kinds of subjects in New Spain. The Bourbon reformers set out to change New Spain's dominant political culture, its colonial hegemonic order. However, the Bourbon reforms generated far less change than the reformers' brave intentions suggest. As many authors have shown, some of the centerpiece Bourbon reforms generated fierce resistance from entrenched interest groups.[120] Yet, more importantly for the subject of this book, Bourbon innovations in political culture had a surprisingly muted effect on how relatively poor people in both Antequera and Villa Alta engaged in politics. The Bourbon reforms did not dramatically alter the way people discussed political issues, the arguments they made, or the tactics they used. There are several reasons for the limited impact of the reforms on everyday political life. At times the Bourbon need for order overcame the Bourbon desire for reform. Moreover, even when the Bourbons promoted new policy goals, they often fell back on older tools of policy implementation, setting up contradictions that slowed change in New Spain. However, nothing limited the impact of the Bourbons on popular political culture more than the fact that Bourbon theorists never believed that the mass of the population could help them achieve their goals. This last problem in fact suggests a great deal about how efforts to implant new hegemonic ideologies take root in the populations they seek to control. New hegemonic ideologies become more fully established when subaltern populations begin to routinely seek their own goals by arguing within them. Encouraging this process required more faith in subalterns than Bourbon ideologues could muster.

Although the Bourbons in general believed that they should mobilize the untapped economic potential of New Spain's masses to improve the tax revenues of the Spanish empire, they did not feel that the colony's vast impoverished majority could contribute to the success of their efforts to change society. Bourbon theorists and administrators did not direct their arguments to the population of New Spain. The overt policy debates and argumentation were confined to a relatively small coterie of officials. In fact, the only open appeals Bourbon administrators made to the mass of the population were pleas for donations or loans to fund European wars. Such pleas were passed along from viceroys to intendants and then to subdelegados, who finally sent the appeals to village governments. Generally, the first stages of this correspondence are documented, but we cannot be sure exactly what subdelegados actually transmitted to the indigenous population. However, it seems most likely that the rhetoric closely mirrored that of a viceroy who in 1795 appealed to the king's subjects to "defend Religion, the Fatherland, and the kingdom of our august sovereign at all cost."[121] Needless to say, this was far from an effort to seek the poor's support in the internal effort to reform society.

The Bourbons did not seek the aid of impoverished plebeians and indigenous peasants because they did not see how such people could help them. They viewed the poor as uneducated and traditional, unable to understand the sophisticated arguments of political economy or the need to change customary ways of doing things. Bourbon reformers were extremely wary of the idle, drunken, and scandalous poor they believed to dominate cities. Redeeming this group was something to be accomplished by force, not persuasion.[122] Indigenous peasants were slated for gentler treatment. As William Taylor points out, the Bourbons saw Indians as the objects of improvement, "capable of full 'conversion' into the new Hispanic order."[123] This view infuses the instructions for Spanish officials in the Real Ordenanza de Intendentes. Yet Indians were also seen as particularly fond of tradition, a great obstacle to reform. Moreover, Bourbon administrators were no more immune to racism than their Hapsburg predecessors. Thus even when an anonymous Bourbon functionary counseled the intendant not to use armed force against a village that had rioted, he referred to the villagers as "a few idiotic Indians."[124] Spanish administrators believed that such people could not contribute to the success of crucial state policies.

The evidence suggests that they were wrong. In reality, the Bourbon state lacked the technology and personnel it would have needed to thoroughly enforce any of its policies. For this reason, the state relied on the complaints of common Indian villagers to bring to its attention failures to follow official policy. Again and again in this chapter we have seen how groups of villagers utilized new Bourbon policies for their own goals. Rather than a monolithic mass of traditionalist Indians, the Bourbons in fact faced a diverse and often divided set of individuals, families, and villages. Some factions or individuals saw the new policies as important tools for achieving their own goals. The Bourbons seem never to have understood the significance of this diversity, and their failure to see it dramatically reduced the impact of their reforms.

Other factors also reduced the reach and depth of the Bourbon reforms. Generally, the Bourbons relied on older instruments of power to implement their novel reforms, and this led to severe contradictions. Earlier we saw how the new subdelegados were drawn from the same pool of candidates that had supplied the alcaldes mayores, and that they brought many of the same expectations about how they should be compensated for their service in remote areas. Not surprisingly, they were unwilling to give up the profits and perks of office in exchange for the much smaller salaries offered under the Bourbon system. In theory, Bourbon reformers opposed the power and autonomy of corporatist groups like guilds and Indian villages. In practice, their drive to collect more tribute forced them to rely on Indian villages and guilds. They also introduced new corporatist institutions, including merchant guilds in important provincial cities like Veracruz.[125] In Oaxaca, the clearest example of this continued reliance on corporatism was the establishment of the mining deputation, which proved to be quite ineffective. The deputation, charged with service to "the King, the Public, and the body of mining" proved to be a toothless body whose members avoided meeting as much as possible. When the provincial administration called for a meeting in 1804, most members cited begged off by empowering one of two colleagues to represent them. After those two also refused to attend, the meeting was canceled.[126]

Mine owners may not have felt that the Bourbon offer of corporate representation served their interests, but they were quite willing to take advantage of the Bourbon fascination with mining. The Bourbon desire to increase the production of precious metals overwhelmed their individualist philosophical bent, providing the most poignant example of the contradictions that limited the impact of the Bourbon reforms on the way that subalterns engaged in politics. As various Bourbon economic initiatives took hold, Juan Francisco Echarri, a merchant resident of Antequera, began investing money in Santa Gertrudis, a mine in Villa Alta. Santa Gertrudis was not a very rich claim, and it was much smaller than the great mines of Taxco, the Bajío, or northern Mexico, yet Echarri was able to work this marginal operation for decades precisely because the Bourbon appetite for silver led them to lend key state support to his operation. Echarri was granted the right to force workers from nearby indigenous communities to work his claim. These communities were required to supply up to 137 miners at a time to the mine and processing plant, and, although workers were paid a nominal wage, they had no choice about performing the difficult and dangerous work.[127]

Echarri became one of the most hated men in the district, although the evidence suggests that he rarely visited it. His corrections also made him a particularly formidable opponent for the indigenous peasants forced to work for him. Although earlier he had been involved in commerce, his involvement with Santa Gertrudis soon led him to shift most of his capital into mining there and at other small mines in Villa Alta or nearby districts. In addition to his often-reluctant officeholding in the mining deputation, he was a colonel in the militia, another corporatist institution the Bourbons strengthened to promote their goals. Although he was often at odds with Intendant Antonio Mora y Peysal, his other contacts in the Bourbon administration combined with the Bourbon goal of maximizing mine output helped him maintain his labor draft from 1783 until his death in 1807 despite fierce opposition from local Indians.[128] A brief examination of the arguments about this institution will help show some of the limits and contradictions of the Bourbon reforms.

The origins of the labor draft and the disputes about it are obscure, but in 1783 the problem began to generate copious documentation. That year the Audiencia issued a decree regulating the draft. Echarri was required to pay the Indians an unspecified "just" wage. Village governments had to send up to 4 percent of their population each week to work at the mine. That year Echarri wrote to the bishop in Antequera, accusing two parish priests of encouraging their parishioners to resist the labor draft. The bishop scolded these priests and ordered them not to get involved and above all not to encourage disobedience. Pedro Joseph Avendaño, parish priest of Tabaa, responded by complaining that Echarri had posted men on the roads to Oaxaca, kidnapping his parishioners on the pretext that they were fleeing their mine service. He also pointed out that his parishioners feared death in the mine, as several men had been killed in accidents. According to Avendaño, the Indians argued that if the king and the pope loved them, "why did they want to treat them as if they were slaves." After the Indians' complaints were pushed aside, they fled to the bush, "missing Mass on Sundays, and losing their work."[129] The indigenous peasants did not confine themselves to this everyday form of resistance. As mentioned earlier, in January 1784, the elders of San Juan Tabaa, complaining of the "slavery and servitude" to which they were subjected, insisted that their newly elected officers continue the legal battle with Echarri, and tried to depose the officers when they refused. The new officers agreed to continue the case, and again the village lost.[130] Indigenous peasants turned once more to everyday forms of resistance. The villagers due to give labor service simply refused to go. When the authorities of various villages were criticized for this, they explained that they always escorted the peasants due to give service to the limits of their villages' territories. There the authorities sent the draftees on to the mine, but the peasants instead disappeared. Again Echarri blamed parish priests for encouraging this behavior.[131]

Continued evasion of service at the mine makes it seem unlikely that Echarri could ever count on the number of workers he was legally entitled to. In fact, Echarri was forced to compromise even to get the workers he did get. Indigenous peasants often paid substitutes to take turns at the mine, a practice that Echarri opposed because he believed the peasants did not pay their substitutes well or on time and as a consequence the substitutes did not work hard.[132] In fact, peasants paid substitutes a peso per week in addition to whatever wage Echarri provided, so his objection is effectively an admission that he did not pay these forced workers enough to compensate them for the precious time they lost. Echarri's complaint about substitution underlines the way in which labor at his mine was rotated among the indigenous peasants of the villages obligated to provide service. Service at Echarri's mine was but one of the many labor obligations of indigenous peasants. Most of those obligations were to the village. As we have seen, villagers served in the cargo system, and they worked in the tequio, periodic labor for public works projects. In villages where the payment of priests had not been placed on a strict fee schedule, villagers also labored periodically for the priest. Elaborate customary systems were designed to distribute these burdens equitably among the residents of each village. However, these customs, far from consensual, were often very conflictive. Not surprisingly, in at least one village required to provide workers for Echarri, some inhabitants tried to reduce their own burdens by subjecting mine service to the same kinds of rules that governed community service. In 1791, the commoners of Santiago Lalopa complained to Bernardo Bonavia that years before village officers had begun to exempt the principales from service in the mines. The exemption of course increased the frequency with which the "poor youths," those villagers who had not reached high office in the cargo system, had to work for Echarri. Pablo de Ortega, the previous alcalde mayor, had accepted this arrangement and even forced the commoners to agree to it. Fortunately for the commoners, Bonavia did not want the royal requirement for mine service to be subject to indigenous customs, and he overturned Ortega's decision, ordering all villagers to take their turns in the mine.[133]

The bitter disputes about indigenous labor service in the mines suggest some important things about the Bourbon reforms and their limits. The Bourbons worked to change colonial society, and in general terms they sought to move it in directions that would make it more "modern." They sought to rationalize public administration and free decisions of state from the web of custom that restricted them. The Bourbons also worked to reduce the thicket of corporate rights and privileges that prevented individuals from making their economic choices freely. However, these long-term goals were always subordinated to the more immediate goal of maximizing royal revenue. As we have seen, corporate bodies usefully increased royal revenue. Moreover, even the purely economic freedom sought by the indigenous peasants who opposed service in Echarri's mining operation was less important to the Bourbons than increasing silver production and the taxes derived from it. For these indigenous peasants, the contradiction was stark. Royal decrees abolishing the repartimiento insisted that peasants should be allowed to make their own economic choices, but almost simultaneously they were required to provide forced labor, leading some of them to say, "Mr. Colonel Echarri is rich, and because we are poor you have beaten us down."[134]

CHAPTER Four

Loyalty, Liberalism, War, and Independence

❦ Bourbon officials had worked to reform Spain's empire, and they had introduced important innovations in the way that empire functioned. Yet, as we have seen, Bourbon initiatives did not have a particularly profound impact on the way ordinary urban plebeians or rural indigenous peasants acted or argued in politics. The same cannot be said about the events of 1808–1821. When Napoleon removed the royal family from imperial politics in 1808, he inadvertently set in motion intense political conflicts in Spain and Spanish America, and these conflicts had lasting effects on Hispanic political culture. Moreover, change accelerated when Spanish liberal politicians, who often saw themselves as revolutionary innovators in public affairs, temporarily replaced the relatively conservative royal family at the head of the empire. The liberals' disdain for older forms of Hispanic political culture was manifest, and the constitution they promulgated in 1812 threatened to sweep away the foundation of colonial political culture in Mexico. Events and trends in Spain had a profound effect on the way politics were conducted in Oaxaca and other parts of Mexico.

For the people of Mexico, Spain's struggle against Napoleon was not a spectator event. At the urging of colonial officials, individuals and groups stepped forward to aid Spain in its time of need. The defense of the monarchy required the mobilization of resources in the overseas possessions, and, to accomplish this, leaders had to make political arguments to the general population. Later, the Spanish liberal drive to remake society required other arguments to build support for such radical change. After 1810, however, the inhabitants of New Spain also had their own war to fight. Again politicians and ideologues stepped forward to convince people to subscribe to their visions of what New Spain should be, and what their enemies were up to. The stakes in this civil war were enormous, and both insurgent and royalist groups appealed to New Spain's populations on a scale that would have been unimaginable just a few years before. Absolutists took up this search for popular support after Fernando VII suspended the liberal experiment in 1814.

From 1808 on, the more or less conscious and planned efforts of Spanish liberals, insurgents, royalists, and later absolutists to shape the empire's political culture were supplemented by a more amorphous but perhaps no less powerful pressure toward change. The struggle against Napoleon and the civil war in Mexico inspired not only programmatic efforts to convince people to lean one way or another but also a prodigious rumor mill.[1] In a culture where most people were illiterate, rumors flourished, especially in times of crisis.[2] In hindsight, we often see these rumors as static, meaningless noise that sometimes interferes with our efforts to clearly "hear" the story of actual events. However, these rumors also shaped events. They heightened the sense of crisis that pervaded politics in the period, and they shaped the beliefs of individuals and groups. These often-anxious rumors also help us understand political culture by demonstrating what people saw as possible and plausible events or positions. As Ranajit Guha points out, rumors recorded political consciousness even as they served as a medium for its transmission.[3]

In combination, the conscious innovations of politicians and ideologues, their need to mobilize the populace to support their diverse goals, and the rumor mill of crisis created an unusually apt environment for changes in political arguments, tactics, and strategies. The result was a kind of hothouse that led to a proliferation of exotic and sometimes riotous growth in the strands of political discourse. The political culture that grew under these conditions was neither totally new nor an incremental change from colonial political culture. The arguments and actions fostered by this altered political environment were also much more diverse than anything Mexico had seen before. Notably, the most important changes had relatively little to do with independence from Spain, the event that most historians still place at the center of the 1808–1821 period.

All of the issues outlined above affected both the city of Antequera and the indigenous villages of Villa Alta. However, different arguments and changes resonated with local conflicts and earlier preoccupations in these two locations. As a result, the political cultures of Antequera and Villa Alta tended to diverge in this period. Conflicts over social class that were already latent in the city became more salient under the rapidly changing political conditions of the period. As we will see in the next chapter, these conflicts and arguments would continue to shape politics in the city for the next several decades. Social class did not generate important political conflicts in Villa Alta, most of all because indigenous society was remarkably socially homogeneous. Instead, in Villa Alta the key clashes both before and after 1821 revolved around service and patriarchy, themes we will take up in chapter 6. In comparison to the conflicts in urban Antequera, Villa Alta's were much more muted in the 1808–1821 period, and it is much more difficult to see clear connections to the changes that were to come later.

𝕾❧ The Shadow of Napoleon

When Napoleon Bonaparte imprisoned the Spanish royal family and tried to set his brother in its place in 1808, he inadvertently set off far-reaching changes throughout the Hispanic world. By 1808 Fernando VII had already become an important symbol of hope for the empire's future. Over the previous few years groups and individuals had begun to look to Fernando VII, "el Deseado" or desired one, to save the Hispanic world from the bumbling of his father, Carlos IV, and the royal favorite, Manuel Godoy.[4] Carlos IV and Godoy had allied Spain with France against England, weakening the seaborne communications that held the empire together even as they brought French heresy closer. In March 1808, Fernando's followers forced Carlos IV to abdicate in his favor, but Napoleon soon imprisoned the royal family and forced them to cede their rights to the throne. Fernando VII's imprisonment triggered a powerful reaction against French influence and French troops even as it raised crucial questions about whom his subjects should obey. In Spain, the crisis energized opposition to Napoleon. In Mexico, the crisis brought political uncertainty and efforts to aid the Spanish opposition to Napoleon. More dramatically, it generated fears about Napoleon's designs on the New World as well as suspicions that groups or individuals in New Spain might cooperate with those designs.

The Iberian events of 1808 brought an extreme sense of crisis to New Spain, but it is important to realize that many of the elements of anti-Napoleonic arguments were already familiar to the population. They had been deployed over a decade earlier when Catholic Spain first clashed with the French revolutionary state.[5] Beginning in 1793, the leaders of New Spain issued a series of appeals for donations to aid the Spanish crown in its war against France. Such donations were voluntary, and thus the calls for support stressed arguments that played to the most cherished values of the population. For instance, in 1793, when Bishop Gregorio Omaña called on Oaxaca's parish priests to contribute money for the war, he spoke of "the atrocious crime the French committed by laying their sacrilegious hands on their legitimate King, and Lord, the implacable hate that they have showed toward the empire's Sacred Religion, and the audacious way they have insulted the Ministers and wife and the King, the images of the Saints and the Virgin Mary and even the Holy Eucharist."[6] Omaña then worked through a procession of outrages, finishing with insults to the Holy Eucharist, the very body of Christ. Civil authorities also stressed the need to defend Catholicism. In 1795, Viceroy Miguel de la Grúa Talamanca y Branciforte appealed to the need to defend "at all cost Religion, the Fatherland, and the property of the dominion of the empire's august sovereign." Regional officials passed this call for donations on to villages in Villa Alta.[7]

Throughout the 1790s, authorities repeatedly called on the population of Oaxaca to provide funds to support Spain's foreign wars. These appeals reached groups throughout society, and they responded by emptying their pocketbooks. For instance, in 1795 the indigenous villagers of the district of Villa Alta forwarded over 60,000 pesos in response to Viceroy Branciforte's appeal. This sum probably represented the fruits of several days' labor for each family.[8] The urban population of Antequera was not left behind. The record of donations collected after a 1798 appeal lists 298 individuals. They range from the wealthiest men of the city, who each donated hundreds of pesos, to artisans who did not own even the dignity of a last name, and who contributed as little as a fraction of a peso each. The list includes members of the city council and members of various guilds — silversmiths, painters, carpenters, blacksmiths, and tailors. Generally male heads of households are listed, although in some cases the widows of artisans contributed also. Thirty-eight master tailors contributed for their forty-six unnamed journeymen, considered members of their households.[9] All of these members of New Spain's polity, whether indigenous peasants, wealthy merchants, or humble artisans, were participating in a collective effort to aid the king against his enemies. Their actions prepared the ground for other forms of collective political behavior that would be unleashed after 1808.

In 1795 Spain lost its war with France and was forced into a sometimes-uneasy alliance with its former enemy. This alliance lasted until 1808, and of course while it was in effect there was no official criticism of revolutionary France. Whatever lasting effect the earlier propaganda may have had was forced underground until Napoleon's effort to impose his brother as king of Spain sparked massive resistance. In 1808 authorities again launched a propaganda effort to collect funds for the war in Europe. Some of the elements were the same as those seen in the early 1790s. On 13 October 1808, Bishop Antonio Bergoza y Jordán argued that donations were needed to save both the Catholic religion and the monarchy. However, Bergoza heightened the sense of crisis by claiming that the capture of Fernando VII was punishment for the sins of the empire's populace. Moreover, in 1808 authorities made the danger seem more immediate. Authorities suggested that French ships were preparing for an invasion of the New World, and Bergoza warned of other conspiracies.[10]

In 1808, the official voices of the viceroy, bishops, and intendants were seconded by a chorus of unofficial propagandists. Generally, these often-anonymous propagandists mirrored the official pronouncements and appeals for funds, but they did so through poetry, wit, and sarcasm. They aimed praise at Fernando VII and insults at Napoleon in verses that were then posted in public places. These anonymous messages, called pasquines, were read aloud for the illiterate and often discussed at length.[11] Combined with the oral messages in homilies delivered at Mass and the public readings of official messages, the unofficial discourse contributed to a rich stew of news, rumors, and opinion.[12] The pervasive sense of crisis was deepened by persistent rumors that Napoleon had sent emissaries to subvert New Spain. In May 1810, Bishop Bergoza ordered Oaxaca's parish priests to be alert to Joseph Bonaparte's "seductive emissaries that try to pervert loyal Americans with tricks" and make them accomplices of "their enormous crimes, of the usurpation of the Crown of our legitimate Sovereign, of their own apostasy of the Catholic Religion, of the violation, profanation and robbery of Churches, of the looting of Cities and villages, of the burning of houses, the death of our brothers, and of all the crimes imaginable."[13] These rumors became even more credible after the wealthiest Spaniards of the colony deposed the viceroy in 1808, and they persisted even after Hidalgo began the great insurrection against their rule in 1810.[14]

The rumors, the propaganda, and the drive to collect funds to aid the king all had a decidedly inclusive and sometimes even egalitarian edge. The rumors were the objects of public discussion, and they thrived on street corners, in village squares, and in the small retail shops that dispensed alcohol to Antequera's urban residents.[15] As we have seen, the wealthy donated money to aid the king, but so did Indian villagers and humble artisans. Often the propaganda itself emphasized the idea that all should demonstrate their loyalty to the king and Catholicism. Thus, for instance, an anonymous poet wrote:

> The Yndios and the Yndianos
> We are Vassals of the King
> We will Defend the Law
> Like two strong Brothers.[16]

Here, *Yndios* refers to Indians, and *Yndianos* refers to all the inhabitants of Spain's New World possessions. Expressions like this were designed to unify the people of New Spain against the traitorous emissaries of Napoleon. Their authors did not intend to corrode the social barriers of race, class, and corporation that organized colonial society. However, the drive for unity led both officials and the writers of anonymous pasquines to emphasize the common bonds of loyalty to the king and Catholic faith shared by all residents of New Spain.[17] The emphasis on unity and the constant appeals to all loyal subjects had an unintended consequence. They led some people of inferior caste, class, or corporate status to view themselves as the equals of their betters, or at least equal in their loyalty to the king.

Public spectacles emphasized the drama of the unique situation being lived by the empire. After the 1808 coup in Mexico City, officials throughout New Spain organized ceremonies pledging loyalty to Fernando VII. In Antequera, authorities led by the interim intendant, José María Izquierdo, began planning an elaborate ceremony, but their efforts were short-circuited by a group of merchants who held a private oath-swearing ceremony on 17 August. This group then marched to the cathedral chapter and town council, forcing both bodies to swear oaths.[18] This relatively hasty set of ceremonies was followed two weeks later by a more elaborate effort. The merchants paid for a mass to honor Fernando VII. They also financed the publication of the sermon Ramón Casaus Torres y Las Plazas preached on the occasion. Casaus emphasized the bonds that tied "Spaniards and Americans" as one chosen nation. He pointed out that the afflictions of the empire were part of God's eternal plan, and good would triumph in the end. Following these relatively upbeat arguments, Casaus stated that Napoleon had plans for Antequera, suggesting the need for vigilance. Casaus, like many authors of the period, emphasized unity in loyalty to the king, arguing that the king's name resonated "in everyone's mouth, without distinction of ages, classes, or sexes."[19] Notice again how this statement suggests that all people of the city could be equal in their loyalty if nothing else.

Rumors of pro-French conspiracies in New Spain persisted, keeping authorities busy tracking them down. In 1809, José Aparicio, a Dominican monk in Oaxaca, was accused of participating in a French plot to assassinate the viceroy. An investigation revealed that Aparicio was in fact only spreading rumors of such a plot. Notably, however, Aparicio's denouncer also reported him to be a Creole enemy of the European Spaniards.[20] The inclusion of this information in the denunciation suggests how the struggle against France could be mapped onto fissures in colonial society. Also in 1809, Bernardo Galvez, a traveler from Spain, was arrested for arriving in Antequera without the proper documents. Soon authorities suspected him of being an emissary from France, and they imprisoned him indefinitely in the royal jail.[21] Other social problems contributed to the tensions. In Oaxaca, the 1809 harvest had been small, and by March 1810 the poor of the city began complaining about the high price of food. In May, Interim Intendant Izquierdo criticized landowners in the valley who had kept their corn from the market to drive the price up, and he ordered them to sell it to the town council's granary at a just price. Despite this measure, in August Izquierdo reported that the poor were complaining that the granary was selling green corn at the same price as ripe corn. These complaints were expressed in anonymous letters posted in public places.[22]

Antequera was already awash in social tensions, rumors, and denunciations when news of the Hidalgo revolt reached the city in the autumn of 1810. Immediately the city's militiamen were ordered to remain on alert in their barracks. This order soon mutated into a rumor that conspirators were planning to ring the church bells to gather a crowd and then behead the city's European Spaniards.[23] The news of Hidalgo's revolt was also closely followed by two of Hidalgo's emissaries, Miguel López de Lima, a muleteer, and José María Armenta, a tailor. The other guests at the inn where they stayed soon denounced them. The guests had noticed that their clothes and accents identified López and Armenta as residents of the Bajío, Hidalgo's original base of operations. When officials interrogated the pair they denied any link to Hidalgo, and they were freed. Soon afterward, López and Armenta made the mistake of attempting to suborn Intendant José María Lazo. Authorities tried the unlucky pair and publicly executed them on the last day of the year. Their bodies were dismembered, and the parts were distributed for display in various public places as visible symbols of the fate that awaited traitors.[24]

The punishment of two unlucky outsiders proved ineffective as a warning. Less than a month later, Latin teacher José María Corro convinced his student, Mariano Suarez, to copy and post a proinsurgent pasquín in an effort to further frighten the already rattled European Spaniards of the city. The pasquín was posted in four of the city's barrios. In fourteen lines of witty verse, it praised insurgent leader Ignacio Allende and called on the city's residents to expel, wound, rob, and kill the *gachupines*, a pejorative term for European Spaniards. Officials imprisoned the unlucky student for eighteen months despite the efforts of his wealthy father to portray the incident as a boyish joke. The young man also lost his post as a sublieutenant in the city's militia.[25] The climate of fear and suspicion persisted. In February 1811, María Francisca Chavez denounced her neighbor Manuel Breña, the city's postmaster. She had heard Breña deny that Hidalgo was a heretic, pointing out that Hidalgo's message was "against the gachupines, Long Live Our Lady of Guadalupe, Death to the Bad Government." Breña insisted that the Inquisitors that had labeled Hidalgo a heretic had done so because they themselves were gachupines. Called to answer for his statements, Breña at first denied uttering them. When that failed Breña stated that he could not remember and that if he had said such things he did so thoughtlessly. Breña professed his adhesion to Catholicism and was released with a warning.[26]

The pasquines of Suarez might have been a bad joke, and Breña might have simply been indiscreet, but a real conspiracy soon followed these episodes. In June 1811, authorities imprisoned a group of young Creoles led by Felipe Tinoco, a revenue official, and José Caterino Palacios, a merchant and militia officer. The two men had enlisted the group to organize an urban insurrection against the city's European Spaniards, who they called the "owners of everything" and accused of preparing to turn Oaxaca over to Napoleon. Tinoco and Palacios insisted that official propaganda stating that Hidalgo had been captured and Morelos defeated was untrue. They also insisted, like Breña had earlier, that Hidalgo was not a heretic. Palacios hinted that several of the city's most prominent Creoles were backing the conspiracy. Evidence suggests that Tinoco and Palacios recruited followers at cockfights, a popular form of entertainment in the city.[27] Tinoco and Palacios arranged for leaders in each barrio to convoke the city's plebeians. After the hated gachupines were beheaded, their wealth would be confiscated, and the plebeians would be rewarded with alcohol. Here we can see that the conspirators were building on accumulated resentment against the wealthy European merchants of the city even as they tapped into fears that

European Spaniards were involved in their own conspiracy to turn Antequera over to the godless Napoleon. Tinoco and Palacios were both publicly executed, but before their deaths Palacios stated that he had lied about the involvement of several prominent Creoles. Several other members of the group received prison sentences. Among them was the priest Ignacio María Ordoño, who would be important in urban politics for the next two decades. Ordoño defended himself by insisting that he had tried to talk the conspirators out of their plans, and that failing that he was going to denounce them to the authorities.[28]

The Tinoco and Palacios conspiracy only heightened the climate of suspicion, and denunciations continued. Even those already imprisoned in the royal jail were not immune. Ignacio María Ordoño, perhaps seeking to curry favor with the authorities who would decide his fate, soon denounced the luckless Bernardo Galvez, who we earlier saw had been imprisoned on suspicion of being a Napoleonic emissary. According to Ordoño, Galvez supported the insurgents and attacked Catholicism. Ordoño was probably not a particularly trustworthy witness, but a series of common prisoners also testified against Galvez. They noted that he frequently cursed the king, God, and the Virgin in vulgar terms, and said that religious icons were nothing but painted caricatures. The witnesses added that Galvez eagerly awaited the arrival of Morelos. These expressions made Galvez unpopular with the prisoners. As an outsider, Galvez was already at a great disadvantage, because prisoners in the royal jail relied on their families to feed them. Galvez was slowly starving to death, receiving only a little food from charity. He soon disappears from the historical record, probably a victim of malnutrition. It is worth noting, however, how far out of touch Galvez's apparent lack of allegiance to Catholicism was from the sample of Oaxacan society with whom he shared the royal jail.[29] A little later a less prominent prisoner, Ygnacio Ximenez, was also denounced for saying he defecated on the king. Five prisoners corroborated this story. Ximenez, a butcher imprisoned for homicide, defended himself by explaining that he had cursed the king during a card game, and he was in fact referring to the card, not the royal personage, for whom he would give his very life. Apparently authorities accepted his version of the story.[30]

The Tinoco and Palacios incident shows how insurgent supporters in the city played off of the sense of crisis engendered by Napoleon's invasion of Spain and imprisonment of the royal family. The insurgents claimed to be working to save New Spain from a gachupín conspiracy to turn it over to Napoleon. Not surprisingly, propaganda directed against the insurgents played essentially the same tune. The most vociferous and vocal enemy of the insurgency in Oaxaca was Antonio Bergoza y Jordán, the Spanish bishop. He had worked hard to insure the province's loyalty to Fernando VII, and after news of the Hidalgo revolt reached Oaxaca he turned his literary skills and religious prestige against the insurgents. At the end of November 1810, he published a letter to his entire flock, apparently in response to the arrest of Armenta and López. In this pastoral letter he argued that agents of Napoleon had promoted the sedition in the Bajío. He also stated that Hidalgo denied the divinity of Christ and the virginity of Mary.[31] In the middle of December Bergoza wrote a new letter to his parish priests, accusing Hidalgo of apostasy and ordering the priests to turn in any pro-Hidalgo propaganda they found.[32] In early 1811, Bergoza published another pastoral letter directed to the coasts of southern Oaxaca, where some villages had joined Morelos's forces, arguing that Morelos was a sacrilegious priest.[33] After the discovery of the Tinoco and Palacios conspiracy, Bergoza wrote a long pastoral letter, denouncing it as a cabal that recruited in gambling houses. He called Hidalgo the "representative of the tyrant Napoleon, of Satan, and of hell," saying that Hidalgo had tried to ruin Catholicism and the Spanish monarchy in America. Bergoza also denied reports that Spain no longer existed because Napoleon had won the war.[34]

ᔓ Antequera Mobilizes for War

The crisis in Spain and, more directly, the Hidalgo insurrection, led to efforts to put Antequera on a war footing. Many felt the need to mobilize, arm, and clothe members of local society. However, like every other initiative of the period, the organization of new troops took place in a local context already shaped by social tensions and the social pretensions of various groups. In effect, members of the elite saw the work of mobilizing new forces as the key to their own survival and another opportunity for them to distance themselves from the mass of the urban population. Conversely, many relatively poor mixed-race men saw the need for new part-time soldiers as a chance for them to demonstrate that they could make equal sacrifices for the king. The short but sharp clash that resulted provides us with a window on social tensions. It also prepared the ground for future conflicts.

Some local notables were interested in organizing new militia forces even before the Hidalgo insurrection, but as can be expected news of Hidalgo's uprising brought home to Oaxacans the fact that they faced potential military threats even in their own region. In October 1810, the viceroy issued a call for the formation of companies of "distinguished" men, composed of wealthy Creoles and European Spaniards. Later, military and social necessities led to the organization of larger units that recruited men from all groups.[35] Yet although these units were justified by a rhetoric that emphasized the unity of all inhabitants, their organization was a contentious affair.

On 8 October 1810, a group of Antequera's merchants asked the viceroy to allow them to establish two companies of volunteers in the city. The appeal emphasized the unity of Creoles and European Spaniards, and the merchants suggested that although they trusted the loyalty of the city's inhabitants they feared that outsiders might introduce insubordination. The merchants' request was followed by a list of forty-seven master artisans willing to join the companies. A few days later the merchants submitted a roll for each company. The officers were all Creoles or European Spaniards, but the ethnic backgrounds of the men were not listed. Some of the officers were from prominent families, but their selection was not a smooth process. At first the merchants who would finance the forces elected a slate of officers, but some volunteers were unhappy with their choices. The frustrated merchants then chose new officers through a lottery, but again they faced dissent. The final slate of officers submitted to the viceroy was elected by the enlisted soldiers, a very different procedure. Bernardo Bonavia, commander of the city's regular established militia force, soon raised objections to some of the officers. According to him, the problem was not a question of aptitude, but that each officer "should have the means to maintain themselves with decorum and splendor."[36] In other words, Bonavia, like many wealthy officers of the day, felt that it was important that officers demonstrate position in a social class higher than that of their troops.[37]

Bonavia's views would soon be tested. In the following month, as military policy shifted toward the organization of larger and more inclusive part-time forces, a large force of artisans was organized into military units in Antequera. Bonavia did not want these new units to wear the same uniform as the original companies of volunteers organized by the merchants, ostensibly because paying for such uniforms would unduly burden humble artisans. Instead, Bonavia ordered them to wear simple uniform jackets and round hats. Faced with this attitude, the artisans wrote to the viceroy: "[This is] in a way unseemly due to the distinction given to the other companies of volunteers from the city's merchants, which is painful to us because we defend the same cause and serve the same Monarch, thus we should not be made unequal."[38] The artisans were not willing to concede social prestige to the merchant elite. Their demand for equality, however, seems to owe less to the Enlightenment or the French Revolution than to the history of crises of the previous twenty years, during which all members of New Spain's society had been asked to contribute to the defense of the king and the Catholic religion. The artisans followed this appeal with a detailed list of artisan volunteers for two companies, including 17 silversmiths, 21 tailors, 17 barbers, 17 carpenters, 16 shoemakers, 11 weavers, 7 painters, 2 tinsmiths, 41 fireworks makers, 3 hatmakers, 38 bakers, and 16 members of the guild of candlemakers, matchmakers, and candy makers. All of these 206 men insisted they could pay for their own uniforms, except for 29 fireworks makers, 32 bakers, and 8 men from the guild of candlemakers, matchmakers, and candy makers. The artisans also listed other volunteers who were willing to fight but were not needed for the ranks of the organized companies. This list included 12 more candlemakers, matchmakers, and candy makers, as well as 4 leather workers, 12 potters, 2 shoemakers, and 47 inhabitants who did not belong to guilds.[39] The artisans, like the merchants before them, elected their own officers.[40]

Bishop Bergoza organized another volunteer force of priests, friars, and sacristans through his chaplain, José de San Martín. This group also had a distinctive uniform.[41] Yet even as these efforts took shape, insurgent leader José María Morelos defeated a militia force from Oaxaca in the mountains of Guerrero. Bergoza responded by trying to increase Antequera's will to fight. He argued that if the rebels ever took Oaxaca they would rape the city's women and girls and sack its churches, especially that of the Virgin of Soledad, the beloved patroness of the city.[42] Civil officials also played up the danger, collecting funds to fortify the approaches to the city. Again, these efforts stressed the idea that individuals of all classes and conditions should participate.[43] Yet, in the end, the thousands of pesos spent fortifying Antequera and arming its men could not prevent the rebels from taking the city.

❧ The Insurgents in Antequera, 1812–1814

In November 1812, the forces of José María Morelos attacked Antequera. After a short fight they overpowered the city's defenses. Despite the fierce rhetoric of the city's elite and the efforts spent organizing resistance, the actual battle was minimal. The key royalist leaders, including Bishop Bergoza and militia commander Bernardo Bonavia, fled. In the previous months royalist leaders had feared that Antequera's artisans and other poor would not fight to defend it from Morelos, but the evidence suggests that no social group in the city had much heart for the struggle.[44]

By November 1812 Morelos had been fighting against the government of the viceroyalty for two entire years. Beginning as an obscure parish priest in a remote posting, he had led insurgent forces over a wide area of Mexico. With the help of provincial intellectuals, including Antequera's own Carlos María de Bustamante, Morelos had produced dozens of documents explaining his goals and denouncing the viceregal government. Of course, at the same time viceregal authorities had produced countless messages criticizing the insurgents. Although the authorities had an advantage in this propaganda war because they could read documents aloud and preach from pulpits in relative safety, the evidence suggests that the basics of Morelos's message were discussed in cockpits, stores, and on the street, and that they were sometimes posted publicly in the form of anonymous pasquines. We can safely assume that by November 1812 most of Antequera's inhabitants were reasonably familiar with the thrust of Morelos's message. Those who may not have been were soon exposed to it through ceremonies, speeches, and sermons, as well as the publication of decrees and a newspaper in the city.

Although the insurgents were not above pointing out the potential material benefits of their regime, such as lower taxes, references to higher political values far outnumber this kind of practical argument.[45] Some key elements of insurgent discourse mirrored those of their opponents. In 1812 the insurgents still insisted that they were loyal to Fernando VII, and they argued that the viceregal authorities were preparing to hand Mexico over to Napoleon Bonaparte.[46] Two weeks after the arrival of the insurgent army, its principal generals led a ceremony featuring the city's royal banner and a portrait of Fernando VII. In this ceremony, the city recognized the role of the insurgents' Suprema Junta Nacional as the custodian of Fernando VII's rights. After the ceremony the insurgents fired cannons, rang all the city's bells, and tossed coins from the stage. The royal banner was paraded, and the officials of all the guilds and nearby villages participated. Some villagers performed indigenous dances, and that night there was an official banquet and fireworks.[47] The insurgents were, in effect, replicating the ceremony and festivities usually used to swear allegiance to a newly crowned monarch.

Insurgent discourse also shared other characteristics with earlier colonial ones. The most obvious similarity is the emphasis on religion, not surprising for a movement whose first two important leaders were parish priests. Here the insurgents disputed the high ground with their enemies. In a message for Antequera written on 23 December 1812, Morelos wrote that "far from being heretics, we protect our Holy, Catholic, Apostolic Roman Church better than our enemies do." Morelos went on to point out that the viceregal government had trampled ecclesiastical rights.[48] It was not uncommon for insurgent propaganda to stress the idea that theirs was a holy war against a government in league with French heretics.[49] In their struggle against the government, the insurgents also incorporated two other elements common in late colonial political culture. First, they characterized their enemies as tyrants, unjust rulers who had imposed themselves on an innocent populace.[50] The rebels also accused the viceregal government of keeping New Spain's people in slavery. Insurgent documents generally linked this slavery to the government's loyalty to Napoleon, but occasionally they made more direct references.[51]

The insurgents owed much to colonial political culture and more recent discourse used to mobilize society against Napoleon, but they also introduced some crucial new wrinkles into the political ferment of the day. The most striking was their condemnation of Spain's colonial experience in America. In one of his first messages to the city, Morelos criticized the Spanish for keeping New Spain in "the chains of an ominous serfdom for almost three centuries." The idea of the colonial period as one of slavery or servitude was often repeated, especially on special occasions such as the August 1813 election of insurgent representatives.[52] Another striking new element in the discourse of the insurgency was the rebels' devotion to Our Lady of Guadalupe. As William Taylor has argued, Guadalupe was not popular on a colony-wide scale before the insurgency, but the insurgents spread her fame everywhere they campaigned.[53] In Antequera, the feast of Guadalupe had previously been overshadowed by the annual feast of the Virgin of Soledad, patroness of the city, held less than a week later on 18 December. Yet on 12 December 1812, a month after they captured Antequera, the insurgents held an elaborate celebration of Guadalupe's feast. A year later the insurgents staged an even grander homage, carrying Guadalupe's image in procession from the central plaza of the city to the Belemnite convent outside of town. The image was accompanied by a military escort and indigenous dancers. After her mass the city held a celebration with music and a fireworks display.[54]

The insurgents were involved in a long and bloody war against the viceregal government, and some of their actions after occupying the city brought this home to the population. In the days following the battle the insurgents captured several high-ranking royalists, some of whom had fled the fighting.

Their prisoners included Lieutenant General Antonio González y Sarabia, Lieutenant Colonel José María Régules y Villasante, Colonel Bernardo Bonavia, and Captain Nicolás Aristi. All were executed. José María Barrientos, a boy who had burned an insurgent decree posted in the center of the city, was also shot.[55] González y Sarabia and Régules y Villasante were executed in the same location where the viceregal authorities had executed Tinoco and Palacios, while Bonavia's death took place in the plaza where Hidalgo's emissaries Miguel López and José María Armenta had been killed in 1810. Morelos also ordered that the skulls and other bones of López and Armenta be collected from the various public places where they were displayed. They were placed in coffins, paraded through the center of the city, and interred in the cathedral.[56]

The official insurgent attitude that probably resonated most with Antequera's plebeians was the rebels' condemnation of the European Spaniards. One of the first messages of Morelos in Antequera condemned the gachupines as traitors and brutes.[57] Insurgent discourse had for years labeled the European Spaniards as Napoleon's agents in Mexico. Gachupines were sometimes identified as heretics, an argument that followed logically from their close association with atheist France. Insurgent discourse also identified the European Spaniards as monopolists and economic parasites.[58] With the insurgent occupation, these arguments came to a city where wealthy, often Spanish, merchants had dominated the economy and society, stressing their Spanish roots and identity to differentiate themselves from the racially diverse mass of the population. There is some evidence that Antequera's plebeians seconded insurgent ire against the European Spaniards. A reporter noted in 1813 that on the publication of news of insurgent victories, the assembled crowd not only shouted "vivas" for the insurgents, but also "Death to the Jackets," a term commonly applied to European Spaniards due to their wealthy style of dress.[59]

After occupying the city, the rebel forces did not limit themselves to purely rhetorical attacks on the resident European Spaniards. They made a concerted effort to search out and confiscate the wealth of all gachupines. This effort began with looting on the day of the battle, but it continued for months. On the first day of looting, the rebel troops also robbed Creoles, but later Morelos placed their wealth off-limits even as he ordered all European Spaniards to turn theirs in. He also publicly invited the city's inhabitants to denounce any valuables the gachupines tried to hide. Many people apparently accepted this offer. In the words of María Micaela Frontaura, wife of the Spanish official Antonio María Izquierdo, "there were an infinite number of denouncements."[60] The rebel officers gathered Spanish arms, money, jewels, and even cochineal to finance their war, not sparing wealth the owners had hidden in convents. Some observers placed this booty at more than three million pesos. This attack on the wealth of European Spaniards sometimes left their Creole wives destitute. María Josefa Gonzalez Mimiaga, wife of a Spaniard, Manuel del Solar Campero, tried to recover her dowry from the authorities who had confiscated it along with her husband's goods. In her words, without the 4,820 pesos of the dowry, her property under Hispanic law, she was reduced "in substance to the class of miserable widows."[61] During their occupation of the city, insurgent officers continued to seek out the hidden wealth of European Spaniards. For instance, in February 1813 a patrol led by Ignacio Ordoño, the priest who had earlier been imprisoned for conspiring with the insurgents Tinoco and Palacios, searched a house occupied by an elderly Spanish woman. Her complaint implied that the patrol was actually made up of local plebeians.[62]

The evidence about whether some of Antequera's mixed-race plebeians cooperated with insurgent authorities in their attack on the wealth of European Spaniards is tantalizing but far from decisive. Still, another of Morelos's initiatives almost certainly met with their approval. As we saw in the previous chapters, for years plebeians had been downplaying the issue of race in the way they lived their lives, even as the city's elite played it up as a major component of their identity. Morelos was also of mixed race, and from the beginning of his movement he had striven to abolish racial categories. Soon after arriving in Antequera he issued a sarcastically pointed denunciation of racial differentiation. He decreed: "The very beautiful gibberish of qualities *Indian, mulatto or mestizo, suspended in air*, etcetera is abolished, and we will only recognize regional distinctions, calling all generally *Americans*, with which word we distinguish ourselves from the *English*, the *French*, or even more from the *European Spaniard* that harms us, from the *African* and the *Asian* who occupy other parts of the world."[63] The documents of the insurgent government and petitions addressed to them no longer listed the racial identity of individuals.[64] The insurgents resolutely avoided racial references, even when describing the participation of indigenous villagers in official public celebrations. They instead identified these dances as "rustic-style dances" or remarked that the dancers' costumes recalled the age of the Aztecs.[65]

The end of racial distinctions did not find favor with wealthy Creoles, and in general the insurgent occupation put them in a very uncomfortable position. Morelos actively sought out and even required their continued participation in government. After the royalists regained control, many Creoles who had cooperated with Morelos emphasized this coercion. Yet official coercion on the part of the insurgent authorities explains only part of the scene. In the days after the rebels occupied the city, María Micaela Frontaura confronted her nephew about his cooperation with the rebels. He replied, in her words, that "any man of honor who did not join the rebels would soon find himself ordered around by blacks, and for this reason many men of honor have embraced the rebel cause."[66] Faced with an occupying army composed of people they considered their racial inferiors, and an urban population of similar composition that was sympathetic to the insurgents, wealthy Creoles may have cooperated with Morelos to maintain their privileged place in society.[67]

Morelos may have understood this dynamic, but he did not rely on it. He worked to convince Creoles that the European Spanish were their true enemies, and even the enemies of the king. Creoles that had held posts in the previous administration were promoted to fill the places of their European superiors. Morelos also strove to involve every prominent Creole in his government, hoping that by forcing them to choose sides he would leave them without the future option of supporting his enemies. Soon after his arrival he named a new town council and did not allow any of the men named to demur.[68] Later the insurgents solicited donations to buy uniforms for the new rebel force based in the city, and they published the names of the donors in their newspaper, the *Correo Americano del Sur*.[69]

Many prominent Creoles found themselves trying to negotiate treacherous and shifting terrain. Perhaps the best-known example is the cleric José de San Martín, subject of a recent study by Ana Carolina Ibarra. San Martín was Bishop Bergoza's closest aide in the latter's efforts to defend the city against the insurgents. San Martín established the militia company of clerics and also organized the city's fortifications. However, unlike many other prominent royalists, he did not flee the insurgent army. San Martín soon was collaborating closely with the insurgents. He preached sermons on important occasions like the feast of Guadalupe, and he was eventually named principal chaplain of the insurgent army. Even so, during the occupation San Martín worked both openly and behind the scenes to protect the lives and property of European Spaniards and other known royalists, moving like other members of the cathedral chapter to mediate between the demands of the insurgent authorities and the city's elite. When the royalists retook the city in 1814, San Martín again refused to flee. As Ibarra points out, San Martín's vacillations stemmed from the "ambiguities of the period."[70]

Under the insurgent government, the town council and cathedral chapter, each staffed by respectable Creoles, retained their preponderant role in the political life of the city, and indeed of the entire province. Perhaps the best evidence of this is seen in the way the province elected its representative to the insurgents' Suprema Junta Nacional. Although the electors on this occasion included those representing eight parishes near the city and seventeen districts in the province as well as eight urban neighborhoods, the sum of these electors barely balanced the fact that each member of the town council and cathedral chapter also had a vote.[71] Unfortunately, no record has survived of the method used to select electors from the city's neighborhoods or any of the areas outside the city. Generally, however, various discussions preceding the election suggest that the insurgents continued to rely on the corporatist ideal under which people belonged to society through their membership in various corporate bodies. Ana Carolina Ibarra points out that the city's elite worked with the revolutionary ideals of the moment "within a traditional context," continuing to rely on previous formulas.[72] This reliance distinguished them somewhat from the liberals, who, as we will see, were rapidly rewriting the rules of the political game for both Spain and all areas of the empire still under Spanish control.

The insurgent leaders never believed that they had fully captured the hearts and minds of Antequera's wealthy Creoles. From early in their occupation they felt threatened by negative rumors and the correspondence that some inhabitants maintained with royalists who had fled. The rebels soon identified the cathedral chapter as the epicenter of the rumors and the local nexus of correspondence with the royalists. In July 1813 Morelos admonished the cathedral chapter in a letter he ordered read aloud in their meeting. Later Carlos María de Bustamante sent a similar warning. Two members of the chapter were exiled for their pro-royalist activities. This move inspired, however, the posting of a pro-royalist pasquín in the city. The pasquín compared the insurgents' profession of loyalty to Catholicism to their harsh treatment of these clerics.[73]

The insurgents controlled Antequera from November 1812 to April 1814. The insurgents lacked the manpower to resist a powerful royalist force led by Colonel Melchor Alvarez, and they abandoned the city on his advance. According to Juan Bautista Carriedo, writing thirty years later, as the insurgents retreated they were insulted by "the mob, egged on by the gachupines." Carriedo also wrote that the population prepared flowers and triumphal arches for the arriving royalists. Alvarez reported to his superiors that on his arrival in the city he was met by demonstrations of joy.[74] The insurgent experiment in Antequera was over. Unfortunately for the city's wealthy, the same could not be said for their political troubles.

꩜ The War in Villa Alta

Antequera's experience during the war is relatively well-known, especially since it was the only major city the rebels held for such a long period. The district of Villa Alta had a much shorter but also significant involvement in the fighting that convulsed New Spain. Many parts of the district had better communication with Veracruz than they did with the Valley of Oaxaca. In the summer of 1812, a small rebel force from the Gulf coast of Veracruz invaded the district, and indigenous peasants from several villages cooperated with them. The commander of the local royalist militia soon drove them off, but the dust had not yet settled when the rebels took the city of Antequera that autumn.

Very few documents describe this rebel incursion and people's reaction to it. Clearly news of the insurgency worried the few Spanish and Creole administrators, merchants, and priests who lived among the thousands of indigenous peasants of the district. By early 1812, at least some peasants had apparently learned enough about the issues of the war to begin to take advantage of that nervousness. Evidence for both these propositions abounds in a long, rambling, fearful letter written to the viceroy in March 1812 by Joseph María de Paz y Mendoza, parish priest of Santa María Yahuive. Paz was engaged in complicated disputes with his parishioners over clerical fees, but he also demonstrated fear of a general insurrection, and he accused his opponents of being sympathetic to the insurgents. Paz argued that many Indians believed that they could free themselves by killing the European Spanish. He even reproduced an anonymous pasquín found outside his door. The pasquín, which Paz attributed to the young men of the village, criticized the priest, and said, "Now we have no government, now we have no king, they've already thrown him out, because now the time has arrived for our crown to return, a crown that belongs to we Indians, a crown that does not belong to the Gachupines. The Gachupines stole it, they made a great effort to take it, but now that time is over, it is another thing now." After this millenarian interpretation of Fernando VII's captivity, the pasquín went on to add, "The insurgents are in favor of poor Indians like us, they are coming to look for the Gachupines, to kill them and throw them out. We are also ready to accompany the insurgents, who are good friends, who defend us against the Gachupines."[75] The vast bulk of the available evidence on indigenous political culture before and after the war of independence makes it seem unlikely that these views could have become widespread among the district's indigenous peasants, and it seems possible that even the authors of the pasquín were not truthfully recording their political beliefs. Even if this was the case, it is interesting to see how they used their knowledge of the general political situation to their advantage in what appears to be a relatively routine argument with their pastor over fees. They seem, in fact, determined to frighten him into resigning his parish.

Fears and hopes that the rebels would invade the district were realized a few months later. In June, a rebel force approached, apparently invited by the authorities of the village of Santiago Jalahui, near Yahuive. The insurgents, mulattos from the Veracruz coast and Mixes from the lower elevations of Villa Alta, were met near Jalahui by the residents and officials of that village and those of Latani and Santiago Sochiapan, along with many villagers from Choapan. These combined forces waited for a mule train with goods and its European Spanish owners. They then looted the train and captured its owners and muleteers. Together with the insurgents the villagers celebrated with music, dance, and drinking.[76] A few days later another mule train met a similar fate in Solaga. Its owner and muleteers were intercepted by a crowd of indigenous peasants led by Solaga's mayor, Antonio Matias. They surrounded the mules and threw stones at the train's attendants, forcing them to drop their weapons. The peasants imprisoned the muleteers and merchant and stole their goods. Up to this point both the Jalahui and Solaga incidents look very much like colonial village riots, although on a larger scale.[77] Here things began to differ. A merchant, Juan José Gómez, asked insurgent leader Pedro Flores, an Indian from Jalahui, the motive of this treatment, and he responded that there was no king there and that he would defecate on the king of Spain. Flores then ordered nearby villages to join his forces, and his troops looted Zoochila, a village that had defied his order under the influence of the resident priest, Francisco María Ramirez. Royalist militia arrived in the area two days later and soon put the rebel troops and villagers to flight.[78]

Nicolás Aristi, royalist militia captain and a prominent merchant of the district, took charge of the subsequent repression. He executed some leaders and searched for those who had fled. Aristi warned all villages in the district that they should imprison any Indian or other travelers who did not carry a pass from him. He also used the practical power he gained from this small skirmish in the war to pursue his own interests. In particular he tried to pressure villages into repaying him for cochineal that the rebels had stolen from him. Aristi deposed village authorities and named their successors, aiding his commercial contacts in the villages. He continued interfering with village governments into October, arousing the ire of the district's subdelegado, Julian Nieto Posadillo. Posadillo complained that Aristi was usurping his powers, and the royal government agreed, reprimanding Aristi in November 1812. Within weeks Antequera itself had fallen to the rebels, and Aristi, captured there, died at their hands.[79] Unfortunately there is no evidence available to investigate whether the insurgents extended more than nominal control over the district of Villa Alta during their occupation of Antequera. Thus there is no way of knowing whether they made any significant changes in government there.

ꕜ Liberal Innovation in the Midst of War

Even as insurgents and defenders of the viceregal government jockeyed for support in Oaxaca, the government was undergoing a process of conscious reform that would soon outstrip decades of Bourbon innovations. The first of these reforms were actually announced in Oaxaca before the rebel forces attacked Antequera and Villa Alta, but for simplicity's sake we have not considered them until now. After the 1808 coup, the new viceregal government proclaimed its adherence to the groups fighting against Napoleon in Spain, not realizing that soon some of the most radical men in Spanish politics would come to lead that Spanish resistance. These radicals rose to power after a long series of Spanish defeats at the hands of Napoleon's armies. Although the government these men organized was legitimized by its claim to rule in the name of the captive and therefore voiceless Fernando VII, it embarked on a series of changes that Fernando eventually found quite objectionable. The reforms enacted by these Spanish liberals were also intended for, and sometimes implemented in, Spain's overseas dominions. Their application left colonial authorities in a strange situation. They were leading a struggle against the local insurgency even as they received orders envisioning changes that were in important ways much more radical than anything Hidalgo or Morelos contemplated. Note, for instance, the horror of the insurgents when the Spanish Cortes abolished the Inquisition, an institution the insurgent leader Benito Rocha y Pardiñas saw as "the bronze wall against which the impetuous waves of heresy dashed themselves." Rocha y Pardiñas argued that this measure was evidence that the Spanish liberals were agents of Napoleon and "Jacobin terrorists."[80]

How did this dramatic turn of events in Spain play out in Oaxaca? The series of bulletins that informed Oaxacans of French victories in Spain augmented the palpable sense of crisis that had grown since 1808, and by the time the Spanish resistance began to organize the new central government it seemed clear that the new government would play a crucial role in deciding the fate of the Spanish world. Thus, in March 1810 the town council of Antequera, learning that the viceroy had ordered a special mass to pray for guidance for the new Cortes, immediately ordered a similar ceremony for Antequera. Official documents generally stressed optimism, suggesting that the Cortes would successfully unite Spaniards and Americans as a single people to stop Napoleon's aggression. Yet in August 1810, when the town council of Antequera chose the province's representative to the Cortes, there was considerable ambivalence. The election was celebrated by a Te Deum, the pealing of all the city's church bells, and three nights of special lighting in the streets, but those elected were not pleased with the honor. According to the electoral procedure, the names of the three men with the greatest number of votes were placed in an urn, and a young child chose the winner. Two of the top three candidates resigned the post, perhaps unwilling to face a months-long voyage to a war-torn Spain, and a new election had to be held before Juan María Ybañez accepted the post.[81]

Among other dramatic decrees, the Cortes soon abolished tribute, a step that had profound implications in heavily indigenous districts like Villa Alta. Evidence of the attitude of indigenous peasants in Villa Alta toward the abolition of tribute is scarce, but the limited evidence available suggests a certain ambivalence, stemming in part from economic considerations. Apparently some peasants suspected that the end of tribute would soon lead to them being forced to pay *alcabala*, the tax already levied on the sale of goods by non-Indians. Their suspicions were entirely on target.[82] Notably, this complaint suggests that tribute payments were smaller than the alcabala at least some indigenous household economies would have to pay. Particularly after the abolition of the repartimiento, many indigenous households raised scarce cash by producing cotton mantas and selling them in Antequera, with or without the intervention of small-scale indigenous traders.

In the 1950s, Nellie Lee Benson began to argue that the Constitution of 1812 had crucial importance in the formation of Latin American political culture, but only recently have many historians followed her lead and begun to probe the constitution's impact on different social groups and regions. In this historiography, Spanish liberals have taken their place alongside Bourbon ideologues and the liberal politicians of the eventually independent Latin American states as reformers whose controversial measures had a deep influence on the relationship between society and government in Latin America. Historians have examined the impact of the liberals on both urban and rural groups, showing how they introduced new kinds of authority and novel forms of argument to Latin America's political culture.[83] In the case of Oaxaca, Spanish liberal measures were only in effect for three very brief periods. The first, as we have seen, was from 1810 to 1812, before the insurgent occupation of the territory. When Melchor Alvarez recuperated Oaxaca for the royalists in March 1814, he immediately implemented the Constitution of 1812, but when Fernando VII returned to the throne in May 1814 he abolished the constitution and other liberal measures. Although it took some time for this dramatic turn of events to become known in Oaxaca, the 1814 liberal experience was very brief. The constitution was again put into effect in 1820 after a liberal coup in Spain, and it remained in vigor in a modified form from the fall of the royal government in Mexico in 1821 until the new state of Oaxaca wrote rules replacing it in 1824. Despite the relative brevity of the constitution's reign in the region, it had a profound impact on the arguments and tactics of Oaxacan politics. That impact was deeper in Antequera, where the constitution provided new opportunities for people of mixed race to assert themselves in politics, but the document also had a significant, if more muted influence, in Villa Alta.

In Antequera the new constitution was published on 12 April 1814, soon after the royalists recuperated the city. The residents of the city were ordered to light and decorate their balconies for three consecutive nights. Special stages were set up in the four most important plazas of the city. A notary read the constitution out loud on each stage, an exercise that took more than two hours. Applause punctuated the reading, and when it ended cannon fired and the bells of the city's churches pealed. On 13 April authorities attended a mass in the cathedral, and the new intendant, Melchor Alvarez, and all officials swore allegiance to the constitution. The bells rang out again after this ceremony.[84]

Melchor Alvarez moved immediately to organize the election of a new city council under the constitutional rules. In doing so he stirred up a hornet's nest. The key provision of the constitution extended citizenship to "those Spaniards who by both lines descend from the Spanish dominions of both hemispheres." In other words, indigenous origins or blood did not disqualify one from voting or holding office, a point Alvarez clarified in his decree regulating the election, stating that "every Spaniard and Indian, every castizo and mestizo" could both vote and hold office. The city was divided into four quarters. In each citizens would vote for eight electors, and the thirty-two electors would in turn select the councilmen. The order was issued the day before the election, and the constitution had been published only a few days before.[85] Although general ideas about the new rules for citizenship might have filtered into Antequera during the previous two years of insurgent occupation, it is unlikely that any group was able to organize to influence the results of this first election.

Records of this election are unfortunately sparse. We know that more than 400 men voted in the third quarter in front of the Bethlemite monastery, and we know that more than 900 voted in the central quarter in the cathedral cemetery. The thirty-two electors chosen in this first election then selected the eighteen town councilmen. Eight of these eighteen men are identified in primary documents as European Spaniards. Eight appear to have been Creoles. Two councilmen, however, belonged to the groups newly empowered by the constitution. Casimiro Cruz Hernandez was an Indian, and Angel Calvo was definitely an artisan and probably a mestizo. Silke Hensel suggests that the electors, whose meetings took three days, may have come to an agreement to split the posts between Spaniards and Creoles. Such agreements had occurred in the past, and it seems possible that an arrangement was worked out in 1814. However, this does not explain the seating of Cruz Hernandez and Calvo. The average number of votes received by winning candidates was 23.4. Calvo received 25, and Cruz Hernandez 19. In other words, the two members of previously excluded groups polled well among secondary electors.[86]

The election of two nonwhite members on a council of eighteen may seem insignificant, since the vast majority of men in Antequera were not white. The apparent insignificance can only be heightened by the short tenure of this council, which was removed from office a few months later when Fernando VII abolished the constitution. However, this election showed the city's elite that under wide suffrage they could not replicate their complete control of municipal office, a control that had in fact helped them define themselves as a group before 1812. For the city's elite, the Cortes's earlier abolition of the distinction between Spaniards, Creoles, mestizos, and Indians had been a minimal concern. Often families included both Spaniards and Creoles, and the nominal equality of Indians and mestizos had made little difference while council vacancies were still filled by purchase or internal elections. Allowing Indians and mestizos not only to vote for council members but to take seats on the council was another matter altogether. In the late colonial period, men acquired posts on the city council less out of a political ambition than a social one. As Silke Hensel points out, its officers were not really members of the city's most prestigious families, but wealthy men who purchased their posts in an attempt to join the elite.[87] Now, under the new constitution, these officers were elected, and the racial purity the elite had prized as part of its identity was no longer a criterion for office. Moreover, although the Spanish constitution excluded from citizenship men who had African blood, most of the city's population of African or partial African origin had moved itself into the mestizo category in the eighteenth century. There were few identifiable mulattos or Africans to exclude. The 1814 election was a wakeup call for the city's elite. In effect, these men could no longer consider membership in the city council an effective way to demonstrate their social prestige. When a similar result occurred in the 1820 election also held under the Spanish constitution, the elite began to organize Oaxaca's first political party, which will be discussed extensively in the next chapter.

The Constitution of 1812 also had a significant impact in Villa Alta, although that impact was certainly less important there than in some rural areas of Spanish America.[88] In Villa Alta, the subdelegado, Julian Nieto Posadillo, published the constitution in June 1814, two months after its publication in Antequera. This delay most likely resulted from the fact that Nieto Posadillo had to travel to Villa Alta from wherever he had taken refuge during the insurgent occupation of 1812–1814. However, it may represent some reluctance on his part, for we will see that Nieto Posadillo saw the constitution as a threat to his powers. In any event, on 16 June he read it aloud from a balcony overlooking the plaza of the small village of Villa Alta. The officials of each village in the parish attended the event, and they proceeded to swear allegiance to the constitution. The bells were tolled and music was played for three nights, and the parish pastor said a Te Deum mass.[89] It seems likely that similar ceremonies were held in the other parishes of the district, but the records are silent on this point.

In Antequera, Melchor Alvarez had moved immediately to elect a new city council, perhaps because the town council previously elected for 1814 had been chosen under the insurgents. Nieto Posadillo took no such action in Villa Alta. Apparently he was waiting for the end of the year, when the villages would normally elect new authorities. However, it is also possible that he simply did not see a need for change, as according to the constitution a settlement needed 1,000 inhabitants to elect a town council, and probably only four of the districts' more than one hundred villages were that large in 1814.[90] In any event, the impact of wide suffrage on village government in Villa Alta was delayed until the next decade. Villa Alta's authorities did, however, implement another measure that resulted from the ethnic equality enshrined by the constitution. Nieto Posadillo began collecting alcabala from indigenous villagers, prompting complaints.[91]

The failure to set up constitutional local governments before Fernando VII abolished the constitution later in 1814 muted the impact of the constitution in Villa Alta, but its brief reign did not go entirely unnoticed. Julian Nieto Posadillo was a relatively greedy subdelegado, and his behavior after he took up his post again in 1814 aroused many complaints. Several villages, backed by their parish priests, complained that Nieto Posadillo was charging them for the feria de varas, the ceremony in which newly elected village officials were inaugurated. In June 1814 Nieto Posadillo defended this practice to Intendant Melchor Alvarez, and he added that "very few of the Indians ([in] this district) will enjoy the right of citizenship granted by the political Constitution of the Monarchy" because few parents sent their children to schools. He added that "most will not become citizens due to their lack of industry and their very old custom of being idle, lax, and slovenly." Apparently Nieto Posadillo assumed that literacy was required to exercise citizenship, while the constitution actually postponed that requirement until 1830.

This reply seems to have infuriated Melchor Alvarez. He answered that "today's Government is not that of the past, and anyone who reads the Constitution knows this." Alvarez argued that the custom of the feria de varas was a corruption that officials had designed to fill their pockets, and that schools would be established in rural areas "to slowly educate and civilize, following the Constitution, these Spaniards who form no less than an integral part of the Monarchy."[92] Here we see a clash over the role of indigenous peasants in the new order established by the constitution. For Nieto Posadillo, nothing could change the lazy and slovenly Indians, who did not deserve the rights of citizenship, and whom in another document he called "naturally rebellious, conspiratorial, rumor-mongering."[93] For Alvarez, the Indians were an integral part of the monarchy, who could be civilized by schooling.[94]

The debate between Nieto Posadillo and Alvarez and the immediate threat to the Antequeran elite's monopoly on city government were both cut short later in 1814. Fernando VII recovered his throne, and on 4 May 1814 he abolished the Spanish Cortes and all its works, including of course the constitution. On 15 June he dissolved the town councils erected under the constitution.[95] These measures were published in Antequera on 17 September. Alvarez, who had earlier trumpeted the notion that government was no longer what it had been, was forced to explain that according to Fernando VII the Constitution of 1812 had copied "the revolutionary and democratic principles of the French Constitution of 1791."[96] A few months later Antequera held a mass of thanksgiving for Fernando's return to the throne. The homilist, Ignacio Mariano Vasconcelos, again held up Fernando as a king destined to save the empire from its troubles. The priest insisted that God, not the people, was the origin of sovereignty. He stridently argued that Fernando was king through the specific will of God. Vasconcelos argued that Spain's liberals had tried to tie Fernando's hands, and the king had broken those bonds.[97] The liberal experiment appeared to be over in Oaxaca.

꧁ *A Return to Calm?*

The end of the liberal experiment combined with the ebbing of the insurgent military threat brought a period of relative calm to Oaxacan politics, but even then it was a nervous sort of calm. The people of both Antequera and Villa Alta faced a series of problems that unsettled political life. Despite the best efforts of Fernando VII, it was impossible to return to the values and ideas that had regulated politics before 1808. Fernando VII could abolish the laws written by the liberals, he could imprison their leaders, and he even could punish otherwise loyal officials who had accepted posts from them.[98] However, he could not erase people's memories of the liberal experiment, and he could not turn back the clock. Likewise, royalist armies succeeded in driving the insurgents out of most of the province, and eliminated the direct military threat to cities. Still, the insurgents lived on in tenacious groups in many regions of New Spain, and their presence was a constant drain on the royal treasury and the economy as a whole. Moreover, even in relatively secure Oaxaca the authorities could not banish the terrifying specter of a world turned upside down that the insurgents had introduced.

One of the first problems royalist authorities faced after retaking Antequera was the status of important officials and families that had collaborated with the rebels during the insurgent occupation. Generally the royalist authorities were lenient. They accepted the basic argument that many people had served the insurgents against their will, and noted that some had even been forced to take military posts with the rebels. A few individuals who had provided funds for the rebels were exiled to Havana, but the authorities stopped far short of anything resembling a witch-hunt. The men Morelos had forced to serve on the city council were eventually pardoned.[99] José de San Martín, the cleric whose ambiguous career was discussed earlier, was exempted from the death penalty but was still placed under investigation. Despairing of exoneration, San Martín fled royalist custody and joined the insurgent forces in the field.[100] Institutionally, the authorities replaced the insurgent city council with a new one elected under the provisions of the Constitution of 1812. After Fernando VII abolished the constitution, they reinstalled the city council that had been in office before the insurgent occupation.[101]

The authorities and the city's elite continued to fear pro-insurgent conspiracies, and this fear combined with the presence of royal troops from other parts of Mexico magnified personal disputes. In 1817 a tax official accused Manuel Nicolás de Bustamante, his unnamed wife, Angel Alvarez, Francisco Pimentel, and José Lazo of conspiring against the king. His only evidence was that he had seen them conversing publicly and they were "all suspicious people."[102] In 1817 a parish priest denounced Belemnite Friar José Monserrate for speaking in favor of the insurgents. Monserrate successfully defended himself against the charge, showing that in fact during the insurgent occupation he had hidden a European Spaniard from the insurgents.[103] These apparently spurious accusations did not mean that there was no sympathy in the city for the insurgents. In August 1817 a proinsurgent pasquín was posted in a prominent public space.[104] Moreover, the political vocabulary of the war injected itself into everyday disputes. Authorities tried to prevent violence by prohibiting urban residents from carrying arms, but their efforts were not totally successful. An 1816 argument over who could buy the last charcoal in an urban store escalated to a near riot after a weaver called a soldier from outside Oaxaca a "licker of gachupín asses."[105] Even monasteries were not immune from these tensions. An 1819 election for the city's Dominicans was marred by a fierce dispute between the friars who were born in Spain and those who were born in Mexico. This problem led to the resignation of the newly elected prior.[106]

Even as these tensions persisted, the city's residents struggled to earn their livings in an economy that was at best anemic. The fact that their young men had been impressed into military service diminished the earning power of many families. Artisans were under a double burden. They faced competition from women, Indians, and other people who had not passed through an examination process and did not contribute to the expenses of their guilds. At the same time, authorities had become very reluctant to defend guild prerogatives. The insurgents had actually abolished guilds, but they became legal again when the royalists retook the city in 1814. That October the shoemakers' guild complained of unexamined journeymen who not only set up unauthorized independent shops but also outbid the masters for the services of other journeymen. In 1815 a weaver resisted the efforts of his guild to make him take the master's exam, claiming that it was too costly.[107] At first authorities tried to back up the guilds, but in 1816 Intendant Francisco Rendón delivered them a terrible blow. Rendón criticized the efforts of guilds to prevent women from exercising their trades, and in response he published royal orders from 1779 and 1784 that allowed women to exercise "all manufactures compatible with the decency, strength, and disposition of their sex."[108] In 1817 the intendant went even further. He actually enforced an 1813 liberal decree opening up any trade to all residents of the empire, even though theoretically Fernando VII had abolished such decrees after his return to the throne.[109] The rearguard action of the guilds became a rout. In 1818 the rope makers complained of competition from indigenous villagers who brought rope to the Saturday market. Rather than trying to enforce their previous monopoly, the rope makers asked to be relieved of some of the obligations of their guild. In particular they wanted to stop preparing and carrying an angel in the funeral procession held for Christ each Good Friday. The authorities granted this wish.[110] Few young men bothered to take the expensive guild exams anymore. Although the guilds continued their social activities, their economic role was essentially over.[111] Antequera had become a much harder place for artisans to make a living. In 1820 the pastry makers of the city complained that merchants in the city's center had obtained a municipal order preventing them from stopping to sell their goods on the streets and plazas there. The merchants had argued that the sweets attracted flies, which then dirtied the merchants' expensive wares. The artisans complained that the "effeminate" merchants should simply put their wares under glass or pay someone to scare away the flies. The town council ruled in favor of the merchants.[112]

The war also heated up political rhetoric in Villa Alta. The issue of loyalty to the king and government, and particularly the stands people had taken or failed to take during the insurgent incursion in the summer of 1812 or their later 1812–1814 administration of the district, became weapons in more mundane disputes. The stakes were high. People convicted of playing leading roles for the insurgents were subject to execution. Those who had distinguished themselves opposing the insurgents sought special privileges that would give them an edge in local conflicts. Thus Calixto Perez, Ursulino Perez, and Vizente Mata of Puxmetecan wanted credit for maintaining the loyalty of their village during the 1812 insurgent incursion. They had led a group of volunteers from their village against the insurgents in several skirmishes, and they had been named militia commanders. The intrepid three complained that during the later insurgent occupation they were forced to hide in the bush. In 1814 they asked for the return of their previous titles as militia leaders in order to root out insurgent corruption in the area.[113] However, insurgent corruption could be defined various ways. Juan José Cruz of Yovego complained in 1814 that he was imprisoned unjustly "due to the hate that the cited José Santiago holds for my entire generation, who he calls insurgents." In late 1815 José Santiago again accused Juan José Cruz of being an insurgent, and he succeeded in having the latter's election as alcalde annulled on these grounds. Cruz tried to turn the rhetorical tables, arguing that this false accusation was itself a form of disloyalty to the king.[114] Here a generational conflict within a village was being interpreted in the wider context of Mexican politics. In 1812, Joseph Vicente María de Paz, a priest, had argued that a similar generational conflict was taking place in Yahuive. According to Paz, the young men of the village were locked in a struggle with their elders, and the young favored the insurgency.[115]

Individuals also used the new political labels in struggles that were apparently not originally political at all. Timoteo Bargas, jailed on suspicion of homicide, tried to reduce the prestige of his accusers by charging them with being insurgents who kept shotguns to use against royalist soldiers. Marcelino Hernandez, accused of abandoning his wife, was also criticized for speaking in favor of the insurgents. Crisanto Alfaro of San Miguel Reagui was involved in a complicated dispute with the village authorities in 1815. They accused him of failing to provide obligatory community labor and then lying about his absence. He was also denounced for supporting the insurgents.[116] Although most of these cases were inconclusive, and it is therefore impossible to say how much weight authorities put on these accusations, clearly the political culture in which village politics and personal disputes operated had become more confrontational.

The nervous calm that began in 1814 came to an end in 1820. In March a group of liberal Spanish officers organized a coup and forced Fernando VII to reinstate the Constitution of 1812.[117] This news reached Oaxaca in June, and the sitting town council recalled the constitutionally elected city council of 1814. The city council arranged for another oath of allegiance to the constitution, a thanksgiving mass, and the constitution's publication in the main plaza of the city.[118] It also published a flyer defending the constitution. The flyer drew both from concerns that predated 1808 and those of more recent vintage. The authors argued that if the constitution had existed before 1808, Godoy would never have risen to power and Fernando VII would never have fallen captive to Napoleon. It also stated that the constitution "makes all equal; but not with a fanciful equality that destroys but instead with an equality that builds and conserves, that orders everything to reciprocal benefit, and with respective attributes, cooperating with their mutual duties, helping one another mutually."[119] The argument here outlines the problem that would bedevil Oaxaca's wealthy for the next several decades. How could the elite embrace the idea that all men were equal while simultaneously preserving the social order that allowed them to exploit the mass of the population?

The problem was to become more difficult in the months to follow. In early 1821 Agustín de Iturbide, a royalist military officer, abandoned the royalist cause, allying himself with the insurgent Vicente Guerrero in a bid to make Mexico independent. Their Plan de Iguala represented an interesting compromise. It left the Constitution of 1812 in place with two substantial exceptions. The first specifically protected the Mexican clergy, while the second extended the rights of citizenship to people with African ancestry. The plan guaranteed adherence to the Roman Catholic religion, independence, and equal treatment for those born in Spain and those born in the New World. As Timothy Anna points out, the new compromise fit the ideas of many of New Spain's urban wealthy. It provided for "monarchy, the constitution of 1812, and home rule."[120] However, apparently Antequera's elite were less than enthusiastic about this compromise. When Iturbide sent the city council a copy of the plan, the councilmen forwarded it immediately to the central government in Mexico City.[121] They also criticized the Plan de Iguala in a public statement, arguing that it would introduce anarchy. Silke Hensel suggests that the mercantile origins of the councilmen led to this opposition. They feared damage to trade with Spain, and they also worried about the prospect of renewed civil war.[122] In the end, the Plan de Iguala would triumph in Oaxaca by force of arms.

The victory of the Plan de Iguala in Oaxaca originated in an unlikely source. Antonio de León was a young mestizo cattleman from the northern district of Huajuapan. He had served in the royalist militia since 1811, and in 1820 he was also elected to the local municipal council. In March 1821, León and his brother agreed to support the Plan de Iguala. After months of planning and recruitment he publicly embraced the plan in June 1821. León began his campaign with a mere thirty men but rapidly accumulated recruits after a series of victorious skirmishes with the royalists. On 21 June he took the town of Huajuapan, and from there he began campaigning along the route to the city of Antequera. The campaign ended on 30 July when León defeated the major royalist force in the province at Etla, a few miles from the city. The next day he entered the city.[123] The rapid progression of events suggested that, more than anything else, the province's population and economy were exhausted by the years of uncertainty and war that had followed 1808. In fact, despite their initially fierce opposition to Iturbide, the city councilmen had refused to supply royalist troops with extra funds as León closed in.[124] In effect, independence arrived in the province relatively quietly, more an anticlimax than a climax.

℘ Conclusion

The years between 1808 and 1821 were pivotal in Oaxaca's transition from an Old Regime colonial political culture characterized by corporatism under the leadership of the Spanish monarchy to a more modern political culture of individual citizenship and popular sovereignty. On the face of it, this is not a surprising statement, and it coincides with a Mexican nationalist historiographical tradition that stretches back to the 1820s.[125] Nevertheless, the similarity between the argument here about political culture and the nationalist historiography is misleading. Actually the most important changes in the 1808–1821 period were not directly related to Mexico's independence from Spain. Even when the war of independence briefly washed across the region, the key issues of political discussion did not include any project to make Mexico a sovereign nation. In 1812 the insurgents who occupied Antequera did not openly advocate independence. Moreover, Spanish liberals who never had such intentions were more important innovators in Oaxaca than the rebel leaders, even after the latter began to argue for independence.

Two tendencies had the most lasting impact in the region. The first of these was the increasingly popular idea that all adult men were in some fundamental sense political equals, with a shared stake in the political system. Certainly even equality's most ardent supporters considered it necessary to limit equality's potentially revolutionary effects, generally by filtering the will of the majority through electoral systems designed to insure that distinguished men held a preponderance of influence. However, the basic notion of equality was extremely corrosive to traditional politics and society in the colonial city of Antequera. Delays in converting the ideal to political practice prevented that corrosion from becoming obvious before 1821, but as we will see in the next chapter the concept of equality set in motion a virulent party politics that would define the city for decades. The pedigree of this idea can be traced to the Enlightenment, and the pressures toward equality became manifest through a series of outsiders, first officials who sought support for Spain and Spain's rule in America, then insurgent leaders, and finally Spanish liberals. However, the initiatives of these outsiders fed into a latent conflict between a small social elite that defined itself by its racial purity and control of government institutions and a large population of mixed-race people who had little interest in race as a category and little patience for the social and political pretensions of the elite. The movement toward political equality was not linked in any fundamental way to the question of whether Mexico should be an independent nation. Although Morelos promoted equality, Spanish liberals advanced an even more radical version of egalitarianism.

The emergence of the ideal of political equality was important in Europe and other parts of the Americas. It is also a development that seems to have at least some positive aspects when viewed from our perch at the beginning of the twenty-first century. Neither of these statements can be made about the second important trend of the 1808–1821 period in Oaxaca. These years saw the emergence of a much more disturbing and at the same time much more amorphous tendency. From 1808 on, rumors, often of different kinds of political apocalypse, took on great force in Oaxaca. These rumors, combined with the very real violence of the independence war, caused many personal disasters, beginning with the luckless traveler Bernardo Galvez, who probably died of malnutrition in the royal jail, and continuing with many victims who were imprisoned, executed, or killed in battles both in Villa Alta and Antequera. Yet beyond these individual tragedies the rumors and violence also cast a very negative influence over the next decades, especially in the city. Although certainly conspiracy rumors had occasionally surfaced in the politics of New Spain before 1808, two new developments, neither of which was explicitly related to the question of national sovereignty, gave such rumors much greater weight. The first was the French Revolution and the way it was portrayed in New Spain as an assault on religion and the royal person. The second was Napoleon's imprisonment of the royal family, in effect a symbolic beheading of the political body. The combination had striking effects. The very foundations of society were at stake. Throughout New Spain, groups disputed the right to represent the king and the mantle of defenders of Catholicism in a world gone mad.[126] The stakes of politics became enormously higher in 1808, and for some people expectations became almost millennial.[127] We have seen how these suspicions and expectations changed the way even common prisoners in the royal jail viewed each other. An even more striking example was found in the pasquines some indigenous peasants used in an 1812 conflict over parish fees in Yahuive. A relatively routine conflict led to expressions that the Indians no longer had a government or a king, the crown now belonged to the Indians, and the time of the Spaniards was over.[128] Although these statements may have actually represented a savvy attempt to scare away an unpopular priest rather than widespread beliefs, either way it is impossible to imagine a return to the political culture that existed before 1808.

Despite the example from Yahuive, as of 1821 both the adoption of equality as an ideal and the salience of conspiracy fears and apocalyptic political thinking affected the city of Antequera far more than they did the relatively isolated and heavily indigenous district of Villa Alta. In fact, conspiracy fears and the feeling that the stakes of politics had become enormous never really took hold in Villa Alta after the brief rebel incursion of 1812. Moreover, although the idea that all men were equal made a dramatic transformation of indigenous village politics in Villa Alta possible, that possibility remained latent before 1821 because no government had yet attempted to hold elections governed by the new ideal. The pattern of political change was for the moment predictable. The most dramatic innovations showed their effects in the city long before they began to impact politics in the countryside.

CHAPTER Five

Oil and Vinegar: The Construction and Dissolution of Republican Order in the City of Oaxaca

ᕙ When Mexico became independent the colonial city of Antequera changed its name to Oaxaca. Authorities did not document their reasons for dropping a name that had been used for almost three hundred years. Clearly, though, the change had more than a little to do with the triumphant emotions of the moment. The colonial years were seen as a time of darkness, and the new epoch as one of rebirth. Nevertheless, the authorities did not choose just any name. In Michoacán, Valladolid had adopted the name of one of the insurgency's great heroes, becoming Morelia. In Oaxaca, in contrast, politicians claimed the name of the region as the new name for its largest city. This choice sent a message about the city's place in the new political order. The city's elite expected to revive and renew its economic and political domination of the surrounding territory. As we saw in previous chapters, the Bourbon reforms had weakened the urban elite's economic domination of the region even as the city's political status as the capital was formalized for the first time. Now the urban elite hoped to both recover what it had lost and consolidate what it had gained.

The successes and failures of that urban elite will be one of the subjects of this chapter, but the focus will be on politics in the city of Oaxaca, and how the formation of a republic changed popular political culture. The republic brought new forms of making politics, and new ways of envisioning society. National sovereignty, with elections based on virtually universal male suffrage, was combined with earlier beliefs about the ends and means of politics, and this fusion created a virulent partisan politics. One group of Oaxacans heralded a new age of egalitarianism, federalism, and nationalism, and feared that sinister forces threatened Mexico's independent existence. Their opponents worried about disorder and social dissolution, and were particularly wary of the danger posed by impiety. Political mobilizations and political passions came to dominate urban society to an astonishing degree. The majority of voters were relatively poor men, and not surprisingly parties experimented with discourses and tactics to mobilize the support of this majority. Eventually, though, this relatively democratic political trend was limited by the repeated application of military force, often for purposes that had much more to do with national events than the relative strength of local political forces. These outside interventions in local politics did not end urban mobilizations, but they limited the role of elections in determining who controlled political offices. The period after independence was a time of great fluidity in social and especially political life that at first seemed to present important opportunities for various groups to pursue their ends. This perception of possibility underlay strong political optimism early in the period. Eventually most of these possibilities were foreclosed, and many Oaxacans became much more cynical.

Soon after Latin American nations became independent, observers, both internal and external, noted that the newly fashionable politics of elections did not lead to political stability. On the contrary, the politics of most Latin American nations soon came to be dominated by a whirlwind of civil wars and coups. For nearly two hundred years now intellectuals and politicians have put forward a variety of theories to explain this phenomenon. In recent years, one of the most interesting and influential approaches to the problem has been that of François-Xavier Guerra. Guerra argued that the root of the disorder lay in the incompatibility between modern forms of politics and a social structure dominated by collective entities like corporate bodies, family cliques, and clientalist networks. Guerra developed the basic ideas of this approach in his analysis of the Mexican Revolution, and then turned his attention to the early nineteenth century.[1] His work has been fundamental to the research of his students and collaborators in Europe and Latin America, and it has enjoyed influence far beyond that circle.

Although there is much to praise about Guerra's work, the research presented in this chapter provides some grounds for skepticism on two important points. First, although it seems quite logical to assume the existence of strong corporate bodies, family cliques, and clientalist networks in urban politics after independence, the sources for Oaxaca do not provide much evidence. For reasons I will explore below, it is unlikely that clientalism was capable of mobilizing the large number of voters active in Oaxacan politics. Family cliques were clearly important at the level of officeholding, but again they did not extend to rank-and-file voters. The sources instead suggest that ideology was probably more important in motivating voters in urban Oaxaca. Second, and more importantly, approaches that stress the incompatibility between collective social groups and modern politics do not adequately address the importance of pluralism in establishing stable electoral systems. As we will see, the forms of partisan ideology that emerged in urban Oaxaca after independence precluded political tolerance. These forms of ideology also prevented political actors from gaining the simple but crucial confidence that losing some elections was an acceptable price for maintaining electoral politics. More than anything else, the absence of pluralism stunted electoral politics in urban Oaxaca.

The most important works published on Oaxacan politics after independence are those of Silke Hensel and Carlos Sánchez Silva. Hensel used the techniques of collective biography to examine politics in the period from 1786 to 1835.[2] Her analysis shows that the city's merchant elite supported the movement to make Oaxaca an independent state under the federalist model. This group sought to recover the economic domination of the province they had lost during the Bourbon reforms. Hensel also demonstrates that after independence this mercantile elite gradually lost control of the most important institutions of government. Hensel's analysis focuses on the identity of Oaxaca's political elite, especially their socioeconomic characteristics. While valuable, this approach does not allow her to probe the problem of party conflict, a problem that every Oaxacan politician of the period would probably have placed at the center of his political analysis. In fact Hensel does not even list the party affiliations of politicians in her collective biography. In her defense it can be said that the leaders of both urban parties had broadly similar backgrounds.[3] However, even though the socioeconomic background of many leaders of the populist party did not differ greatly from those of their opponents, they deployed a political discourse that stressed the privileged backgrounds of their adversaries.

Although Carlos Sánchez Silva also employs some collective biography, his work offers a broader vision of continuities in the way the city's political and economic elite dominated and exploited the region's indigenous majority. Sánchez Silva argues that despite significant changes set in motion by the Bourbon reforms and independence, a relatively wealthy few managed to extract profits from the peasantry by renewing old practices and forging new techniques.[4] This is an extremely valuable work, but it does not probe the kinds of issues that interest us here. Like Hensel, Sánchez Silva leaves aside the problem of party conflict in the city, and the ways in which postco-lonial politicians and groups constructed discourses to justify their political actions. Moreover, continuities in the relationship between the city and the surrounding region did not translate into continuities in the city itself, where political innovation and ferment were the order of the day.

Oaxaca was one of the birthplaces of the Reform, the political move-ment that eventually broke the back of Mexican conservatism and laid the groundwork for the peculiarly liberal forms of authoritarianism that domi-nated Mexican political life for most of the last 150 years. The politics and political culture we will explore in this chapter nurtured the early career of Benito Juárez, the most famous politician of the Reform. Juárez immi-grated to the city from the nearby mountains right at the beginning of the period discussed in this chapter, and by its end he had become governor of the state. Many liberal politicians later argued that nothing had changed in Mexico in the first decades after independence. For them, Mexico in the mid-1850s was essentially still a colonial place. Their view of the period after independence has informed much of the historiography of the pe-riod.[5] But in fact much changed in the period immediately after indepen-dence. The Reform also plays a determining role in another set of works on the period. Some historians, both nationally and in Oaxaca, tend to see the period after independence as one whose events and people represent a set of precursors to the great events of the Reform.[6] Yet this way of conceptualiz-ing the period overlooks some of the most important developments. More-over, the political dividing lines and issues of the postindependence period were not identical to those of the Reform.

𝔣ℕ Religion and Politics

Conflict between church and state was crucial to the Reform, so historians searching earlier periods for the Reform's antecedents tend to emphasize that conflict. Although such clashes became crucial to politics in 1833–34 and 1846–47, on both occasions the measures that offended the church were national laws that had few supporters in Oaxaca. Both clerics and government officials in Oaxaca tended to be very moderate on such issues. Even politicians who would later be associated with the Reform, includ-ing Benito Juárez, accepted the fact that Catholicism and the institutional church were central to Oaxacan society and politics. The church maintained an important presence in Oaxaca, and throughout the first half of the nine-teenth century most people saw religion as basic to politics, while religious metaphors abounded in the political discourse of all major groups.[7] The first constitution of the state of Oaxaca enshrined Catholicism as the religion of the state, and when the constitutional congress introduced the constitution to the populace, the congress argued that "nothing is better to shape customs (without which no laws can survive) than the Christian religion which preaches social duties."[8]

Prayer was an integral part of political ceremonies. Politicians also cooperated with religious authorities to arrange special public prayers and masses in moments of crisis, including droughts, epidemics, and wars.[9] In other words, politicians and society saw appeals for divine assistance as plausible responses to pressing problems. Many also believed that divine intervention was important to Mexico's very existence as a nation. The most obvious example of this is the cult of the Virgin of Guadalupe. Guadalupe, a relatively minor figure in colonial Oaxaca's religious affairs, became an important symbol of Mexican independence, and her feast gained a prominent place on the civic and religious calendar of the city.[10] Religious references also underpinned nationalist speeches at civic events. Benito Juárez's independence day speech of 1840, for instance, referred to Hidalgo as "a new Moses" who rescued the Aztec people from captivity.[11] Many of these speeches put forward a providentialist view of Mexico's history and identity, arguing that God had given Mexico a unique role to play in the political and religious affairs of the globe. Mexican sovereignty would, for these writers, redeem a world turned irreligious and immoral.[12]

Catholicism not only was a fundamental component of Mexican nationalism, it was woven thoroughly into everyday life in places like Oaxaca. Church bells and religious devotions set the pace for many an inhabitant's day. More importantly, Catholicism was a common denominator in society, uniting rich and poor, Indians and whites, old and young.[13] Thousands of adults, for instance, continued to belong to confraternities or cofradías, which provided their members with funeral expenses and masses after their deaths. The cofradías also organized special devotions for their patron saints. It is impossible to know how many Oaxacans attended mass regularly at one of the city's many churches, but it seems likely that religious participation was quite common.

Civil politicians and clerics usually cooperated on both civil and religious issues. In 1826, when the government expelled a monk who refused to swear allegiance to the national constitution, it received complete cooperation from the prior of his convent. When the national government sought to reduce the number of holy days in 1840, it received papal and diocesan support. In 1842 the government decreed that all burials should take place in cemeteries rather than church buildings, violating well-established religious customs. Although many Oaxacans protested this decree, the diocese cooperated completely with the government.[14] Only occasionally did echoes of earlier Bourbon attitudes about clerical political action filter into political debates in early postindependent Oaxaca. For instance, when some legislators proposed that parish priests be asked to teach their parishioners about the new state constitution, others objected that priests should not involve themselves in political questions.[15]

The most important tension between church and state in the 1820s and early 1830s was the issue of the *patronato*, the authority Spain's kings had enjoyed to name clerics in the New World. The 1824 Mexican constitution claimed this right for the independent state, but the Vatican feared that ceding this point would alienate Spain. Although the church refused to officially give way on the issue, in practice it conceded what Brian Connaughton calls a "virtual patronato." The church allowed state governors to approve clerical appointments and did not contest the state's insistence that all new bishops be Mexicans. Church authorities were careful to cooperate with state governments in these matters.[16]

❧ Urban Political Culture: The Means of Change

The first decades after independence saw many new ideas, tropes, and tactics in urban politics. These novelties were introduced to the mass of the populace through means that were often themselves new. One of the most important was the periodical press. No newspaper was published in Oaxaca during the colonial period, and the 1810s saw the publication of only one short-lived paper, *El Correo Americano del Sur*. In contrast, many newspapers appeared in the 1820s, 1830s, and 1840s. Copies exist of more than twenty separate titles, and references to several more survive.[17] Many of these papers had relatively short runs, existing for only a few months or even a few weeks. All were printed on very fragile paper, and it is possible that some copies were destroyed for political reasons. Nevertheless, the surviving newspapers are an important source of information on political events and discourses. Perhaps more importantly, they themselves shaped both events and discourses.

Those who edited or contributed to newspapers typically remained nameless, used initials, or made up fanciful pseudonyms. For us they seem curiously disembodied, but it seems likely that many people of the period knew who they were. At the very least certain newspapers were associated with particular political groups, especially during electoral campaigns. Newspapers relied on, and simultaneously created, a body of common knowledge about the actors of Oaxacan politics and their political positions. On occasion this knowledge even allowed a newspaper to ridicule a political figure without naming him outright, particularly strong evidence of readers' political acuity.[18]

Often two different printing presses operated at the same time in Oaxaca.[19] Usually the government owned one. In the late 1820s and early 1830s this press printed political papers that were not officially associated with the government. From middle of the 1830s on, the government press published an official newspaper that ran laws and decrees as well as editorials. The government press was entrusted to a printer who put out the official newspaper and also had the right to use the equipment for commercial purposes, publishing books and pamphlets. The printer who ran the government press typically competed with at least one privately owned press that published one and sometimes two newspapers as well as books and pamphlets.[20] In the late 1830s and early 1840s no fewer than five newspapers were published simultaneously in Oaxaca, a city with around 20,000 inhabitants.[21] Newspapers came out one to three times per week. The business parameters of newspaper publishing are difficult to establish. Sometimes newspapers ran advertisements, but it seems that relatively high subscription prices generated most of their revenue. It also seems likely that political groups or figures subsidized the publication of newspapers.

Newspapers and their editors sometimes paid a heavy price for their exposed political position. In 1835 the national government decreed that all newspaper articles must be written on the premises of the press that published them, preventing the owners of presses from claiming that unknown authors were responsible for the contents of the papers they printed. The three papers publishing in Oaxaca at that moment immediately quit the business. Similar restrictions in 1840 drove four newspapers from circulation, leaving only the official newspaper of the state government.[22] Legal restrictions were not always effective. In 1834 the government prosecuted José Ines Sandoval, editor of *La Voz del Pueblo*, for sedition. It succeeded in forcing the printer Juan Oledo to identify Sandoval, but a jury decided that the editorial in question was not seditious.[23] Sometimes the worst threats were not official ones. During a heated election campaign in 1828, the director of the state press, Antonio Valdés y Moya, was arrested for domestic abuse, a charge his supporters claimed was trumped up. His party won the election, but Valdés y Moya fled town after his rivals took power through extralegal means. While he was gone the new state government broke down the door to his office and placed another printer in charge of the press.[24]

Oaxacan printers also published a variety of locally written pamphlets and broadsides. Others were imported from other states or reprinted in Oaxaca. The quantity of these works is astounding. Oaxaca printers published at least 116 such works between 1820 and 1850, and they reprinted at least 7 pamphlets originally published in other parts of Mexico. Undoubtedly this count is incomplete, as broadsides and pamphlets, like newspapers, were relatively ephemeral publications, printed on cheap paper and often tied to the events of the day. Individual writers entered into partisan debates about policy, elections, and civil wars. Laws were also published in broadside form. However, many pamphlets were religious sermons, and others were efforts to influence public opinion in legal or commercial disputes.

The politicians who worked to set up a functioning government in the 1820s were very aware that they could not expect most of the populace to be able to read laws. Thus they followed colonial precedent in promulgating legislation. Laws were not only printed and distributed to judges and administrators, they were also publicly proclaimed in ceremonies in every town or village. A local official would parade around the principal square accompanied by an escort, a drummer, and a bugler. In each corner a secretary would read the law "in a loud, slow, and clear manner."[25]

Local politicians believed that literacy was crucial to Mexico's future, and as Victor Raul Martínez Vázquez points out, politicians from all parties supported primary education. Education was seen as an antidote to barbarism as well as an opportunity to inspire respect for law and authority in the population.[26] Basic responsibility for schooling belonged to the city council, and sometimes it educated respectable numbers of students. In 1829, 855 boys were enrolled in municipal primary schools, 242 more students took classes in elementary schools supported by convents or run by private teachers as business enterprises, and 250 were enrolled in the state's Lancasterian school, where in a popular cost-saving system more experienced students taught younger students.[27] However, funds to pay for primary schools were sometimes limited, and therefore the number of students enrolled varied. In 1837, total enrollments ebbed to around 200, while in 1845 there were 1,311 male students in primary schools. Although no document reports school-age population, a rough extrapolation from an 1849 census suggests that the number of males between ages five and fifteen could not have been much greater than 2,500. Probably boys attended primary school for only a few years, but altogether it appears that many youths attended for at least a short time.[28] Girls had access to education in *escuelas amigas*. In 1852 there were 286 girls registered in these private "friendly schools," where they learned the rudiments of reading and writing along with household skills.[29]

Although education was seen as vital to the important new task of forming citizens, the content of primary education changed little from that of the colonial period. Benito Juárez, the most famous person to pass through the city's elementary schools, reported that in the early 1820s he was taught to read, write, and recite the venerable catechism of Padre Ripalda by rote. Soon thereafter the state congress added elementary arithmetic and the study of a political catechism to this curriculum. Students at the Lancasterian school established a few years later progressed through grammar, spelling, and even some universal history.[30] Perhaps the most interesting book mentioned in school inventories is the political catechism, which the state legislature commissioned in 1826. Unfortunately no copy of this work seems to have survived the ravages of time. Other political catechisms of the period were designed to teach the basics of republicanism by presenting questions and answers suitable for rote learning in classrooms. An 1827 federal political catechism, for instance, included the following:

> Question: What does citizen mean?
> Answer: A good man: an individual who belongs to the republic, participates in the sovereign authority, and contenting himself with his rights does not aspire to anything but the good of the patria.[31]

Although the subject here differs significantly from those of religious instruction, the form follows that of religious catechisms, including the famous catechism of Ripalda.

Carlos Sánchez Silva estimates that despite these educational efforts 90 percent of the state's populace could not read, but the literacy rate may have been a bit higher for urban males.[32] However, illiteracy did not entirely sever people from print culture. Literate people read newspapers or pamphlets aloud to groups of their illiterate peers, and from there the news and arguments they contained circulated orally on street corners, in stores, and in homes.[33] In 1828, for instance, José Llano arrived at the cockpit with the latest opposition broadside from Mexico City and read it aloud for, in his words, "these co-citizens my friends." Fortunately for us Llano was put on trial a few days later for sedition. Although he was acquitted of seditious intent, first eighteen witnesses testified, fixing Llano's act in the archival eye.[34] Usually these types of actions were beneath the notice of the state or the literate commentators who described events for the record, but it seems likely that the scene was repeated multiple times during the period in question. Angel Alvarez, a populist politician of note, was famous for buying pamphlets, newspapers, and broadsides for citizens too poor to afford them.[35] One surprising result of the rise of print culture was a decline in the earlier tradition of pasquines or pasquinades, handwritten political commentaries or verses that were usually posted anonymously in public places. The only reference I have seen to pasquines in the city after independence was a set that appeared in 1837, at a moment when the publication of newspapers and pamphlets was severely restricted.[36]

As Hugh Hamill points out, most people probably received political information and ideas through sermons, ceremonies, informal conversations, and rumors.[37] The scenes of political conversations varied. We have seen already how José Llano used a cockfight as a political forum in 1828. Cockfights were particularly popular among Oaxacan males. Other forms of gambling such as cards and dice typically took place more privately, but there is some evidence that conversation turned to politics even in these venues.[38] Acrobats also gathered crowds for diversion. A theater operated in the city periodically beginning just before the War of Independence. Although its plays were subject to the scrutiny of both the city council and newspaper editors, the theater seems to have been quite popular. The owners also sponsored a masked ball in 1848.[39] One suspects that all of these events provided opportunities for political discussion among friends.

Civic ceremonies presented officials with opportunities to shape people's attitudes towards government and authority. These elaborately staged pageants were planned in minute detail, and they have drawn the attention of a number of scholars in recent years. Researchers who focus on colonial ceremonies have often emphasized the ways in which they physically and spatially demonstrated colonial hierarchies. Generally scholars do not see these ceremonies as occasions in which subalterns had more than a passive role, as spectators or as the recipients of official largesse.[40] In contrast, Richard Warren, in his work on postindependence ceremonies in Mexico City, suggests that the gathering of crowds for these ceremonies presented subalterns with opportunities to contest the lessons ceremonies were supposed to impart.[41] Either way, it is impossible to ignore the expense and effort that governmental authorities put into civic ceremonies. Clearly they were considered to be crucially important in legitimating the state and upholding its dignity and authority.

Civic ceremonies were conducted on a variety of occasions. Elaborate rituals were used to swear allegiance to new constitutions at both the state and national levels. Whenever government officials took office they took oaths in public ceremonies whose pomp and attendance varied according to the rank of the official. Public funerals were held for important leaders, even those who lived and died far from Oaxaca. The city also celebrated Mexico's national independence each year, and part of this event consisted of a funeral for the heroes of the independence war. In some periods anniversary festivities commemorated the adoption of the federal constitution. Civic ceremonies were also held when Mexico or Oaxaca faced extraordinary challenges, such as civil or foreign wars, or the inauguration of new constitutional congresses. All of these ceremonies included important religious elements, and most involved a special mass. Of course, more directly religious occasions also had political connotations. This was particularly true of the annual feasts of Corpus Christi, the Virgin of Soledad (patroness of the city), and the Virgin of Guadalupe.[42]

The attention that authorities paid to these ceremonies has bequeathed us with descriptions that are often very elaborate. Reading these descriptions can be fascinating, but if they are read in series what quickly comes to the fore is just how similar the ceremonies were to each other. For each type of ceremony the same basic acts were repeated year after year. Although, in his research on the Yucatán, Marco Bellingeri sees a gradual change in which religious elements became less important over time, such change is arguably less important than the impressive continuity in forms.[43] For example, the basic form of the ceremonies in which the populace received and swore oaths to new constitutions evolved directly from those of ceremonies that celebrated the ascension of new monarchs in the colonial period.[44] Authorities modified the royal ceremony when they first adapted it for the oath to the Constitution of 1812, but thereafter essentially the same ceremony was repeated in 1824 for both the temporary "Constitutive Act" and the Constitution of 1824, in 1835 for the new "Constitutional Bases," in 1837 for the Seven Laws, in 1843 for another set of constitutional bases, and again in 1846 for the federal constitution.[45] Civic funerals had a slightly less direct connection to past practice, but generally in republican civic funerals heroes replaced the godlike figures of kings in royal funerals.[46] It almost seems like officials feared that substantially modifying ceremonial patterns might damage an occasion's credibility in the eyes of the populace, a serious concern when you are planning to swear allegiance to the seventh constitution in thirty years.[47]

Obviously there was some variation, and whatever political group was in power at a given moment staged celebrations that would stress its own political values to the unlettered majority. Independence celebrations, for instance, varied for political reasons. In Oaxaca and elsewhere, populist politicians stressed 16 September, celebrating the anniversary of Hidalgo's revolt. The speeches given under their control focused on Hidalgo and criticized Spain.[48] Beginning in the 1830s, more conservative groups emphasized 27 September, the day Iturbide's Army of Three Guarantees entered Mexico City.[49] In 1846, when the federalists restored the Constitution of 1824, they marked the occasion with a particularly elaborate ceremony and even pardoned some criminals, and for the next few years they made a point of celebrating the anniversary of that constitution's original proclamation.[50] In 1833 Oaxaca's populists exhumed the corpse of their betrayed hero, Vicente Guerrero, and buried him in the cathedral after an elaborate funeral.[51]

Describing each and every civic ceremony that took place in Oaxaca would be tedious, but the importance that officials placed on such acts suggests that an example is warranted. One of the first important civic ceremonies of the postindependence era was the oath of allegiance to the Constitutive Act in 1824. The act was a temporary constitution that would be replaced later that year by the more complete federal constitution. The process that moved Mexico from the empire of Iturbide to this essentially federalist blueprint for the nation was a very contentious one, and Oaxaca took a prominent role.[52] The city council committee that planned the ceremony explicitly wanted to surpass the festivities that had accompanied the earlier oath of allegiance to Emperor Iturbide. The committee ordered all inhabitants to adorn and illuminate their houses for the occasion. Artillery and infantry salutes would precede a procession to the city center where the city council would mount a large and lavishly decorated stage constructed for the event. There the members would swear allegiance to the act, and then throw coins from the four corners of the stage amid the pealing of all of the city's church bells. The city hall would be illuminated and decorated with allegorical paintings for the next three nights, and an orchestra would play each night. On the day after the ceremony, officials and the public would attend a Te Deum mass and then a splendid banquet. On the following day the festivities would conclude with a "sumptuous dance" in the city hall. The cost of the ceremonies was estimated at 10,000 pesos. This proved too expensive, and the ceremonies were scaled back. Bonfires replaced the banquet, but two new stages were added, making the cost a more reasonable 1,600 pesos.[53]

The next turn of events brings up the question of the relative passivity of the urban masses during such ceremonies. The city council heard rumors that the "people and troops" would use the occasion to demand that all Spaniards be expelled and that the state's military commandant, Antonio de León, be elevated to the governorship. The council ordered liquor stores to close for the day and severely limited the military presence at the ceremony. As Warren suggests, the presence of crowds provided a potential opportunity for contestation.[54] However, the rumored movement did not develop, and the ceremony went off without a hitch. The minutes of the city council report that the role of the pueblo was limited to its spontaneous eruption in vivas for "the Sacred Religion, the Sovereign Congress, the Supreme Executive Power of the Nation, and the Sovereign Power of this State."[55] In fact none of the dozens of civic ceremonies that took place between 1820 and 1850 seems to have resulted in disorder or subversive political activity. In Oaxaca at least, these events remained for, but not by, "el pueblo."

The same cannot be said for elections. In recent years a number of historians have begun serious research on early-nineteenth-century elections in Latin America. Their perspectives have varied significantly, but they coincide in criticizing a previous consensus that insisted that these elections were invariably fictions, designed to mask the continued rule of colonial oligarchies. As Richard Warren points out, the elections varied from occasions of mass mobilization that led to the transfer of significant political power to fraudulent or even fictitious events.[56] Electoral turnouts also varied greatly from election to election and place to place. Historians report turnouts as low as 5 percent of the total population and as high as 15 percent.[57] Both of these figures represent much higher proportions of the eligible voters. Available records rarely allow us to make reasonably accurate estimates of turnouts. In Oaxaca, for instance, documents typically report the vote totals of the winning candidates but not the number of overall votes. Elections also sometimes involved people beyond those eligible to vote, as women or minors could participate in campaigns.[58]

Elections were in an important sense another kind of civic ceremony. In elections the "people" symbolically conferred power on their rulers, acting out the ideal of popular sovereignty.[59] These elections thus fortified the bonds between government officials and society. Elections also resembled civic celebrations in that they drew together crowds to make political statements.[60] Most of the basic elements of nineteenth-century election procedures and laws were set out by the Spanish liberals who wrote the Constitution of 1812, and those liberals set up an electoral system that stressed the symbolic transfer of power to representatives. Under these procedures, elections were not supposed to be competitive. Potentially divisive political campaigns or parties were to be prevented by filtering the people's will through a series of indirect elections. On the lowest level, voters would choose honorable and virtuous men as electors rather than choosing men pledged to promote a particular set of policies. As Antonio Annino puts it, "citizens would not vote according to their political opinions, but instead on the basis of the confidence they had in a person."[61] Political elections in this conception would be similar to the electoral practices of such Old Regime corporations as cofradías or guilds. In those elections members of a corporate body voted for prominent and honest men who would manage the affairs of the group.[62] In many places, including Oaxaca, electoral procedures in the postindependence period were modeled directly after those devised by the Spanish liberals. In this vision, electors were chosen to exercise power on behalf of the people. In Oaxaca at least, they were actually given formal, written powers of attorney testifying to this fact. If a person chosen for office was unable to complete his term, the electors met again to choose his successor, even if many months had passed since their own election. The protocol the state government set up in 1825 for civic ceremonies assigned electors an important place in the proceedings.[63]

The basic model for elections set out by the Spanish liberals did not grant electoral organizing or political parties any place. Even so, electoral organizing and partisan politics began almost immediately. Political organizing and parties played a prominent role in many Latin American countries even as they made most Hispanic political theorists quite uncomfortable.[64] In Oaxaca no group seems to have organized for the 1814 elections that were the first held under the Spanish constitution. The constitution was soon suspended. When it was reintroduced in 1820, Oaxaca apparently experienced electoral organizing for the first time. The mobilization for this election escaped the notice of electoral authorities, and it has left little documentary evidence. Four men elaborated lists of individuals they apparently considered to be apt candidates for electors.[65] By December 1822 the scale of electoral organizing was so great that officials began to report its increasing role in urban politics.[66]

From the 1820s on, parties worked hard to organize large numbers of voters for parochial elections, the first stage of the electoral process where all men could vote. Nevertheless, successful organizing in these initial elections was not sufficient to secure victory. Elections took place in various stages. The process through which state legislatures were chosen in the late 1820s and early 1830s can serve as an example. Citizens met in the middle of August to choose parochial electors. In early September the parochial electors then met with those chosen in other parishes in their district to select a second set of electors. At the beginning of October this second group of electors met with their counterparts from all over the state to actually choose the legislators.[67] To be successful a party had to organize three times, first to select and support slates of electors for each parish, then to do the same for each district, and finally to support particular candidates for the legislature. Each occasion was also an opportunity for fraud, and often activities that the winning party construed as successful organizing were seen by its opponents as fraud. If anything, it was more effective to organize for the district and state stages, when a relatively small number of electors could be promised government jobs or plied with lists of apt candidates.[68]

Elections did not in practice work out to be the smooth, nonpartisan affairs that lawmakers had envisioned. Elections in Oaxaca were intensely competitive. Often they generated significant political conflict stretching from months before elections to weeks afterward. Partially as a result, elections tended to become less and less important as mechanisms for determining who held office, but they remained significant emblems of the symbolic connection between the people and the state. Although from 1820 on many groups actually attained governmental power by more forceful means, no group in power before the 1850s ever felt that it could legitimate that power without elections.

The importance of elections in legitimating authority often led the political group in power at a given moment to try to expand or contract suffrage to enhance its electoral prospects. Oaxacan politics, as we will see in detail in the following pages, featured a populist party and a more conservative party. Generally the more conservative party worked to reduce suffrage, usually arguing that restrictions were necessary to prevent fraud and disorder.[69] Whenever possible the populist party rescinded restrictive rules. Early in the 1820s Mexico allowed extremely ample suffrage. The Plan de Iguala declared all Mexicans equal, eliminating the last racial distinction retained by the Spanish liberals, who had excluded people with African ancestry from politics. In the 1823 election for state congress, for instance, all men over eighteen years of age were allowed to vote except for imprisoned criminals or those delinquent in paying their taxes.[70] The state constitution enacted in

1825 made all married men citizens at the age of eighteen while single men had to wait until they reached twenty-one. Two weeks before the 1830 legislative elections, politicians from the more conservative of Oaxaca's parties passed a new law requiring voters to pick up a ballot from the municipal offices before the election. This measure allowed municipal authorities to decide who was eligible to vote on an individual basis, when they would not be subject to pressures from a crowd of the citizen's friends. Moreover, voters would need to be previously registered as citizens, something few had bothered to do. The law also required voters to obey the orders of electoral authorities during the election and penalized those who arrived drunk, insulted officials, carried arms, or attempted to "suborn" voters. Later the law was extended to town council elections, and in a telling move the legislature restricted its application to the city of Oaxaca and those other municipalities where the governor considered it necessary.[71]

Opponents of this law pointed out that it violated the state constitution, which gave the electoral authorities, elected by those present when the polls opened, the exclusive right to determine voter eligibility. They also argued that it was an obvious effort to prevent many Oaxacans from exercising their right to vote. The law's supporters said that it would prevent parties from preparing preprinted ballots and distributing them to voters on election day.[72] When the populists took control of the state legislature in 1833 they abolished the offending decree.[73] After national politics took a more conservative turn in the mid-1830s the national government took over electoral regulation. It required voters to demonstrate a minimum annual income of one hundred pesos, effectively cutting much of the population off the voter rolls. In 1842, for instance, 2,670 of the city's 4,394 adult males were given ballots.[74] The next year the national government further restricted suffrage, limiting voting to those who earned two hundred pesos annually, and the regulations for the 1846 election of a new constitutional congress restricted voting by occupational group.[75] When the federalists regained power in 1846 they revived the 1824 federalist constitution, returning the power to regulate suffrage to the states. Regional federalists once again embraced virtually universal male suffrage.[76]

ꕥ Political Values

The press and elections provided new political means, but the period was also characterized by new political values. Probably the most important of these was egalitarianism. The notion that all Oaxacans, or at least male

Oaxacans, were fundamentally equal had taken root in the period just before independence. As we have seen, egalitarianism had three parallel and mutually reinforcing origins. The first was the effort of the Spanish absolutist state to mobilize the entire population during foreign wars and the civil war against the Mexican insurgency. The second was the anticolonial project of the insurgents themselves, who sought to replace the complex hierarchies of the colonial period with a relatively simple division between Mexicans and foreigners. The third was Spanish liberalism, which combined the mobilizational motives of the absolutist state with a new commitment to enlightened political theory. By the early 1820s egalitarianism was a fundamentally entrenched political value in Oaxaca, and it retained its force in subsequent decades.

Oaxaca's first constitution stressed egalitarianism, and the constitutional congress that composed the document displayed egalitarian sympathies on many other occasions.[77] Most members of this congress were government bureaucrats, lawyers, and priests, and their commitment to egalitarianism was fervently ideological.[78] Although they may have been influenced directly or indirectly by the Enlightenment or the egalitarian ideals of the American or French Revolutions, the representatives did not cite these influences at all. Instead the legislators argued in the preamble to the constitution that their egalitarianism was based on Christianity, which in their words "taught the Greeks and the Romans that the Helots and the slaves were not beasts, but instead men and their own brothers."[79] The racial reference here was not casual. In the 1820s the members of the constitutional congress and other Oaxacan politicians showed repeated and explicit concern for the rights of the state's indigenous majority. In a controversial move, they freed "Indian citizens" from the obligation of constructing arches for the annual Corpus Christi feast in the city of Oaxaca and other parish seats. The bishop opposed this measure, insisting that the practice was necessary for a proper celebration of the feast. Eventually a compromise was reached under which a canopy paid for by the city council replaced the arches previously constructed by Indians.[80] The congress also criticized the military for forcing "the citizens previously called Indians" to fetch firewood or carry supplies for them.[81]

Nevertheless, politicians could not leave behind Oaxaca's legacy of racism. Their high ideals could neither eliminate their own prejudices nor overcome their anxieties about the indigenous population. In 1827, José Ignacio Morales, the governor of the state, criticized the "rusticity" of the rural population. He also claimed that Indians who accepted advances to work on the haciendas of the valleys later failed to report to work. Courts refused to punish this behavior due to the "august cloak of liberty." Morales asked the state legislature to obligate villages to "give the people that the estate owners and farmers request."[82] Two months later the state legislature passed a law regulating relations between agricultural workers and their employers. The law established penalties for laborers who accepted advances and refused to work. It also allowed estate owners to confine repeat offenders to prevent them from fleeing.[83] This law, unlike the governor's report, referred to its subjects as "workers" rather than "Indians," but all involved knew exactly to whom the law would apply. In another twist of the egalitarian ideal, in 1824 the state constitutional congress abolished the practice under which Indian villages had rights to a minimum amount of territory, claiming that by establishing a distinction between Indians and others it violated the idea that all were equal.[84]

Oaxaca also remained a patriarchal society, even though the king had been removed from his role as ultimate patriarch. The end of royal sovereignty made it imperative that government be both "paternal and representative," a task that was less difficult than one would suspect.[85] The question of women's suffrage never came up, most likely because women were seen as natural dependents whose will would follow that of their husbands.[86] The egalitarianism that permeated political discourse simply did not extend to women. Women were not addressed in the vast number of political proclamations and decrees produced after independence. The power of individual male heads of families remained intact, allowing them control they could not always exert on the public level. A humorous dialogue in an 1832 newspaper suggested that men who were frustrated by political events might take their anger out on their wives. The intent here was satirical, but it does suggest something about the ways men struggled for a pretense of control.[87] Sarah Chambers argues that in early republican Peru the new rights enjoyed by men were linked to increased control over women's behavior.[88]

Women could act politically, but typically they did so only as petitioners. Most often they petitioned on behalf of their husbands. Women whose Spanish husbands were expelled for political reasons argued that separating their families would lead to hardship for Oaxacan children.[89] Women asked that their imprisoned husbands be freed or treated better.[90] Sometimes the role of women was more public. Pious women organized to aid the sick in epidemics, or to assist in religious functions for prisoners in the state jail. In these cases male politicians sought to harness what they saw as the womanly qualities of piety and compassion to serve the interests of society. Women interested in these roles could of course mobilize this image to preserve or expand their foothold in public service. For instance, in 1829, María Josefa Ogazon de Varela, leader of the city's Women's Charity Committee, suggested that similar committees be established in the rest of the state or at least the major towns. Ogazon de Varela argued that women's humanity was unequalled, presumably by that of men. There is no evidence that the state government followed up on her idea.[91]

The roles of women in charity and religion were sanctioned or at least tolerated, but some evidence suggests that women sometimes took on unsanctioned public roles that made men uncomfortable. In early elections women accompanied men to the polls, forming part of the crowds that sought to influence who should be allowed to vote. This practice was common enough that an 1828 law prohibited it.[92] The participation of women on election day was seen as contributing to party conflict and disorder in general. Here we see the common notion that women were undisciplined and had the potential to make men disorderly. In 1849 a number of Oaxacan women sent the national congress a petition asking that Protestant denominations not be tolerated in Mexico. This petition was by far the largest collective intervention Oaxacan women made in early-nineteenth-century politics, and it came at a key moment of debate about how Mexico might have a future after its disastrous defeat by the United States. This feminine intervention in politics bypassed the local authorities, but it did not go unnoticed. Two months later a Oaxacan newspaper reprinted a satirical poem about the event. The poem, entitled "Womanly rebellion," suggested that women wanted to "govern the universe." Another republished piece suggested that women take into account the fact that religious tolerance, designed to increase immigration, would bring to Mexico "many good young men and there will be many weddings."[93] In this incident the behavior of a group of women reinforced the idea that they were especially pious, but they took a position in a contentious national debate. The reward for their effort was ridicule that played on other common beliefs about women.

Although women were sometimes called *ciudadana* (citizens), the title was less a political statement than a rarely used attempt to replace the older honorific *doña*.[94] Although the effort to educate Oaxaca's population was extended to women, this education was not intended to facilitate women's own political participation. Schools taught women feminine crafts like making artificial flowers and sewing along with religious catechism and reading.

Writing was taught only on demand.[95] The objective was to prepare women for their natural role, that of raising their male children to be good citizens. Although education to serve as "republican mothers" raised the political profile of women, they themselves were not expected to take any active role in politics.[96] As Sarah Chambers points out, even in times of war women were most often seen not as practical contributors but as symbols of what needed to be protected from the enemy. In 1847 Benito Juárez argued that men should fight to keep American soldiers from raping their wives and daughters.[97] Republican egalitarianism was for the most part a male affair.

🍃 Society and Economy in Republican Oaxaca

The new emphasis on equality could not erase the practical reality of corporatism. A variety of corporations continued to exist in the republican city, and undoubtedly they exercised both practical political influence and a subtle brake on the emergence of strictly individual identities.[98] The city's confraternities or cofradías continued to fulfill social and religious functions deep into the republican period. People still needed the things that cofradías provided, particularly the security of knowing that they would receive adequate funerals and that someone would pray for their souls after death.[99] Despite this fundamentally religious role, during at least one election cofradías also played a significant part in politics, as we will see later.

Guilds likewise continued to exist despite the best efforts of believers in the new economic orthodoxy of the free market. The government no longer granted the guilds economic rights. In 1841 the candlemakers' guild asked the city council to uphold its traditional schedule of candle sizes, weights, and prices. For the next four years its petition was batted around among several municipal authorities. Although the councilman entrusted with regulating guilds supported the request, the city attorney pointed out in 1844 that the guild's petition violated the Spanish liberal law of 1813 that declared that any object could be sold at the price that most benefited its owner. In January 1845 the city council approved this conclusion, denying the petition.[100] Nevertheless, the guilds retained social and political roles. In 1823 politicians solicited their views during a political crisis, and in 1849 a newspaper editor suggested that they march in the independence day parade.[101] Each guild still carried the statue of an angel in the funeral procession of Christ on Good Friday.[102] Corporate identity mattered in practical ways. In 1824 guilds prevented their members from being drafted into the army by testifying to their honest occupation. Guilds could protect their members from some government demands, but the government sometimes relied on corporate identity to enforce other demands. In 1844 the state government made masters responsible for the personal tax owed by their employees, and in 1847 authorities made the guilds of water carriers and masons responsible for fighting fires in the city.[103]

Even if authorities had been more favorable to the continued economic role of guilds, it is unlikely that the guilds could have protected much of the population from the economic problems that followed independence. Estimates of the city's population varied from 20,500 to 25,000, and there were 4,394 adult males in 1842. It is unlikely that the occupations for which guilds existed employed more than 1,500 workers.[104] More importantly, the principal industries were vulnerable to the international economic forces set in motion by the Industrial Revolution. This was particularly true of the production of cheap cotton textiles. Oaxacan farmers, whether wealthy landowners or indigenous peasants, found it difficult to compete with cotton grown by slaves in the United States, especially since U.S. plantations used cotton gins to process their product. Moreover, in the actual production of textiles both indigenous women in rural areas and plebeian men in the city were forced to compete with factory-woven cloth from Europe. The contest in both cases was a futile one. The state produced around 200,000 arrobas of cotton per year in the late colonial period, but by 1830 it produced only 55,000. There were five hundred working looms in the city in 1812 and thirty in 1827.[105] Although some politicians advocated protectionism, others instead suggested that the state modernize its textile industry by buying modern cotton gins and looms.[106]

The decline of Mexico's textile industry and the role of urban plebeians in politics did eventually bring protectionism to Mexico. In 1838 the government banned the importation of cotton cloth, and an unrelated French blockade made the action effective. The government also supported the establishment of modern spinning and weaving factories in Mexico. To appease handloom weavers like those of Oaxaca, only enough power looms were put in operation to use half of the machine-spun yarn.[107] This protectionism allowed the recovery of the city's textile industry. By 1842 there were 378 weavers working in the city. These men were probably producing their cloth with machine-spun yarn, since in 1843 the city imported almost 35,000 pounds of yarn from Puebla, site of many power spindles.[108] Thereafter, though, the effectiveness of protectionism declined rapidly. Contraband cloth was simply too inexpensive to keep out of the country, and as a result the weavers of Oaxaca found their livelihood slipping away. They bought less and less yarn from Puebla, and the brief textile boom faded away. By 1846 hardly a vestige remained, as the city's weavers imported only 571 pounds of yarn.[109]

The city's other great colonial export had been cochineal. Urban merchants had bought cochineal from indigenous peasants through the repartimiento or other arrangements, and then sold it on the lucrative European market, where the red dye was highly prized. Eventually this natural dye was replaced with chemical ones, but Oaxaca's cochineal trade suffered long before that. Guatemala became an important producer of cochineal, and it was able to offer the dye at prices that made it difficult for Oaxaca to compete. Oaxacan cochineal sales fell from 1,695,375 pesos in 1819 to 419,248 pesos in 1831, and despite a limited recovery later in the decade cochineal never regained its colonial glory.[110] Moreover, cochineal had never generated much employment in the city of Oaxaca. Indigenous peasants in outlying villages provided the labor that went into the trade, and the profits remained in the hands of a few merchants. In its limited impact on the urban labor market cochineal was a typical primary material in a colonial system.

Manuel Esparza has compared the occupations listed in the 1792 and 1842 censuses. The census of 1842 shows that the occupational structure of the city had not changed much from that recorded in 1792. Artisans and merchants were clearly the two largest groups, and, thanks to protectionism, textiles in 1842 again constituted the largest single sector of the economy. The two biggest changes were related. Priests and monks fell from 11.7 percent of the population in 1792 to 2.8 percent in 1842, while professionals rose from 4.5 percent to 7.9 percent. In essence, postindependence society allowed lettered men to make a living outside the church.[111] Of course incomes within occupational groups could vary drastically. According to 1847 data, blacksmiths could make 8.5 reales daily while a hat maker might make 2.5 and a weaver 2.25. Merchants usually made much more, but some made as little as the wealthier artisans.[112] Economic opportunities were very unevenly distributed. Although the wealthiest men perhaps dreamed of recovering the economic glories of the late colonial period, they were still far better off than the bulk of the population, an economic fact that seemed to clash with the new political ideal of republican egalitarianism. The least fortunate members of society were single women. Some worked in the cigar factory, but most were domestic servants or street vendors. The fate of the latter is summed up by the testimony of a doctor, Juan N. Bolaños, in 1847. Bolaños sought a free funeral for Teresa Jimenes, who he stated was "poor to such a degree, that her wealth consisted of four reales that she invested in making *atole* [a common corn beverage] to sell. She always lived in a miserable shanty at the foot of the Cerro de la Soledad . . . She did not leave any relatives except one daughter, as miserably poor as she."[113]

𝕱❧ Politics in the City, 1820 to 1828

Political culture is a dynamic product of historical trends and contingencies. Thus we can only understand how political culture changes by tracing the political history of an era. The narrative that follows focuses on the tactics and discourses of politics during a period when the city was dominated by the development of two virulently opposed parties. These parties arose directly from the introduction of new political means, particularly elections and the development of a political print culture. Although often elections and the introduction of mass media are seen as harbingers of democracy and pluralism, in Oaxaca the panorama is much less positive. The parties lived in great suspicion and fear of one another, and as a result elections became less and less important in determining who would actually govern. Both parties soon became adept at riding the coattails of a national politics where power was distributed through a succession of coups and civil wars. Elections and mass media did not bring democracy to urban Oaxaca.

Although eventually Oaxaca's two parties became linked to groups on the national level, they actually originated before any national political group. Observers of the local political scene agreed that the parties began in the early 1820s, when the Spanish Constitution of 1812 was put into effect in Mexico for the second time. They also agreed that the political parties grew from concerns over membership in the city council. Before 1808 the city council had not been a source of political power in the region. Instead it was a vehicle for social prestige. The wealthiest families did not bother to buy offices on the city council because they already had sufficient social capital. Families that were slightly less well off used city council office to demonstrate their growing prestige. When the city council was made subject to elections in 1814, two of those elected were from racial groups previously excluded from Oaxaca's high society. Angel Calvo was a mestizo artisan, and Casmiro Cruz Hernández was an Indian landlord who owned over a hundred houses in the city.[114] For the city's elite this election was a distressing warning about the potential social costs of virtually universal male suffrage. When Fernando VII abrogated the constitution later that year the wealthiest merchant families of the city began to take an interest in city government, and they bought the offices that had fallen vacant due to emigration. Since these offices brought little political power or economic opportunity, it seems that the elite families were mostly concerned with preventing any decline in their social prestige. These families held the vast majority of city council posts until 1820.[115]

In 1820 the Spanish constitution was again put into practice. First the 1814 city council was called back, and the electors from 1814 filled seats that had been vacated by emigration. In July 1820 the city held an election for a new city council. Race immediately came to the fore. The Spanish constitution granted citizenship to all men born in Spanish possessions unless they had African blood. Apparently working to avoid the distressing result seen in 1814, the electoral authorities used this provision to prevent many relatively humble Oaxacans from voting. The electoral authorities seem to have used simple appearance as a guide to ancestry, and they excluded those with dark skin. Observing this process, many people who approached the polls did not even try to cast their ballots. Wealthy Creole and Spanish merchants again dominated the resulting city council.[116] Here we can see how the city's elite worked to maintain the two values that had defined their group in the colonial period: their Spanish identity and their control of the prestige of officeholding. However, this open use of racial exclusion would haunt them for the next decades.

When the royalist Agustín de Iturbide tried to interest the insurgent Vicente Guerrero in his plan to make Mexico independent, the latter insisted on abolishing racial limitations on citizenship. Iturbide acquiesced, and the Plan de Iguala extended citizenship to all the inhabitants of Mexico. In the December 1821 city council elections all men over eighteen were allowed to vote, and the city's elite lost the tool that had allowed them to keep their racial inferiors off the council.[117] The newly enlarged electorate had immediate effect. Four councilmen who were not Creoles or Spaniards were elected. These men also seem to have been relatively poor, since they do not show up in any notary records of the period.[118]

As we saw in chapter 1, urban plebeians and many other Oaxacans who were not of pure Spanish blood had long ceased to believe that race should govern their social relations, and thus they were quite ready to accept the nominal egalitarianism of nineteenth-century liberal constitutionalism.[119] However, this was not the case for the city's elite. For the December 1822 city council election the city's wealthy organized what was essentially a political party, calling themselves *aceites* or "oils" and their opponents *vinagres* or "vinegars" to emphasize the idea that they would always come out on top, as oil will in any mixture with vinegar. Although *vinagre* was intended to be a pejorative term, those to whom it was applied soon proudly appropriated it for their own uses. The aceites argued that the ceremonial garb expected of councilmen was too costly for people of humble extraction, a striking echo of the 1810 arguments about the uniforms of the various militia forces of the city. In effect the aceites, whose real concern seems to have been as much the race of the council members as their class, fell back on a discourse of class because the new racial egalitarianism of the era permitted them nothing else. The vinagres responded that in fact the Indians and mestizos elected to the council had dressed themselves as well as any member.[120] Both groups mobilized for the election. Notably, their interest throughout focused on municipal elections. Neither group showed any interest in elections for the provincial deputation, where their votes would be counted along with those of rural areas of the province. The provincial deputation as a result came to be dominated by rural priests, government administrators, landowners, and small merchants.[121]

In the December 1822 council elections each group campaigned for its own slate of electors. Despite some success in parochial elections, the vinagres received a lesson in the importance of also organizing in the secondary elections. The electors met beforehand to try to reach consensus on a slate of councilmen. They failed, and subsequently the aceite electors met separately and lined up their own slate. This act was crucial, because as the positions were filled one by one, the weight of the aceite electors voting in unison was enough to allow them to win every single post on the council. The vinagres immediately protested to the governor, José María Murguía y Galardi. When he arrived home from the secondary election, he was met by a group so large that it filled his house and spilled into the street outside. Asked to overturn the election, Murguía y Galardi responded that he could consider only written petitions. Five days later he was again surprised at his house by a crowd that overflowed into the street. They put into his hands a petition signed by 163 men and on the behalf of 200 who could not write their names. The city's military commander had limited the number by preventing the militia under his command from signing the document, but even so this was an impressive feat of political organizing. The signatures were apparently collected by the informal leaders of the city's barrios, and men visited the shops of many artisans seeking support. Although eight electors signed, the vast bulk of the petitioners were clearly relatively poor. Few of them, for instance, were wealthy enough to own property or even rent entire houses. The petition claimed that the meeting of the aceite electors before the actual election amounted to a conspiracy. The vinagres also claimed that several of the men elected were not "addicted to Independence," a quality that the decree convoking the election had stated was essential for officeholders. The vinagres believed that the election had been tainted by the maneuvering of a few "noble families" who had worked to prevent the election of honorable artisans, thus "demonstrating themselves too discontented with the system that judged people by virtue and merit, and not by money and prestige."[122] They also directly associated this group with opposition to independence and allegiance to Spain, pointing out "among them are some that splutter while speaking in order to show a Spanish style as if this were a virtue."[123] In other words, some aceites even affected exaggerated Spanish accents. Here the vinagres' concern with class became tied to the ethnic origins of their opponents and whether they represented a threat to Mexican independence. Although the petition was an entirely legal maneuver, rumors also surfaced that on the day the new authorities were sworn into office the plebeians and the military garrison would rise up, dragging the alcaldes through the streets until they were dead. Those discussing the conspiracy also highlighted the potential threat the aceites posed to Mexican independence.[124]

Governor Murguía y Galardi asked the national government for advice on how to proceed, and the language he used in his report suggests that he had considerable sympathy for the vinagres. Other officials were less positive. Bishop Manuel Pérez Suárez, who was rumored to be one of the founders of the aceites, worked with military commander Celso de Yruela against three militia officers who they accused of whipping up the fervor of plebeians and conspiring to impose republicanism. They arranged to have military authorities call the officers to Mexico City.[125] In the end authorities upheld the aceite victory.

Soon after the contentious election Emperor Iturbide was driven from office, and politicians in several provinces worked to make their regions more independent of Mexico City. In Oaxaca both aceites and vinagres wanted more autonomy from the center, but they wanted it for different reasons. Aceites, who included the wealthiest merchants of the province, saw a strong state government as an instrument they could use to regain past economic glories. They could promote exports and form policies that would help them reactivate the economy, recovering the kind of autonomy they had enjoyed before the Bourbon reforms. An anonymous pamphlet criticized Oaxaca's subordination to Mexico City and then laid out a series of policies designed to make Indians more economically active. The author accused Indians of literally burying their money and refusing even to buy clothes to dress decently.[126]

The vinagres also espoused federalism, but for them independence from Mexico City was linked to the larger issue of who would govern Oaxacan society. Working with Antonio de León, the popular military politician who in 1821 had led Oaxacan support for Mexican independence, the vinagres struck on 1 June 1823. Large groups of plebeians gathered in the center of the city and demanded that Oaxaca separate itself from Mexico. León, military commander of the city, called the city council together. The city council sounded out the opinion of the military, the guilds, the chamber of commerce, and the city's clergy. The first three groups were all enthusiastic in their support for a sovereign state. Bishop Pérez Suárez and his subordinates were undecided. They claimed that the rest of the province should be consulted, and noted that even in the city the crowds demanding the province's independence represented "only one part of the People of Oaxaca, which everyone knows did not represent a majority." Carlos María de Bustamante, Oaxaca's conservative representative in the national congress, claimed that the demonstration had been arranged by only a hundred agitators, led by the vinagre Ignacio María Ordoño.[127] These qualms did not slow down events. Oaxaca's politicians declared the province independent from Mexico, and they prepared to defend that independence with arms if necessary. A military clash was avoided only when the national government gave in and arranged for the election of a new congress, one likely to support the federalist pretensions of the provinces.[128] Notably, although the role of the chamber of congress suggests aceite support for federalism, Ignacio María Ordoño, one of the vinagre organizers, argued later that the movement "made the State sovereign, made the rich equal to the poor, and gave all inhabitants their rights."[129] For vinagres like Ordoño, federalism was not only about relations between the provinces and the national capital; it was about social relations within Oaxaca.

After further political maneuvering, Mexico adopted a new federalist constitution. Oaxaca elected a constituent congress, composed for the most part of government functionaries from outlying districts, clergymen, and lawyers. The few merchants in the congress tended to be from outside the city.[130] The election for this congress was a relatively quiet affair, and there is no evidence of campaigning by either party. Apparently the congress was balanced between members sympathetic to both parties. The parties' relative lack of interest in the state congress did not last, as the new state constitution made it a very powerful institution. Soon elections for the state congress became the principal battlegrounds of partisan politics. The incumbent party always had great advantages in these electoral contests. For reasons I will explore in the next chapter, Oaxaca's indigenous majority tended to choose parish priests and state government functionaries as electors. These men were very vulnerable to pressure from the state governor, who controlled the livelihood and future prospects of government functionaries. Thus the state governor had important influence over the actual composition of each legislature.

In 1826 the state held elections for a new state legislature, and both parties worked hard to win. Apparently the aceites decided that the best way to oppose the power the vinagres had demonstrated in urban elections was to accuse the vinagres of anticlericalism and heresy. According to vinagre accounts, the aceites organized through the city's cofradías, leading cofradía processions through the streets and preaching to cofradía members about the dangers posed by Masonic organizations. The implication here is that the vinagres had established contacts with the York rite masons who were espousing similar political views in Mexico City. Some aceites also mobilized a crowd to attack the house of Manuel Santaella, a prominent vinagre merchant and state senator whose house was used for electoral meetings. In elections, the first voters to arrive chose the electoral officials who determined whether a given individual could vote. On the day of the election a large crowd of aceite voters arrived early and chose the electoral officials. They also threatened vinagre voters and officials, calling them heretics. Intimidated vinagre voters left without casting ballots.[131] Of course, aceite accounts of the same election paint a different picture. The aceites claimed the election was orderly and spontaneous, and they denied using religious rhetoric against the vinagres.[132] However, one aceite pamphlet published before the election suggests the importance of electing men who would respect Oaxaca's religion. The publication also criticizes those who believed that only the poor or artisans should be elected.[133] Leaving aside the partisan accounts, clearly the aceites dominated the congress elected in 1826, and they used their power against their enemies, proscribing vinagre politicians Ignacio Ordoño and José Mariano Toro.[134]

The struggle between aceites and vinagres continued, and the next major act in this drama was intertwined with local and national efforts to expel Spaniards from Mexico. For decades the principal families of the city of Oaxaca had defined themselves by stressing their Spanish ancestry and contrasting it with the mixed racial heritage of many urban middle- and lower-class people as well as the indigenous peasantry of the surrounding region. Not surprisingly, the urban poor were not particularly sympathetic to the Spaniards who continued to live in the city. We saw in the previous chapter how Morelos persecuted the Spaniards with the aid of at least part of the urban populace. The evidence suggests that some artisans retained their prejudice against the Spaniards after the royalists retook the city.[135]

The Plan de Iguala under which Mexico obtained its independence guaranteed the rights of those Spaniards who chose to remain in Mexico. Nevertheless, many Oaxacans remained fiercely suspicious of Spaniards, and none was more so than Antonio de León, the military officer whose activities were crucial in both promoting the Plan de Iguala and making Oaxaca an independent state. At a local theater in January 1824 some of his troops, accompanied by civilians who were probably vinagres, shouted death to the gachupines and put up a banner threatening the Spaniards. The state legislature responded by passing a law reaffirming the right of Spaniards to remain in Mexico and threatening to punish those who demonstrated against them. On the eve of the April ceremony in which the city swore allegiance to the Constitutive Act rumors surfaced that León, his troops, and part of the "pueblo" would use the occasion to demand that all Spaniards be expelled from the state. The ceremony proceeded in calm, but in June León struck the long-awaited blow. He arrested several Spaniards he accused of conspiring against Mexico's independence and demanded that the state legislature expel all Spaniards from the state. Moreover, he commandeered the state's own printing press to publicize his demands. León failed to intimidate the congress into compliance. His troops retired to his home territory in the Mixteca, where they murdered a Spanish employee of the state government. The men directly responsible were executed, and León himself was removed to Mexico City for a military trial that kept him out of circulation for several years.[136]

Throughout Mexico anti-Spanish feelings were rooted in the notion that Spaniards were monopolists whose business practices exploited Mexicans. Spaniards became scapegoats for a postindependence economy in which the economic opportunities of many Mexicans were limited.[137] In Oaxaca this strain of thought was less direct. Many Spanish residents were merchants, and occasionally vinagres made references to pernicious business activities.[138] However in Oaxaca the Spaniards were not accused of monopolizing commerce. Instead vinagre propaganda linked them to the aceites, who in turn were accused of constituting an oligarchy.

Anti-Spanish prejudice in Oaxaca was tied much more closely to the idea that the state's Spaniards were conspiring to overthrow Mexico's government and facilitate a Spanish reconquest of Mexico. Sometimes even relatively conservative politicians fomented these rumors. In 1822 Carlos María de Bustamante suggested that the Spanish government would try to recover Mexico "by secret and dangerous means."[139] This fear was fanned in Oaxaca by what appear to have been conspiracies to do exactly that. An 1822 pamphlet breathlessly describes a thwarted rebellion by Spanish soldiers with aid from a high cleric and "all the merchants."[140] In 1826 a conspiracy was discovered on the Pacific coast. According to testimony, its leaders hoped to raise troops there to collaborate with a Spanish expedition launched from Havana.[141] Although it is impossible to determine whether these conspiracies were serious threats, their discovery stoked anti-Spanish prejudice. For some vinagres, confronting the city's Spaniards was another opportunity for them to prove their loyalty to the community against an external threat. The importance of this loyalty, and the role of subalterns in defending the community, had been pressed on them repeatedly since the 1790s. Calls for financial support against Spain's enemies in the late colonial period had given way to the physical mobilization of subalterns after 1808, but the basic pattern was similar. Those seeking subaltern support had repeatedly emphasized the danger of conspiracies. In the past, colonial officials had publicized threatening conspiracies, but now that role was filled by vinagre politicians and pamphleteers.

The anti-Spanish movement came to a head in 1827. In November Colonel Santiago García issued a call to expel the Spaniards from Mexico. Like León before him, García commandeered the state government's press to print copies of his initiative. He claimed that the Spanish were conspiring against Mexican independence. According to this plan, all unmarried Spaniards and all those who had entered the country since independence without government permission would be expelled. Married Spaniards and widowers would be allowed to stay as long as they were not "marked by public opinion as notoriously disloyal to the cause of the Patria." Although at first glance the initiative might seem a purely military affair, there is a great deal of evidence that civilian vinagres took an important part in this movement. Ignacio María Ordoño signed the plan, and crowds of civilians petitioned officials to back the plan.[142] The vinagres accused state governor Ignacio Morales of protecting the Spaniards, and he fled. The state legislature resisted adopting García's plan and instead passed a weaker expulsion law that contained more exceptions. Laws were typically published in a procession accompanied by a military escort. García refused to provide an escort for the law passed by the legislature. Instead he sent a group of troops in dress uniform who published his own plan "with the noise of the church bells, fireworks, and much attendance by the People who had come together in the square." García also refused to let the government press print the legislature's decree. In the weeks that followed Santiago García and the vinagres pressured authorities to issue a more severe expulsion. Vinagre José Mariano Toro led large groups of civilians to petition the city council and state legislature. On one occasion the acting state governor reported that more than 1,500 men attended a city council session.[143] In December tensions eased when the national government passed an expulsion law. Santiago García accepted an amnesty for his men and was transferred out of state.

The congress, dominated by the aceites, refused to persecute the Spaniards. It also tried to prevent anti-Spanish propaganda and similar propaganda aimed at English merchants from circulating in the state. This defense of foreigners, however, ran counter to the growing sense of many urban Oaxacans that the Spaniards were oligarchs who stood between them and prosperity. It also contradicted their impression that the Spaniards were a threat to the independence of the new nation. The actions the legislature took to protect the Spaniards may have been motivated by the close familial and cultural ties between the principal families of the city and the Spaniards, by a principled stand against ethnic persecution, or perhaps by both. However, to many urban Oaxacans the aceites' defense of the Spaniards suggested that they themselves might welcome a Spanish reconquest of Mexico.[144]

ꙮ Party Identity and Ideology in Early Republican Oaxaca

Despite their strange names, by the beginning of 1828 the aceite and vinagre parties had each shown considerable mobilizational capacity. The aceites had gained control of the state legislature and governorship, and they had obtained large numbers of votes in the 1826 election. The vinagres had been less successful at electoral organizing, but they had shown the ability to put hundreds and perhaps thousands of people into the street for political demonstrations. Who did these political parties represent, and how did they mobilize their constituencies? These questions cannot be answered solely by analyzing the socioeconomic backgrounds of the leaders. The political leaders of both parties tended to include priests, professionals, government employees, and a few merchants. These socioeconomic groups dominated

Oaxacan officeholding in the period directly after independence.[145] However, this similarity should not lead us to assume that the two parties represented the same interest groups. Priests, professionals, government employees, and merchants were the literate, articulate men who could give voice to different political aspirations. Individuals in these broad categories had very different personal histories and political beliefs. For this reason it makes sense to outline the political careers of a few prominent vinagres and aceites.

Probably the most important vinagre was Angel Alvarez. Born in 1792, Alvarez earned a bachelor's degree and served in the colonial militia before losing his sight in 1812. Blindness did not prevent Alvarez from having a unique political career. In 1817 he was accused of conspiring to aid the insurgents, and his political profile grew rapidly after the reintroduction of the Spanish constitution in 1820. Angel Alvarez immediately demonstrated a fierce egalitarianism. He began working for voting rights for men with African ancestry, the only group denied citizenship by the Spanish constitution. In the year before Iguala made the issue moot Alvarez wrote two pamphlets on this topic, pointing out that the constitution stressed virtue rather than birth everywhere except where it arbitrarily excluded a large portion of the population from voting.[146] Not surprisingly Alvarez was one of the first vinagres. He helped organize the protest against the December 1822 municipal elections, and in response the opposition used his status as a retired military officer to temporarily remove Alvarez from the state. Bishop Manuel Pérez Suárez called him "proud, unruly, and revolutionary," while Governor José María Murguía y Galardi said Alvarez was "a popular young man who has influence over the plebeians, because they ask him questions in order to understand the measures of the government and the state of our independence."[147]

Alvarez was a proud and confrontational man, famous for public arguments with the aceites. Alvarez's prominence and refusal to back down from a fight made him a target on numerous occasions. When Vicente Prieto spoke up against a candidate Alvarez favored in the 1823 congressional elections, Alvarez insulted him, in Prieto's words, "without considering the great distance between his rank and mine." Prieto threatened to defend his honor physically if the authorities did not imprison Alvarez. During the 1830 election campaign Alvarez was threatened with clubs. After the aceites regained control of the legislature Alvarez continued to attend sessions as a spectator, leading one aceite legislator to suggest that someone break his legs. In 1839 thugs destroyed his printing press. Several times during his career aceite officials refused to let Alvarez serve as a secondary elector, citing the rule that secondary electors must be able to read, something the blind Alvarez could no longer do.[148] The vinagres, on the other hand, never missed an opportunity to elect Alvarez to office. He served repeatedly as secondary elector, city councilman, and state congressman.[149] Alvarez survived until at least 1849. Throughout his political career Alvarez emphasized the core political values of the vinagres. He stressed federalism, the threat Spaniards posed to independence, and the injustice of the continued predominance of "oligarchs."[150] However, his ideas about how these values might be put into practice shifted over time. The staunch electoral warrior continued to work in elections throughout his life, but by the 1830s he also had an appreciation of the importance of military force in deciding political issues. When a new military commander sympathetic to the vinagres arrived in 1833 Alvarez greeted him with a poem, and Alvarez wrote another poem for Antonio de León's birthday in 1843.[151]

Ignacio María Ordoño was the only early vinagre whose prominence rivaled that of Alvarez. Ordoño was also born around 1792. He became a priest, but soon after finishing his studies Ordoño turned to politics. As we saw in chapter 4, in 1811 he was arrested for involvement in a proinsurgent conspiracy. Ordoño claimed that he was preparing to denounce the conspirators, and he later informed against fellow prisoners in the royal jail. Unable to get his sentence reduced, he instead joined the insurgents when they took Oaxaca in 1812. Working with the insurgents, he led plebeians who searched the houses of Spaniards for money and valuables, and he became known for scandalous behavior.[152] In 1823 Ordoño was one of the principal leaders of the crowds who lobbied for Oaxacan independence from Mexico City, and he was elected to the first state congress. His political activities soon brought him unwanted attention from the aceites. In 1824 Ordoño's enemies forced him to leave the state. In 1826 he returned, but the aceites continued to harass him, following him in the streets, publicly accusing him of heresy, and shouting, "Death to Ordoño." The aceites also ordered the prior of the convent where Ordoño lived to prevent him from holding political meetings there. After the aceites won the 1826 election they again exiled Ordoño from the state. When he returned in 1828 the aceites continued their harassment in print.[153] The criticism the aceites heaped on Ordoño did not prevent the vinagres from electing him to office. In 1829 he became a state senator, and in 1833 he became a senator in the national congress. He was also chosen as an elector various times.[154] In his writings Ordoño, like Alvarez, emphasized federalism and warned of threats to Mexico's independence.[155]

Alvarez and Ordoño were men that the city's elite disdained as lowly and disreputable. Other vinagre leaders were less easy to dismiss. The most socially prominent vinagre was Ramón Ramírez de Aguilar, member of a distinguished family. Born in 1792, Ramírez de Aguilar inherited his family's lands and also earned money as a merchant. He was an elected city councilman in the early 1820s and then served as a representative in the first state congress. In 1827 he was vice governor of the state when Santiago García's rebellion temporarily drove the governor out. Acting as interim governor, Ramírez de Aguilar negotiated with García. Here Ramírez de Aguilar's sympathies became clear. He agreed with García about the threat posed by the Spaniards and repeatedly emphasized the popular support for their expulsion. From then on Ramírez de Aguilar was firmly associated with the vinagres, and in the 1830 election the aceites even accused him of manipulating the ballot count. He was a vinagre candidate for elector in 1830 and 1833, a city councilman in 1829, and acting governor when the vinagres controlled state offices in 1829–30 and 1833–34.[156] Ramírez de Aguilar never enjoyed Alvarez's or Ordoño's popularity with plebeians, and he never wrote much in the periodical or pamphlet press, but he became the respectable face of the vinagres. Notably, other members of his family were identified with the aceites. The difference seems to have been that he sincerely believed that the Spaniards threatened independence and that a more egalitarian politics would be more just and stable.

José María Pando, born around 1798, was another vinagre from a prominent Oaxacan family. Pando, a sometime merchant, owned a small sugar hacienda, but he was best known as a politician and civil servant. He served in the federal congress in 1821–22 and 1825–26, was a city councilman in 1824 and a state congressman in 1825. By 1828 he was an important figure in the vinagre party, and during the tragic election of 1828, when an electoral dispute led to violence, he was one of two leaders who led a delegation to seek the intervention of the state governor. Even this incident shows Pando's family connections, since the governor, Joaquín Guerrero, was his uncle. In 1829, however, Pando's political career took a drastic turn. He was appointed district administrator of Villa Alta, and he served in that post throughout the 1830s. During much of his term in Villa Alta the aceites ran the state government, but Pando apparently had little objection to this and even drew official praise from aceite governor José López de Ortigosa.

Pando was an energetic official who visited all 112 villages of his district and compiled a statistical abstract that was later published in the state's official newspaper. In the early 1840s Pando returned to the city of Oaxaca and served on the state's supreme council and as governor of the central district. In 1842 he was elected to the national congress. Pando died in May 1843 at the age of 45.[157] Pando's cooperation with the aceites later in his life does not mean his earlier radicalism was feigned. His testimony about the election of 1828 was impassioned in its defense of the vinagres. Pando also was convinced that Spanish residents of Mexico were a threat to independence. In 1829 he denounced the suspicious behavior of the Spaniard Francisco Arenas, arguing that Mexico's internal enemies "are conspiring to ruin the Patria to facilitate the triumph of the invaders."[158] His career apparently follows the pattern Michael Costeloe has outlined for "hombres de bien," who were attracted to the ideal of democratic, representative government in the 1820s but later became convinced that too much democracy had brought political instability.[159]

The aceites were more tightly knit than the vinagres. Many of the most prominent aceite politicians and civil servants were related to each other, and they used their family connections to support their political ambitions.[160] In the late 1820s one of the most important aceites was Manuel María Fagoaga. Although his brother, the priest Ignacio Fagoaga, was a vinagre in the late 1820s, most members of the Fagoaga family were aceites.[161] Manuel María Fagoaga, son of a prominent Oaxacan family, was a relatively wealthy landowner who served the royalist and later republican governments as a tax official. In 1822–23 Fagoaga was accused of agitating for the vinagres, but soon his political sympathies clearly lay in the other direction. Fagoaga was a state senator in 1824–26 and a national congressman in 1843. However, he was best known for his activities as administrator of central Oaxaca in 1828, when he was accused of rigging the election to favor the aceites and then ordering troops to fire on protesters. The vinagres hated him for this, and forced him to leave the state the next time they held power. Later Fagoaga served as administrator of central Oaxaca on other occasions under aceite governments.[162]

Juan José Quiñones was another aceite who many vinagres hated. He was likewise accused of complicity in the 1828 massacre. When the vinagres took power in 1829 they exiled Quiñones, and in 1830 a vinagre newspaper published a biting satire in which two artisans composed verses accusing him of emptying the people's pockets, poisoning their hearts, persecuting vinagres, and protecting thieves. Later Quiñones served as elector at various times for the aceites, as a justice on the state supreme court, and as a national congressman. When Quiñones died in 1849 a federalist newspaper offered a sarcastic prayer asking pardon for his sins.[163]

Antonio Valdés y Moya was born around 1808. He was still a very young man when the aceites put him in charge of the state government press in the late 1820s. This press published official decrees as well as an aceite newspaper and pamphlets attacking the vinagres in the heated election campaign of 1828. During this campaign the vinagres controlled the municipal government, and they arrested Valdés y Moya for abusing his wife. He was released before the election, but later that year the vinagres took power and Valdés y Moya fled in fear of his life. The vinagres took over the press while Valdés y Moya lived in exile in another state. By 1832 he was back in Oaxaca and served as an aceite candidate for elector in that year's elections. He also took charge of the government press again, but in 1833 Valdés y Moya was arrested for attempted homicide after he threatened a man during an argument. This arrest may also have had political motives, as at that moment the vinagres again controlled the municipal government. Apparently he was sentenced to three years prison but never entered jail, probably because the aceites took over the state government immediately thereafter. Valdés y Moya continued to live in Oaxaca and work as a printer and newspaper publisher until at least 1849. Although he toned down his political activities after his unpleasant experiences of the late 1820s and early 1830s, in his later years he was an ally of the increasingly conservative Antonio de León.[164]

José López de Ortigosa was perhaps the most powerful aceite. Member of a very prominent Oaxaca family, he led a tight family network that sometimes filled many of the most important posts of state government. In the late 1820s he served as a representative in the national congress, but soon he returned to more local politics, becoming vice governor in 1828. López de Ortigosa served as governor or interim governor in 1830–33, 1834–36, 1837–38, 1839–41, and 1846. He also was elected to the national congress in 1842 and the state congress in 1847.[165] López de Ortigosa was a relatively moderate aceite who believed that only order would allow Oaxaca to progress. López de Ortigosa was willing to collaborate with talented men of radical antecedents, including Pando and even Benito Juárez. Like many urban politicians, he disdained Oaxaca's indigenous majority, whose customs he called "rancid" and whose lands he wanted to privatize.[166]

Aceite and vinagre politicians shared some basic characteristics. Generally they were educated professionals. Certainly Angel Alvarez and Ignacio Ordoño were not as wealthy as Ramón Ramírez de Aguilar and José López de Ortigosa, but in a purely occupational analysis they held similar positions in Oaxacan society. None of them were indigenous peasants, urban artisans, or plebeians. However, clearly both the aceites and vinagres mobilized relatively poor men from the city to support their political positions. An analysis of the fierce political rivalries of urban Oaxaca requires us to consider the relationship between the leaders of political parties and their followers. The most tempting hypothesis is that of patronage, particularly because analyses of twentieth-century Mexican politics attribute so much power to it.[167] As mentioned above, François-Xavier Guerra has recently focused attention on this aspect of politics in the early nineteenth century.[168] Certainly family ties and clientalism determined appointments to government posts, but those posts were available only to the same literate and educated minority that dominated party leadership. It is difficult to imagine what benefits these politicians could have offered the urban poor. Wealthy Oaxacans did not employ poor Oaxacans beyond their own domestic servants, who constituted less than 8 percent of the city's adult males in 1842.[169] Most Oaxacans rented living space, but thanks to an 1824 census we know who owned all of it. None of the most prominent politicians of the period appear as urban landlords. The wealthiest landlord in the city was Casmiro Cruz Hernández, whose 1814 election to the city council was cited as one spark contributing to the formation of the aceite party, but after 1814 Hernández stayed out of politics. The second wealthiest was José María Gris, who also was a member of the 1814 city council and held council office again in 1817, 1820, and 1822 before leaving politics.[170] Although it remains possible that political parties offered their supporters access to housing, this seems very unlikely, and neither party ever denounced its rival on these grounds.

The role of corporatism presents another possibility. Guilds may have been important in political organizing. The city council consulted them during the 1823 federalist movement, and later the city council consulted the guilds on the advisability of protectionism.[171] Moreover, the vinagres often referred to the importance of honorable artisans and their problems. However, there is no evidence that guilds took any role in electoral organizing. Cofradías were more widespread than guilds in early-nineteenth-century Oaxaca, and we know they played some political role. In 1826 the aceites apparently used cofradías as organizational vehicles during their electoral campaign. Yet even then the sources do not stress corporate identity but rather the use of cofradía meetings and processions to present ideological arguments about the threat the vinagres posed to Oaxacan Catholicism.[172] In this way they were not terribly different from the clubs the vinagres organized for the 1828 election, which we will examine in more detail below.[173]

Party allegiances undoubtedly also intersected with networks of friends and relatives among the city's poor. Evidence of this intersection is hard to come by. We know, for instance, that the informal leaders of several of the city's barrios collected the signatures for the vinagres' 1822 electoral protest. In 1830 Rito García Pensamiento, on trial for carrying an illegal weapon, stated that he had suffered due to the "party system, because I am from the Barrio of Coyula, and they hate us for this."[174] The political could be very personal indeed. Timoteo Castañeda, a vinagre involved in fighting in the city in 1828, was walking with his wife when Manuel Reyes publicly professed his love for her. After Castañeda tried to warn Reyes off, Reyes proclaimed his aceite allegiance and attacked. Castañeda fought back and killed Reyes.[175] In 1830 a drunken Rafael Jimenez shouted his allegiance to Vicente Guerrero, claiming that since his son had died fighting for Guerrero, he would also fight for Guerrero, in effect taking a political stance in favor of the vinagres.[176] The political opinions of even common people seem to have been well known. Manuel Pinelo, a policeman, accused a twenty-year-old leatherworker, José Bolaños, of participating in a violent vinagre demonstration in 1838. After Bolaños denied the charge, Pinelo insisted he had seen him there and told Bolaños "besides which you can not deny that you are of that opinion."[177]

Although cofradías, clubs, and personal networks helped political parties organize groups of voters or a presence in the streets, in urban Oaxaca party allegiance was most likely inspired by the political discourses elaborated by each party. Each party developed an ideology that tapped into some of the core values of Oaxacan society. The vinagres aligned themselves with relatively novel values. In 1824 egalitarianism, federalism, and nationalism may have been new touchstones of political identity, but they were very firm touchstones. The concepts were enshrined by the laws and constitutions developed in the period of relative consensus immediately after the fall of Iturbide. Both aceites and vinagres agreed on these basic values. However, by the early 1830s the vinagres had succeeded in appropriating these ideals as the basis of their partisan identity. They were able to do this because, unlike the aceites, the vinagres argued that egalitarianism, federalism, and nationalism were threatened by powerful political forces. The aceites also tapped values important to all Oaxacans, but the key allegiance they singled out was a much older one. The aceites argued that Catholicism was under attack, and they called on Oaxacans to defend it by turning against the vinagres.

The vinagres stressed their commitment to true egalitarianism in opposition to what they saw as aceite hypocrisy on the issue. Certainly the aceites had supported the egalitarian principles of the state constitution, but in the 1822 city council election they had openly organized to keep people of the lower classes and mixed race off the council, and the vinagres never let them forget it. In 1826 the vinagre newspaper *Sociedad de Amigos del País* criticized a councilman for arresting a musician who had refused to take off his hat when the councilman passed on patrol. The paper alluded to the existence of local families who preserved genealogical trees to show that they were descendants of Mexico's conquerors.[178] From the 1820s to the 1840s, the vinagres repeatedly referred to the aceites as "oligarchs" and "aristocrats," and they constantly argued that, since all Mexicans were equal, talent and virtue should be the only criteria for selecting officials.[179] Although the vinagre party was basically urban, its leaders understood that the city was surrounded by dozens of Indian villages that could be important in deciding elections even in the central district of the state. Thus they tried to reach out to indigenous villagers. The vinagre newspaper published in 1832–33 was called *El Zapoteco*, and its pages featured a continuing dialogue between an Indian from a neighboring village and a wise vinagre from the city. In October 1832 the newspaper published a letter in Zapotec denouncing the aceite government for forcing villagers to work on the roads. Literacy in Zapotec was probably extremely rare by the 1830s, but the authors were probably trying to make a point about their openness to the problems of rural Indians. Later the newspaper printed a pro-vinagre speech supposedly given by an indigenous villager in a nearby village.[180] Despite these efforts, secondary electors chosen by the indigenous voters of outlying districts tended to favor whichever party held the governorship of the state, and evidence from Villa Alta suggests that indigenous peasants there were basically indifferent to the party politics that dominated the city. It is possible that partisan politics were much more important in the valley villages close to Oaxaca or in other districts of the state, but that question can be answered only by further investigation.

The vinagres argued constantly that sinister external and internal forces threatened Mexican independence. In the 1820s the external threat was quite obvious. Spain had refused to recognize Mexico's independence and many Spaniards still dreamed of recapturing the colony. In 1829 the Spanish government sponsored a military force that invaded Mexico only to be forced into an ignominious surrender. For years thereafter the vina-gres warned of a continued threat from Spain, and during Mexico's 1838 clash with France they recycled the same rhetoric to use against a new enemy. Throughout the period, however, the vinagres also linked the exter-nal threat to an internal threat. Years of warnings and denunciations fol-lowed the discovery of pro-Spanish conspiracies in the early 1820s. Begin-ning in 1824 the vinagres constantly argued that the Spanish residents of Oaxaca were a threat to Mexican independence. In 1829 a city council committee opined that resident Spaniards could "never be attached to our Independence and system of government."[181] A vinagre poem from 1830 called Spaniards miserable cowards who did not deserve to be born.[182] The vinagres' denunciations of the threat to Mexican independence were crucial to their partisan identity, and they often referred to themselves as the party of the patriots.[183] An 1828 vinagre pamphlet called the aceites "unnatural-ized Americans" and "Vile Americans . . . sold out to the enemy."[184] In 1832 the vinagres accused President Anastasio Bustamante of being an instru-ment of the Spaniards.[185] Yet as we saw in the protest against the 1822 municipal election, anti-Spanish feelings also incorporated an element of class conflict. The city's elite had long stressed its identity as a Spanish group surrounded by nonwhite colonial subjects, and now that effort to draw stark boundaries connected them to a foreign enemy. The tendency to tie domestic political enemies to external threats continued even after the Spanish threat receded, and in 1839 a pamphlet claimed that the govern-ment of Anastasio Bustamante was preparing to make a French king ruler of Mexico.[186]

The vinagres were also committed federalists. They took pride in their role in the 1823 demonstrations that had helped force the national government to adopt a federalist model, and they insisted that centralism amounted to tyranny.[187] However, in the 1820s the aceites also supported federalism. Federalism became an identifying trait of the vinagres only when it lost favor with the aceites and their national allies. This process began during the 1830–32 regime of Anastasio Bustamante. Although this government did not openly espouse centralism, its critics often accused it of centralism, and vinagre propagandists participated in this criticism.[188] In 1835, when it became clear that politicians in Mexico City would abolish the 1824 federal-ist constitution, 123 Oaxacans signed a petition arguing that federalism was still the best system for Mexico. The petitioners included many prominent vinagres and not one person identified with the aceites.[189] In 1836 the vinagres supported a federalist rebellion, and throughout the following decade the vinagres argued for the restoration of federalism.[190] In the 1830s the term *vinagre* was replaced by *federalist*. Federalism was restored in August 1846, and Manuel Iturribarría's speech for the independence commemorations of the following month praised federalism as the most secure guarantee of liberty and called on Oaxacans to oppose privileges, centralization, and dictatorship.[191] Manuel Pasos argued in 1849 that the federalist constitution brought equality and freedom to Oaxaca, linking it to other cherished vinagre values.[192]

The aceites rejected the notion that they were allies of Spanish efforts to subvert Mexico. In the 1820s the aceites criticized Spanish colonialism but argued that Spanish residents of Mexico had the right to stay as long as they were loyal to the new nation.[193] Later, the efforts of Lucas Alamán to emphasize the Spanish roots of Mexican culture made praising the Spanish more acceptable. In 1845, for instance, Vicente Márquez y Carrizosa pointed out that Mexico had "relations of blood, customs, and religion" with Spain.[194] Likewise, after 1822 the aceites often denied the idea that they somehow represented an oligarchy or aristocracy. The aceites did not criticize egalitarianism until the idea that political participation should be limited became more popular on the national level. In 1834, for instance, the newspaper *El Broquel de las Costumbres* criticized those who advocated a "misunderstood equality" that would allow people to claim places in society they did not deserve, insulting or supplanting those who deserved more respect due to their honesty, courage, wealth, age, religion, birth, or education.[195] When the national government introduced income qualifications for suffrage in 1836 and 1843 the aceites did not protest.

The most important argument the aceites offered to voters was that they were defending Catholicism from the threat of impiety and heresy. We have already seen their use of cofradías to spread this notion in 1826. The vinagres constantly accused the aceites of cynically exploiting the religiosity of Oaxaca's people.[196] Whatever the aceites might have been saying in cofradía meetings or shouting on the streets in the 1820s, their printed propaganda on this point was relatively sparse. An 1826 pamphlet pointed out the need to elect pious men but did not directly criticize the vinagres. In 1828 the aceite newspaper *Cartas al Pueblo* described how the vinagres had hoped to prove their piety during Holy Week by seizing control of the carriage carrying the Holy Eucharist. The newspaper pointed out that the carriage broke down, because "doubtless God did not want to be dragged as a result of a decree given in the shadows of iniquity." The paper also accused the vinagres of heresy and said they yelled "death to priests" in the streets. On election day the paper argued that the vinagres "do not love the religion of the Crucified, nor independence." The paper pointed out that the vinagres were using Masonic lodges to organize for the election even though membership was a violation of church law.[197] By associating the supposed impiety of the vinagres with Masonic lodges the aceites implied that the vinagres formed part of an international conspiracy to undermine piety by promoting rationalism and skepticism.[198] The ill-fated liberal experiment in national politics of 1833–34 provided the aceites with a great deal of ammunition. The aceites led a local reaction against the anticlericalism of the national administration, and afterwards they castigated the vinagres for contributing to the "abandonment of religious principles" and criticized them as the "Anti-Christian faction."[199] This last epithet was extremely powerful, combining as it did a defense of religion with the idea that the vinagres were dividing the polity for their own gain.

✺ 1828–1835: Elections and Civil Wars

In late 1827 Santiago García used regular army troops to take control of the city's streets, pressure the state legislature to expel the state's Spaniards, and encourage vinagre demonstrations. In the middle of this crisis the city held its annual elections for the city council, and not surprisingly the vinagres won. After García's troops left, the state legislature, dominated by the aceites, overturned the city council election, claiming that it was unconstitutional and that "lack of liberty" prevented "the vast majority of citizens from voting."[200] New elections were held, and both parties organized extensively. The vinagres again won these elections.[201] Even as the vinagres celebrated their victory, Ignacio Morales, the aceite governor who had been driven out by the García affair, returned. According to the aceite newspaper, a crowd met him on the road to the city, unhitched the horses from his coach, and pulled him to his house amid fireworks.[202] This expression of aceite popularity may have been staged, but there is no doubt that in 1828 the vinagres controlled the city council, and the aceites controlled the state government, including the legislature, the governorship, and the government's printing press. This split between the two governments would contribute to the extraordinary tension of the 1828 campaign for the state legislature.

The August 1828 elections for the Oaxacan state legislature also became linked to a controversial contest in national politics. A new president would be elected in 1828, and the national campaign pitted Vicente Guerrero, a radical populist allied with the vinagres, against Manuel Gómez Pedraza, a former royalist officer whom the aceites supported. Gómez Pedraza's supporters did not make overt policy proposals, but his candidacy suggested that he would slow down the national movement against the Spaniards in Mexico and provide more order for Mexico's wealthy. Guerrero's supporters stressed his background as an insurgent and played up the threat that resident Spaniards posed to Mexico's survival. Some supporters also suggested that Guerrero would use protectionism to revive Mexico's industries. However, it is important to note that the presidential campaign was not aimed at ordinary voters. The president would be chosen by the state legislatures, and each state would have just one vote.[203] Although Oaxaca's legislative elections would take place a few weeks before the presidential election, Oaxaca's presidential vote would actually be cast by the outgoing legislature. Nevertheless, the unspoken hope of the vinagres was that an overwhelming victory in the August legislative elections would convince the outgoing legislature to vote for Guerrero.

The vinagres also borrowed some tactics from national politics to aid their campaign. The most important was the use of Masonic groups and other electoral clubs. The vinagres founded two York rite lodges in March 1828. Later they founded a series of "Guadalupan" clubs or societies. It seems likely that the Masonic lodges were vehicles for the vinagre leadership, while the larger Guadalupan clubs were efforts to reach rank-and-file voters. Some meetings were held in the Convent of Belen, and vinagre priests presided over the meetings of the Guadalupan societies. According to testimony received by Governor Ignacio Morales, in one lodge meeting the vinagres placed their newspaper on a standard and toasted it with drink. They then conducted a mock trial of the aceite newspaper and burned it along with effigies of the governor and another aceite.[204] In meetings of the Guadalupan societies, members swore allegiance to the Virgin and fidelity to the vinagre cause.[205] The Guadalupan societies were apparently an effort to counteract the cofradías the aceites had used for similar purposes in the previous election. The electoral organizing spilled out into the streets. Parties of vinagres gathered at night on the street corners, shouting electoral slogans.

One month before the legislative election, the state senate met to elect the state governor for the next term. The aceites had a solid majority, but the vinagres tried to deny them a quorum. One of the two vinagre senators left, feigning illness. The second, José Lucas Almogavar, then publicly declared that the election was unconstitutional because two of the gubernatorial candidates the lower house had proposed were currently members of the state congress. Almogavar swept out of the chamber, and was met at the door by a large crowd of vinagres who prevented authorities from physically compelling him to stay. Only two weeks later did the state authorities succeed in forcing Almogavar to attend a session where Joaquín Guerrero was elected to the governorship.[206] As in November 1827, the aceites controlled the state government, but the vinagres controlled the streets.

In the weeks leading up to the election both the vinagres and the aceites tried to repress their opponents. A vinagre crowd broke into an aceite meeting, and another vinagre crowd assaulted an aceite legislator. The vinagres controlled the city council that policed the city, and a city official arrested Antonio Valdés y Moya, director of the state government press and publisher of the aceite newspaper, for abusing his wife. Another city official supposedly assaulted an aceite politician and his wife. The aceites, in turn, took advantage of their control of state government. In November 1827 they had arrested civilians who attempted to bring complaints against resident Spaniards to Santiago García. They exiled Ignacio Ordoño from the state, and they prevented the publication of vinagre pamphlets. As the election neared the aceite-dominated state legislature banned nocturnal meetings of four or more men, and prohibited citizens from shouting "long live" or "death" to causes or people in the streets.[207]

The rhetoric of the election campaigns was extremely heated. As we saw above, the vinagres accused the aceites of virtual conspiracy with the Spanish government. In other words, for them a vote for the aceites was a vote against Mexican independence. The aceites, on the other hand, repeatedly accused the vinagres of attacking Catholicism. Both parties presented apocalyptic visions of what a victory for their rivals would mean. To the vinagres, an aceite victory would facilitate a return to Spanish rule. To the aceites, a vinagre victory would lead to the decline of Catholicism in Oaxaca. Mutual distrust heightened these stark visions. Each side accused the other of cheating in previous elections. The vinagres cited the 1826 state legislature elections, and the aceites cited the January 1828 city council election.[208] The implication for each side was that the other would cheat, and the consequences for Oaxaca would be unthinkable.

Ten days before the election the aceite-dominated state legislature passed a law that shows how far Oaxacan elections had come from the joyous affirmation of popular sovereignty first envisioned by Hispanic legislators. The law prohibited anyone from bringing weapons to the polls unless they were on military duty. It provided for extra electoral officials to help prevent individuals from voting more than once. The law prohibited citizens from shouting down the decisions of electoral officials and excluded women and boys from the plazas where the elections were to be held. Finally, it gave electoral officials the power to issue any order they considered necessary for safeguarding the election.[209] Perhaps more importantly, the aceites moved to staff the militia with their own partisans. Before 1828, the militia had not been particularly popular among the citizenry, and those drafted into it had often sought to be exempted from service. In July 1828, the aceites made property a prerequisite for militia officers, and it seems that by August they had firm control of the institution.[210]

Ignacio Ordoño, writing just before the election, stated that election-day violence was inevitable. Unfortunately his prediction was correct. In elections, the first voters to arrive at the central plaza chose the officials who would accept and count the ballots. On 15 August, the aceites won this crucial first stage. According to the vinagres, Manuel Fagoaga, the administrator of the state's central district, ended the voting for electoral officials before many vinagres could vote. Aceite electoral officials were thus in a position where they could refuse to accept the ballots of any voter who did not meet their approval. The vinagres protested this decision vociferously, and Fagoaga ordered the imprisonment of several vinagre leaders. The vinagres immediately sent a delegation to the house of the state governor seeking his intervention. This delegation was led by the state governor's nephew, José María Pando, and the district governor's brother, Ignacio Fagoaga. After the delegation departed the electoral officials began to accept ballots, and again the vinagres in the crowd began shouting protests. At this point events become less clear. According to the vinagres, the militia guard Manuel Fagoaga had organized for the election opened fire on the crowd. According to the aceites, people in the crowd fired pistols at the voting table, and the militia responded in self-defense. In any event, several people were killed or wounded in the central plaza.[211]

Meanwhile, at the governor's house Ignacio Fagoaga and Pando tried unsuccessfully to convince Governor Joaquín Guerrero to restrain Manuel Fagoaga's partiality. Guerrero argued that he had no legal authority to give Manuel Fagoaga orders. As they conversed a crowd of vinagre voters arrived at the governor's door, where they were prevented from entering by a small militia guard. When Pando and Ignacio Fagoaga left, they heard the firing begin a few blocks away in the plaza. According to Pando a militia patrol arrived immediately and attacked the crowd at the governor's house with firearms, bayonets, and swords. In contrast the aceite militia claimed that Ignacio Fagoaga fired two pistols at the patrol, which responded in self-defense. In either case several men were killed and wounded right in front of the governor's house. Guerrero prevented more deaths by ordering the militia guarding his door not to fire and letting some of the wounded vinagres take refuge in his house.[212]

At least five vinagres were killed or mortally wounded that day, and several received lesser wounds. José María Pando and several other vinagres were arrested. The election was suspended, but several days later the governor ordered the secondary elections to continue without the contingent of electors from the city. The aceites argued that according to law only two thirds of the secondary electors needed to be present, and the outlying districts of the state provided more than enough to make the election legal. The aceites won this election handily and dominated the next state legislature. Meanwhile the sitting legislature cast Oaxaca's vote in the presidential election, voting for Manuel Gómez Pedraza despite rumors that more disorder would result. Gómez Pedraza won the national election, eleven to nine.[213]

The bitter events of August 1828 would be remembered for years, and the election was often held up as an event Oaxaca should never again repeat. In the immediate aftermath, of course, the two parties accused each other of causing the tragedy, and their different versions prevent any clear vision of the actual events of that day. The day shattered whatever remaining trust the two parties might have had in the basic good intentions of their political adversaries. Moreover, the very notion that elections could be used to achieve power was also severely weakened.

The importance of military force was demonstrated immediately. The dust of the election had hardly settled when Antonio López de Santa Anna began a rebellion in Veracruz against the election of Gómez Pedraza. He argued that a pro-Spanish, aristocratic conspiracy had tainted the election results. Although militia units in the present-day state of Guerrero seconded this plan, Santa Anna initially received little support elsewhere. Soon he began a long march to Oaxaca with his troops. Santa Anna probably chose Oaxaca precisely because he could expect support from the vinagres. He arrived on 6 November 1828 and fortified several points in the city. Santa Anna ordered the authorities to release the vinagre leaders imprisoned after the election. A little more than a week later government troops arrived and began their attack. After bloody fighting the government cornered Santa Anna and his remaining troops in the convent of Santo Domingo. There some vinagres joined his men, while others provided intelligence and provisions during the siege that followed. The civil war was cut short when rebels took over Mexico City. Although the state legislature at first refused to recognize Vicente Guerrero as president, in the end Oaxaca could not resist. Governor Joaquín Guerrero resigned, Santa Anna became the temporary military commander of the city, and the civil war was over.[214]

The events of 1828 constituted a watershed in Oaxacan political history. The electoral massacre suggested that elections were no longer a viable route to power for those who did not already hold office. Later, the arrival of Santa Anna's army showed that power could be won through alliances forged between civilian politicians and regular army officers. Antonio de León in 1824 and Santiago García in 1827 had used troops to pressure the state legislature, but in neither case was there actual fighting, and in both cases backing from the national government helped the legislature resist pressure. In 1828 Santa Anna's revolt became linked to a successful rebellion on the national level. Moreover, in 1828 the streets of Oaxaca saw bloody combat for the first time since 1812. From 1828 on, military might was more important than electoral strength in determining who would hold office in Oaxaca. Elections continued to be important for legitimating rulers already in office, but they were not the means of choosing officeholders. Instead national politics determined who would command the regular army in Oaxaca, and the regular army effectively determined which party would hold local office. In elections after 1828, usually the group with the most military power attempted to intimidate the other side into avoiding the polls while turning out the maximum number of its own supporters.

The new importance of Mexico's regular army in Oaxacan state politics was ironic. The army was far from an icon of republican citizenship, and it was not popular with the civilian populace of the city. Oaxaca was responsible for providing the federal army with a certain number of recruits, and this "contigente de sangre," or "blood quota," was very difficult to provide. Recruits were supposed to be at least eighteen years of age and at least five feet tall. The army wanted recruits who could speak Spanish, and if that was not possible it desired the most intelligent recruits possible.[215] It was extremely difficult to get Indians to serve. They viewed military service as a sentence of social death, and ran away at the first opportunity. Moreover, even in the relatively prosperous central valleys indigenous recruits often did not reach the minimum height or speak Spanish. In the city itself the guilds vouched for any member caught up in the draft, arguing that he was not a vagrant but instead an honorable artisan. Hence, in practice, officials running the draft found most of their recruits in the jail. The list of recruits for 1824 suggests just who the city government was eager to rid itself of. The list included Bruno Ximenez, a single tailor who did not work at his craft "because he invested his time in gambling and drinking," Andres Reynoaga, "professional gambler . . . his lover prefers jail to putting up with him," and many other gamblers, drunks, and wife-beaters.[216] Of course sending these men to the army did not end the problems they caused. Although recruits were usually sent to serve in other parts of Mexico to reduce the risk of desertion, other states sent their own troublemakers to Oaxaca as federal troops. They harassed shopkeepers and generally made the lives of those who tried to keep order miserable.[217]

Although sometimes Oaxaca's civilian politicians eulogized the various "liberating armies" that became so important in politics after 1828, usually they worked less with the troops as common citizens and more with the officers who led them. These officers often had well-defined political allegiances and were not the politically cynical careerists of legend. Antonio de León, for instance, was in the first half of his career a committed vinagre, and Santa Anna was also first associated with the radical yorkinos and later federalists who were the counterparts of the vinagres on the national level. Both men evolved considerably in the 1830s, moving steadily away from their previous commitments to popular politics. Mexico's political instability led them to believe that a strong hand was necessary for political peace.[218] Oaxaca's civilian politicians worked hard to curry favor with military politicians. In 1833, after yet another national rebellion, Isidro Reyes, considered a populist, arrived to become the new military commander of the city's garrison. A committee of vinagre politicians met him at the edge of the city, and, amid the sounds of fireworks and church bells, escorted him to a plaza where a very large crowd shouted vivas. This demonstration was followed by a banquet, a dance, and a play in his honor.[219] These alliances with military men were difficult to end even after political differences developed. The vinagre agitator Angel Alvarez was one of those who toasted Reyes, and he had collaborated with Antonio de León in the 1824 proclamation of Oaxaca's independence and other movements of the 1820s. León drifted to the right, and Alvarez remained a staunch populist federalist. Even so, Alvarez recited a poem at León's birthday party in 1843.[220]

The August 1828 debacle and the violent ascension of Vicente Guerrero to the national presidency also led to a significant decline in political tolerance in Oaxaca. Again, this was an incremental change. Before 1828 each party had used exile, imprisonment, and street violence against its opponents. However, when the vinagres took power locally at the end of that year many feared that a Spanish invasion of Mexico was imminent. The vinagres were extremely sensitive to the idea that the resident Spaniards or the aceites were prepared to cooperate with a Spanish invasion. During the next year a number of people were denounced for treason. They included two men, at least one of them drunk, who supposedly shouted "Long live Spain" in public, a man and woman arrested for selling sweets that were embossed with "Long Live Fernando VII," and another drunk who shouted that he would defecate on the eagle (the symbol of Mexican independence), and that all those who favored it were "pimps."[221] In July 1829 a Spanish force landed in Tampico on Mexico's Gulf coast. In August, when news of the Spanish invasion reached Oaxaca, José María Pando denounced the Spaniard Francisco Arenas for his suspicious conversations. Pando reported that he knew Arenas as an "enemy of order and disloyal to the cause of Independence."[222] Yet despite this supercharged atmosphere Arenas and most of the other accused people were released for lack of evidence. The courts were generally not disposed to take these allegations seriously. One set of men was much less lucky. Friars Margarito Morán and Diego de San José had been in prison since 1827 for involvement in a pro-Spanish conspiracy. After the Spanish actually invaded in 1829 they were sentenced to death. Some fellow clerics called on their parishioners to prevent the execution, but the authorities smuggled the prisoners out of jail and executed them.[223] The vinagres also repressed their aceite enemies. They accused Manuel María Fagoaga and several other aceites of responsibility for the August 1828 massacre, and refused to let them return to the state.[224]

The Spaniards residing in the state were victimized by this intolerance. Some asked vinagre friends to certify their political activities in favor of independence and the vinagres.[225] However, the national government passed laws expelling Spaniards in 1827 and again in 1829. The 1827 law targeted single men, those considered dangerous to independence, and those who lacked proper papers. The 1829 law was much more inclusive and had fewer exceptions. Following the provisions of the 1827 law, 103 Spaniards were expelled from Oaxaca, and a further 154 were expelled under the 1829 law.[226] These expulsion laws tore families apart, and it was extremely difficult for Spaniards to reenter the country even if they had left voluntarily.[227] Although some Spaniards returned, and others immigrated to Mexico in the following years, at moments of tension the vinagres continued to focus on the Spaniards and other foreigners, playing a nationalist card in local politics. They criticized the Spaniards in their newspapers and in 1833 expelled a number from the state. The vinagres often accused their political enemies of collaborating with foreign governments.[228]

After Vicente Guerrero became president the vinagres gained control of local politics. The city council was dominated not by the city's principal families but by vinagres of middle-class origins. Still, there remained the problem of the state congress elected in 1828. The city council immediately began lobbying the governor and national congress to annul the 1828 elections, citing the election-day violence. In March 1829 the vinagres succeeded, and a new state congress was elected despite the bitter protests of the aceites. A vinagre, Ramón Ramírez de Aguilar, became governor.[229] Meanwhile, rumors of the impending Spanish invasion kept political temperatures at the boiling point. After they turned out to be true, authorities kept an eye on travelers, and a Spaniard was murdered in the Mixteca. Priests were ordered to excite the patriotism of the people, and the city council issued a call to arms.[230]

In December 1829 national events again shook Oaxacan politics. General Anastasio de Bustamante rebelled against President Guerrero, and his supporters took Mexico City. Guerrero retreated to his home region in southern Mexico, and Bustamante became president. He purged the state governments, and Oaxaca was no exception. Thus another legislature was dissolved, and the one elected in 1828 finally took office.[231] By now the pattern was clear. Despite the brave words of federalism, in effect local politics was hostage to pressure from the national scene, and for the most part that pressure was transmitted through the regular army garrison of the city.

Still, the 1830 elections for the state legislature were hotly contested. A few minor characters switched parties, and seeing this each party gave the other a new derogatory title. The vinagres were now called the *lamparilla*, or night-lights, apparently referring to their lack of intelligence. The aceites became the "ever oily" or "scorpion oil." Little else changed between the two parties. The vinagres accused the aceites of using the militia to organize voters. The aceites accused the vinagres of collecting gifts of alcohol and sweets to bribe voters and reported that the vinagres were organizing in the Indian villages near the city as well as in the capital itself.[232] The aceites enacted a new law designed to reduce electoral participation and make fraud more difficult. The law required citizens to pick up ballots from municipal authorities before the elections. Only those already registered as citizens could vote. The law also prohibited voters from bringing weapons to the polls and crowding around the voting tables after their ballot was cast. It did not however, outlaw electoral clubs, a measure some legislators favored. Clubs were simply too useful to both parties.[233] The popular election was quite calm, and the lamparilla or vinagres won the primary elections. In the district level elections they also dominated, and the aceites accused them of fraudulently manipulating the count by stuffing the urns and suborning indigenous electors from nearby villages.[234] However, the vinagres were again disappointed when the district's electors met with those from other regions of the state to actually choose the state legislators. The electors from outlying districts supported the aceite party in office, and the new legislature was again dominated by the aceites.[235] This represented another barrier to the use of elections to gain power. Even if the opposition party won the vote in the central district, the indigenous voters from outlying parts of the state who selected the vast bulk of the electors almost always chose state government officials and priests. These men were very likely to throw their support to whichever party already controlled the legislature and governorship, often because their political futures depended on it.

Meanwhile national politics were dominated by the War of the South, in which populist leaders from southern Mexico worked to restore Vicente Guerrero to the presidency. This extremely bloody civil war dragged on throughout 1830. The national press demonized the rebels as fanatical enemies of order, and the vinagres did not dare to openly support them, although there were occasional hints that Guerrero was popular in the city. Some fighting spilled over into adjacent areas of the state of Oaxaca, but for the most part the war seemed far away.[236] However, in January 1831 Vicente Guerrero was captured, and the Bustamante regime arranged his transfer to the city of Oaxaca. There he was convicted of rebellion and treason. The authorities moved him to the nearby village of Cuilapam in the middle of the night to forestall popular resistance, and Guerrero was executed on 13 February 1831.[237]

In the 1832 elections for the state legislature the vinagres apparently concentrated their efforts on the indigenous villages of the central district. The newspaper *El Zapoteco*, which featured efforts to get indigenous secondary electors to vote for the vinagres as well as a defense of indigenous rights, appeared after the first stage of the election had already concluded, and it seems to have been aimed at indigenous secondary electors, who were likely to be literate. The vinagres won the district elections, where the electors of the city met with those of the nearby villages to choose another set of electors. However, once more the power of the governor to influence electors from outlying parts of the state allowed him to determine the final results.[238] The new state legislature was again tilted heavily toward the aceites. Unfortunately for the aceites, this time national events conspired against them. A rebellion led by Antonio López de Santa Anna forced the Bustamante regime from office, and the agreement ending the revolt stipulated that the states would hold new elections. Oaxaca held new elections in January 1833, and the vinagres won.[239]

The new legislature did not waste much time. It abolished the 1830 law under which voters had to pick up ballots from municipal authorities before elections. It also annulled the city council elections of December 1832, elected Ramón Ramírez de Aguilar governor, and replaced all state authorities from the previous regime. The latter move infuriated the aceites, as many of them lost government employment they had come to depend on.[240] Vicente Guerrero's remains, buried in a simple grave at the place of his execution, were exhumed and reburied in the cathedral following an elaborate procession and funeral.[241] The vinagres also organized other symbolic acts. The government confiscated the Oaxacan properties of the Duke of Monteleone, heir of Hernán Cortés, and officials kept a wary eye on the Spaniards and other foreigners present in the state.[242] In their political discourse the vinagres called their opponents oligarchs, stressed nationalism, and praised federalism.

Unfortunately for the vinagres, many members of the national congress had more expansive ideas of what could and should be accomplished in Mexico. Beginning in 1833 the national government led by Vice President Valentín Gómez Farías reduced the privileges of the army and passed several measures that affected the interests of the Catholic Church. The national congress expropriated the properties of some religious orders, shut down the national university and other Catholic institutions of learning, abolished the civil obligation to pay tithes, and reasserted its right to appoint church officials.[243] The Oaxacan clergy immediately attacked the measures. Priests published several pamphlets criticizing the national government for overstepping its bounds and facilitating the growth of impiety in Mexico. Governor Ramón Ramírez de Aguilar and the editors of *El Zapoteco* responded, arguing that the government was within its rights and denying that the measures were antireligious.[244] Tensions were heightened by the cholera epidemic that shook the city that year, and some opponents of the government suggested that the epidemic was a punishment for the impiety of the government.[245] As we have seen, Oaxaca's vinagres had been accused of heresy and impiety despite the presence of many priests in their ranks. When the vinagres regained power in 1833 they had made a conscious effort to put these accusations to rest, and vinagre priests preached publicly that there was no basis to that accusation. Now through no fault of their own the vinagres found themselves at loggerheads with the church. Moreover, they feared that clerics would conspire with regular army officers to overthrow the government. The latter fear was realized in the summer of 1833, when Valentín Canalizo invaded the state and once again fighting took place in the streets of Oaxaca. Canalizo argued that he would protect religion as well as the privileges of the church and the army. His forces were defeated only when the national government sent reinforcements.[246]

The vinagres' control of state government survived this episode, but they remained vulnerable. The vinagres feared conspiracy, and in January 1834 they arrested a group of aceites and clerics who had met in the house of a priest, ostensibly to gamble. A neighbor had noticed that the group did not contain even one vinagre.[247] The real threat, however, was external to the state. In May 1834 military officers in Cuernavaca rebelled against the national government and convinced President Santa Anna to abolish many of the measures passed in the preceding year. In June the garrison of Oaxaca seconded the movement and soon Governor Ramírez de Aguilar resigned, and the legislature was dissolved. Almost immediately the aceites launched a newspaper, *El Broquel de las Costumbres*, which criticized the vinagres for supporting the impious laws of the national government. The city council was dissolved, and the aceite-dominated council of early 1833 returned to office. In August the aceites won the elections for a new state legislature.[248] The political wheel had come full circle once more, and again the motive power was located not in local politics but in the vagaries of the national political climate.

✈ *1835–1845: The Seduction of Order*

The downfall of Valentín Gómez Farías in Mexico City and the vinagres in Oaxaca was not just another of the periodic political upsets that had plagued Mexico since independence. Within months Mexico's new leaders had abandoned the federal constitution and replaced it with a radically different system. Centralism strengthened, of course, the center of the country against the periphery. The states lost their power to make their own laws on a variety of issues, and they also lost their right to elect their own officials. At least on paper, the government in Mexico City was placed firmly in control. Centralism also explicitly placed political power in the hands of people who were relatively well-off, establishing income qualifications for voting that effectively removed both peasants and the urban poor from the electorate.[249] Obviously some public support for centralism was a direct response to the anticlerical measures of the previous regime, and the centralists emphasized this in their propaganda. However, in Oaxaca and elsewhere the principal benefit many people saw in centralism was political stability. People were tired of fighting, and the violence that had broken out in the streets of Oaxaca in 1828 and 1833 had made many people believe that trading some political participation for peace was a good bargain. The official acts of adhesion to centralism stressed the problem of order. As Oaxaca's congress put it, the federal system "divided [Mexicans] instead of uniting [them]."[250] In Oaxaca and other parts of the country some of the relative calm that followed the end of the first federal republic was undoubtedly also due to initiatives to protect Mexican manufactures from foreign competition. Protectionism was designed to short-circuit some of the political activity of urban artisans and, to a lesser extent, coastal cotton-growers. In Oaxaca it temporarily revived the moribund textile industry.[251]

Nevertheless, it would be wrong to assume that the national turn to centralism ended party conflict in Oaxaca. The aceites became known as centralists, while the vinagres' efforts to prevent the adoption of centralism and later to overthrow it soon led them to replace the name *vinagre* with *federalist*. In 1835 the vinagres published a call to reform rather than abolish federalism. The question of federalism was raised in street brawls and in veiled comments in newspapers and pamphlets.[252] In 1836 Francisco Enciso and Miguel Acevedo led a federalist rebellion. After recruiting troops in the Mixteca they marched to Oaxaca and besieged government forces fortified in the Dominican monastery and other buildings. The rebels sacked several commercial establishments before attacking the enemy strong points. Government troops held out until a relief column arrived from central Mexico. The relief column defeated the rebels in a bloody battle outside the city, and Acevedo was executed. Governor José López de Ortigosa reported that many urban Oaxacans had joined Acevedo's force. After the fighting ended the government prosecuted a number of Oaxacans for collaborating with the rebels. Most were exonerated for lack of evidence, as in the confusion of civil war certainties were hard to come by. In a rather poignant case, Juan Manuel Leyva was prosecuted for shouting insults at the defenders of the government positions. Leyva explained that when he saw the Spaniard Juan Casalduero firing at the retreating rebels, calling them "robbers, shirtless ones, sans culottes," he became angry at seeing "a Spaniard, enemy of national independence like all Spaniards" participating in domestic affairs and taking pleasure from the spilling of Mexican blood. Leyva shouted at Casalduero to stop, calling him a "crooked Gachupín." Leyva insisted that although his actions may not have been prudent they were not criminal.[253] The court agreed. Here we see, though, some of the anguish of the vinagres as they were again defeated by the application of military force sent by the national government.

The federalists continued to agitate even after the defeat of Acevedo. During the night of 4 October 1837 one of the city's night watchmen found two pasquines. The first read, "Follow necessity, imitate New Mexico," while the second read, "Oaxacans: Hunger continues, punish the merchants." The author was apparently calling on Oaxacans to follow the example of the impoverished people of New Mexico, who had revolted in August against centralism and the wealthy of the province.[254] Events in December 1838 brought the federalists more hope. President Anastasio Bustamante actually agreed to restore federalism and nominated two federalists to his cabinet. The congress refused to comply, but in the meantime large groups of protesters had gathered in the streets of Mexico City. When the news of this uproar reached Oaxaca, local federalists began their own demonstrations demanding federalism. Although in Mexico City authorities had tolerated the demonstrations, in Oaxaca the night watchmen charged with keeping order broke up the protest.[255]

Bustamante went back on his word, but the federalists still hoped to use their popular support in the city to promote political change. In 1841 they tried to weaken the centralists by taking advantage of a monetary crisis. Since the 1810s various Mexican governments had coined copper money, and by the 1830s this money, available in smaller denominations than silver money, was the currency most poor people used on a daily basis. Some retail stores gave tokens of wood or glass as change, but the problem with tokens was that they were redeemable for merchandise only at the stores that issued them. If the store went out of business, all its tokens became useless. Copper coins were acceptable everywhere. Still, copper money had its own problems. It was easy to counterfeit, and governments covered fiscal shortfalls by issuing more coins. Not surprisingly, copper money lost its value steadily, and merchants accepted it only at a discount. In 1837 the national government devalued the currency by 50 percent, and the sudden doubling of prices this caused led to a massive riot in Mexico City.[256] In 1841 the national government tried to solve the problem once and for all by issuing new silver money in small denominations and redeeming all copper coins quickly. However, when the mail carrier with this news reached Oaxaca, a rumor conflated it with the unpopular measures of 1837. According to the rumor, which the government blamed on the federalists, existing copper money was to be immediately devalued 50 percent. Storeowners and vendors suddenly doubled their prices. Oaxacan plebeians were faced with the loss of half of the value of whatever cash they had accumulated, and they refused to buy goods at the new prices. The ensuing arguments soon took on the appearance of a noisy riot. Governor Antonio de León immediately ordered storekeepers to accept the copper money at its official value and keep their stores open. He also publicly denied that a devaluation was coming. These measures forestalled the riot and kept the situation calm during the next sixty days, during which time the state treasury was able to exchange most of the copper money in circulation for the new silver coins.[257]

The federalists also continued to organize for elections. In December 1841 they worked to win the city council election, a step that León, now working with the centralists, tried to prevent. They arrived at the polls early in force and were able to nominate the election officials of many voting tables. Once installed, these officials denied the right to vote to soldiers, citing a law that stated that soldiers who lived in a place only because they were stationed there could not vote in city council elections. Many soldiers refused to leave the voting tables, and a tense standoff resulted. León appealed to the national government for a legal interpretation, and the government decided that since most of the soldiers denied the vote had been born in the city the elections should be repeated. The new election was held under tightly controlled circumstances. Voters had to explain how they earned their living. They then had to either write out their ballots in their own hand or ask the official secretary of the table to do it. This measure effectively short-circuited the most important electoral technique of the federalists or vinagres, who had in the past written out hundreds of ballots to pass out to their supporters. Not surprisingly, the centralists won the election handily.[258]

Little information is available on the 1842 election for the national constitutional congress. The available sources suggest that the parties did not organize heavily for this election. The list of primary electors chosen in the city contains many names from each party. The secondary electors these men chose seem to have been compromise candidates. José María Pando and Tiburcio Cañas were both men who had begun their political careers as vinagres but had accepted government posts from the aceites. In the state-wide elections that followed both also became national congressmen, along with other figures noted as moderates.[259] The spirit of cooperation did not last long. Santa Anna and his allies found it impossible to control the 1842 congress, so they dissolved it and wrote a new constitution, the Organic Bases. This 1843 document set up a corporatist political system in which different interest groups would have their own representatives in congress. These representatives would be chosen by new state congresses after the state congress elections of the summer of 1843. Editorials called for the end of party organizing, and newspapers reported that very little organizing took place. The results of the city's primary election, the election of the state congress, and its choice of national representatives all favored the centralists.[260] Apparently the failures of past vinagre electoral efforts to actually win power were discouraging further attempts.

ᶾᴥ The Next Generation

By 1845 it was clear that centralism had failed to end the seemingly endless series of coups and civil wars Mexico experienced after 1821. Centralism had not brought the political stability it promised, and just about every other national problem also worsened between 1834 and 1845.[261] Moreover, many people continued to believe that federalism made more sense in a nation whose regions varied so much. A very important subset of these federalists also believed that more inclusive forms of government, in which even poor Mexicans had a formal role in choosing leaders, were not only just but also more effective for making public policy for the country as a whole. By 1845, then, centralism was on its last legs. Actually, centralism had probably enjoyed greater success in Oaxaca than it had in most places. Although the vinagres or federalists remained committed to change, many had served in the administration of the province, and generally they had sought reform by working within the various electoral systems set up by centralist regimes in Mexico City. Even so, the political fate of Oaxaca would once again be tied to events on the national scene.

Another factor in that political fate had already begun to surface in the first part of the 1840s. Many of the key leaders of Oaxaca's two urban political parties were growing old, and a new generation was rising to take their place. Some members of the new generation of vinagres, now federalists, would later become very famous as radical or moderate liberals. One of the most important was Juan Bautista Carriedo. Carriedo was born around 1813, and he first appears in the records as a schoolteacher in 1833. By the 1840s he had moved into a career in printing and journalism. Carriedo edited several newspapers in the 1840s, and his press also published books. Carriedo himself wrote a two-volume work on the history and current situation of Oaxaca. Carriedo was a staunch federalist who opposed the influence that Antonio de León exercised over Oaxacan politics. By the 1840s, León, who had previously been an ally of the vinagres, had made his move to the right, following the lead of his sometime patron, Santa Anna.[262]

Carriedo's political career was entirely local. The same cannot be said of Benito Juárez. Juárez was a Zapotec Indian from the nearby mountains who as a youth had migrated to the city in search of an education. The numerous biographies of Juárez usually focus on his later career as Mexico's most famous liberal. Even those that devote serious attention to his role in Oaxacan politics usually argue that Juárez was a political liberal very early in his career.[263] In doing so they take a cue from Juárez's own autobiography. In this work Juárez essentially portrays the vinagres as liberals, something that was far from the case. The vinagres had no particular interest in reducing the power of the Catholic Church or in breaking up the communal lands of indigenous villages, policies that became signatures of the liberals later on. Moreover, unlike some later liberals, the vinagres emphasized egalitarian values. When we keep this in mind, the early career of Juárez makes more sense. Juárez's interest in intellectual matters led him to the diocesan seminary, but later he transferred to the new, secular Instituto de Ciencias y Artes. Juárez studied law, and soon moved into politics. He served on the city council and then as a congressman in 1833–34. Juárez argued for the preservation of federalism in 1835, but even so the local centralists nominated this talented vinagre to important judicial posts in the late 1830s.[264] In the early 1840s Juárez was definitely identified with the moderate federalists who were gradually infiltrating the centralist regime on the local level. In 1844 he even became the secretary of government under Governor León.[265] Like most of the moderates, Juárez preserved a clear emotional connection to past vinagre struggles to preserve independence and federalism, but he was worried about the vehement partisan politics that had accompanied those struggles.

By 1845 the centralist regime was disintegrating, but it was difficult to predict just how it would end. Santa Anna had been overthrown in December 1844, and the federalists were pressing for a restoration of federalism. Oaxaca's state assembly, manifesting the general cooperation between moderate federalists and moderate centralists that prevailed at the time, proposed a constitutional reform that would be a compromise between federalism and centralism. In this formulation the states would not be sovereign but they would receive new police powers, and their laws would no longer be subject to review by the national congress.[266] Later in 1845, elections for the state and national congresses were held. Calm prevailed, the winners included notable figures from both parties, and political rhetoric emphasized the importance of ending the era of parties and revolutions.[267] Soon another national rebellion halted the country's drift back toward federalism. The new president, Mariano Paredes y Arillaga, was a staunch centralist and conservative who even flirted with the idea of making Mexico a monarchy.[268] He set up an electoral system in which various interest groups would each separately elect representatives to a national constituent congress. For most interest groups, voting rights were gained based on the amount of taxes paid, and so this type of election effectively shut out all but the wealthiest.[269]

In August 1846 Paredes y Arillaga was overthrown by a coup in Mexico City, and the country prepared for the restoration of federalism many had long suspected was coming. The Mexico City coup had an echo in Oaxaca, where on 9 August the military garrison and a group of civilians pronounced against the Paredes regime. The successful rebels set up a temporary triumvirate consisting of Benito Juárez, Luis Fernandez del Campo, and José Arteaga. Fernandez del Campo was basically a supporter of Santa Anna, Juárez a federalist, and Arteaga an independent. The proposal united the supporters of Santa Anna, who now would return to the presidency, and those of federalism, which now would again become the official political system of the country. The signers of the call to arms in Oaxaca included men from both groups, but perhaps the one who stands out the most is the old vinagre Ignacio Ordoño. His signature appears far down on the list, and he had been politically inactive since the establishment of centralism in the 1830s. For Ordoño this must have been a long-awaited day.[270]

Yet the shadow of international conflict hung over this moment of triumph. Francisco Enciso, the only leader of Oaxaca's 1836 federalist rebellion who had escaped execution, was selected to give an independence day speech in September 1846. He eulogized his fallen comrades and argued that their deaths had been ordained by a tyrannical party that now advocated monarchy. According to Enciso, federalism was the optimal political system for Mexico. He also argued that it would give Mexico the best chance to defeat the United States, and his argument was repeated in other speeches commemorating independence.[271] Over the previous years aggressive American expansionism and the political dysfunction of centralism had led Mexico into a confrontation with the United States that would define its nineteenth-century history.

Both the clergy and civilian politicians, including many who would soon become liberals, saw the United States as a religious threat to Mexico. Governor José Arteaga argued in 1846 that if the United States won the war Mexican Catholicism would be destroyed. In 1848, when Benito Juárez was governor, the official government newspaper of Oaxaca published a special edition detailing the outrages American troops had committed against churches. In a similar vein, the priest Bernadino Carbajal criticized the United States for harboring "a frightful miscellany of heretical sects." He argued that if the United States defeated Mexico it would establish these Protestant denominations in Mexico, saying, "Considered this way, the cause we defend is that of God."[272] The Catholic Church supported the war effort with this kind of exhortation, with public prayer, with money, and sometimes even with church bells that were melted down and turned into arms.[273]

This cooperation between church and state faltered in January 1847 when the national government passed a law to provide funds for the war by mortgaging or selling church property. Clerics immediately argued that this measure could have been passed only by an impious government.[274] Bishop Antonio Mantecón and other local clergymen contended that the decree infringed on the liberty of the clergy and placed too much of the financial responsibility of the war effort on the shoulders of the church.[275] On 14 February the garrison and militia of Oaxaca deposed Governor Arteaga and suspended the offensive decree. Throughout, the rebels insisted that if it were not for this decree they would support the national government and the war effort. Even so, they soon held elections for a new legislature, and that legislature elected Antonio de León as governor. Throughout all of this the national government stood aside.[276] This attitude is not surprising, since a similar rebellion in Mexico City had driven Vice President Valentín Gómez Farías from office and led to the suspension of the January decree.

The events of 1847 were an important antecedent for the Reform, the movement that a decade later would definitively alter church-state relations in Mexico. However, tensions over church-state relations had existed in Oaxaca for decades. Some of these tensions stemmed from Bourbon preoccupations with the need to subordinate the church to civil government. Generally, though, conflicts between church and state only heated up over two issues. The first was property, as we saw in 1833–34 as well as in 1847.

The church saw control over its finances as essential to its long-term mission of saving souls. The second difficult issue was religious freedom. Mexico's various constitutions had established Catholicism as the official religion of the country. Many Mexicans saw other religions as a serious threat to the souls of Mexicans, and they opposed all attempts to enact religious tolerance.[277] As the century wore on some politicians came to believe that church property should be sold off to foster the formation of a real estate market and that religious tolerance would help Mexico attract foreign immigrants, but even in the late 1840s their views were very much in the minority.

In 1847 Benito Juárez, the man who would push through the major realignment of church-state relations that defined the 1850s and 1860s, became governor of Oaxaca. Juárez had originally attended a seminary and later transferred to the new Instituto de Ciencias y Artes, where he studied law. Some historians have identified the Instituto as a hotbed of liberalism, but many of the faculty were priests, and even most secular professors had been educated in seminaries. The Instituto certainly did not, as Brian Hamnett argues, encapsulate "the Liberal aim of eliminating the clergy from higher education."[278] The first three directors were distinguished priests, and one of them, Florencio del Castillo, also defended church property as acting bishop during the church-state crisis of 1833–34. Moreover, many of the public ceremonies of the Instituto were dedicated to saints or clerics. Certainly some priests also wanted to change the role of the church in Mexican life, but it seems reckless to assume that the Instituto was somehow an incubator for anticlericalism. It undoubtedly introduced young men to egalitarian and republican ideas, and many of these men became vinagres, but we must keep in mind that the vinagres included numerous priests and that they actively denied association with anticlericalism throughout the 1820s, 1830s, and 1840s.[279]

When Benito Juárez became governor for the first time, his clerical counterpart was Antonio Mantecón. Mantecón was a Oaxacan from one of the city's wealthy families. He worked as a lawyer for several years, and served on the city council before he entered the priesthood. His talent and family brought him quickly to the heights of diocesan politics. His first post was at the cathedral, and he soon became a member of the cathedral chapter, essentially the cabinet of the bishop. Unlike some clerics, for the most part Mantecón stayed out of civil politics with the exception of a brief term as a state senator in 1832. The timing here suggests that he was then associated with the aceites, not surprising given his background. Mantecón became bishop in 1844. Like many clerics, Mantecón was concerned by what he saw as the increasing impiety of his times.[280] In fact, this was arguably the most important attitude he had in common with Juárez.

The Benito Juárez who became governor in 1847 was apparently a religious man who in his own words looked to "Divine Providence" to help him govern. He was also a politician who believed that religion was an important source of unity for Mexico, providing the moral values needed to make society work. Judging by his correspondence, Juárez seems to have seen clerics more as collaborators in moral reform than as rivals for power. Congratulating a priest on an honor bestowed by the pope, Juárez wrote in 1850 that public order resulted "precisely from the reform of customs and the rise of good morality."[281] Perhaps the best demonstration of this attitude came during Lent in 1850. Juárez decided on his own initiative that prisoners in the state jail should participate in Lenten spiritual exercises, and he asked Mantecón to assign clerical personnel to the duty. Mantecón complied happily, and the priest who led the clerical team reported that the exercises, which involved days of prayer, confessions, and then a mass where all the prisoners could take Communion, were a huge success.[282]

There is no evidence that when Juárez took office in 1847 he deviated from the common belief that Catholicism was the primary bond unifying all Mexicans. Governor Juárez was responsible for organizing civic ceremonies. This duty generated a great deal of correspondence with the bishop, as Juárez arranged religious services for civic celebrations like the commemorations of Mexican independence and the promulgation of the 1824 constitution.[283] Juárez also ordered government officials to attend the festivities for the Virgins of Guadalupe and la Soledad, respective patronesses of Mexico and Oaxaca.[284] Juárez and other government officials likewise played a prominent role in religious celebrations, including Holy Week and Corpus Christi.[285]

Juárez and the diocese also collaborated on more mundane matters. Mantecón insisted that priests respect civil authority, and Juárez reminded Oaxacans that priests had a right to their parish fees and the state would enforce that right. Juárez asked Mantecón to order parish priests to collaborate in the compilation of statistical and geographical information to aid development, and Mantecón complied.[286] Oaxaca's Dominican monastery was riven by dissension in the late 1840s and early 1850s. Apparently a dissident group opposed the financial mismanagement of the administrators that had served since the mid-1840s. The only thing that is abundantly clear in this complicated dispute is that Juárez and Mantecón cooperated in supporting the dissident group.[287] Even the patronato, the question that had been so important in church-state relations after independence, was handled in a spirit of cooperation. In 1848 the cathedral chapter sent Juárez a list of candidates to fill its vacant seats. Juárez had the right to exclude any candidate he wanted to, but he responded that all the candidates were acceptable.[288] When Mantecón died in 1852, the cathedral chapter nominated José Agustín Domínguez as his successor. Juárez sent this nomination to the national government with his support, and Domínguez became the next bishop.[289] Juárez was sensitive to the preoccupations of clerics. When the prior of the Merced monastery complained to him that a police official had followed a suspect into the monastery's cemetery, violating church immunity, Juárez assured the prior that he would not allow it to happen again.[290] In 1848 the cathedral chapter asked for permission to bury one of its members in the cathedral despite a controversial law prohibiting such burials, and Juárez raised no opposition.[291]

Juárez governed Oaxaca from October 1847 to August 1852, first on an interim basis and then as the constitutionally elected governor. Church-state relations seem to have occupied little of his time, and little of the attention of the urban populace. During the first part of this period Juárez struggled to raise funds and troops for the war with the United States, a war that was winding down after the great battles fought in central Mexico. Juárez also worked to organize state finances. However, perhaps his biggest challenge was unrest, both in the capital and in the Isthmus of Tehuantepec.[292] Close to home, Juárez found himself in a fierce but often silent battle for political supremacy with José Arteaga, the governor who had been deposed in the proclerical reaction of early 1847. First Juárez worked through the federal government to prevent Arteaga from returning to Oaxaca. That effort failed, and soon Arteaga was jailed on suspicion of conspiring against public order.[293] Arteaga was apparently released, and the political crisis Juárez had been trying to prevent finally broke out in 1849. On 1 April a group of civilians entered the barracks of a National Guard battalion and began taking the arms they found there while shouting, "Viva Arteaga!" National Guard troops subdued the rebels, and Juárez hurried to the scene to accept demonstrations of support. Arteaga and a number of his followers were imprisoned or investigated, among them the old vinagre Angel Alvarez.[294] Apparently this rebellion stemmed from a split within the old vinagre/federalist group, as the conspirators clearly worked to recruit from the federalist rank and file.[295] However, little is known about the political beliefs of the conspirators. One document suggests that some may have opposed recent proposals to tolerate other religions in Mexico. An alleged conspirator toasted federalism, religion, and the death of Juárez.[296] Moreover, José Arteaga's wife, Dolores Soto de Arteaga, had recently led a group of women who petitioned the national congress against religious tolerance.[297] Nevertheless, this intriguing possibility remains uncorroborated. José Arteaga spent the next several months in prison before disappearing from Oaxacan politics.[298]

Juárez and his collaborators remained staunch defenders of federalism. Manuel Pasos pointed out in an 1849 speech that federalism made more sense in such a diverse country, and federalist regimes had proven stronger when faced with foreign aggression. Politicians criticized monarchists, who were working to convince Mexico's elite to support a monarchy. Pasos responded, "There is no other king but the people and no other sovereignty but the nation."[299] Newspapers criticized a rumored alliance between Santa Anna and the monarchists. They claimed that Santa Anna had always put his own interests ahead of those of the country, leading Mexico into chaos time and again.[300]

Juárez finished his term as governor in August 1852. Barely two months later the garrison of Guadalajara rebelled, beginning a sequence of events that would end Mexico's second federal republic. As a result, the federalists led by Juárez lost control of state politics in Oaxaca, and military authorities began a fierce period of repression, imprisoning or exiling many people, including Juárez himself.[301] This turn of events ended an era of Oaxacan urban politics that stretched back in some respects to 1808.

The new era would be dominated by the rapid emergence of Mexican liberalism. Mexican liberalism was associated with a series of major changes in Mexican politics and society. Liberals worked to reshape church-state relations, first making the church subordinate to the state and then separating the church from the state. Liberals also sought to improve Mexico's economic prospects by putting the real estate held by the church and indigenous villages onto the market. Notably, Oaxacan vinagres did not advocate either of these two great reforms before the mid-1850s.[302] Neither the anticlericalism of the 1833–34 administration nor the 1847 attempt to mobilize church property for the war effort received more than the most perfunctory defense from Oaxacan vinagres. Although in the 1820s and 1830s the aceites accused the vinagres of anticlericalism, the latter denied the accusation vigorously, often using the voices of priests to do so. Oaxaca's liberals grew out of the tradition of the vinagre party centered in the city of Oaxaca, but it is incorrect to see the vinagres as liberals. The notion that the vinagres were liberals was first introduced by the liberals themselves, particularly Juárez in the autobiography he wrote years after his direct participation in Oaxacan politics.[303] Juárez had by then reinvented himself, projecting onto his earlier self and his peers a precocious and anachronistic anticlericalism.[304] It is simply incorrect to conflate the vinagres of the 1820s and 1830s with the liberals of the 1850s and 1860s.[305] Both groups were fiercely nationalist, and both espoused federalism. However, many important liberals denied any connection to the popular politics of the 1820s that spawned the vinagres.[306] The liberals in general did not particularly favor a widely inclusive political system; in contrast Oaxacan vinagres and federalists emphasized the point right to the end of the 1840s.[307]

꧁ Conclusion

Probably the feature of Oaxacan political life that both most surprised and most dismayed contemporary observers was the development of fierce partisan politics. The two parties that disputed political power began as the aceites and vinagres, and they persisted under other names into the middle of the century. The aceites became centralists, then conservatives or even monarchists, and sometimes they were called *chaquetas*, both by their enemies and by their own faithful. The vinagres later called themselves federalists, and then at least some became liberals. Partisanship persisted throughout the period, and it continued to distress observers. In May 1850 a Oaxacan was heard to exclaim loudly "that he was an old chaqueta and that it was necessary to fight the Federal System and the federalists until they were exterminated." Critics argued that he was abusing his right to an opinion by making it manifest in such a public manner.[308] In 1850, partisanship was still a dangerous issue.

Politicians and authors repeatedly called on the Oaxacan populace to eschew partisan politics. These condemnations began early, and they continued throughout the period. In 1828, for instance, Juan José Quiñones quoted George Washington on the danger that the disorder and insecurity brought by factionalism would lead to dictatorship. Calls to end Oaxaca's fierce partisanship continued throughout the 1830s and 1840s.[309] Politicians also tried to legislate partisan politics out of existence. In 1829 the city council even prohibited the use of the words *aceite* and *vinagre*.[310] Figures from both parties condemned party politics. Thus in the summer of 1830 both Angel Alvarez, a dedicated vinagre, and José López de Ortigosa, the aceite leader of the state, denounced party politics.[311] Politicians and pundits preferred to distance themselves from party politics in print even as they continued party organizing. Every group that gained power suggested that it was nonpartisan, and party politics had thus lost their grip on the populace.[312] These arguments, typically made after elections, suggested that elections in which parties organized were less legitimate than elections where, in the words of an 1845 government newspaper, Oaxacans "formed a single party."[313] Governments that argued this were claiming that they represented a unified popular will. Rhetoric against party politics was itself often used in partisan ways. In 1849 José Gamboa y Aldeco criticized factions in the abstract, and then specifically criticized every manifestation of aceite, centralist, or conservative politics during the previous twenty years, conveniently avoiding any mention of the opposing political tradition to which he himself belonged.[314]

Oaxacan political culture abhorred parties even though partisan feelings ran deep. One clue that helps us unravel this contradiction is the fact that Oaxacans did not criticize the existence of ideological differences as much as they objected to groups organizing to shape elections and thereby policy. Thus in 1830 the aceite legislator José María Regules argued for a law against the "clubs" that met before elections, and he proposed that those who attended "secret societies that try to direct or regulate" the elections be judged as traitors.[315] The common practice of organizational meetings before elections was generally viewed with suspicion. Groups in power tried to keep a close eye on these activities, and sometimes they prohibited meetings.[316] The general sense that emerges from the documents is that a phenomenon that a twentieth-century observer might see as perfectly normal partisan political activity was construed in early-nineteenth-century Oaxaca as conspiracy against public order.

The idea that factions were subversive was deeply rooted in the Hispanic political culture of the old regime. The electoral process was designed to lead to the selection of individuals on the basis of their talent and honesty rather than their identification with a particular program.[317] Indirect elections would minimize not only the dangers of popular radicalism but also the action of organized interest groups. However, the newer political notions coming into vogue likewise did not favor political parties. We have already seen how a Oaxacan politician cited George Washington's argument against factionalism. In the Anglo-American political world some Oaxacans looked to for clues to the way forward, electoral organizing was linked to factionalism, which implied mobilization for private rather than public interests.[318] Moreover, the ideal of popular sovereignty seemed to suggest popular unity, and led to a tendency to marginalize political oppo-nents as conspirators of one kind or another.[319] Both the Hapsburg abhor-rence of factionalism and the fear of conspiracies against popular sover-eignty were heightened by the events of 1808–21, when conspiracies and conspiracy rumors permeated political consciousness in Mexico.

When elections became the path to power in Oaxaca, those who wanted to win power found political parties essential. Politicians needed to ally themselves with colleagues with similar visions of what Oaxaca and Mexico could and should be. Moreover, they had to mobilize popular support. Under these circumstances, both political parties soon developed ideolo-gies that were capable of mobilizing significant numbers of common voters. However, the very ideologies the vinagres and aceites developed made pluralism implausible. The vinagres argued that the aceites threatened Mex-ican independence. The aceites responded by claiming that the vinagres would lead Mexico away from Catholicism. Each party portrayed the con-sequences of a possible victory by its opponents as catastrophic, even apoca-lyptic. Moreover, each party quickly came to believe that its opponents lied in order to cynically manipulate a naive pueblo, cheated in the elections themselves, and used force to gain power. Once these ideologies crystal-lized, how could either party gracefully concede elections to its rival? The ideologies that developed in postindependence Oaxaca made it impossible for electoral pluralism to develop.

Marie-Danielle Demélas and François-Xavier Guerra have argued that modern political life and elections did not smoothly take root in Spanish America due to the persistence of the collective entities of the old society, including family cliques, clientalist networks, and municipal bodies. Only a few people were really individual citizens. The principal result of this was *caciquismo*, Spanish America's persistent clientalist politics.[320] Although the authors do not use the word *failure*, in essence they are comparing an ideal, pure form of modern politics with the reality Spanish America experienced after independence. In contrast, I would argue that at least for the case of urban politics in Oaxaca, the principal problem was less the persistence of old forms of corporatist or clientalist politics than it was the absence of respect for pluralism. Party politics were denied legitimacy just as elections made popular mobilization essential to political success. The result was sobering. Although Oaxaca experienced fierce partisan politics for decades, very soon the most important determinants of who would actually govern the city and state came to be located in the vagaries of national politics.

CHAPTER Six

The Reconstruction of Order in the Countryside

ʄꙮ In the 1820s Oaxaca's lawmakers faced a daunting prospect. Even as they participated in the political euphoria that followed independence and Oaxaca's achievement of autonomy within a federalist system, they realized that the vast majority of the regions' inhabitants were indigenous peasants who did not read, write, or even speak Spanish. Moreover, although some Oaxacan politicians were attracted to the novel ideal that all men were political equals, all of them had also been indoctrinated from their earliest youth to see indigenous people as both alien and inferior. The men who constructed and later amended the official political rules of the new era thus felt they had to both govern this alien population and make it more like themselves. It was a task some believed would take centuries.

Indigenous peasants faced a situation that was potentially even more difficult. Over the centuries of Spanish colonial rule they had alternatively adapted, cooperated, and resisted, building a set of social and political understandings that allowed them to survive. Indigenous society, culture, and politics continued to change, but at the end of the colonial period they were still recognizably indigenous. Village life was far from utopian and harmonious, and indigenous families faced the constant challenges posed by their poverty, the vagaries of the weather, and the impositions of colonial society. Now, however, they faced a new and sometimes more vexing set of problems. The newly empowered Mexican elite wrote important new laws that aimed to change indigenous society and ultimately to make it disappear.

The drama of this historical moment has drawn the attention of several historians of the region. The questions involved are very complicated, and the answers historians have provided vary greatly. In his seminal ethnohistory of the Mixteca, Rodolfo Pastor paints a somber picture of the effect of postindependence reforms on indigenous society and politics. He believes that the state government succeeded in disarticulating indigenous communities beginning in the 1820s.[1] Marcello Carmagnani suggests a similar outcome but different timing in his own ethnohistory of the state. According to Carmagnani, ethnic society was resilient during the first decades after independence, but that changed in the late 1840s when a more determined state government succeeded in a veritable second conquest of indigenous society. Notably, Carmagnani did not conduct detailed research on this second conquest, instead citing laws without probing their reception on the ground.[2] Others who have looked at the period are less confident in the power of the state to make drastic changes. In his analysis of institutional change Ronald Spores suggests that local communities retained an important degree of autonomy well into the independence period.[3] Moisés Bailón Corres believes that indigenous peasants had a great capacity "to use the legal framework to defend themselves in disputes over their local autonomy and control of resources."[4] Carlos Sánchez Silva also argues for continuity with the colonial period, but his analysis focuses less on politics and more on the basic patterns of economic interaction between the regional elite and the indigenous population.[5]

In the crucial decades between independence and the Reform, the communities of Villa Alta maintained a high degree of autonomy even as they continued to provide important fiscal resources to the government. My research on Villa Alta confirms the argument Sánchez Silva put forward for the entire state and also parallels the institutional analysis of Spores. However, the autonomy of indigenous communities was relative. Although in general communities were able to govern themselves, the ways in which they did so changed quite dramatically. Succeeding state governments enacted shifting sets of rules about local governments. These rules were interpreted within communities that were already divided in important ways, and not surprisingly significant conflicts erupted. In other words, the efforts of some elite politicians to implant a new political culture in Mexico had important consequences in indigenous villages.

Even more so than during earlier periods, after independence the political elite worked consciously to drastically alter a hegemonic political culture. Here we can see how these changes from above affected the complicated series of understandings and misunderstandings that had governed the relationship between the indigenous peasant majority and the colonial order. To understand this kind of transition historians must carefully research both the laws that encode the desires of political elites and the archival documents that show how people interpreted and used those laws. Without careful research on laws and regulations it is impossible to understand the strategies and discourses that both authorities and indigenous peasants deployed in disputes. Yet we can never assume that these laws were implemented in ways that their authors would recognize as successful. Only research on specific sites and concrete interactions will allow us to see the actual operations of hegemony.[6]

✺ The Economy of Villa Alta after Independence

Independence brought significant change to the economy of the district. In the colonial period villagers produced a wide variety of agricultural products and handicrafts, and some also were drafted to work in an important mine. The most significant economic tie to the outside was the production of textiles. Indigenous women wove thousands of yards of coarse cotton cloth each year. This cloth was sold in the city of Oaxaca, where it clothed most of the population. Merchants working with the colonial alcaldes mayores also sent vast quantities of cloth to the Bajío to clothe mineworkers there. Through the colonial repartimiento alcaldes mayores and subdelegados advanced money and goods to indigenous families and collected their debts in cloth. These officials and their merchant partners enjoyed high profits due to their monopoly position in the credit and product markets.

Numerous reports on the economy of Villa Alta after independence agree that cotton textile production declined severely. Most state that the region fabricated roughly a quarter of the cloth it had manufactured in the colonial period. The reports present widely varied opinions about the timing of the decline and its origins. Most authorities blamed the decay of cloth production on the foreign textiles that flooded Mexico after independence. However, some believed that the end of the repartimiento was also an important factor. Moreover, according to one 1856 report the region also lost market share to the new textile factories that opened in Puebla beginning in the 1830s.[7] In an 1837 report José María Pando, the longtime administrator of the district, argued that local production had stabilized around the middle of the 1820s even though few merchants lent money or goods against the delivery of textiles. He pointed out that although the handwoven cloth was more expensive to purchase, poor Mexicans often preferred it because it lasted much longer than the cheap textiles of England's factories. Pando also suggested that most of the impact of foreign competition had been absorbed by merchants rather than the actual producers. He noted that the impoverished consumers of cheap textiles were clearly beneficiaries of all this competition.[8]

In 1852, one of Pando's successors, Nicolás Férnandez y Muedra, made an important point about textile production in the district. Like many of his peers, he lamented the decline of the industry, but he added that the Indians "have not abandoned it because it is work that only women do."[9] In economic terminology, the opportunity cost of weaving cloth for the market was low, because the women who provided the labor lacked profitable alternatives. In these villages, the agriculture that fed families was men's work. Women contributed economically by maintaining households, marketing in tianguis, or weekly markets, and earning cash in the textile trade. Since there was no other way for women to earn cash, they continued to weave even though their profits were low. In the words of Antonio Salvador de Vargas, an indigenous official from Yalalag, "the only occupation of its women as likewise that of the majority or almost all women of the district, is weaving mantas to help in the expenses of their husbands."[10] Families needed cash to pay taxes and buy the goods they could not produce with their own labor. The reports of district administrators repeatedly pointed out that the women of various villages did the weaving and spinning, and in criminal cases where female witnesses were asked to state an occupation they usually identified themselves as weavers or spinners.[11] Although the manufacture of coarse cotton textiles was not profitable for urban artisans or even the new factories established beginning in the 1830s, it remained a practical way for indigenous peasant women to earn cash.[12]

The textile industry generated large amounts of commerce. Only some villages cultivated cotton, and after harvesting it the owners brought it to the various tianguis of the district. Indigenous families bought raw cotton in tianguis, and then transported it to their homes where women separated out the seeds by flailing it. Some women apparently produced yarn only for sale to their peers, but clearly many women both spun yarn and wove it into finished cloth. The finished cloth was brought again to tianguis where it was sold to indigenous merchants from local villages that specialized in commerce. These merchants and their employees transported the cloth to the city of Oaxaca either on their own backs or those of mules. There indigenous merchants sold it to consumers or to white or mestizo merchants who sent it overland to other markets in Mexico.[13] Although production was down from colonial levels, the women of these indigenous villages continued to weave for consumers outside the district. The decline in production did not signal a retreat to autarky.

Several features of this postindependence commercial system merit comment. The first is the prevalence of indigenous merchants.[14] Although certainly some indigenous merchants had traded in the colonial period, even well into the Bourbon era colonial officials and their Spanish or Creole merchant partners had dominated the trade, using the repartimiento to buy raw cotton and advance it to indigenous families against the production of finished cloth.[15] Documents show that colonial officials often owned thousands of yards of Villa Alta cloth. Their postindependence successors do not seem to have traded in cloth at all. The repartimiento that the Bourbons had tried to eliminate was definitively gone, and indigenous merchants expanded their activities to take advantage of the resulting opportunities.

The commerce associated with cloth production sometimes led to controversies. The tianguis held in several of the villages of the district were crucial, and thousands of pesos exchanged hands there through innumerable minor transactions.[16] In the tianguis indigenous families could sell their cotton, cloth, or other products and buy what they needed. It was also there that families acquired the cash needed to pay taxes. As the village of Yalahui put it in 1831, "[In the tianguis] we buy and sell everything necessary for our taxes and the survival of our families."[17] Of course this meant that these weekly markets were often thronged, and the villages allowed to hold them were jealous of this economic privilege. Early in the independence period only three district villages, Villa Alta, Choapan, and Yalalag, held regular weekly markets. A few other villages held markets irregularly, probably in association with patron saint or other religious celebrations. In the middle of 1830 Zoogocho also was granted the privilege of a regular weekly market.[18] Later in the 1830s the weekly tianguis of Villa Alta was moved to Lachiroag, and in 1841 Zoogocho's tianguis was moved to Zoochila. The motives of the state officials who made these decisions remain obscure, but in each case the change led to resistance. In 1841 Zoogocho continued to hold a market, and state officials felt that force might be needed to close it.[19] Villa Alta, the district's only nonindigenous village, particularly resented losing its tianguis. In 1834 its residents took advantage of a raging cholera epidemic to try to recover their commercial prominence. Cholera, an originally Asian disease, was making its first frightening appearance in Mexico. On the day of the Lachiroag tianguis the mayor of Villa

Alta forbade his constituents from attending, claiming that Lachiroag was contaminated by cholera. He also posted messengers on all the roads into Lachiroag to warn the indigenous families traveling there from other villages about the epidemic, diverting them to Villa Alta for their sales and purchases. This action precipitated a near riot and tense confrontations in both villages and on the nearby roads.[20] The indigenous commerce associated with the cotton cloth trade led to other problems. Indigenous merchants bringing cloth to the city of Oaxaca were exposed to the same risk of robbery that so many elite observers of nineteenth-century Mexico have remarked on.[21] The officials of villages that specialized in commerce repeatedly asked the state government to provide better security for their travel. They pointed out that their commerce generated the cash indigenous peasants throughout the district used to pay their taxes.[22]

As important as the cloth trade was, it was neither the only commercial activity of indigenous merchants, nor was cloth the only product of the district. Indigenous merchants from several villages took goods south to the Isthmus of Tehuantepec, where they bought salt as well as salted meat and fish.[23] In the 1820s and 1830s the district still produced a little cochineal, although this product diminished quickly due to competition from other sources of dye. The tianguis were also sites of a lively trade in local products like sandals, sugar, lime, fish, rope, fruits, and livestock. Such trade was driven by village specialization based on each village's ecological niche and artisanal history.[24] This rich tapestry of economic activity was of little interest to state officials, however, partially because, like their Bourbon predecessors, they were more interested in the potential the mountainous region held for mining. *Potential* is the important word here, however, because many of the mines carefully listed in administrative reports seem to have existed only on paper or in the fertile imaginations of those who staked claim to them.[25] Although a few mines were actually explored or worked, most never developed significant or long-lasting production. The sole exception seems to have been the mining complex of Santa Gertrudis near Talea, which not coincidentally had been the site of the Bourbon era's most productive mines. By the late 1840s and early 1850s this enterprise employed between 250 and 300 men.[26] Nevertheless, the economic motor that district officials searched for throughout the early 1800s did not surface until the 1850s. In the early 1850s indigenous peasants began growing coffee, which was well-suited to some of the temperate ecological niches available in the district.[27] However, the story of coffee in Oaxaca really belongs to the second half of the century, and therefore it remains outside the scope of this book.

❧ *Indigenous Peasants and Local Government*

In the 1990s historians of Mexico became intensely interested in the role of municipalities in the political life of indigenous peasants after independence. In regional and local studies historians have found that the municipalities first institutionalized under the Spanish Constitution of 1812 and later modified in various ways were crucial to the fate of indigenous peasants after independence and their participation in political movements.[28] Some historians traced tight connections between colonial village governments and their municipal successors, pointing out continuities in the discourse and functioning of local government. Alicia Hérnandez took this idea the farthest when she stated that "doubtless it was the old solidarities, their uses and customs, which made it possible for the transition to the new to be realized more softly and with less instability than that of the state or federal governments."[29] Generally the following pages will confirm the importance of municipal government for indigenous peasants, although we will see that in Villa Alta the transition to republican forms of local government was less smooth than Hérnandez suggests.

Of course, not all historians have argued that municipal government in independent Mexico favored the autonomy of indigenous peasants. Rodolfo Pastor argued that colonial village governments were far more autonomous than their municipal successors, which were conceived as administrative agents of state governments.[30] Pastor faithfully captures here the intentions of lawmakers, but there is a significant gap between their intentions and the way local governments actually played out in practice. Pastor and others have also noted how the institution of municipal government allowed the nonindigenous residents of villages to exert political power that had been denied them in the colonial period.[31] Although this certainly occurred in many parts of Mexico, in Villa Alta there were very few residents who were not Indians, and therefore this dynamic never became important.

Municipalities were first established in Mexico under the Spanish Constitution of 1812, but this step was delayed in Oaxaca. When the constitution was first promulgated Oaxaca was in the hands of the insurgents. After the royalists recaptured the province in April 1814 they set up a new constitutional city council in Antequera, but in Villa Alta officials were slow to take similar steps. They were spared the trouble a few months later when Fernando VII returned to the throne and abolished the constitution. Thus the constitutional provisions for local government were not implemented until the document was published again in 1820. These provisions mandated the establishment of municipalities in all settlements that, together with their outlying areas, contained at least one thousand inhabitants, and allowed for their establishment in smaller locations where officials judged municipalities to be convenient.[32] These rules remained in effect even after Mexico became independent, and by 1822 authorities had established 232 municipalities in Oaxaca.[33] In Villa Alta the rules led to the creation of municipalities in the six largest villages, which had populations varying from 1,972 to 829, as well as the district capital of Villa Alta with its relatively tiny population of 379.[34] As a result, over 100 district villages that had enjoyed colonial *repúblicas* did not become municipalities under the Spanish constitution.

In his study of the Mixteca, Rodolfo Pastor noticed a similar disparity between the number of villages with colonial repúblicas and those that became municipalities under the Constitution of 1812. This disparity led him to conclude that the introduction of municipalities reduced the autonomy of many villages.[35] In the short term this was indeed true, but Pastor failed to realize that when Oaxaca became a state it took over the regulation of local government, and the state constitution adopted in 1825 radically altered the municipal organization set up by Spanish liberals. The constitution decreed the establishment of large town councils, called ayuntamientos, in settlements with at least 3,000 inhabitants, and smaller town governments, called repúblicas, in all other settlements in the state. The use of the term *república* was probably a conscious reference to the colonial república de indios. Repúblicas were not in any way subject to the ayuntamientos of the larger towns, and in fact there was little difference in the duties and powers of the two forms of local government.[36] This basic set of ground rules set the pattern that resulted in the tremendous number of municipalities still found in Oaxaca. Today Oaxaca has 570 municipal governments, about one quarter of all the municipalities in Mexico, a ratio that is entirely out of proportion to its population.[37] In providing for local governments in all settlements the writers of Oaxaca's first state constitution distanced themselves from their peers in other states, who generally reduced the number of municipalities below that provided for by the Spanish constitution.[38] In Oaxaca, having municipalities in all of its numerous villages was a concession to its social geography. How else could the state expect to govern isolated mountain villages? Moreover, large landholdings were much less important in Oaxaca than they were in most other states, and thus landowners probably did not feel that they needed new political tools to wield in their disputes with neighboring villages. The constitutional congress that wrote the state constitution also included many men who had experienced the realities of life and politics in the indigenous countryside, including rural priests, local government officials, merchants from outlying areas, and lawyers.[39] More than anything else, the provision for repúblicas was the first of a long series of concessions that Oaxacan lawmakers made to indigenous traditions of government, a fact that can be seen even in the name they assigned to the local governments.

These concessions did not imply that Oaxaca's political elite had great confidence in the abilities of indigenous leaders. Like their counterparts in other states, they constantly criticized indigenous municipal officials.[40] Juan Bautista Carriedo recorded one of the most common stereotypes in the 1840s when he ridiculed Indian officials as drunkards. This supposed lack of decorum extended to indigenous dress, as legislator Joaquín de Miura y Bustamante pointed out in 1826.[41] More often state politicians complained of the illiteracy of Indian officials, and their frequent inability to even speak Spanish.[42] In 1827 the state governor, José Ignacio Morales, publicly stated that indigenous officials were "submerged in rusticity and ignorance" and argued that "they usually understand nothing, nor will they understand for many years, until the advance of civilization lifts them out of barbarism."[43]

Indigenous peasants were not as uncomprehending as state officials supposed. Many soon realized that the new system contained both promises and perils. In Villa Alta, one of the principal ways that the new state constitution and subsequent laws changed indigenous political life also eliminated a potent source of controversy. During the late colonial period dozens of families that had achieved principal status through climbing cargo ladders sought to pass that status on to their sons, in effect joining an older hereditary nobility whose membership and privileges were already debatable. The attempts of new families to gain the already disputed privileges of noble families had generated dozens of court cases between 1750 and 1820. These conflicts were the greatest source of tension within the indigenous communities of Villa Alta. After 1820 these conflicts, and indeed the indigenous nobility itself, disappeared without a trace. Claims to inherited status no longer made their way into the archives.

John Chance believes that Spanish administrators seeking clients in communities had propped up the nobility and encouraged families to seek inherited status. In his view the disappearance of the nobility and disputes over inherited status flowed directly from the absence of Spanish administrators.[44] My own research indicated that Spanish administrators only upheld the pretensions of nobles or would-be nobles in about half the cases, suggesting that their role in encouraging suits might have been less important than Chance believes. More importantly, Chance's argument about the end of the disputes leaves aside the role of the state officials who replaced Spanish administrators. After all, wouldn't they also have desired clients in the villages?

Unfortunately, one of the most striking problems of researching this issue is that the demise of inherited privileges was both swift and silent. An issue that had generated dozens of lawsuits in the previous decades seemingly vanished into thin air, and cargo systems earlier characterized by inherited privileges became nominally egalitarian, much as they still are today. How could the demise of such a controversial and important element of indigenous political life leave no trace in the archives? To approach this question we need to realize that essentially all the colonial documentation on these issues is found in judicial archives, especially the district judicial archive of Villa Alta. This documentation was generated because individuals and groups took their cases to the Spanish courts. The absence of documentation on these issues after 1820 indicates that people stopped pursuing these claims in the district and state courts. However, why would they do so, considering that for many families this meant giving up privileges that they had already spent important financial resources and political capital upholding?

The answer to this question seems to lie not in any change initiated within the communities but instead in the new constitution the state adopted in 1825. Article 18 of the constitution states that "there cannot be in the State hereditary distinctions, authority, or power."[45] This constitution was published in every village, and primary schools were required to teach it through a "political catechism."[46] Moreover, indigenous peasants began to cite the constitution in disputes in the district court as early as 1826, the year following its adoption.[47] The importance of this article to the struggle over hereditary privileges within villages was clear, and its existence meant that it was impossible to successfully claim hereditary privileges in any court case. Undoubtedly some families still felt they should be exempted from the lower steps of the cargo ladder, and others desired the same treatment. These families may even have convinced some villages to honor these privileges, but if any village balked there was no point in spending money pursuing a hopeless lawsuit. Thus the lawsuits that generated records simply dried up. Moreover, although it is possible that some villages still honored hereditary status, even that seems unlikely given the long history of resistance to such privileges.

The end of hereditary privileges was a transcendent moment in the political and social histories of these communities. It ended a long series of expensive and divisive disputes, and it also fundamentally altered the system of service obligations that was central to village political life and ideas about community membership. However, neither the constitution nor subsequent laws abolished the cargo system or other forms of obligatory service. In fact, the 1825 law that regulated local government actually codified municipal governments' power to demand unpaid service from community members.[48] This codification probably did not stem from any conscious desire to preserve cargo systems in indigenous communities but rather originated in the older Hispanic legal tradition of *cargas consejiles*, defined by an 1840 legal dictionary as the posts "that all the residents of a town should take turns serving."[49] In this way the 1825 law on local government suggests again the Hispanic roots of the indigenous system of cargos. Moreover, the prohibition on personal service that was decreed by the Spanish Cortes in November 1812 and continued after independence was never interpreted as applying to the cargo system.[50]

In the years after 1826, individuals in the district of Villa Alta sometimes took disputes about the cargo system to the courts, especially when a man who had already served in a high office was nominated to fill a lower one. However, these cases were rare, and their very absence suggests that the cargo system functioned much more smoothly after the removal of the thorny issue of hereditary privileges. Moreover, when asked to enforce customs about the cargo system, district and state judges refused. Instead they cited the provision of the 1825 law on local government that stated that municipal governments should distribute obligations among all inhabitants.[51] In effect, judges left the regulation of the cargo system in the hands of villagers. Yet, when state lawmakers codified the right of village governments to demand labor service from community members, they allowed villages to preserve the notion that service in the cargo system, for public works through the tequio, and to the priest were the key components of village membership. In effect this allowed villages to preserve their corporate identities, undermining in an important way the nineteenth-century effort to convert Indians into individual citizens.[52] As Brian Hamnett points out, the new system did not officially recognize Indian villages as corporate entities.[53] However, by allowing all villages to have municipal governments, and by allowing these municipal governments to demand service from community members, lawmakers inadvertently reinforced the same corporate identities that they wanted to do away with. The preservation of the cargo system was probably inadvertent. As we saw above, the right to demand services from residents was a Hispanic municipal tradition, and as a practical matter lawmakers could never have expected local governments to have the funds to pay employees to accomplish the essential tasks handled through obligatory service. In practice, though, the preservation of obligatory service was a significant concession to indigenous political traditions.

The preservation of obligatory service did not mean that indigenous forms of local government were always carried over smoothly from the colonial period. In fact, nothing could be further from the truth. The fundamental features of indigenous politics in the late colonial period are clear. Through the cargo system men served the village in a series of posts of ascending importance, and when they reached the top they became principales or ancianos, exempt from future service. As we have seen, state law allowed this practice to continue. However, those who had climbed to the top also became the key decision-makers in the community, and in fact they chose all officeholders, including the gobernador, the highest official. Under first the Spanish liberal constitution and then republican law this changed drastically. First, the highest officials of the village were now alcaldes, and depending on the size of the village there might be more than one alcalde. Like earlier village officials they were elected annually for one-year terms. Second, and more importantly, the principales no longer chose the holders of the highest offices. The alcaldes and the regidores, or councilmen, who served directly below them were now chosen through indirect elections in which all men older than twenty-one and all married men older than eighteen were allowed to vote.[54] Since marriage was nearly universal and typically early in these villages, essentially all males were allowed to vote, and there is ample evidence that elections were actually held under these rules.[55] Moreover, there was no provision mandating that alcaldes and regidores were required to serve in lower offices before being elected, and the minimum age for election to these offices was twenty-five. Individuals whom indigenous culture considered to be mere boys could not only vote, they could occupy the highest offices. This change was an earthshaking event in an indigenous political culture that prized age and patriarchal authority. Not surprisingly, it led to violent controversy in at least some villages. In ending hereditary privileges liberal republicanism had eliminated a major source of conflict in Villa Alta's villages; in mandating universal male suffrage it introduced a new source of conflict.

One clash occurred in San Pablo Ayutla in late 1832 and early 1833. In late November 1832 the principales of the village met and decided that Domingo Juan should be the alcalde for 1833. However, according to law communities should hold their first-stage elections for municipal government on the first Sunday in December. On that day a number of villagers, who according to witnesses included "both youths and adults," met and chose electors. Following state law, these electors met the next Sunday and selected Thomas Pasqual Quintana, the village's 33-year-old schoolteacher, as alcalde. A group of principales sent a bitter complaint to the district governor. They claimed that Quintana was their enemy, and the electors who had chosen him included his brothers and brothers-in-law. The principales argued that Quintana had dispossessed one of the electors they had chosen in November to make sure he won the election. They also complained that he was one of several "boys who stir up villages." The principales did not confine their resistance to legal means. When Quintana arrived at the village hall on 1 January 1833 to take possession of his office they led a riot against him, shouting, "Let's take the staff of office from Quintana." His supporters were attracted by the noise, and a huge brawl was narrowly avoided. When asked to justify his election Quintana pointed out that the November meeting of the principales had no legal standing, and if he had disqualified one elector in the December election it was because the man was drunk. Various witnesses denied that any electoral fraud had taken place, and state authorities not only upheld Quintana's election, they ordered his opponents to pay the court costs of the dispute.[56]

In San Pablo Ayutla, the principales clearly sought to continue their electoral role, but they were thwarted by the severe divisions in the village and the fact that one faction was willing to follow the constitutionally mandated electoral procedures. Their adherence to these procedures gave them the winning hand when the dispute moved from the village plaza to the district court. Moreover, note that the 33-year-old Quintana was in the eyes of at least some a mere boy, too young to exercise legitimate authority, and men who were obviously old enough to vote according to state law were called "youths." The basic oppositions here, between youth and age, and between adherence to state law and older customs, would crop up in numerous disputes in the next twenty years.

A more deadly drama played out in San Juan Yatzona in 1834. In late

September the village was besieged by cholera, an Asian disease they as yet had no experience with. This epidemic of an unknown illness must have been particularly frightening for the villagers. Unlike other epidemic diseases with which villagers had more experience, cholera killed its victims quickly and attacked people of all ages, killing about 4 percent of the inhabitants of the district. The epidemic affected most of the state, and state officials, including the governor of Villa Alta district, dispatched medical advice and drugs to every village.[57] In the midst of this epidemic the alcaldes of Yatzona, Juan Tomás Velasco and Juan Medina, began to treat those who had fallen ill. Not surprisingly, they both soon contracted the disease. As Velasco lay ill, the principales sent a regidor to see him, asking for the eight pounds of lard he had accumulated for the Fiesta del Rosario, and criticizing him for not having bought pigs for the fiesta. Velasco sent along the lard but answered that he had not bought pigs because pork was damaging to victims of cholera. Witnesses testified later that the principales were already the political enemies of Velasco, and in questioning him about the fiesta they seem to have established themselves as the guardians of tradition. The principales sent the regidor back, asking for the alcalde's staff of office. They said that they wanted to keep it on the table during their meeting to add gravity to their proceedings, and they added that Velasco should be replaced. Velasco acquiesced, believing that they meant to temporarily replace him with the senior regidor, a measure allowed by state law. The principales sent the regidor back a third time, this time to ask for the money the alcalde had accumulated for the head tax. Velasco resisted but eventually gave in. Even then he had second thoughts, and arose from his sick bed to attend the meeting.

Velasco arrived at the meeting, greeted the principales, and went to take his seat, picking up his staff of office from the table where it lay. As he did so Antonio Bautista stood up and challenged Velasco, saying, "Who has given you the right to take that staff, trampling my authority?" Velasco answered that he did not recognize Bautista's authority because he was "a constitutionally elected Alcalde." In other words, faced with the defiance of the principales, Velasco appealed to the authority granted him by the state constitution. In the short run it did him little good. The principales and Bautista, the new alcalde they had named, arrested Velasco and put him in the stocks.

José Vargas held Velasco responsible for the deaths of his wife and two daughters, apparently victims of the epidemic. Vargas beat the bound Velasco and kicked him as he lay helpless. Velasco reported angrily that as this went on "no one defended me, not due to my authority, nor because of my illness." Later that night Velasco's wife convinced the two principales on guard duty to let her take Velasco home and treat his illness on the condition that he return to jail before morning. Velasco did so, and the next day his travails continued. Juan Medina, the other constitutional alcalde, was also arrested, even though he was so ill he had to be carried to the jail. After the village inhabitants gathered, José Vargas and Antonio Bautista accused the two alcaldes of bringing cholera to the village either by not being vigilant enough or through acts of witchcraft. The two alcaldes were beaten and, on the advice of a shaman from another village, they were drenched with cold water to punish them for their witchcraft. Villagers also cut off Velasco's braids and burned them along with his shirt, again to counteract his witchcraft. They stoned Velasco and arrested his daughter when she came to his defense. They also removed from his house the firewood he had collected for the fiesta.

Several days later Velasco was released from jail, and he immediately complained to state authorities. The judge interviewed witnesses but the case ended without resolution, possibly because Antonio Bautista had died before he could be questioned. None of the principales were punished, and Velasco, near the end of his term anyway, disappears from the records.[58] Although the cholera epidemic and witchcraft accusation add drama and ethnographic detail to the account, the heart of the affair is clearly the conflict between the principales and the constitutionally elected authorities. The principales apparently had not backed the election of Velasco and Medina, and when Velasco became vulnerable they acted. When the principales and their allies arrested Velasco and Medina the alcaldes became the focus of the village's terror and grief, against which state law gave little protection.

The dramatic challenges that alcaldes faced in San Pablo Ayutla and Yatzona seem to have been the exceptions rather than the rule. Somehow most villages negotiated the transition from gobernadores chosen by the principales to alcaldes chosen through universal male suffrage without conflict severe enough to reach the attention of the district authorities. In fact, the case of San Pablo Ayutla suggests one way in which villages may have managed the transition. Notably, this was the eighth year of elections with universal male suffrage, yet the first in which a controversy occurred in Ayutla, a fact that suggests that somehow the village had already reached an understanding on the issue. The principales met to decide whom they wanted to serve as alcalde before the elections set by state law for early December.[59] It seems likely that the elders expected their decision to be honored by either the entire male population slated to vote in the first-stage election or the electors who would later choose officers. This pattern, in which the principales would advise about an election or perhaps even determine its outcome, might have been common, and if so it would reach official notice only when villages were strongly divided and one group took its case to the district court. There is stronger evidence to support this speculation. In 1837 José María Pando, who had been district governor since 1830, presented a lengthy report to the state government. In discussing village government, Pando stressed the persistence of the cargo system and the respect accorded the principales, whom he called "the only directors of the village." According to Pando, "The elections for municipal posts have always been won by individuals that already lent services to the village, and none . . . could be alcalde or regidor, if he had not been constable, sacristan, messenger or servant to carry papers, and if he had not filled other posts they consider to be low."[60] Not surprisingly, the moral prestige of the principales had not disappeared, and neither had the ethic of community service.

This initial adjustment to the new norms introduced from outside the district did not end the story. In the middle of the 1830s, conservative Mexican politicians abolished the federalist system of government and introduced a centralist constitution. The most obvious effects of this development were felt on the state level, where governors were now appointed and states, now called departments, lost their power to make laws. However, the national government now took over responsibility for regulating local governments, and the centralists restricted municipalities to cities where they had existed in the colonial period: departmental (state) capitals, ports with at least 4,000 residents, and other cities with at least 8,000.[61] The powers of previously existing municipalities were to be exercised by appointed officials. Oaxaca's hundreds of indigenous villages thus lost all right to self-government.

This centralist ideal had to be reconciled with the problem of governing the countryside. For this reason the centralists allowed district governors, now called prefects, to appoint *jueces de paz*, or justices of the peace, to help them administer isolated areas. In Oaxaca, the departmental government decided that there should be jueces de paz in all the villages where there had been ayuntamientos or repúblicas under Oaxaca's federalist constitution. It added that jueces de paz would be aided by "as many principal and subordinate helpers as the Prefect arranges with the approval of the Departmental Government, following the customs of the very same villages to the degree they are useful and convenient."[62] In other words, although the prefect would choose jueces de paz to replace the previously elected alcaldes, the cargo system would persist for lower offices, and presumably the principales would continue to appoint villagers to these lower offices. Despite the pretensions of the centralists on the national level, the centralist government of Oaxaca had made yet another concession to indigenous traditions of government.

Many documents show that in the villages of Villa Alta the cargo system continued to function under the jueces de paz, and some clearly indicate that the principales chose men to fill cargo posts.[63] Even more evidence shows that the principales continued to exert their prestige in village political life.[64] Moreover, in Villa Alta the jueces de paz were chosen from among the indigenous villagers, and they clearly took over the symbolic and practical role exercised recently by the alcaldes and previously by village governors. Jueces de paz carried staffs of office, and in fact like colonial gobernadores they were handed these staffs when they were sworn in by the district administrator.[65]

However, the transition from elected alcaldes to appointed jueces de paz was far from seamless. The district administrator who first implemented the centralist reforms, José María Pando, was critical of what he called the "magic prestige" of the principales. Pando believed that "the internal government of the villages is truly patriarchal, and it will only end when the Indians advance in the course of civilization." Pando was seriously interested in helping the Indians "advance," and thus he reported that he would take steps to make the jueces de paz more independent of the power of the principales.[66] Pando had also been a frequent critic of the Indians elected as alcaldes. In 1834 he bitterly described the "idiocy" of officials, who read "the decrees and messages that are sent to them, without understanding even their spirit."[67] Now he was allowed to select jueces de paz for all villages. Although jueces de paz were unpaid, and thus realistically could be selected only from among the inhabitants of the villages where they served, Pando did not have to limit himself to the older peasants often favored by the principales. The evidence suggests that he and his successors in the district administration favored younger men who were literate and presumably more familiar with the norms of Hispanic government. These choices often led to conflict.

The problems began almost immediately. In 1838, Miguel Gomes, the first juez de paz chosen under the new system for the village of San Miguel Reagui, asked the district administrator to send soldiers to uphold his authority. Gomes reported, "I find myself held in contempt and trodden on because all my arms and helpers, and constables, none of these obeys my orders . . . they say that I was not elected by the village, and for this reason I am trodden on . . . I am like a schoolboy."[68] Gomes lacked the basic legitimacy of having been chosen by the village. More practically, without the help of the cargo holders who did the physical work of policing the village, a juez de paz was powerless. In 1840 Crisanto de Vargas, the juez de paz of Yalalag, became involved in a drunken brawl. Defending himself, Vargas reported, "I am in a terrible situation because the principales named two haughty and arrogant constables who, proud of having served in order in all the posts that are customary in this village, treat me and the councilmen as pests, constantly disobeying us and insulting us." The implication here is that Vargas did not climb the cargo system properly, and those who had were jealous of the authority conferred on him by the district administrator.[69]

Village leaders could not govern effectively if cargo holders did not cooperate, but they were even worse off if they faced the active opposition of the principales. In Santiago Lalopa, the juez de paz, Juan María Santiago, faced this dilemma in 1841. In Lalopa tradition dictated that the highest village officers would serve the principales a feast after the officers accepted their staffs of office. The principales chose this occasion to resist his appointment. They refused to go to the feast, even though he invited them six times. Later the principales convinced the village to passively resist Santiago's administration, alleging that Santiago and his colleagues had violated custom by not serving them the feast. In Santiago's words, "The principales therefore said they don't know who we are." Villagers refused to perform the tequio, or labor service for public works. They also resisted paying the head tax. Faced with this defiance Santiago complained to the district court. The principales agreed to cooperate with the juez de paz only when faced with legal action.[70] In December 1845, as the juez de paz of Lachixila, Fabian de la Cruz, left the community office, Julian Gomez began to insult him. Gomez said that Cruz "should not rule because he was very young and had not yet paid any expense in the village." In other words, he had not served in the cargo system with its financial duties. Later Gomez went to Cruz's house, and in a confrontation there Gomez stated that Cruz "was a little girl, not manly, that he did not know how to govern because he was a boy and he (Gomez) was an elder and principal of the village." The district judge sentenced Gomez to fifteen days of hard labor.[71] At least some jueces de paz were viewed as usurpers appointed by an alien authority. In

1844 Jose Domingo Villegas of Totontepec criticized the juez de paz Pascual Manuel María Reyes. Villegas said that Reyes was "a pimp . . . who should not have the post of Juez de Paz and whoever had given it to him had not known what they were doing."[72]

The problems of the jueces de paz were not always as severe as the above cases suggest. At least one district administrator let slip in an official document that he had allowed a village to name its own juez de paz, and state officials sometimes had the impression that even appointed jueces de paz were as interested in protecting their villages from state demands as they were in following the mandates of their superiors.[73] Yet judging from the district court records, jueces de paz faced defiance far more often than the elected alcaldes they had succeeded. Often relatively young, literate men who had served as scribes, schoolteachers, or members of the church choir, jueces de paz did not fit well into older patterns of indigenous political culture. At the very least, alcaldes had been elected by villages which still respected the opinions of the elders who had earned their voice through service. District administrators did not always respect those opinions when they appointed jueces de paz. The resulting friction is not very surprising.

Mexico's centralist era ended in August 1846. The federalist laws enacted in the 1820s and early 1830s were again enforced, and among these were the laws that had established elected repúblicas in every village. The national rebellion against centralism thus turned out to be important even for indigenous peasants in isolated Oaxacan districts. This significance was noticed even by Governor Benito Juárez, a politician not known for his sympathy for indigenous peasants. In his 1848 report to the state congress Juárez spent considerable time on the issue. In his words,

> Since before the establishment of the federal system the villages of the state have had the democratic custom of electing on their own the functionaries who with the names of alcaldes and regidores kept the villages clean, kept order, and administered the communal funds. This beneficial custom was strengthened by the federalist system, giving the villages the power to elect the members of their ayuntamientos and repúblicas, and codifying the duties and rights of these bodies. For this reason the republican representative federal system was well-received in the villages of the State, and the centralist system that abolished those bodies caused universal disgust, contributing to the fall of that system that damaged us so much. With the reestablishment

of federalism the villages have recovered not only their ayuntamientos and repúblicas, but also the right to elect them following their past customs, leaving local government organized in a way that, far from obstructing, instead expedites the march of the general administration of the State.[74]

Juárez, born in the Zapotec mountain village of Guelatao, is often described as having turned definitively away from his indigenous roots as he pursued a career in law and politics. Even so, he recognized the practical utility of melding republican state formation with indigenous political culture. Men like Juárez may have wanted to change indigenous culture to bring it into line with the liberal individualism they saw as modern and efficient. However, they still needed indigenous peasants to live quietly and pay the taxes that formed the backbone of the state treasury, and these needs led them to compromise their longer-term ideals.

The restoration of elected village governments seems to have allowed the indigenous peasants of Villa Alta to return to the political pattern many villages probably followed in the earlier federalist period. In this pattern villagers chose the highest officials every year in early December according to the official rules laid down in the state constitution and laws, but they did so following the advice of the principales. The principales also decided who held the lower posts that helped elected officials govern effectively. The evidence of this compromise between state laws and indigenous custom is weak precisely because after 1846 village government became less controversial. Still, when the village of Temaxcalapan tried to depose its alcalde in 1853, its petition was presented to the district governor by "citizens Juan Morales, Juan Velasco and Salvador Velasco, in their own name and the name of the principales" of whom 42 are named. The petition claimed that Alcalde Juan Molina had become an abusive drunk no longer worthy of the post the village had conferred on him.[75] In a similar case a year earlier, Alcalde Hermengildo Ayala of Lachixila was accused of drunkenness, sexual harassment, and fornication. The nominal authors of the petition, the "principales and all the commons," asked "according to the votes of the principales and votes of the village that Mateo de Luna serve as first Alcalde." Although the Spanish here is not exactly standard, it seems to suggest that both the principales and other villagers had already chosen Mateo de Luna to replace Ayala.[76] In both these cases the principales assert their role as guides for village politics, and in the second they seem to see that role as at least in part an electoral one.

Both under federalism and under centralism the indigenous political culture that associated leadership with service and age remained important. However in at least two villages, San Pablo Ayutla and Yalalag, the documents generated by repeated disputes suggest the emergence of a new form of leadership that in contemporary Oaxaca would be called caciquismo. Caciquismo is a Mexican political shorthand for situations where a powerful individual uses patronage, friends in higher offices, and sometimes violence to dominate the politics of an area for long periods of time. In Oaxacan villages today it is often associated with literacy, bilingualism, and corruption. The same appears to have been true in early-nineteenth-century San Pablo Ayutla and Yalalag. In important ways these caciques seem to have been practitioners of what William Taylor calls legal entrepreneurship, in which young men impatient for power used their bilingualism, literacy, legal knowledge, and contacts to pursue lawsuits on behalf of the village.[77] Only in their longevity did caciques differ from Taylor's portrait of legal entrepreneurs.

In the case of San Pablo Ayutla the person who seemed to develop these forms of power was Thomas Pasqual Quintana, whom we have already met. As we saw above, in 1832 the 33-year-old Quintana became alcalde in a controversial election in which the first-stage voters and then the electors seem to have gone against the will expressed by the principales. The latter rioted against his authority, but state officials upheld Quintana's right to hold the office.[78] Quintana next shows up in the records in 1836, when he was serving as village scribe, an appointed post that was of course typically held by bilingual and literate men. In this case the parish priest accused Quintana of leading a riot against him. The issue here was the amount of wax the village should give the priest for Holy Week services, and the dispute ended a year later with an agreement between the two sides.[79] When the district administrator, José María Pando, began choosing jueces de paz in 1838 he selected the young, literate, and bilingual Quintana to fill this post in San Pablo Ayutla. Quintana decided that as a parish seat Ayutla should have a decent church rather than the rickety building that served that purpose. He began working along parallel tracks to secure his goal. On the one hand he lobbied the parish priest to pay masons from cofradía funds and convinced the villagers to contribute labor and lime for the project. On the other hand he sought and received orders from the diocese and the district administrator to achieve the same goal. This appeal to outside authority put muscle behind his drive but also irritated Quintana's enemies, who included some of the men who had opposed him in 1832–33. They hired a lawyer to complain about his behavior and convinced many villagers to refuse to provide materials and labor for the project. Quintana's opponents began to organize resistance to his collection of the head tax, and they openly defied Quintana and other village officers who sought to collect it. In petitions to higher authority they accused Quintana of imprisoning his opponents, of having led an 1826 riot against the priest and of having in the same year brought religious images to the village from the city of Oaxaca and collected donations from believers until the priest stopped the practice. Notably, they also claimed that Quintana faked orders from higher authorities, reading aloud papers in village meetings. In the end state authorities decided that Quintana had been imprudent but had broken no laws, and the series of accusations and counteraccusations found in the file ended.[80] In 1839 Quintana was still juez de paz, and he became involved in a dispute over the sale of corn the villagers had grown to meet communal expenses. This dispute ended with an agreement that was not recorded.[81] Only four years later Quintana filed suit against Pedro Pablo, who was then juez de paz. According to Quintana, Pablo had reestablished an illegal village custom under which three "captains" fed forty dancers for an entire week during the village's patron saint feast. Pablo responded that the captains had volunteered. He also criticized Quintana for "the dominion he always wants to have in the village." A lengthy complaint from Pablo and the principales of the village detailed Quintana's disputes with parish priests going back to the 1820s. These enemies of Quintana claimed that since his 1833 term as alcalde Quintana had arranged to dominate the village by serving as alcalde, juez de paz, or scribe, and by manipulating others who held those offices. The state court refused to rule on this dispute, saying the parties had introduced too many irrelevant events.[82]

The detailed narrative of Quintana's activities is more than the history of a series of squabbles in a remote Mexican village. What emerges here is a new kind of local political power that in some sense defies the orderly progression laid out in custom, where every ambitious young man had to serve in a long series of menial posts before reaching the highest office, and after one year was forced to step into a new role as just one among many other elders who had followed the same pattern. Whether or not we believe all the charges leveled at Quintana by his enemies, the very fact that he surfaces repeatedly in various posts over such a long period of time indicates that he had found ways to sustain a form of political power. In a village that was politically divided, Quintana made the most of his literacy and contacts with the district administration, alternately clashing and negotiating with the principales, the parish priest, and his enemies in the village. A relatively young man when he first became involved in disputes in the 1820s, generally Quintana seems to have been less than respectful of village traditions, as seen in 1832 when he ran for election against the candidate favored by the principales and in 1843 when he criticized the revival of a customary feature of the patron saint feast. He also came into conflict with some priests even as he promoted Catholicism and remained almost fanatically committed to building a new church.

In the more populous village of Yalalag, not one but three such figures appeared in multiple disputes between 1831 and 1857. During this period, and perhaps beyond, Yalalag was a very divided village. The village shows up in judicial and administrative records more than any other in the district, and almost always the documents were generated by internal conflicts. There was competition between barrios and families, and severe conflicts with parish priests. Several times the documents record riots or near-riots. Two political figures, Antonio Vargas and Crisanto de Vargas, came from the same barrio and perhaps the same family, and they were often opposed by Antonio Maldonado, who was from a competing barrio. Again, all three were literate and bilingual, and they began their careers at relatively young ages. They served in various years as alcaldes and jueces de paz. Here, though, both Antonio Vargas and Antonio Maldonado solidified their power by serving as *apoderados*, people to whom the community had given a formal power of attorney. Powers of attorney were common in colonial disputes but were typically given to Spanish or Creole lawyers. Now Vargas and Maldonado used their knowledge of written Spanish and perhaps their practical legal expertise to convince villagers to grant them the right to act as legal representatives. Notably, unlike offices in the cargo system, a power of attorney lasted indefinitely. Antonio Vargas also organized the village's principal revenue source for years. In Yalalag, villagers were obliged to donate their labor to make roof tiles that the village sold to finance public works, lawsuits, and religious celebrations. Vargas managed this operation for more than ten years, and his opponents accused him of not justifying his accounts. Maldonado was also young by village political standards. He was born around 1806 and also served as juez de paz and apoderado until at least 1848. Crisanto de Vargas, possibly the son of Antonio Vargas, first appeared as a juez de paz in 1840 and after repeated involvement in disputes served as alcalde in 1857, leading a riot against a district official.[83] Again, what is notable in all of this is how these individuals kept their political power for long periods of time.

Gender remained central to the social and political lives of these communities, and it was the dimension of power that changed the least after independence. As we have seen, the challenge to patriarchy posed by universal male suffrage and the ascension of young men to high office was eventually turned back. Although the national and state governments made some important innovations regarding formal village politics, they did not introduce any new laws that changed the lives of women, their role in village politics, or the salience of gender in village political discourse. Young women continued to spend the first few years of their married life in the homes of their in-laws, an important custom that caused problems for many brides. A district judge called on to mediate a dispute between young Juana María of Zoogocho and her husband Alejo Vicente Hernandez agreed with María that the principal problem was the interference of her mother-in-law, who had accused her of infidelity. In the words of the judge, the interference of mothers-in-law was "usually the origin of bad marriages."[84] Of course the young groom provided reciprocal service in the house of his bride's parents, but his service ended with the wedding. If a wedding was called off he had lost considerable time, labor, and sometimes goods, but he was still better off than a woman marooned with a spiteful mother-in-law.[85] One problem young couples faced was the high cost of elaborate wedding celebrations. A young couple could not hope to start their slow advance up the village's gendered hierarchy without marrying, but marrying was expensive, and not all families could bear the cost. Thus young couples and their families borrowed money from relatives and friends. Those without recourse to family might have to save for years to afford marriage. State officials saw these costly customary obligations as a pernicious drag on the peasant economy, but their orders to limit costs were simply ignored.[86]

Marriage was among other things an economic partnership. Men tended the fields and in some villages tried to earn money through trading trips. Women cared for children, gathered wood, fetched water, washed and mended clothes, and prepared food. Most also earned cash by spinning or weaving. These activities were all crucial to the peasant economy. Although perhaps the roots of marital discord lay in emotional issues, when such problems came to the attention of the judicial system both men and women tended to bring up their economic claims on one another. Men argued that their wives had failed in their domestic duties. During a domestic argument Francisco Ygnacio of Lachiroag called his wife María José Geronimo "a lazy woman who does not fulfill her obligations and does not prepare enough food."[87] Women complained that men had failed to support them and the children. In 1828 Casilda Torres of Santa María Lachixila complained that her husband Francisco Mendez had failed to provide "corn salt everything necessary in the house as is the custom among . . . natives."[88] Although sexual jealousy also surfaced in many of these disputes, it was usually interwoven with economic issues.[89] Most marital disputes were probably handled verbally by village officials. Even when problems were so intractable they ended up before the district judge, authorities sought above all to reconcile the two parties so that they would live "as God orders."[90] The efforts of the authorities to reconcile couples were aided by the economic facts of life in these communities. Apparently weaving and spinning were not profitable enough to allow women to support themselves and their families without a man to grow food. Few women could earn enough to live without their husbands for extended periods of time.[91] The same was true for men. Men who did not marry or who were widowed found it necessary to informally contract women to care for their domestic interests, sometimes including child-rearing.[92] Neither men nor women could legally remarry after a failed marriage, so both had great incentive to reunite after arguments or even physical abuse.

Village officials had an important role in regulating gender relations. In many villages they were required to attend wedding celebrations. In at least Tanetze they also played a central part in ceremonies formalizing betrothals. In the words of Alcalde Juan Bautista Martinez, village officials "following an ancient custom" attended such ceremonies. After a meal, the alcalde was required to give "said couple a speech about how Citizens should preserve the Sacred Sacrament of marriage."[93] The role of officials was not limited to their wise counsel. They also punished infractions of gender norms. Couples who lived together without benefit of marriage were sometimes jailed, as were men who seduced young women.[94] Women who bore illegitimate children were sometimes beaten despite the official prohibition of corporal punishment, while a man who refused to support his wife ran the risk of being drafted into the army.[95]

Sometimes officials themselves violated gender norms. Jueces de paz or alcaldes were accused of sexually harassing women.[96] These were damaging accusations precisely because villages were acknowledged patriarchies, and therefore officials were expected to act like wise fathers. Thus some documents suggest that officials were supposed to be married, although it is not clear how much this had to do with the theoretical underpinnings of government and how much with the more practical problem of the domestic help officials needed to fulfill their duties.[97] Because villages were explicitly patriarchal, many of the metaphors used to describe good and bad government were heavily gendered. In 1838, when the juez de paz Antonio Vargas of Yalalag felt that his authority was being challenged, he insisted that he wore pants. Five years later, when Julian Gomez of Lachixila sought damaging words to direct at the juez de paz Fabian de la Cruz, he criticized his youth and added that Cruz was a "little girl."[98]

Of course women could and did engage in political action themselves. Unmarried women defended their economic interests by going to court.[99] Yet given the importance of married couples in village economic life, it is not surprising that women also sought to defend their male relatives. Thus Juana de Fernando of Yalalag complained about the village juez de paz when he decided to draft her son into the army. Although certainly emotions played a part, since it was unlikely that she would see him again after he left, the son also represented economic security for her, and she began to suffer economically as soon as he was jailed, a routine precaution taken to prevent draftees from fleeing.[100] Women also engaged in physical confrontations in defense of their husbands. These seem to have been more common when a woman's husband served in a village office. When Alcalde Francisco Mendez of Lahoya had trouble arresting some drunks in 1857 his wife rushed to his aid, bringing him the staff that symbolized his office and served as a handy weapon as well.[101] In 1841, when José Antonio Martinez, the former juez de paz of Yatee, was assaulted during an argument about his administration, his wife, Francisca Antonio, rushed to his defense. She was knocked down and beaten.[102] Even if her husband did not serve in an office a woman might be punished in his absence. When the authorities of Xagalazi could not find Patricio Mendoza in 1828 they jailed his wife, Juana Perez, and refused to let her nurse their young daughter.[103]

Following the colonial pattern, after independence women continued to play an extremely prominent role in village riots. We will consider these riots more thoroughly in the pages that follow, but it seems that after independence as in the colonial period women's participation in riots was a strong symbol of village solidarity. However, we should not forget that women could contribute significantly during physical confrontations. Sixteen years after an 1822 riot Tomás Vicente of San Pablo Ayutla testified vividly about how during the riot he was placed in the stocks, surrounded by women, and beaten severely.[104] More than one official expressed mortal fear of the violence women might do them with clubs or stones during a riot.[105] In violent confrontations between villages women added to the available strength of each village.[106] In these situations women were as important to the political relationship between the village and outsiders as they were to the economic relationship between the village and the larger economy.

༄ Indigenous Peasants and Government beyond the Village

Surprisingly, some important features of the ways villagers saw and interacted with the state and national governments are not as well-documented as the workings of village society and government. The most important of these mysteries is the symbolic dimension of the transition from monarchism to republican forms of government. As we saw in chapter 2, in the colonial period the monarchy had been crucial to the legitimation of village territory, village government, and the taxes villagers paid to higher authorities. The king and his officers played prominent roles in the narrative of the primordial titles that symbolized village territories. Moreover, in the colonial tributary pact, the king guaranteed village territories in exchange for the faithful payment of tribute. Village government was also linked to the king. The government building where indigenous officials conducted business, judged disputes, and jailed miscreants was known as the "royal house." The staffs that served as the crucial insignia of authority were seen as emanating from the king, and the king's representative in the district handed the staffs to new officers every year in a key ceremony. Given all of this, the end of the monarchy was an important moment in the political histories of indigenous communities. Unfortunately, it is a moment that did not leave very much evidence.

Indigenous communities probably handled this transition in two ways. First, they may have replaced the relationship to the abstract king with a relationship to the hardly more abstract constitution, or perhaps to the nation. As we saw in chapter 5, this equation was precisely what lawmakers sought when they modeled the ceremonies for swearing allegiance to constitutions after those for swearing allegiance to new kings. There is some more direct evidence for this in Villa Alta. As we saw above, in 1834 an alcalde, Juan Tomas Velasco, argued to the principales of his village that his own authority was derived from the constitution.[107] Moreover, although the former "royal house" was usually referred to as the "national house" after independence, sometimes it was called the "constitutional house."[108]

As the reference to national houses suggests, to some extent the idea of the nation replaced the king. For instance, sometimes a village official referred to himself as a "national authority."[109] Yet, in the end there was another possibility that was not foreseen by lawmakers. Perhaps the demise of the monarchy increased the symbolic authority of the elders or principales. However, the documents do not suggest this, and in fact we have seen that at least sometimes their practical authority became problematic due to the establishment of universal male suffrage. Thus for the moment the possibility of a stronger role for the principales remains difficult to confirm.

The transition to a dramatically new form of government left state and national authorities with a thorny problem. Why should indigenous peasants in the mountains of Oaxaca obey the national and state governments? After all, it was unlikely that these new entities would be able to compel obedience with force, as even the relatively solvent colonial government had never been able to field respectable military contingents in interior areas. The short answer to this question is fairly obvious. Indigenous peasants in fact often disobeyed the orders of the state and national governments. Moreover, they demonstrated significant displeasure with indigenous authorities that they considered too solicitous of higher officials.

Villagers who collaborated too closely with state authorities were often called *alcahuetes*, literally pimps or go-betweens. For example, when Juan Martinez Velasco of Santiago Lalopa allowed visiting government officials to stay at his house in 1832 he was accused of "pimping."[110] This insult was more often leveled at village officials. Sometimes the behavior that led to the accusation is not specified in the documents, and *pimp* was also one of a number of popular insults leveled at officials attempting to jail drunks.[111] On other occasions the epithet was associated with an indigenous official's relationship with the state government. In these cases the gendered dimension of the insult is clearer, as rather than acting as a good father the official is portrayed as facilitating the exploitation of his family by a stranger.[112] When José Domingo Villegas of Totontepec criticized the appointment of Pascual Manuel María Reyes as juez de paz, Villegas called Reyes a "pimp."[113] The usage here was not exclusively the property of Indians. When Alcalde Mariano Bravo of Lachitao followed the order of a judge and refused to use his authority to collect payments owed the parish priest José María Iturribarría, Iturribarría assaulted Bravo and called him "pimp of the government."[114]

Of course one way to avoid being labeled a pimp was to withhold cooperation from the government. Sometimes village authorities openly defied state officials. In 1823 the authorities of Yalalag refused to remit witnesses to the state judge and stopped signing off on orders sent to them. The judge sent a messenger to urge their compliance, and Mateo Estila, the secretary of Yalalag, told the messenger that the village government had as much authority as the judge. Estila told his comrades not to fear the judge: "Here no one orders us around; we are the Judge of this municipal court." Estila also told the judge's messenger, "What you do is rob, you as well as the Judge."[115] During an 1832 dispute in Santiago Lalopa the village government defied another messenger from the district judge, saying that the orders he brought were "papers of no importance" with which the village officials "will clean our asses, that's why we are in the time of Liberty."[116] Even appointed village officials were sometimes defiant. In a similar situation in 1838 Antonio Vargas, the juez de paz of Yalalag, insisted to a messenger from the district judge, "We are not planning on following the order of the judge, because I have as much authority as he does."[117] Perhaps the most severe case of such defiance occurred in Zoogocho in 1851. When the subprefect, Francisco Beltran, tried to collect a new tax at the village tianguis he soon faced a terrifying mob of women. Beltran implored the village authorities to intervene, but they refused, explaining that the members of the mob wanted to kill Beltran because "they were already sick of him and of the government, as both were just robbers." Beltran survived to describe the incident, and toward the end of his report Beltran complained that during the riot some members of the crowd had stolen the meal he was about to eat. According to Beltran the alcaldes of the village ate the meal, and then the crowd broke the dishes and threw them at Beltran.[118]

One way the government and elite politicians hoped to avoid incidents like these was by using oaths and ceremonies to show peasants where their political allegiance should lie. There is no evidence that strictly indigenous villages were asked to swear allegiance to any of the various political proclamations that signaled major changes in Mexican politics in the first few years after independence. Instead authorities seem to have been content to arrange these political acts in the few relatively large villages that served as residences for nonindigenous officials.[119] By the middle of the 1840s all villages seem to have been required to swear allegiance to successful political movements, and this continued in the 1850s.[120] Authorities were less hesitant about the benefits of arranging village ceremonies and celebrations marking the establishment of new constitutions. Each village received instructions to celebrate the occasion with the best pomp and circumstance possible. Villages also had to provide evidence of their obedience, describing their ceremonies in signed documents. Under federalism, these documents were apparently destined for eventual oblivion in state archives, but the centralist fixation on Mexico City has bequeathed to us two complete sets of such documents for Villa Alta.

The first set is from 1835, when Mexico's political elite was turning from federalism to centralism, partially in response to the efforts of some radical politicians to alter church-state relations. In Oaxaca the governor ordered all villages to swear allegiance to the new Constitutional Bases, and all the villages of Villa Alta did so. Although each village apparently received copies of both the Constitutional Bases and the decree ordering them to swear allegiance, the documents they sent back show interesting diversity in their reactions. Many of the documents carefully cite the relevant decree without mentioning anything about centralism or even the notion that the form of the government had changed, a reaction that irked the district administrator.[121] Two were more specific about the content of the new Constitutional Bases, but even they focused not on centralism but on the idea that in the new system, in the words of the authorities of San Melchor Betaza, the government would not "profess or protect any other religion but the Apostolic Roman Catholic one, nor tolerate the exercise of any."[122] One reason for the emphasis was that in fact the decree called for the celebrations to be held in parish seats where the priest could offer a Te Deum mass. Thus most of the documents indicate that outlying villages swore their oaths in the parish seat even though under both Oaxacan law and local tradition they were not politically subordinate to such head towns.[123] Generally the documents stress obedience to authority rather than details about the form of government.[124] Descriptions of the festivities differed. In addition to the Te Deum, these included in various villages the pealing of bells, "music and other instruments of which use is made in the first class festivities," fireworks, and "public acclamations and vivas."[125] As Antonio Annino suggests for ceremonies in which villages swore allegiance to the Spanish Constitution of 1812, some of these activities are very similar to those offered for patron saint feasts.[126] A similar set of documents exists for 1842–43. Villages were ordered to swear their allegiance to December 1842 decrees in which Antonio López de Santa Anna dissolved a constitutional congress and replaced it with a handpicked set of notables who would write yet another constitution. In the next two months every village in Villa Alta remitted the corresponding document. On this occasion relatively few villages specified the festivities associated with their oaths, and one assumes that such festivities were muted at best.[127]

One question that has been important in recent studies of nineteenth-century Mexican peasants has been to what degree peasants developed a sense of themselves as members of a Mexican nation. The evidence for the district of Villa Alta suggests that this kind of identity had definite limits. As we will see later, the indigenous peasants of Villa Alta did not participate in the partisan politics and civil wars that developed a sense of nationalism in places like Guerrero, Morelos, or Puebla.[128] At moments of crisis the national and state government asked for voluntary contributions from citizens, and in Villa Alta it was common for district officials, priests, and other non-Indians to contribute.[129] Yet indigenous peasants in Villa Alta also made contributions, typically through their village governments. These contributions were modest, but may have been enough to represent significant sacrifices for impoverished peasants. They included not only cash but, in the case of the war against the United States, dried tortillas to feed the troops.[130]

Although willing to contribute financially to wars, the indigenous peasants of Villa Alta were not willing to participate directly. Oaxaca, like the other states, was required to contribute a certain *contingente de sangre*, or blood quota, of recruits to the military, and the state government distributed this number proportionally among the districts.[131] For an indigenous male, forced recruitment into the national military was a death sentence. If physical death did not result from the violence, malnutrition, and diseases that ravaged the troops, then social death was inevitable when the man was taken from the community and thus could not marry or begin climbing the cargo ladder. State officials were well aware of this problem, and frequently remarked on how much indigenous peasants abhorred military service. In 1829 Vice Governor Ramón Ramírez de Aguilar even suggested that the draft was a serious impediment to convincing indigenous peasants to accept republican institutions, while in the same year Nicolás Fernandez y Muedra, the district governor of Villa Alta, feared that the draft would lead villagers to desert their villages, undermining tax collection.[132] Moreover Fernandez y Muedra and others pointed out that recruits from the villages were not particularly useful to the army. Many lacked the minimum height required for service, and few could speak Spanish.[133]

The fact that few recruits could speak Spanish suggests that villages were not sending the bilingual and literate young men who were assuming more prominent roles in village governments. These men were powerful enough to avoid selection, and they were also valuable to the villages. Faced with the requirement to send recruits, villages engaged in a number of strategies.

According to law, they should first send vagrants and troublemakers. If they could not find enough they should then send single men, and if more were required, married but childless men. Of course in villages where men married very young, single recruits were often rejected because they were mere boys.[134] When the quota was first implemented in 1824 the village of Tepuxtepec did something that seemed quite logical. Since they could not find any vagrants or troublemakers in their village, they asked two nearby villages to send Tepuxtepec theirs.[135] Villages quickly realized that the social cost of the draft would be minimized if they could draft men who did not live in the village. Sometimes villages jailed and then remitted to the army men from rival villages. Other times villages drafted men who had already emigrated from the village.[136] Indigenous authorities also used the draft to punish their political enemies or men who had abandoned their wives.[137] Another way village officials sought to minimize the impact of the draft on their communities was by deliberately selecting men who they knew would be rejected due to lack of height or intelligence.[138]

Individuals also strategized to avoid the draft. The law allowed them to hire replacements, although there are few references to this practice. Several administrators complained that individuals who were likely to be drafted married to avoid it. Villages were sometimes able to recover even single men if they could show that the men had other relatives to support. Many men simply deserted at the first opportunity and made their way back to their villages. Village governments did not turn these men in, and with luck by the time the next draft contingent was due they would be married fathers who were essentially untouchable. It was no less a personage than Antonio López de Santa Anna that ended this burden on villagers. In August 1853 he exempted indigenous men from military recruitment.[139]

The state government was often critical of indigenous peasants, and politicians believed that only through legislation and effort could they gradually make the peasants into more useful citizens. Their efforts to reform indigenous culture closely followed the initiatives of the Bourbons before them. One of their principal tools was education. The state constitution adopted in 1825 decreed that all villages should have primary schools, "in which children will be taught to read, write, and count, the catechism of the Catholic religion, and another catechism which will consist of a brief exposition of civil and political rights and obligations as well as criminal laws."[140] At first it seemed like this educational effort would be successful. In 1829 there were forty-nine schools in the district, and 3,844 of the 44,750 inhabitants of the district attended school. However, the district governor reported that in fact the vast majority of these schools did not follow the mandated curriculum. Instead, indigenous teachers taught children only the religious catechism and perhaps the very rudiments of reading. There were basic problems with the educational system. As in the colonial period, parents needed the labor of their children either in the house or guarding the fields. Many parents felt that the religious catechism was just about the only useful schooling for children. Moreover, villages were too poor to employ well-educated teachers. Most were able to provide only a small stipend, perhaps some corn from village communal plantings, and exemption from village service requirements.[141] Nevertheless, we know that a significant proportion of indigenous peasants did learn to read and write. These literate men provided the core of officials who served as cantors, scribes, and schoolteachers, and as we have seen some achieved greater power with the help of new laws after independence. They formed a kind of educational elite, able to write legal petitions, handle correspondence, and translate laws and orders for the village. It is difficult to say what percentage of the male population acquired this knowledge, but an 1860 census of one village lists sixty adult men and notes that seven were literate.[142] The evidence suggests that these men received private education from tutors hired by their parents. These tutors included cantors and, of course, schoolteachers.[143] In other words, the kind of education the state government saw as essential for all citizens was viewed in indigenous villages as a private investment some families might choose to make. The government's efforts to provide it to all were viewed as costly interference, and this led to resistance.[144] Notably, larger villages and the nonindigenous village of Villa Alta boasted significantly better schools, and these schools provided the various minor functionaries needed by the district courts and administration.[145] There public education along the lines envisioned by the government made more sense to parents.

Like their colonial predecessors, alcaldes and jueces de paz often confronted defiance and insults as they sought to collect taxes, resolve domestic disputes, and scold or arrest men for public drunkenness.[146] Unlike their predecessors, alcaldes and jueces de paz did not have the legal right to mete out corporal punishment.[147] Instead they were forced to refer defiant and insulting individuals to the district court. This court would often decline to punish men for simply defying village officials, especially if the men were drunk at the time. Thus in an important way village officials after independence exercised less power than their colonial predecessors. Moreover, if indigenous officials did resort to corporal punishment, they themselves became vulnerable to sanctions. However, although district judges and administrators often investigated accounts of floggings, they do not appear to have actually punished any official for administering a flogging.[148]

State politicians moved to end practices important to indigenous celebrations. In many villages of the state it was traditional to stage bullfights on religious holidays. In 1826 the state legislature banned them for humanitarian reasons, and villages that flouted this law were fined.[149] Indigenous villages also put on various kinds of dances during religious celebrations. From colonial times villages had been required to pay for a license for each occasion, and the state government apparently continued this practice until 1844, when it prohibited the dances outright.[150] In 1846 this prohibition was lifted for all but "the ancient feather dance in which was represented some scenes of the Conquest." Apparently this enactment of indigenous submission was seen as embarrassingly out of step with the official interpretation of Mexican independence as a recovery from Spanish domination. In any event, the state went back to selling licenses for indigenous dances, converting an effort to reform an indigenous custom into a fiscal opportunity.[151]

State politicians and other literate urban Oaxacans were particularly hostile to indigenous customs under which so-called stewards or captains expended large amounts of their personal wealth providing food and drink to groups during religious celebrations. Urban Oaxacans believed that these periodic expenses prevented indigenous peasants from accumulating the capital they needed to better themselves.[152] The state government prohibited the practice, but this prohibition was difficult to enforce. Villages continued the custom, claiming that participation was voluntary and thus legal. In fact, government authorities could take official notice of the practice only when a group within a particular village complained. Like their Bourbon predecessors, independent officials relied on indigenous allies to help them enforce the law. Yet even when officials found out about such cases they limited their efforts to repeating the prohibition. No one was punished, and one assumes that the practice simply continued.[153]

Again and again the efforts of state officials to change indigenous customs were subordinated to their desire to continue exacting taxes from peasants. Carlos Sánchez Silva has emphasized the enormous importance of the taxes paid by Indians to the state's fiscal health.[154] All inhabitants of the state paid a personal tax that for indigenous peasants effectively replaced the colonial tribute. Although according to law this tax was collected from all inhabitants regardless of their ethnic identity, the state government had much more difficulty collecting it from urban people. Urban people resented paying the tax, while in indigenous villages the new repúblicas inherited from the colonial period very effective institutional mechanisms for collecting the tax.[155] Village leaders were personally responsible for paying it, and they had broad if informal powers to punish resisters. Moreover, each alcalde or juez de paz had to turn into the district administration the full amount owed when he left office at the end of December.[156] The District of Villa Alta was a particularly valuable source of revenue for the state government, and in fact the state government sometimes used the steady income it provided to secure emergency loans.[157]

Although indigenous peasants usually paid the personal tax promptly, problems and even resistance sometimes arose. Droughts and epidemics occasionally delayed payment at least until the end of the year, at which point the indigenous officials made up any shortfall.[158] In 1831 the alcalde of Yatzachi fell six months behind in the village's payments, and he defied the commissioner sent by the district administrator to collect the back taxes, claiming that the villagers had refused to pay. The alcalde was removed from office, and the commissioner organized the lower-ranking officials of the village to collect the tax.[159] Years later the village of San Andres Yaa likewise fell months behind. In June 1853 the district administrator sent a commissioner to oversee collection of the back taxes. Villagers paid the tax for March, but when the commissioner began organizing collection for April Pedro Manuel Agustin, the regidor assigned to collect the April tax, argued that they should wait since "the village did not have any money tree that could be shaken whenever the Government wanted." After this argument Agustin's wife began advising her neighbors to refuse to pay. One woman threatened the official collecting the tax, and when he arrested her a mob of women followed officials to the jail threatening to stone them.[160] However, this kind of resistance against the head tax was very uncommon in Villa Alta. Villa Alta did not experience anything like the massive revolt against the head tax that shook Guerrero in the 1840s and spilled into the neighboring Mixteca in Oaxaca.[161]

Probably no one was more grateful for this than the district administrators who oversaw Villa Alta. These administrators were called district governors under federalism from 1825 to 1835 and 1846 to 1853, and prefects in the intervening centralist period. The governor of the state named the administrators, and they served for four-year terms. These men occupied a key position in the new postcolonial political system. They provided the state and national government with information about the inhabitants of the district even as they explained the desires of those governments to local residents. Administrators were charged with the often contradictory imperatives of preserving order and fostering change, working to make the new liberal republican system a reality even as they kept taxes flowing to the state coffers. District administrators in Villa Alta also found themselves isolated among thousands of cultural others, separated from them by barriers of distrust and language difference. Altogether, it was a difficult job. These officials lacked the judicial duties and powers of their colonial predecessors, but they still had broad responsibilities. District administrators were supposed to keep public order, execute laws, oversee tax collection, preserve public health, supervise municipal governments, and promote economic development. Each was required to visit all the villages of his district soon after taking up the post in order to collect data about population, resources, and public necessities. These administrators were also responsible for collecting the head tax and remitting it to Oaxaca. District administrators were aided by subprefects in the different parts of their district.[162] Like colonial alcaldes mayores or subdelegados, district administrators also commissioned men to visit villages on specific administrative errands.

District administrators in Villa Alta often served for long periods. Nicolás Fernandez del Campo, who had previously been the last colonial subdelegado, served as administrator during the second half of the 1820s. After Fernandez del Campo was promoted to a more central district, he was replaced by José María Pando, who held the post from 1830 to 1841. Antonio García Camacho took over in the early 1840s, and then he was replaced by Francisco Franco. Nicolás Fernandez y Muedra, son of Nicolás Fernandez del Campo, filled the post from 1847 to 1853 and returned to it in 1856.[163] District administrators received significant compensation for their labors. This compensation at first included 1,000 pesos annually and 3.5 percent of the head tax collected, but the salary was later increased to 1,300 pesos.[164] Although the position of district administrator may have positioned these men for commercial activities in the district, there is so little evidence of this activity that it seems impossible that they could have engaged in commerce on the same massive scale as colonial alcaldes mayores and subdelegados.[165]

Although the various administrators who governed the district acted in broadly similar ways, José María Pando was the most interesting for two reasons. First, his long service spanned both the federalist and centralist periods. Second, he came to the district after playing a very prominent role in the urban politics of the city of Oaxaca. Pando became governor of the district in 1830 at the age of thirty-two. His family was well-known in

Oaxaca, although he himself does not seem to have been very wealthy. Pando was a minor government functionary in 1828, and he was also a radical vinagre. As we saw in the previous chapter, Pando took a leading role in the electoral protests that resulted in the August 1828 massacre. He was imprisoned as a result and then freed after the vinagres won control of state government a few months later. Pando briefly became a state congressman before the acting governor, a vinagre, named Pando to the Villa Alta post in late 1829 or early 1830. When the aceites achieved power a few months later they apparently did not view Pando's strong identification with the vinagres as a handicap. In fact in his 1831 report to the state congress the aceite governor José López de Ortigosa singled Pando out for praise. López de Ortigosa was especially impressed by Pando's treks to every one of the district's over one hundred villages.[166] Pando continued in his post during both vinagre and aceite administrations in the years that followed. Pando's political allegiance does seem to have been of some interest in the district capital of Villa Alta, where he quickly became involved in a dispute between the parish priest and some of the more prominent residents. Pando supported the priest, and eventually moved the district capital to the larger village of Zoochila and the tianguis to the neighboring village of Lachiroag. Pando's principal enemy in Villa Alta, the merchant Francisco Gonzalez, was reputed to be an aceite who hoped in vain that an aceite administration would remove Pando from his post.[167] Like many vinagres, Pando was far from anticlerical. He ordered the village of San Pablo Ayutla to rebuild its derelict church and called on parish priests to bless public works projects. Pando also erected a cross in a remote mountain location where he believed Indians had been conducting pagan rites.[168] A few months of service in the mountains also seems to have softened Pando's radical anti-Spanish stance. In 1829 Pando was convinced that all Spaniards living in Mexico represented a risk to Mexico's sovereignty. However, in 1831 Pando discovered that two Spanish former soldiers had lived in the indigenous village of Comaltepec since the early 1820s. There they had married indigenous women and fathered children. In Pando's words, the two Spaniards

> adopted the customs of the natives not only regarding the miserable lives they live and the difficult occupations in which they work, but also their dress and food, such that upon seeing them dressed in white pants of coarse cotton cloth, with their blankets on their shoulders, with sandals, their loads on their backs and eating tortillas with salt, it is difficult to believe that they are Spaniards.

Faced with this sight and the realization that their indigenous families could not survive without them, Pando asked the governor to allow the men to remain despite the expulsion laws.[169]

In the 1830s some radical vinagres emphasized the hope that with proper education Oaxaca's indigenous peasants could become informed citizens who would help bring progress. Pando himself at first blamed the Indians' deficiencies on Spanish colonialism, but his years dealing with the indigenous peasants of the district clearly wore on him.[170] Like many educated Oaxacans, he believed the Indians were too attached to customs that were pernicious to republicanism, and at times he lost hope of ever making them more like himself. In 1837 he wrote that "these Indians govern themselves according to hardened uses and old customs more than by laws and decrees."[171] He even doubted their economic rationality.[172] Soon after Pando arrived in the district he struggled to set up a militia company in the district capital to put down village riots and make village authorities follow orders. Yet he soon became convinced that such activities were not a serious threat to public order, and he praised the Indians for their obedience and love of peace. In 1837 he wrote that even during civil wars that divided the city of Oaxaca the district "always has enjoyed in its territory an Octavian peace," calling the Indians naturally peace-loving.[173] Like many public officials, Pando drew a sharp distinction between the localized resistance seen in village riots and the more "political" civil wars that periodically rocked Mexico.

Leticia Mayer Celis has written on the role of statistical thought in the creation of a "national imaginary" in nineteenth-century Mexico.[174] José María Pando was an enthusiastic collaborator in this process. Like other district administrators, he was charged with compiling statistics on the population and resources of Villa Alta. This kind of scientific knowledge was considered essential to governing Mexico and helping it progress to the new glory that awaited it. The mania for compiling statistics was tied very closely to Pando's hopes for the future, and his reports often mention initiatives to improve the economic and social conditions of the district. District governors were also asked to send to Oaxaca items of interest such as unusual trees and antiquities from pre-Hispanic times. The process of collecting all of this information was a very tangible one. In the first year of his administration Pando visited each of the over one hundred villages in the district. Even today that would be an enormous task, and when Pando accomplished it he would have had to spend endless days on the backs of mules. In 1836, after six years of living in the district, Pando topped off this scientific marathon by climbing with several friends to the top of the highest mountain in the district, the famous Cempoaltepec, which rises to an altitude of over 12,000 feet. There he found various artifacts related to pre-Hispanic religious rites and erected a cross that he later reported being able to see from his office in Zoochila. Pando also noted the tremendous view of the surrounding countryside available from the rarified height of Cempoaltepec, and suggested that it would be an ideal vantage point for drawing part of the map of the state.[175]

Although much of the information Pando collected was put away in a still uncatalogued section of the state archive, at various times state governors referred to it in their annual reports to the state congress. In 1837 Pando wrote a lengthy report to his superiors that distilled much of the information he had compiled. It contained geographic and climatic information as well as archeological data and summaries of the stories told in the primordial titles held by several villages. Pando described indigenous customs and the schools he hoped would eventually change them. The administrator included a detailed analysis of the region's economy and his hopes for its improvement as well as data on public health and speculations about the cholera that had recently attacked the district. This fabulous report was apparently also archived, but after Pando left the district his political fortunes led to its publication. He became a congressman and later served as administrator of the state's central district, including the city of Oaxaca. The official newspaper of the state published the 1837 report in various issues during the spring of 1843 as Pando suffered from a long illness. Pando died on 15 May, less than two months after the publication of his report was complete.[176]

🦚 Priests, Religion, and Indigenous Society

Priests greatly outnumbered civil administrators in Villa Alta, and their religious role also meant they loomed larger in the lives of indigenous peasants. Although villages employed the services of indigenous religious specialists like cantors for official Catholic practice and shamans for unofficial indigenous rites, Catholic priests were necessary for the sacraments. Individual sacraments like baptism, marriage, and last rites marked the major passages of life for Catholics, although of course their particular significance for indigenous peasants is hard to gauge from the available documents. Priests were also central to the collective religious life of villages. Villagers attended Sunday mass periodically, and masses were crucial to the collective village celebrations of general Catholic holidays and the specific feasts of the patrons of villages, cofradías, or barrios.[177] As we saw in chapter 2, barrios in Villa Alta were not residential neighborhoods but religious groups that each organized and financed the costly worship of a separate patron saint. As John Chance points out, by the late colonial period they were virtually synonymous with indigenous cofradías.[178] Barrios jealously defended their funds and lands, insisting that they be devoted only to the worship of their particular patron.[179] Unlike cofradías, barrios seem to have developed rivalries within villages. These rivalries were related to the different religious obligations of the members of distinct barrios, but they often spilled over into conflicts over elections and community service. Barrio rivalries in some villages became severe and prolonged, contributing to the problems of indigenous village leaders who struggled to maintain village unity.[180]

Although most priests apparently managed to avoid involvement in barrio rivalries, their position in villages could still become uncomfortable. As in the colonial period, priests depended on their parishioners to pay them for their services. In some villages these payments were determined by custom or agreements between priests and their parishioners, while in others payments were regulated by a fee schedule published by the diocese. Neither arrangement actually guaranteed that a priest would be paid, and often even within villages parishioners disagreed over which form of payment should be used. Government authorities were frequently drawn into these disputes. Although they generally tried to mediate, they steadfastly upheld the general principle that parishioners were required to support their priests.[181] As a lawyer Benito Juárez had represented villagers in similar disputes, and when he became governor he suggested that the best way to minimize these costly and divisive conflicts would be for the diocese to update the fee schedule and make it mandatory for all villages. Juárez noted in 1852 that the adoption of liberal republicanism did not free parishioners from the obligation to pay their priests.[182] Notably, even after independence village officials were made responsible for actually collecting customary fees, and at the ends of their terms they were required to pay priests all that was owed.[183] Yet if a priest charged according to the fee schedule he himself would have to collect sums from individual peasants for services like baptism and last rites, and the priest's demand for payment on these occasions could lead to ugly feelings.[184] Generally, the movement to republican laws and forms of government did not substantially change the economic relationship between priests and their parishioners.

Conflict between priests and parishioners could also arise over religious issues. Parishioners sometimes severely criticized priests who did not provide the sacraments in timely fashion.[185] Pastors also ran afoul of the religious devotion of their parishioners in other ways. In 1836 the priest Francisco María Gonzalez planned to use an image of San Antonio for a procession and mass. When his envoys arrived at the chapel where it was kept its devotees refused to allow its removal, apparently because they feared that the priest would place it in the main village church. Gonzalez responded that he only wanted to use it for a vigil, procession, and mass. He angrily cried, "Tell those drunks that I do not want to take the saint, I have enough saints in the Church." Later the priest admitted that in fact he was trying to gain control of the religious celebration of the saint, since the annual celebration in the chapel was a drunken affair, with music, fireworks, and shouts. Apparently Gonzalez sought to substitute a more orthodox or modern religious ceremony for the indigenous custom. His plan was foiled by the near-riot.[186] Six years later Juan María Carreño, parish priest of Lachiroag, also faced resistance provoked by the attempt to modernize religious practices. The state government had, with the support of the diocese, decreed that all burials should take place not inside churches but instead in cemeteries outside populated areas. When the infant child of Doroteo Lorenzo died, Carreño refused to bury the body in the church. A crowd of parishioners gathered, shouting that if they could not be buried in the church they would stop paying taxes and clerical fees. After the ringleaders were punished the matter was resolved with the inauguration of a properly blessed cemetery.[187]

Priests occupied an ambiguous position in the local political terrain. Priests and their dependents were the only people who lived in villages but did not believe themselves to be subject to village governments. Both priests and village authorities were very sensitive to this problem, and as a result many conflicts included incidents that either priests or village officials believed showed a lack of proper respect. In 1839 a priest, Vicente Antonio Brioso, complained that José María Isidro, the alcalde of Betaza, had approached Brioso while drunk and failed to remove his hat. Brioso reported that when he scolded Isidro for this, Isidro raised his staff of office and said that "he was the Alcalde, and that he ruled in the whole village and he would put me in the jail." In his testimony Isidro admitted that he had been drinking when the priest called him to ask about something. When Isidro asked to kiss the priest's hand the priest responded by slapping him. Isidro raised his staff of office to protect his face and said, in his words, "Sir priest,

I warn you that I am an authority of the Village and you should not abuse me this way, because if I have committed some crime, I have a court where I should be judged according to law just as you have your own court." The state judge assigned the case closed it immediately, pointing out that even if the priest's version was true no crime had been committed. He did, however, suggest that state authorities scold the alcalde.[188]

Agustín María Castillejos, parish priest of Yae, complained in 1853 of the villagers' lack of respect. Castillejos had forced the alcalde's wife to clean up the mess she made while ginning cotton on his porch. The next day Castillejos found an anonymous letter in his window, criticizing him for abusing the woman and living off the work of the villagers. The writer insisted to Castillejos that "we all have hearts and souls and are children of God" and suggested that Castillejos did not treat the villagers as well as his predecessor had. Castillejos launched an investigation into who had written the letter, but he was never able to get the most likely suspect to confess, and village authorities refused to punish the man. Later villagers refused to doff their hats to Castillejos, and several mocked him while they were drunk or pretending to be drunk. Castillejos asked judicial authorities to prosecute his tormentors, but they declined.[189] On many other occasions priests complained to civil authorities when villagers refused to show the respect they thought was their due. Although certainly many priests were esteemed or at least tolerated by their flocks, when disputes arose they often included symbolic battles over respect.[190]

✿ Peasants and Politics Beyond the Village

In the previous pages we have seen how villagers' relationships with state regulations, district administrators, and parish priests could often be conflictive. Yet, in elections the villagers of Villa Alta never forged political alliances with the parties that disputed state power. When villagers were asked to vote in elections for state office, their votes, once filtered through district secondary elections, invariably favored the party already in office regardless of its political orientation. In other words, villagers of Villa Alta district did not exert significant electoral pressure in the political struggles that divided the state, and they apparently made no effort to bargain their votes in exchange for favorable treatment on local issues. The support that whichever party was in power received from the district of Villa Alta cannot be explained by patron-clientalism. Richard Graham has shown the importance of patronage for impoverished rural voters in nineteenth-century Brazil, where landowners could offer clients food, access to land, and exemption from the draft.[191] However, in Villa Alta villages controlled almost all the cultivated land, and each village only had to send a handful of men to the draft. Moreover, there is no evidence of powerful whites or mestizos extending patronage to poor villagers. Conceivably judges or district administrators might have been able to extend aid in land disputes to entire villages in exchange for their support, but since all the disputes were between villages, any aid offered to one village hurt another. Therefore we have to look elsewhere to explain the solid support the district offered to sitting governors.

First, it is clear that elections were not entirely a farce. Villagers voted regularly, and they appear to have generally followed electoral regulations.[192] Each parish routinely sent electors to the district capital to participate in the next stage of elections. According to the state constitution, parish electors were required to be literate, but the constitution delayed enforcement of this provision until 1840. Parish electors were also required to possess "territorial property, or real estate, or a profession, job, or other productive industry."[193] Moisés Bailón Corres suggests that this effectively excluded indigenous peasants, but the evidence shows that most parish electors in Villa Alta were in fact indigenous peasants.[194] Apparently, either communal ownership of land was accepted as sufficient, or authorities believed that the spirit of the law required simple economic independence. In these district elections indigenous electors chose district electors who would actually cast the ballots for state legislators. The multiple stages for this process were in fact the key to the support state governors were able to muster. State governors could not offer patronage to the indigenous voters who voted at the earliest stage, but as contemporaries well understood, governors had much they could offer to a reduced number of district electors.[195] Moreover, the indigenous electors who voted for district electors repeatedly selected men who were vulnerable to pressure from sitting governments. As we have seen, they chose people who were not indigenous peasants, including priests, district administrators, judges, and sometimes merchants. This pattern began with elections held in 1820 under the Spanish constitution, and continued throughout the period considered in this book.[196]

Why did indigenous peasants chosen by their peers as parish electors turn around and choose nonpeasants to represent the district in statewide elections? Literacy does not seem to have been an issue, as even the indigenous men chosen as parish electors were literate enough to handle ballots.[197] Instead one problem seems to have been that indigenous electors faced a rather limited pool of choices. They had to choose residents of the district, but they were not likely to know, or especially to trust, indigenous peasants from villages other than their own. Since the villages were quite small, no Indian peasant could have become a district elector on the basis of votes from his village alone. Given this, most indigenous electors seem to have selected people they knew outside the peasantry, in other words, priests, government officials, and sometimes merchants. Moreover, there were no political issues capable of uniting peasants from more than one village in an alliance. Land disputes, for instance, typically pitted village against village. State authorities in Oaxaca, unlike those in other states, never made a concerted effort to limit indigenous village government, and in Villa Alta indigenous peasants never expressed the kind of widespread resistance to new taxes that drove political movements in Guerrero in the 1840s.[198] In other words, indigenous peasants in Villa Alta lacked any motive for trying to shape the membership of the state legislature. Although the evidence that Villa Alta's indigenous peasants were aware of party divisions in the state is quite limited, it is likely they had some awareness.[199] Many peasants traveled to the city of Oaxaca to market their textiles, and emigration to the city meant that some had relatives there. However, indigenous political culture abhorred factionalism and political organizing within villages, and this might have made indigenous peasants shy away from similar struggles on the state or national levels. Ironically, indigenous peasants acted the way that the writers of the state constitution believed that all voters should act: they exercised their popular sovereignty by selecting men of prestige to actually choose government personnel.

The district did not remain entirely untouched by state political conflicts. In 1828 it, like most districts in the state, returned an aceite slate of electors. When the vinagres took power in the state after the Revolution of the Acordada, they named Nicolás Fernandez del Campo, a vinagre, as interim administrator of the district. Fernandez del Campo apparently tried to lend the district's weight to the effort to have the 1828 state election annulled. Soon after he took office the governments of fourteen different villages signed petitions to annul the elections. The lone surviving example, produced in the relatively Hispanicized village of Analco, alleges that the district election was manipulated to favor the aceites.[200] Despite Fernandez del Campo's role here, the political opinions of the district administrator do not seem to have determined how district electors voted in state elections. José María Pando followed Fernandez del Campo in district office, and he was a radical vinagre. Although this fact was occasionally mentioned in disputes during the early part of his term, Pando apparently did not try to influence district electors to support the vinagres, and even aceite governments placed great confidence in him. Either the patronage power held by the government was enough to keep Pando in line, or Pando, like many radicals, drifted to the right as his political career continued. The latter seems very likely.

ℑ⅋ *The Political Repertoires of Indigenous Peasants*

Although the political culture of Villa Alta's indigenous peasants was not static in the period after independence, older parts of the political repertoire retained their relevance. Indigenous peasants had long been known as litigious, and the peasants of Villa Alta continued to take cases to court. Many of the documents used to research this chapter were generated through lawsuits and criminal cases about a variety of issues. Lawsuits of course required money for court costs, and groups of villagers raised money for court actions by soliciting voluntary donations or involuntary quotas from villagers. Not all indigenous peasants wanted to participate in lawsuits, but dissidents faced great pressure. In 1831 Miguel Ylarto of Yalalag was threatened with exile in such a case, while in 1826 villagers from Tabaa threatened to exile three such dissidents and burn down their houses. In the late 1830s the nation's centralist administration tried to limit lawsuits by requiring the approval of district administrators, but judging from the number of cases in the archive this measure was ineffective.[201]

Village riots also continued to form an important part of the indigenous political repertoire. In many parts of Mexico large, multivillage peasant rebellions became common after independence, and the assumption up to now has been that these more general movements replaced village riots.[202] This was definitely not the case in Villa Alta. There were at least thirty-three riots in the district of Villa Alta between 1821 and 1857. This large number is not far from the total of fifty-two that John Coatsworth calculated for the entire country between 1820 and 1860.[203] The difference probably arises from the research process. Coatsworth based his total on the secondary sources that were available in the middle of the 1980s, and most of those sources relied on national-level archives. Yet, by their very nature riots were usually considered minor and local affairs, and thus many never came to the attention of officials in Mexico City or even state capitals. In the case of Villa Alta even state-level archives only mention three of the thirty-three riots known to have taken place, and not one appears in the Archivo General de la Nación. The vast majority are documented only in the district archive. Because they were not considered threats to the security or legitimacy of the state, district officials often did not even report them to their superiors.[204] It remains quite possible that riots also remained common in other regions.[205] Riots may have continued to occur when the local character of grievances or the absence of dissident elites prevented larger alliances.

Riots after independence remained very similar to their colonial counterparts. For instance, women continued to take leading roles in riots.[206] As we have seen, women's participation was a symbol of village unity and also a vital contribution to the physical threat posed by rioters. In fact, the latter motive was important enough that women also were prominent in most riots that pitted village factions against each other.[207] Yet riots continued to feature threats more than actual physical violence. During an 1851 riot in Zoogocho, Subprefect Francisco Beltran faced an angry crowd of women and men for several hours. They chased him from the plaza to the government offices, broke down the doors, threatened to kill him, threw rocks, sticks, and mud at him, spat on him, and stole his belongings. Yet despite the obvious danger, his testimony admitted that in the end the only wounds he had received were bruises.[208] As intimidating as riots were, no one was killed in a riot in the district.

Riots often occurred during internal disputes. In electoral disputes and other cases the principales used riots to defend their influence in the face of new laws that appeared to marginalize them.[209] At other times rioters sought to hold officials responsible for their management of village funds or labor projects. These disputes were sometimes linked to barrio rivalries.[210] Rioters also acted against people who refused to follow community decisions, snuffing out dissidence within villages.[211] Riots were sometimes even brawls between families over basically private economic disputes.[212] In all of these cases rioters sought to settle crucial internal issues with physical force or the threat of force, and each therefore suggests the limits of the legitimacy of village government.

Conversely, riots often took place as a result of rivalries between villages. Territorial disputes often underlay these rivalries. Usually territorial disputes were fought out in the arena of the judicial system, but in many cases these disputes also led to physical confrontations.[213] These riots or brawls almost always took place at the margins of village territories. Indians who farmed or herded ran the risk of physical confrontation with mobs from neighboring villages.[214] Other times a land dispute led to confrontations on the roads and paths that linked the villages of the region. In 1824 the officials of Yatoni presented a petition in the district capital describing their complaints against the neighboring village of Talea. As the officials were walking home they ran into a group of men from Talea who were repairing the road, and a battle ensued. A similar confrontation took place between work parties of Yaganiza and San Mateo Cajonos in 1830. In 1831 a group of villagers from Temaxcalapan confronted rivals from Yalahui who were on their way to a nearby tianguis.[215] Disputes between villages frustrated higher authorities. The rivalry between Lachiroag and the district capital of Villa Alta led to several battles and innumerable complaints in the 1830s. A territorial dispute soon led to a tug of war over the residence of their shared parish priest and even the location of the local tianguis. Judges, the district administrator, and even the state legislature tried to mediate without results.[216]

Village riots also targeted people from outside the region. Priests found themselves isolated in rural villages, and as we have seen their role in village life often led to economic or religious conflicts. These disputes sometimes led to threatening riots, although in the end priests' injuries were always confined to their pride.[217] On a few occasions efforts to collect taxes also led to riots, and on two occasions we have already seen the riots or near-riots directed at outsiders. In 1853 in San Andres Yaa a representative from the district administration was trying to collect head taxes that the village had fallen behind on, and only the timely intervention of village officials saved him from a mob of women. In 1851 Francisco Beltran's effort to collect taxes at the tianguis of Zoogocho led to a terrifying riot. Village officials refused to intervene, and in the end he was rescued by a group of men from a neighboring village. Later witnesses stated that many of the rioters were women from other villages who were at the tianguis to buy and sell.[218]

The continued importance of village riots in Villa Alta suggests significant continuities between the colonial and postindependence political repertoires of indigenous communities. Other continuities are visible in key symbols, values, and language. Varas or bastones, the staffs of office, continued to be the most important symbols of village authority. Villagers sometimes disputed the right of various officials to carry this important insignia. In a heated reference to popular sovereignty several men of Lahoya insisted to the Alcalde Francisco Mendez in 1857 that "they had given him the staff he carried."[219] State politicians understood the importance of this crucial symbol. In federalist periods elected alcaldes carried staffs openly, and during the centralist interlude the government arranged for appointed local officials to also carry them because otherwise villagers would not respect their authority. As the state governor, Antonio de León, put it in 1844, it was difficult to "make a hardened custom disappear." Moreover, the centralists also replicated the colonial feria de varas, a ceremony under which village officials were sworn in by the district administrator and handed their staffs of office.[220] Documents likewise remained potent political symbols, often taking a central role in disputes, even though most villagers were illiterate. For instance, when the villagers of Juquila complained to the bishop against their priest, the bishop gave them a document to deliver to him. The priest not only refused to open the document, he threw it to the ground, an act that caused consternation.[221]

Village unity was still one of the most important political values. The archives for both the republican and colonial periods repeatedly portray conflicts within villages over a variety of issues. Yet through all of this villages struggled to present unified faces to the outside world. Villagers continued to frown on meetings to organize political groups within the village.[222] They also threatened dissidents with exile.[223] Yet it should be noted that villagers often made strenuous efforts to find compromise solutions to controversial problems. In 1821 San Miguel Talea split over the way the village paid its priest. After a long struggle the two sides agreed that the issue "should not be a reason to live divided into bands since they were one Village and all relatives," and they ended their dispute symbolically with a mutual embrace.[224]

Political discourse also showed some continuity with the past. Sometimes indigenous peasants referred to colonial laws in disputes.[225] More often the carryovers were less specific. We have seen, for instance, multiple references to the elders and commons even though state laws did not recognize their relevance to contemporary politics.[226] Although specific words from the colonial political culture found their way into the documents of republican archives, the most striking continuities were in the forms of discourse. Indigenous peasants in Villa Alta continued to present the same kinds of documents. Legal petitions or escritos were still the most common documents, and like their colonial predecessors they provided first-person narration of disputes. Sometimes escritos were formed with the help of lawyers or other outsiders with legal expertise, but more often they seem to have been composed by village scribes and other literate villagers. Indigenous peasants also continued to testify in court. In effect, the fact that court procedures did not change significantly with independence meant that the forms of indigenous political discourse, or at least those forms that are available to us, did not change either.

New political terms entered the indigenous vocabulary even as traditions continued and older terms remained common. The result was, in the words of Michael Ducey, "a complicated duality."[227] This duality emerged immediately and continued for many years. Moreover, it was not always confined to documents definitely composed by Indians. For instance, in 1821, right after the Spanish constitution was implemented, Joaquín Villasante, a lawyer, prepared a petition on behalf of a group in San Miguel Talea. Villasante identified the petitioners as "the commons and Citizens of the Village." Yet Villasante's clients were not ignorant of the change in the forms of government. Later in the same file, they refer to the "Constitution" repeatedly in a petition written by the village scribe.[228] The identifying terms of the colonial indigenous culture were repeatedly mixed with those of the new republican order. These can best be seen in escritos, which commonly began by identifying the party submitting the document. Thus an 1827 petition from San Pablo Ayutla begins with the phrase, "We the Citizens, Alcaldes, Regidores, Principales, and rest of the commons of this Village."[229] The first two terms were introduced by the constitution and postindependence laws, while the last three were carryovers from older traditions. Yet the petitioners saw no contradiction. These types of phrases are evident in the majority of petitions directed to authorities. Moreover, similar mixtures of political identities were common in the documents describing oaths to the centralist constitution in 1835. On this occasion, villages varied in how they identified those who had participated in the act of allegiance. For instance, in Talea the document was headed by "We the Constitutional Republic"; in Zochistepec, "all the Citizens that make up the republic of this municipality the principales and commons"; in Latani, "the Republic . . . in union with many residents"; in Jalahui, "the entire corporation"; in Juquila, "all the citizens"; in Cacalotepec, " the commons and principales for all the authorities"; in Tagui, "all the children [of the village]"; in Comaltepec, "the Republic and all the native citizens"; in Zoogocho, "the justice and principales"; in Lalopa, "principales and all inhabitants and residents"; and in Teotalcingo, "all the Republic Principales and other residents."[230] These phrases suggest the way that villages stretched beyond the visions of political identity offered by urban politicians to incorporate their traditions. Many villages explicitly mentioned the participation of the principales, showing the continued political importance of this group even in each village's relationship with higher government.[231] In 1842–43 villages were ordered to swear allegiance to a new set of supreme decrees. As in 1835, the identities of those who participated in the acts varied, including for example "the justices of the peace of this village and the helpers"; "many residents"; "the justices of the peace helpers and principales many residents"; "the justice of the peace municipality and principal"; " the justice of the peace, helpers, principales and rest of the municipal corps and other residents"; "the principal citizens and commons"; "commons of natives"; and "we the judges justice of the peace in union with all the sir principales and all the commons."[232] For several years the highest village authorities had been selected by the district administrator, but more expansive visions of village political life remained vibrant. By the 1830s the term *citizen* had entered indigenous political vocabulary and can be seen in a variety of documents. At least once it was even applied to a woman.[233]

The new political language was also featured prominently when indigenous officials described their authority. Under the state's federalist constitution the highest village officials were elected alcaldes, and these alcaldes stressed how their authority derived from the constitution. In 1833 Thomas Quintana of San Pablo Ayutla called himself the "constitutional alcalde," while in 1834 Tomas Velasco of Yatzona reminded his opponents that he was a "constitutionally elected Alcalde."[234] Colonial village officials had seen their authority as emanating from the king, and their republican counterparts replaced the king with the constitution or sometimes an abstract nation.[235] Thus, as we have seen, the government offices at the center of each village mutated from being the "royal house" to the "constitutional house" or "national house."[236] Of course someone had to actually issue the orders that arrived from outside the village, and villagers at least occasionally saw those orders as those of the "Sovereign Congress," which replaced the king.[237] Notably, this formulation in indigenous documents matches closely the political theories that guided Hispanic politicians. Apparently the pessimism that some Hispanic politicians expressed about the ability of indigenous peasants to understand and adapt to political change was not warranted. Perhaps the yawning cultural gap most Hispanic politicians saw as separating themselves from indigenous peasants was not as wide as it appeared.

ꜰ꒰ Conclusion

Enrique Florescano eloquently describes what he calls the "obsessive aspiration" of Mexico's nineteenth-century politicians: their ambition to create "a nation of citizens governed by the same laws, united by common values and animated by the idea of creating a sovereign state."[238] Autonomous indigenous village governments governed by local custom were of course a serious obstacle to this effort, and many politicians sought to eliminate them from the political and social landscape. However, this drive for uniformity was much weaker in Oaxaca than it was in many other states. Oaxaca's elite, perched on top of a largely indigenous population on which it depended economically, "always understood that they would have to build bridges between themselves and the Indians," in the words of Carlos Sánchez Silva. The means of mediation involved a trade-off: Oaxaca's elite maintained its economic supremacy but in turn had to tolerate a great deal of indigenous political autonomy.[239]

Oaxacan lawmakers and other politicians thus made a series of concessions to indigenous social customs and political traditions. The earliest and perhaps the most important was the 1825 provision for governments in all the villages of the state, no matter what their size. This decision shaped the Oaxacan political landscape in profound ways, and it underlies the relatively strong tradition of indigenous autonomy that Oaxaca still enjoys. Although the centralists later eliminated these locally chosen governments, even they made many concessions to indigenous traditions. The appointed jueces de paz carried out the same duties as the previous officials, and they also used the same symbols.

Hispanic lawmakers and politicians also failed to eliminate the community service that had long dominated political and social life in indigenous communities. The preservation of the cargo system was a practical decision. After all, even Hispanic municipal governments relied heavily on unpaid but obligatory offices, and it is difficult to imagine how local governments could have functioned without such posts. However, in districts like Villa Alta the continuation of the cargo system and obligatory service fatally undermined the republican effort to create a nation of equal, individual citizens because community service was the central feature of indigenous corporate identity. Belonging to a village, being a good "child of the village," required participation in the cargo system and its sister institutions, the tequio and service for the priest. Those who did not participate lost their membership in the village. The survival of the cargo system was as important in preserving indigenous identity as the provision for local governments in every village. Yet even the cargo system changed significantly in the republican period. The republican abolition of hereditary distinctions ended the colonial disputes over inherited exemptions and privileges that had bitterly divided many villages.

Hispanic politicians did not casually sanction the continuance of indigenous governments. They introduced new procedures for choosing village officers, and they also gave repúblicas new duties that were designed to make them administrative arms of the state rather than centers of indigenous identity. The nature of the interplay between these two roles is of course a key question, and it is particularly difficult to answer because most documents about what village governments actually did were generated by conflict. The relatively quiet negotiation of the old and new that must have been the norm remains largely out of the reach of historians. However, one interesting document provides some suggestive answers. From the colonial period on, indigenous authorities kept scrupulous accounts of village expenditures because they had to prove that there were no shortfalls at the end of their terms. These internal documents rarely appear in state or even district archives. However, during a dispute over parochial fees Solaga's juez de paz forwarded to the court his accounts for 1842. His list of expenditures shows how village government both continued indigenous traditions and served as an administrative agent for the state. It includes sums spent for pulque and cigars for officials; incense, candles, holy water, and parochial fees for religious occasions; and expenses for the traditional feria de varas. The government also spent money on paper, ink, pens, helpers for the village scribe, and visits to the district capital to see the administrator about various affairs. None of these expenditures would have stood out in an account from the colonial period. Yet the 1842 account also contains evidence of the new role of village governments. The juez de paz spent significant sums during the election of a new constitutional congress. These expenditures included paper for ballots, helpers to write out voters' choices, and pulque to refresh those counting ballots as well as trips to the district capital to receive instructions for the election and later to participate in the district secondary election. The village government also elaborated a census to determine who was eligible for the draft, and then made yet another visit to the district capital to try to gain the village an exemption from this burden.[240] Was the government of Solaga the old, colonial, depository of village identity or was it the new administrative arm of a government that sought to forge national unity? In some sense it was both.

CONCLUSION

꙳ In the middle of the nineteenth century Mexico was poised on the brink of an intense period of political change that has come to be known as the Reform. During the Reform a group of liberals whose most prominent leader was Benito Juárez struggled against the Church hierarchy, conservatives, and eventually the French empire to construct a new liberal national state in Mexico. This ultimately successful authoritarian liberal state set a pattern which would endure throughout the remainder of the nineteenth century and would only be modified by the great upheaval of the 1910–20 Mexican revolution and subsequent attempts at state formation. For many Mexicans the Reform stands between the War of Independence and the Revolution as one of the three great epochs in the formation of Mexican nationality. Although interpretations of the Reform do not always grant it a heroic character, historians of many perspectives see it as crucial.[1]

During and after the Reform liberal politicians and historians constructed a vision of politics in early republican Mexico. This vision served both as an analytical tool for Reform thinkers and legitimation for their often-authoritarian methods. Generally the liberals argued that as of the middle of the nineteenth century Mexico was still an essentially colonial place, with a promising economy held back by traditional forms of collective property and a political system still controlled by the privileged groups and institutions that had dominated the colonial period. In the liberals' view, the mass of Mexican society had been left essentially untouched by political change and largely at the margins of Mexico's putatively republican and democratic politics.[2] In constructing this vision, liberals filtered their knowledge of

Mexican society through a set of political interests and ideals that empha-sized the need for dramatic reform.

The evidence from the city of Oaxaca and the district of Villa Alta sug-gests that the liberals' portrait of that early republican period was extremely flawed. Certainly politics and political culture did not match the ideals of republican theorists, and Mexico was already notorious for political in-stability. Moreover, the distribution of wealth in both Oaxaca and the coun-try as a whole remained skewed, and most Mexicans were mired in poverty. Yet much had indeed changed over the previous century, and nothing had changed more than the practice of politics. Even the coups and civil wars themselves were evidence of change, as the colonial period had seen noth-ing like them. Efforts to develop a new hegemonic political culture for Mexico influenced the lives of Oaxaca's urban poor and Villa Alta's indige-nous peasants even though they did not become the idealized citizens that political culture raised to iconic status.

Understanding how popular political culture changed in these two loca-tions can help us answer some fundamental questions. First, why was the transition to republicanism so difficult in Mexico and other parts of Spanish America? Why did it not bring the peace and prosperity its missionaries promised? How did the new political system change the ways in which Mexico's impoverished majorities engaged the state? Second, on a more theoretical plane, what happens when political elites work to replace a hegemonic political culture? How does change conceived at the highest levels in the sociopolitical system become the new basis of legitimacy that allows political elites to continue their dominance of the mass of society?

ʃ❧ Urban politics

The central story we saw in urban Oaxaca was that of the rise and fall of electoral politics. In Oaxaca electoral politics were introduced in a socially polarized milieu, where a proud urban elite with a strong racial identity shared urban space warily with a diverse population ready to embrace the more egalitarian social visions offered by Bourbon reformers, Spanish liber-als, and insurgent leaders. The result was intense partisan conflict. This conflict was initially defined in the electoral arena, but ultimately it could not be confined there. Political conflict became inseparable from political intolerance, and in a few years both parties came to rely on military forces that originated from outside the city. Elections no longer determined who would govern in the city. The electoral politics that seemed so crucial to Mexican republicanism ultimately failed in the city of Oaxaca.

The failure of electoral politics in Oaxaca did not stem from any indifference on the part of the populace. Although the sources do not allow accurate calculations of electoral turnouts, clearly many people voted, and anecdotal evidence suggests that these voters varied widely in their socioeconomic status. Electoral politics in Oaxaca, at least in the first decade after independence, were hardly a democratic fiction. François Xavier-Guerra and Marie-Danielle Demélas-Bohy have argued that in nineteenth-century Latin America the only true citizens were members of the elite who internalized modern notions of democracy.[3] Yet in cities like Oaxaca and Mexico City, and even in some rural areas, many impoverished Mexicans claimed and exercised their right to vote. Guerra and Demélas-Bohy explain this contradiction by arguing that these voters participated due to clientalism and older corporatist structures of politics, and that these older social patterns made elections in places like Mexico farces that did not determine who was to hold power.[4]

The evidence from the city of Oaxaca contradicts this view. There was simply no social basis for a clientalist politics because the economic ties between urban elites and the mass of the population were extremely tenuous. More importantly, the breakdown of electoral politics in Oaxaca arose not from a failure to foster democratic participation but from a lack of pluralism and political tolerance. The origins of this political intolerance were several. As Guerra points out, in premodern Hispanic political culture power was seen as unitary, and unanimity remained an important political ideal. Organized interest groups were criticized as factions who threatened social harmony.[5] Yet as François Furet, among others, has shown in the case of the French Revolution, the more modern notion of a general political will arising from popular sovereignty also contained the seeds of intolerance, as each side claimed to represent the will of the true people and accused its enemies of plotting against that will.[6] Moreover, in the case of Oaxaca the development of this political intolerance proceeded step by step as elections were disputed and each party came to see the other as a threat to core political values. Eventually, Oaxacan political groups developed such apocalyptic visions of the goals of their adversaries that they came to not only accept but also actively court military aid from outside the region. At that point elections were no longer important in determining who would rule, and democracy had essentially become a fiction.

Even today the district of Villa Alta has the reputation of being physically remote and culturally traditional. Yet the evidence we have seen from the late eighteenth century and the early nineteenth shows that, despite a reverence for tradition, indigenous society was far from static. Political innovations introduced by governing elites were alternatively resisted, embraced, and modified by distinct groups within the many villages of Villa Alta. Manuel Ferrer Muñoz and María Bono López have argued recently that the new political norms introduced beginning in the late eighteenth century had nothing to offer Mexico's Indians, who simply were not in a position to take advantage of legal equality.[7] They offer a reasonable interpretation based on comparing the new juridical norms with a largely idealized indigenous society. But by actually researching how these norms shaped politics in even a place as traditional as Villa Alta, we realize that some of the innovations found constituencies within indigenous communities, and a few of these changes were naturalized to become fundamental features of indigenous political culture. At the same time, indigenous peasants certainly struggled with some of the innovations, but they were able to preserve key aspects of earlier political traditions through their own efforts and through the pragmatism of elites who placed political stability and tax revenue ahead of the goal of changing indigenous cultures.

Thus, indigenous politics were not unchanged in the period. At least some communities experienced the emergence of new and more lasting forms of political leadership by individuals familiar with the Spanish language, writing, and the administrative norms of the state. More importantly, all the communities of Villa Alta appear to have used the new ideal of political equality to abolish the privileges of village nobles, ending controversies that had wracked many communities in the last sixty years of the colonial period. Steve Stern argues that the political culture of Mexican peasant communities has long included strong tendencies toward both hierarchy and egalitarianism.[8] In this case we can see how the postindependence ideals of republican lawmakers, products of an Enlightenment political culture often seen as antithetical to indigenous traditions, helped villagers raise the more democratic side of indigenous political culture to unquestioned supremacy in at least one institution. When anthropologists began investigating politics in these communities in the first half of the twentieth century, they found, in the words of pioneer ethnographer Julio de la Fuente, that "strong egalitarian thinking" governed both the cargo system and relations between groups within villages.[9]

The ability of indigenous communities to alternatively shape and re-sist the norms of republican local government has been stronger in Oaxaca than in any other Mexican state. Today just about every indigenous com-munity has its own municipal government. Moreover, during the twentieth century indigenous communities have generally been able to choose their own leaders autonomously following various local customs centered on the cargo system. The emergence of the twentieth century's dominant national party did not change this pattern, as the PRI itself deferred to village elders. The PRI simply accepted their choices as its own candidates for municipal office, in effect offering local autonomy in exchange for indigenous electoral support on the state and national levels.[10] Thus the PRI followed the lead of nineteenth-century elite Oaxacan politicians. In 1995 the state legislature of Oaxaca enacted a municipal reform that effectively granted legal status to this indigenous autonomy, allowing 412 of the state's 570 municipalities to choose their own authorities following their local "uses and customs." No-tably, even then these uses and customs were not set in stone. They con-tinued to adjust themselves to the circumstances and balances of forces in various villages. In 2001, for instance, the village of Santa María Camotlán began allowing villagers resident in Mexico City and the United States to vote in municipal elections.[11] Thus traditional village "uses and customs" embraced the contemporary reality of massive immigration and transna-tional communities.

ʃ◑ Urban Plebeians and Indigenous Peasants

The changing political cultures of Oaxaca's urban plebeians and Villa Alta's indigenous peasants in the late eighteenth century and early nineteenth are difficult to compare because the sources for the two groups are so different. As mentioned in the introduction, urban plebeians do not show up in the documents as often, and the ways in which they appear are not nearly as articulate. Generally, though, indigenous peasants seem to have been better able to shape the new political norms to achieve their own goals. They enjoyed strong collective organization in the shape of the village, an institu-tion whose legitimacy few Indian peasants ever questioned. Moreover, po-litical elites were much more willing to make concessions to indigenous peasants because they were seen as representing little, if any, threat to political order or the fortunes of either of the two political parties in the state. Thus Oaxaca's political elites initially allowed for municipalities in every indigenous community and legalized the demands communities made on the labor of their members through the cargo system. Even under the centralists Oaxacan politicians made informal concessions that were not common in states where elites and peasants had more conflictive relationships. For their part, indigenous peasants seem to have accepted this de facto bargain. They voiced few opinions about state politics, but their votes invariably aided whoever held the governorship because peasant primary electors always nominated district electors who were potential clients of the governor. Indigenous peasants also paid their taxes with greater regularity than any other group in the state.

Oaxaca's urban plebeians were in a much less favorable position. Their collective organizations were considerably weaker. Guilds never incorporated more than a fraction of the urban work force, and their economic privileges were eroded to near nullity very early in the nineteenth century. Urban plebeians faced fierce economic competition from both the indigenous peasant artisans of outlying villages and the factories of the industrializing world. Even then urban plebeians did not withdraw from politics. They worked toward protectionism in the late 1820s, and from the 1810s on they seem to have fiercely embraced the egalitarian promise of liberal republican politics. Yet the symbolic gains they attained were outweighed in the end by the practical difficulties of republican politics. Because the electors returned by indigenous peasants of the state consistently favored whichever party was in power, urban plebeians usually found their electoral weight nullified precisely at the crucial moments when they sought to exert it to effect a change in government. More importantly, urban plebeians were exposed to the possibility of military intervention and political repression, and the city endured several civil conflicts. In addition, the economic goals of urban plebeians were probably unobtainable in the Atlantic world in which they lived. A dignified living was hard to come by as the urban poor throughout the Atlantic world were buffeted by the rising winds of the Industrial Revolution.

Ironically, both the massive and sometimes violent participation of plebeians in party politics and the apparent disinterest of indigenous peasants in that same party politics played into the hands of those who wanted to reduce opportunities for popular participation or even entirely remove elections from the political repertoire. The politicians who worked to reduce electoral participation, separate elections from the way political decisions were actually made, or simply eliminate elections altogether were probably motivated by the electoral defeats of their generally conservative and centralist political groups. Yet they needed more disinterested arguments to justify their positions, and they based those arguments on the behaviors observed in elections. Both the unruly urban crowds who thronged the polling places and the seemingly stolid and alien masses of indigenous peasants who lent their electoral weight to groups already in power seemed too far removed from the ideal of a sovereign people rationally exercising its will through the ballot. Like many historians now, politicians who wanted to reduce the importance of elections held the living, breathing people of the nineteenth century up against a basically fictitious ideal they believed to be prevalent in Europe or North America. In both cases Mexico's population appeared to come up short.

ꝳ Oaxaca and Guerrero

My earlier research on Guerrero in the early nineteenth century suggests some fruitful comparisons to the developments traced here for urban Oaxaca and rural Villa Alta. Oaxaca and Guerrero were both overwhelmingly rural regions with indigenous majorities and important coastal populations of African Americans. The two regions were also both later known for their contributions to the Reform, contributions that were symbolized by Juan Alvarez of Guerrero, who led the Revolution of Ayutla that began the Reform and briefly became president, and Benito Juárez, president during much of the period. In Guerrero I studied rural social mobilization and state formation over a fifty-year period from the War of Independence to the Revolution of Ayutla. Over time both indigenous and nonindigenous peasants began to form alliances that spanned village boundaries and even included politicians who were not peasants. In the case of the mulatto sharecroppers of the coast, these alliances sought to punish monopolistic merchants and support protectionist policies. Some indigenous peasants of mountainous regions rebelled over land, but most became involved when taxes skyrocketed. In both cases local autonomy was an important issue, especially after it was eliminated under the centralists. By the 1840s Guerrero's peasants were participating in national political alliances, supporting popular federalists and expressing their own concerns with the rhetoric of that national movement. Peasants' support for popular federalists allowed them to achieve many of their political aims, at least in the short run.[12]

The politics of Oaxaca's urban plebeians were more like those of Guerrero's peasants than were the politics of Villa Alta's peasants. To the extent one can tell from sources that still leave them quite voiceless, Oaxaca's urban plebeians became heavily involved in party politics. They used the rhetoric of the vinagres, the local variant of the popular federalists, to express their concerns and pursue their interests, and they provided the vinagres with crucial electoral and military support. However, compared to Guerrero's peasants Oaxaca's plebeians were much less able to achieve their goals through political alliances. As mentioned above, economic circumstances made the effort to achieve prosperity through protectionism a lost cause.[13] Although plebeians did succeed in making egalitarianism a key value in Oaxacan politics, international and national trends would probably have led to this outcome anyway, and the victory was largely symbolic in a society characterized by such stark economic stratification. Oaxaca's plebeians and their vinagre leaders also faced much more effective opposition than did Guerrero's peasants and popular federalists. Their national opponents worked hard to keep the city out of their hands, sending troops when necessary. Moreover, Oaxaca's plebeians found such military force more difficult to resist, as guerrilla warfare was not an option in the city.

The political experiences of the indigenous peasants of Villa Alta were very different from those of their counterparts in Guerrero. As we have seen, Villa Alta's peasants did not engage in large rebellions that united several villages. Moreover, these indigenous peasants did not build political alliances with urban politicians or engage in party politics. Although it is tempting to look for ethnographic explanations based on differences between indigenous cultures in the two locations, the contrast can be explained without them. The indigenous peasants of Guerrero simply faced a very different situation. Oaxacan elites conceded local autonomy to peasants right from the beginning of the independence period, and although the national turn to centralism in the middle of the 1830s seemed to end that autonomy it was implemented very cautiously in Oaxaca. Certainly the replacement of elected alcaldes with appointed jueces de paz was controversial in some villages, but prefects soon began bowing to the wishes of village elders. Moreover, in Villa Alta there were no landowners to challenge village elders for control of local government, and there was no widespread threat to village lands. Villages often clashed with neighboring villages over territory, but this problem was not conducive to forming alliances. As we have seen, taxation sometimes sparked resistance in Villa Alta, but taxes never became the huge issue they did in Guerrero. This difference seems to result from the history of legislation in the two areas. In Guerrero head taxes dropped after independence and then were raised to colonial levels in the early 1840s.[14] In Oaxaca head taxes were always maintained at the same basic level established by the colonial tribute.[15] Thus Villa Alta's indigenous peasants never experienced the kind of sudden and universal tax increase that might have led to simultaneous resistance in various villages.

Finally, one other factor separated Villa Alta's peasants from their counterparts in Guerrero. In Guerrero Juan Alvarez led a group of popular federalist politicians, often veterans of the independence war, who actively sought alliances with the region's peasantry. These popular federalists, of rural origin themselves, had both a vision of how poor rural people could benefit from increased local autonomy and the practical drive to organize in remote areas. Oaxaca nurtured a local variant of the popular federalists, the vinagres, and the vinagres engaged in fierce partisan battles in the city of Oaxaca. Vinagre politicians made strenuous efforts to proselytize among the urban poor. However, they did not often reach out to the vast rural majorities of the state. There is some evidence that in the early 1830s the vinagres attempted to organize among the valley villages near the city, and in 1836 they apparently allied themselves with peasants from the Mixteca in an abortive attempt to restore federalism.[16] However, both incidents remain obscure for the moment, pending future research. Even if these limited efforts were as they appear, the vinagres still seem to have ignored the great masses of peasants in Oaxaca's outlying regions. Vinagre political pamphlets and newspapers did not mention these indigenous peasants or their problems. Unlike Guerrero's popular federalists, the vinagres were themselves products of a traditional urban center that dominated its hinterland. The vinagres did not seek to change this dynamic, and perhaps could not imagine the inhabitants of the outlying regions of the state as a potential source of political power. The motives for this omission are difficult to fathom, because the electoral weight of these rural villagers was so overwhelming it was simply impossible for anyone to win statewide elections without them. Perhaps the vinagres believed that such an effort would not pay off because the electors chosen by peasants would still be subject to pressure from whatever party held the state's governorship. Yet the vinagres may have simply believed that the task of organizing the seemingly alien peasants in Oaxaca's hundreds of villages was impossible. After all, the vinagres could not offer municipal autonomy because it had already been granted, they could not offer tax relief because peasant taxes were too crucial to state finances, and they could not offer support against landowners because most indigenous peasant villages did not face such a threat. In any case, the vinagres stayed away from elections in the outlying districts. Generally one gets the impression that the vinagres did not even imagine reaching out to the indigenous peasants of outlying districts like Villa Alta, and that such an effort would have been doomed because they had little to offer indigenous peasants. The bridge between urban and rural politics remained in Oaxaca's future.[17]

ꕤ *Looking In or Looking Out?*

Recently Eric Van Young published an eagerly anticipated study of popular ideology and popular violence during Mexico's long war of independence. This fascinating book examines some of the same issues of political culture considered here, and it provides a variety of important insights into how peasant interpretations of the international events of 1808–10 led to a widespread millenarian rebellion. One central concept in the book is Van Young's conviction that peasant politics were inwardly oriented and communally driven. The author summarized this neatly by coining a new term, *campanillismo*, which he defines as "the tendency of villagers to see the social and political horizon as extending metaphorically only as far as the view from their church bell tower."[18] This memorable image contrasts sharply with the recent findings of several scholars of nineteenth-century Mexican peasant politics. Working in distinct periods and regions, these scholars have argued that some groups of peasants both participated in far-reaching alliances and developed interpretations of the political ideologies debated in national politics.[19] These historians have worked in different regions and sometimes different periods than those examined by Van Young, yet I believe that these starkly contrasting views are mostly a product of the authors' distinct analytical perspectives. Generally, Van Young has focused on the social and cultural aspirations of peasants, while scholars like Florencia Mallon and Guy Thomson have stressed their political behavior and the discourses associated with it. These perspectives can actually be reconciled if we carefully consider the connections between these phenomena.

Most scholars agree that peasants, or at least most peasants, were primarily concerned with securing a decent subsistence and living culturally satisfying lives, and that the activities and relationships needed to achieve these goals were often internal to their communities. This view correlates with both a multitude of ethnographic observations and copious amounts of historical evidence. However, to fulfill these desires peasants also sometimes required activities and relationships that extended beyond community boundaries. Even peasants in the most isolated villages were connected to the wider economy as both consumers and producers, a fact made most evident in the case of Villa Alta through the textile trade. Peasants were also members of supralocal political entities both before and after independence, something seen both in taxes and symbols like the staff of office carried by village leaders. Peasant village religion existed within Catholicism, and key ceremonies required religious specialists who were neither Indians nor peasants, specialists who worked hard to keep village religion in line with the larger church.

The connections between indigenous peasants and the wider world in all of these areas fostered a geographic mobility that was much greater than one would suppose. Economically, peasants of all kinds traveled to regional markets or tianguis, some worked for wages outside their home village, and others earned income as petty traders. Politically, male peasants walked to district capitals like Villa Alta, provincial capitals like Oaxaca, and even Mexico City to receive their staffs of office and present legal petitions or testimony, either on their individual behalf or that of their communities. Religiously, peasants attended ceremonies in their parish seat and perhaps other villages.

The world outside the village presented indigenous peasants with burdens and threats, but also resources and opportunities. Very often, their ability to live the lives they wanted to live within their communities depended on their capacity to lessen external burdens, resist external threats, use external resources, and seize external opportunities. Even internally, peasant communities were neither seamless nor timeless. They contained divisions, struggles, histories, and vibrant political cultures. Thus a new law or political argument encountered outside the village sometimes resonated with the particular interests and cultural predispositions of an individual or group, and reaching out to a new potential ally might make sense to one faction or perhaps to a more unified village leadership. When peasants from several villages simultaneously made connections with ideas and people from the wider political world they sometimes precipitated large-scale rebellions and alliances with outsiders like those seen in Guerrero in the 1840s and the Sierra de Puebla in the 1850s and 1860s.[20] These mobilizations occurred when pressures affected many villages at once and available political discourses suggested that redress could be obtained through collective action. The movements could seriously affect national politics. Yet they were also fragile, as local concerns pulled the actors in alliances in different directions and sapped their stamina.

Historically such widespread mobilizations were rare in the sense that most indigenous peasants in nineteenth-century Mexico probably lived their lives without even a glimpse of this kind of social drama. Even so many indigenous peasants still pursued disputes in courts outside their villages, sold and bought goods, negotiated the form and costs of religious observances with the parish priest, and tried to make sense of, and sometimes use, the decrees and laws of outside authorities to pursue their own economic, political, and cultural goals. Peasants did not necessarily try to shape these outside actors and forces, but they needed to engage them on some level to live their lives inside their communities the best they could.

Returning to Van Young, although he is more than correct in emphasizing the fact that peasant social and cultural aspirations were centered on life in the village, it seems to me that he underestimates how often peasants needed recourse to allies, discourses, or symbols from the outside world to fulfill those aspirations. Whether peasants acted within grand social movements or through seemingly petty lawsuits, they were involved in a political system that extended much farther than one could see from the top of the village bell tower. Recognizing the connection between the local preoccupations of peasants and the wider political, social, and cultural environment in which they sometimes pursued those concerns does not require us to naively believe that words, ideas, or symbols were being understood the same way by peasants and outsiders. There was tremendous potential for what Van Young calls dialogues of the deaf, where neither side really heard what the other was saying.[21] Yet as James Lockhart suggests with his similar concept of double mistaken identity, misunderstanding could be quite useful for both sides as long as they did not come into direct conflict.[22] The fact that they could use the same language was enough to facilitate alliances or make legal arguments, and if the dialogue continued long enough the two interpretations sometimes even began to approach one another. This process of interaction formed the indigenous communities that existed in the late colonial period, and it has continued to the present.

ƒ҇ *Hegemony and Popular Political Cultures*

Beginning in the middle of the eighteenth century the ways in which politics were conceived and justified shifted dramatically in Mexico. The Enlightenment, the Bourbon Reforms, the independence wars, and the introduction of republicanism together transformed the polity, making it very different from the monarchical corporatism that had characterized the mature colonial order. The urban plebeians of Oaxaca and the indigenous peasants of Villa Alta did not remain on the margins of this transformation. As we have seen, the ways in which they acted and spoke politically changed in important ways. Plebeians embraced the ideal of political equality and participated in a fierce partisan politics. Indigenous peasants reformed their communities even as they worked to find ways to preserve important elements of their political culture. Examining the experiences of these marginalized groups can help us understand how the introduction of republican states changed the political activities of Latin American majorities.

The principal innovations of the era originated in philosophical trends from the greater Atlantic world, and for the most part it was elite or middle-class officials and politicians who adopted these new ideas in efforts to reform Mexico's social and political system. Mexico's hegemonic political culture was in this case subject to change from above. Thus one obvious step in researching the process is to investigate the intentions of elites, intentions that were codified in laws and constitutions but also expressed in a variety of other documents. However, the effort cannot stop there, because as we have seen in this book often the intentions of elites were not fulfilled in political practices on the ground. Therefore the present study has also probed in depth the subaltern responses to this era of political innovation. To understand the real impact of such innovation from above we need to understand what subalterns, in this case urban plebeians and indigenous peasants, actually did. How did they react to new laws and new arguments? How did they hear what elites had to say? Which elements of the new laws and ideas did they see as useful for pursuing their goals and able to fit with their own cultural preoccupations? Similarly, which elements of the new political philosophies did subalterns resist and why? Lastly, what parts of these new laws and ideas did they simply ignore as irrelevant? Such silence can also be eloquent, as it shows where the gaps between the concerns of policymakers and those of subalterns were so wide that they could not be bridged at all.

During the decades covered in this book, change was most rapid and far-reaching when efforts were made to mobilize the bulk of the population. This point becomes most clear when we compare the Bourbon Reforms with the period of Spanish liberalism and the independence war. The Bourbons prefigured liberalism and even republicanism in important ways, a point many historians have made. Yet Bourbon policymakers never believed that the ragged plebeians and alien peasants who dominated New Spain's population could actually help them reform colonial society. Bourbon ideologues worked to convince colonial officials and even New Spain's elite of the justice and efficacy of change, but their policy debates were never disseminated to the populace, who Bourbon thinkers expected to obey superiors without question. In contrast, beginning in 1808 Spanish liberals, viceregal authorities, and insurgent leaders all worked to mobilize mass support for their programs. Their arguments sometimes conflicted and sometimes were surprisingly compatible, and together these groups had an enormous impact on the ways in which politics were conceived in Mexico.

Obviously, when politicians sought to mobilize support for any political program they searched for allies by trying to explain the advantages their ideas had for specific groups. What is less obvious is the fact that even when governments were firmly in power they had to engage in similar processes in order to actually implement their programs. Government programs and new legislation did not really become meaningful to people until they were implemented, and given the relative weakness of the state in the era such implementation required allies on the ground. However, in this traditional, Old Regime society, where would the promoters of more "modern" forms of government find such allies? This question more than anything else has led many historians and political scientists to assume that a vast gulf remained between the theories of government and society embraced by Latin Amerca's political elites and the lives of the vast majority of the population.[23]

In contrast, the research presented here suggests that important constituencies for change did exist even in the most remote and apparently traditional areas. The key to understanding why some groups seized on elements of the new laws and the political philosophies that inspired them is the fact that political culture is always changing, and politics are always contested, even in what at first glance seem to be stagnant backwaters. Hegemony does not prevent conflict; it instead shapes the way conflicts are expressed.[24] There were significant conflicts in the streets of Antequera and the villages of Villa Alta even before Enlightenment ideas began to catch the fancy of policymakers in the Hispanic world. When these ideas began to modify the ways in which policymakers made decisions, subalterns began to employ the novel notions and attitudes in already existing struggles.

The point is particularly striking in the indigenous communities of Villa Alta. Even in these most "traditional" of communities there existed groups who seized on the new, "modern" ideas and tactics because they resonated with their own experiences or concerns. Some new laws were obeyed much more quickly and thoroughly than others. These seemingly homogeneous communities were already the sites of political conflict and division, especially about how the burdens of community life were distributed. Thus some peasants were poised to take advantage of Bourbon laws regulating village festivities or payments to priests. A few years later other indigenous peasants quickly adopted the egalitarianism that became so central to laws and political discourse in early-nineteenth-century Mexico. Peasant commoners used the new ideal of equality mandated in the state constitution to eliminate hereditary privileges that had divided their communities. In doing so they ended a history of conflict that extended back over fifty years. Moreover, in some communities younger men who had chafed in the rigid patriarchy that regulated village politics used universal male suffrage to challenge the power of their elders. Yet as we have seen the traditional power of the elders was not as weak as that of the nobles, and the elders were soon able to turn back this threat.

Developments that were in some ways similar took place in the city. Here, also, some subalterns already possessed social and cultural preoccupations that resonated well with the new political ideals. The city's large mixed-race plebeian population did not emphasize race as a significant measure of individual worth. They transacted business, socialized, and reproduced across the rigid racial lines that meant so much to the city's urban elite. It is impossible to know what these plebeians were saying to each other about the airs put on by the elite, but plebeians' actions beginning in 1808 suggest that they were ready for change. The plebeians quickly embraced the new rhetoric of racial equality and the new means of elections to assert their worth against an urban elite that disdained them. The opposition of the urban elite to this effort only goaded the plebeians and their allies into more strenuous efforts, fueling a partisan politics that dominated the city for decades.

Notably in neither case were those who exploited the "modern" ideals and institutions of the new "time of liberty" necessarily the literate, urban elite or middle-class groups that one would expect to be most attracted to republicanism and individualism.[25] This pattern suggests that there are significant limits to the utility of our macrosociological theorizing about the affinity of different social groups for particular forms of ideology or politics.[26] A number of different schools of thought, from forms of Marxist or Marxian analysis to modernization theory, have shared the notion that certain classes favor specific ideologies.[27] Since the early 1960s Marxian studies of working-class identity and politics have steadily moved away from this assumption, and during roughly the same period modernization theory has lost more than a little of its luster. Yet the impulse to tie particular social sectors to certain worldviews remains strong, and it has influenced the recent analyses of nineteenth-century politics that focus on forms of sociability and the transition from traditional corporatism to modern liberalism typified by François-Xavier Guerra.[28] However, the empirical evidence simply does not support this kind of theoretical assumption about the historical actors.

At this point it will be clear to many readers that the historiographical and theoretical questions that have driven this research have collapsed into each other, becoming essentially unified. In other words, to understand what happens when ruling elites change the hegemonic framework that shapes their relationship with subalterns we need to look at the very specific ways in which hegemonic discourses are disseminated, contested, and modified. Judging from the experiences detailed in this book, it seems that newly introduced ideas about the shape of society and the relationship between the state and social groups are likely to take hold more quickly when the state or political elites work not only to insure their control over populations but also to mobilize those populations against foreign or domestic enemies. This was clearly the case during the accelerated changes of the 1810s, especially in the city of Oaxaca. Moreover, the establishment of new hegemonic political cultures depends ultimately on the actions of subaltern people and groups. Subalterns must think critically and creatively about the ways in which dominant groups portray society and government in order to pursue their own interests and address their own concerns. Yet, like most groups and individuals, subalterns pursue their interests by appealing to elites, the state, or at the very least potential allies from beyond their own immediate peers. In doing so they must shape their discourse for maximum effect, working with whatever knowledge they have about the kinds of arguments policymakers, judges, and potential allies are likely to accept. In other words, subalterns must engage the hegemonic political culture.

Ultimately, what matters most in probing the theoretical question of what happens when elites abandon one hegemonic political culture in favor of another is the methodology of inquiry. Abstract and elegant logic will advance the cause only so far, because societies are too complex to be more than approximately explained by social theory. As much research has shown in the past decades, the social position of actors does not make their actions predictable because people work and struggle in culture and history rather than on chalkboards. The complicated lives that people actually live mean that understanding how they react to attempts to shift hegemonic frameworks requires us to conduct detailed research into their experiences and struggles. This kind of research is essential to understanding not only the past but also the present in which we live, both in Latin America and wealthier parts of the world. Moreover, the effort can also be emotionally rewarding because it provides telling glimpses of the very human experiences of people who were, like most, both ordinary and extraordinary at the same time.

NOTES

Notes to Introduction

1. Perhaps the definition of political culture that has most influenced me is that of Keith Baker. See Baker, introduction to *The Political Culture of the Old Regime*, vol. 1 of *The French Revolution and the Creation of Modern Political Culture* (New York: Pergamon Press, 1987), xii.

2. Charles Tilly, "Social Movements and National Politics," in *Statemaking and Social Movements: Essays in History and Theory*, edited by Charles Bright and Susan Harding (Ann Arbor: University of Michigan Press, 1984), 307–9.

3. Historians based in Europe have included Antonio Annino, Marco Bellingeri, Marie-Danielle Demélas, Will Fowler, Pilar González Bernaldo, François-Xavier Guerra, and Annick Lempérière. Those based in North America include Timothy Anna, Sarah Chambers, Arlene Díaz, Michael Ducey, Peter Guardino, Cecilia Méndez, Vincent Peloso, Jaime Rodríguez, Mark Thurner, Victor Uribe-Uran, Charles Walker, and Richard Warren. Those based in Latin America include Alfredo Avila, Brian Connaughton, Antonio Escobar Ohmstede, Virginia Guedea, Alicia Hernández Chávez, Marco Antonio Landavazo, Carole Leal Curiel, Jorge Myers, Victor Peralta Ruíz, José Antonio Serrano Ortega, and Torcuato Di Tella. See their works in the bibliography.

4. François-Xavier Guerra was the most influential historian to make this basic argument. See, for instance, Guerra, *Modernidad e independencias: Ensayos sobre las revoluciones hispánicas* (Mexico City: Fondo de Cultura Económica, 1993), especially 1, 92, 108, 231.

5. On the emergence of a liberal tradition, see Jaime Rodríguez, *The Independence of Spanish America* (New York: Cambridge University Press, 1998), 243–46. Antonio Annino has offered the interesting argument that the transition was in fact too

far-reaching (Annino, "Ciudadanía 'versus' gobernabilidad republicana en México: Los orígenes de un dilema," in *Ciudadanía política y formación de las naciones: Perspectivas históricas de América Latina*, edited by Hilda Sabato [Mexico City: El Colegio de México/Fideicomiso Historia de las Américas/Fondo de Cultura Económica, 1999], 63).

6. Antonio Annino, "Nuevas perspectivas para una vieja pregunta," in *El primer liberalismo* mexicano (Mexico City: Museo Nacional de la Historia, 1995), 74; Annick Lempérière, "Reflexiones sobre la terminología del liberalismo," in *Construcción de la legitimidad política en México en el siglo XIX*, edited by Brian Connaughton, Carlos Illades, and Sonia Pérez Toledo (Mexico City: El Colegio de Michoacán/ Universidad Autónoma Metropolitana/Universidad Nacional Autónoma de México/El Colegio de México, 1999), especially 51; Marco Bellingeri, "Las ambigüedades del voto en Yucatán. Representación y gobierno en una formación interétnica 1812–1829," in *Historia de las elecciones en Iberoamérica, siglo XIX*, edited by Antonio Annino (Buenos Aires: Fondo de Cultura Económica, 1995), 260; Michael Ducey, "Hijos del pueblo y ciudadanos: Identidades políticas entre los rebeldes indios del siglo XIX," in *Construcción*, edited by Connaughton, Illades, and Pérez Toledo, 143.

7. This idea is implicit in much of Guerra's interesting work. See for instance Guerra, *Modernidad*, 108 and 360. See also David Bushnell and Neill Macaulay, *The Emergence of Latin America in the Nineteenth Century* (New York: Oxford University Press, 1988), 35; and Fernando Escalante Gonzalbo, *Ciudadanos imaginarios*, (Mexico City: El Colegio de México, 1992), 56.

8. Antonio Annino, "Cádiz y la revolución territorial de los pueblos mexicanos 1812–1821," *Historia*, 178; Annino, "Ciudadanía," 63; Sarah Chambers, *From Subjects to Citizens: Honor, Gender and Politics in Arequipa, Peru 1780–1854* (University Park: Penn State University Press, 1999); Arlene Díaz, *Female Citizens, Patriarchs, and the Law in Venezuela, 1786–1904* (Lincoln: University of Nebraska Press, 2004); Ducey, "Hijos," 1999; Peter Guardino, "Identity and Nationalism in Mexico: Guerrero, 1780–1840," *Journal of Historical Sociology* 7, no. 3 (1994): 314–42; Guardino, *Peasants, Politics and the Formation of Mexico's National State: Guerrero, 1800–1857* (Stanford: Stanford University Press, 1996); J. Samuel Valenzuela, "Building Aspects of Democracy before Democracy: Electoral Practices in Nineteenth Century Chile," in *Elections before Democracy: The History of Elections in Europe and Latin America*, edited by Eduardo Posada-Carbó (New York: St. Martin's Press, 1996), 225; and Richard Warren, *Vagrants and Citizens: Politics and the Masses in Mexico City from Colony to Republic* (Wilmington, Del.: Scholarly Resources, 2001).

9. Guardino, *Peasants*.

10. See for instance, the criticisms of Eric Van Young in Van Young, "The Cuatla Lazarus: Double Subjectives in Reading Texts on Popular Collective Action," *Colonial Latin American Review* 2, nos. 1–2 (1993): 16; and James Scott in *Domination*

and the Arts of Resistance: Hidden Transcripts (New Haven: Yale University Press, 1990), 71.

11. William Roseberry, "Hegemony and the Language of Contention," in *Everyday Forms of State Formation: Revolution and the Negotiation of Rule in Modern Mexico*, edited by Gilbert Joseph and Daniel Nugent (Durham, N.C.: Duke University Press, 1994), 360–61.

12. See for instance, many of the essays in Joseph and Nugent, *Everyday Forms*, as well as Guardino, *Peasants*, 9; and Connaughton, Illades, and Pérez Toledo, introduction to *Construcción*, 14, 28. Notably similar concepts are important to some works that do not explicitly refer to the theoretical term. Thus, in describing the social order of New Spain, Felipe Castro Gutiérrez speaks of "a kind of script" on which characters improvised their everyday performances (Castro Gutiérrez, *Nueva ley y nuevo rey: Reformas borbónicas y rebelión popular en Nueva España* [Zamora: El Colegio de Michoacán/Universidad Autónoma de México, 1996], 21).

13. The exception to this seems to be the literature on the French Revolution, where for over twenty years diverse historians such as François Furet and Lynn Hunt have examined a drastic transformation of political culture. See Furet, *Interpreting the French Revolution* (New York: Cambridge University Press, 1981); and Hunt, *Politics, Culture and Class in the French Revolution* (Berkeley: University of California Press, 1984). Yet, to my knowledge these historians have generally left aside the question of how this transformation of political culture changed the way subalterns engaged in politics.

14. Florencia Mallon, *Peasant and Nation: The Making of Postcolonial Mexico and Peru* (Berkeley: University of California Press, 1995), especially p. 6; Roseberry, "Hegemony," 365.

15. Mallon, *Peasant and Nation*, 15.

16. Sergio Serulnikov, "Customs and Rules: Bourbon Rationalizing Projects and Social Conflicts in Northern Potosí during the 1770s," *Colonial Latin American Review* 8, no. 2 (1999): 246.

17. I could not possibly cite every work in this exploding trend, but the articles in Joseph and Nugent, *Everyday Forms*, are often recognized as pioneering.

18. In a different spin on the construction metaphor, Serulnikov states that elite hegemonic projects are "less an ideological blueprint than a series of contested practical interpretations" (Serulnikov, "Customs and Rules," 246).

19. Van Young, "Cuatla," 4, 17

20. Scott, *Domination*.

21. Van Young, "Cuatla," 17.

22. Richard Warren, "Ashes and Aerostats: Popular Culture Meets Political Culture in Nineteenth Century Mexico" (paper presented at the Latin American Studies Association, Chicago, 25 September 1998), 7.

23. Ranajit Guha notes the connection between rumors and political conscious-

ness in nineteenth-century India. See *Elementary Forms of Peasant Insurgency in Colonial India* (Delhi: Oxford University Press, 1983), 265.

24. Felipe Castro Gutiérrez makes this point about lies (Castro Gutiérrez, *Nueva*, 251). For a case of a "telling" lie, see Ignacio Ordoño's jailhouse accusations against his fellow prisoner in Archivo General de la Nación (AGN), Infidencias, vol. 2 exp. 2, discussed in chapter 4.

25. Eric Van Young provides some wonderful metaphors for this kind of method in Van Young, *The Other Rebellion: Popular Violence and Ideology in Mexico, 1810–1816* (Stanford: Stanford University Press, 2001), 27–28.

26. Eric Wolf, "Aspects of Group Relations in a Complex Society: Mexico," *American Anthropologist* 58, no. 6 (1956): 1065–78. See also William Taylor, "¿Era campesinos los indios? El viaje de un norteamericano por la historia colonial mesoamericana," *Relaciones* 20, no. 78 (1999): 84; and Guardino, *Peasants*, 15.

27. See, for instance Archivo de Villa Alta, (AVA), Civil, exp. 1283, 1848.

Notes to Chapter 1: Society, Economy, and Politics in Colonial Antequera

1. The definitive history of colonial land tenure in the valleys is William Taylor, *Landlord and Peasant in Colonial Oaxaca* (Stanford: Stanford University Press, 1972).

2. For the rental of costumes, see AVA, Penal, exp. 414, 1798. For occupations listed (for non-Indians) in 1792 see Chance, *Race*, 160.

3. Silke Hensel, "Los orígenes del federalismo en México. Una perspectiva desde la provincia de Oaxaca de finales del singlo XVIII a la Primera República," *Ibero-Amerikansches Archiv* 25, nos. 3–4 (1999): 221.

4. Chance, *Race*, 147–48.

5. Hugo Altamirano Ramírez, *La ciudad de Oaxaca que conoció Morelos* (Oaxaca: n.p., 1992).

6. Studies of this group abound. See Silke Hensel, *Die Enstehung des Foderalismus in Mexiko: die politische Elite Oaxacas zwischen Stadt, Region und Staat, 1786–1835* (Stuttgart: Franz Steiner Verlag, 1997) 246–56; Brian Hamnett, "Between Bourbon Reforms and Liberal Reforms: The Political Economy of a Mexican Province — Oaxaca, 1750–1850," in *The Political Economy of Spanish America in the Age of Revolution, 1750–1850*, edited by Kenneth Andrien and Lyman Johnson (Albuquerque: University of New Mexico Press, 1994), 39, 42; Taylor, *Landlord*; Chance, *Race*, 106.

7. Archivo General del Estado de Oaxaca, (AGEO), Alcaldías Mayores, vol. 17, exp. 12.

8. Ann Twinam, *Public Lives, Private Secrets: Gender, Honor, Sexuality and Illegitimacy in Colonial Spanish America* (Stanford: Stanford University Press, 1999); and Lyman Johnson and Sonya Lipsett-Rivera, eds., *The Faces of Honor: Sex, Shame and Violence in Colonial Latin America* (Albuquerque: University of New Mexico Press, 1998).

9. For a couple of examples, see AGEO, Real Intendencia I, vol. 14, exp. 7; AGEO, Real Intendencia I, vol. 14, exp. 9.

10. AGEO, Real Intendencia II, vol. 5, exp. 11.

11. AGEO, Alcaldías Mayores, vol. 3, exp. 11. For another case, see AGEO, Alcaldías Mayores, vol. 27, exp. 36.

12. AGEO, Alcaldías Mayores, vol. 22, exp. 14.

13. Twinam, *Public Lives*, 32–33.

14. AGEO, Alcaldías Mayores, vol. 1, exp. 14.

15. AGN, Ayuntamientos, vol. 95. For a comparison to Michoacán and the Bajio in the same period see Castro Gutiérrez, *Nueva*, 223.

16. See, for instance, AGEO, Alcaldías Mayores, vol. 22, exp. 11; and AGEO, Alcaldías Mayores, vol. 26, exp. 13.

17. For references to dress, see AGEO, Alcaldías Mayores, vol. 13, exp. 5; and AGEO, Alcaldías Mayores, vol. 14, exp. 23.

18. AGEO, Alcaldías Mayores, vol. 1, exp. 8; AGEO, Alcaldías Mayores, vol. 1, exp. 11; AGEO, Alcaldías Mayores, vol. 2, exp. 41; AGEO, Colonial, vol. 1, exp. 80; AGEO, Colonial, vol. 4; Manuel Esparza, *Relaciones Geográficas de Oaxaca 1777–1778* (Oaxaca: Centro de Investigaciones y Estudios Superiores en Antropología Social/Instituto Oaxaqueño de las Culturas, 1994), 397–400; Chance, *Race*, 112–23.

19. The list is from AGEO, Alcaldías Mayores, vol. 2, exp. 42. See also Chance, *Race*, 123, 133–34; AGEO, Alcaldías Mayores, vol. 2, exp. 17.

20. Theodore Vincent eloquently and imaginatively evokes this social and cultural world for the case of Mexico City (Vincent, *The Legacy of Vicente Guerrero, Mexico's First Black Indian President* [Gainesville: University of Florida Press, 2001], 34–40).

21. For the nicknames, see AGEO, Alcaldías Mayores, vol. 22, exp. 17; AGEO, Alcaldías Mayores, vol. 14, exp. 3. Savedra's will is found in AGEO, Alcaldías Mayores, vol. 1, exp. 8. For other examples, see AGEO, Alcaldías Mayores, vol. 22, exp. 15; AGEO, Alcaldías Mayores, vol. 25, exp. 21.

22. AGEO, Alcaldías Mayores, vol. 1, exp. 1.

23. R. Douglas Cope makes a similar if less drastic argument for Mexico City (Cope, *The Limits of Racial Domination: Plebeian Society in Colonial Mexico City, 1660–1720* [Madison: University of Wisconsin Press, 1994], 162–63).

24. Chance, *Race*, 127–38.

25. AGEO, Alcaldías Mayores, vol. 3, exp. 1.

26. This is similar to what Cope found in Mexico City (Cope, *Limits*, 161–63).

27. Brian Hamnett, *Politics and Trade in Southern Mexico, 1750–1821* (Cambridge: Cambridge University Press, 1971) is still the best source on the economic connections of Oaxaca's merchants.

28. Cope, *Limits*, 86–105.

29. For the ownership of urban real estate, see Manuel Esparza, *Padrón de casas de la ciudad de Oaxaca, 1824* (Oaxaca: Centro Regional de Oaxaca, Instituto Nacional

de Antropologia e Historia, 1981), especially Esparza's introduction. For loans in small amounts made by people of relatively modest means, see, for example, AGEO, Alcaldías Mayores, vol. 1, exp. 6; and AGEO, Alcaldías Mayores, vol. 1, exp. 8.

30. See for example, AGEO, Real Intendencia II, vol. 5, exp. 11. Chance provides a more complete image of the class structure of the city in *Race*, 159–64.

31. I thank Michael Ducey for pointing this out to me in a personal communication.

32. Lempérière, "Reflexiones," 40; Annino, "Cádiz," 179–80; William Taylor, *Magistrates of the Sacred: Priests and Parishioners in Eighteenth-Century Mexico* (Stanford: Stanford University Press, 1996), 13, 362, 433.

33. Lempérière, "Reflexiones," 44; Alfredo Avila, *En nombre de la nación. La formación del gobierno representativo en México (1808–1824)* (Mexico City: Taurus/Centro de Investigación y Docencia Económica, 2002), 21; Marco Antonio Landavazo, *La máscara de Fernando VII: Discurso e imaginario monárquicos en una época de crisis, Nueva España, 1808–1822* (Mexico City: El Colegio de México/Universidad Michoacana de San Nicolás de Hidalgo/El Colegio de Michoacán, 2001), 23.

34. Colin MacLachlan, *Spain's Empire in the New World* (Berkeley: University of California Press, 1988), 6–9, 22, 40–41; Carole Leal Curiel, *El discurso de la fidelidad. Construcción social del espacio como símbolo del poder regio (Venezuela, siglo XVIII)* (Caracas: Biblioteca Nacional de la Historia, 1990), 211–21; Castro Gutierrez, *Nueva*, 27, 213.

35. Dorothy Tanck de Estrada, *Pueblos de indios y educación en el México colonial, 1750–1821* (Mexico City: El Colegio de México, 1999), 439.

36. Carlos R. Espinosa, "The Portrait of the Inca: Aesthetics and Politics in the Audiencia of Quito, 1630–1750," (Ph.D. diss., University of Chicago, 1990), 91–93. For the king's presence, see Victor Minguez, *Los reyes distantes: Imágenes del poder en el México virreinal* (Castello de la Plana: Universitat Jaume I/Diputacio de Castello, 1995), 17. For patron saint feasts, MacLachlan, *Spain's Empire*, 22–23; for Corpus Christi, Enrique Florescano, *Etnia, estado y nación: Ensayo sobre las identidades colectivas en México* (Mexico City: Nuevo Siglo Aguilar, 1997), 235; Juan Pedro Viquiera Alban, *¿Relajados o reprimidos? Diversiones públicas y vida social en la ciudad de México durante el siglo de las luces* (Mexico City: Fondo de Cultura Económica, 1987) 117–18; and Linda Curcio-Nagy, "Giants and Gypsies: Corpus Christi in Colonial Mexico City," in *Rituals of Rule, Rituals of Resistance: Public Celebrations and Popular Culture in Mexico*, edited by William Beezley, Cheryl English Martin, and William French (Wilmington, Del.: Scholarly Resources, 1994). For celebrations in Oaxaca of the arrival of bishops, the accession of popes, and victories in international wars, see Eutemio Pérez, *Recuerdos históricos del episcopado oaxaqueño* (Oaxaca: Imprenta de San German, 1888), 80; and AGN, Historia, vol. 437.

37. Sonia Lombardo de Ruiz, "La presencia del rey en la vida pública de la ciudad de México," in *Las ciudades y sus estructuras. Población, espacio, cultura en México, siglos XVIII y XIX*, edited by Sonia Pérez Toledo, René Elizade Salazar, and Luis Pérez

Cruz (Mexico City: Universidad Autónoma Metropolitana/Universidad de Tlax-cala, 1999), 211–12.

38. Archivo Histórico de la Ciudad de Oaxaca, (AHCO), Actas, 1746, fols. 90, 100, 154–57. The viceroy cancelled this second celebration on the grounds that it was both excessive and late.

39. Leal Curiel, *El Discurso*, 171–210; Avila, *En nombre*, 22–23; Curcio-Nagy, "Giants," 810. On the pedagogy of ceremonies, see Curcio-Nagy, "Giants," 2–4.

40. Minguez, *Los Reyes*, 17.

41. Reinhard Liehr describes the basic norms for acquiring and transfering mu-nicipal posts (*Ayuntamiento y oligarquía en Puebla*, 2 vols. [Mexico City: Secretaría de Educació Pública, 1976], 1: 92–94, 99–111). For Oaxaca, see AHCO, Actas, 1746, fols. 1–7; AHCO, Actas, 1806, fols. 7, 34–35; AHCO, Actas, 1809, fols. 50–54; AHCO, Actas, 1810, fols. 58–61; AGEO, Real Intendencia I, vol. 10, exp. 15; AGEO, Real Intendencia II, vol. 37, exp. 22.

42. AHCO, Actas, 1746, fols. 78, 85.

43. AHCO, Actas, 1806, fols. 9–12.

44. For the auction, see AGEO, Real Intendencia I, vol. 10, exp. 15. For complaints about the duties of Oaxaca's alcaldes ordinarios, see AGN, Ayuntamientos, vol. 175; and AGN, Ayuntamientos, vol. 191.

45. AGEO, Real Intendencia II, vol. 31, exp. 6.

46. For a ranking of occupations found in the 1792 census, see Chance, *Race*, 160.

47. AGEO, Alcaldías Mayores, vol. 32, exp. 3.

48. AGEO, Alcaldías Mayores, vol. 37, exp. 3.

49. Lempérière, "Reflexiones," 39. See, for example, the 1810 electoral records in AGEO, Real Intendencia II, vol. 31, exp. 5.

50. Juan Bautista Carriedo, *Estudios histórico y estadísticos del Departamento de Oaxaca* (Oaxaca: Imprenta del Autor, 1849), 123.

51. AGEO, Alcaldías Mayores, vol. 32, exp. 3. Ecclesiastical authorities acceded to this petition.

52. Lempérière, "Reflexiones," 39.

53. Taylor, *Magistrates*, 5.

54. Francisco Canterla y Martin de Tovar, *La iglesia de Oaxaca en el siglo xviii* (Sevilla: Escuela de Estudios Hispano-Americanos de Sevilla, 1982), 10–13.

55. Leal Curiel, *El discurso*, 21.

56. For the history of the convent, see Luis Castañeda Guzmán, *Templo de los Príncipes y Monasterio de Nuestra Señora de los Angeles* (Oaxaca: Instituto Oaxaqueño de las Culturas, 1993).

57. AGEO, Legajos Encuadernados, Eclesiástico, vol. 8, 1771.

58. AGEO, Real Intendencia I, vol. 2, exp. 6; Florescano, *Etnia*, 233.

59. Juan Javier Pescador, *De bautizados a fieles difuntos: Familia y mentalidades en una parroquía urbana: Santa Catarina de Méxuco, 1568–1820* (Mexico City: El Colegio de México, 1992), 294–98.

60. AGEO, Legajos Encuadernados, Eclesiástico, vol. 7, 1766.

61. Archivo Histórico del Obispado de Oaxaca, (AHAO), Parroquial, Disciplinar, Cofradías, 1765–97.

62. Pamela Voekel provides a useful explanation of the beliefs and practices surrounding death in the period in *Alone Before God: The Religious Origins of Modernity in Mexico* (Durham, N.C.: Duke University Press, 2002), 27–30.

63. AGEO, Alcaldías Mayores, vol. 5, exp. 23.

64. AGEO, Alcaldías Mayores, vol. 2, exp. 19.

65. AHAO, Parroquial, Disciplinar, Cofradías, 1765–97.

66. For examples, see AHAO, Parroquial, Disciplinar, Cofradías, 1765–97; and AHAO, Parroquial, Disciplinar, Cofradías, 1804. These contracts were often printed with blanks for names, signatures, and dates.

67. AHAO, Parroquial, Disciplinar, Cofradías, 1791.

68. AGEO, Legajos Encuadernados, Eclesiástico, vol. 6, 1752.

69. AGEO, Legajos Encuadernados, Eclesiástico, vol. 8, 1772a.

70. Chance, *Race*, 139; AGEO, Legajos Encuadernados, Eclesiástico, vol. 1, 1686.

71. Pescador, *De bautizados*, 322, 342.

72. For Cofradía del Señor de los Desamparados, see AGEO, Legajos Encuadernados, Eclesiástico, vol. 7, 1766; for Cofradía del Patriarcha Señor San Joseph, AGEO, Legajos Encuadernados, Eclesiástico, vol. 7, 1766b; for Cofradía de San Antonio de Padua, AGEO, Legajos Encuadernados, Eclesiástico, vol. 10, 1782; for Cofradía de la Consolación, AHAO, Parroquial, Disciplinar, Cofradías, 1746–85.

73. AGEO, Legajos Encuadernados, Eclesiástico, vol. 4, 1725.

74. AGEO, Legajos Encuadernados, Eclesiástico, vol. 12, 1788b.

75. AGEO, Legajos Encuadernados, Eclesiástico, vol. 12, 1788b.

76. AHAO, Parroquial, Disciplinar, Cofradías, 1804.

77. See, for example, Dagmar Bechtloff, *Las cofradías en Michoacán durante la época colonial* (Toluca: El Colegio Mexiquense/El Colegio de Michoacán, 1996); Asunción Lavrín, "World in Contrasts: Rural and Urban Confraternities in Mexico at the End of the Eighteenth Century," in *The Church and Society in Latin America*, edited by Jeffrey Cole (New Orleans: Tulane University Center for Latin American Studies, 1984), 99–122; and even Taylor, *Magistrates*, 304–16.

78. See the vote totals for the Cofradía del Rosario del Peñaso in AGEO, Legajos Encuadernados, Eclesiástico, vol. 15, 1828.

79. AGEO, Legajos Encuadernados, Eclesiástico, vol. 7, 1766.

80. Taylor, *Magistrates*, 301; AHAO, Diocesano, Gobierno, Mandatos, 1784–1805. Lavrín states that urban cofradías were relatively free of supervision by priests ("World in Contrasts," 101).

81. Pescador, *De bautizados*, 337, 340.

82. AGEO, Real Intendencia I, vol. 1, exp. 25.

83. Stephanie Wood, "Adopted Saints: Christian Images in Nahua Testaments of Late Colonial Toluca," *The Americas* 47, no. 3 (1991): 264–65; 270.

84. See, respectively, AGEO, Real Intendencia I, vol. 13, exp. 1; AGEO, Alcaldías Mayores, vol. 13, exp. 15; AGEO, Alcaldías Mayores, vol. 1, exp. 8; and AGEO, Real Intendencia II, vol. 12, exp. 23.

85. Chance, *Race*, 160.

86. MacLachlan, *Spain's Empire*, 6.

87. Steve Stern, *The Secret History of Gender: Men, Women and Power in Late Colonial Mexico* (Chapel Hill: University of North Carolina Press, 1985), 19, 21.

88. AGEO, Alcaldías Mayores, vol. 12, exp. 10.

89. AGEO, Real Intendencia I, vol. 11, exp. 19.

90. AGEO, Real Intendencia II, vol. 29, exp. 26.

91. AHCO, Tesorería, 1764–1829.

92. AGEO, Real Intendencia II, vol. 26, exp. 4.

93. AGEO, Real Intendencia I, vol. 1, exp. 17.

94. AGEO, Alcaldías Mayores, vol. 1, exp. 1. The Spanish is, "Siendo una India neofita, y muger al fin me admiro se le haiga tanto asensio, y se haiga santificado de tal modo."

95. AGEO, Alcaldías Mayores, vol. 14, exp. 3.

96. AGEO, Alcaldías Mayores, vol. 27, exp. 31.

97. AGEO, Alcaldías Mayores, vol. 27, exp. 30.

98. AGEO, Alcaldías Mayores, vol. 26, exp. 13.

99. Probably the most famous works are Lyle McAllister, "Social Structure and Social Change in New Spain." *Hispanic American Historical Review* 43, no. 3 (1963): 349–70; and John Leddy Phelan, *The People and the King: The Comunero Revolution in Colombia, 1781* (Madison: University of Wisconsin Press, 1978). Two more recent works that include these themes are MacLachlan, *Spain's Empire*; and Cope, *Limits*.

100. After around 1780 the sermons delivered on these political occasions were often printed, but this was less common in earlier years.

101. On this point see especially Stern, *Secret History*, ix, 20–21, 302.

Notes to Chapter 2: Society, Economy, and Political Culture in Colonial Villa Alta

1. John Chance, *Conquest of the Sierra: Spaniards and Indians in Colonial Oaxaca* (Norman: University of Oklahoma Press, 1989).

2. Scarlett O'Phelan Godoy, *Un siglo de rebeliones anticoloniales: Peru and Bolivia 1700–1783* (Cusco: Centro de Estudios Rurales Andinos Bartolomé de las Casas, 1988), 175–86; Taylor, *Magistrates*, 83–86.

3. Julio de la Fuente, "Ocho años de experiencia en el medio rural," *El Maestro Rural* 12 (1939): 10–12; de la Fuente, *Yalalag. Una villa zapoteca serrana* (Mexico City: Museo Nacional de Antropología, 1949); Laura Nader, *Harmony Ideology: Justice and Control in a Zapotec Mountain Village* (Stanford: Stanford University Press, 1990); Phillip Parnell, *Escalating Disputes: Social Participation and Change in the Oaxacan Highlands* (Tucson: University of Arizona Press, 1988); Etzuko

Kuroda, *Bajo el Zampoaltépetl: La sociedad mixe de las tierras altas y sus rituales* (Oaxaca: Centro de Investigaciones y Estudios Superiores en Antropología Social/Instituto Oaxaqueño de las Culturas, 1993).

4. María de los Angeles Romero Frizzi, *El sol y la cruz: Los pueblos indios de Oaxaca colonial* (Mexico City: Centro de Investigación y Estudios Superiores en Antropología Social/Instituto Nacional Indigenista, 1996), 213.

5. Chance, *Conquest*, 39 (for the nonnative population), 62 (for the entire population).

6. Chance, *Conquest*, 87, 112; AGEO, Real Intendencia II, vol. 11, exp. 9.

7. Chance, *Conquest*, 11; Nader, *Harmony*, 16.

8. Chance, *Conquest*, 5, 7; Nader, *Harmony*, 98. For older descriptions see Esparza, *Relaciones*, 153–54; and Carriedo, *Estudios*, 155.

9. Romero Frizzi, *El sol*, 159. See the pioneering work of Andeanist John Murra on Andean economic responses to the vertical terrain (John Murra, *Formaciones económicas y políticas del mundio andino* [Lima: Instituto de Estudios Peruanos, 1975]).

10. Chance, *Conquest*, 106–7.

11. Hamnett, "Between Bourbon Reforms," 41–43; Esparza, *Relaciones*, 400.

12. Esparza, *Relaciones*, 31; Chance, *Conquest*, 108; AVA, Civil, exp. 610, 1799.

13. See, for instance, AGEO, Real Intendencia I, vol. 5, exp. 4.

14. Notably, Indians used the verbs *azotar* and *escarmentar*, usually reserved for punishment, to describe how they separated the seeds from the cotton (AVA, Penal, exp. 439, 1805; AGEO, Real Intendencia II, vol. 6, exp. 11, 1801).

15. Romero Frizzi (*El sol*, 184) suggests the figure of one month, while Chance, (*Conquest*, 109–10) cites sources suggesting that by working constantly the process could be completed in a week. The inhabitants of several villages claimed in 1791 that a single manta took as long as a month and a half to produce (AGN, Indios, vol. 88, exp. 3, fol. 29).

16. For scattered references to merchants see AGEO, Alcaldías Mayores, vol. 16, exp. 10; AGEO, Real Intendencia I, vol. 8, exp. 15; Romero Frizzi, *El sol*, 183.

17. Chance, *Conquest*, 108–9; AVA, Penal, exp. 274, 1768; AVA, Civil, exp. 206, 1750.

18. Hensel, "Los orígenes," 221; Anselmo Arellanes Meixuero, "Un anónimo y su circunstanca," *Acervos* 1 (1996): 15; Chance, *Conquest*, 104.

19. Chance, *Conquest*, 104, 107; Hamnett, *Politics*, 45.

20. Jeremy Baskes, "Coerced or Voluntary?: The 'Repartimiento' and Market Participation of Peasants in Late Colonial Oaxaca," *Journal of Latin American Studies* 28, no. 1 (1996): 1–28.

21. Romero Frizzi, *El sol*, 188; Chance, *Conquest*, 103–11.

22. Arellanes Meixuero, "Un anónimo," 15; AGEO, Real Intendencia II, vol. 2, exp. 25; AGEO, Real Intendencia II, vol. 2, exp. 27; AGN, Clero Regular y Secular, vol. 188, exp. 6.

23. Often in the complaints Indians made about the repartimiento this surfaces as

a key issue. See, for example, AGEO, Real Intendencia II, vol. 2, exp. 27; AGN, Clero Regular y Secular, vol. 188, exp. 6.

24. AGEO, Real Intendencia II, vol. 2, exp. 27; AGN, Criminal, vol. 206, fols. 144–45v.

25. AVA, Penal, exp. 274, 1768; AGEO, Real Intendencia II, vol. 5, exp. 17.

26. Romero Frizzi, *El sol*, 190–91.

27. Baskes, "Coerced," 20–22.

28. Chance, *Conquest*, 97–102. On the difficulties of debt collection for independent merchants see AGEO, Alcaldías Mayores, vol. 16, exp. 10.

29. Chance, *Conquest*, 117–21, 178.

30. Chance, *Conquest*, 40, 117. Laura Nader mistakenly suggests that Villa Alta was a market town. See Nader, *Harmony*, 162–63.

31. Esparza, *Relaciones*, 176, 293; Chance, *Conquest*, 92–97.

32. Gonzalo Aguirre Beltrán, *Formas de gobierno indígena* (Mexico City: Imprenta Universitaria, 1953), 31–39.

33. Castro Gutiérrez, *Nueva*, 217; Guardino, *Peasants*, 27–28.

34. Dorothy Tanck de Estrada lays these activities out in a useful table (*Pueblos*, 57).

35. Chance did find evidence of this pattern for some areas in the sixteenth and seventeenth centuries (*Conquest*, 133–34). By 1730, though, most villages had gobernadores, and references to cabecera/sujeto relationships stopped appearing in the documents.

36. These figures are calculated from Table 9 of Chance, *Conquest*, 48–63.

37. See Romero Frizzi, *El sol*, 222–24 and 266–69; Chance, *Conquest*, 13, 75–76. For the absence of head and subject towns in the contemporary era see Parnell, *Escalating Disputes*, 88.

38. AGN, Gobernación, vol. 134, caja 1, exp. 134, 1835; AVA, Civil, exp. 566, 1797; AGEO, Real Intendencia II, vol. 16, exp. 4, 1814.

39. For recent studies emphasizing the lack of democracy in indigenous villages see Florescano, *Etnia*, 189–90; Castro Gutiérrez, *Nueva*, 238–39; and Taylor, *Magistrates*, 89.

40. William Taylor suggests this in his key 1979 book, *Drinking, Homicide, and Rebellion in Colonial Mexican Villages* (Stanford: Stanford University Press, 1979), 123.

41. AVA, Civil, exp. 207, 1750; AVA, Penal, exp. 278, 1769.

42. AVA, Civil, exp. 402, 1781a; AVA, Civil, exp. 452, 1789.

43. AVA, Civil, exp. 453, 1789. Anthropologist Laura Nader points out that contemporary Zapotecs often challenge authority when they believe it is being abused (*Harmony*, 274–75). For more examples of verbal confrontations see AVA, Penal, exp. 448, 1806; and AVA, Penal, exp. 449, 1806.

44. AVA, Penal, exp. 449, 1806.

45. In 1769 Juan Mendoza, the fiscal, or church warden of San Juan Tabaa as-

saulted Regidor Salvador Vicente when the latter sought to defend a woman who had missed mass due to the illness of her family (AVA, Penal, exp. 278, 1769).

46. AVA, Penal, exp. 324, 1789.

47. AVA, Penal, exp. 326, 1789.

48. Felipe Castro Gutiérrez argues the same for villages elsewhere in New Spain (*Nueva*, 238).

49. AVA, Civil, exp. 204, 1750.

50. AGEO, Real Intendencia II, vol. 6, exp. 11, 1801.

51. For women, see AGEO, Real Intendencia II, vol. 6, exp. 11, 1801; AVA, Penal, exp. 278, 1769. For former officials, see AVA, Penal, exp. 349, 1792; AVA, Penal, exp. 409, 1798; AVA, Penal, exp. 334, 1791.

52. AVA, Civil, exp. 463, 1791.

53. For a description see AVA, Civil, exp. 258, 1760. The offices varied slightly from village to village.

54. In some villages one became a principal before reaching the office of gobernador.

55. For comments of eighteenth-century lawyers about the Spanish origins of the cargo system, see AVA, Civil, exp. 394, 1779; AVA, Civil, exp. 513, 1796.

56. John Chance and William Taylor, "Cofradías and Cargos: An Historical Perspective on the Mesoamerican Civil-Religious Hierarchy," *American Ethnologist* 12 (1985): 1–26.

57. Romero Frizzi, *El sol*, 125.

58. AVA, Civil, exp. 258, 1760. The Spanish reads, "Topiles, assi de Yglesia como de casas reales."

59. AVA, Penal, exp. 409, 1798.

60. For cantores, see AVA, Civil, exp. 453, 1789; and AVA, Penal, exp. 409, 1798. For schoolteachers, see AVA, Penal, exp. 449, 1806.

61. AGN, Indios, vol. 66, exp. 10, fol. 14v.

62. Chance, *Conquest*, 13, 125–32, 181.

63. AVA, Civil, exp. 258, 1760.

64. AVA, Civil, exp. 759, 1814; AVA, Civil, exp. 790, 1816. In 1751 Juan Bautista of Zoogochi argued that nobles were "legitimos patrimoniales," descendants from the "primeros de dicha fundacion de Nuestro Pueblo" (AVA, Civil, exp. 212, 1751). In 1814 the nobles of Santiago Lalopa referred to themselves as "originarios" (AVA, Civil, exp. 759, 1814).

65. For examples of these documents see Romero Frizzi, *El sol*, 257–60; and AGEO, Colonial, vol. 13, exp. 32, fols. 19–25. For an individual noble telling the same kind of story, see Yanna Yannakakis, "'Indios Ladinos': Indigenous Intermediaries and the Negotiation of Local Rule in Colonial Oaxaca, 1660–1769" (Ph.D. diss., University of Pennsylvania, 2003), 154–55.

66. AVA, Civil, exp. 293, 1766. See also Stern, *Secret History*, 80.

67. AVA, Civil, exp. 790, 1816; AVA, Civil, exp. 513, 1796.

68. For an example, see AVA, Civil, exp. 730, 1811. In 1798 the village of Temax-calapan highlighted the fact that not all elders could vote in elections by calling those with voting rights "ancianos reservados" (AVA, Civil, exp. 573, 1798). For the role of age in community politics in the Andes, see Espinosa, "Portrait," 74.

69. AVA, Civil, exp. 258, 1760.

70. AVA, Civil, exp. 434, 1787.

71. AVA, Civil, exp. 573, 1798.

72. AVA, Civil, exp. 212, 1751; AVA, Penal, exp. 349, 1792; AVA, Penal, exp. 425, 1801.

73. AVA, Penal, exp. 349, 1792. In 1805 the village government accused the school-master, Juan Miguel, of being "muy muchacho," or very much a boy, because he had not served a single post in the cargo system (AVA, Civil, exp. 657, 1805).

74. Chance, *Conquest*, 147–48.

75. AVA, Civil, exp. 293, 1766. The Spanish reads, "Todos casiques y personas nobles y como tales exemptos por Leyes del Reyno de ocuparse en Tequios y oficios vajos de Gobases, y otros de esta naturaleza, en que se exersisan los Masehuales." For other examples see AVA, Civil, exp. 212, 1751; AVA, Penal, exp. 334, 1791(1802); AVA, Civil, exp. 513, 1796; AVA, Civil, exp. 625, 1802; AGN, Indios, vol. 66, exp. 10, fols. 14v–17.

76. John Chance found a higher success rate in his analysis, but I believe that his figures include the cases where agreements were reached (*Conquest*, 143–44).

77. See the very detailed agreement reached in Yae in 1774. Note this is an agree-ment reached after a lawsuit, and there is no evidence that the children of principales had any special status before the conflict (AVA, Civil, exp. 363, 1774).

78. AVA, Civil, exp. 258, 1760. A careful examination of the documents reveals that sometimes it was Spanish officials or lawyers who began referring to people claiming cacique status as principales. See AVA, Penal, exp. 334, 1791 (1802).

79. AVA, Civil, exp. 372, 1775. See AVA, exp. 573, 1798; AGEO, Real Intendencia I, vol. 7, exp. 26; and AGEO, Real Intendencia II, vol. 41, exp. 26 for similar cases.

80. AVA, Civil, exp. 759, 1814.

81. Luis Chávez Orosco, *Las instituciones democráticas de los indígenas mexicanos en la época colonia* (Mexico City: Instituto Indigenista Interamericano, 1943), 14–15; Romero Frizzi, *El sol*, 125; Taylor, *Magistrates*, 347. Aguirre Beltrán suggests that Bourbon officials abetted these efforts, but I have seen no evidence of this in the district of Villa Alta (*Formas*, 49, 50).

82. A great example of this is found in AGN, Indios, vol. 66, exp. 10, fols. 14–17, where the 1776 complaint of the commoners of San Juan Yae first describes the efforts of some families to exempt themselves from labor for the village, then con-tinues about their efforts to control village elections.

83. AVA, Civil, exp. 790, 1816; AVA, Civil, exp. 362, 1774.

84. Romero Frizzi, *El sol*, 33; Chance, *Conquest*, 8–9. In her ethnographic research Laura Nader found that people in the Rincón, a geographic region of the district, did not refer to themselves as Zapotecs until very recently (*Harmony*, 16).

85. Chance, *Conquest*, 9–10, 24. For other parts of New Spain, see Florescano, *Etnia*, 326; Tanck de Estrada, *Pueblos*, 588; and Eric Van Young, "Paisaje de ensueño con figuras y vallados: disputa y discurso cultral en el campo mexicano de fines de la Colonia," in *Paisajes rebeldes: Una larga noche de rebelión indígena*, edited by Jane Dale-Lloyd and Laura Pérez Rosales (Mexico City: Universidad Iberoamerican, 1995), 153–54. In fact at least one village, Santa María Lachixila, was composed of both Zapotec speakers and Chinantec speakers (AVA, Penal, exp. 414, 1798). There is some historical evidence that different villages had distinct ways of dressing, although the historical evidence is surprisingly weak compared to the detail noted by more recent observers. See AVA, Penal, exp. 460, 1822; Esparza, *Relaciones*, 159, 293.

86. Chance, *Conquest*, 124.

87. Yannakakis, "Indios," 69–72, 165.

88. AGEO, Real Intendencia II, vol. 11, exp. 4. The quote reads, "El comun de Naturales de Santiago Amatepec, Xaltepec, y demás de la Jurisdiccion de Villa alta."

89. AGEO, Real Intendencia II, vol. 16, exp. 21.

90. AGEO, Real Intendencia I, vol. 11, exp. 19.

91. AVA, Penal, exp. 387, 1796. In the fifth case, the governments of three villages complained against the subdelegado in 1791 (AGN, Indios, vol. 88, exp. 3, fols. 28–29v).

92. Romero Frizzi, *El sol*, 222.

93. The examples are limitless, but see for instance AGEO, Colonial, vol. 1, exp. 64.

94. For examples see AVA, Penal, exp. 387, 1796; and AVA, Civil, exp. 656, 1805; AGEO, Real Intendencia I, vol. 5, exp. 4.

95. AGEO, Real Intendencia I, vol. 5, exp. 9; AGEO, Real Intendencia I, vol. 11, exp. 19; AGEO, Real Intendencia II, vol. 5, exp. 10; AGEO, Colonial, vol. 14.

96. Robert Haskett, "Paper Shields: The Ideology of Coats of Arms in Colonial Mexican Titles," *Ethnohistory* 43, no. 1 (1996): 101. See the 1815 comments of Luis Castellanos, a lawyer, in AGEO, Colonial, vol. 13, exp. 32.

97. AGEO, Colonial, vol. 13, exp. 32. In 1715 the village of Tanetze submitted a less elaborate but otherwise similar document as evidence of its land claims. This document is reproduced in Romero Frizzi, *El sol*, 257–60.

98. Romero Frizzi, *El sol*, 225–26. Primordial titles for villages elsewhere in New Spain were similar in these respects (Haskett, "Paper," 101).

99. AGEO, Colonial, vol. 2; AGEO, Real Intendencia I, vol. 6, exp. 12; Romero Frizzi, *El sol*, 222.

100. Tanck de Estrada, *Pueblos*, 306. For descriptions of patron saint festivities in Villa Alta see AVA, Penal, exp. 334, 1791 (1789). In a few villages the different barrios also had patron saints. See AVA, Penal, exp. 326, 1789.

101. For various activities in the colonial period see for example AVA, Penal, exp. 407, 1798; AVA, Penal, exp. 442, 1805; AVA, Penal, exp. 44, 9, 1806. Notably, the tequio remains a vibrant institution in many villages today. See David Arriaga, "El tequio," *México Indígena* 6 (1990): 32–36.

102. For such a case see AVA, Penal, exp. 414, 1798. The Bourbon reforms and their effects on popular political culture will be the subject of chapter 3.

103. AVA, Penal, exp. 591, 1832. I have found two other cases where authorities either dismantled or threatened to dismantle a house. In one a government threatened such punishment for an abusive Spaniard resident in their community. In the other the houses of two men were taken apart to compensate the village for a shortfall in community accounts during their term in office (AGN, Clero Regular y Secular, vol. 188, exp. 6; AVA, Civil, exp. 204, 1750). For other examples of sanctions against those who did not serve, see AVA, Civil, exp. 842, 1821; and AVA, Penal, exp. 441, 1805. The centrality of community service to village membership helps explain the severe sanctions many communities have meted out to families that convert to Protestantism and refuse to labor for religious functions in the twentieth century. See Parnell, *Escalating Disputes*, 74–75; Nader, *Harmony*, xv; and Yannakakis, "Indios," 15–16.

104. A parish priest, Joseph Mariano Davila Bustamante, pointed out in 1783 that in Latani there was not a single unmarried male (AGEO, Obispado, vol. 13, exp. 13).

105. To finance their 1791 Lenten celebration, the villagers of San Cristóbal Lachirioag taxed married couples two reales and widowers one real (AGEO, Real Intendencia II, vol. 21, exp. 12). Widows did not even pay royal tribute (AGEO, Real Intendencia II, vol. 21, exp. 11). In a rare case where a widower paid a nonrelative to do his domestic labor, he paid her three pesos per month (AVA, Civil, exp. 773, 1815).

106. AVA, Penal, exp. 441, 1805. In a similar fashion, a complaint the officials of Santiago Yagayo raised against Salvador Hernandez changes in mid-sentence into a complaint against his wife (AVA, Civil, exp. 463, 1791). Recently, Dorothy Tanck de Estrada found an unusual document for the Central Mexican town of Actopan that listed husband-and-wife pairs as the holders of cargos (*Pueblos*, 424).

107. AVA, Civil, exp. 625, 1802.

108. AVA, Civil, exp. 430, 1786. The Spanish reads, "No tiene que le assista."

109. AVA, Civil, exp. 258, 1760; AVA, Civil, exp. 414, 1798.

110. AVA, Penal, exp. 407, 1798.

111. Stern, *Secret History*, 80, 100, quote from 302. Ethnographers confirm that these basic features of village life continue in the region. Laura Nader found that village leaders are still called fathers, while Philip Parnell notes that in the 1980s women were still not allowed to vote in municipal assemblies, presumably because they would have simply added their votes to those of their husbands (Nader, *Harmony*, 64; Parnell, *Escalating Tensions*, 5).

112. Stern, *Secret History*, 19–20, 202.

113. AVA, Penal, exp. 449, 1806. The Spanish reads, "No hera mujer para que los Justicias lo andana que las mujeres davan gusto como lo dava el comun a dichos Justicias."

114. AVA, Civil, exp. 463, 1791; AVA, Civil, exp. 453, 1789. The quote reads, "A la mierda." For another case, see AVA, Penal, exp. 449, 1806.

115. AGEO, Real Intendencia II, vol. 6, exp. 11. For a similar case see AVA, Civil, exp. 452, 1789.

116. AVA, Penal, exp. 324, 1789.

117. Taylor was the first to notice this (*Drinking*, 116). See also Castro Gutiérrez, *Nueva*, 224. For cases in colonial Villa Alta see AGN, Indios, vol. 88, fol. 296v; AGEO, Real Intendencia II, vol. 3, exp. 28; AVA, Civil, exp. 656, 1805.

118. Stern, *Secret History*, 205–9.

119. AVA, Civil, exp. 1310, 1855; AVA, Civil, exp. 773, 1815. Florencia Mallon found a similar pattern in the Sierra de Puebla in the nineteenth century (*Peasant*, 66–74).

120. Stern, *Secret History*, 80–85. For some examples from Villa Alta see AVA, Penal, exp. 390, 1796; and AVA, Penal, exp. 445, 1806. The nineteenth-century records preserve couples' voices on these matters much better than the colonial records do. I suspect that the district court became much more active in adjudicating domestic violence cases and other kinds of marital disputes, no longer leaving them in the hands of the community religious officials. For examples see AVA, Penal, exp. 515, 1827; AVA, Penal, exp. 520, 1828; AVA, Penal, exp. 529, 1829; AVA, Penal, exp. 536, 1830; AVA, Penal, exp. 554, 1831; AVA, Penal, exp. 891, 1844; and AVA, Penal, exp. 911, 1848.

121. AVA, Penal, exp. 683, 1838; AVA, Penal, exp. 699, 1839; AVA, Penal, exp. 706, 1840; AVA, Penal, exp. 1241, 1857.

122. AVA, Penal, exp. 390, 1796; AVA, Penal, exp. 439, 1805; AVA, Penal, exp. 441, 1805; AVA, Penal, exp. 449, 1806. Compare to the somewhat similar attitudes of twentieth-century officials in Nader, *Harmony*, 113–15, 185–218.

123. AGEO, Alcaldes Mayores, vol. 14, exp. 28, 1751; AVA, Penal, exp. 324, 1789. This was more difficult if the offender was not an Indian native of the village. See AGN, Clero Regular y Secular, vol. 188, exp. 6.

124. AVA, Civil, exp. 730, 1811.

125. Chance, *Conquest*, 164–68.

126. For descriptions, see AGN, Indios, vol. 58, fols. 195–95v; AVA, Penal, exp. 334, 1791 (1789).

127. Chance, *Conquest*, 169; Tanck de Estrada, *Pueblos*, 23.

128. Chance, *Conquest*, 170.

129. The constitutions of two early cofradías are found in AGEO, Legajos Encuardenados, Eclesiástico, vol. 5, 1732. For later ones, see AVA, Penal, exp. 278, 1769; AGEO, Obispado, vol. 5, exp. 17; AVA, Civil, exp. 699, 1807.

130. Chance, *Conquest*, 156.

131. Taylor, *Magistrates*, 88.

132. Taylor, *Magistrates*, 88, 199, 202; Chance, *Conquest*, 175.

133. Romero Frizzi, *El sol*, 224.

134. See the comments of the leaders of Santa Cruz Yagavila in AGEO, Obispado, vol. 14, exp. 3.

135. For more on the sacramental duties of parish priests and the hardships involved in fulfilling them, see Taylor, *Magistrates*, 191–97.

136. AGEO, Obispado, vol. 13, exp. 13; AGEO, Obispado, vol. 13, exp. 32; Tanck, *Pueblos*, 407. Zapotec villages may have used a seventeenth-century Zapotec translation of the famous sixteenth-century catechism of Padre Ripalda. See Rosendo Pérez García, *La Sierra Juárez* (Mexico City: Gráfica Cerventina, 1956), 311.

137. AVA, Civil, exp. 749, 1811.

138. It was not uncommon for schoolteachers to serve as village scribes (AVA, Civil, exp. 657, 1805).

139. Taylor, *Magistrates*, 333–34. The quote is from AVA, Penal, exp. 409, 1798. The original reads, "Para que supiessen Cantar nuestros hiyos, nos havi Gastado Nuestro Dinero el que los enseñasen." See also Tanck de Estrada, *Pueblos*, 412–13.

140. Chance, *Conquest*, 154, 158.

141. For a classic case see AVA, Penal, exp. 278, 1769. See also AGEO, Obispado, vol. 1, exp. 20; AGEO, Obispado, vol. 1, exp. 21; and AVA, Penal, exp. 416, 1799.

142. Romero Frizzi, *El sol*, 223; Chance, *Conquest*, 156–57.

143. Taylor, *Magistrates*, 358–59.

144. For the reference to Maldonado, see the 1763 complaint of Santiago Jocotepec reproduced in Romero Frizzi, *El sol*, 266–69. For other references to the circulation of the arancel, see AGEO, Obispado, vol. 1, exp. 7; AGEO, Alcaldías Mayores, vol. 14, exp. 28; and AVA, Civil, exp. 362, 1774.

145. AVA, Civil, exp. 362, 1774.

146. AGEO, Obispado, vol. 15, exp. 10.

147. AGEO, Obispado, vol. 14, exp. 3.

148. AGEO, Colonial, vol. 2.

149. Chance, *Conquest*, 157; Taylor, *Magistrates*, 367; AGN, Clero Regular y Secular, vol. 188, exp. 6, fol. 88v; AGN, Indios, vol. 88, fols. 295–96v, 301; AGEO, Real Intendencia I, vol. 8, exp. 11.

150. AGEO, Obispado, vol. 13, exp. 32.

151. AGEO, Real Intendencia II, vol. 24, exp. 28.

152. AGEO, Obispado, vol. 13, exp. 13.

153. Chance, *Conquest*, 159–68.

154. AVA, Civil, exp. 215, 1753; AVA, Civil, exp. 463, 1791.

155. AGEO, Obispado, vol. 2, exp. 5.

156. Taylor, *Magistrates*, 273.

157. Chance, *Conquest*, 37.

158. AVA, Civil, exp. 206, 1750.

159. Taylor, *Magistrate*, 401.

160. Chance, *Conquest*, 33–34, 42–43; Yannakakis, "Indios," 47–53.

161. For example, see AGEO, Real Intendencia II, vol. 3, exp. 28.

162. AVA, Civil, exp. 259, 1761. The Spanish reads, "Por aber venido nuestros antepasados en compania de los españoles conquistadores conquistando todo este Reino." The claims here are similar to those made by presidio soldiers and their descendants in northern New Spain. See Ana María Alonso, *Thread of Blood: Colonialism, Revolution, and Gender on Mexico's Northern Frontier* (Tucson: University of Arizona Press, 1995), 30–36.

163. AGEO, Real Intendencia II, vol. 3, exp. 28; AGEO, Real Intendencia II, vol. 27, exp. 4.

164. AGEO, Real Intendencia II, vol. 6, exp. 19; AGEO, Real Intendencia II, vol. 7, exp. 6; AGEO, Real Intendencia II, vol. 15, exp. 34.

165. AGEO, Real Intendencia I, vol. 1, exp. 40; AGEO, Real Intendencia I, vol. 11, exp. 19; AVA, Civil, exp. 498, 1795.

166. Chance, *Conquest*, 41–42; Curcio-Nagy, "Giants," 3–4.

167. AVA, Civil, exp. 402, 1781b.

168. Chance, *Conquest*, 136; Tanck de Estrada, *Pueblos*, 23.

169. Today in at least some parts of Oaxaca it is a respected elder who hands the vara to the newly elected official, suggesting a very different origin for the authority it symbolizes. See Carmen Cordero Avendaño de Duran, *La vara del mando: Costumbre jurídica en la transmisión de poderes* (Oaxaca: Ayuntamiento Constitucional, 1997), 36.

170. The basic definition used here is derived from Baker, in his introduction to *The Political Culture of the Old Regime* (xii). He also discusses change over time. For more on change over time, see Taylor, *Magistrates*, 4.

171. We know very little about those means. For a study of dispute resolution in a local village in the twentieth century, see Nader, *Harmony*, 1990.

172. Chance, *Conquest*, 123.

173. Michael Scardaville, "(Hapsburg) Law and (Bourbon) Order: State Authority, Popular Unrest, and the Criminal Justice System in Bourbon Mexico City," *The Americas* 50, no. 4 (1994): 516. For a detailed explanation of legal procedures see Charles Cutter, *The Legal Culture of Northern New Spain, 1700–1810* (Albuquerque: University of New Mexico Press, 1995), 109–13.

174. See, for example, the first document in AVA, Penal, exp. 407, 1798.

175. Florescano, *Etnia*, 289.

176. The Spanish had apparently developed a standardized written form of Zapotec that was adequate for the three mutually unintelligible dialects spoken in the district. John Chance found only one document written in Mixe during his research (*Conquest*, 125), and I was unable to locate even that document because the district archive had been reorganized between his research and my own.

177. The legal petition, which actually is directed against the village scribe, is in

AVA, Civil, exp. 773, 1815. For the primordial title see AGEO, Colonial, vol. 13, exp. 32.

178. In order, AVA, Civil, exp. 699, 1807; AGEO, Alcaldías Mayores, vol. 14, exp. 28; AGEO, Alcaldías Mayores, vol. 24, exp. 16; AVA, Civil, exp. 713, 1809; and AVA, Civil, exp. 771, 1815.

179. Chance, *Conquest*, 124. For an example of people from several villages testifying without interpreters, see AGEO, Real Intendencia II, vol. 16, exp. 1. An Indian with adequate Spanish was described as "ladino" (AGEO, Real Intendencia II, vol. 40, exp. 30). Tanck de Estrada estimates that about 20 percent of the indigenous population of New Spain was bilingual (*Pueblos*, 582).

180. Tanck de Estrada, *Pueblos*, 585.

181. For examples see AGEO, Colonial, vol. 2; AGN, Indios, vol. 88, fol. 309.

182. A couple of early-nineteenth-century documents refer evocatively to pens and inkpots as weapons. See AVA, Penal, exp. 473, 1823; AVA, Penal, exp. 591, 1832. Colonial Spanish authorities also recognized the power of literacy. After the 1767 rebellions of northern New Spain, authorities severed the heads of village governors and the hands of village scribes and posted them in prominent places as a reminder to the populace (Castro Gutiérrez, *Nueva*, 195).

183. See for instance AVA, Civil 495, 1795.

184. For the contemporary descendants of colonial tinterillos, see Nader, *Harmony*, 79. I owe thanks for Nader's precise and concise definition of tinterillos as "lay lawyers."

185. AGEO, Colonial, vol. 1, exp. 80; AGEO, Impresos, 4 February 1842; Tanck de Estrada, *Pueblos*, 527.

186. AVA, Civil, exp. 699, 1807. A 1768 document by the village of S. Andres Yaa refers to its lawyer as its "patrono" (AVA, Penal, exp. 274, 1768). For a similar reference, see AGN, Indios, vol. 88, fol. 298. Some examples of documents that lawyers composed for indigenous clients include AGEO, Real Intendencia I, vol. 5, exp. 4; AVA, Penal, exp. 407, 1798; AVA, Civil, exp. 759, 1814; AVA, Civil, exp. 790, 1816.

187. See, respectively, AGN, Indios, vol. 88, fol. 298; AGEO, Real Intendencia II, vol. 16, exp. 21; AGN, Clero Regular y Secular, vol. 188, exp. 6.

188. Romero Frizzi, *El sol*, 191.

189. Taylor, *Magistrates*, 370, 380, 382.

190. AVA, Civil, exp. 453, 1789; AVA, Penal, exp. 334, 1791 (1802).

191. AGEO, Obispado, vol. 1, exp. 7. The case of Martínez is detailed in AVA, Penal, exp. 425, 1801. The original reads, "Su Padre le dijo que habia de haser algunas comparencias a nombre del comun, y defenderlo en quanto se ofreciera, que era preciso ovedecer y agachar la Cabeza en quanto se ofreciera."

192. In general, see Florescano, *Etnia*, 280–81; and MacLachlan, *Spain's Empire*, 29, 48. For officials criticizing the propensity of Indians to seek redress in court see

AGEO, Colonial, vol. 2; AGEO, Real Intendencia II, vol. 4, exp. 11; and AGN, Indios, vol. 88, fol. 302v. After independence Oaxacan officials made repeated efforts to limit lawsuits by Indians. See AGEO, Legajos Encuadernados, Decretos, vol. 71, 1832b; AGEO, Legajos Encuadernados, Decretos, vol. 73, 1845; AGEO, Legajos Encuadernados, Decretos, vol. 74, 1850a; AGEO, Legajos Encuadernados, Gobernación, vol. 32, 1842i; AGEO, Legajos Encuadernados, Gobernación, vol. 38, 1846f; AGEO, Legajos Encuadernados, Gobernación, vol. 43, 1850n.

193. AGN, Indios, vol. 88, fols. 302v–303.

194. AGEO, Obispado, vol. 1, exp. 17; AVA, Civil, exp. 204, 1750; AVA, Civil, exp. 207, 1750; AVA, Civil, exp. 452, 1789; AVA, Penal, exp. 334, 1791 (1802); AVA, Penal, exp. 407, 1798.

195. Florescano, *Etnia*, 289.

196. MacLachlan, *Spain's Empire*, 28.

197. Tanck de Estrada, *Pueblos*, 526.

198. AVA, Civil, exp. 566, 1797; AGEO, Real Intendencia II, vol. 16, exp. 4; AGEO, Real Intendencia II, vol. 21, exp. 2.

199. AVA, Civil, exp. 793, 1816. Even Spanish officials sometimes demonstrated an astonishing grasp of older laws. In 1812 the priest Joseph Vicente de Paz cited an order issued by Spain's King Philip II, who ruled from 1556 to 1598 (AGN, Indios, vol. 88, fol. 298v).

200. Taylor, *Drinking*, 133–34; Castro Gutiérrez, *Nueva*, 155; Ducey, "Hijos," 134.

201. Spanish officials lay out this policy explicitly in response to an 1807 riot in Tabaa in AGEO, Real Intendencia I, vol. 9, exp. 11. See also the quote in Castro Gutiérrez, *Nueva*, 155.

202. AVA, Penal, exp. 474, 1823. The quote reads, "El caracter tumultuoso de esta clase de gente." See also the comments of another priest in AGN, Indios, vol. 88, fol. 302v.

203. AGN, Criminal, vol. 306, fol. 145v; AGN, Clero Regular y Secular, vol. 188, exp. 6; AGN, Indios, vol. 88, fol. 300v; AVA, Penal, exp. 425, 1801.

204. Taylor, *Drinking*, 115–16.

205. AGN, Historia, vol. 132, exp. 14, fol. 14. Church bells are rung for the same purpose in the district today (Parnell, *Escalating*, 79).

206. AVA, Civil, exp. 204, 1750; AGN, Criminal, vol. 306, fol. 146v; AVA, Civil, exp. 1027, 1833; AVA, Penal, exp. 739, 1841; AVA, Penal, exp. 1046, 1853.

207. Others have observed this in other parts of New Spain (Taylor, *Drinking*, 116; Castro Gutiérrez, *Nueva*, 224).

208. AGEO, Real Intendencia II, vol. 3, exp. 28.

209. AVA, Civil, exp. 656, 1805.

210. Taylor, *Drinking*, 133–34; Romero Frizzi, *Nueva*, 204; Van Young, "Cuatla," 19.

211. Romero Frizzi, *El sol*, 186; Taylor, *Magistrates*, 399, 422.

212. AVA, Civil, exp. 400, 1780; AVA, Civil, exp. 207, 1750. According to a parish priest in 1812, respect for the king flowed from respect for God (AGN, Indios, vol. 88, fol. 294v).

213. AGEO, Real Intendencia I, vol. 6, exp. 12. The Spanish reads, "Que hai Dios primeramente, y despues de Dios al Rey que es el que esta votado y nombrado para el superior Govierno, para que los hijos no se perjudiquen." See also AVA, Civil, exp. 259, 1761.

214. AVA, Penal, exp. 274, 1768; AGEO, Real Intendencia II, vol. 21, exp. 12.

215. The only reference I have seen for the area was written by a priest (AGN, Indios, vol. 88, fol. 293v).

216. AGEO, Colonial, vol. 13, exp. 32.

217. *Real ordenanza para el establecimiento e instrucción de intendentes de ejercito y provincia en el Reino de la Nueva Espana* (Mexico City: Universidad Nacional Autonoma de Mexico, Instituto de Investigaciones Historicas, 1984), 21. The Spanish reads, "El Real Tributo que pagan á mi Soberanía en reconocimiento del vassallage y suprema proteccion que les está concedida."

218. Taylor, *Magistrates*, 13, 433; MacLachlan, *Spain's Empire*, 28.

219. AVA, Civil, exp. 723, 1810.

220. AVA, Penal, exp. 414, 1798.

221. AVA, Civil, exp. 452, 1789.

222. For examples see AVA, Civil, exp. 212, 1751; AVA, Penal, exp. 349, 1792; AVA, Penal, exp. 425, 1801. Keep in mind, however, that some men did not advance in the system due to their lack of commitment or incompetence in the lower rungs of the cargo ladder or due to their illegitimate birth (AVA, Civil, exp. 730, 1811).

223. Guerra, *Modernidad*, 361. See also Taylor, *Magistrates*, 374.

224. Nader, *Harmony*, 1.

225. For a case of deference to the majority, see AVA, Penal, exp. 425, 1801; and AVA, Penal, exp. 278, 1769.

226. AVA, Penal, exp. 414, 1798. The original reads, "Ellos rebeldes siempre particularmente Narsizo Cruz, con los mencionados arriba comenzaron a alvoratar el Pueblo haciendos Juntas nocturnas en Casa de Narsizo Cruz, para irse apresentar contra nosotros."

227. See, for example, AVA, Penal, exp. 678, 1838; AVA, Penal, exp. 887, 1848; AVA, Penal, exp. 894, 1848; AVA, Penal, exp. 1070, 1853; AVA, Penal, exp. 1079, 1853.

228. Taylor, *Magistrates*, 374.

229. AVA, Civil, exp. 452, 1789. For parcialidades as kinship groups, see Yannakakis, "Indios," 172–75.

230. Chance, *Conquest*, 130.

231. The villages in question are San Juan Bautista Comaltepec and Santa María Yahuive (Esparza, *Relaciones*, 108, 148).

232. Chance, *Conquest*, 171–72.

233. AVA, Penal, exp. 414, 1798. Chance identifies this village as unambiguously

Chinantec (*Conquest*, 56). For references to barrios as religious organizations, see AVA, Penal, exp. 326, 1789; and AVA, Civil, exp. 699, 1807.

234. For more on "harmony ideology" and its consequences in contemporary villages, see Nader, *Harmony*, xx, 2, 6, 307; as well as Parnell, *Escalating Disputes*, 5–6.

235. AVA, Civil, exp. 771, 1815. The quote reads, "Casa del Dios y del Rey." For the more common formulation see AVA, Civil, exp. 258, 1750.

236. Taylor, *Drinking*, 118–19.

237. One exception to this rule consisted of riots during boundary disputes, which were likely to take place at the margins of the village territory.

238. Aguirre Beltrán, *Formas*, 43–44; Cordero Avendaño, *La vara*, 49–52.

239. Cheryl English Martin, *Governance and Society in Colonial Mexico: Chihuahua in the Eighteenth Century* (Stanford: Stanford University Press, 1996), 97. See, for example, AGN, Ayuntamientos, vol. 136.

240. For varas in contemporary Oaxaca see Cordero Avendaño, *La vara*. For varas in Colombia see Joanne Rappaport, *Cumbe Reborn: An Andean Ethnography of History* (Chicago: University of Chicago Press, 1994), 77–79; and Rappaport, *The Politics of Memory: Native Historical Interpretation in the Colombian Andes* (Durham, N.C.: Duke University Press, 1998), 171–73.

241. AVA, Civil, exp. 206, 1750. The Spanish reads, "Para que quitara las varas a dichos Alcaldes por ser contra el bien comun."

242. Aguirre Beltrán, *Formas*, 42.

243. Martin, *Governance*, 97; AVA, Penal, exp. 407, 1798; AGN, Criminal, vol. 306, fols. 144–45v.

244. AVA, Civil, exp. 259, 1761.

245. AVA, Penal, exp. 448, 1806. The original reads, "De mirar por el honor y respecto de la vara que portamos y por el buen Gobierno y sobordinacon de los sugetos a ella."

246. Eric Van Young found the same to be true in central Mexican communities (*Other*, 445–46).

247. AGN, Criminal, vol. 306, fols. 144–45v. The original reads, "La vara que tenía era del Rey."

248. AVA, Penal, exp. 324, 1789. The original reads, "Esas baras abia muchas en el monte."

249. AVA, Penal, exp. 407, 1789. The original reads, "De que serviran las varas que el Rey nos ha dado, y Vuestra Magestad en su nombre, sino fuera mas arbitros a castigar a los defectos de los subalternos?"

250. Romero Frizzi, *El sol*, 112; Alicia Hernández Chávez, *Anenecuilco: Memoria y vida de un pueblo* (Mexico City: El Colegio de México/Fideicomiso Historia de las Américas/Fondo de Cultura Económica, 1991), 19.

251. Again, for central Mexico, see Van Young, *Other*, 446–47.

252. See, for instance, AVA, Penal, exp. 479, 1824, where the villagers of Yatoni

complain that their neighbors in Talea have appropriated disputed land "sin mas documento que una informacion simple, y sin aprovacion del superior Govierno."

253. Romero Frizzi, *El sol*, 176. See also Taylor, *Magistrates*, 433; and Yannakakis, "Indios," 134–35.

254. AVA, Civil, exp. 453, 1789. The Spanish reads, "A la mierda . . . con sus papeles que tiene en el jusgado que no bale nada."

Notes to Chapter 3: Bourbon Intentions and Subaltern Responses

1. David Brading, *Miners and Merchants in Bourbon Mexico, 1763–1810* (Cambridge: Cambridge University Press, 1971), 31–92.

2. O'Phelan Godoy, *Un siglo*, 175–221.

3. Brooke Larson, *Cochabamba, 1550–1900: Colonialism and Agrarian Transformation in Bolivia*, expanded ed. (Durham, N.C.: Duke University Press, 1998), 288–89.

4. Susan Deans-Smith, *Bureaucrats, Planters, and Workers: The Making of the Tobacco Monopoly in Bourbon Mexico* (Austin: University of Texas Press, 1992), xii.

5. Pamela Voekel, "Peeing on the Palace: Bodily Resistance to the Bourbon Reforms in Mexico City," *Journal of Historical Sociology* 5, no. 2 (1992): 183.

6. In addition to Voekel, see in particular Viquiera Alban, *Relajados*; and Susan Deans-Smith, "The Working Poor and the Eighteenth-Century Colonial State: Gender, Public Order, and Work Discipline," in *Rituals*, edited by Beezley, Martin, and French, 47–75.

7. Castro Gutiérrez, *Nueva*, 175. See also p. 213.

8. Serulnikov, "Customs," 246.

9. Josefina Vázquez, "De la crisis monárquica a la Independencia (1808–1821)," in *Interpretaciones de la Independencia de México* (Mexico City: Nueva Imagen, 1997), 13.

10. The quote is from Serulnikov, "Customs," 247.

11. Hensel, "Los orígenes," 220.

12. Hensel, *Die Enstehung*, 89.

13. *Real ordenanza*, 163–64.

14. For the Andes, see Larson, *Cochabamba*, 288–89.

15. *Real ordenanza*, 164.

16. Chance, *Race*, 155–57, 175.

17. Chance, *Race*, 178.

18. Tribute, however, remained a very potent social stigma. In 1795 Luis Santibañez and his wife struggled mightily to avoid being classified as mulattos subject to tribute. They had both been adopted by Spanish families when they were infants, although an official described Santibañez as a mulatto and his wife as a mestizo. (AGEO, Real Intendencia II, vol. 27, exp. 48).

19. Silvia Arrom, *The Women of Mexico City, 1790–1857* (Stanford: Stanford University Press, 1985), 28–29.

20. AGEO, Real Intendencia II, vol. 31, exp. 4; AGEO, Real Intendencia I, vol. 7, exp. 10.

21. Arrom, *Women*, 27–28; AGEO, Real Intendencia II, vol. 31, exp. 8.

22. AGEO, Real Intendencia II, vol. 21, exp. 6.

23. Christon Archer, *The Army in Bourbon Mexico, 1760–1810* (Albuquerque: University of New Mexico Press, 1977), 12, 90–93, 145, 147.

24. AGN, Criminal, vol. 532, exp. 3, fol. 152–52v.

25. For the composition of the militia, see Archer, *Army*, 238.

26. Archer, *Army*, 121–22, 145–47. For North America, see Edmund Morgan, *Inventing the People: The Rise of Popular Sovereignty in England and America* (New York: Norton, 1988), 169–73.

27. Archer, *Army*, 122, 146, 238.

28. Hensel, *Die Enstehung*, 82; Hamnett, *Politics*, 48–52; Canterla, *La iglesia*, 107, 204; Ricardo Rees-Jones, *El despotismo ilustrado y los indendentes de la Nueva España* (Mexico City: Universidad Nacional Autónoma de México, 1983), 168–69; *Real ordenanza*, 18–20.

29. Hamnett, *Politics*, 73–75; Hensel, *Die Enstehung*, 87–89; Hensel, "Los orígenes," 221.

30. Archer, *Army*, 122.

31. AHCO, Delitos contra la Autoridad, 1790.

32. Brading, *Miners*, 83.

33. AGN, Clero Regular y Secular, vol. 188, exp. 8, fol. 149; AGN, Clero Regular y Secular, vol. 188, exp. 12, fol. 208v; AGN, Historia, vol. 132, exp. 14; Hamnett, *Politics*, 76–81; Chance, *Conquest*, 102, 110.

34. Hamnett, *Politics*, 87–88.

35. AGEO, Real Intendencia II, vol. 7, exp. 6. The original Spanish reads, "Mediante la aprobacion de su Magestad y el Expediente concluido para que los Justicias reparten como ante lo hacian guardando Justicia."

36. AGEO, Real Intendencia II, vol. 5, exp. 1; AGEO, Real Intendencia II, vol. 5, exp. 17; AGEO, Real Intendencia II, vol. 40, exp. 8.

37. Romero Frizzi, *El sol*, 271–73.

38. AGEO, Real Intendencia II, vol. 4, exp. 21; AGEO, Real Intendencia II, vol. 7, exp. 6.

39. AGEO, Real Intendencia II, vol. 6, exp. 19; AGEO, Real Intendencia II, vol. 22, exp. 25.

40. AGN, Clero Regular y Secular, vol. 188, exp. 6.

41. AVA, Penal, exp. 442, 1805.

42. AGN, Indios, vol. 88, exp. 3, fol. 29.

43. AGN, Historia, vol. 132, exp. 14, fol. 36v; AGEO, Real Intendencia I, vol. 1, exp. 40.

44. AGEO, Real Intendencia I, vol. 10, exp. 37.

45. AGEO, Real Intendencia II, vol. 6, exp. 19.

46. AVA, Penal, exp. 449, 1806.

47. Chance, *Conquest*, 136.

48. *Real ordenanza*, 21–23.

49. AGN, Indios, vol. 88, exp. 3, fols. 28–28v; AGEO, Real Intendencia I, vol. 11, exp. 19; AGEO, Real Intendencia II, vol. 11, exp. 4; AGEO, Colonial, vol. 4.

50. AGEO, Real Intendencia II, vol. 3, exp. 28; Romero Frizzi, *El sol*, 271–73; AGEO, Real Intendencia II, vol. 6, exp. 19.

51. AGEO, Real Intendencia II, vol. 6, exp. 19.

52. AGN, Indios, vol. 88, exp. 3, fol. 29v; AGEO, Real Intendencia II, vol. 11, exp. 4.

53. Voekel provides a very convincing explanation of the rise of an Enlightenment-era Catholicism that led many clerics toward the reform of Baroque religious practices, making them sometime allies of the Bourbons (*Alone*, especially 104–5).

54. Taylor, *Magistrates*, 14.

55. AGN, Clero Regular y Secular, vol. 188, exp. 8.

56. AGN, Clero Regular y Secular, vol. 188, exp. 12, fols. 196–215v.

57. Taylor, *Magistrates*, 415; AVA, Civil, exp. 498, 1795.

58. AGEO, Real Intendencia II, vol. 11, exp. 4; AGEO, Real Intendencia II, vol. 10, exp. 1.

59. Ana Carolina Ibarra, *Clero y política en Oaxaca: Biografía del Doctor José de San Martín* (Oaxaca: Instituto Oaxaqueño de las Culturas/Universidad Nacional Autónoma de México/Fondo Estatal para la Cultura y las Artes, 1996), 53.

60. Taylor, *Magistrates*, 13.

61. *Real ordenanza*, 308–9.

62. On Bergoza y Jordan, see Hamnett, *Politics*, 164; Cristina Gómez Alvarez and Francisco Téllez Guerrero, "Los libros de Antonio Bergosa y Jordan, Obispo de Antequera de Oaxaca, 1802," *Acervos* 2 (1996): 8–12. For his arancel decision, see AGEO, Obispado, vol. 5, exp. 11; AGEO, Obispado, vol. 14, exp. 13. Bergoza y Jordan shared many other assumptions with Bourbon officials. In 1804 he criticized parish priests for not doing enough to promote agriculture and the arts (AHAO, Fondo Diocesano, Sección Gobierno, Serie Mandatos, 1804).

63. AGN, Clero Regular y Secular, vol. 178, exp. 12.

64. Taylor, *Magistrates*, 369.

65. AVA, Civil, exp. 498, 1795. Similarly terse documents written on behalf of whole villages are found in AGN, Indios, vol. 69, exp. 325, fols. 246–46v; AGN, Clero Regular y Secular, vol. 39, exp. 6. More forthcoming petitions that were also written on behalf of whole villages are found in AGEO, Obispado, vol. 5, exp. 11; and AGEO, Obispado, vol. 14, exp. 13.

66. AVA, Civil, exp. 576, 1798.

67. See AVA, Civil, exp. 697, 1802, as well as the 1774 agreement of San Juan Yae discussed in chapter 2 and reproduced in AVA, Civil, exp. 362, 1774.

68. Florescano, *Etnia*, 315–16; Serge Gruzinski, "La 'segunda aculteración': El estado ilustrado y la religiosidad indígena de la Nueva España (1775–1800)," *Estudios de Historia Novohispana* 8 (1985): 187–88; Tanck de Estrada, *Pueblos*, 23.

69. Gruzinski, "La 'segunda aculteración,'" 176; Chance, *Conquest*, 170–71.

70. AVA, Penal, exp. 334, 1791 (1789).

71. AGN, Clero Regular y Secular, vol. 88, exp. 8, fol. 141. The Spanish reads, "El Rey no quiere que los Yndios con motibo de tales fiestas se empeñen, pues no se limitan a solo la de Yglesia, sino que asi danzas, convites, y otros gastos."

72. AGN, Clero Regular y Secular, vol. 188, exp. 12, fols. 203v, 214.

73. For Parra y Arteaga, see AGN, Clero Regular y Secular, vol. 88, exp. 8, fols. 142–42v. For the quote, see AGN, Clero Regular y Secular, vol.188, exp. 12, fol. 213v. The Spanish quote reads, "Tan debiles fundamentos entre estos Neofitos llegue a flaquear, y caer en esta juridiccion."

74. Chance, *Conquest*, 165–72.

75. AGN, Indios, vol. 88, fols. 300–300v.

76. Gruzinski, "La 'segunda aculteración.'"

77. AVA, Penal, exp. 334, 1791 (1789).

78. AGN, Clero Regular y Secular, vol. 188, exp. 12, fols. 203v–204.

79. AVA, Civil, vol. 576, 1798; AVA, Penal 414, 1798. The Spanish reads, "Unas corruptelas . . . con el titulo de costumbre."

80. AGEO, Colonial, vol. 11.

81. AHCO, Actas, 1806, fol. 26v; AGEO, Real Intendencia II, vol. 35, exp. 38.

82. Pérez, *Recuerdos*, 44; Canterla, *La iglesia*, 93, 99, 101–2; Deborah Kanter, "Indian Education in Late Colonial Mexico: Policy and Practice," (master's thesis, University of Virginia, 1987), 23–24.

83. Canterla, *La iglesia*, 209.

84. AGN, Clero Regular y Secular, vol. 188, exp. 12, fol. 210; Tanck de Estrada, *Pueblos*, 385.

85. AVA, Civil, exp. 657, 1805; AVA, Penal, exp. 449, 1806.

86. AVA, Civil, exp. 749, 1811. This was often a goal of villagers. See AGN, Indios, vol. 88, exp. 3, fol. 29v.

87. Canterla, *La iglesia*, 196.

88. Taylor, *Magistrates*, 340.

89. AGN, Indios, vol. 88, exp. 3, fol. 29v. The Spanish reads, "Maltraten mucho a los niños y niñas por no ser de su calidad." I believe that in this case *ethnicity* is the best direct translation of *calidad*.

90. Tanck de Estrada, *Pueblos*, 337.

91. Tanck de Estrada, *Pueblos*, 339–40.

92. AGEO, Obispado, vol. 13, exp. 32. See also AVA, Civil, exp. 829, 1820; AGN, Indios, vol. 88, fol. 299v.

93. Tanck de Estrada, *Pueblos*, 412.

94. AGN, Clero Regular y Secular, vol. 188, exp. 12, fol. 210.

95. AGEO, Real Intendencia II, vol. 40, exp. 32; AVA, Civil, exp. 749, 1811.

96. AVA, Penal, exp. 419, 1799.

97. Tanck de Estrada, *Pueblos*, 407, 410.

98. Benito Juárez, "Apuntes para mis hijos," in *Archivos privados de D. Benit Juárez y D. Pedro Santacilia*, vol. 1 (Mexico City: Secretaría de Educación Pública, 1928), 229.

99. Tanck de Estrada, *Pueblos*, 408. For evidence of its use in Villa Alta, see AVA, Civil, exp. 749, 1811.

100. Juan María Domínguez, *Caton christiano de la santa escuela de Christo Nuestro Seño: Lo escribe en la de Teanquiztengo el minimo discípulo Lic. D. Juan María Dominguez, Colegial de Oposicion en el Real y mas Antiguo Colegio de San Ildefonso* (Mexico City: Don Mariano de Zúñiga y Ontiveros, 1805), 3, 20, 21; Tanck de Estrada, *Pueblos*, 408.

101. Taylor, *Magistrates*, 363.

102. Florescano, *Etnia*, 289; Taylor, *Magistrates*, 363.

103. Cutter, *Legal Culture*, 130–31.

104. Scardaville, "(Hapsburg) Law," 516.

105. Taylor, *Magistrates*, 13.

106. *Real ordenanza*.

107. Taylor, *Magistrates*, 13.

108. Castro Gutiérrez, *Nueva*, 214.

109. On bishops and priests, see Gómez Alvarez and Téllez Guerrero, "Los libros," 11–12; and Taylor, *Magistrates*, 92, 451, 455.

110. AGEO, Colonial, vol. 13, exp. 32.

111. Lempérière, "Reflexiones," 36.

112. AGEO, Real Intendencia II, vol. 4, exp. 11.

113. AVA, Civil, exp. 419, 1784. Here I translated *vocales* as *committee members* for lack of a better term in English. The original Spanish of the other quotes reads, "En todas nuestras Naciones, y casi en todas distintas a las nuestras" and "Jusgar segura la defensa de la Patria y de la livertad de sus patricios."

114. AGEO, Real Intendencia I, vol. 11, exp. 19. The original Spanish reads, "Personales servicios contra toda ley Justicia y equidad."

115. AGN, Indios, vol. 69, exp. 325, fol. 246; AVA, Civil, exp. 576, 1798; AVA, Penal, exp. 414, 1798.

116. Leal Curiel, *El discurso*, 207.

117. AHAO, Fondo Diocesano, Sección Gobierno, Serie Mandatos, 1793. The quotes are from Omaña's first pastoral letter, Gregorio José de Omaña y Sotomayor, *Carta pastoral instructiva y exhortatoria sobre el origen, necesidad y justicia de la presente guerra, que con el fin de excitar y alentar al clero de su diócesi á las oraciones y subsidios que pide S. M. le dirigió el ilustrisimo señor doctor don Gregorio Joseph de Omaña y Sotomayor,*

obispo de Antequera, publicándola en forma de edicto en la santa Iglesia Catedral de Oaxaca el dia domingo veinte y tres de junio de 1793 (Mexico City: F. De Zúñiga y Ontiveros, 1793), 5, 8. The original Spanish is "Guerra Santa, porque en ella se interesa tambien la causa de Dios" and "Franceses modernos y mundanos."

118. AGN, Clero Regular y Secular, vol. 188, exp. 12, fol. 213v.

119. AVA, Penal, exp. 407, 1798. The Spanish reads, "Las pasadas funestas revoluciones de la Nacion francesa."

120. Brian Hamnett's study of the repartimiento, *Politics and Trade in Southern Mexico, 1750–1821,* is a classic in this vein.

121. AVA, Civil, exp. 503, 1795. The Spanish reads, "Defender a toda costa la Religion, la Patria, y la propiedad del dominio de nuestro augusto soberano." For similar appeals by Oaxaca's bishop, see AHAO, Fondo Diocesano, Sección Gobierno, Serie Mandatos, 1793; and Omaña y Sotomayor, *Carta.*

122. As I pointed out earlier in this chapter, this effort was much more serious in Mexico City than it was in Antequera. See Voekel, "Peeing"; Scardaville, "(Hapsburg) Law"; Viquiera Alban, *Relajados.*

123. Taylor, *Magistrates,* 19.

124. AGEO, Real Intendencia I, vol. 9, exp. 11. In a like vein, Antonio Ramirez de Omaña, parish priest of Tontontepec, referred to his Mixe flock in 1820 by saying, "La Yndiada Mige . . . toda ella es mala," or "The Mije rabble is all bad" (AVA, Civil, exp. 829, 1820).

125. Lempérière, "Reflexiones," 48.

126. AGEO, Real Intendencia II, vol. 22, exp. 22. The Spanish reads, "Servicio del Rey, de Público y al Cuerpo de Minería."

127. Chance, *Conquest,* 94–96.

128. For biographical information see Hamnett, *Politics,* 159; Archer, *Army,* 121–22; AHCO, Actas, vol. 42v, 1807.

129. AVA, Civil, exp. 458, 1789; AGEO, Obispado, vol. 13, exp. 13; AGEO, Obispado, vol. 15, exp. 10. The Spanish quotes are "Para que les querian tratar como si fueran esclavos" and "Quedandose sin misa en domingos, y perdiendo su trabajo."

130. AVA, Civil, exp. 419, 1784. The Spanish reads, "Esclavitud, y servidumbre."

131. AVA, Civil, exp. 444, 1788; AGEO, Colonial, vol. 10.

132. AVA, Civil, exp. 469, 1791; AVA, Civil, exp. 444, 1788.

133. AVA, Civil, exp. 469, 1791. The Spanish reads, "Pobres mosos."

134. AVA, Civil, exp. 656, 1805. The Spanish reads, "Señor Coronel Echarri que es rico, Y a nosotros por Pobres nos han avatido."

Notes to Chapter 4: Loyalty, Liberalism, War, and Independence

1. Christon Archer, "The Bite of the Hydra: The Rebellion of Cura Miguel Hidalgo, 1810–1811," in *Patterns of Contention in Mexican History,* edited by Jaime E.

Rodríguez O. (Wilmington, Del.: Scholarly Resources, 1992), 72–73; Van Young, *Other Rebellion*, 328–34.

2. Charles Walker, *Smoldering Ashes: Cuzco and the Creation of Republican Peru, 1780–1840* (Durham, N.C.: Duke University Press, 1999), 90.

3. Guha, *Elementary Forms*, 265.

4. Rodríguez O., *Independence*, 50–51.

5. Jean René Aymes, "La 'Guerra Gran' como prefiguración de la 'Guerra del Francés' (1808–1814)," in *España y la Revolución Francesa* (Barcelona: Editorial Crítica, 1989), 345–50; Rodríguez O., *Independence*, 51.

6. AHAO, Fondo Diocesano, Sección Gobierno, Serie Mandatos, 1793. Another copy exists in the Fondo Martínez Gracida, vol. 68. The Spanish original reads, "El atroz delito cometido por los Franceses poniendo sus sacrilegas manos sobre su legitimo Rey, y Señor, el odio implacable que hase mostrado a nuestra Sagrada Religion, y los audaces insultos que han hecho a los Ministros y esposa del Señor, a las imagenes de los Santos y Madre Santisma y aun al Divinismo Señor Sacramentado."

7. AVA, Civil, exp. 503, 1795. The Spanish reads, "A toda costa la Religion, la Patria, y la propiedad del dominio de nuestro augusto soberano."

8. AVA, Civil, exp. 503, 1795. In 1797, the subdelegado visited each parish seat, called the officials of all the parish villages together and appealed to them through an interpreter for funds to use against the English (AVA, Civil, exp. 566, 1797). On these and other occasions the district's parish priests also contributed money. See AGN, Donativos y Préstamos, vol. 2, exp. 3, fols. 23–27; AGEO, Obispado, vol. 13, exp. 28; AGEO, Real Intendencia II, vol. 26, exp. 26.

9. AGN, Donativos y Préstamos, vol. 18, exp. 34, fols. 458–69.

10. Fondo Manuel Martínez Gracida, vol. 68.

11. For an extensive collection, see Maribel Larraga, "Indios, blancos y mulatos: 'Si todos somos Hermanos Y, todos bamos Fin ya no ay criollo ó, Gachupin, todos sean Americanos,'" *Colonial Latin American Historical Review* 5, no. 1 (1996): 47–73.

12. Hugh Hamill, "'¡Vencer o morir por la patria!' La invasión de España y algunas consecuencias para México, 1808–1810," in *Interpretaciones*, edited by Vázquez, 89–99; Avila, *En nombre*, 78–79.

13. Fondo Manuel Martínez Gracida, vol. 68. The Spanish reads, "Emisarios seductores que traten de pervirtir con engaños a los fieles Americanos," and "Sus enormes delitos, de la usurpacion de la Corona de nuestro legitimo Soberano, de su propia apostacia a la Religion Catolica, de la violacion, profanacion y robos de las Yglesias, del saqueo de las Ciudades y aldeas, del indendio de las casas, de la muerte de nuestros hermanos, y de todos los delitos imaginables."

14. Juan Ortiz Escamilla, *Guerra y gobierno. Los pueblos y la independencia de México* (Mexico City: Instituto Mora / El Colegio de México / Universidad Internacional de Andalucia / Universidad de Sevilla, 1997), 23, 27–30. For such a rumor in Oaxaca, see AGN, Operaciones de Guerra, vol. 103, fol. 6v.

15. Rodríguez O. makes this point for Spanish America more generally (*Independence*, 41).

16. Larraga, "Indios," 59. The Spanish reads,

"Los Yndios, y Los Yndianos
Somos Vasallos del Rey,
Defenderemos, la Ley
Como dos, fuertes Hermanos."

17. Landavazo, *La máscara*, 76–85.

18. The merchants, enemies of Izquierdo, complained that his hesitation was a symptom of his lack of loyalty to the king. They also accused Izquierdo and the recently deceased Intendant Antonio Mora y Peysal of running a lax regime in Oaxaca. Hamnett (*Politics*, 122–24) and Ibarra (*Clero*, 65–66) state that Izquierdo's hesitation stemmed from a desire to prevent a public commotion in a city unsettled by rivalries between Creoles and European Spaniards. Hensel argues in a more convincing manner that Izquierdo and his colleagues simply wanted a more elaborate ceremony, and their merchant enemies invented the tensions they claimed divided the city ("Los orígenes," 223–25). The merchants wanted to restore the repartimiento, an institution that Intendant Mora and his protégé Izquierdo both opposed. It was not unusual for political ceremonies to be postponed until they could be celebrated properly. In fact, a few months later, in March 1809, Izquierdo and Bishop Bergoza arranged to postpone the city's oath of loyalty to Spain's Supreme Junta until after Easter. See AGEO, Real Intendencia II, vol. 37, exp. 28.

19. Ramón Francisco Casaus y Torres, *Sermon en accion de gracias a Dios nuestro senor por las gloriosas hazanas de la invicta nacion espanola para la restauracion de la monarquia, y restitucion de nuestro amado soberano el Sr. D. Fernando VII. a su trono. Predicado el dia 10 de septiembre de 1808 en la iglesia de San Agustin de Antequera de Oaxaca* (Mexico City: Por D. M. de Zuñiga y Ontiveros, 1808), 2, 17, 18. The Spanish reads, "En boca de todos, sin distincion de edades, clases, y sexos." There also was apparently another, similar mass in the Iglesia de Santa María de los Angeles. This mass was preceded by the burning of a *castillo*, an elaborate framework festooned with fireworks that is often part of patron saint feasts in Mexico. See AGEO, Colonial, vol. 7.

20. AGN, Infidencias, vol. 10, exp. 1.

21. AGN, Infidencias, vol. 2, exp. 13.

22. AHCO, Actas, 1810, fols. 89, 98; AHCO, Tesorería, 1764–1829.

23. Manuel Esparza, ed., *Morelos en Oaxaca: Documentos para la Historia de la Independencia* (Oaxaca: Archivo General del Estado de Oaxaca, 1986), 184–91.

24. Manuel Martínez Gracida, "Reseña histórica de algunos hechos de la Guerra de Independencia," (Guadalajara, 1908, manuscript), 73–79; Carlos María de Bustamante, *Cuadro histórico de la revolución mexicana de 1810*, vol. 1 (Mexico City: Instituto Nacional de Estudios Históricos de la Revolución Mexicana, 1985), 355–57.

25. AGN, Infidencias, vol. 11, exp. 1, fol. 1v; AGN, Infidencias, vol. 10, exp. 5, fols. 213–13v.

26. AGN, Infidencias, vol. 14, exp. 7. The quote is from fols. 195–95v, and the original is, "Venía diciendo, que viva nuestra Señora de Guadalupe; muera el mal gobierno y en contra de los Gachupines."

27. Bishop Bergoza reports this. See Martínez Gracida, "Reseña," 111–16. The notion also entered popular legend. See Altamirano Ramírez, *La ciudad*, 51.

28. AGN, Infidencias, vol. 10, exp. 2, fols. 30–56v; AGN, Infidencias, vol. 10, exp. 4; AGN, Infidencias, vol. 11, exp. 6, fols. 3–4. The quotes are from AGN, Infidencias, vol. 10, exp. 2, fol. 31v; and AGN, Infidencias, vol. 11, exp. 6, fol. 3.

29. AGN, Infidencias, vol. 2, exp. 2. In 1812 Ordoño turned in another fellow prisoner for treason. See AGEO, Real Intendencia I, vol. 1, exp. 1.

30. AGN, Infidencias, vol. 2, exp. 6.

31. Antonio Bergoza y Jordán, *Nos el doctor don Antonio Bergosa y Jordan por la gracia de dios y de la Santa Sede Apostolica: obispo de Antequera de Oaxaca, electo arzobispo de Mexico, Caballero de la real y distinguida orden española de Carlos Tercero, del consejo de S. M. &c* (Oaxaca: n.p., 1810).

32. Fondo Manuel Martínez Gracida, vol. 68.

33. Bergoza y Jordán, *Nos el doctor don Antonio Bergosa y Jordan por la gracia de dios y de la Santa Sede Apostolica: obispo de Antequera de Oaxaca, electo arzobispo de Mexico, Caballero de la real y distinguida orden española de Carlos Tercero, del consejo de S. M. & c* (Oaxaca: n.p., 1811).

34. Martinez Gracida, "Reseña," 111–16, quote from 115. The Spanish reads, "Proto-apoderado del tirano Napoleon, de Santanás, y del infierno." The town councilmen of Antequera also suggested that the Hidalgo revolt was anti-Catholic when they offered funds for its suppression in November 1810. See their letter in Esparza, *Morelos*, 1–2.

35. AHCO, Actas, 1810, fol. 95; Ortiz Escamilla, *Guerra*, 69–72.

36. AGN, Operaciones de Guerra, vol. 103, fols. 6–46, quote from fol. 46. The Spanish reads, "Debe tener facultades con que poderse sostener con el decoro y esplendor."

37. Edmund Morgan points out that in colonial British America militias often served as a crucial support for the social status of local elites (*Inventing*, 169–73).

38. AGN, Operaciones de Guerra, vol. 103, fol. 61v. The Spanish reads, "En cierto modo indecoroso por la distincion en que queda la otras companias de voluntarios del comercio que estan de formarse en esta Ciudad lo que nos es dolorosa respecto a que siendo igual la causa que defendemos y uno el Monarca a quien servimos no se nos debe desigualar."

39. AGN, Operaciones de Guerra, vol. 103, fols. 63–69. For more on the number of troops organized in Oaxaca, see Ortiz Escamilla, *Guerra*, 191, 195.

40. AGN, Operaciones de Guerra, vol. 103, fol. 63. See also fol. 54.

41. Carriedo, *Estudios*, 33; Martínez Gracida, "Reseña," 217–18; Ibarra, *Clero*, 82.

42. Francisco Ruiz Cervantes and Carlos Sánchez Silva, *Pensamiento político y social oaxaqueño* (Oaxaca: Instituto Estatal de Educación Pública de Oaxaca/Proyecto Editorial Huaxyácac, 1998), 3–4.

43. AHCO, Actas, 1812, fol. 115v. See also Ibarra, *Clero*, 82, 85.

44. Ibarra, *Clero*, 79; AGN, Ayuntamientos, 160.

45. For an example of such a practical argument, see the *El Correo Americano del Sur*, 6 October 1813.

46. See the long diatribe in Ernesto Lemoine, *Morelos: su vida revolucionaria a través de sus escritos y otros testimonios de la época* (Mexico City: Universidad Nacional Autónoma de México, 1965), 251, 254, 255.

47. Altamirano Ramírez, *La ciudad*, 11; Esparza, *Morelos*, 3–5; Lemoine, *Morelos*, 235–39.

48. Lemoine, *Morelos*, 242. The Spanish reads, "Lejos de ser nosotros herejes, protegemos más que nuestros enemigos la religión santa, católica, apostólica romana."

49. Guardino, *Peasants*, 63; Taylor, *Magistrates*, 462; Lemoine, *Morelos*, 185–86.

50. References to this tyranny are ubiquitous. See, for example, Lemoine, 243, 245, 247, 249.

51. Lemoine, *Morelos*, 246, 247, 250, 255.

52. The original message is found in Lemoine, *Morelos*, 230–32. The quote is from 231. The Spanish reads, "Las cadenas de una ominosa servidumbre de casi tres siglos." The message was reproduced in the insurgent newspaper, *El Correo Americano del Sur*, on 20 May 1813. The reference to three centuries of slavery was also used on the occasion of the election, found in *El Correo Americano del Sur* of 5 August 1813, and in a description of the feast of Guadalupe in *El Correo Extraordinario del Sur*, 28 December 1813. Rodríguez O. notes that in the Spanish Cortes, American deputies used similar rhetoric, while their Spanish counterparts also cited three hundred years of slavery, although they were referring to the period since the Hapsburgs had crushed Spain's mythical democracy (*Independence*, 93).

53. William Taylor, "The Virgin of Guadalupe in New Spain: An Inquiry into the Social History of Marian Devotion," *American Ethnologist* 14 (1987): 9–33.

54. For 1812, see the report of María Micaela Frontaura in Esparza, *Morelos*, 90. For 1813, see Esparza, *Morelos*, 159–60; *El Correo Extraordinario del Sur*, 28 December 1813.

55. Altamirano, Ramírez, *La ciudad*, 8–9.

56. Esparza, *Morelos*, 88; Lemoine, *Morelos*, 233–34.

57. Lemoine, *Morelos*, 248, 250.

58. Guardino, *Peasants*, 61–65; AGN, Operaciones de Guerra, vol. 939, fol. 684.

59. Esparza, *Morelos*, 149. The Spanish reads, "Mueran los chaquetas."

60. Esparza, *Morelos*, 87. The Spanish reads, "Las denuncias fueron infinitas."

61. AGEO, Real Intendencia I, vol. 13, exp. 1. The Spanish reads, "En substancia a la clase de las viudas miserables."

62. AGN, Infidencias, vol. 10, exp. 6.

63. Lemoine, *Morelos*, 264. The Spanish reads, "Quede abolida la hermosísisima jerigonza de calidades *indio, mulato, o mestizo, tente en el aire,* etcétera, y sólo se distinga la regional, nombrándolos todos generalmente *americanos,* con cuyo epíteto nos distinguimos del *inglés, francés,* o más bien del *europeo* que nos perjudica, del *africano* y del *asiático* que ocupan las otras partes del mundo." For Morelos's earlier abolition of the caste system see Lemoine, *Morelos*, 162–63.

64. See for example, AGEO, Real Intendencia I, vol. 14, exp. 12.

65. Esparza, *Morelos*, 4; *El Correo Extraordinario del Sur*, 28 December 1813. The Spanish reads, "Danzas al estilo rústico."

66. Esparza, *Morelos*, 87. The original reads, "El hombre de honor que no tomaba partido en su causa, se vería dentro de poco tiempo mandado por los negros, y por este motivo lo habían abrazado muchos."

67. For a local Creole's view of the racial composition of the insurgent army, see again María Micaela Frontaura. She reported that there were about one hundred "decent" officers and troops, and the rest of the large army were "pura negrería" (Esparza, *Morelos*, 91).

68. Esparza, *Morelos*, 89–90.

69. *El Correo Americano del Sur*, 22 April 1813, 6 May 1813, and 24 June 1813.

70. Ibarra, *Clero*. The phrase is used repeatedly in this biographical study. See for instance p. 105. San Martín's political twists and turns continued after the royalist reoccupation of Antequera. He fled while under investigation for his activities under the insurgents. He then joined the insurgents, where he served in various posts during the remaining years of the war. After the war he was elected as a representative of Oaxaca to Mexico's first Constitutional Congress.

71. Virginia Guedea provides an extensive analysis of this election ("Los procesos electorales insurgentes," *Estudios de historia novohispana* 11 [1991]: 214–22). See also AGEO, Real Intendencia I, vol. 13, exp. 28; Lemoine, *Morelos*, 285–86, 317–21; and *El Correo Americano del Sur*, 5 August 1813.

72. Ibarra, *Clero*, 90. For an example of this see Lemoine, *Morelos*, 299–313.

73. *El Correo Americano del Sur*, 29 April 1813; Lemoine, *Morelos*, 329–31, 400–403; Francisco Lorenzo de Velasco, *Francisco Lorenzo de Velasco Mariscal de Campo de los Exercitos Nacionales por Nombramiento del serenismo Sr. José María Morelos* (Oaxaca: n.p., 1814); AGN, Infidencias, vol. 10, exp. 6.

74. Carriedo, *Estudios*, 61; AGN, Operaciones de Guerra, vol. 2, fol. 39. The original is, "El populacho, excitados por los gachupines."

75. AGN, Indios, vol. 88, fols. 293–313. The quotes are from fol. 312v. The original Spanish reads, "Ya no tenemos govierno, ya no tenemos rey, y a lo hecharon fuera, por que ya yego el tiempo, que vuelva nuestra corona, que son de nosotros

índios, no son de los Gachupines ese nuestra corona. Esta rovado los gachupines, no son suya, tanta fuersa hizo, lo llevo; pero ya acavo todo ese tiempo, otra cosa ahora"; and "Los insurgentes vienen de nuestro favor que somos pobres Yndios; lo que viene avuscar los Gachupines, para matarlos y hecharlos fuera. Tambien estamos pronto nosotros de acompañarlos insurgentes, que son buenos amigos, lo defienden a nosotros contra los Gachupines."

76. See the report of witness Miguel Jacinto, a peasant from Zacapetec, in AGEO, Real Intendencia II, vol. 41, exp. 14.

77. Michael Ducey informed me in a personal communication that the outbreak of the insurgency in Chicontepec, Veracruz, in 1811 also had significant similarities to a colonial village riot.

78. AHCO, Delitos Contra la Seguridad Interior del Estado, 1812. On the identity of Flores see *El Regenerador*, 6 March 1843, 75. For the activity of Ramírez see AGEO, Real Intendencia II, vol. 24, exp. 28.

79. AHCO, Delitos Cometidos por Autoridades, 1812; AGEO, Real Intendencia II, vol. 1, exp. 4; AGEO, Real Intendencia II, vol. 24, exp. 22; Esparza, *Morelos*, 79.

80. See his order in Esparza, *Morelos*, 155. The Spanish reads, "El muro de bronce contra el que se estrellaban las olas impetuosas de la herejía"; and "Jacobinos terroristas."

81. AHCO, Actas, 1810, fols. 83–83v; AHCO, Tesorería Municipal, 17641829, 26 June 1810, 10 August 1810.

82. Manuel Ferrer Muñoz and María Bono López, *Pueblos indígenas y estado nacional en México en el siglo XIX* (Mexico City: Universidad Nacional Autónoma de México, 1998), 210, 276. In 1814 the village of Lachiroag raised a similar complaint. See AGEO, Colonial, vol. 12.

83. Benson's contribution was not coincidentally republished in 1992 as interest in the constitution revived. See Benson, *The Provincial Deputation in Mexico* (Austin: University of Texas Press, 1992). In 1966 Benson edited an important volume on the theme, *Mexico and the Spanish Cortes, 1810–1822* (Austin: University of Texas Press, 1966). Then in the 1990s the Spanish liberal reforms occupied a central place in an enormous quantity of works. See Antonio Annino, "The Ballot, Land, and Sovereignty: Cádiz and the Origins of Mexican Local Government," in *Elections*, edited by Posada-Carbó, 61–86; "Cádiz y la revolución territorial de los pueblos mexicanos 1812–1821," in *Historia*, 177–226; and "Prácticas criollas y liberalismo en la crisis del espacio urbano colonial: El 29 de noviembre de 1812 en la ciudad de México," *Secuencia* 24 (1992): 121–58; Bellingeri, "Las ambiguidades"; Marie-Danielle Demélas, "Modalidades y significación de las elecciones generales en los pueblos andinos, 1813–1814," in *Historia*, edited by Annino, 291–313; Ducey, "Hijos"; Antonio Escobar Ohmstede, "Los ayuntamientos y los pueblos de indios en la Sierra Huasteca: Conflictos entre nuevos y viejos actores, 1812–1840," in *La reindianización de América, siglo xix*, edited by Leticia Reina (Mexico City: Siglo XXI / Centro de Investigación y Estudios Superiores de Antropología Social, 1997), 294–316; and

"Del gobierno indígena al ayuntamiento constitucional en las huastecas hidalguense y veracruzana, 1780–1853," *Mexican Studies/Estudios Mexicanos* 12, no. 1 (1996): 1–25; Guardino, *Peasants*; Virginia Guedea, "Las primeras elecciones populares en la ciudad de México: 1812–1813," *Mexican Studies/Estudios Mexicanos* 7, no. 1 (1991): 1–28; François-Xavier Guerra, *México: del Antiguo Régimen a la Revolución* (Mexico City: Fondo de Cultura Económica, 1988); and *Modernidad*; Alicia Hernández Chávez, *La tradición republicana del buen gobierno* (Mexico City: El Colegio de México / Fideiscomiso Historia de las Americas / Fondo de Cultura Económica, 1993); Ortiz Escamilla, *Guerra*; Victor Peralta Ruiz, "Elecciones, constitucionalismo y revolución en el Cusco, 1809–1815," in *Partidos políticos y elecciones en América Latina y la Peninsula Ibérica, 1830–1930*, vol. 1, edited by Carlos Malamud (Madrid: Instituto Ortega y Gasset, 1995), 83–111; Rodríguez O., *Independence*; Terry Rugeley, *Yucatán's Maya Peasantry and the Origins of the Caste War* (Austin: University of Texas Press, 1996); Walker, *Smoldering Ashes*; and Richard Warren, "Elections and Popular Political Participation in Mexico, 1808–1836," in *Liberals, Politics, and Power: State Formation in Nineteenth-Century Latin America*, edited by Vincent Peloso and Barbara Tennenbaum (Athens: University of Georgia Press, 1996), 30–58.

84. AGN, Historia, vol. 403, fols. 293–96.

85. The constitution is reproduced in Antonio Padilla Sierra, ed., *Constituciones y leyes fundamentales de España (1808–1947)* (Granada: Universidad de Granada, 1954). The quote is from p. 12. The Spanish reads, "Aquellos españoles que por ambas líneas traen su origen de los dominios españoles de ambos hemisferios." The bando is in AGEO, Real Intendencia I, vol. 13, exp. 36. The Spanish reads, "Todo español e yndio puro todo castizo o mestizo."

86. AGEO, Real Intendencia II, vol. 38, exp. 13; AGN, Historia, vol. 403, fol. 297; AGN, Gobernación, vol. 1936, exp. 6, fol. 4; Hensel, *Die Enstehung*, 136, 232.

87. Hensel, "Los orígenes," 225–26.

88. See in particular the case of the Yucatán, analyzed in Rugeley, *Yucatán's Maya Peasantry*, 33–48; and Marco Bellingeri, "De una constitución a otra: Conflicos de jurisdicciones y dispersión de poderes en Yucatán (1789–1831)," in *El liberalismo en México*, edited by Antonio Annino and Raymond Buve (Hamburg: Lit, 1993), 65. See also the case of rural Quito in Rodríguez O., *Independence*, 101.

89. AGN, Historia, vol. 403, fol. 351.

90. See Chance, *Conquest*, 63.

91. AGEO, Colonial, vol. 12.

92. The quotes in this and the previous paragraph are all from AGEO, Real Intendencia II, vol. 15, exp. 38. The Spanish originals for Nieto are, "Pocos seran señor los Yndios (hablo de este partido) que gocen del derecho de ciudadanos, como probiene la Constitucion politica de la Monarquia"; and "Se pribarán de ser ciudadanos la mayor parte de los Yndios por su falta de aplicacion y por una costumbre antiguisma de ser desidiosos, flojos y abandonados." The original Spanish of Alvarez's replies is, "El Gobierno del dia no es el de antes, y lo conoce todo el que lee la

Constitucion politica de la Monarquia"; and "El Gobierno del dia no es el de antes, y lo conoce todo el que lee la Constitucion politica de la Monarquia." Alvarez's use of the word *Spaniard* for the Indians was imitating the formulation found in the constitution, which declared that the Indians were now Spaniards in the sense of citizens of the Spanish monarchy.

93. AGEO, Colonial, vol. 12. The Spanish is, "Naturalmente tumultario, cabiloso, fomentador de especies."

94. Nieto Posadillo's problems continued. He tried to solve the problem of the feria de varas by calling the officials of a series of villages to testify to his good character and the fact that any gift they gave him on the occasion was voluntary. He also refused to publish the intendant's orders abolishing the practice and again abolishing the use of sahuiches, who were discussed in chapters 2 and 3. See AGEO, Real Intendencia II, vol. 16, exp. 1; AGEO, Real Intendencia II, vol. 16, exp. 4; AGEO, Real Intendencia II, vol. 16, exp. 21.

95. AGEO, Real Intendencia II, vol. 24, exp. 38

96. Melchor Alvarez, *Ciudad Capital de Antequera. Habitantes del Valle de Oaxaca y de todos los partidos dependientes de aquella, no ignorais ya, que nuestro soberano, si, nuestro amado, suspirado, y deseado FERNANDO VII DE BOURBON, ocupa su trono* (Oaxaca: n.p., 1814), found in AGN, Historia, vol. 280, fol. 75. The quote in Spanish reads, "Los principios revolucionarios y democraticos de la constitucion francesa de 1791."

97. Ignacio Mariano Vasconcelos, *Sermon que en la solemne función de accion de gracias que hicieron los curas del Obispado de Oaxaca en la santa Iglesia Catedral de aquella ciudad, el dia 6 de febrero de 1815, por la libertad del señor Don Fernando VII Rey Católico de ambas Españas, predicó el Señor Licenciado Don Ignacio Mariano Vasconcelos, dignidad de Chantre de la misma Santa Iglesia, dedicado al Rey Nuestro Señor por el Obispo de Oaxaca* (Mexico City: Impreso en la Oficina de la Calle De Santo Domingo, y esquina de Tacuba, 1816), 4, 6, 15, 16.

98. The best example of this is Antonio Bergoza y Jordán. This Spanish cleric had been a rising star, and as bishop of Oaxaca he had defended royal prerogatives against his own clergy and then defended the viceregal government against the insurgents. The Spanish liberals, recognizing his talent, named him archbishop of Mexico. Fernando VII cancelled this promotion before Bergoza could take up his post, and Bergoza was instead named to a small diocese in Spain (Gómez Alvarez and Téllez Guerrero, "Los libros," 9).

99. AGEO, Real Intendencia I, vol. 13, exp. 42; AGEO, Real Intendencia I, vol. 13, exp. 43; AGEO, Real Intendencia II, vol. 24, exp. 40; AGN, Criminal, vol. 629, exp. 5, fols. 128–74.

100. Ibarra, *Clero*, 99–100.

101. They also replaced the mining tribunal elected under the insurgents. See AGEO, Real Intendencia II, vol. 29, exp. 50.

102. AGEO, Real Intendencia II, vol. 25, exp. 35. The Spanish is, "Todos sospechosos."

103. AGN, Infidencias, vol. 158, exp. 19.

104. AGN, Infidencias, vol. 32, exp. 13, fol. 296.

105. AGN, Operaciones de Guerra, vol. 56, fol. 75. The quote is from AGEO, Colonial, vol. 8, and in Spanish it reads, "Lame culos de los gachupines." Soldiers from outside the city continued to be unpopular. In 1820 soldiers from Guanajuato arrested four Antequeran plebeians at a party. Twenty men from the city went to their barracks, shouted insults, and threw stones. An officer ordered his troops to arrest them and open fire if necessary. After the troops opened fire, the plebeians fled unharmed. See AGN, Criminal, vol. 514, exp. 6, fols. 103–49.

106. AGN, Clero Regular y Secular, vol. 87, exp. 6, fols. 276–88.

107. AGEO, Colonial, vol. 14; AGEO, Real Intendencia II, vol. 14, exp. 12; AGEO, Colonial, vol. 9; AGEO, Real Intendencia II, vol. 29, exp. 17.

108. AGEO, Real Intendencia II, vol. 3, exp. 8; Arrom, *Women*, 27–28. The Spanish reads, "Todas aquellas manufacturas compatibles con la decencia, fuerzas, y disposicion de su sexo."

109. AGEO, Real Intendencia II, vol. 25, exp. 30.

110. AGEO, Real Intendencia I, vol. 36, exp. 9.

111. Apparently only six men went through the examination process between 1814 and 1819. Four did so in 1814, immediately after the guilds were reestablished, and two did so in 1819. See AGEO, Real Intendencia II, vol. 31, exp.7.

112. AHCO, Actas, 1820, fol. 37, fols. 65–68.

113. AGEO, Real Intendencia I, vol. 13, exp. 7.

114. AGEO, Colonial, vol. 4; AVA, Civil, exp. 776, 1815. The original is, "Por odio que tiene el sitado Jose Santiago a toda mi generacion que nos intitula de Ynsurgentes."

115. AGN, Indios, vol. 88, fols. 300, 301, 302v, 303v, 304, 304v, 305v, 312.

116. AGEO, Real Intendencia II, vol. 40, exp. 32; AVA, Civil, exp. 768, 1815; AVA, Civil, exp. 773, 1815.

117. Rodríguez O., *Independence*, 194–95.

118. Hamnett, *Politics*, 144–45; AHCO, Actas, 1820, fol. 226v.

119. The flyer can be found in AHCO, Actas, 1820. The Spanish reads, "Hace a todos iguales; pero no con una igualdad quimerica, con una igualdad que destruya sino con una que edifique y conserve, que lo ordene todo con reciproci beneficio, y con respectiva atribucion, cooperando todos a sus peculiares deberes, aucxiliandandose mutuamente."

120. Guardino, *Peasants*, 77–78; Timothy Anna, *Forging Mexico 1821–1835* (Lincoln: University of Nebraska Press, 1998), 68.

121. AGEO, Real Intendencia II, vol. 26, exp. 21.

122. Hensel, *Die Enstehung*, 147.

123. Guillermo Rangel Rojas, *General Antonio de León: Consumador de la Indepen-dencia de Oaxaca y Benemérito del Estado de Oaxaca* (Oaxaca: Ayuntamiento Con-stitucional, 1997), 21–28.

124. Hensel, *Die Enstehung*, 148.

125. Probably the first important contribution to that tradition was made by Oaxaca's native son, Carlos María de Bustamante (*Cuadro*, 1985).

126. Rodríguez O., *Independence*, 161.

127. Eric Van Young, "Millenium on the Northern Marches: The Mad Messiah of Durango and Popular Rebellion in Mexico, 1800–1815," *Comparative Studies in Society and History* 28 (1986): 386–413; and "Quetzalcóatl, King Ferdinand, and Ignacio Allende Go to the Seashore; or Messianism and Mystical Kingship in Mex-ico, 1800–1821," in *The Independence of Mexico and the Origins of the New Nation*, edited by Jaime Rodríguez O. (Los Angeles: University of California at Los Angeles Latin American Center, 1989), 109–27.

128. AGN, Indios, vol. 88, fol. 312v.

Notes to Chapter 5: Oil and Vinegar: The Construction and Dissolution of Republican Order in the City of Oaxaca

1. See the works by Guerra in the bibliography.

2. Hensel, *Die Enstehung*.

3. Hensel, "Los orígenes," 217.

4. Carlos Sánchez Silva, *Indios, comerciantes y burocracia en la Oaxaca poscolonial, 1786–1860* (Oaxaca: Instituto Oaxaqueño de las Culturas/Fondo Estatal para la Cul-tura y las Artes/Universidad Autónoma Benito Juárez de Oaxaca, 1998).

5. For Oaxaca, see, for instance, Charles Berry, *The Reform in Oaxaca: A Microhis-tory of the Central District, 1856–1876* (Lincoln: University of Nebraska Press, 1983), 1–26.

6. The two best local examples of this are Jorge Fernando Iturribarría, *Historia de Oaxaca* (Oaxaca: Ediciones E. R. B., 1935); and Brian Hamnett, *Juárez* (New York: Longman, 1994), 1–48.

7. For Catholicism's institutional presence, note that there were a total of 548 regular clergy, nuns, and secular clergy in 1829, compared to 568 in 1849. See *Memoria que el Vice-gobernador en Ejercicio del Estado de Oaxaca presentó al Tercer Congreso Constitucional del mismo al abrir sus primeras sesiones ordinarias el 2 de Julio de 1829* (Oajaca: Imprenta del Gobierno, 1829), appendix; *Esposición que en cumpli-miento del articulo 83 de la Constitución del Estado hace el Gobernador del mismo al soberano Congreso al abrir sus sesiones el 2 de julio del año de 1849* (Oaxaca: Impreso por Ignacio Rincón, 1849), appendix. On religion and legitimacy see Van Young, "Cuatla," 9; Brian Connaughton, "Conjuring the Body Politic from the 'Corpus Mysticum': The Post-independent Pursuit of Public Opinion in Mexico, 1821–1854," *The Americas* 55, no. 3 (1999): 459–79.

8. *Colección de leyes y decretos del estado libre de Oaxaca*, vol. 1 (Oaxaca: Imprenta del estado en el Ex obispado, 1861), 49; Ruiz Cervantes and Sánchez Silva, *Pensamiento*, 28. The original Spanish reads, "Nada es más conveniente para formar las costumbres, (sin las cuales ningunas leyes pueden subsistir) que la religión cristiana que predica los deberes sociales."

9. AHCO, Actas, 1824, fol. 509; J. Iturribarría, *Historia*, 28, 243; AGEO, Gobernación, vols. 13, 27; AHCO, Actas, 1829, fol. 95.

10. José M. Alvarez y Castillejos, *Sermón patriótico moral que predicó en la Iglesia de Nuestra Señora de Guadalupe de esta capital el día 12 de diciembre de 1850* (Oaxaca: Impreso en la oficina de Francisco O. y Quintas, 1851). Evidence of the emergence of Guadalupanism can also be seen in census records. In 1842 there were two men named Guadalupe living in the city, one born in 1822 and one in 1823. See Manuel Esparza, ed., *Padrón general de los habitantes de la ciudad de Oaxaca, 1842* (Mexico City: Instituto Nacional de Antropología e Historia, 1981), 61, 101.

11. Benito Juárez, *Discurso que el C. Benito Juárez pronunció el día 16 de septiembre de 1840, en el aniversario del glorioso grito de independencia* (Oaxaca: Impreso por Ignacio Rincon, 1840), 3.

12. Brian Connaughton, "Agape en disputa: Fiesta Cívica, cultura política regional y la frágil urdimbre nacional antes del Plan de Ayutla," *Historia Mexicana* 45, no. 2 (1995): 284; "La sacralización de lo cívico: La imagen religiosa en el discurso cívico-patriótico del México independiente. Puebla (1827–1853)," in *Estado, Iglesia y sociedad en Mexico, siglo XIX*, edited by Alvaro Matute, Evelia Trejo, and Brian Connaughton (Mexico City: Universidad Nacional Autónoma de México/Miguel Angel Porrua, 1995), 232; and "Conjuring," 472–73.

13. Berry, *Reform*, 5–6, 9.

14. For these incidents, see, respectively, AGEO, Gobernación, vol. 1; AGEO, Legajos Encuadernados, Gobernación, vol. 30, 1839h; AGN, Gobernación, s/s, caja 186, exp. 4; J. Iturribarría, *Historia*, 277–79. Bishops in other regions also cooperated with the effort of authorities to change burial practices. See Anne Staples, "Secularización: Estado y iglesia en tiempos de Gómez Farías," *Estudios de Historia Moderna y Contemporánea de México* 10 (1986): 118.

15. AGEO, Legajos Encuadernados, Decretos, 1826d, 13 July 1826. The same question came up earlier regarding the Spanish liberal constitution. See AHCO, Actas, 1820, fol. 364v.

16. For an Oaxacan defense of the church's position, see *Contestación del Obispo y Cabildo de la Santa Iglesia Catedral de Oajaca, al oficio del Señor Ministro de Justicia y Negocios Eclesiásticos, con que les remitió el dictamen sobre instrucciones al Enviado a Roma* (Guadalajara: Reimpreso en la Oficina de la viuda de Romero, 1827). Connaughton found a similar response in Jalisco. See *Ideología y sociedad en Guadalajara (1788–1853)* (Mexico City: Universidad Nacional Autónoma de México/Consejo Nacional para la Cultura y las Artes, 1992): 318–21. See also AGEO, Gobernación, vol. 2. For the virtual patronato, see Connaughton, "El ocaso del proyecto de 'Nación Cató-

lica': Patronato virtual, préstamos, y presiones regionales, 1821–1856," in *Construc-ción de la legitimidad política en México en el siglo XIX*, edited by Brian Connaughton, Carlos Illades, and Sonia Pérez Toledo (Mexico City: El Colegio de Michoacán/ Universidad Autónoma Metropolitana/Universidad Nacional Autónoma de México/El Colegio de México, 1999), 229.

17. This is similar to what Charles Walker calls a "journalistic orgy" in Cuzco during the same period ("'La orgía periodística': Prensa y cultura política en el Cuzco durante la joven república," *Revista de Indias* 61, no. 221 [2001]: 7).

18. See, for example, the editorial by "Medio Million de no caval de oajaqueños" in *El Oaxaqueño Constitucional*, 8 July 1830. Newspapers, it should be noted, could also be used to air out personal or legal disputes that did not have direct political connections. For the use of papers for personal disputes see *La Bocina de la Justica*, 28 June 1846; *La Prensa*, 31 July 1846; and *La Centinela*, 23 July 1843.

19. Carlos Sánchez Silva, "La imprenta en Oaxaca, 1821–1876: De la especulación a la certidumbre," in *La historia de la imprenta en Oaxaca* (Oaxaca: Biblioteca Francisco Burgoa/Universidad Autónoma Benito Júarez de Oaxaca, 1999), 27; Carriedo, *Estudios*, 133.

20. In 1830 the printer José Felipe Matos published both *El Oajaqueño Federalista* and *El Oajaqueño Constitucional*.

21. J. Iturribarría, *Historia*, 244–45; *La Muralla*, 22 October 1839.

22. J. Iturribarría, *Historia*, 212, 244–45.

23. AHCO, Delitos Contra la Seguridad Interior del Estado, 1834.

24. Peter Guardino, "'Toda libertad para emitir sus votos': Plebeyos, campesinos, y elecciones en Oaxaca, 1808–1850," *Cuadernos del Sur* 15 (2000): 100; Fondo Martínez Gracida, vol. 72.

25. AGEO, Legajos Encuadernados, vol. 70, 1826e. The Spanish reads, "En voz alta, pausada y perceptible."

26. Victor Raul Martínez Vázquez, "La educación primaria y la formación de docentes en Oaxaca (1825–1869)," *Testimonios de Oaxaca* 3, no. 7, (1992): 17, 19.

27. AGEO, Gobernación, vol. 12.

28. Carriedo, *Estudios*, 132, 172–73. The census is found in AGEO, Colonial, vol. 15. It reports 7,718 children. If we assume half were female, and the rest were distributed equally across ages, there would be 2,573 between the ages of five and fifteen.

29. *Esposición que el Gobernador del Estado hace en cumplimiento del articulo 83 de la Constitución al Soberano Congreso al abrir sus primeras sesiones ordinarias el día 2 de julio del año de 1852* (Oaxaca: Impreso por Ignacio Rincón, 1852), appendix.

30. Juárez, "Apuntes," 229; J. Iturribarría, *Historia*, 57; AGEO, Gobernación, vols. 4 and 27.

31. M. M. Vargas, *Catecismo de República o Elementos del gobierno republicano popular federal de la nación mexicana* (Mexico City: Imprenta y Librería a Cargo de Martin Rivera, 1827), 21. The Spanish reads:

Pregunta: ¿Que quiere decir ciudadano?

Respuesta: Un hombre de bien: un individuo que pertenece a la república, que participa de la autoridad soberana, y que contendandose con sus derechos no ambiciona ni aspira mas que al bien de la patria.

The provision for a Oaxacan political catechism is seen in AGEO, Legajos Encuadernados, vol. 70, 1826d.

32. Sánchez Silva, "La imprenta," 30.

33. Again, this is similar to what Walker found in Cuzco ("La orgía," 9, 14–15).

34. AGEO, Juzgado, vol. 14, exp. 2.

35. Un Oaxaqueño, *La calumnia confundida o sea Carta escrita al editor del Semanario político y literario, por un Oaxaqueño, sobre elección de Diputados en Oajaca a 10 de Febrero de 1822* (Mexico City: Imprenta de D. Mariano Ontiveros, 1822).

36. AHCO, Seguridad Interior del Estado, 1837.

37. Hamill, "¡Vencer," 89.

38. Carriedo, *Estudios*, 122, 133; J. Iturribarría, *Historia*, 39. For politics at a private gambling party see AGEO, Juzgado, vol. 22, exp. 4.

39. For acrobats, see *El Zapoteco*, 25 October 1832. For the theater see AGEO, Colonial, vol. 13; AHCO, Actas, 1824, fol. 120; *El Oajaqueño Constitucional*, 7 and 11 November 1830; *El Guajalote Periodista*, 25 June 1849.

40. Leal Curiel, *El discurso*; Florescano, *Etnia*, 235; Martin, *Governance*, 113.

41. Warren, *Vagrants*, 165–66.

42. J. Iturribarría, *Historia*, 185–91; *Colección de leyes y decretos del estado libre de Oaxaca*, vol. 1, 371; AHCO, Seguridad Pública, 1836; J. Iturribarría, *Historia*, 251; Francisco Ortiz de Zarate, *El general de Brigada graduado Francisco Ortiz de Zarate, vice-gobernador en ejercicio del poder ejecutivo del Estado de Oaxaca, a sus habitantes* (Oaxaca: Impreso por Ignacio Rincon, 1847); *El Guajalote Periodista*, 2 August 1849; AGEO, Gobernación, vol. 4; AGEO, Juárez, vol. 1, exps. 30–31; AGEO, Gobernación, vol. 1; AGEO, Legajos Encuadernados, Decretos, vol. 70, 1825b; Berry, *Reform*, 8–9; Carriedo, *Estudios*, 122–23; Canterla, *La Iglesia*, 93; J. Iturribarría, *Historia*, 287–88; Francisco José Ruiz Cervantes, "La Semana Santa en la Oaxaca de 1866, Crónica Periodista" *Acervos* 1 (1996): 18–20; *El Oajaqueño Constitucional*, 24 October 1830.

43. Bellingeri, "Las ambiguidades," 279–80.

44. Annino, "Ballot," 76–77; Warren, "Ashes," 9. Antonio Annino also suggests that these ceremonies were modified on patron saint feasts ("Ciudadanía," 83).

45. AGN, Historia, vol. 403, fol. 293; AHCO, Actas, 1824, fols. 102–4, 178, 252c, 255–56v, 565, 626; AGN, Gobernación, vol. 134, caja 1, exp. 134; AGEO, Legajos Encuadernados, Gobernación, vol. 30, 1839h; *El Regenerador*, 6 July 1843.

46. For royal funerals see Minguez, *Los reyes*, 141–42. An excellent example of a republican hero's funeral in Oaxaca is that of Vicente Guerrero in 1833. See Hamnett, *Juárez*, 24; J. Iturribarría, *Historia*, 185–91.

47. Sometimes officials made explicit references to previous ceremonies that they wanted to surpass or at least equal in magnificence. See, for instance, AHCO, Actas, 1824, fol. 102; AGEO, Gobernación, vol. 1.

48. See for example Juárez, *Discurso*. For Mexico City see Warren, "Ashes," 14–15.

49. See for instance Vicente Fermin Márquez y Carrizosa, *Oracion funebre que en memoria de las victimas sacrificadas por la independencia mexicana pronuncio en la Santa Iglesia Catedral de Oaxaca Vicente Marquez y Carrizosa: el dia 17 de septiembre de 1845* (Oaxaca: Impreso por I. Rincón, 1845). For Mexico City see Warren, *Vagrants*, 167–68.

50. AGEO, Juárez, vol. 9, exp. 4; AGEO, Juárez, vol. 1, exps. 30, 31.

51. Iturrbarría, *Historia*, 185–91; Hamnett, *Juárez*, 24.

52. Anna, *Forging Mexico*, 73–175. For Oaxaca's role, see Jaime Rodríguez O., "'Ningun pueblo es superior a otro': Oaxaca y el federalismo mexicano" (paper presented at the Seminario Internacional sobre Construcción de la legitimidad política en México, siglo XIX: Instituciones, cultura política y poder,Universidad Autónoma Metropolitana-Iztapalapa, Mexico City, 19 May 2000).

53. AHCO, Actas, 1824, fols. 102–4, 178. Compare this to the description of the 1789 oath ceremony for Carlos IV in Lombardo de Ruiz, "La presencia," 212–16.

54. Warren, *Vagrants*, 165–66; AHCO, Actas, 1824, fols. 252v–256.

55. AHCO, Actas, 1824, fol. 256v.

56. Antonio Annino, introduction to *Historia*, 7; Valenzuela, "Building," 224; José Antonio Serrano Ortega, "Reforma municipal y elecciones en Guanajuato, 1820–1836," in *Historia y nación: Actas del Congreso en homenaje a Josefina Zoraida Vázquez*, vol. 2, *Política y diplomacia en el siglo xix mexicano*, edited by Luis Jáuregui and José Antonio Serrano Ortega (Mexico City: El Colegio de México, 1998), 99; and *Jerarquía territorial y transición política: Guanajuato, 1790–1836* (Zamora: El Colegio de Michoacán/Instituto Mora, 2001), 202; Warren, "Ashes," 23.

57. Hilda Sabato, introduction to *Ciudadanía*, 23; Annino, "Cádiz," 206–7.

58. Valenzuela, "Building," 225.

59. Sabato, introduction to *Ciudadanía*, 18; Guardino, "Toda," 24; Morgan, *Inventing Mexico*, 207.

60. Warren, "Ashes," 19.

61. Annino, "Cádiz," 195. See also Marie Danielle Demélas-Bohy and François Xavier Guerra, "The Hispanic Revolutions: The Adoption of Modern Forms of Representation in Spain and America (1808–1810)," in *Elections*, edited by Eduardo Posada-Carbó, 40; Annino, "Ballot," 64; Sabato, introduction to *Ciudadanía*, 22. The procedures in the Constitution of 1812 can be seen in Padilla Sierra, *Leyes*, 14–23.

62. AHAO, Fondo Parroquial, Sección Disciplinar, Serie Cofradías, 1815–1822, 1823b; Pescador, *De bautizados*, 337, 342.

63. *Colección de leyes y decretos del estado libre de Oaxaca*, vol. 1., 58–64; AGN, Gobernación, vol. 129, caja 1, exp. 1; AHCO, Actas, 1824, fol. 45.

64. Guedea, "Las primeras," 9–13; Warren, "Elections," 34–36; Annino, "Ballot,"

67–73; Bellingeri, "De una constitución," 75; Valenzuela, "Building," 240–41; Sabato, introduction to *Ciudadanía*, 21.

65. Fondo Luis Castañeda Guzmán, 636, caja 21.

66. AGN, Gobernación, vol. 1836, caja 2, exp.6.

67. See articles 38–66 of the state constitution in *Colección de leyes y decretos del estado libre de Oaxaca*, vol. 1, 58–64.

68. For differing views of this process in the 1830 legislative election see *El Oajaqueño Federalista*, 14 September and 5 October 1830; and *El Oajaqueño Constitucional*, 8 September 1830. For a later election see *El Zapoteco*, 23 September, 4 October, and 11 October 1832.

69. Mexico City went through a very similar process. See Warren, "Elections," 44–46; and *Vagrants*, 102–4.

70. AGN, Gobernacón, vol. 129, caja 1, exp. 1.

71. *Colección de leyes y decretos del estado libre de Oaxaca*, vol. 1, 344–53, 357–58, 375; AGEO, Legajos Encuadernados, Decretos, vol. 71, 1832b. This is quite similar in some ways to the 1830 electoral reform in Mexico's Federal District. See Warren, *Vagrants*, 102–4.

72. *El Oajaqueño Constitucional*, 24 June and 15 July 1830; *El Oajaqueño Federalista*, 3 August 1830.

73. AGN, Gobernación, vol. 129, caja 1, exp. 2.

74. AGEO, Legajos Ecuadernados, Gobernación, vol. 30, 1839h. The number of ballots is reported in *El Regenerador*, 24 January 1842, and the population figure is in Esparza, *Padrón general*, xiv.

75. Guardino, *Peasants*, 100. The 1846 rules severely restricted suffrage in the city of Oaxaca. See *Lista de los ciudadanos que por la clase de propiedad raiz, rústica, urbana y de agricultores tienen derecho de votar en las prócsimas elecciones, con arreglo al art. 28 de la ley de convocatoria espedidia en 27 de enero del corriente año* (Oaxaca: Ignacio Rincon, 1846) for the list of people who owned enough property to vote for representatives of the propertied class.

76. For Oaxaca, see AHCO, Tesorería, 1840–48.

77. See the constitution in *Colección de leyes y decretos del estado libre de Oaxaca*, vol. 1, 50–57.

78. For the composition of the congress see Hensel, "Los orígenes," 235.

79. Ruiz Cervantes and Sánchez Silva, *Pensamiento*, 28. The original Spanish reads, "Enseñó a los griegos y romanos, que los ilotas y los esclavos no eran bestías, sino hombres y hermanos suyos."

80. AGEO, Legajos Encuadernados, vol. 70, 1825b; AHCO, Actas, 1824, fols. 308, 339; *Memoria que el Gobernador del Estado de Oaxaca presentó en la apertura de las sesiones ordinarias del Segundo Congreso Constitucional del mismo, verificado el 2 de julio de 1827* (Oaxaca: Imprenta del Gobierno, 1827), 15.

81. AGEO, Legajos Encuadernados, Decretos, vol. 70, 1826c. The Spanish reads, "Los ciudadanos llamados antes Yndios."

82. *Memoria que el Gobernador*, 7–8.

83. *Colección de leyes y decretos del estado libre de Oaxaca*, vol. 1, 324–28.

84. *Colección de leyes y decretos del estado libre de Oaxaca*, vol. 1, 16–18.

85. The quote is from the noted populist politician Angel Alvarez, of whom we will hear more below. See AGN, Gobernación, Legajo 58, exp. 16, fols. 19–19v.

86. Chambers, *From Subjects to Citizens*, 214.

87. *El Zapoteco*, 23 September 1832.

88. Chambers, *From Subjects to Citizens*, 214.

89. AGN, Expulsión de Españoles, vol. 56, exp. 35; AGEO, Gobernación, vol. 7.

90. AGEO, Legajos Encuadernados, Decretos, vol. 71, 1826d; AGEO, Juárez, vol. 12, exp. 1.

91. For the Women's Charity Committee see AHCO, Actas, 1829, fols. 94–97, 106, 120. For women assisting religious functions in the state jail see AGEO, Juárez, vol. 14, exp. 7.

92. *Colección de leyes y decretos del estado libre de Oaxaca*, vol. 1, 337–38.

93. *El Guajalote Periodista*, 12 April 1849.

94. AHCO, Homicidios, exp. 168, 1835; Donald F. Stevens, "Lo revelado y lo oscurecido: La política popular desde los archivos parroquiales," in *Construcción*, edited by Connaughton, Illades, and Pérez Toledo, 208–12.

95. See the advertisements for women's schools in *El Oajaqueño constitucional*, 12 August 1830; and *El Regenerador*, 2 May 1842. In 1852 there were 724 boys and 286 girls in primary school in the city. See *Esposición que el Gobernador del Estado hace en cumplimiento del articulo 83 de la Constitución al Soberano Congreso al abrir sus primeras sesiones ordinarias el día 2 de julio del año de 1852* (Oaxaca: Impreso por Ignacio Rincón, 1852), appendix.

96. The phrase *republican mothers* is from Linda Kerber's work on the somewhat similar U.S. case (*Women of the Republic: Intellect and Ideology in Revolutionary America* [Chapel Hill: University of North Carolina Press, 1980], 283–88). For the Peruvian case see Chambers, *From Subjects to Citizens*, 201–2. See also Sylvia Arrom on Mexico more generally (*Women*, 15–20).

97. Chambers, *From Subjects to Citizens*, 204; AGEO, Juárez, vol. 1, exp. 21.

98. Antonio Escobar Ohmstede, "El discurso de la 'inteligencia' india en los primeros años posindependientes," in *Construcción*, edited by Connaughton, Illades, and Pérez Toledo, 263.

99. AHCO, Actas, 1824, fols. 36v–37; AHAO, Fondo Parroquial, Sección Disciplinar, Serie Cofradías, 1815–22, 1823, 1823b, 1846, 1855.

100. AHCO, Tesorería, 1840–48.

101. Fondo Manuel Martínez Gracida, vol. 38; *El Guajalote Periodista*, 2 August 1849.

102. Ruiz Cervantes, "La Semana," 20.

103. AHCO, Actas, 1824, fol. 308v; AGN, Gobernación, vol. 129, caja 1, exp. 3.

104. For population estimates see Eduardo Muhlenpfordt, *Ensayo de una descripción fiel de la República de Méjico, con especial referencia a su geografía, etnografía y estadística, Estado de Oaxaca* (Mexico City: CODEX Editores, 1993), 33; Esparza, *Padrón*, xiv; AGEO, Colonial, vol. 15. For an occupational breakdown see Esparza, *Padrón general*, xv–xvi.

105. Muhlenpfordt, *Ensayo*, 16, 21; *Memoria que el Gobernador*, 8.

106. *Memoria que el Gobernador*, 8; *Esposición que el Tercer Gobernador del Estado hizo en cumplimiento del Artículo 83 de la Constitución Particular del mismo a la 4a Legislatura Constitucional al abrir sus segundas sesiones ordinarias el 2 de julio de 1832* (Oaxaca: Impreso por Antonio Valdés y Moya, 1832), 29–30.

107. Guy Thomson, "Protectionism and Industrialization in Mexico, 1821–1854: The Case of Puebla," in *Latin America, Economic Imperialism and the State: The Political Economy of the External Connection from Independence to the Present*, edited by Christoper Abel and Colin Lewis (London: Athlone Press, 1985), 134–36; Guardino, *Peasants*, 141–42.

108. Esparza, *Padrón general*, xv; *Balanza mercantil del departamento de Oaxaca, correspondiente al año de 1843* (Oaxaca: Impresa por I. Candiani, 1844).

109. *Balanza Mercantil de la Plaza de Oaxaca correspondiente al año de 1844, formada y publicada por la Junta de Fomento* (Oaxaca: Oficina de Antonio Valdés y Moya, 1845); *Balanza Mercantil de la Plaza de Oaxaca correspondiente al año de 1845, formada y publicada por la Junta de Fomento* (Oaxaca: Ignacio Rincon, 1846); *Balanza Mercantil de la Plaza de Oaxaca correspondiente al año de 1846, formada y publicada por la Junta de Fomento* (Oaxaca: Oficina de Antonio Valdés y Moya, 1847).

110. Hamnett, "Between," 51–52.

111. Esparza, *Padrón general*, xv–xix.

112. AGEO, Padrones, vol. 1, exp. 2. For data on construction trades see AGEO, Gobernación, vol. 20.

113. AHAO, Fondo Diocesano, Sección Gobierno, Serie Autoridades Civiles, 1847. The Spanish reads, "Pobre hasta tal grado, que su capital consistia en cuatro reales que invertía en hacer atole para vender. Vivió siempre en un jacalito miserable al pie del Cerro de la Soledad . . . No dejó mas parientes que una hija, en tanta miseria como ella." Four reales would be about two days' wages for a working-class man of the city.

114. Manuel Esparza, ed., *Padrón de casas, 1824* (Oaxaca: Instituto Nacional de Antropología e Historia, 1981), iv. According to this census of houses, Casmiro Cruz Hernández earned more than 9,000 pesos in rent in 1824.

115. Hensel, "Los orígenes," 225–26.

116. AHCO, Actas, 1820, fols. 222v, 223, 251, 257–58; AGN, Gobernación, vol. 1936, caja 2, exp. 6, fols 19v–20; AGEO, Real Intendencia I, vol. 5, exp. 25.

117. Guardino, *Peasants*, 77; the Plan de Iguala is found in Bustamante, *Cuadro*, vol. 5, 115–18. For the rules governing the 1821 election see Fondo Manuel Martínez Gracida, vol. 38.

118. AGN, Gobernación, vol. 1936, exp. 16, fol. 4v; Hensel, *Die Enstehung*, 233, 262.

119. Michael Ducey points out that in nineteenth-century popular rebellions in Veracruz it was usually the government or the local targets of popular ire who brought up the issue of race, not the rebels themselves (personal communication). Again, for a telling evocation of the social and cultural world of the urban plebeians of various races in the early nineteenth century, see Vincent, *Legacy*, 34–40.

120. AGN, Gobernación, vol. 1936, exp. 16, fol. 5. For the 1810 dispute see chapter 4. For the significance of the party names, see *El Oajaqueño Constitucional*, 12 August 1830.

121. Hensel, *Die Enstehung*, 264; Hensel, "Los orígenes," 227; AGN, Gobernación, s/s, caja 27, exp. 10; Rodríguez O., "Ningún," 18–19.

122. Most of the information on the incident is from AGN, Gobernación, vol. 1936, exp. 16, which contains Murguía's report and the original petition itself. For the quote see AGN, Gobernación, vol. 1936, exp. 16 fol. 13v. The original Spanish reads, "Adictos a la independencia"; and "Manifiestandose demasiada descontento con el sistema que igualaba por el virtud y el merito, y no por el dinero y grandeza." The names on the petition do not show up on the 1824 census of houses (Esparza, *Padrón de casas*).

123. AGN, Gobernación, vol. 1936, exp. 16, fol. 13. The Spanish reads, "Entre ellos hay algunos que se atropeyan al esplicarse por producirse con estilo peninisular como si esta fuese una virtud."

124. AGN, Gobernación, vol. 1936, exp. 16, fols. 9v, 31v–32v; AGN, Gobernación, s/s, caja 58, exp. 16, fols. 14–17.

125. AGN, Gobernación, s/s, caja 58, exp. 16. It is worth noting that one of the officers ordered to Mexico City due to his republican sympathies was Manuel Fagoaga, who at least later would be a noted aceite.

126. Y. M. O., *Invitacion que hace un oaxaqueño a su suelo patrio* (Oaxaca: n.p., 1823), 10–14; Hensel, "Los orígenes," 217, 230–32; Brian Hamnett, "Oaxaca; Las principales familias y el federalismo de 1823," in *Lecturas Históricas del Estado de Oaxaca*, vol. 3, *Siglo XIX*, edited by María de los Angles Romero Frizzi (Mexico City: Instituto Nacional de Antropología e Historia/Gobierno del Estado de Oaxaca, 1990), 58–59.

127. Rodríguez, "Ningún," 28–32; Fondo Manuel Martínez Gracida, vol. 38; J. Iturribarría, *Historia*, 18–23; Carlos María de Bustamante, *Diario Histórico de México*, vol. 1 (Mexico City: Instituto Nacional de Antropología e Historia, 1980), 279. The quote is from AGN, Gobernación, s/s, caja 48, exp. 12, fol. 53. The original Spanish is, "Una sola parte del Pueblo de Oaxaca, que como era público y notorio no formaba la mayoría de él."

128. J. Iturribarría, *Historia*, 28; Rodríguez O., "Ningún," 40–41.

129. Ignacio María Ordoño, *Vindicación del Padre Cortés* (Oaxaca: Imprenta Liberal a Cargo de Nicolás Idiáquez, 1826). The original Spanish reads, "Hizo so-

berano al Estado, igualó al rico con el pobre, y le concedió a todos los habitantes sus derechos y guarantías."

130. Hensel, "Los orígenes," 235.

131. El Enemigo Irreconciliable de los Pícaros, *¿Si tendremos monarquía a pretesto de heregía?* (Mexico City: Imprenta del Aguila, dirigida por José Ximeno, 1826); Ignacio María Ordoño, *Manifiesto al público imparcial* (Oaxaca: Imprenta Liberal a Cargo de Nicolás Idiáquez, 1826), 5; and *Acusación al público contra el Supremo Gobierno* (Mexico City: Imprenta del Correo por C. C. Sebring, 1828), 16; *Dos clérigos y un coyote pueden más que un batalón, ó sea Diálogo entre un Sensato y un Mayordomo Oajaqueño* (Mexico City: Imprenta de Mariano Galván, 1826); Pablo Villavicencio (El Payo del Rosario), *Ya tenemos in Oaxaca parte de la Santa Liga*, reproduced in James C. McKegney, *The Political Pamphlets of Pablo Villavicencio "El Payo del Rosario,"* vol. 2 (Amsterdam: Rodopi N. V. 1975), 598–607; *Si en Oaxaca hay azeiteros aqui sobran vinateros: Por el que no es aspirante* (Mexico City: Alejandro Valdés, 1828). Electoral violence and intimidation were also common in eighteenth-century England and colonial British America, especially in the southern colonies. See Morgan, *Inventing Mexico*, 182–89.

132. Un Espectador Imparcial, *Elecciones parroquiales de Oajaca en los dias 15 y 16 del corriente* (Oaxaca: n.p., 1826); *Cartas al Pueblo*, 12 April 1828.

133. Un ciudadano, *A mis conciudadanos de Oajaca y todo el Estado* (Oaxaca: n.p., 1826).

134. *El Oajaqueño Constitucional*, 12 August 1830.

135. AGEO, Colonial, vol. 8.

136. J. Iturribarría, *Historia*, 36–37, 44–53; José María Bocanegra, *Memorias para la historia de México independiente* (Mexico City: Instituto Nacional de Estudios Históricos de la Revolución Mexicana, 1985), 351, 353; AGEO, Gobernación vol. 1; *Colección de leyes y decretos del estado libre de Oaxaca*, vol. 1, 13–14.

137. Guardino, "Identity," 329–36; and *Peasants*, 115–20.

138. Ruiz Cervantes and Sánchez Silva, *Pensamiento*, 33. For the occupations of Spaniards see AGN, Expulsión de Españoles, vol. 4, exp. 9.

139. Carlos María de Bustamante, *A los habitantes de la provincia de Oaxaca* (Mexico City: Imprenta Imperial de D. Alejandro Valdés), 1822.

140. [José Joaquín Fernández de Lizardi], *La Revolución de Oajaca, o sean los efectos de la revolución que intentaron hacer en aquella provincia los deconocidos españoles, el día 9 del presente, en que se hizo la Jura de nuestro digno emperador. Carta particular. Oajaca diciembre 8 de 1822* (Puebla: La Liberal de Moreno Hermanos, 1822). The original Spanish reads, "Todo el comercio."

141. AHCO, Seguridad Interior del Estado, 1826; AGN, Gobernación, s/s, caja 96, exps. 2, 6; J. Iturribarría, *Historia*, 81–83.

142. J. Iturribarría, *Historia*, 83–89, quote from 85. The original Spanish reads, "Marcados por la opinión pública como notoriamente desafectos a la causa de la Patria."

143. AGN, Gobernación, leg. 66, caja 1; Fondo Luis Castañeda Guzmán, 113/C14; Hensel, *Die Enstehung*, 172; AGEO Legajos Encuadernados, Decretos, vol. 70, 1826e; *Manifiesto que los oaxaqueños dirigen a sus compatriotas de los Estados, por los acontecimientos de Matamoros* (Puebla: Reimpreso en la Oficina del Patriota, 1827). The original Spanish reads, "Con el estruendo de campana, coetes y mucho concurso de Pueblo que se había juntado en dicha plaza."

144. See, for instance, A. F. A., *Los déspotas quisieran impedir la libertad de escribir* (Mexico City: Imprenta de la Aguila, 1825).

145. This is a key finding of Hensel, *Die Enstehung*, and Carlos Sánchez Silva, "Patrimonialismo y poder político en Oaxaca, 1786–1860," *Cuadernos del Sur* 3, no. 10 (1995): 57–89.

146. The 1817 accusation is seen in AGEO, Real Intendencia II, vol. 25, exp. 35. For 1820, see *Cañon de a cuatro disparado a metralla contra las reflécciones de D. Manuel Yglesias, y crítica burlesca de ellas en este segundo diálogo de los Morenos, y gracias que se dan al Exmô. Sôr. Virrey por haber concedido la igualdad á estos* (Puebla: Imprenta Liberal, 1820); AGN, Gobernación, vol. 1936, caja 2, exp. 6, fol. 19v.

147. AGN, Gobernación, s/s, caja 58, exp. 16. Quotes from fols. 25, 28.

148. The quote is from AGEO, Gobernación, vol. 7. The Spanish reads, "Sin consideracion a la gran distancia que media de su graduacion a la mia." The other threats and attacks are found in *El Oajaqueño Constitucional*, 22 July and 9 September 1830; *La Muralla*, 30 November 1839. Efforts to prevent him from serving as an elector are seen in *El Zapoteco*, 11 October 1832; AHCO, Actas, 1829, fols. 53–53v.

149. Hensel, *Die Enstehung*, 293, 370, 381; *El Oajaqueño Constitucional*, 24 June 1830; *El Zapoteco*, 20 January, 31 January, 14 February 1833; Esparza, *Padrón general*, 115; *El Regenerador*, 7 March 1842.

150. AHCO, Seguridad del Estado, 1829; *El Oajaqueño Constitucional*, 22 July 1830; Tiburcio Canãs et al., *Representación que los ciudadanos Oajaqueños que subscriben dirigen al congreso nacional Mexicano* (Mexico City: Impreso por Francisco C. y Torres en las Escalerillas Num. 13, 1835).

151. *El Zapoteco*, 24 January 1833; *El Centinela*, 20 June 1843.

152. Esparza, *Padrón general*, 74; AGN, Infidencias, vol. 2, exp. 2; AGN, Infidencias, vol. 10, exps. 1, 2, 5, 6; Ibarra, *Clero*, 95.

153. Bustamante, *Diario Histórico*, vol. 1, 279; J. Iturribarría, *Historia*, 26; Hensel, *Die Enstehung*, 375; Ordoño, *Manifiesto*; *Vindicación*; and *Acusación*; AGEO, Gobernación, vol. 1; Villavicencio, *Ya tenemos*; *Cartas al Pueblo*, 15 March 1828.

154. Hensel, *Die Enstehung*, 375, 435–36; *El Zapoteco*, 11 October 1832; 20, 24, and 31 January 1833; 14 February 1833.

155. Ordoño, *Manifiesto*; *Vindicación*; and *Acusación*.

156. A summary of his career is found in Hensel, *Die Enstehung*, 440. See also Hensel, *Die Enstehung*, 263; Hamnett, *Juárez*, 20, 23–24; Muhlenpfordt, *Ensayo*; Brian Hamnett, "Benito Juarez, Early Liberalism, and the Regional Politics of Oaxaca, 1828–1853," *Bulletin of Latin American Research* 10, no. 1 (1991): 6; AHCO,

Actas, 1829, fol. 39; Fondo Martínez Gracida, vol. 71; Sánchez Silva, "Patrimonialismo," 69; *El Oajaqueño Constitucional*, 12 August 1830; *El Zapoteco*, 20 January 1833. For his role in the 1827 García affair see AGN, Gobernación, leg. 66, caja 1. For the 1830 accusation see *El Oajaqueño Federalista*, 14 September 1830.

157. Muhlenpfordt, *Ensayo*, 34; Hensel, *Die Enstehung*, 271, 279, 293, 375, 436–37; AGEO, Gobernación, vols. 2, 3; *Esposición que el Vice-gobernador en Ejercicio del Supremo Poder Ejecutivo del Estado hizo en cumplimiento del Artículo 83 de la Constitución Particular del mismo a la 4a Legislatura Constitucional al abrir sus primeras sesiones ordinarias el 2 de julio de 1831* (Oaxaca: Impreso por Antonio Valdés y Moya, 1831), 6; AHCO, Actas, 1824, fol. 495v; *El Regenerador*, 7, 21, and 31 March 1842; 11 April 1842; 18 May 1843; *La Centinela*, 30 July 1843; Sánchez Silva, "Patrimonialismo," 65–66.

158. For Pando's testimony about 1828 see AGEO, Gobernación, vol. 2. For the 1829 denunciation see AHCO, Seguridad Interior del Estado, 1829. The quote reads, "Maquinen la ruina de la Patria para facilitar el triunfo a que aspiran los inbasores."

159. Michael Costeloe, *The Central Republic in Mexico, 1835–1846* (New York: Cambridge University Press, 1993), 29–30.

160. Sánchez Silva, "Patrimonialismo," 68, 80–85.

161. For Ignacio see Hensel, *Die Enstehung*, 293, 371, 396. He also played a prominent role in the 1828 election debacle. See AGEO, Gobernación, vol. 2. In 1830 Ignacio Fagoaga flirted with the aceites, but by 1833 he was back in the vinagre fold (*El Oajaqueño Constitucional*, 12 August 1830; *El Zapoteco*, 14 February 1833).

162. Hensel, *Die Enstehung*, 270, 396–97; Muhlenpfordt, *Ensayo*, 34; Esparza, *Padrón de casas*, 65; AGN, Gobernación, s/s, caja 58, exp. 16; AHCO, Actas, 1829, fols. 125–28; *El Oajaqueño Federalista*, 14 September 1830; *El Oajaqueño Constitucional*, 27 June 1830, *El Regenerador*, 7 March 1842; J. Iturribarría, *Historia*, 293–94.

163. Juan José Quiñones, *Discurso que pronunció el ciudadano Dr. Juan José Quiñones, fiscal de la Escma. Corte de Justicia, en la capital del estado de Oajaca el 16 de septiembre de 1828, aniversario del Grito de Dolores, por encargo de la Junta Patriótica* (Oaxaca: Imprenta del Superior Gobierno, dirigida por Antonio Valdés y Moya, 1828); AHCO, Actas, 1829, fols. 125–28; *El Oajaqueño Constitucional*, 12 August 1830; *El Zapoteco*, 16 September 1832; *El Regenerador*, 7 March and 11 April 1842. The 1830 satire is from *El Oajaqueño Constitucional*, 15 July 1830, and the 1849 prayer is in *El Guajalote Periodista*, 26 April 1843.

164. *El Zapoteco*, 16 September 1832; Esparza, *Padrón general*, 105; AGEO, Padrón de Capitación, leg. 1, exp. 2, 1849, 3; *La Prensa*, 31 July 1846. For his legal troubles see Guardino, "Toda," 100; AHCO, Homicidios 1833; *El Regenerador*, 6 March 1845.

165. Muhlenpfordt, *Ensayo*; Hensel, *Die Enstehung*, 420–21; Sánchez Silva, "Patrimonialismo," 68, 83–85; Hamnett, *Juárez*, 20; J. R. Fortson, *Los gobernantes de Oaxaca: Historia (1823–1985)* (Mexico City: J. R. Fortson Editores, 1985).

166. For the connection to Juárez see Hamnett, *Juárez*, 24. For López de Ortigosa's views on Indians see *Esposición que el Vice-gobernador*, 12, 24.

167. For patronage in Latin American elections more generally see Sabato, introduction to *Ciudadanía*, 21. For a comprehensive study of patronage in Brazilian politics in this period see Richard Graham, *Patronage and Politics in Nineteenth-Century Brazil* (Stanford: Stanford University Press, 1990).

168. See the works by Guerra in the bibliography, especially Guerra, *México*.

169. Esparza, *Padrón general*, xix.

170. Esparza, *Padrón de casas*, iv; Hensel, *Die Enstehung*, 408.

171. Fondo Manuel Martínez Gracida, vol. 38; J. Iturribarría, *Historia*, 18–23; AGN, Gobernación, s/s, caja 48, exp. 12, fol. 53; *Esposición que el Tercer Gobernador*, 30.

172. Villavicencio, *Ya tenemos*.

173. For clubs in Chile see Valenzuela, "Building," 241.

174. AHCO, Homicidios, exp. 106, 1829. The Spanish reads, "Sistema de partidos, que como yo soy del Barrio de Coyula, y a estos nos tienen algun odio."

175. AHCO, Homicidios, exp. 98, 1829.

176. AGEO, Juzgado, vol. 17, exp. 10.

177. AHCO, Delitos Contra la Seguridad Interior del Estado, 1838. The Spanish reads, "Amas de que no puedes negar que eres de esa opinión."

178. *Alcance al Número 6 del Periódico Sociedad de Amigos del Pais*, found in Fondo Manuel Martínez Gracida, vol. 38.

179. See for instance, *El Zapoteco*, 16 September 1832; 7, 11, and 14 October 1832; and 10 January 1833; Manuel M. Pasos, *Discurso prononuciado en la ciudad de Oaxaca el día 4 de octubre de 1849, aniversario de la promulgación de la Constitución Federal* (Oaxaca: Impreso por Ignacio Rincón, 1849).

180. *El Zapoteco*, various issues. For the letter in Zapotec see the issue of 14 October 1832. The speech is in *El Zapoteco*, 13 January 1833.

181. AHCO, Actas, 1829, fol. 133.

182. *El Oajaqueño Constitucional*, 15 July 1830. The original reads, "Jamas puedan ser afectos a nuestra independencia y sistema de gobierno."

183. Ordoño, *Acusación*, 16; and *Manifiesto*, 5.

184. *Si en Oaxaca hay azeiteros aqui sobran vinateros*. The Spanish reads, "Desnaturalizados americanos"; and "Viles americanos . . . vendidos a los enemigos."

185. *El Zapoteco*, 15 October 1832. For more vinagre efforts to link their domestic enemies to the Spaniards see Villavicencio, *Ya tenemos*; and *El Zapoteco*, 15 November 1832; and 6, 12, and 16 December 1832.

186. Unos Mexicanos, *¿El General Bustamante, es traidor a la nación?* (Oaxaxa: Reimpreso por José Cresencio Valverde, 1839).

187. Ordoño, *Vindicación*; AGN, Gobernación, leg. 1540, exp. 3.

188. Guardino, *Peasants*, 135–36; *El Zapoteco*, 15 November 1832.

189. Cañas, *Representación*. The one possible exception was Joaquín Guerrero, a former governor who often stood between the two parties.

190. Muchos Mexicanos, *Viva la Federación. Alcance al núm. 12 del Restaurador*

Mexicano (Oaxaca: Reimpreso por José Rafael España, 1838); El Vigía, *Federación* (Oaxaca: Reimpreso por José R. España, 1838); Los patriotas oaxaqueños, *Venganza piden los buenos sobre los viles serenos* (Oaxaca: Impreso por José Rafael España, 1838); José Juan Canseco, *Proposicion que el Dr. D. Jose Juan Canseco presentó en la Camara de Senadores de la H. Legislatura del Estado Libre de Oaxaca para que se dirija iniciativa al soberano Congreso General sobre que se conserve vigente la Constitucion Federal de 1824 con las reformas necesarias* (Oaxaca: Impreso por Ignacio Rincón, 1846).

191. Manuel Iturribarría, *Arenga cívica pronunciada en el aniversario de la consumación de la independencia, el día 28 de septiembre de 1846, en la capital del estado de Oaxaca* (Oaxaca: Impreso por I. Rincón, 1846), 20–21. See also Francisco S. de Enciso, *Oracion civica que el ciudadano Lic. Francisco Enciso pronuncio en la capital del Estado libre y soberano de Oaxaca el 16 de septiembre de 1846, aniversario de la gloriosa proclamacion de la Independencia en el ano de 1810* (Oaxaca: Impresa por Ignacio Rincón, 1846).

192. Pasos, *Discurso*, 3. See also *El Guajalote Periodista*, 18 and 25 June 1849.

193. *Colección de leyes y decretos del Estado de Oaxaca*, vol. 1, 13–14; Quiñones, *Discurso que pronunció el ciudadano Dr. Juan José Quiñones*, 3.

194. Vicente Fermin Márquez y Carrizosa, *Oracion funebre que en memoria de las victimas sacrificadas por la independencia mexicana pronuncio en la Santa Iglesia Catedral de Oaxaca Vicente Marquez y Carrizosa el dia 17 de septiembre de 1845* (Oaxaca: Impreso por I. Rincón, 1845), 4. The original quote reads, "Relaciones de sangre, costumbres, y culto." On Alamán see Will Fowler, *Mexico in the Age of Proposals, 1821–1853* (Westport, Conn.: Greenwood Press, 1998), 75–84.

195. *El Broquel de las Costumbres*, 13 July 1834. The Spanish reads, "Igualdad mal entendida."

196. *Dos clérigos y un coyote*; El Enemigo de los Despotas, *No queremos dictador ni en Oajaca un gran señor*, (Mexico City: Imprenta de las Escalerillas, a cargo de Manuel Ximeno, 1828); Ordoño, *Manifiesto*; Villavicencio, *Ya tenemos*; El Zapoteco, 22 November 1832 and 10 February 1833.

197. Un ciudadano, *A mis conciudadanos. Cartas al Pueblo*, 12 and 23 April 1828; 9 and 16 July 1828; and 16 August 1828. The quotes are from 23 April, 16 July, and 16 August. In Spanish they read, "Sin duda no quería el Ser Eterno ser arrastado mediante un decreto que se espedió entre las sombras de la iniquidad"; "Mueran los clerigos"; and "No amen a la religion del crucificado, ni a la independencia."

198. Guardino, "Toda," 96.

199. *El Broquel de las Costumbres*, 6 and 13 July 1834. The originals read, "Abandono de los principios religiosos"; and "Faccion anticristiana."

200. AGEO, Impresos, 1 January 1828. The Spanish reads, "La falta de libertad"; and "La inmensa mayoria de ciudadanos a dar sufragios."

201. AGEO, Decretos, Legajos Encuadernados, vol. 70, 1825a.

202. *Cartas al Pueblo*, 16 January 1828.

203. Guardino, *Peasants*, 124–25.

204. AGN, Gobernación, leg. 76, exp. 1.

205. *Cartas al Pueblo*, 9 July and 20 August 1828; Un principista, *Muerte del Estado de Oaxaca, decretada por el ciudadano Miguel Ignacio Iturribarría vice gobernador interino de este estado, a sus habitantes hago saber* (Mexico City: Imprenta de Galvan, 1829).

206. *Cartas al Pueblo*, 19 July 1828; AGN, Gobernación, leg. 76, exp. 1.

207. AGN, Gobernación, leg. 76, exp. 1; *Cartas al Pueblo*, 21 June and 16 July 1828; Ordoño, *Acusación*, 21; AHCO, Tesorería Municipal, 1764–1829.

208. *Cartas al Pueblo*, 12 April 1828.

209. *Colección de leyes y decretos del Estado de Oaxaca*, vol. 1, 337–38.

210. *Colección de leyes y decretos del Estado de Oaxaca*, vol. 1, 23, 100–1; Fondo Manuel Martínez Gracida, vol. 72; AHCO, Tesorería, 1764–1829; Ordoño, *Acusación*, 21; AGEO, Legajos Encuadernados, Decretos, vol. 70, 1826e.

211. Ordoño, *Acusación*, 28; *Cartas al Pueblo*, 16 August and 10 September 1828; AGEO, Gobernación, vol. 2; AGN, Gobernación, leg. 76, exp. 1. Later an aceite pamphleteer claimed that the vinagres had arrived at the voting place drunk and armed (Un principista, *Muerte*, 6).

212. AGEO, Gobernación, vol. 2; AGN, Gobernación, leg. 76, exp. 1.

213. AGN, Gobernación, leg. 76, exp. 1; *Cartas al Pueblo*, 8 October 1828; *Defenza de los empleados oaxaqueños* (Oaxaca: n.p., 1833), 10–11; Un principista, *Muerte*; J. Iturribarría, *Historia*, 99; Fondo Manuel Martínez Gracida, vol. 72.

214. Carriedo, *Estudios*, 78–79; J. Iturribarría, *Historia,* 120–41; AGEO, Impresos, 14 September 1829; Fondo Manuel Martínez Gracida, vol. 72; Fondo Luis Castañeda Guzmán, 115/c14; AHCO, Homicidios, exp. 98, 1829.

215. AHCO, Actas, 16 September 1824. The quotes read, "Por inbertir el tiempo en Juegos y Pulquerias"; and "Jugador de profecion . . . su amacia pidio el ir primero a los recojidas que sufrirlo."

216. AHCO, Actas, 1824, fols. 549v, 660–61.

217. AHCO, Actas, 1824, fols. 340, 372v.

218. For a lucid account of the political evolution of Santa Anna's supporters, see Fowler, *Mexico*, 219–54. In this way they did not differ from the civilian "hombres de bien" studied by Costeloe (*Central*, 1993).

219. *El Zapoteco*, 24 January 1833.

220. *El Centinela*, 20 June 1843.

221. AGEO, Juzgado, vol. 14, exp. 13; vol. 15, exp. 4; vol. 16, exp. 1. The quote is from the last expediente. In 1832 the drunken Seferino Sanchez was arrested for similar expressions. See AGEO, Juzgado, vol. 20, exp. 7.

222. AHCO, Seguridad del Estado, 1829. The original reads, "Enemigo del orden y sospechoso a la causa de Yndependencia."

223. J. Iturribarría, *Historia*, 148–51.

224. AHCO, Actas, 1829, fols. 125–28v; Fondo Manuel Martínez Gracida, vol. 72.

225. AHCO, Actas, 1829, fols. 131–33.

226. Harold Sims, *Descolonización en México: El conflicto entre mexicanos y españoles* (Mexico City: Fondo de Cultura Económica, 1982), 120; AGN, Expulsión de Españoles, vol. 4, exp. 9; and vol. 55, exp. 39; *Memoria que el Vice-gobernador*.

227. AGN, Expulsión de Españoles, vol. 49, exp. 4; and vol. 56, exp. 35; AGEO, Gobernación, vol. 7; AGN, Gobernación, vol. 134, caja 1, exp. 2.

228. *El Zapoteco*, 25 October and 15 November 1832; AHCO, Seguridad Pública, 1833; AHCO, Delitos Contra la Autoridad, 1833; *La Muralla*, 30 October 1839; Unos Mexicanos, *¿El General Bustamante*.

229. Hensel, *Die Enstehung*, 263; AHCO, Actas, 1829, fols. 63v–64v, 79, 81v–83, 100v; J. Iturribarría, *Historia*, 147; Un principista, *Muerte*; *El Oajaqueño Constitucional*, 12 August 1830.

230. Fondo Manuel Martínez Gracida, vol. 72; AGEO, Gobernación, vol. 2; AHCO, Actas, 1829, fols. 231–34.

231. Fondo Manuel Martínez Gracida, vol. 72; J. Iturribarría, *Historia*, 154; *El Oajaqueño Constitucional*, 12 August 1830.

232. *El Oajaqueño Constitucional*, 15 August 1830; *El Oajaqueño Federalista*, 3, 10, and 31 August 1830. The originals of the epithets applied to the aceites are "Oleum Sempentorum" and "aceite de Alacranes."

233. *Colección de leyes y decretos del Estado de Oaxaca*, vol. 1, 346–53; *El Oajaqueño Federalista*, 20 July, 3 August 1830; *El Oajaqueño Constitucional*, 24 June, 1, 11, and 15 July 1830.

234. *El Oajaqueño Federalista*, 17 August, 14 September, 5 and 12 October, and 9 November 1830; *El Oajaqueño Constitucional*, 9 September 1830.

235. *El Oajaqueño Federalista*, 5 October 1830.

236. *Aunque corran rios de sangre Guerrero no ha de triunfar* (Oaxaca: Reimpreso por la Imprenta liberal a cargo del ciudadano José Felipe Matos, n.d.); *El Oajaqueño Federalista*, 30 November 1830; El Novel, *Recuerdos de gratitud al inmortal Iturbide* (Oaxaca: Reimpreso in la Imprenta Liberal, a cargo del ciudadano José Felipe Matos, 1830); AGEO, Juzgado, vol. 17, exp. 10.

237. J. Iturribarría, *Historia*, 157–75.

238. *Diálogo entre Jose Toribio indigena y Don Clarion valiente vecino de esta ciuda* (Oaxaca: Imprenta a Cargo del C. Juan Oledo, 1832); *El Zapoteco*, 16, 20, and 23 September 1832; 11 and 14 October 1832.

239. *El Zapoteco*, 25 October 1832; 15, 22, and 25 November 1832; 6, 9, 13, 16, and 20 December 1832. One of the vinagres elected was Benito Juárez.

240. AGN, Gobernación, leg. 129, caja 1, exp. 2; J. Iturribarría, *Historia*, 184; *Defenza*; *El Zapoteco*, 20 December 1832; 6, 10, 13, 17, 20, 31 January 1833.

241. AGN, Gobernación, leg. 129, caja 1, exp. 2; J. Iturribarría, *Historia*, 184–92.

242. AGEO, Legajos Encuadernados, Gobernación, vol. 30, 1839h; AGN, Gobernación, vol. 134, caja 1, exp. 2; AGCO, Delitos contra la Autoridad, 1833.

243. For a chronology see Will Fowler, "Valentín Gómez Farías: Perceptions of

Radicalism in Independent Mexico, 1821–1847," *Bulletin of Latin American Studies* 15, no. 1 (1996): 194–95.

244. AGN, Gobernación, s/s, caja 166, exp. 8; J. Iturribarría, *Historia*, 200–2; *El Zapoteco*, 23 June 1833; Fondo Manuel Martínez Gracida, vol. 71; *Contestacion que los editores del Zapoteco dan al papel titulado Defensa del Fuero Eclesiastico* (Oaxaca: Imprenta Municipal de C. A. V. y Moya, 1833); *Defensa del fuero eclesiástico contra varios artículos del periódico titulado el Zapoteco* (Oaxaca: Imprenta Municipal del ciudadano Antonio Valdés y Moya, 1833); *Contestaciones habidas entre el gobernador del estado de Oaxaca, y el de la mitra del mismo, sobre la ley de 17 de diciembre ultimo, y decreto de 22 de abril proximo pasado, y representacion de dicho gobernador del obispado, para que las camaras deroguen las citadas leyes* (Mexico City: Imprenta de la testamentaria del finado Valdes, 1834); *Exposición que el gobernador del obispado de Oaxaca, dirige al Supremo Gobierno, en defensa de los bienes eclesiásticos* (Mexico City: Imprenta de la testamentaria de Valdes, a cargo de Jose María Gallegos, 1834).

245. J. Iturribarría, *Historia*, 198–200; *Esposición que el Gobernador Constitucional del Estado hizo en cumplimiento del Artículo 83 de la Constitución Particular del mismo a la Sexta Legislatura en sus segundas sesiones ordinarias el mes de julio de 1835* (Oaxaca: Impreso por Antonio Valdés y Moya, 1835), 7–8.

246. J. Iturribarría, *Historia*, 194–96; Fondo Manuel Martínez Gracia, vol. 71.

247. AGEO, Juzgado, vol. 22, exp. 4.

248. *El Broquel de las Costumbres*, 6, 10, 13, and 20 1834; AGN, Ayuntamientos, vol. 17, fol. 257; AGEO, Gobernación, vol. 27.

249. Anna, *Forging Mexico*, 262; Guardino, *Peasants*, 99–100.

250. *El Día*, 13 December 1837; *La Muralla*, 22 October 1839; *El Ocaso de las Revoluciones*, 28 September 1841; *La Centinela*, 23 July 1843; *El Aurora de la Libertad*, 21 September 1845. The quote is from AGN, Historia, vol. 562, exp. 14. In Spanish it reads, "Nos dividió en lugar de unirnos."

251. Thomson, "Protectionism," 134–36; Guardino, *Peasants*, 141–42; Esparza, *Padrón general*, xv; *Balanza mercantil del departamento de Oaxaca, correspondiente al año de 1843*. Later protectionist measures were generally justified by their potential effect on urban artisans. See *La Centinela*, 27 August 1843.

252. Cañas, *Representación*; *El Día*, 31 December 1837; Muchos Mexicanos, *Viva*; *La Muralla*, 22 October 1839.

253. J. Iturribarría, *Historia*, 218–22; Un Amigo de la Patria, *Manifestacion de verdades que desengañaran a los incautos* (Oaxaca: Impreso por el ciudadano Antonio Valdés y Moya, 1836); Luís Quintanar, *El Comandante General del Departamento de Oaxaca a las tropas de la guarnicion* (Oaxaca: Impreso por el ciudadano Antonio Valdes y Moya, 1836); AGN, Gobernación, leg. 162, caja 1, exp. 3; AHCO, Seguridad Interior de Estado, 1836; AGEO, Juzgado, vol. 24, exp. 14; AGEO, Juzgado, vol. 25, exp. 4; AGEO, Juzgado, vol. 26, exp. 2. The quotes are from AGEO, Juzgado, vol. 24, exp. 13. The Spanish reads, respectively, "Ladrones, descamisados, sansculotes";

"Un español enemigo como todos los de su origen de la independencia nacional";
and "Oajaqueños el hambre sigue, castigad a los trafacantes."

254. AHCO, Seguridad Interior del Estado, 1837. The Spanish reads, "Sigue la
nesidad imitad a nuebo Mexico"; and "Oajaqueños el hambre sigue, castigad a los
traficantes." On the New Mexico revolt see David J. Weber, *The Mexican Frontier,
1821–1846: The American Southwest under Mexico* (Albuquerque: University of New
Mexico Press, 1982), 260–66.

255. Costeloe, *Central Republic*, 141–44; Muchos Mexicanos, *Viva*; Los patriotas
oaxaqueños, *Venganza*; El Vigía, *Federación*; AHCO, Seguridad Interior del Estado,
1838.

256. For the problems with copper money and tokens in Oaxaca see AGEO, Lega-
jos Encuadernados, Gobernación, vol. 16, 1817a; AHCO, Actas, 1829, fols. 172v–
173; AGEO, Legajos Encuadernados, Gobernación, vol. 30, 1839h, fol. 103; *La
Centinela*, 5 June and 30 July 1843. For the Mexico City riot see Richard Warren,
"'El congreso por su gusto hizo de un Justo un ladrón' el cobre, 'la chusma' y el
centralismo, 1837," in *Instituciones y ciudad: Ocho estudios históricos sobre la Ciudad de
México*, edited by Carlos Illades and Ariel Rodríguez Kuri (Mexico City: Ediciones
Unios, 2000), 61–79; Costeloe, *Central*, 79–82.

257. AGEO, Legajos Encuadernados, Gobernación, vol. 40, 1849b; J. Iturribarría,
Historia, 248–59.

258. J. Iturribarría, *Historia*, 260–62; *El Regenerador*, 24 January and 17 February
1842.

259. *El Regenerador*, 7 March 1842. For Cañas see Hensel, *Die Enstehung*, 386;
and Hamnett, *Juárez*, 23–24, 27.

260. *El Regenerador*, 17 July 1843; 14 August 1843; 7 and 21 September 1843; and
2 October 1843; *La Centinela*, 23 and 30 July 1843; 6, 13, and 20 August 1843; and
24 September 1843; J. Iturribarría, *Historia*, 293–94.

261. Costeloe, *Central*, 298–301.

262. AHCO, Tesorería, 1830–34; *El Regenerador*, 6 March 1845; AGEO, Padrón de
Capitación, leg. 1, exp. 2, 1849, 3; Carriedo, *Estudios*. Carriedo published the newspapers *El Pasatiempo*, *El Guajalote Periodista*, and *El Cócura*. For his federalist views
see *El Guajalote Periodista*, 18 June and 31 August 1849.

263. This is the basic argument in Hamnett, *Juárez*; and "Benito."

264. Juárez, "Apuntes," 234; Hensel, *Die Enstehung*, 373, 414; *El Zapoteco*, 14
February 1833; Cañas, *Representación*; *El Guajalote Periodista*, 10 July 1849.

265. J. Iturribarría, *Historia*, 302.

266. *Iniciativa que la Asamblea departamental de Oaxaca elevo en 19 de febrero de 1845
al soberano Congreso nacional sobre reformas de las bases orgánicas de la republica* (Oaxaca: Impreso por I. Rincón, 1845).

267. *La Voz de la Patria*, 5 and 12 August 1845; and 7 October 1845. See the
independence day speech of Francisco Rincón for a taste of the antiparty rhetoric.

See Francisco Rincón Ríos, *Arenga cívica que el 16 de septiembre de 1845, aniversario de la gloriosa proclamación de la independencia, pronunció en la ciudad de Oaxaca el ciudadano Francisco Rincón* (Oaxaca: Imprenta por Ignacio Rincón, 1845).

268. Costeloe, *Central*, 284–89.

269. Costeloe, *Central*, 286–87; *Lista de los ciudadanos*.

270. J. Iturribarría, *Historia*, 326–27; Reynaldo Sordo Cedeño, "Benito Juárez y el Soberano Congreso Constituyente, 1846–1847," in *Historia*, edited by Luis Jáuregui and José Antonio Serano Ortega, 356–57; AGN, Gobernación, leg. 129, caja 2, exp. 5; AHCO, Tesorería Municipal, 1840–48.

271. Enciso, *Oracion civica*; M. Iturribarría, *Arenga cívica*.

272. Manuel Esparza, "El difícil camino de sentirse nación: Oaxaca y la guerra contra Estados Unidos," in *México en guerra (1846–1848)*, edited by Laura Herrera Serna (Mexico City: Consejo Nacional para la Cultura y las Artes, 1997), 507; *El Espíritu de la Independencia*, 18 February 1848; Bernadino Carbajal, *Discurso que en la funcion de la bendicion de la bandera del Batallon guerrero pronunció el presberito C. Bernadino Carbajal en 28 de diciembre de 1847* (Oaxaca: Impreso por Ignacio Rincon, 1848), 17, 21. See also Esparza, "El difícil," 515. The Spanish quotes are, "Una miscelánea espantosa de sectas heréticas"; and "La causa que defendemos, considerada bajo este aspecto, es la causa de Dios."

273. AGEO, Juárez, vol. 1, exp. 38; AGEO, Juárez, vol. 10, exp. 1; Ortiz de Zarate, *El general de Brigada*; Esparza, "El difícil," 509–17.

274. Esparza, "El difícil," 511–14, 517.

275. *Protestas de los Illmos. señores Obispos de Durango y Oaxaca* (Guadalajara: Reimpresa en la Oficina de Dionisio Rodríguez, 1847).

276. Brian Hamnett, "El estado de Oaxaca durante la Guerra contra los Estados Unidos: 1846–1848," in *México al tiempo de su guerra con Estados Unidos (1846–1848)*, edited by Josefina Zoraida Vázquez (Mexico City: Fondo de Cultura Económica/Colegio de México/Secretaría de Relaciones Exteriores, 1997), 365; Sordo Cedeño, "Benito," 369–76.

277. For these issues in Oaxaca see AGEO, Legajos Encuadernados, Decretos, 1826d; *Contestacion*; *Exposición que el gobernador del obispado de Oaxaca*; Carlos María de Bustamante, *Defensa de los bienes eclesiásticos* (Oaxaca: Reimpresa por Antonio Valdés y Moya, 1837); *Protestas*; T. T. C., *Inconvenientes de una colonización indiscreta, o sea impugnación al establecimiento de la libertad de cultos en la República Mexicana* (Oaxaca: Impreso por Ignacio Rincón, 1848); Sánchez Silva, "La imprenta," 30; Jose M. Alvarez y Castillejos, *Sermón patriótico moral que predicó en la Iglesia de Nuestra Señora de Guadalupe de esta capital el día 12 de diciembre de 1850* (Oaxaca: Impreso en la oficina de Francisco O. y Quintas, 1851); *El Guajalote Periodista*, 15 February and 12 April 1849.

278. Hamnett, "Benito," 5.

279. The general interpretation of the history of the Instituto that I am following here is that of Ramón Pardo, "Breve estudio sobre la evolución del Instituto de

Ciencias y Artes de Oaxaca," in *El Instituto de Ciencias y Artes del Estado: Los años de formación* (Oaxaca: Universidad Autónoma "Benito Juárez" de Oaxaca, Instituto de Investigaciones en Humanidades, 1990), 30–46. On the leadership of the institution see J. Iturribarría, *Historia*, 76; Hamnett, *Juárez*, 22, 25; Pardo, "Breve," 31–32. Apparently basing his views on Juárez's memoirs, Hamnett buys into the idea that the Instituto was a hotbed of liberalism and says it was "anathematized by the clergy" (*Juárez*, 22).

280. Pérez, *Recuerdos*, 105–7; Hensel, *Die Enstehung*, 425–26; *El Regenerador*, 26 August 1844.

281. For "Divine Providence," see his first speech as governor in AGEO, Juárez, vol. 1, exp. 21. The second quote is from AGEO, Juárez, vol. 14, exp. 7a. The Spanish reads, "Precisamente de la reforma de las costumbres y del aumento de la buena moral."

282. AGEO, Juárez, vol. 14, exp. 7b. On Juárez and religion in this period see also J. Iturribarría, *Historia*, 397–99.

283. AGEO, Juárez, vol. 4, exps. 224, 226; AGEO, Juárez, vol. 12, exp. 9; AGEO, Juárez, vol. 1, exps. 30, 31.

284. AGEO, Juárez, vol. 4, exps. 229–31, 233.

285. AGEO, Juárez, vol. 12, exp. 7; AGEO, Juárez, vol. 13, exp. 2; AGEO, Juárez, vol. 15, exp. 5.

286. AGEO, Juárez, vol. 4, exp. 222; AGEO, Juárez, vol. 12, exp. 9a; AGEO, Juárez, vol. 4, exp. 235; *Esposición que el Gobernador del Estado hace en cumplimiento del articulo 83 de la Constitución al Soberano Congreso al abrir sus primeras sesiones ordinarias el día 2 de julio del año de 1852* (Oaxaca: Impreso por Ignacio Rincón, 1852), 33.

287. Connaughton, "El ocaso," 247–50; AGEO, Juárez, vol. 4, exps. 218, 220–21; AGEO, Juárez, vol. 5, exp. 247; AGEO, Juárez, vol. 1, exp. 1; AGEO, Gobernación, vol. 36.

288. AGEO, Gobernación, vol. 28.

289. Perez, *Recuerdos*, 114–15; Connaughton, "El ocaso," 250–51.

290. AGEO, Juárez, vol. 15, exp. 3.

291. *El Espíritu de La Independencia*, 27 February 1848. On the debates surrounding church burials see Voekel, *Alone*.

292. For the Tehuantepec events, see John Tutino, "Rebelión indígena en Tehuantepec," *Cuadernos políticos* 24 (1980): 88–101; and Hamnett, *Juárez*, 40–43.

293. AGN, Gobernación, s/s, caja 335, exp. 2; AGEO, Juárez, vol. 12, exp. 1.

294. AGN, Gobernación, s/s, caja 370, exps. 10 and 26; *El Guajalote Periodista*, 5 April, 24 August 1849; *Esposición que en cumplimiento del articulo 83 de la Constitución del Estado hace el Gobernador del mismo al soberano Congreso al abrir sus sesiones el 2 de julio del año de 1849* (Oaxaca: Impreso por Ignacio Rincón, 1849), 6–7.

295. AHCO, Delitos contra Seguridad Interior del Estado, 1849.

296. AHCO, Delitos Contra la Autoridad, 1849.

297. *El Guajalote Periodista*, 15 February and 12 April 1849.

298. AGEO, Juárez, vol. 12, exp. 7; *El Guajalote Periodista*, 24 August 1849.

299. Pasos, *Discurso*, 6–8, quote from 13. The original reads, "No hay más rey que el pueblo ni mas soberanía que la de la nacion."

300. *El Guajalote Periodista*, 16 and 29 March 1849; 12 April 1849; and 25 June 1849; *La Crónica*, 15 September 1848; *El Vigilante*, 8 and 15 March 1849; *El Cócura*, 3 November and 23 December 1849.

301. AGN, Gobernación, s/s, caja 425, exp. 7; J. Iturribarría, *Historia*, 408–22.

302. In the mid-1820s Governor Ignacio Morales suggested that dividing up indigenous lands would be a good idea, but the notion was apparently abandoned without debate, probably because it was manifestly impractical. See *Memoria que el Gobernador*, 4.

303. See in particular Juárez, "Apuntes," 234.

304. Charles Berry notes the problem even in the section of the autobiography about Juárez's second term as governor in 1857 (*Reform*, 39–41).

305. For a recent interpretation that does just that see Hamnett, "El estado," 362.

306. Warren, "Elections," 51.

307. Pasos, *Discurso*, 3, 14.

308. AGEO, Juárez, vol. 13, exp. 2. The Spanish reads, "El era chaqueta antiguo y que habia de combatir contra el Sistema Federal y contra los federalistas hasta esterminarlos." For another comment on the persistence of partisanship see Berry, *Reform*, 8.

309. Quiñones, *Discurso*, 11; Aurelio Bolaños, *Discurso cívico pronunciado en el aniversario de la Independencia Mexicana el 16 de septiembre de 1837* (Oaxaca: Impreso por el ciudadano Antonio Valdés y Moya, 1837), 8; *El Ocaso de las Revoluciones*, 28 September 1841; *El Regenerador*, 17 July 1843; Rincón, *Arenga*, 17; AGEO, Juárez, vol. 1, exp. 20.

310. J. Iturribarría, *Historia*, 141.

311. *El Oajaqueño Constitucional*, 24 June and 11 July 1830.

312. See, for instance, *El Oajaqueño Federalista*, 30 July and 9 November 1830; Un Amigo de la Patria, *Manifestacion*, 2; *El Regenerador*, 7 September 1843; *La Voz de la Patria*, 7 October 1845; AGEO, Juárez, vol. 1, exp. 19; *El Guajalote Periodista*, 17 July 1849; *Esposición que en cumplimiento del articulo 83 de la Constitución del Estado hace el Gobernador del mismo al soberano Congreso al abrir sus sesiones el 2 de julio del año de 1849*, 3, 7; Hamnett, "Benito," 4–5.

313. *La Voz de la Patria*, 12 August 1845. The Spanish reads, "Formaron un solo partido."

314. José A. Gamboa y Aldego, *Arenga cívica pronunciada el día 27 de septiembre de 1849 en la capital del Estado de Oaxaca por el profesor de medicina y cirugía C. José A. Gamboa y Aldego en memoria de la gloriosa consumación de la independencia de México en el año de 1821* (Oaxaca: Impreso por Ignacio Rincón, 1849), 8.

315. *El Oajaqueño Federalista*, 20 July 1830. The quote reads, "Sociedades secretas en que se trate de dirigir, o de reglamentar." See also *Iniciativas*.

316. AGEO, Gobernación, vols. 1 and 24; AHCO, Actas, 1824, fols. 106–7; AHCO, Actas, 1829, fol. 52; AGEO, Legajos Encuadernados, Decretos, vol. 70, 1825a; *El Oajaqueño Federalista*, 3 August 1830; AGEO, Juzgado, vol. 22, exp. 4; *El Regenerador*, 6 March 1845.

317. Demélas and Guerra, "The Hispanic," 40; François-Xavier Guerra, "El soberano y su reino: Reflexiones sobre la génesis del ciudadano en América Latina," in *Ciudadanía*, edited by Hilda Sabato, 53–55; Connaughton, "Agape," 288; Sabato, introduction to *Ciudadanía*, 22; Avila, *En nombre*, 285.

318. Morgan, *Inventing Mexico*, 304.

319. For analysis of how this worked during the French Revolution, see Furet, *Interpreting*, 53–56; and Hunt, *Politics*, 39–45.

320. Demélas and Guerra, "The Hispanic," 56–57.

Notes to Chapter 6: The Reconstruction of Order in the Countryside

1. Rodolfo Pastor, *Campesinos y reformas: La Mixteca, 1700–1856* (Mexico City: El Colegio de México, 1987), 13, 447. The term *disarticulate* is Pastor's. It seems to refer to the dissolution of the strongest ties that held communities together.

2. Marcello Carmagnani, *El regreso de los dioses: La reconstitución de la identidad étnica en Oaxaca, siglos xvii y xviii* (Mexico City: Fondo de Cultura Económica, 1988), 230–37.

3. Ronald Spores, "Relaciones gubermentales y judiciales entre los pueblos, los distritos, y el estado en Oaxaca (siglo XIX)," in *Lecturas Históricas del Estado de Oaxaca*, vol. 3, *Siglo XIX*, edited by María de los Angles Romero Frizzi (Mexico City: Instituto Nacional de Antropología e Historia/Gobierno del Estado de Oaxaca, 1990), 254–55.

4. Moisés Bailón Corres, *Pueblos indios, élites y territorio: Sistemas de dominio regional en el sur de México: Una historia política de Oaxaca* (Mexico City: El Colegio de México, 1999), 122.

5. Sánchez Silva, *Indios*, especially 87 and 205. See also Karen Caplan, "The Legal Revolution in Town Politics: Oaxaca and Yucatán, 1812–1825," *Hispanic American Historical Review* 83, no. 2 (2003): 260.

6. Obviously, this theoretical argument is not totally separate from the historiographical perspectives outlined above. One place that Pastor goes astray in his generally very good book is that he assumes that the set of rules about local government enacted by Spanish liberals and implemented starting in 1820 remained unchanged thereafter, when actually they were modified in important ways beginning in 1825. See Pastor, *Campesinos*, especially 420–21 and 427. Carmagnani runs into a different kind of problem. After conducting significant archival research for the colonial period, for his analysis of the period after independence he relies entirely on the extant legislation (*El regreso*, 230–37).

7. *Esposición que el Vice-gobernador*, 3; *Esposición que el Tercer Gobernador*, 32; AGEO,

Gobernación, vol. 3; Muhlenpfordt, *Ensayo*, 16; Fondo Martínez Gracida, vol. 12; Ronald Spores, Irene Huesca, and Manuel Esparza, eds., *Benito Juárez Gobernador de Oaxaca: Documentos de su mandato y servicio público* (Oaxaca: Archivo General del Estado de Oaxaca, 1987), 127–28.

8. *El Regenerador*, 23 February 1843, 64.

9. AGEO, Gobernación, vol. 4. The original reads, "No lo han abandonado por que es un trabajo esclusivo de mujeres."

10. AGEO, Gobernación, vol. 16. The original reads, "El unico oficio de sus mugeres como tambien de la mayor parte o casi todas las del Distrito es tejer mantas para alludar en los gastos de sus maridos."

11. For reports on the economic activities of various villages, see Fondo Martínez Gracida, vol. 12 for 1826; and AGEO, Gobernación, vol. 12 for 1832. For women's self-identification as spinners and weavers see AVA, Penal, exp. 890, 1848; AVA, Penal, exp. 891, 1848; AVA, Penal, exp. 911, 1848; AVA, Penal, exp. 1023, 1852. For descriptions of women producing textiles see AVA, Penal, exp. 1062, 1853; AVA, Penal, exp. 800, 1844; AVA, Penal, exp. 521, 1828.

12. On the profitability of the new factories, see Araceli Ibarra Bellon, *El Comercio y el poder en México, 1821–1864* (Mexico City: Fondo de Cultura Económica/ Universidad de Guadalajara, 1998), 217.

13. The amount of cloth sent to other parts of Mexico seems to have been small and this trade is poorly documented. For reports, see *Balanza mercantil del departamento de Oaxaca, correspondiente al año de 1843*; *Balanza Mercantil de la Plaza de Oaxaca correspondiente al año de 1844*; *Balanza Mercantil de la Plaza de Oaxaca correspondiente al año de 1845*; *Balanza Mercantil de la Plaza de Oaxaca correspondiente al año de 1846*.

14. There were a handful of mestizo or white merchants in the villages of Choapan and Villa Alta, but their activities seem to have been quite limited. See AGN, Expulsion, vol. 3, exp. 4. References to indigenous merchants are myriad. See for example AGEO, Gobernación, vol. 12; Fondo Martínez Gracida, vol. 12; *El Regenerador*, 23 February 1843; and the various documents about robberies cited below.

15. For indigenous merchants in the colonial period, see AGEO, Real Intendencia I, vol. 11, exp. 9; AGEO, Real Intendencia I, vol. 14, exp. 22; AGEO, Real Intendencia II, vol. 35, exp. 42; Chance, *Conquest*, 110–13. The commercial activities of alcaldes mayores and subdelegados are discussed in detail in chapters 2 and 3 of this book.

16. Records for the alcabala or excise tax give a sense of the overall dimensions of commerce, but since these small transactions were not recorded singly it is impossible to know their specific nature with any precision. See AGEO, Legajos Encuardenados, Alcabalas, 1830c, 1831b, 1832g, 1838a.

17. AVA, Penal, exp. 565, 1831. The original reads, "Deligenciamos todo lo nesario para nuestras contrivuciones y mantencion de nuestras familias."

18. AGEO, Legajos Encuardenados, Alcabalas, 1830c.

19. AGEO, Legajos Encuardenados, Decretos 73, 1841; AGEO, Gobernación, 27.

20. AVA, Penal, exp. 627, 1834.

21. For an overview of banditry in early-nineteenth-century Mexico see Paul Vanderwood, *Disorder and Progress: Bandits, Police and Mexican Development* (Lincoln: University of Nebraska Press, 1981), especially 3–38.

22. AVA, Penal, exp. 460, 1822; AGEO, Gobernación, vol. 3; AGEO, Gobernación, vol. 16; AGEO, Gobernación, vol. 9.

23. *El Regenerador*, 23 February 1843; AVA, Civil, exp. 1310, 1855.

24. This diversity is described in Fondo Martínez Gracida, vol. 12; and AGEO, Gobernación, vol. 12.

25. For such lists see AGEO, Gobernación, vol. 35; J. Iturribarría, *Historia*, 368–74; *Esposición que en cumplimiento del articulo 83 de la Constitución del Estado hace el Gobernador del mismo al Noveno Congreso Constitucional al abrir sus segundas sesiones ordinarias el día 2 de julio del año de 1851* (Oaxaca: Impreso por Ignacio Rincón, 1851), 51.

26. *Esposición que en cumplimiento del articulo 83 de la Constitución del Estado hace el Gobernador del mismo al soberano Congreso al abrir sus sesiones el 2 de julio del año de 1849*; *Esposición que en cumplimiento del articulo 83 de la Constitución del Estado hace el Gobernador del mismo al Noveno Congreso Constitucional al abrir sus segundas sesiones ordinarias el día 2 de julio del año de 1851*. I have deliberately left the mines of Ixtlan, a parish that was temporarily part of the District of Villa Alta, out of this analysis. Because Ixtlan was administered with Villa Alta for only a few years I have instead confined my research to the area that was part of the district in the colonial period.

27. AGEO, Gobernación, vol. 4.

28. See, for example Antonio Escobar Ohmstede, "El federalismo en las Huastecas durante la primera mitad del siglo XIX," in *Historia*, edited by Luis Jáuregui and José Antonio Serano Ortega, 79; Guardino, *Peasants*, 85–94; Caplan, "Legal," 2003.

29. Alicia Hernández Chávez, *Anenecuilco: Memoria y vida de un pueblo* (Mexico City: El Colegio de México/Fideicomiso Historia de las Américas/Fondo de Cultura Económica, 1991), 65.

30. Pastor, *Campesinos*, 419–20.

31. Pastor, *Campesinos*, 422–24; Pablo Valderrama Rouy and Carolina Ramírez Suárez, "Resistencia étnica y defensa del territorio en el Totonacapan serrano: Cuetzalan en el siglo XIX," in *Indio, nación y comunidad en el México del siglo XIX*, edited by Antonio Escobar Ohmstede (Mexico City: Centro de Estudios Mexicanos y Centroamericanos/Centro de Investigaciones y Estudios Superiores en Antropología Social, 1993), 193–94; Guardino, *Peasants*, 96.

32. See the constitutional articles in Padilla Sierra, *Leyes*, 49.

33. Florescano, *Etnia*, 345; Annino, "Ciudadanía," 72; Annino, "Ballot," 74; Hensel, *Die Enstehung*, 223.

34. AGN, Ayuntamientos, vol. 120; AGI, Mexico, vol. 1679, exp. 30, carta no. 132,

fols. 566–69, 582–83; AGI, Mexico, vol. 1679, exp. 132, carta no. 114, fols. 735–36, 739–40.

35. Pastor, *Campesinos*, 420–21.

36. *Colección de leyes, decretos y circulares del estado libre y soberano de Oaxaca*, vol. 1, 85–89, 106–10, 210–17; Spores, "Relaciones," 245; Bailón Corres, *Pueblos*, 124; Caplan, "Legal Revolution," 273. Manuel Ferrer Muñoz and María Bono López noted the cut-off of 3,000 inhabitants for ayuntamientos but somehow failed to notice the establishment of local governments in smaller settlements (*Pueblos*, 380, 383).

37. Moisés Bailón Corres, "Elecciones locales en Oaxaca en 1980," *Nueva Antropología* 7, no. 25 (1984): 74–76; and *Pueblos*, 25, 28; and *La Jornada*, 25 March 1998.

38. For Puebla and Mexico, see Guardino, *Peasants*, 94; for Guanajuato, see Serrano Ortega, "Reforma," 90; and for the Yucatán see Bellingeri, "De una constitución," 71. This difference probably explains the high proportion of all Mexican municipalities that are found in Oaxaca today.

39. Hensel, "Los orígenes," 235.

40. Antonio Escobar Ohmstede, *De la costa de la sierra: Las huastecas, 1750–1900* (Mexico City: Centro de Investigaciones y Estudios Superiores en Antropología Social, 1998), 70.

41. Carriedo, *Estudios*, 126; AGEO, Legajos Encuardenados, Decretos 70, 1826c, fol. 27v.

42. See, for example, AGEO, Gobernación, vol. 20; AGEO, Gobernación, vol. 27; *La Centinela*, 20 June 1843; Un principista, *Muerte*; AGEO, Legajos Encuardenados, Gobernación, vol. 32, 1841a.

43. *Memoria que el Gobernador*, 5, 13. The original reads, "Sumergidos en la rusticiad y la ignorancia"; and "Por lo comun nada entienden, ni entenderán en muchos años, hasta que el curso de la civilizacion los saque de la barbarie."

44. Chance, *Conquest*, 146.

45. *Colección de leyes, decretos y circulares del estado libre y soberano de Oaxaca*, vol. 1, 52. The original reads, "No podrá haber en el Estado distinciones, autoridad, ni poder hereditario."

46. See the law governing local administration in *Colección de leyes, decretos y circulares del estado libre y soberano de Oaxaca*, vol. 1, 210. For the use of political catechisms in the district see AGEO, Gobernación, vol. 29.

47. See, for example, AVA, Penal, exp. 502, 1826.

48. *Colección de leyes, decretos y circulares del estado libre y soberano de Oaxaca*, vol. 1, 213.

49. Joaquín Escriche, *Diccionario razonado de legislación civil, penal, comercial y forense* (Caracas: Imprenta de Valentín Espinal, 1840), 87. The Spanish reads, "Que deben servir por su turno todos los vecinos de un pueblo."

50. On this prohibition see Ortiz Escamilla, *Guerra*, 116; Rugeley, *Yucatán's Maya Peasantry*, 39.

51. For such cases see AVA, Civil, exp. 1079, 1834; AVA, Civil, exp. 1199, 1840; AVA,

Penal, exp. 786, 1843. Notably, as late as 1821, when the Spanish liberal constitution was still in force, judges did enforce the custom. See AVA, Civil, exp. 842, 1821.

52. Peter Guardino, "'Me ha cabido en la fatalidad': Gobierno indígena y gobierno republicano en los pueblos indígenas: Oaxaca, 1750–1850," *Desacatos* 5 (2000): 130.

53. Brian Hamnett, "Liberales y conservadores ante el mundo de los pueblos, 1840–1870," in *Los pueblos indios y el parteaguas de la independencia de México*, edited by Manuel Ferrer Muñoz (Mexico City: Universidad Nacional Autónoma de México, 1999), 170.

54. *Colección de leyes, decretos y circulares del estado libre y soberano de Oaxaca*, vol. 1, 54, 88.

55. For a couple of examples, see AVA, Civil, exp. 1027, 1833; and AGN, Gobernación, vol. 154, caja 1, exp. 4, fol. 314. The evidence about municipal elections under the similar rules of the Spanish constitution is more limited, but see AGN, Ayuntamientos, vol. 120 for the 1820 election in Zoogocho.

56. The petitions and testimony are found in AVA, Civil, exp. 1027, 1833. The Spanish quotes read, respectively, "Tanto chicos como grandes"; "Muchachos alborotadores de pueblos"; and "Vamos a quitarle la bara a Quintana." Quintana's age is extrapolated from the age he reported in 1838. See AVA, Penal, exp. 678, 1838.

57. For the cholera epidemic in Villa Alta, see the reports of the district governor published in *El Regenerador*, 2 and 20 March 1843. For the epidemic in the city of Oaxaca and elsewhere in the state, see Lourdes Marquez and Leticia Reina Aoyama, "La cólera en Oaxaca en el siglo XIX," *Cuadernos del Sur* 1 (1992): 71–98; and *Esposición que el Gobernador Constitucional*, 7–8.

58. The description of the event in the preceding paragraphs comes entirely from the petitions and testimony contained in AVA, Penal, exp. 631, 1834. The quotes are, in order, "Con que orden ha tomado usted ese vaston, atropellando mi autoridad"; "Un Alcalde electo constitucionalmente"; and "No fuese defendido de nadie, no por su autoridad, ni por el citado de enfermedad en que estaba."

59. AVA, Civil, exp. 1027, 1833.

60. The report was published several years later in the state's official newspaper (*El Regenerador*, 16 February 1843). The original Spanish reads, "Esclusivamente los directores del pueblo"; and "Las elecciones para los cargos municipales, han recaido siempre en individuos que ya prestaron servicios al pueblo, y ninguno . . . podía ser alcalde o regidor, si no habia sido topil, sacristan, gobace o mozo para conducir cordilleras, y si no habia desempeñado otros oficios que ellos estiman por bajos."

61. Guardino, *Peasants*, 100.

62. AGEO, Legajos Encuardenados, Gobernación, vol. 30, 1839h, fol. 133. The Spanish reads, "Auxiliares principales y subalternos electos en el numero que dispongan los Prefectos con aprobacion del Gobierno Departamental, siguiendose en cuando se juzgue util y conveniente las costumbres de los mismos pueblos."

63. For examples see AVA, Penal, exp. 673, 1838; AVA, Penal, exp. 706, 1840; AVA, Penal, exp. 786, 1843.

64. See, for example, AGEO, Gobernación, vol. 35; AGEO, Gobernación, vol. 37; and many of the actas in AGN, Gobernación, s/s, caja 268, exp. 1.

65. Spores, "Relaciones," 265–66; AGEO, Legajos Encuardenados, Gobernación, 1841e, 30 March 1842; AGEO, Gobernación, vol. 35.

66. All this is from Pando's 1837 report published in *El Regenerador*, 16 February 1843. The Spanish quotes are, "Prestigio mágico"; and "El gobierno interior de los pueblos es verdaderamente patriarcal, y solo acabará, cuando los indígenas avancen en la carrera de la civilización."

67. AGEO, Gobernación, vol. 12. The Spanish reads, "Idiotismo"; and "Los decretos y cordilleras que les remiten, sin entender ni siquiera el espiritu de ellas."

68. AVA, Penal, exp. 673, 1838. The Spanish reads, "Me allo con gran desprecio ultrajado y atropellado por que todos mis braso u ausiliares mayor, y topil, ninguno de estos se me ovedese en mis mandado . . . dice que no fui Electo del Pueblo, y por eso soy atropellado . . . estoy como muchacho de Escuela."

69. AVA, Penal, exp. 706, 1840. The quote reads, "Me ha cabido en la fatalidad de aber los principales nombrado por topiles a dos hombres soberbios y altivos que orgullosos por haber echo por su orden y escala los serbicios que en este pueblo se acostumbra, me traten a mi a y los Regidores de moscosos desobediciendonos e injuriandonos a cada paso." In a similar case the juez de paz is described as having ascended "por salto," literally jumping up the ladder (AVA, Penal, exp. 786, 1843).

70. AVA, Penal, exp. 739, 1841. The Spanish reads, "No conosen quien somos."

71. AVA, Penal, exp. 828, 1845. The quotes read, "No debia mandar por que era muy muchacho y no habia hecho en el pueblo ningun gasto"; and "Era mugercita, machinado, que no sabia governar por que era muchacho y que el (Gomez) era anciano y principal del pueblo."

72. AVA, Penal, exp. 808, 1844. The Spanish reads, "Un alcahuete . . . que no le correspondia tener el encargo de Juez de Paz y que quien se lo habia dado no savia lo que hacia."

73. See, respectively, AGEO, Gobernación, vol. 17; and AGEO, Gobernación, vol. 27. For these issues in Guerrero see Guardino, *Peasants*, 102–3.

74. *Esposición que en cumplimiento del articulo 83 de la Constitución del Estado hace el Gobernador del mismo al soberano Congreso al abrir sus sesiones el 2 de julio del año de 1848* (Oaxaca: Impreso por Ignacio Rincón, 1848), 12. The Spanish reads, "Desde antes del establecimiento del sistema federal los pueblos del Estado han tenido la costumbre democrática de eligir por sí mismos á los funcionarios que con el nombre de alcaldes y regidores cuidaban de la policia, de la conservacion de la paz y de la administracion de los fondos comunales. Esta costumbre benéfica fue robustecida por el sistema federativo, otorgándose á los pueblos la facultad de eligir á los miembros de sus ayuntamientos y repúblicas, y reglamentándose las obligaciones y derechos de estas corporaciones. Por este motivo el sistema republicano representivo

popular federal fue bien recibido por los pueblos del Estado, y el sistema central que abolió aquellas corporaciones causó un disgusto universal que contribuyó á la caida de ese sistema que nos fue tan fatal. Restablecida la federación los pueblos han recobrado no solo sus ayuntamientos y repúblicas, sino el derecho de elegirlas conforme á sus antiguas costumbres, quedando así organizada la administración local de las municipalidades, de una manera, que lejos de obstruir, espedita la marcha de la administración general del Estado."

75. AVA, Penal, exp. 1046, 1853. The quote reads, "Los ciudadanos Juan Morales, Juan Velasco y Salvador Velasco, por sí y á nombre de los principales."

76. AVA, Penal, exp. 1023, 1853. The quotes read, "Nosotros principales y con todos del comun"; and "Votos todos los principales voto de los pueblo que ban Alcalde primero Mateo de Luna."

77. Taylor, *Magistrates*, 382.

78. AVA, Civil, exp. 1027, 1833.

79. AVA, Penal, exp. 667, 1837.

80. AVA, Penal, exp. 678, 1838.

81. AVA, Penal, exp. 687, 1839.

82. AVA, Penal, exp. 785, 1843. The Spanish reads, "El dominio que quiere tener siempre en el pueblo."

83. AVA, Penal, exp. 582, 1831; AVA, Penal, exp. 683, 1838; AVA, Penal, exp. 706, 1840; AVA, Penal, exp. 885, 1848; AVA, Penal, exp. 887, 1848; AVA, Penal, exp. 894, 1848; AVA, Penal, exp. 1070, 1853; AVA, Penal, exp 1257, 1857; AVA, Penal, exp. 1303, 1857; AGEO, Gobernación, vol. 16; AGEO, Gobernación, vol. 20; AGEO, Gobernación, vol. 28.

84. AVA, Civil, exp. 956, 1832. The Spanish reads, "Por lo comun origen de los malos matrimonios."

85. AVA, Civil, exp. 1310, 1855.

86. AVA, Civil, exp. 956, 1832; AVA, Civil, exp. 1310, 1855; AGEO, Legajos Encuardenados, Gobernación, vol. 37, 18450, 11 August 1845.

87. AVA, Penal, exp. 911, 1848. The quote reads, "Una floja que no cumplia con sus obligaciones a mas de que le escaseaba sus alimentos." For other examples see AVA, Civil, exp. 956, 1832; AVA, Penal, exp. 515, 1827; AVA, Penal, exp. 529, 1829; AVA, Penal, exp. 891, 1848.

88. AVA, Penal, exp. 520, 1828. The quote reads, "Mais sal todo lo necesario en la casa como acostumbramos nosotros los naturales." For other examples see AVA, Penal, exp. 521, 1828; AVA, Penal, exp. 554, 1831.

89. Here again we see Steve Stern's "contested patriarchal pact" (*Secret History*, 80–85).

90. AVA, Penal, exp. 515, 1827. The quote is, "Como Dios manda."

91. For one who did succeed, see the case of María Torivia, who was able to earn money working as a domestic servant for one of the few non-Indian officials who lived in the district (AVA, Penal, exp. 536, 1830).

92. AVA, Civil, exp. 956, 1832; AVA, Civil, exp. 1283, 1848.

93. AVA, Penal, exp. 1241, 1857. The Spanish reads, "En cumplimiento de una costumbre antigua"; and "Dichos novios alguna reconvencion del modo que deben los Ciudadanos guardar el Santo Sacramento del matrimonio." See also AVA, Penal, exp. 683, 1838.

94. AGEO, Legajos Encuardenados, Gobernación, vol. 32, 1842i, 13 September; AVA, Civil, exp. 1330, 1857.

95. See, respectively, AVA, Penal, exp. 885, 1848; AVA, Penal, exp. 714, 1840; and AGEO, Gobernación, vol. 16.

96. AVA, Penal, exp. 800, 1844; AVA, Penal, exp. 1023, 1852.

97. See, for instance AVA, Civil, exp. 1027, 1833.

98. See, respectively, AVA, Penal, exp. 683, 1838; and AVA, Penal, exp. 828, 1845. The quote reads, "Mugercita."

99. See, for instance, AVA, Penal, exp. 591, 1832.

100. AGEO, Gobernación, vol. 16.

101. AVA, Penal, exp. 1246, 1857.

102. AVA, Penal, exp. 741, 1841.

103. AVA, Penal, exp. 521, 1828.

104. AVA, Penal, exp. 678, 1838.

105. AVA, Penal, exp. 651, 1836; AVA, Penal, exp. 995, 1851; AVA, Penal, exp. 1095, 1853.

106. AVA, Penal, exp. 533, 1830; AVA, Penal, exp. 565, 1831.

107. AVA, Penal, exp. 631, 1834. For another reference to constitutional alcaldes see AGN, Gobernación, leg. 154, caja 1, exp. 4, fol. 273.

108. AVA Penal, exp. 538, 1830; AGN, Gobernación, leg. 154, caja 1, exp. 4, fol. 273. The Spanish quotes are, "Casas reales"; "Casas nacionales"; and "Casa constitucional." For some reason in the colonial period the building in each village was always referred to in the plural, as "royal houses."

109. AVA, Penal, exp. 739, 1841. The quote is, "Autoridad nacional."

110. AVA, Penal, exp. 591, 1832. The Spanish reads, "Alcahueteria."

111. AVA, Penal, exp. 977, 1850; AVA, Penal, exp. 1246, 1857.

112. Eric Van Young provides a somewhat different interpretation of this term. Van Young suggests that instead of connoting a sexual go-between, *alcahuete* suggested the feminization of the person the term was applied to (*Other*, 314–15).

113. AVA, Penal, exp. 808, 1844.

114. AVA, Penal, exp. 1204, 1856. The quote reads, "Un alcahuete del gobierno."

115. AVA, Penal, exp. 473, 1823. The quotes read, "Aqui ninguno nos manda somos Jues de este Jusgado de Ayuntamiento"; and "Ustedes lo que tratan es robar dinero tanto tu como el Jues."

116. AVA, Penal, exp. 591, 1832. The quotes read, "Papeles de ningun ymportancia"; and "Nos limpiaremos el culo, que para eso estamos en tiempo de Libertad." See also AVA, Penal, exp. 577, 1831.

117. AVA, Penal, exp. 683, 1838. The Spanish is, "No estamos pensando lo de Juez pues tanta autoridad tengo yo como el." For another case, see AVA, Penal, exp. 732, 1841.

118. AVA, Penal, exp. 995, 1851. The Spanish reads, "Estaban ya fastidiades con el que declara y con el gobierno, por que tanto uno como el otro era unos ladrones."

119. For the 1821 Plan de Iguala, see Fondo Manuel Martínez Gracida, vol. 38. For the 1835 Plan de Orizaba that led to the establishment of federalism, see *Esposición que el Gobernador Constitucional*, 11; and *El Regenerador*, 16 June 1835.

120. AGEO, Legajos Encuardenados, Gobernación, vol. 38, 1846f, 6 October 1846.

121. AGEO, Gobernación, vol. 12. For an example, see AGN, Gobernación, leg. 154, caja 1, exp. 4, fol. 248.

122. AGN, Gobernación, Leg. 154, caja 1, exp. 4, fol. 265. The quote reads, "Profesa ni protege otra Religion que la Catolica, apostolica Romana ni tolera el ejercicio de otra alguna." See also Cacalotepec in AGN, Gobernación, Leg. 154, caja 1, exp. 4, fol. 275.

123. For a few examples, see AGN, Gobernación, leg. 154, caja 1, exp. 4, fol. 263–64; AGN, Gobernación, leg. 154, caja 1, exp. 5, fols. 323, 349.

124. For an example, AGN, Gobernación, leg. 154, caja 1, exp. 4, fol. 273.

125. AGN, Gobernación, leg. 154, caja 1, exp. 4, fols. 257–58, 276, 280, 308. The quotes read, "Musica y otros instrumentos de que se hase huso en las festividades de primera clase"; and "Publicas aclamaciones y vivas."

126. Annino, "Ciudadanía," 83.

127. AGN, Gobernación, s/s, caja 268, exp. 1.

128. For Guerrero, see Guardino, "Identity"; and *Peasants*. For Morelos see Florencia Mallon, "Peasants and State Formation in Nineteenth-Century Mexico: Morelos, 1848–1858," *Political Power and Social Theory* 7 (1988): 1–54. For Puebla see Mallon, *Peasant and Nation*; and Guy Thomson, *Patriotism, Politics, and Popular Liberalism in Nineteenth-Century Mexico: Juan Francisco Lucas and the Puebla Sierra* (Wilmington, Del.: Scholarly Resources, 1999).

129. AGEO, Gobernación, vol. 2; *El Regenerador*, 5 January 1843.

130. *Union Nacional*, 23 June 1846; AGEO, Gobernación, vol. 20.

131. The process is described in depth in José Antonio Serrano Ortega, *El contigente de sangre: Los gobiernos estatales y departmentales y los métodos de reclutamiento del ejército permanente mexicano, 1824–1844* (Mexico City: Instituto Nacional de Antropología e Historia, 1993).

132. *Memoria que el Vice-gobernador*, 5; AGEO, Gobernación, vol. 11. See also *Memoria que el Gobernador*, 24; *Esposición que en cumplimiento del articulo 83 de la Constitución del Estado hace el Gobernador del mismo al soberano Congreso al abrir sus sesiones el 2 de julio del año de 1848*, 30.

133. AGEO, Gobernación, vol. 11; AGEO, Legajos Encuardenados, Gobernación, vol. 17, 1831a, 30 June 1831; *El Regenerador*, 19 February 1844.

134. AGEO, Gobernación, vol. 35; Serrano Ortega, *El contingente*, 111.

135. AVA, Penal, exp. 509, 1826.

136. AGEO, Gobernación, vol. 17; AGEO, Gobernación, vol. 21; AGEO, Gobernación, vol. 35; AGEO, Legajos Encuardenados, Gobernación, vol. 32, 1842a.

137. AGEO, Gobernación, vol. 16; AVA, Penal, exp. 678, 1838.

138. AGEO, Gobernación, vol. 27.

139. Esparza, "El difícil," 504, 508; AGEO, Legajos Encuardenados, Gobernación, vol. 31, 1842i; AGEO, Legajos Encuardenados, Gobernación, vol. 43, 1850n; AGEO, Gobernación, vol. 13; AGEO, Gobernación, vol. 21.

140. *Colección de leyes, decretos y circulares del estado libre y soberano de Oaxaca*, vol. 1, 101. The original reads, "En las que se enseñará a los niños, a leer, escribir y contar, el catecismo de la religion católica, y otro catecismo político que comprenderá una breve exposición e los derechos y obligaciones civiles y políticas, y de las leyes Penales."

141. AGEO, Gobernación, vol. 2; AGEO, Gobernación, vol. 35; *El Regenerador*, 16 February 1843; AGEO, Gobernación, vol. 17; AGEO, Juárez, vol. 15, exp. 6.

142. AGEO, Padrones, vol. 21, exp. 31.

143. See, for instance AVA, Penal, exp. 800, 1844.

144. AVA, Penal, exp. 995, 1851.

145. AGEO, Gobernación, vol. 20; AGEO, Gobernación, vol. 36; AVA, Penal, exp. 1322, 1858; AGEO, Gobernación, vol. 29.

146. AVA, Penal, exp. 968, 1850; AVA, Penal, exp. 977, 1850; AVA, Penal, exp. 1155, 1855; AVA, Penal, exp. 1177, 1855; AVA, Penal, exp. 1178, 1855; AVA, Penal, exp. 1241, 1757; AVA, Penal, exp. 1246, 1857; AVA, Penal, exp. 1296, 1857.

147. For Spanish liberals see AGEO, Real Intendencia II, vol. 15, exp. 34; Pastor, *Campesinos*, 431.

148. AVA, Penal, exp. 521, 1828; AVA, Penal, exp. 540, 1830; AVA, Penal, exp. 714, 1840; AVA, Penal, exp. 828, 1845; AVA, Penal, exp. 885, 1848; AVA, Penal, exp. 1307, 1857.

149. *Colección de leyes, decretos y circulares del estado libre y soberano de Oaxaca*, vol. 1, 299; AGEO, Legajos Encuardenados, Decretos, vol. 71, 1826d, 19 August 1826; AGEO, Gobernación, vol. 21.

150. AGN, Indios, vol. 58, fols. 195–95v; AGEO, Legajos Encuardenados, Gobernación, vol. 38, 1846f, 23 June 1844; AGEO, Legajos Encuardenados, Gobernación, vol. 32, 1844a, 8 July 1844; AGN, Gobernación, vol. 129, caja 1, exp. 3; AGEO, Legajos Encuardenados, Decretos, vol. 73, 1846.

151. *Colección de leyes, decretos y circulares del estado libre y soberano de Oaxaca*, vol. 1, 44. The quote reads, "La danza antigua de pluma en que se representaban algunas escenas que llamaban de la conquista."

152. Carriedo, *Estudios*, 127. This attitude continued in the twentieth century. See Nader, *Harmony*, 46.

153. AVA, Penal, exp. 502, 1826; AVA, Penal, exp. 785, 1843; AVA, Civil, exp. 999, 1832.

154. Carlos Sánchez Silva, ed., *Las lecturas de Juárez* (Oaxaca: Amigos de los Archivos y Bibliotecas de Oaxaca, 1998), 111–25.

155. AHCO, Copiador de Oficios, 1822–1825, 14 July 1825; Sánchez Silva, *Lecturas*, 123.

156. AGEO, Gobernación, vol. 3; AGEO, Gobernación, vol. 16; AGEO, Legajos Encuardenados, Gobernación, vol. 32, 1842a.

157. AGEO, Legajos Encuardenados, Tesorería, vol. 133, 1841b; *Esposición que en cumplimiento del articulo 83 de la Constitución del Estado hace el Gobernador del mismo al soberano Congreso al abrir sus sesiones el 2 de julio del año de 1849*; *Esposición que en cumplimiento del articulo 83 de la Constitución del Estado hace el Gobernador del mismo al Noveno Congreso Constitucional al abrir el primer período de sus sesiones ordinarias el día 2 de julio del año de 1850* (Oaxaca: Impreso por Ignacio Rincón, 1850); AGEO, Gobernación, vol. 7; J. Iturribarría, *Historia*, 140, 269.

158. AGEO, Gobernación, vol. 3; AGEO, Gobernación, vol. 7; AGEO, Gobernación, vol. 12.

159. AVA, Penal, exp. 577, 1831.

160. AVA, Penal, exp. 1095, 1853. The Spanish reads, "No tenia en su pueblo ningún árbol de dinero para estarlo sacudiendo a cada momento que el Gobierno quisiera." During the 1851 Sogocho riot against the tax on tianguis slated to finance a school, the female rioters also demanded that the subprefect return the money he had collected for the head tax and alcabala.

161. Guardino, *Peasants*, 147–77; Leticia Reina, *Las rebeliones campesinas en México (1819–1906)* (Mexico: Siglo XXI, 1980), 235–37.

162. *Colección de leyes, decretos y circulares del estado libre y soberano de Oaxaca*, vol. 1, 22, 27–32, 217–22; Spores, "Relaciones," 1990, 248.

163. *Esposición que en cumplimiento del articulo 83 de la Constitución del Estado hace el Gobernador del mismo al soberano Congreso al abrir sus sesiones el 2 de julio del año de 1848*, 11; Hensel, *Die Enstehung*, 264, 398; AGN, Gobernación, vol. 104, caja 1, exp. 3; AGEO, Legajos Encuardenados, Decretos, vol. 73, 1840; AGEO, Gobernación, vol. 7; AGEO, Gobernación, vol. 37.

164. *Esposición que en cumplimiento del articulo 83 de la Constitución del Estado hace el Gobernador del mismo al soberano Congreso al abrir sus sesiones el 2 de julio del año de 1848*, 11; *Esposición que en cumplimiento del articulo 83 de la Constitución del Estado hace el Gobernador del mismo al soberano Congreso al abrir sus sesiones el 2 de julio del año de 1849*; AGEO, Gobernación, vol. 12.

165. I have found only two references to such economic activities. In 1834 a resident of the village of Villa Alta accused Pando of moving the tianguis to neighboring Lachiroag because "era conveniente a sus intereses" (AVA, Penal, exp. 627, 1834). In 1852 Francisco Franco, who would become prefect in 1853, owned a farm in Choapan (AGEO, Gobernación, vol. 21).

166. Hensel, *Die Enstehung*, 271, 437; AGN, Gobernación, vol. 104, caja 1, exp. 3; *Esposición que el Vice-gobernador*, 6.

167. AVA, Civil, exp. 1076, 1834; AGEO, Gobernación, vol. 3.

168. AVA, Penal, exp. 678, 1838; *Esposición que el Tercer Gobernador*, 14–15; AGEO, Gobernación, vol. 12.

169. The quote is from AGEO, Gobernación, vol. 3. It reads, "Adoptaron no solamente las costumbres de los naturales por lo respectivo a la vida miserable que llevan y los ejercicios penosos en que se ocupan, sino el trage y alimentos por manera que al verlos en calzoncillos blancos de manta, con su chomosreta al hombro, con sandalias, su carga en la espalda y comiendo tortilla con sal, hacese difícil creer que son españoles." The documents do not specify the ultimate fate of the men, suggesting that Pando was allowed to make the decision on his own. For Pando's earlier beliefs about Spaniards, see AHCO, Delitos Contra la Seguridad Interior del Estado, 1829.

170. *El Zapotec*, 16 September 1832; AGEO, Gobernación, vol. 35.

171. *Esposición que el Vice-gobernador*, 12, 24; AGEO, Gobernación, vol. 12; AVA, Penal, exp. 682, 1838; AGEO, Gobernación, vol. 35. The quote is from *El Regenerador*, 16 February 1843. It reads, "Mas que por las leyes y decretos, se dirigen estos indigenas en su gobierno económico por usos inveterados y costumbres añejas."

172. *Esposición que el Tercer Gobernador*, 32; *El Regenerador*, 23 February 1843.

173. AGEO, Gobernación, vol. 3; AGEO, Gobernación, vol. 12. The quote is from *El Regenerador*, 6 March 1843. It reads, "Siempre se ha disfrutado en sus territorio de una paz octaviana."

174. Leticia Mayer Celis, *Entre el infierno de una realidad y el cielo de un imaginario: Estadística y comunidad científica en el México de la primera mitad del siglo xix* (Mexico City: El Colegio de Mexico, 1999).

175. AGEO, Gobernación, vol. 2; AGEO, Gobernación, vol. 3; AGEO, Gobernación, vol. 12; AGEO, Gobernación, vol. 16.

176. *El Regenerador*, 13, 16, and 23 February 1843; 2 and 20 March 1843. Pando's obituary is found in the same newspaper on 18 May 1843.

177. For some examples from the period see AVA, Penal, exp. 670, 1837; AVA, Penal, exp. 699, 1839; AVA, Penal, exp. 739, 1841; AVA, Penal, exp. 741, 1841; AVA, Civil, exp. 1196.

178. Chance, *Conquest*, 171. For instance an 1845 document from San Juan Tanetze equates the barrio of "nuestra Señora de la Soledad" with the cofradía of the same name (AVA, Civil, exp. 1255, 1845).

179. AVA, Civil, exp. 1255, 1845; AVA, Civil, exp. 985, 1832; AVA, Civil, exp. 999, 1932.

180. See, for example, AVA, Civil, exp. 985, 1832; AVA, Civil, exp. 999, 1832; AVA, Penal, exp. 502, 1826; AVA, Penal, exp. 887, 1848; AVA, Penal, exp. 894, 1848; AVA, Penal, exp. 968, 1850.

181. AGEO, Legajos Encuardenados, Decretos, vol. 73, 1841; AGEO, Legajos Encuardenados, Gobernación, vol. 32, 1841a, 31 December; AGEO, Legajos Encuardenados, Gobernación, vol. 32, 1844a, 20 January; AGEO, Legajos Encuardenados, Gobernación, vol. 32, 1844d, 30 January; AVA, Civil, exp. 1240, 1842.

182. *Esposición que el Gobernador del Estado hace en cumplimiento del articulo 83 de la Constitución al Soberano Congreso al abrir sus primeras sesiones ordinarias el día 2 de julio del año de 1852*, 33–34, appendix 31.

183. AVA, Civil, exp. 1223, 1842; AVA, Civil, exp. 1233, 1843.

184. AVA, Civil, exp. 840, 1821.

185. AVA, Penal, exp. 1315, 1857.

186. AVA, Penal, exp. 651, 1836. The quote reads, "Digale a esos borrachos que no me quiero coger al santo, santos tengo en la Yglesia."

187. AVA, Penal, exp. 753, 1842. On the debates surrounding burial practices, see Voekel, *Alone*.

188. AVA, Penal, exp. 699, 1839. The quotes read, "El era el Alcalde, y que mandaba en todo el Pueblo y que me pondría a mi mismo en la carcel"; and "Señor cura, advierto vuestra majestad que soy un autoridad del Pueblo y vos no debe ultrajarme de ese modo pues si en algo he faltado, Tribunal tengo a donde con arreglo a la Ley se me deve juzgar así como Vos tiene sus tribunal." This wasn't the first problem Brioso had had in Betaza. In an 1837 case the authorities sought to arrest Brioso's nephew for fighting with village officials and trying to seduce the village girls. The nephew fled to the priest's house, but the next day the alcalde led a group of villagers who tried to remove him from the house. The villagers stopped only after the priest ordered the village elders to intervene (AVA, Penal, exp. 670).

189. AVA, Penal, exp. 1062, 1853. The Spanish reads, "Todos tenemos corazon y almas y somos hijos de Dios."

190. AVA, Penal, exp. 474, 1823; AVA, Penal, exp. 475, 1823; AVA, Penal, exp. 642, 1835; AVA, Penal, exp. 786, 1843; AVA, Penal, exp. 1204, 1856.

191. Graham, *Patronage*, 20–22, 29.

192. See, for instance, AVA, Civil, exp. 1240, 1842; AVA, Penal, exp. 1303, 1857.

193. *Colección de leyes, decretos y circulares del estado libre y soberano de Oaxaca,* vol. 1, 60.

194. Bailón Corres, *Pueblos*, 92. The quote reads, "Una propiedad territorial, ó en bienes raíces, ó una profesión, empleo ó industria productiva."

195. *El Zapoteco*, 20 and 23 September 1830.

196. AVA, Civil, exp. 830, 1820; *Cartas al Pueblo*, 13 September 1828; AGEO, Gobernación, vol. 11, [1829]; AGEO, Gobernación, vol. 27, [1834]; AGEO, Gobernación, vol. 36 [1846]; AGEO, Gobernación, vol. 7, [1847]; AGEO, Gobernación, vol. 28, [1847]; AGEO, Gobernación, vol. 4, [1848]; *El Regenerador*, 31 March 1842.

197. AVA, Civil, exp. 830, 1820.

198. For attacks on indigenous government and resistance to taxation in Guerrero see Guardino, *Peasants*, 152–64.

199. For some of the evidence see AVA, Penal, exp. 549, 1831; AVA, Civil, exp. 1076, 1834.

200. *Cartas al Pueblo*, 13 September 1828; AGEO, Gobernación, vol. 16; AHCO, Actas, 1829, fol. 42.

201. For Ylarto see AVA, Penal, exp. 592, 1831. For the Tabaa case see AVA, Civil, exp. 861, 1826. For the centralist effort to limit suits see Guardino, *Peasants*, 107; and AGEO, Gobernación, vol. 18, 1850.

202. John Coatsworth, "Patterns of Rural Rebellion in Latin America: Mexico in Comparative Perspective," in *Riot, Rebellion, and Revolution: Rural Social Conflict in Mexico*, edited by Friedrich Katz (Princeton: Princeton University Press, 1988), 35; Guardino, *Peasants*, 7. Two important works that cover many of these rebellions are Jean Meyer, *Problemas campesinas y revueltas agrarias (1821–1910)* (Mexico City: Secretaría de Educación Pública, 1973); and Reina, *Las rebeliones*. Van Young shows that riots continued in central Mexico even during the decade of the independence war (*Other*, 386).

203. Coatsworth, "Patterns," 34.

204. See Pando's 1837 report in *El Regenerador*, 6 March 1843. Pando reported an enduring "Octavian peace" in the district even though there had been at least six riots between Pando's arrival in 1830 and 1836.

205. Rodolfo Pastor found this to be the case in the Mixteca (*Campesinos*, 435).

206. AVA, Penal, exp. 533, 1830; AVA, Penal, exp. 565, 1831; AVA, Penal, exp. 582, 1831; AVA, Penal, exp. 627, 1834; AVA, Penal, exp. 651, 1836; AVA, Penal, exp. 678, 1838; AVA, Penal, exp. 753, 1842; AVA, Penal, exp. 799, 1844; AVA, Penal, exp. 995, 1851; AVA, Penal, exp. 1095, 1853.

207. See, for instance, AVA, Penal, exp. 799, 1844.

208. AVA, Penal, exp. 995, 1851.

209. For the San Pablo Ayutla case see AVA, Civil, exp. 1027, 1833. For other cases see AVA, Penal, exp. 631, 1834; and AVA, Penal, exp. 739, 1841.

210. AVA, Penal, exp. 687, 1839; AVA, Penal, exp. 741, 1841; AVA, Penal, exp. 887, 1848; AVA, Penal, exp. 894, 1848.

211. AVA, Penal, exp. 582, 1831.

212. AVA, Penal, exp. 799, 1844.

213. AVA, Civil, exp. 1215, 1841; *El Regenerador*, 16 February 1843; *Memoria que el Gobernador*, 13; *Esposición que el Vice-gobernador*, 24.

214. AVA, Penal, exp. 551, 1831; AVA, Penal, exp. 660, 1837; AVA, Penal, exp. 1007, 1852; AGEO, Gobernación, vol. 13.

215. AVA, Penal, exp. 479, 1824; AVA, Penal, exp. 533, 1830; AVA, Penal, exp. 565, 1831.

216. AVA, Penal, exp. 551, 1831; AVA, Penal, exp. 627, 1834; AVA, Penal, exp. 644, 1835; AVA, Penal, exp. 648, 1836; AVA, Penal, exp. 656, 1837; AVA, Penal, exp. 660, 1837; AGEO, Legajos Encuardenados, Decretos, vol. 71, 1832b, 18 July; AGEO, Gobernación, vol. 12.

217. AVA, Penal, exp. 474, 1823; AVA, Penal, exp. 582, 1831; AVA, Penal, exp. 651, 1836; AVA, Penal, exp. 667, 1837; AVA, Penal, exp. 670, 1837; AVA, Penal, exp. 678, 1838; AVA, Penal, exp. 753, 1842; AVA, Penal, exp. 768, 1842.

218. AVA, Penal, exp. 1095, 1853; AVA, Penal, exp. 995, 1851. For a riot against a village official collecting the head tax see AVA, Penal, exp. 678, 1838.

219. AVA, Penal, exp. 1246, 1857. The quote reads, "El bastón que tenía se lo habían dado ellos." See also AVA, Penal, exp. 968, 1850.

220. AGEO, Gobernación, vol. 35. The quote is from AGEO, Legajos Encuardenados, Gobernación, vol. 32, 1844a, 9 December. It reads, "Hacer desaparecer una costumbre inveterada."

221. AVA, Penal, exp. 475, 1823. See also AVA, Penal, exp. 479, 1824.

222. AVA, Civil, exp. 840, 1821.

223. AVA, Penal, exp. 582, 1831. See also AVA, Civil, exp. 861, 1826.

224. AVA, Civil, exp. 840, 1821. The Spanish reads, "No debe ser motivo para vivir divididos en bandos siendo uno mismo Pueblo y todos parientes."

225. AVA, Penal, exp. 1257, 1857.

226. See also Guardino, *Peasants*, 93.

227. Ducey, "Hijos," 143.

228. AVA, Civil, exp. 840, 1821. The quote reads, "El comun y Ciudadanos del Pueblo." After the Spanish constitution was replaced by Oaxaca's state constitution it was referred to in many documents submitted by indigenous peasants. See for example AVA, Penal, exp. 502, 1826; AVA, Penal, exp. 521, 1828; AVA, Penal, exp. 590, 1832.

229. AGEO, Gobernación, vol. 1. The quote reads, "Nosotros Los Ciudadanos, Alcaldes, regidores, Principales, y de mas comun de este Pueblo." An 1833 petition from the same village shows a similar combination (AVA, Civil, exp. 1027, 1833).

230. Respectively, AGN, Gobernación, leg. 154, caja 1, exp. 4, fols. 80, 248, 250, 251, 273, 275, 283, 290, 293, 307, 308. The quotes read, respectively, "Nosotros la Republica Constitucional"; "Todos los Ciudadanos que componen la republica de esta municipalidad los principales y comun"; "La Republica . . . en union de una muchedumbre de becinos"; "Toda la corporacion"; "Todos Los ciudadanos"; "Los comunes y principales para todas las hautoridades"; "Todos los hijos"; "La Republica y demas ciudadanos naturales"; "La justicia y principales"; "Principales y todos havitantes y vesinos"; and "Toda la Republica Principales y de mas becinos."

231. In addition to the above, see AGN, Gobernación, leg. 154, caja 1, exp. 4, fols. 298, 309–13, 350.

232. AGN, Gobernación, s/s, caja 268, exp. 1, fols. 126, 369, 488, 493, 495–96, 506, 546. The quotes read, "Los Jues de Paz de este Pueblo y los auxiliares"; "Muchos vecinos"; "Los jues de paz auciliares y principales y muchos vecinos"; "Juez de paz municipalidad y prinsipal"; "El Jues de paz, hauxiliares, principales y demas cuerpo municipal y demas vecinos"; "Los ciudadanos principales y comun"; "Comun de naturales"; and "Nosostros Justicias Juez de paz en union de todos los Señores Principales y todo el comun."

233. For some examples, see AGEO, Gobernación, vol. 1; AVA, Penal, exp. 521,

1828; AVA, Penal, exp. 579, 1831; AVA, Penal, exp. 590, 1832; AVA, Penal, exp. 678, 1838. For a "ciudadana," see AVA, Penal, exp. 591, 1832.

234. AVA, Civil, exp. 1027, 1833; AVA, Penal, exp. 631, 1834.

235. For the colonial period see AVA, Civil, exp. 207, 1750; and AVA, Penal, exp. 278, 1769.

236. AVA, Penal, exp. 538, 1830; AVA, Penal, exp. 521, 1828; AVA, Penal, exp. 549, 1831.

237. AVA, Civil, exp. 1027, 1833; AVA, Penal, exp. 648, 1836.

238. Florescano, *Etnia*, 17.

239. Sánchez Silva, "Patrimonialismo," 78.

240. AVA, Civil, exp. 1240, 1842.

Notes to Conclusion

1. Compare, for example, Enrique Semo, "Las revoluciones en la historia de México," in *Historia mexiana: Economía y lucha de clases* (Mexico City: Era, 1978), 279–98, with Jan Bazant, *A Concise History of Mexico* (New York: Cambridge University Press, 1977), 62–94.

2. These views were expressed repeatedly in the debates of the liberals' great 1856–57 constitutional congress. See Francisco Zarco, *Historia del Congreso Extraordinario Constituyente (1856-7)* (Mexico City: El Colegio de México, 1956).

3. Demélas and Guerra, "The Hispanic," 57; Guerra, *Modernidades*, 361.

4. Demélas and Guerra, "The Hispanic," 55–57; Guerra, *Modernidades*, 361.

5. Guerra, *Modernidades*, 361.

6. Furet, *Interpreting*, 53–56.

7. Ferrer Muñoz y Bono López, *Pueblos*, 620.

8. Stern, *Secret History*, 194–97.

9. Fuente, *Yalalag*, 211.

10. Fuente, *Yalalag*, 225; *El Imparcial*, 23 August 1998; Bailón Corres, "Elecciones," 81–84; Bailón Corres, *Pueblos*, 217–20.

11. Bailón Corres, *Pueblos*, 220; *La Jornada*, 30 March 2001.

12. Guardino, *Peasants*.

13. Guerrero's mulatto sharecroppers of cotton shared this disadvantage.

14. Guardino, *Peasants*, 101–2.

15. Sánchez Silva, *Indios*, 111–24.

16. For the electoral organizing of the early 1830s see *El Zapoteco*. For the 1836 rebellion see J. Iturribarría, *Historia*, 218–23.

17. Recent research on the second half of the nineteenth century provides some tantalizing evidence about how that bridge was eventually built. See in particular Patrick McNamara, "Sons of the Sierra: Memory, Patriarchy, and Rural Political Culture in Mexico, 1855–1911" (Ph.D. diss., University of Wisconsin, 1999); and Paul Garner, "Federalism and Caudillismo in the Mexican Revolution: The Gene-

sis of the Oaxacan Sovereignty Movement (1915–20)," *Journal of Latin American Studies* 27 (1985): 111–33.

18. Van Young, *Other*, 483. Van Young first introduced this concept in "The Raw and the Cooked: Elite and Popular Ideology in Mexico, 1800–1821," in *The Middle Period in Latin America*, edited by Mark Szuchman (Boulder, Col.: Lynne Reiner, 1989), 88.

19. Mallon, *Peasant and Nation*; Guardino, *Peasants*; Guy Thomson, *Patriotism*; Ducey, "Hijos."

20. Mallon, *Peasant and Nation*; Guardino, *Peasants*; Thomson, *Patriotism*.

21. Van Young, *Other*, 493, 500.

22. James Lockhart, *The Nahuas After the Conquest: A Social and Cultural History of the Indians of Central Mexico, Sixteenth through Eighteenth Centuries* (Stanford: Stanford University Press, 1992), 445–46.

23. Guerra has been the most eloquent and effective advocate of this view, which can be found in essentially his entire corpus of work on the nineteenth century. A similar argument runs through Fernando Escalante Gonzalbo's stimulating *Ciudadanos imaginarios*.

24. Roseberry, "Hegemony," 360–61.

25. The phrase "time of liberty" was used by Luis Martínez, an indigenous peasant of Santiago Lalopa, in 1832. See AVA, Penal, exp. 591, 1832.

26. For a similar point about which groups adopt nationalist ideas see Guardino, "Identity," 336.

27. Many Latin Americanist historians and other social scientists could be cited here, but just for example one could consult John J. Johnson, *"Political Change in Latin America: The Emergence of the Middle Sectors* (Stanford: Stanford University Press, 1958), the classic expression of modernization theory in Latin American studies; and Heraclio Bonilla, "The Indian Peasantry and 'Peru' during the War with Chile," in *Resistance, Rebellion and Consciousness in the Andean Peasant World, 18th to 20th Centuries*, edited by Steve J. Stern (Madison: University of Wisconsin Press, 1987), 219–31, a very clear and relatively late expression of the Marxian tenet linking nationalism to the bourgeoisie.

28. See for instance, Guerra, *Modernidades*, 98–102.

BIBLIOGRAPHY

Archives

Archivo General del Estado de Oaxaca (AGEO)
Archivo General de Indias (AGI)
Archivo General de la Nación (AGN)
Archivo Histórico del Arzobispado de Oaxaca (AHAO)
Archivo Histórico de la Ciudad de Oaxaca (AHCO)
Archivo de Villa Alta (AVA)
Fondo Manuel Martínez Gracida (FMG)
Fondo Luis Castañeda Gúzman (FCG)

Printed Primary Sources

A. F. A. *Los déspotas quisieran impedir la libertad de escribir*. Mexico City: Imprenta de la Aguila, 1825.

Alvarez y Castillejos, Jose M. *Sermón patriótico moral que predicó en la Iglesia de Nuestra Señora de Guadalupe de esta capital el día 12 de diciembre de 1850*. Oaxaca: Impreso en la oficina de Francisco O. y Quintas, 1851.

Un Amigo de la Patria. *Manifestacion de verdades que desengañaran a los incautos*. Oaxaca: Impreso por el ciudadano Antonio Valdés y Moya, 1836.

Aunque corran rios de sangre Guerrero no ha de triunfar. Oaxaca: Reimpreso por la Imprenta liberal a cargo del ciudadano José Felipe Matos, n.d.

Balanza mercantil del departamento de Oaxaca, correspondiente al año de 1843. Oaxaca: Impresa por I. Candiani, 1844.

Balanza Mercantil de la Plaza de Oaxaca correspondiente al año de 1844, formada y publicada por la Junta de Fomento. Oaxaca: Oficina de Antonio Valdés y Moya, 1845.

Balanza Mercantil de la Plaza de Oaxaca correspondiente al año de 1845, formada y publicada por la Junta de Fomento. Oaxaca: Ignacio Rincon, 1846.

Balanza Mercantil de la Plaza de Oaxaca correspondiente al año de 1846, formada y publicada por la Junta de Fomento. Oaxaca: Oficina de Antonio Valdés y Moya, 1847.

Bergoza y Jordan, Antonio. *Nos el doctor don Antonio Bergosa y Jordan por la gracia de dios y de la Santa Sede Apostolica: obispo de Antequera de Oaxaca, electo arzobispo de Mexico, Caballero de la real y distinguida orden española de Carlos Tercero, del consejo de S. M. & c.* Oaxaca: n.p., 1810.

Bergoza y Jordan, Antonio. *Nos el doctor don Antonio Bergosa y Jordan por la gracia de dios y de la Santa Sede Apostolica: obispo de Antequera de Oaxaca, electo arzobispo de Mexico, Caballero de la real y distinguida orden española de Carlos Tercero, del consejo de S. M. &c.* Oaxaca, 1811.

Bocanegra, José María. *Memorias para la historia de México independiente.* Mexico City: Instituto Nacional de Estudios Históricos de la Revolución Mexicana, 1985.

Bolaños, Aurelio. *Discurso cívico pronunciado en el aniversario de la Independencia Mexicana el 16 de septiembre de 1837.* Oaxaca: Impreso por el ciudadano Antonio Valdés y Moya, 1837.

Bustamante, Carlos María de. *A los habitantes de la provincia de Oaxaca.* Mexico City: Imprenta Imperial de D. Alejandro Valdés, 1822.

———. *Defensa de los bienes eclesiásticos.* Oaxaca: Reimpresa por Antonio Valdés y Moya, 1837.

———. *Diario Histórico de México.* Mexico City: Instituto Nacional de Antropología e Historia, 1980.

Canãs, Tiburcio, et al. *Representación que los ciudadanos Oajaqueños ques subsriben dirigen al congreso nacional Mexicano.* Mexico City: Impreso por Francisco C. y Torres en las Escalerillas Num. 13, 1835.

Cañon de a cuatro disparado a metralla contra las reflécciones de D. Manuel Yglesias, y crítica burlesca de ellas en este segundo diálogo de los Morenos, y gracias que se dan al Exmô. Sôr. Virey por haber concedido la igualdad á estos. Puebla: Imprenta Liberal, 1820.

Canseco, José Juan. *Inconvenientes de una colonización indiscreta, o sea Impugnación al establecimiento de la libertad de cultos en la Republica Mexicana.* Oaxaca: Impreso por I. Rincon, 1848.

———. *Proposicion que el Dr. D. Jose Juan Canseco presentó en la Camara de Senadores de la H. Legislatura del Estado Libre de Oaxaca para que se dirija iniciativa al soberano Congreso General sobre que se conserve vigente la Constitucion Federal de 1824 con las reformas necesarias.* Oaxaca: Impreso por Ignacio Rincón, 1846.

Carbajal, Bernadino. *Discurso que en la funcion de la bendicion de la bandera del Batallon guerrero pronunció el presberito C. Bernadino Carbajal en 28 de diciembre de 1847.* Oaxaca: Impreso por Ignacio Rincon, 1848.

Carriedo, Juan Bautista. *Estudios históricos y estadísticos del Departamento de Oaxaca*. Oaxaca: Impr. del autor, 1840–1849.

Casaus y Torres, Ramón Francisco. *Sermon en accion de gracias a Dios nuestro senor por las gloriosas hazanas de la invicta nacion espanola para la restauracion de la monarquia, y restitucion de nuestro amado soberano el Sr. D. Fernando VII. a su trono. Predicado el dia 10 de septiembre de 1808 en la iglesia de San Agustin de Antequera de Oaxaca*. Mexico City: Por D. M. de Zuñiga y Ontiveros, 1808.

Un ciudadano. *A mis conciudadanos de Oajaca y todo el Estado*. Oaxaca: n.p., 1826.

Colección de leyes, decretos y circulares del estado libre y soberano de Oaxaca. Oaxaca: Imprenta del Estado en el Instituto, 1851.

Colección de leyes y decretos del estado libre de Oaxaca. Vol. 1. Oaxaca: Impr. del estado en el Ex obispado, 1861.

Contestación del Obispo y Cabildo de la Santa Iglesia Catedral de Oajaca, al oficio del Señor Ministro de Justicia y Negocios Eclesiásticos, con que les remitió el dictamen sobre instrucciones al Enviado a Roma. Guadalajara: Reimpreso en la Oficina de la viuda de Romero, 1827.

Contestacion que los editores del Zapoteco dan al papel titulado Defensa del Fuero Eclesiastico. Oaxaca: Imprenta Municipal de C. A. V. y Moya, 1833.

Defenza de los empleados oaxaquenos. Oaxaca: n.p., 1833.

Defensa del fuero eclesiástico contra varios artículos del periódico titulado el Zapoteco. Oaxaca: Imprenta Municipal del ciudadano Antonio Valdés y Moya, 1833.

Diálogo entre Jose Toribio indigena y Don Clarion valiente vecino de esta ciudad. Oaxaca: Imprenta a Cargo del C. Juan Oledo, 1832.

Domínguez, Juan María. *Caton christiano de la santa escuela de Christo Nuestro Seño. Lo escribe en la de Teanquiztengo el minimo discípulo Lic. D. Juan Maria Dominguez, Colegial de Oposicion en el Real y mas Antiguo Colegio de San Ildefonso*. Mexico City: Don Mariano de Zúñiga y Ontiveros, 1805.

Dos clérigos y un coyote pueden más que un batalón, ó sea Diálogo entre un Sensato y un Mayordomo Oajaqueño. Mexico City: Imprenta de Mariano Galván, 1826.

Enciso, Francisco S. de. *Oracion civica que el ciudadano Lic. Francisco Enciso pronuncio en la capital del Estado libre y soberano de Oaxaca el 16 de septiembre de 1846, aniversario de la gloriosa proclamacion de la Independencia en el ano de 1810*. Oaxaca: Impresa por Ignacio Rincón, 1846.

El Enemigo de los Despotas. *No queremos dictador ni en Oajaca un gran señor*. Mexico City: Imprenta de las Escalerillas, a cargo de Manuel Ximeno, 1828.

El Enemigo Irreconciliable de los Pícaros. *¿Si tendremos monarquía a pretesto de heregía?* Mexico City: Imprenta del Aguila, dirigida por José Ximeno, 1826.

Escriche, Joaquín. *Diccionario razonado de legislación civil, penal, comercial y forense*. Caracas: Imprenta de Valentín Espinal, 1840.

Esparza, Manuel, ed. *Morelos en Oaxaca. Documentos para la Historia de la Independencia*. Oaxaca: Archivo General del Estado de Oaxaca, 1986.

———. *Padrón de casas de la ciudad de Oaxaca, 1824*. Oaxaca: Centro Regional de Oaxaca: Instituto Nacional de Antropologia e Historia, 1981.

———. *Padrón general de los habitantes de la ciudad de Oaxaca, 1842*. Mexico City: Instituto Nacional de Antropología e Historia, 1981.

———. *Relaciones geográficas de Oaxaca 1777–1778*. Oaxaca: Centro de Investigaciones y Estudios Superiores en Antropología Social/Instituto Oaxaqueño de las Culturas, 1994.

Un Espectador Imparcial. *Elecciones parroquiales de Oajaca en los dias 15 y 16 del corriente*. Oaxaca: n.p., 1826.

Esposición que el Gobernador Constitucional del Estado hizo en cumplimiento del Artículo 83 de la Constitución Particular del mismo a la Sexta Legislatura en sus segundas sesiones ordinarias el mes de julio de 1835. Oaxaca: Impreso por Antonio Valdés y Moya, 1835.

Esposición que el Tercer Gobernador del Estado hizo en cumplimiento del Artículo 83 de la Constitución Particular del mismo a la 4a Legislatura Constitucional al abrir sus segundas sesiones ordinarias el 2 de julio de 1832. Oaxaca: Impreso por Antonio Valdés y Moya, 1832.

Esposición que el Vice-gobernador en Ejercicio del Supremo Poder Ejecutivo del Estado hizo en cumplimiento del Artículo 83 de la Constitución Particular del mismo a la 4a Legislatura Constitucional al abrir sus primeras sesiones ordinarias el 2 de julio de 1831. Oaxaca: Impreso por Antonio Valdés y Moya, 1831.

Esposición que en cumplimiento del articulo 83 de la Constitución del Estado hace el Gobernador del mismo al soberano Congreso al abrir sus sesiones el 2 de julio del año de 1848. Oaxaca: Impreso por Ignacio Rincón, 1848.

Esposición que en cumplimiento del articulo 83 de la Constitución del Estado hace el Gobernador del mismo al soberano Congreso al abrir sus sesiones el 2 de julio del año de 1849. Oaxaca: Impreso por Ignacio Rincón, 1849.

Esposición que en cumplimiento del articulo 83 de la Constitución del Estado hace el Gobernador del mismo al Noveno Congreso Constitucional al abrir el primer período de sus sesiones ordinarias el día 2 de julio del año de 1850. Oaxaca: Impreso por Ignacio Rincón, 1850.

Esposición que en cumplimiento del articulo 83 de la Constitución del Estado hace el Gobernador del mismo al Noveno Congreso Constitucional al abrir sus segundas sesiones ordinarias el día 2 de julio del año de 1851. Oaxaca: Impreso por Ignacio Rincón, 1851.

Esposición que el Gobernador del Estado hace en cumplimiento del articulo 83 de la Constitución al Soberano Congreso al abrir sus primeras sesiones ordinarias el día 2 de julio del año de 1852. Oaxaca: Impreso por Ignacio Rincón, 1852.

Exposición que el gobernador del obispado de Oaxaca, dirige al Supremo Gobierno, en defensa de los bienes eclesiásticos. Mexico: Imprenta de la testamentaria de Valdes, a cargo de Jose Maria Gallegos, 1834.

[Fernández de Lizardi, José Joaquín]. *La Revolución de Oajaca, o sean los efectos de la revolución que intentaron hacer en aquella provincia los deconocidos españoles, el día 9 del presente, en que se hizo la Jura de nuestro digno emperador. Carta particular. Oajaca dicembre 8 de 1822*. Puebla: La Liberal de Moreno Hermanos, 1822.

Gamboa y Aldego, José A. *Arenga cívica pronunciada el día 27 de septiembre de 1849 en la capital del Estado de Oaxaca por el profesor de medicina y cirugía C. José A. Gamboa y Aldego en memoria de la gloriosa consumación de la independencia de México en el año de 1821*. Oaxaca: Impreso por Ignacio Rincón, 1849.

Huesca, Irene, Manuel Esparza, and Luís Castañeda Guzmán, eds. *Cuestionario de Don Antonio Bergoza y Jordán, Obispo de Antequera a los señores curas de la diócesis*. Oaxaca: Archivo General del Estado de Oaxaca, 1984.

Iniciativas dirigidas al soberano congreso de la union, por la honorable legislatura tercera constitucional del Estado. Oaxaca: Imprenta del Gobierno, 1830.

Iturribarría, Manuel. *Arenga cívica pronunciada en el aniversario de la consumación de la independencia, el día 28 de septiembre de 1846, en la capital del estado de Oaxaca*. Oaxaca: Impreso por I. Rincón, 1846.

Juárez, Benito. "Apuntes para mis hijos." In *Archivos privados de D. Benito Juárez y D. Pedro Santacilia*. Vol. 1. Mexico City: Secretaría de Educación Pública, 1928.

———. *Discurso que el C. Benito Juárez pronunció el día 16 de septiembre de 1840, en el aniversario del glorioso grito de independencia*. Oaxaca: Impreso por Ignacio Rincon, 1840.

———. *Esposición que en cumplimiento del artículo 83 de la Constitución del Estado hace el Gobernador del mismo al Soberano Congreso al abrir sus sesiones el 2 de julio del año de 1848*. Oaxaca: Impreso por Ignacio Rincón, 1848.

Lista de los ciudadanos que por la clase de propiedad raiz, rústica, urbana y de agricultores tienen derecho de votar en las prócsimas elecciones, con arreglo al art. 28 de la ley de convocatoria espedidia en 27 de enero del corriente año. Oaxaca: Ignacio Rincon, 1846.

Manifiesto que los oaxaqueños dirigen a sus compatriotas de los Estados, por los acontecimientos de Matamoros. Puebla: Reimpreso en la Oficina del Patriota, 1827.

Márquez y Carrizosa, Vicente Fermin. *Oracion funebre que en memoria de las victimas sacrificadas por la independencia mexicana pronuncio en la Santa Iglesia Catedral de Oaxaca Vicente Marquez y Carrizosa el dia 17 de septiembre de 1845*. Oaxaca: Impreso por I. Rincón, 1845.

Memoria que el Gobernador del Estado de Oaxaca presentó en la apertura de las sesiones ordinarias del Segundo Congreso Constitucional del mismo, verificado el 2 de julio de 1827. Oaxaca: Imprenta del Gobierno, 1827.

Memoria que el Vice-gobernador en Ejercicio del Estado de Oaxaca presentó al Tercer Congreso Constitucional del mismo al abrir sus primeras sesiones ordinarias el 2 de Julio de 1829. Oaxaca: Imprenta del Gobierno, 1829.

Muchos Mexicanos. *Viva la Federación. Alcance al núm. 12 del Restaurador Mexicano*. Oaxaca: Reimpreso por José Rafael España, 1838.

Muerte del estado de Oaxaca. Mexico City: Imprenta de Galvan a cargo de Mariano Arevalo, 1829.

Muhlenpfordt, Eduardo. *Ensayo de una descripción fiel de la República de Méjico, con especial referencia a su geografía, etnografía y estadística, Estado de Oaxaca*. Mexico City: CODEX Editores, 1993.

El Novel. *Recuerdos de gratitud al inmortal Iturbide*. Oaxaca: Reimpreso in la Imprenta Liberal, a cargo del ciudadano José Felipe Matos, 1830.

Oaxaca (Mexico). Congreso. *Iniciativa hecha al Congreso de la Union por la Legislatura del estado libre de Oaxaca*. Oaxaca: Impr. del Gobierno, 1827.

Oaxaca (Mexico). Gobernador (Ramírez de Aguilar). *Contestaciones habidas entre el gobernador del estado de Oaxaca, y el de la mitra del mismo, sobre la ley de 17 de diciembre ultimo, y decreto de 22 de abril proximo pasado, y representacion de dicho gobernador del obispado, para que las camaras deroguen las citadas leyes*. Mexico City: Imprenta de la testamentaria del finado Valdes, 1834.

Oaxaca, Mexico (State). *Asamblea departamental. Iniciativa que la Asamblea departamental de Oaxaca elevo en 19 de febrero de 1845 al soberano Congreso nacional sobre reformas de las bases organicas de la republica*. Oaxaca: Impreso por I. Rincón, 1845.

Un Oaxaqueño. *La calumnia confundida o sea Carta escrita al editor del Semanario político y literario, por un Oaxaquño, sobre elección de Diputados en Oajaca a 10 de Febrero de 1822*. Mexico City: Imprenta de D. Mariano Ontiveros, 1822.

Omaña y Sotomayor, Gregorio José de. *Carta pastoral instructiva y exhortatoria sobre el origen, necesidad y justicia de la presente guerra, que con el fin de excitar y alentar al clero de su diócesi á las oraciones y subsidios que pide S. M. le dirigió el ilustrisimo señor doctor don Gregorio Joseph de Omaña y Sotomayor, obispo de Antequera, publicándola en forma de edicto en la santa Iglesia Catedral de Oaxaca el dia domingo veinte y tres de junio de 1793*. Mexico City: F. De Zúñiga y Ontiveros, 1793.

Ordoño, Ignacio María. *Acusación al público contra el Supremo Gobierno*. Mexico City: Imprenta del Correo por C. C. Sebring, 1828.

———. *Manifiesto al público imparcial*. Oaxaca: Imprenta Liberal a Cargo de Nicolás Idiáquez, 1826.

———. *Vindicación del Padre Cortés*. Oaxaca: Imprenta Liberal a Cargo de Nicolás Idiáquez, 1826.

Ortiz de Zarate, Francisco. *El general de Brigada graduado Francisco Ortiz de Zarate, vice-gobernador en ejercicio del poder ejecutivo del Estado de Oaxaca, a sus habitantes*. Oaxaca: Impreso por Ignacio Rincon, 1847.

Padilla Sierra, Antonio, ed. *Constituciones y leyes fundamentales de España (1808–1947)*. Granada: Universidad de Granada, 1954.

Pasos, Manuel M. *Discurso prononuciado en la ciudad de Oaxaca el día 4 de cctubre de 1849, aniversario de la promulgación de la Constitución Federal*. Oaxaca: Impreso por Ignacio Rincón, 1849.

Los patriotas oaxaqueños. *Venganza piden los buenos sobre los viles serenos*. Oaxaca: Impreso por José Rafael España, 1838.

Un principista. *Muerte del Estado de Oaxaca, decretada por el ciudadano Miguel Ignacio Iturribarria vice gobernador interino de este estado, a sus habitantes hago saber.* Mexico City: Imprenta de Galvan, 1829.

Protestas de los Illmos. señores Obispos de Durango y Oaxaca. Guadalajara: Reimpresa en la Oficina de Dionisio Rodríguez, 1847.

Quiñones, Juan José. *Discurso que pronunció el ciudadano Dr. Juan José Quiñones, fiscal de la Escma. Corte de Justicia, en la capital dl estado de Oajaca el 16 de septiembre de 1828, aniversario del Grito de Dolores, por encargo de la Junta Patriotica.* Oaxaca: Imprenta del Superior Gobierno, dirigida por Antonio Valdés y Moya, 1828.

Quintanar, Luís. *El Comandante General del Departamento de Oaxaca a las tropas de la guarnicion.* Oaxaca: Impreso por el ciudadano Antonio Valdes y Moya, 1836.

Real ordenanza para el establecimiento e instrucción de intendentes de ejercito y provincia en el Reino de la Nueva Espana. Mexico City: Universidad Nacional Autonoma de Mexico, Instituto de Investigaciones Historicas, 1984.

Rincón Ríos, Francisco. *Arenga cívica que el 16 de septiembre de 1845, aniversario de la gloriosa proclamación de la independencia, pronunció en la ciudad de Oaxaca el ciudadano Francisco Rincón.* Oaxaca: Impresa por Ignacio Rincón, 1845.

Si en Oaxaca hay azeiteros aqui sobran vinateros: Por el que no es aspirante. Mexico City: Alejandro Valdés, 1828.

Spores, Ronald, Irene Huesca, and Manuel Esparza, eds. *Benito Juárez Gobernador de Oaxaca: Documentos de su mandato y servicio público.* Oaxaca: Archivo General del Estado de Oaxaca, 1987.

T. T. C. *Inconvenientes de una colonización indiscreta, o sea impugnación al establecimiento de la libertad de cultos en la República Mexicana.* Oaxaca: Impreso por Ignacio Rincón, 1848.

Unos Mexicanos. *¿El General Bustamante, es traidor a la nación?* Oaxaxa: Reimpreso por José Cresencio Valverde, 1839.

Vargas, M. M. *Catecismo de República o Elementos del gobierno republicano popular federal de la nación mexicana.* Mexico City: Imprenta y Librería a Cargo de Martin Rivera, 1827.

Vasconcelos, Ignacio Mariano. *Sermon que en la solemne función de accion de gracias que hicieron los curas del Obispado de Oaxaca en la santa Iglesia Catedral de aquella ciudad, el dia 6 de febrero de 1815, por la libertad del señor Don Fernando VII Rey Católico de ambas Españas, predicó el Señor Licenciado Don Ignacio Mariano Vasconcelos, dignidad de Chantre de la misma Santa Iglesia, dedicado al Rey Nuestro Señor por el Obispo de Oaxaca.* Mexico City: Impreso en la Oficina de la Calle De Santo Domingo, y esquina de Tacuba, 1816.

de Velasco, Francisco Lorenzo. *Francisco Lorenzo de Velasco Mariscal de Campo de los Exercitos Nacionales por Nombramiento del serenismo Sr. José María Morelos.* Oaxaca: n.p., 1814.

El Vigía. *Federación.* Oaxaca: Reimpreso por José R. España, 1838.

Villavicencio, Pablo (El Payo del Rosario). *Ya tenemos in Oaxaca parte de la Santa Liga*. N.p.: n.p., 1826. Reproduced in James C. McKegney, *The Political Pamphlets of Pablo Villavicencio "El Payo del Rosario"*. Vol. 2. (Amsterdam: Rodopi N.V., 1975), 598–607.

Y. M. O. *Invitacion que hace un oaqueño a su suelo patrio*. Oaxaca: n.p., 1823.

Zarco, Francisco. *Historia del Congreso Extraordinario Constituyente (1856–7)*. Mexico City: El Colegio de México, 1956.

Newspapers

La Aurora de la Libertad
La Bocina de la Justica
El Broquel de las costumbres
Cartas al Pueblo
El Centinela
El Cocura
El Cometa
Correo Americano del Sur
Correo Extraordinario del Sur
La Crónica
El Dia
La Esperanza
El Espíritu de la Independencia
El Guajalote Periodista
El Imparcial
La Jornada
La Muralla
Oaxaqueño Constitucional
Oaxaqueño Federalista
El Ocaso de las Revoluciones
El Pasatiempo
El Payaso de los Periodistas
La Prensa
El Regenerador
El Siglo XIX
Sociedad de Amigos del pais
El Triunfo de la Libertad
La Union Nacional
El Vigilante
El Voz de la Patria
El Zapoteco

Secondary Sources

Aguirre Beltrán, Gonzalo. *Formas de gobierno indígena*. Mexico: Imprenta Universitaria, 1953.

Alonso, Ana María. *Thread of Blood: Colonialism, Revolution, and Gender on Mexico's Northern Frontier*. Tucson: University of Arizona Press, 1995.

Altamirano Ramírez, Hugo. *La Ciudad de Oaxaca que conoció Morelos*. Oaxaca. n.p., 1992.

Anna, Timothy. *The Fall of the Royal Government in Mexico City*. Lincoln: University of Nebraska Press, 1978.

———. *Forging Mexico 1821–1835*. Lincoln: University of Nebraska Press, 1998.

———. "Inventing Mexico: Provincehood and Nationhood after Independence." *Bulletin of Latin American Studies* 15, no. 1 (1996): 7–17.

———. *The Mexican Empire of Iturbide*. Lincoln: University of Nebraska Press, 1990.

———. "Spain and the Breakdown of the Imperial Ethos: The Problem of Equality." *Hispanic American Historical Review* 62 (1982): 254–72.

Annino, Antonio. "The Ballot, Land, and Sovereignty: Cádiz and the Origins of Mexican Local Government, 1812–1820." In *Elections before Democracy: The History of Elections in Europe and Latin America*, edited by Eduardo Posada-Carbó. New York: St. Martin's Press, 1996.

———. "Cádiz y la revolución territorial de los pueblos mexicanos, 1812–1821." In *Historia de las elecciones en Iberoamérica, siglo xix*. Buenos Aires: Fondo de Cultura Económica, 1995.

———. "Ciudadanía 'versus' gobernabilidad republicana en México: Los orígenes de un dilema." In *Ciudadanía política y formación de las naciones: Perspectivas históricas de América Latina*, edited by Hilda Sabato. Mexico City: El Colegio de México/Fideicomiso Historia de las Américas/Fondo de Cultura Económica, 1999.

———. Introduction to *Historia de las elecciones en Iberoamérica, siglo xix*. Buenos Aires: Fondo de Cultura Económica, 1995.

———. "El Jano bifronte mexicano: Una aproximación tentativa." In *El liberalismo en México*, edited by Antonio Annino and Raymond Buve. Hamburg: Lit, 1993.

———. "Nuevas perspectivas para una vieja pregunta." In *El primer liberalismo mexicano*. Mexico City: Museo Nacional de la Historia, 1995.

———. "El pacto y la norma: Los orígenes de la legalidad oligárquica en México." *Historias* 5 (1984): 3–31.

———. "Prácticas criollas y liberalismo en la crisis del espacio urbano colonial: El 29 de noviembre de 1812 en la ciudad de México." *Secuencia* 24 (1992): 121–58.

Archer, Christon. *The Army in Bourbon Mexico, 1760–1810*. Albuquerque: University of New Mexico Press, 1977.

———. "The Bite of the Hydra: The Rebellion of Cura Miguel Hidalgo, 1810–

1811." In *Patterns of Contention in Mexican History*, edited by Jaime Rodríguez. Wilmington, Del.: Scholarly Resources, 1992.

Arellanes Meixuero, Anselmo. "Un anónimo y su circunstancia." *Acervos* 1 (1996): 14–17.

Arriaga, David. "El tequio." *México Indígena* 6 (1990): 32–36.

Arrom, Siliva. *The Women of Mexico City, 1790–1857*. Stanford: Stanford University Press, 1985.

Avila, Alfredo. *En nombre de la nación. La formación del gobierno representativo en México (1808–1824)*. Mexico City: Tauras/Centro de Investigación y Docencia Económica, 2002.

Aymes, Jean-René. "La 'Guerra Gran' como prefiguración de la 'Guerra del Francés' (1808–1814)." In *España y la Revolución Francesa*. Barcelona: Editorial Crítica, 1989.

Bailón Corres, Moisés. "Elecciones locales en Oaxaca en 1980." *Nueva Antropología* 7, no. 25 (1984): 67–98.

——. *Pueblos indios, élites y territorio: Sistemas de dominio regional en el sur de México: Una historia política de Oaxaca*. Mexico City: El Colegio de México, 1999.

Baker, Keith. Introduction to *The Political Culture of the Old Regime*. Vol. 1 of *The French Revolution and the Creation of Modern Political Culture*. New York: Pergamon Press, 1987.

Baskes, Jeremy. "Coerced or Voluntary?: The 'Repartimiento' and Market Participation of Peasants in Late Colonial Oaxaca." *Journal of Latin American Studies* 28, no. 1 (1996): 1–28.

Bazant, Jan. *A Concise History of Mexico*. New York: Cambridge University Press, 1977.

Bechtloff, Dagmar. *Las cofradías en Michoacán durante la época colonial*. Toluca: El Colegio Mexiquense/El Colegio de Michoacán, 1996.

Bellingeri, Marco. "Las ambigüedades del voto en Yucatán. Representación y gobierno en una formación interétnica 1812–1829." In *Historia de las elecciones en Iberoamérica, siglo XIX*, edited by Antonio Annino. Buenos Aires: Fondo de Cultura Económica, 1995.

——. "De una constitución a otra: Conflicos de jurisdicciones y dispersión de poderes en Yucatán (1789–1831)." In *El liberalismo en México*, edited by Antonio Annino and Raymond Buve. Hamburg: Lit, 1993.

——. "El tributo de los indios y el estado de los criollos: las obvenciones eclesásticas en Yucatan en el sigo XIX." In *Sociedad, estructura agraria y estado en Yucatán*, edited by Othón Baños Ramirez. Mérida: Universidad de Yucatán, 1990.

Benson, Nettie Lee. *The Provincial Deputation in Mexico*. Austin: University of Texas Press, 1992.

——, ed. *Mexico and the Spanish Cortes, 1810–1822*. Austin: University of Texas Press, 1966.

Berry, Charles. *The Reform in Oaxaca: A Microhistory of the Central District, 1856–1876.* Lincoln: University of Nebraska Press, 1983.

Bonilla, Heraclio. "The Indian Peasantry and 'Peru' during the War with Chile." In *Resistance, Rebellion and Consciousness in the Andean Peasant World, 18th to 20th Centuries,* edited by Steve J. Stern. Madison: University of Wisconsin Press, 1987.

Brading, David. *Miners and Merchants in Bourbon Mexico, 1763–1810.* Cambridge: Cambridge University Press, 1971.

Bushnell, David, and Neill Macaulay. *The Emergence of Latin America in the Nineteenth Century.* New York: Oxford University Press, 1988.

Bustamante, Carlos María de. *Cuadro histórico de la revolución mexicana de 1810.* Mexico City: Instituto Nacional de Estudios Históricos de la Revolución Mexicana, 1985.

Canterla y Martin de Tovar, Francisco. *La iglesia de Oaxaca en el siglo xviii.* Seville: Escuela de Estudios Hispano-Americanos de Sevilla, 1982.

Caplan, Karen. "The Legal Revolution in Town Politics: Oaxaca and Yucatán, 1812–1825." *Hispanic American Historical Review* 83, no. 2 (2003): 255–93.

Carmagnani, Marcello. *El regreso de los dioses: La reconstitución de la identidad étnica en Oaxaca, siglos XVII y XVIII.* Mexico City: Fondo de Cultura Económica, 1988.

Castañeda Guzmán, Luis. *Templo de los Príncipes y Monasterio de Nuestra Señora de los Angeles.* Oaxaca: Instituto Oaxaqueño de las Culturas, 1993.

Castro Gutiérrez, Felipe. *Nueva ley y nuevo rey: Reformas borbónicas y rebelión popular en Nueva España.* Zamora: El Colegio de Michoacán / Universidad Nacional Autónoma de México, 1996.

Chambers, Sarah. *From Subjects to Citizens: Honor, Gender and Politics in Arequipa, Peru 1780–1854.* University Park: Penn State University Press, 1999.

Chance, John. *Conquest of the Sierra: Spaniards and Indians in Colonial Oaxaca.* Norman: University of Oklahoma Press, 1989.

———. *Race and Class in Colonial Oaxaca.* Stanford: Stanford University Press, 1978.

Chance, John, and William B. Taylor. "Cofradías and Cargos: An Historical Perspective on the Mesoamerican Civil-Religious Hierarchy." *American Ethnologist* 12 (1985): 1–26.

Chávez Orosco, Luis. *Las instituciones democráticas de los indígenas mexicanos en la época colonial.* Mexico City: Ins'tituto Indigenista Interamericano, 1943.

Coatsworth, John. "Patterns of Rural Rebellion in Latin America: Mexico in Comparative Perspective." In *Riot, Rebellion, and Revolution: Rural Social Conflict in Mexico,* edited by Friedrich Katz. Princeton: Princeton University Press, 1988.

Connaughton, Brian. "Agape en disputa: Fiesta cívica, cultura polítca regional y la frágil urdimbre nacional antes del Plan de Ayutla." *Historia Mexicana* 45, no. 2 (1995): 281–316.

———. "Conjuring the Body Politic from the 'Corpus Mysticum': The Post-independent Pursuit of Public Opinion in Mexico, 1821–1854." *The Americas* 55, no. 3 (1999): 459–79.

———. *Ideología y sociedad en Guadalajara (1788–1853)*. Mexico City: Universidad Nacional Autónoma de México/Consejo Nacional para la Cultura y las Artes, 1992.

———. "El ocaso del proyecto de 'Nación Católica': Patronato virtual, préstamos, y presiones regionales, 1821–1856." In *Construcción de la legitimidad política en México en el siglo XIX*, edited by Brian Connaughton, Carlos Illades, and Sonia Pérez Toledo. Mexico City: El Colegio de Michoacán/Universidad Autónoma Metropolitana/Universidad Nacional Autónoma de México/El Colegio de México, 1999.

———. "El sermón, la folletería y la ampliación del mundo editorial mexicano, 1810–1854." *Secuencia* 39 (1997): 55–60.

———. "La sacralización de lo cívico: La imagen religiosa en el discurso cívico-patriótico del México independiente. Puebla (1827–1853)." In *Estado, Iglesia y sociedad en Mexico, siglo XIX*, edited by Alvaro Matute, Evelia Trejo, and Brian Connaughton. Mexico City: Universidad Nacional Autónoma de México/Miguel Angel Porrua, 1995.

Connaughton, Brian, Carlos Illades, and Sonia Pérez Toledo. Introduction to *Construcción de la legitimidad política en México en el siglo XIX*. Mexico City: El Colegio de Michoacán/Universidad Autónoma Metropolitana/Universidad Nacional Autónoma de México/El Colegio de México, 1999.

Cope, R. Douglas. *The Limits of Racial Domination: Plebeian Society in Colonial Mexico City, 1660–1720*. Madison: University of Wisconsin Press, 1994.

Cordero Avendaño de Duran, Carmen. *La vara del mando: Costumbre jurídica en la transmisión de poderes*. Oaxaca: Ayuntamiento Constitucional, 1997.

Costeloe, Michael. *The Central Republic in Mexico, 1835–1846*. New York: Cambridge University Press, 1993.

Curcio-Nagy, Linda. "Giants and Gypsies: Corpus Christi in Colonial Mexico City." In *Rituals of Rule, Rituals of Resistance: Public Celebrations and Popular Culture in Mexico*, edited by William Beezley, Cheryl English Martin, and William French. Wilmington, Del.: Scholarly Resources, 1994.

Cutter, Charles. *The Legal Culture of Northern New Spain, 1700–1810*. Albuquerque: University of New Mexico Press, 1995.

Deans-Smith, Susan. *Bureaucrats, Planters, and Workers: The Making of the Tobacco Monopoly in Bourbon Mexico*. Austin: University of Texas Press, 1992.

———. "The Working Poor and the Eighteenth-Century Colonial State: Gender, Public Order, and Work Discipline." In *Rituals of Rule, Rituals of Resistance: Public Celebrations and Popular Culture in Mexico*, edited by William Beezley, Cheryl English Martin, and William French. Wilmington, Del.: Scholarly Resources, 1994.

Demélas, Marie-Danielle. *Jerusalén y Babilonia. Religión y política en el Ecuador. 1780–1880*. Quito, Ecuador: Corporación Editora Nacional/Instituto Francés de Estudios Andinos, 1988.

——. "Modalidades y significación de las elecciones generales en los pueblos andinos, 1813–1814." In *Historia de las elecciones en Iberoamérica, siglo XIX*, edited by Antonio Annino. Buenos Aires: Fondo de Cultura Económica, 1995.

Demélas, Marie-Danielle, and François-Xavier Guerra. "The Hispanic Revolutions: The Adoption of Modern Forms of Representation in Spain and America (1808–1810)." In *Elections before Democracy: The History of Elections in Europe and Latin America*, edited by Eduardo Posada-Carbó. New York: St. Martin's Press, 1996.

Di Tella, Torcuato. "Ciclos políticos en la primera mitad del siglo XIX." In *La fundación del estado mexicano*, edited by Josefina Zoraida Vázquez. Mexico City: Nueva Imagen, 1994.

——. *National Popular Politics in Early Independent México, 1820–1847*. Albuquerque: University of New Mexico Press, 1996.

Díaz, Arlene. *Female Citizens, Patriarchs, and the Law in Venezuela, 1786–1904*. Lincoln: University of Nebraska Press, 2004.

Ducey, Michael. "Hijos del pueblo y ciudadanos: Identidades políticas entre los rebeldes indios del siglo XIX." In *Construcción de la legitimidad política en México en el siglo XIX*, edited by Brian Connaughton, Carlos Illades, and Sonia Pérez Toledo. Mexico City: El Colegio de Michoacán/Universidad Autónoma Metropolitana/Universidad Nacional Autónoma de México/El Colegio de México, 1999.

——. "Indian Communities and Ayuntamientos in the Mexican Huasteca: Sujeto Revolts, Pronunciamientos and Caste War." *The Americas* 57, no. 4 (2001): 525–50.

——. "Village, Nation, and Constitution: Insurgent Politics in Papantla, Veracruz, 1810–21." *Hispanic American Historical Review* 79, no. 3 (1999): 463–93.

Escalante Gonzalbo, Fernando. *Ciudadanos imaginarios*. Mexico City: El Colegio de México, 1992.

Escobar Ohmstede, Antonio. "Los ayuntamientos y los pueblos de indios en la Sierra Huasteca: Conflictos entre nuevos y viejos actores, 1812–1840." In *La reindianización de América, siglo XIX*, edited by Leticia Reina. Mexico City: Siglo XXI/Centro de Investigación y Estudios Superiores de Antropología Social, 1997.

——. "Los condueñazgos indígenas en las Huastecas Hidalguense y Veracruzana: ¿Defensa del espacio comunal?" In *Indio, nación y comunidad en el México del siglo XIX*. Mexico City: Centro de Estudios Mexicanos y Centroamericanos/Centro de Investigaciones y Estudios Superiores en Antropología Social, 1993.

——. *De la costa de la sierra: Las huastecas, 1750–1900*. Mexico City: Centro de Investigaciones y Estudios Superiores en Antropología Social, 1998.

——. "El discurso de la 'inteligencia' india en los primeros años posindependientes." In *Construcción de la legitimidad política en México en el siglo XIX*, edited by Brian Connaughton, Carlos Illades, and Sonia Pérez Toledo. Mexico City: El

Colegio de Michoacán/Universidad Autónoma Metropolitana/Universidad Nacional Autónoma de México/El Colegio de México, 1999.

———. "El federalismo en las Huastecas durante la primera mitad del siglo XIX." In *Historia y nación: Actas del Congreso en homenaje a Josefina Zoraida Vázquez*. Vol. 2, *Política y diplomacia en el siglo XIX mexicano*, edited by Luis Jáuregui and José Antonio Serano Ortega. Mexico City: El Colegio de México, 1998.

———. "Del gobierno indígena al ayuntamiento constitucional en las huastecas hidalguense y veracruzana, 1780–1853." *Mexican Studies/Estudios Mexicanos* 12, no. 1 (1996): 1–15.

Esparza, Manuel. "El difícil camino de sentirse nación: Oaxaca y la guerra contra Estados Unidos." In *México en guerra (1846–1848)*, edited by Laura Herrera Serna. Mexico City: Consejo Nacional para la Cultura y las Artes, 1997.

Espinosa, Carlos R. "The Portrait of the Inca: Aesthetics and Politics in the Audiencia of Quito, 1630–1750." Ph.D. diss., University of Chicago, 1990.

Ferrer Muñoz, Manuel, and María Bono López. *Pueblos indígenas y estado nacional en México en el siglo XIX*. Mexico City: Universidad Nacional Autónoma de México, 1998.

Florescano, Enrique. *Etnia, estado y nación: Ensayo sobre las identidades colectivas en México*. Mexico City: Nuevo Siglo Aguilar, 1997.

Fortson, J. R. *Los gobernantes de Oaxaca. Historia (1823–1985)*. Mexico City: J. R. Fortson Editores, 1985.

Fowler, Will. *Mexico in the Age of Proposals, 1821–1853*. Westport, Conn.: Greenwood Press, 1998.

———. "Valentín Gómez Farías: Perceptions of Radicalism in Independent Mexico, 1821–1847." *Bulletin of Latin American Studies* 15, no. 1 (1996): 39–62.

de la Fuente, Julio. "Ocho años de experiencia en el medio rural." *El Maestro Rural* 12 (1939): 10–12.

———. *Yalalag. Una villa zapoteca serrana*. Mexico City: Museo Nacional de Antropología, 1949.

Furet, François. *Interpreting the French Revolution*. New York: Cambridge University Press, 1981.

Garner, Paul. "Federalism and Caudillismo in the Mexican Revolution: The Genesis of the Oaxacan Sovereignty Movement (1915–20)." *Journal of Latin American Studies* 27 (1985): 111–33.

Gómez Alvarez, Cristina, and Francisco Téllez Guerrero. "Los libros de Antonio Bergosa y Jordan, Obispo de Antequera de Oaxaca, 1802." *Acervos* 2 (1996): 8–12.

González Bernaldo, Pilar. "Pedagogía societaria y aprendizaje de la Nación en el Río de la Plata." In *De los Imperios a las naciones: Iberoamérica*, edited by Antonio Annino, Luís Castro Leiva, and François-Xavier Guerra. Zaragoza, Spain: Ibercaja, 1994.

———. "Social Imagery and Its Political Implications in a Rural Conflict: The Uprising of 1828–29." In *Revolution and Restoration: The Rearrangement of Power in*

Argentina, 1776–1860, edited by Mark Szuchman and Jonathan Brown. Lincoln: University of Nebraska Press, 1994.

Graham, Richard. *Patronage and Politics in Nineteenth-Century Brazil*. Stanford: Stanford University Press, 1990.

Gruzinski, Serge. "La 'segunda aculteracíon': El estado ilustrado y la religiosidad indígena de la Nueva España (1775–1800)." *Estudios de Historia Novohispana* 8 (1985): 175–201.

Guardino, Peter. "Identity and Nationalism in Mexico: Guerrero, 1780–1840." *Journal of Historical Sociology* 7, no. 3 (1994): 314–42.

———. "'Me ha cabido en la fatalidad': Gobierno indígena y gobierno republicano en los pueblos indígenas: Oaxaca, 1750–1850." *Desacatos* 5 (2000): 119–30.

———. *Peasants, Politics, and the Formation of Mexico's National State: Guerrero, 1800–1857*. Stanford: Stanford University Press, 1996.

———. "'Toda libertad para emitir sus votos': Plebeyos, campesinos, y elecciones en Oaxaca, 1808–1850." *Cuadernos del Sur* 15 (2000): 87–114.

Guedea, Virginia. *En busca de un gobierno alterno: Los guadalupes de México*. Mexico City: Universidad Nacional Autónoma de México, 1992.

———. "Un nueva forma de organización política: la Sociedad Secreta de Jalapa, 1812." In *Un hombre entre Europa y América: Homenaje a Juan Antonio Ortega y Medina*, edited by Amaya Garritz. Mexico City: Universidad Nacional Autónoma de México, 1993.

———. "Las primeras elecciones populares en la ciudad de México: 1812–1813." *Mexican Studies/Estudios Mexicanos* 7 (1991): 1–28.

———. "Los procesos electorales insurgentes." *Estudios de historia novohispana* 11 (1991): 201–49.

Guerra, François-Xavier. "De la política antigua a la política moderna. La revolución de la soberanía." In *Los espacios públicos en Iberoamérica; Ambiguedades y problemas. Siglos XVIII–XIX*, edited by François-Xavier Guerra, Annick Lempiére et al. Mexico City: Centro Francés de Estudios Mexicanos y Centroamericanos/Fondo de Cultura Económica, 1998.

———. "La independencia de México y las revoluciones hispánicas." In *El liberalismo en México*, edited by Antonio Annino and Raymond Buve. Hamburg: Lit, 1993.

———. *México del Antiguo Régimen a la Revolución*. Mexico City: Fondo de Cultura Económica, 1988.

———. *Modernidad e independencias: Ensayos sobre las revoluciones hispánicas*. Mexico City: Fondo de Cultura Económica, 1993.

———. "El soberano y su reino: Reflexiones sobre la génesis del ciudadano en América Latina." In *Ciudadanía política y formación de las naciones: Perpectivas históricas de América Latina*, edited by Hilda Sabato. Mexico: El Colegio de México/Fidecomiso Historia de las Américas/Fondo de Cultura Económica, 1999.

———. "The Spanish-American Tradition of Representation, and its European Roots." *Journal of Latin American Studies* 26, no. 1 (1994): 1–35.

Guerra, François-Xavier, and Annick Lempiére. Introduction to *Los espacios públicos en Iberoamérica; Ambiguedades y problemas. Siglos XVIII–XIX*. Mexico City: Centro Francés de Estudios Mexicanos y Centroamericanos / Fondo de Cultura Económica, 1998.

Guerra, François-Xavier, and Mónica Quijada. *Imaginar la nación*. Munster, Germany: Lit, 1994.

Guha, Ranajit. *Elementary Forms of Peasant Insurgency in Colonial India*. Delhi: Oxford University Press, 1983.

Hamill, Hugh. "'¡Vencer o morir por la patria!' La invasión de España y algunas consecuencias para México, 1808–1810." In *Interpretaciones de la Independencia de México*, edited by Josefina Zoraida Vázquez. Mexico City: Nueva Imagen, 1997.

Hamnett, Brian. "Benito Juarez, Early Liberalism, and the Regional Politics of Oaxaca, 1828–1853." *Bulletin of Latin American Research* 10, no. 1 (1991): 3–21.

——. "Between Bourbon Reforms and Liberal Reforms: The Political Economy of a Mexican Province — Oaxaca, 1750–1850." In *The Political Economy of Spanish America in the Age of Revolution, 1750–1850*, edited by Kenneth J. Andrien and Lyman L. Johnson. Albuquerque: University of New Mexico Press, 1994.

——. "El estado de Oaxaca durante la Guerra contra los Estados Unidos: 1846–1848." In *México al tiempo de su guerra con Estados Unidos (1846–1848)*, edited by Josefina Zoraida Vázquez. Mexico City: Fondo de Cultura Económica / Colegio de México / Secretaría de Relaciones Exteriores, 1997.

——. *Juárez*. New York: Longman, 1994.

——. "Liberales y conservadores ante el mundo de los pueblos, 1840–1870." In *Los pueblos indios y el parteaguas de la independencia de México*, edited by Manuel Ferrero Muñoz. Mexico City: Universidad Nacional Autónoma de México, 1999.

——. "Oaxaca: Las principales familias y el federalismo de 1823." In *Lecturas Históricas del Estado de Oaxaca*. Vol. 3, *Siglo XIX*, edited by María de los Angles Romero Frizzi. Mexico City: Instituto Nacional de Antropología e Historia / Gobierno del Estado de Oaxaca, 1990.

——. *Politics and Trade in Southern Mexico, 1750–1821*. Cambridge: Cambridge University Press, 1971.

——. *Roots of Insurgency: Mexican Regions, 1750–1824*. Cambridge: Cambridge University Press, 1986.

Haskett, Robert. "Paper Shields: The Ideology of Coats of Arms in Colonial Mexican Titles." *Ethnohistory* 43, no. 1 (1996): 99–126.

Hensel, Silke. *Die Enstehung des Foderalismus in Mexiko: die politische Elite Oaxacas zwischen Stadt, Region und Staat, 1786–1835*. Stuttgart: Franz Steiner Verlag, 1997.

——. "Los orígenes del federalismo en México. Una perspectiva desde la provincia de Oaxaca de finales del siglo XVIII a la Primera República." *Ibero-Amerikansches Archiv* 25, no. 3/4 (1999): 215–37.

Hérnandez Chávez, Alicia. *Anenecuilco: Memoria y vida de un pueblo*. Mexico City: El

Colegio de México/Fideicomiso Historia de las Americas/Fondo de Cultura Económica, 1991.

——. *La tradición republicana del buen gobierno*. Mexico City: El Colegio de México/Fideiscomiso Historia de las Americas/Fondo de Cultura Económica, 1993.

Hunt, Lynn. *Politics, Culture, and Class in the French Revolution*. Berkeley: University of California Press, 1984.

Ibarra, Ana Carolina. *Clero y política en Oaxaca: Biografía del Doctor José de San Martín*. Oaxaca: Instituto Oaxaqueño de las Culturas/Universidad Nacional Autónoma de México/Fondo Estatal para la Cultura y las Artes, 1996.

Ibarra Bellon, Araceli. *El Comercio y el poder en México, 1821–1864*. Mexico City: Fondo de Cultura Económica/Universidad de Guadalajara, 1998.

Iturribarría, Jorge Fernando. *Historia de Oaxaca*. Oaxaca: Ediciones E. R. B., 1935.

Johnson, John J. *Political Change in Latin America: The Emergence of the Middle Sectors*. Stanford: Stanford University Press, 1958.

Johnson, Lyman, and Sonya Lipsett-Rivera, eds. *The Faces of Honor: Sex, Shame, and Violence in Colonial Latin America*. Albuquerque: University of New Mexico Press, 1998.

Joseph, Gilbert, and Daniel Nugent, eds. *Everyday Forms of State Formation: Revolution and the Negotiation of Rule in Modern Mexico*. Durham, N.C.: Duke University Press, 1994.

Kanter, Deborah. "Indian Education in Late Colonial Mexico: Policy and Practice." Master's Thesis, University of Virginia, 1987.

Kerber, Linda. *Women of the Republic: Intellect and Ideology in Revolutionary America*. Chapel Hill: University of North Carolina Press, 1980.

Kuroda, Etzuko. *Bajo el Zempoaltépetl: La sociedad mixe de las tierras altas y sus rituales*. Oaxaca: Centro de Investigaciones y Estudios Superiores en Antropología Social/Instituto Oaxaqueño de las Culturas, 1993.

Landavazo, Marco Antonio. *La máscara de Fernando VII: Discurso e imaginario monárquicos en una época de crisis, Nueva España, 1808–1822*. Mexico City: El Colegio de México/Universidad Michoacana de San Nicolás de Hidalgo/El Colegio de Michoacán, 2001.

Larraga, Maribel. "Indios, blancos y mulatos: 'Si todos somos Hermanos Y, todos bamos Fin ya no ay criollo ó, Gachupin, todos sean Americanos.'" *Colonial Latin American Historical Review* 5, no. 1 (1996): 47–73.

Larson, Brooke. *Cochabamba, 1550–1900: Colonialism and Agrarian Transformation in Bolivia*. Expanded ed. Durham, N.C.: Duke University Press, 1998.

Lavrín, Asunción. "World in Contrasts: Rural and Urban Confraternities in Mexico at the End of the Eighteenth Century." In *The Church and Society in Latin America*, edited by Jeffrey Cole. New Orleans: Tulane University, 1984.

Leal Curiel, Carole. *El discurso de la fidelidad. Construcción social del espacio como símbolo del poder regio (Venezuela, siglo XVIII)*. Caracas: Biblioteca Nacional de la Historia, 1990.

———. "Tertulia de dos ciudades. Modernismo tardío y formas de sociabilidad política en la provincia de Venezuela." In *Los espacios públicos en Iberoamérica; Ambiguedades y problemas. Siglos XVIII–XIX*, edited by François-Xavier Guerra and Annick Lempiére et al. Mexico City: Centro Francés de Estudios Mexicanos y Centroamericanos / Fondo de Cultura Económica, 1998.

Lemoine, Ernesto. *Morelos: su vida revolucionaria a través de sus escritos y otros testimonios de la época*. Mexico City: Universidad Nacional Autónoma de México, 1965.

Lempérière, Annick. "Reflexiones sobre la terminología del liberalismo." In *Construcción de la legitimidad política en México en el siglo XIX*, edited by Brian Connaughton, Carlos Illades, and Sonia Pérez Toledo. Mexico City: El Colegio de Michoacán / Universidad Autónoma Metropolitana / Universidad Nacional Autónoma de México / El Colegio de México, 1999.

———. "República y publicidad a finales del Antiguo Regimen." In *Los espacios públicos en Iberoamérica; Ambiguedades y problemas. Siglos XVIII–XIX*, edited François-Xavier Guerra and Annick Lempérière et al. Mexico City: Centro Francés de Estudios Mexicanos y Centroamericanos Fondo de Cultura Económica, 1998.

Liehr, Reinhard. *Ayuntamiento y oligarquía en Puebla, 1787–1810*. 2 vols. Mexico City: Secretaría de Educación Pública, 1976.

Lockhart, James. *The Nahuas After the Conquest: A Social and Cultural History of the Indians of Central Mexico, Sixteenth through Eighteenth Centuries*. Stanford: Stanford University Press, 1992.

Lombardo de Ruiz, Sonia. "La presencia del rey en la vida pública de la ciudad de México." In *Las ciudades y sus estructuras. Población, espacio y cultura en México, siglos XVIII y XIX*, edited by Sonia Pérez Toledo, René Elizade Salazar, and Luis Pérez Cruz. Mexico City: Universidad Autónoma Metropolitana / Universidad de Tlaxcala, 1999.

MacLachlan, Colin. *Spain's Empire in the New World*. Berkeley: University of California Press, 1988.

Mallon, Florencia. *Peasant and Nation: The Making of Postcolonial Mexico and Peru*. Berkeley: University of California Press, 1995.

———. "Peasants and State Formation in Nineteenth-Century Mexico: Morelos, 1848–1858." *Political Power and Social Theory* 7 (1988): 1–54.

Márquez, Lourdes, and Leticia Reina Aoyama. "La cólera en Oaxaca en el siglo XIX." *Cuadernos del Sur* 1 (1992): 71–98.

Martin, Cheryl English. *Governance and Society in Colonial Mexico: Chihuahua in the Eighteenth Century*. Stanford: Stanford University Press, 1996.

Martínez Gracida, Manuel. "Reseña histórica de algunas hechos de la Guerra de Independencia." Guadalajara, 1908. Manuscript.

Martínez Vasquez, Victor Raul. "La educación primaria and la formación de docentes en Oaxaca (1825–1869)." *Testimonios de Oaxaca* 3, no. 7 (1992): 16–25.

Mayer Celis, Leticia. *Entre el infierno de y realidad and el cielo de un imaginario:*

Estadística y comunidad científica en el México de la primera mitad del siglo XIX. Mexico City: El Colegio de Mexico, 1999.

McAlister, Lyle. "Social Structure and Social Change in New Spain." *Hispanic American Historical Review* 43, no. 3 (1963): 349–70.

McNamara, Patrick. "Sons of the Sierra: Memory, Patriarchy, and Rural Political Culture in Mexico, 1855–1911." Ph.D. Diss., University of Wisconsin, 1999.

Méndez, Cecilia. "Los campesinos, la independencia and la iniciacion de la Republica: el caso de los iquichanos realistas." In *Poder y violencia en los Andes*, edited by Henrique Urbano. Cusco, Peru: Centro Bartolomé de las Casas, 1991.

——. "Incas Sí, Indios No: Notes on Peruvian Creole Nationalism and its Contemporary Crisis." *Journal of Latin American Studies* 28, no. 1 (1996): 197–225.

——. "Pactos sin tributo. Caudillos y campesinos en el Perú postindependiente. El caso de Ayacucho." In *La reindianización de América, siglo XIX*, edited by Leticia Reina. Mexico City: Siglo XXI/Centro de Investigación y Estudios Superiores de Antropología Social, 1997.

Meyer, Jean. *Problemas campesinas y revueltas agrarias (1821–1910)*. Mexico City: Secretaría de Educación Pública, 1973.

Minguez, Victor. *Los reyes distantes: Imágenes del poder en el México virreinal*. Castello de la Plana: Universitat Jaume I/Diputacio de Castello, 1995.

Morgan, Edmund S. *Inventing the People: The Rise of Popular Sovereignty in England and America*. New York: Norton, 1988.

Murra, John. *Formaciones económicas y políticas del mundo andino*. Lima: Instituto de Estudios Peruanos, 1975.

Myers, Jorge. *Orden y virtud: el discurso republicano en el régimen rosista*. Buenos Aires: Universidad Nacional de Quilmes, 1995.

Nader, Laura. *Harmony Ideology: Justice and Control in a Zapotec Mountain Village*. Stanford: Stanford University Press, 1990.

O'Phelan Godoy, Scarlett. *Un siglo de rebeliones anticoloniales: Peru y Bolivia 1700–1783*. Cusco, Peru: Centro de Estudios Rurales Andinos Bartolomé de las Casas, 1988.

Ortiz Escamilla, Juan. *Guerra y gobierno. Los pueblos y la independencia de México*. Mexico: Instituto Mora/El Colegio de México/Universidad Internacional de Andalucia/Universidad de Sevilla, 1997.

Pardo, Ramón. "Breve estudio sobre la evolución del Instituto de Ciencias y Artes de Oaxaca." In *El Instituto de Ciencias y Artes del Estado: Los años de formación*. Oaxaca: Universidad Autónoma "Benito Juárez" de Oaxaca, Instituto de Investigaciones en Humanidades, 1990.

Parnell, Philip. *Escalating Disputes: Social Participation and Change in the Oaxacan Highlands*. Tucson: University of Arizona Press, 1988.

Pastor, Rodolfo. *Campesinos y reformas: La Mixteca, 1700–1856*. Mexico City: El Colegio de México, 1987.

Peloso, Vincent. "Liberals, Electoral Reform, and the Popular Vote in Mid-Nineteenth-Century Peru." In *Liberals, Politics, and Power: State Formation in*

Nineteenth-Century Latin America, edited by Vincent Peloso and Barbara Tennenbaum. Athens: University of Georgia Press, 1996.

Peralta Ruíz, Víctor. "Elecciones, constitucionalismo y revolución en el Cusco, 1809–1815." In *Partidos políticos y elecciones en América Latina y la Península Ibérica, 1830–1930*, vol. 1, edited by Carlos Malamud. Madrid: Instituto Ortega y Gasset, 1995.

——. *En pos del tributo: burocracia estatal, elite regional, y comunidades indígenas en el Cusco rural, 1826–1854*. Cusco: Centro de Estudios Regionales Andinos Bartolomé de las Casas, 1991.

Pérez, Eutimio. *Recuerdos históricos del episcopado oaxaqueño*. Oaxaca: Imp. de San German, 1888.

Pérez García, Rosendo. *La Sierra Júarez*. Mexico City: Gráfica Cerventina, 1956.

Pescador, Juan Javier. *De bautizados a fieles difuntos: Familia y mentalidades en una parroquia urbana: Santa Catarina de México, 1568–1820*. Mexico City: El Colegio de México, 1992.

Phelan, John Leddy. *The People and the King: The Comunero Revolution in Colombia, 1781*. Madison: University of Wisconsin Press, 1978.

Rangel Rojas, Guillermo. *General Antonio de León: Consumador de la Independencia de Oaxaca y Benemérito del Estado de Oaxaca*. Oaxaca: Ayuntamiento Constitucional, 1997.

Rappaport, Joanne. *Cumbe Reborn: An Andean Ethnography of History*. Chicago: University of Chicago Press, 1994.

——. *The Politics of Memory: Native Historical Interpretation in the Colombian Andes*. Durham, N.C.: Duke University Press, 1998.

Rees-Jones, Ricardo. *El despotismo ilustrado y los intendentes de la Nueva España*. Mexico City: Universidad Nacional Autónoma de México, 1979.

Reina, Leticia. *Las rebeliones campesinas en México (1819–1906)*. Mexico: Siglo XXI, 1980.

Rodríguez O., Jaime. "From Royal Subject to Republican Citizen: The Role of the Autonomists in the Independence of Mexico." In *The Independence of Mexico and the Origins of the New Nation*. Los Angeles: University of California at Los Angeles Latin American Center, 1989.

——. "La independencia de la América Española: Una reinterpretación." *Historia Mexicana* 42, no. 3 (1993): 571–620.

——. *The Independence of Spanish America*. New York: Cambridge University Press, 1998.

——. Introduction to *The Independence of Mexico and the Origins of the New Nation*. Los Angeles: University of California at Los Angeles Latin American Center, 1989.

——. "'Ningun pueblo es superior a otro': Oaxaca y el federalismo mexicano." Paper presented at the Seminario Internacional sobre Construcción de la legitimidad política en México, siglo XIX: Instituciones, cultura política y poder, Universidad Autónoma Metropolitana-Iztapalapa, Mexico City, 19 May 2000.

———. "Two Revolutions: France 1789 and Mexico 1810." *The Americas* 47, no. 2 (1990) 161–76.

Romero Frizzi, María de los Angeles. *El sol y la cruz: Los pueblos indios de Oaxaca colonial*. Mexico: Centro de Investigación y Estudios Superiores en Antropología Social/Instituto Nacional Indigenista, 1996.

Roseberry, William. "Hegemony and the Language of Contention." In *Everyday Forms of State Formation: Revolution and the Negotiation of Rule in Modern Mexico*, edited by Gilbert Joseph and Daniel Nugent. Durham, N.C.: Duke University Press, 1994.

Rugeley, Terry. *Yucatán's Maya Peasantry and the Origins of the Caste War*. Austin: University of Texas Press, 1996.

Ruiz Cervantes, Francisco José. "La Semana Santa en la Oaxaca de 1866, Crónica Periodista." *Acervos* 1 (1996): 18–20.

Ruiz Cervantes, Francisco José, and Carlos Sánchez Silva, eds. *Pensamiento político y social oaxaqueño*. Oaxaca: Instituto Estatal de Educación Pública de Oaxaca/Proyecto Editorial Huaxyácac, 1998.

Sabato, Hilda. Introduction to *Ciudadanía política y formación de las naciones: Perspectivas históricas de América Latina*. Mexico City: El Colegio de México/Fideicomiso Historia de las Américas/Fondo de Cultura Económica, 1999.

Sánchez Silva, Carlos. "La imprenta en Oaxaca, 1821–1876: De la especulación a la certidumbre." In *La historia de la imprenta en Oaxaca*. Oaxaca: Biblioteca Francisco Burgoa/Universidad Autónoma Benito Juárez de Oaxaca, 1999.

———. *Indios, comerciantes y burocracía en la Oaxaca poscolonial, 1786–1860*. Oaxaca: Instituto Oaxaqueño de las Culturas/Fondo Estatal para la Cultura y las Artes/Universidad Autónoma Benito Juárez de Oaxaca, 1998.

———. "Patrimonialismo y poder político en Oaxaca, 1786–1860." *Cuadernos del Sur* 3, no. 10 (1995): 57–89.

———, ed. *Las lecturas de Juárez*. Oaxaca: Amigos de los Archivos y Bibliotecas de Oaxaca, 1998.

Scardaville, Michael. "(Hapsburg) Law and (Bourbon) Order: State Authority, Popular Unrest, and the Criminal Justice System in Bourbon Mexico City." *The Americas* 50, no. 4 (1994): 501–25.

Scott, James. *Domination and the Arts of Resistance: Hidden Transcripts*. New Haven: Yale University Press, 1990.

Semo, Enrique. "Las revoluciones en la historia de México." In *Historia Mexicana: Economía y lucha de clases*. Mexico City: Era, 1978.

Serrano Ortega, José Antonio. "El ascenco de un caudillo en Guanajuato: Luís de Cortázar, 1827–1833." *Historia Mexicana* 43, no. 1 (1993): 49–80.

———. *El contingente de sangre: Los gobiernos estatales y departmentales y los métodos de reclutamiento del ejército permanente mexicano, 1824–1844*. Mexico City: Instituto Nacional de Antropología e Historia, 1993.

———. "El discurso de la unión: El patriotismo novohispano en la propaganda realista durante el movimiento insurgente de Hidalgo." *Estudios de Historia Novohispana* 14 (1994): 157–77.

———. *Jerarquía territorial y transición política: Guanajuato, 1790–1836*. Zamora: El Colegio de Michoacán/Instituto Mora, 2001.

———. "Reforma municipal y elecciones en Guanajuato, 1820–1836." In *Historia y nación: Actas del Congreso en homenaje a Josefina Zoraida Vázquez*. Vol. 2, *Política y diplomacia en el siglo xix mexicano*, edited by Luis Jáuregui and José Antonio Serano Ortega. Mexico City: El Colegio de México, 1998.

Serulnikov, Sergio. "Customs and Rules: Bourbon Rationalizing Projects and Social Conflicts in Northern Potosí during the 1770s." *Colonial Latin American Review* 8, no. 2 (1999): 245–74.

Sims, Harold. *Descolonización en México: El conflicto entre mexicanos y españoles*. Mexico City: Fondo de Cultura Económica, 1982.

Sordo Cedeño, Reynaldo. "Benito Juárez y el Soberano Congreso Constituyente, 1846–1847." In *Historia y nación: Actas del Congreso en homenaje a Josefina Zoraida Vázquez*. Vol. 2, *Política y diplomacia en el siglo xix mexicano*, edited by Luis Jáuregui and José Antonio Serano Ortega. Mexico City: El Colegio de México, 1998.

Spores, Ronald. "Relaciones gubermentales y judiciales entre los pueblos, los distritos, y el estado en Oaxaca (siglo XIX)." In *Lecturas Históricas del Estado de Oaxaca*. Vol. 3, *Siglo XIX*, edited by María de los Angles Romero Frizzi. Mexico City: Instituto Nacional de Antropología e Historia/Gobierno del Estado de Oaxaca, 1990.

Staples, Anne. "Secularización: Estado y iglesia en tiempos de Gómez Farías." *Estudios de Historia Moderna y Contemporánea de México* 10 (1986): 109–23.

Stern, Steve. *The Secret History of Gender: Women, Men and Power in Late Colonial Mexico*. Chapel Hill: University of North Carolina Press, 1995.

Stevens, Donald F. "Lo revelado y lo oscurecido: la política popular desde los archivos parroquiales." In *Construcción de la legitimidad política en México en el siglo XIX*, edited by Brian Connaughton, Carlos Illades, and Sonia Pérez Toledo. Mexico City: El Colegio de Michoacán/Universidad Autónoma Metropolitana/Universidad Nacional Autónoma de México/El Colegio de México, 1999.

Tanck de Estrada, Dorothy. *Pueblos de indios y educación en el México colonial, 1750–1821*. Mexico City: El Colegio de México, 1999.

Taylor, William B. *Drinking, Homicide, and Rebellion in Colonial Mexican Villages*. Stanford: Stanford University Press, 1979.

———. "¿Eran campesinos los indios? El viaje de un norteamericano por la historia colonial mesomericana." *Relaciones* 20, no. 78 (1999): 79–110.

———. *Landlord and Peasant in Colonial Oaxaca*. Stanford: Stanford University Press, 1972.

——. *Magistrates of the Sacred: Priests and Parishioners in Eighteenth-Century Mexico*. Stanford: Stanford University Press, 1996.

——. "The Virgin of Guadalupe in New Spain: An Inquiry into the Social History of Marian Devotion." *American Ethnologist* 14 (1987): 9–33.

Thomson, Guy. *Patriotism, Politics, and Popular Liberalism in Nineteenth-Century Mexico: Juan Francisco Lucas and the Puebla Sierra*. Wilmington, Del.: Scholarly Resources, 1999.

——. "Protectionism and Industrialization in Mexico, 1821–1854: The Case of Puebla." In *Latin America, Economic Imperialism and the State: The Political Economy of the External Connection from Independence to the Present*, edited by Christopher Abel and Colin Lewis. London: Athlone Press, 1985.

Thurner, Mark. *From Two Republics to One Divided: Contradictions of Postcolonial Nationmaking in Andean Peru*. Durham, N.C.: Duke University Press, 1997.

——. "'Republicanos' and 'la Comunidad de Peruanos': Unimagined Political Communities in Postcolonial Andean Peru." *Journal of Latin American Studies* 27, no. 2 (1995): 291–318.

Tilly, Charles. "Social Movements and National Politics." In *Statemaking and Social Movements: Essays in History and Theory*, edited by Charles Bright and Susan Harding. Ann Arbor: University of Michigan Press, 1984.

Tutino, John. "Rebelión indígena en Tehuantepec." *Cuadernos políticos* 24 (1980): 88–101.

Twinam, Ann. *Public Lives, Private Secrets: Gender, Honor, Sexuality, and Illegitimacy in Colonial Spanish America*. Stanford: Stanford University Press, 1999.

Uribe-Uran, Victor. "The Birth of a Public Sphere in Latin America during the Age of Revolution." *Comparative Studies in Society and History* 42, no. 2 (2000): 425–57.

Valderrama Rouy, Pablo, and Carolina Ramírez Suárez. "Resistencia étnica y defensa del territorio en el Totonacapan serrano: Cuetzalan en el siglo XIX." In *Indio, nación y comunidad en el México del siglo XIX*, edited by Antonio Escobar Ohmstede. Mexico City: Centro de Estudios Mexicanos y Centroamericanos/Centro de Investigaciones y Estudios Superiores en Antropología Social, 1993.

Valenzuela, J. Samuel. "Building Aspects of Democracy before Democracy: Electoral Practices in Nineteenth Century Chile." In *Elections before Democracy: The History of Elections in Europe and Latin America*, edited by Eduardo Posada-Carbó. New York: St. Martin's Press, 1996.

Van Young, Eric. "The Cuautla Lazarus: Double Subjectives in Reading Texts on Popular Collective Action." *Colonial Latin American Review* 2, no. 1–2 (1993): 3–26.

——. "Millenium on the Northern Marches: The Mad Messiah of Durango and Popular Rebellion in Mexico, 1800–1815." *Comparative Studies in Society and History* 28 (1986): 386–413.

——. *The Other Rebelllion: Popular Violence and Ideology in Mexico, 1810–1816*. Stanford: Stanford University Press, 2001.

———. "Paisaje de ensueño con figuras y vallados: disputa y discurso cultural en el campo mexicano de fines de la Colonia." In *Paisajes rebeldes: Una larga noche de rebelión indígena*, edited by Jane Dale-Lloyd and Laura Pérez Rosales. Mexico City: Universidad Iberoamericana, 1995.

———. "Quetzalcóatl, King Ferdinand, and Ignacio Allende Go to the Seashore; or Messianism and Mystical Kingship in Mexico, 1800–1821." In *The Independence of Mexico and the Origins of the New Nation*, edited by Jaime Rodríguez. Los Angeles: University of California at Los Angeles Latin American Center, 1989.

———. "The Raw and the Cooked: Elite and Popular Ideology in Mexico, 1800–1821." In *The Middle Period in Latin America*, edited by Mark Szuchman. Boulder, Col.: Lynne Reiner, 1989.

Vanderwood, Paul. *Disorder and Progress: Bandits, Police and Mexican Development*. Lincoln: University of Nebraska Press, 1981.

Vázquez, Josefina Zoraida. "De la crisis monárquica a la Independencia (1808–1821)." In *Interpretaciones de la Independencia de México*. Mexico City: Nueva Imagen, 1997.

Vincent, Theodore G. *The Legacy of Vicente Guerrero, Mexico's First Black Indian President*. Gainesville: University Press of Florida, 2001.

Viquiera Alban, Juan Pedro. *¿Relajados o reprimidos? Diversiones públicas y vida social en la ciudad de México durante el siglo de las luces*. Mexico City: Fondo de Cultura Económica, 1987.

Voekel, Pamela. *Alone Before God: The Religious Origins of Modernity in Mexico*. Durham, N.C.: Duke University Press, 2002.

———. "Peeing on the Palace: Bodily Resistance to the Bourbon Reforms in Mexico City." *Journal of Historical Sociology* 5, no. 2 (1992): 183–208.

Walker, Charles F. "'La orgía periodística': Prensa y cultura política en el Cuzco durante la joven república." *Revista de Indias* 61, no. 221 (2001): 7–26.

———. *Smoldering Ashes: Cuzco and the Creation of Republican Peru, 1780–1840*. Durham, N.C.: Duke University Press, 1999.

Warren, Richard. "Ashes and Aerostats: Popular Culture Meets Political Culture in Nineteenth Century Mexico." Paper presented at the Latin American Studies Association, Chicago, 25 September 1998.

———. "'El congreso por su gusto hizo de un Justo un ladrón' el cobre, 'la chusma' y el centralismo, 1837." In *Instituciones y ciudad: Ocho estudios históricos sobre la Ciudad de México*, edited by Carlos Illades and Ariel Rodríguez Kuri. Mexico City: Ediciones Unios, 2000.

———. "Elections and Popular Political Participation in Mexico, 1808–1836." In *Liberals, Politics, and Power: State Formation in Nineteenth-Century Latin America*, edited by Vincent Peloso and Barbara Tennenbaum. Athens: University of Georgia Press, 1996.

———. *Vagrants and Citizens: Politics and the Masses in Mexico City from Colony to Republic*. Wilmington, Del.: Scholarly Resources, 2001.

Weber, David J. *The Mexican Frontier, 1821–1846: The American Southwest under Mexico*. Albuquerque: University of New Mexico Press, 1982.

Wolf, Eric. "Aspects of Group Relations in a Complex Society: Mexico." *American Anthropologist* 58, no. 6 (1956): 1065–78.

Wood, Stephanie. "Adopted Saints: Christian Images in Nahua Testaments of Late Colonial Toluca." *The Americas* 47, no. 3 (1991): 259–93.

Yannakakis, Yanna. " 'Indios Ladinos': Indigenous Intermediaries and the Negotiation of Local Rule in Colonial Oaxaca, 1660–1769." Ph.D diss., University of Pennsylvania, 2003.

Index

Athocha, Virgin of, 34
Atlantic world, 280, 287
Audiencia, 28, 58, 78, 101, 103, 112, 119
Avendaño, Pedro Joseph, 119
Ayala, Hermengildo, 242
Ayuntamiento, 28, 96, 230, 238, 241–42
Ayutla, 57, 108, 235, 237, 243, 248, 259,
   271–72
Aztecs, 137, 160

Bajío, 44, 47, 118, 128, 131, 225
Ballados, Doña María, 36
Bando, 84
Bargas, Timoteo, 151
Barrientos, José María, 136
Barrio, 85, 245, 262, 268; "Barrio Chinan-
   teco," 85; "Barrio Zapoteco," 85
Barrio de los Alzados, 24
Baskes, Jeremy, 45, 46
Basquez, Juan Antonio, 72, 76, 102
Bastón. See *Vara*
Bautista, Antonio, 236–37
Bellingeri, Marco, 166
Beltran, Francisco, 251, 268–69
Benson, Nellie Lee, 143
Berdejo, Don Juan, 38
Bergoza y Jordan, Antonio, 103, 126, 131,
   133, 138
Betaza, 99, 102, 252, 263
Blanco y Helguero, Buenaventura, 107
Bolaños, José, 193
Bolaños, Juan N., 177
Bonaparte, Joseph, 126
Bonaparte, Napoleon, 122–27, 129–31,
   134–36, 142–43, 152, 155
Bonavia, Bernardo, 97–102, 104–6, 108,
   110, 115, 120, 132, 136
Bono López, María, 278
Bourbon Reforms, 8, 14–17, 25, 41, 72, 83,
   91–121 passim, 122, 142–44, 156, 158,
   160, 181, 215, 227–28, 254, 256, 276, 287–
   89; and education, 107–11; impact on
   political culture, 15, 25, 41, 111–16, 287;
   and military, 95–96; and race, 15, 95, 117;
   and religion, 101–7, 215

Brading, David, 91; *Miners and Merchants in
   Bourbon Mexico,* 91
Bravo, Mariano, 250
Brazil, 264–65
Breña, Manuel, 129
Brioso, Vicente Antonio, 263
British America, 96
Bucareli, Antonio María de, 23
Bustamente, Anastasio, 195, 205–7, 210
Bustamente, Carlos María de, 134, 139, 182,
   185
Bustamente, Manuel Nicolás de, 149

Cabecera, 48
Cacalotepec, 110, 271
Cacique, 52–56, 58, 68, 82, 231–32, 243, 278,
   289
Caciquismo, 222, 243
Cajonos, San Francisco, 61, 82, 158
Cajonos, San Mateo, 76, 269
Cajonos, San Pedro, 81
Calvo, Angel, 145, 178
Camotlán, 51, 62, 65, 88, 279
Campanillismo, 284
Campo, Manuel del Solar, 137
Canalizo, Valentín, 208
Cañas, Tiburcio, 211
Candayoc, 44
Candelaria, Magdalena de la, 70
Cantor, 51–52, 66, 255, 261
Carbajal, Bernardino, 215
Cargas consejiles. See Indigenous villages: and
   community service
Cargo system, 50–56, 59–61, 66, 68, 83, 108,
   120, 231–33, 239–40, 245, 253, 273, 278,
   280
Carlos IV, 124
Carmagnani, Marcello, 224
Carreño, Juan María, 263
Carriedo, Juan Bautista, 139, 212, 231
Cartas al Pueblo, 196
Casalduero, Juan, 209–10
Casas reales, 86
Casaus Torres y Las Plazas, Ramón, 127
Castañeda, Timoteo, 193

Castellanos, Luis, 113
Castillejos, Agustín María, 264
Castro, Miguel de, 60
Castro Gutiérrez, Felipe, 92
Cempoaltepec, 261
Centralists. See *Aceites*
Ceremonies, 26–31, 33, 35, 39, 48, 59, 64,
   67–68, 70, 73, 86, 90, 96, 100, 102, 104–
   7, 115, 127, 134–35, 138, 143–44, 146–
   47, 150, 160, 165–68, 172, 175, 196, 217,
   227, 236, 240, 243–45, 249, 251–52,
   262–63, 270, 274, 285, 289; civic, 27–28,
   47, 59, 127, 134, 143–44, 146–47, 160,
   165–68, 217, 240, 249, 251–52; and *cofradías*, 33, 35, 64, 107, 175, 243, 262;
   Corpus Christi, 26, 28, 48, 64, 73, 105–6,
   166, 172, 217; Day of All Souls, 96; Feast
   of the Ascension, 28; Feast of Our Lady of
   Guadalupe, 135, 138, 160, 166, 217; Feast
   of the Virgin de los Remedios, 105; Feast
   of the Virgin of the Soledad, 28, 166,
   217; *feria de varas*, 100, 147, 270, 274;
   Good Friday, 150, 175; and guilds, 29–30,
   175; Holy Spirit, 64; Holy Week, 26, 28,
   31, 48, 64–65, 196, 217, 243; Lent, 217;
   Nativity, 64; Purification, 64; Rosary,
   64, 236; San Ildefonso, 73; Santa Rosa,
   105
Cerro de la Soledad, 178
Chambers, Sara, 173, 175
Chance, John, 24, 40, 42, 46, 51–52, 54, 57,
   70, 85, 95, 105, 231–32, 262
Chaquetas. See *Aceites*
Chavez, María Francisca, 129
Chinantec, 48
Choapan, 44, 98, 141, 227
Cholera, 227, 236–37, 261
Citizenship, 144–47, 152–53, 164–65,
   170, 174–75, 179, 187, 200, 202, 205, 233,
   247, 271–72; and race, 144, 146, 154, 179,
   187; and women, 174–75, 200, 247,
   272
Clubs, political, 198, 206, 221; "Guada-
   lupan" clubs, 198
Coatsworth, John, 267

Cofradías, 30–35, 64, 76, 85, 107, 160, 169,
   175, 183, 192–93, 196, 243; Jesus de los
   Desamparados, 33; Jesus Nazareno, 32;
   las Nieves, 32; Nuestra Señora de los
   Angeles, 32; San Anastacio, 31; San Nicolás, 32; Sangre de Cristo, 32; Santa Barbara, 33; Santa Verónica, 32; Santísima
   Trinidad, 32
Comaltepec, 259, 271
Connaughton, Brian, 161
Conquest, 52, 72, 89, 107, 113, 256
Conservatism, 220
Constitutions, 112, 143–49, 152, 160–61,
   166–67, 169, 170–73, 178–79, 182–84,
   187, 193–95, 216, 229–32, 234, 236–38,
   242, 249, 251–52, 254, 265–66, 271–72,
   274, 287, 289; "Constitutional Bases," 166,
   252, 271; "Constitutive Acts," 166–67,
   184; of 1812, 143–46, 148–49, 152, 166,
   169, 178–79, 187, 229–30, 252, 265;
   French Constitution of 1791, 148; of Mexico, 1824, 161, 166–67, 195; of Mexico,
   1846, 166; "Organic Bases," 166, 212;
   Seven Laws, 1837, 166; of state of Oaxaca,
   160, 170, 172–73, 182–83, 194, 230–32,
   236, 242, 254, 265–66, 289
Convents, 31, 36, 107–8, 135, 160, 198;
   Belemnite, 135; Belen, 198; of the Concepción, 36; and education, 107–8; Our
   Lady of Angels, 31
Cope, R. Douglas, 25
Cordero Avendaño, Carmen, 87
Corporatism, 1–2, 12, 25, 29, 38–39, 93, 95,
   118–19, 121, 139, 153, 157, 169, 175, 192,
   212, 222, 230, 233–34, 249, 277, 287, 290;
   colonial, 1–2, 28, 47, 95; and ethnic difference, 1, 15; and indigenous villages, 13,
   15, 118, 233; and mining deputation, 118;
   and monarchy, 12, 153, 249, 287; and
   "Republic of Indians," 25, 47, 230; and
   "Republic of Spaniards," 25; in republican
   Oaxaca, 175, 212, 277; and urban politics,
   14–15, 25, 29, 95, 139, 157, 169, 192, 212,
   222, 277
Corregidor, 19, 27–29, 93

United States of America, 175–76, 214–15, 218, 253, 279

Vacas, Pioquinto, 22
Valdés y Moya, Antonio, 162–63, 191, 199
Valladolid, 156
Van Young, Eric, 10, 284, 286
Vara, 58, 73, 87–88, 236, 239, 249, 263, 269–70, 285
Vargas, Antonio, 245, 251
Vargas, Crisanto de, 240, 245
Vargas, José, 236–37
Vasconcelos, Ignacio Mariano, 148
Vatican, 161
Vázquez, Josefina, 93
Vazquez, Juan Antonio, 114
Velasco, Juan, 242
Velasco, Juan Tomás, 236–37, 249
Velasco, Salvador, 242
Velasco, Tomas, 272
Veracruz, 43, 44, 58, 118, 140–41, 201; Gulf coast of, 140–41
Vicente, Francisco, 61
Vicente, Tomás, 248
Villa Alta, 4, 12, 14–16, 20, 40–90 passim, 94–100, 102–3, 105, 108–9, 114–16, 118–21, 123–25, 140–43, 146, 148, 150, 154–55, 189, 194, 225–32, 235–36, 239, 249, 252–53, 257, 259–62, 264–67, 269–70, 278–79, 281–85, 287–88; and Bourbon Reforms, 15, 94–100, 102–3, 105, 108–9, 114–16, 118–21; economy and geography, 41–47, 225–29; and independence, 16, 123–25, 140–43, 146, 148, 150, 154; and republican era, 189, 194, 225–32, 235–36, 239, 249, 252–53, 257, 259–62, 264–65
Villasante, Joaquín, 271
Villegas, Jose Domingo, 241, 250
Vinagres, 179–201 passim, 208–22, 259–60, 266–67, 282–84
Vitoria, Francisco de, 38
Vocal, 53
Voekel, Pamela, 92

War of Independence (1808–1821), 16, 41, 122–55 passim, 165, 222, 275, 281, 284, 287; in Antequera, 16, 123, 125–40, 142–46, 148, 150, 152, 153–55; and militias, 129, 131–33, 138, 140, 151, 153; in Villa Alta, 16, 41, 123–25, 140–43, 148, 150, 154–55
War of the South, 206
Warren, Richard, 165, 168
Washington, George, 220–21
Women, 33–37, 44, 46, 50, 60–63, 65, 72, 81, 83–85, 89, 95, 104, 106, 114–15, 150, 173–76, 225–27, 246–49, 251, 264, 268–69; and cofradías, 33–34; and elections, 174; and guilds, 33, 95, 150; in republican Oaxaca, 173–76; and riots, 62, 81, 85, 248–49, 268–69; and villages, 44, 46, 50, 60–63, 65, 72, 81, 83–85, 89, 104, 106, 114, 176, 225–27, 246–49, 251, 264
Women's Charity Committee, 174
Wood, Stephanie, 35

Xagalazi, 248
Xaltepec, 57
Ximenes, Joseph Manuel, 37
Ximenes, Juan, 61–62, 108
Ximenes, Raphael, 37
Ximenez, Bruno, 203
Ximenez, Ygnacio, 130

Yaa, 45, 257, 269
Yae, 49, 52, 54, 56, 63, 68, 82, 264
Yagallo, 50, 61–62, 87
Yaganiza, 269
Yagavila, 69
Yahuive, 77, 79, 105, 140–41, 151, 155
Yalahui, 227, 269
Yalalag, 227, 243, 245, 248, 251, 267
Yaneri, 58–59, 75, 113
Yannakakis, Yanna, 57
Yatee, 248
Yatoni, 61, 269
Yatzachi, 80, 257
Yatzachi el Alto, 99
Yatzachi el Bajo, 99

Peter Guardino is an associate professor of history at Indiana University.

Library of Congress Cataloging-in-Publication Data
Guardino, Peter F., 1963–
The time of liberty : popular political culture in Oaxaca,
1750–1850 / Peter Guardino.
p. cm. — (Latin America otherwise)
Includes bibliographical references and index.
ISBN 0-8223-3508-5 (cloth : alk. paper)
ISBN 0-8223-3520-4 (pbk. : alk. paper)
1. Oaxaca Region (Mexico) — History. 2. Government,
Resistance to — Mexico — Oaxaca Region — History.
3. Rural-urban relations — Mexico — Oaxaca Region.
4. Political culture — Mexico — Oaxaca Region.
I. Title. II. Series.
F1391.O12G83 2005
972'.74 — dc22   2004027162